International Law, Museums and the Return of Cultural Objects

While the question of the return of cultural objects is by no means a new one, it has become the subject of increasingly intense debate in recent years. This important book explores the removal and the return of cultural objects from occupied communities during the last two centuries and analyses the concurrent evolution of international cultural heritage law. The book focuses on the significant influence exerted by British, US and Australian governments and museums on international law and museum policy in response to restitution claims. It shows that these claims, far from heralding the long-feared dissolution of museums and their collections, provide museums with a vital new role in the process of self-determination and cultural identity. Compelling and thought-provoking throughout, this book is essential reading for archaeologists, international lawyers and all those involved in cultural resource management.

ANA FILIPA VRDOLJAK is Marie Curie Fellow at the Law Department, European University Institute, Florence and Senior Lecturer at the Faculty of Law, University of Western Australia.

ANA FILIPA VRDOLJAK

INTERNATIONAL LAW, MUSEUMS AND THE RETURN OF CULTURAL OBJECTS

CAMBRIDGE UNIVERSITY PRESS
Cambridge, New York, Melbourne, Madrid, Cape Town, Singapore, São Paulo, Delhi

Cambridge University Press
The Edinburgh Building, Cambridge CB2 2RU, UK

Published in the United States of America by Cambridge University Press, New York

www.cambridge.org
Information on this title: www.cambridge.org/9780521732406

© Ana Filipa Vrdoljak 2008

First published 2006
Reprinted 2007
First published in paperback 2008

Printed in the United Kingdom at the University Press, Cambridge

A catalogue record for this publication is available from the British Library

ISBN 978-0-521-84142-9 hardback
ISBN 978-0-521-73240-6 paperback

for my parents

CONTENTS

ILLUSTRATIONS

Reports of claims for the restitution of cultural objects housed in museums worldwide have increasingly captured the popular imagination in the last two decades. However, the triggers for this book are not directly related to restitution requests. Consequently, this has led to the consideration of the removal and return of cultural objects as not merely physical acts viewed in isolation.

The first trigger took place in October 1991 with the filtering through of images and news reports of the deliberate shelling of the fortified city of Dubrovnik, one of the seminal moments of the early years of the Balkan conflict. This was an example of the indelible link between a people's identity and cultural objects that is made not only by the community itself but also by their would-be occupiers. The violence perpetuated against people because of their membership of a particular ethnic or religious group was also levelled at monuments, historic sites and cultural objects with similarly perceived affiliations.

The physical destruction of the members of the particular group was not sufficient for these belligerents; rather, they hoped to expunge the group's existence from the collective memory of future generations through the systematic removal of their cultural manifestations. The creation of 'eternal silences' in individual and collective memory through the removal or destruction of cultural heritage continues to be a powerful weapon in the occupation and subjugation of peoples.

The second trigger was my visit in late 1995 to the Royal Academy of Arts, London for the 'Africa: The Art of a Continent' show. The aim of the exhibition was to chronicle the arts of an entire continent which was emerging from 'a longing period of humiliation' following decolonisation and the dismantling of the apartheid system in South Africa.[1] The exhibition had been planned and executed at a time when the grand imperial narratives of the past were being challenged by intellectual discourses driven by peoples on the periphery. However, as I walked through the Royal Academy's darkened rooms I was left with a lingering sense of unease despite its laudable aims.

The labelling of the cultural objects on display provided little detailed information of their provenance. The historical voids surrounding the objects accentuated the denial of the colonial past, the present-day effects of former colonial relations and the possible future legacies of this past. In addition, a cursory glance at the exhibition

---

[1] T. Phillips, Introduction, in T. Phillips (ed.), *Africa: The Art of a Continent* (exh. cat., New York, 1995), p.11.

catalogue revealed that exhibits were the 'property' of numerous European, North American or private collections. Only a fraction of the objects were permanently in the possession of African museums. Even these objects were borrowed from institutions located in capital cities of newly independent States. Therefore, it is probable that only a negligible portion of the objects in the exhibition were accessible to the communities from which they originated.

I would not suggest that the exhibition sought to reaffirm the values of the Britain of old. What I do contend is that, even with our growing awareness of colonialism, its effects have not dissipated. Despite the initiatives of various international agencies, a significant portion of the cultural heritage of formerly colonised and indigenous peoples remains housed in foreign museums. These objects continue to be de-contextualised and form a vital part of narratives largely dictated by former colonial powers. And these communities continue to suffer ongoing cultural losses due to the legacies of colonisation and a new wave of globalisation.

The restitution of cultural objects to their community of 'origin' is neither a recent nor rare phenomenon. Since the early nineteenth century, the international community has sanctioned the return of cultural objects to formerly occupied communities following the disintegration of empires or cessation of occupation. Yet why did this not occur during decolonisation in the late twentieth century? In addressing this question, I take up the challenge laid down by Prott and O'Keefe in the penultimate chapter of their work, *Law and the Cultural Heritage*, vol. III: *Movement* (1989). The authors note that despite numerous examples of restitution in the post-conflict situations, very little work has been done to extrapolate these principles and apply them to the circumstances of new States following decolonisation.

In preparing this work, I was fortunate to enjoy the generosity of spirit and experience of the scholars and staff, and draw on the substantial resources of the Lauterpacht Research Centre for International Law, University of Cambridge, which I visited during 1999; the Global Law School, School of Law, New York University, which I visited during 2000; and the Law Department, European University Institute, where I was a Jean Monnet Fellow during 2004 and 2005.

The completion of this project was made possible with the support of Australian Academy of the Humanities, Cooke, Cooke, Coghlan, Godfrey and Littlejohn Fund, the Australian Postgraduate Scheme and the University of Sydney. The illustrations have been reproduced with the kind assistance of Adrienne Kaeppler, Australian Museum, Brooklyn Museum, Leon Morris, Museum of Modern Art, National Library of Australia, Rockefeller Archive Center, Smithsonian Institution, South Australian Museum, State Library of New South Wales, University of Pennsylvania Museum of Anthropology and Archaeology, and Victoria and Albert Museum.

In addition, my journeys both near and far have been reliant on the skills and stamina of numerous library and archives staff. In the United Kingdom, this included Cambridge University Libraries and Archives; the Institute of Advanced Legal Studies Library, University of London; the National Art Library, Victoria and Albert Museum; the Victoria and Albert Museum Archives; the British Library; the British

Museum Library and Archives; and the British Public Records Office. In France, this included the Unesco Archives and Library; the International Council of Museums Library and Archives; and Centre de documentation-bibliothèque, Paris. In Denmark, this included Nationalmuseet library; The Royal Library; and the International Work Group for Indigenous Affairs Resource Centre and Library. In Australia, this included staff of the University of Sydney libraries and archives; University of New South Wales libraries; the Australian Museum Library and Archives; the State Library of New South Wales; the Mitchell Library, Sydney; the South Australian Museum Library and Archives; the State Library of South Australia; the State Library of Victoria; Museum Victoria library and archives; the National Library of Australia; and the United Nations Information Centre, Sydney. In the United States, this included the New York University libraries and archives; the United Nations Archives; the Dag Hammarskjöld and Woodrow Wilson libraries, United Nations, New York; the Museum of Modern Art Library and Archives; the Archives of American Art, Smithsonian Institution; Rockefeller Archive Center; The Brooklyn Museum of Art Library and Archives; American Museum of Natural History Library; the Metropolitan Museum of Art library, New York; New York Public Library; Columbia University libraries; Harvard University Art Museums; and the Roerich Museum Archives.

I am extremely grateful to Jan Brazier, Phil Gordon, Des Griffin, Lynda Kelly, Jude Philp, Jim Specht and Peter White of the Australian Museum; Rosemary Stack of the Macleay Museum; Barry Craig, Phillip Clarke, Colin Pardoe and Aphrodite Vlavogelakis of the South Australian Museum; Lindy Allen, Melanie Raberts, Robert McWilliams and Gary Foley of Museum Victoria; Anthony Burton formerly of the Victoria and Albert Museum; Neil Brodie, MacDonald Institute for Archaeological Research, University of Cambridge; Anita Herle and Robin Boast of the Cambridge University Museum of Archaeology and Anthropology; Stephanie Makseyn-Kelley of the National Museum of the American Indian; Mary Downs of the US National Park Service; Patrick Boylan, City University, London; Torben Lundbaek of the National Museum of Denmark; and Roger O'Keefe, Faculty of Law, University of Cambridge who have been most generous with their time.

The progress, depth and completion of this book would not have been possible without the determination, patience and attention to detail of Ben Boer and Terry Carney of the Faculty of Law, University of Sydney; Patrick O'Keefe, Australian National University; Russel Barsh, Institute of Society and Law, New York University; Terence Smith, Department of History of Art and Architecture, University of Pittsburgh; and Mary Mackay, Department of Art History and Theory, University of Sydney. The guidance and advice of James Crawford, Faculty of Law, University of Cambridge throughout many years is deeply appreciated.

Special thanks to my sister, Katarina Vrdoljak, whose unstinting support has guaranteed the inclusion of images to accompany my words; Annie Parkinson, whose proofreading skills came when they were most needed; and my editor, Simon Whitmore, who patiently guided the book to completion.

One of the most enduring pleasures of this work has been the hospitality and generosity of family and friends in various corners of the globe, especially the Burke, Kramar, Levak, Lingaard-Hansen, Pahović, Rošičič, Stronge and Vrdoljak families, and Teresita Heffernan and her fellow Sisters. Above all, I wish to acknowledge the unfailing physical and emotional support of my parents and sisters, who sparked, fuelled and ensured the realisation of this long-held goal.

TABLE OF CASES

TABLE OF INSTRUMENTS

United States

Australia

Miscellaneous

ABBREVIATIONS

(?)	Original unclear
AAA	Archives of American Art
AAB	Aboriginal Arts Board (Aust.)
AAL	*Art Antiquity and Law*
AAM	American Association of Museums
AAMD	Association of Art Museum Directors
AHB	Alfred H. Barr Jr
AHR	*American Historical Review*
AICRJ	*American Indian Culture and Research Journal*
AILR	*American Indian Law Review*
AIQ	*American Indian Quarterly*
AJICL	*Arizona Journal of International and Comparative Law*
AJIL	*American Journal of International Law*
ALB	*Aboriginal Law Bulletin*
ALJR	*Australian Law Journal Reports*
ALR	*Australian Law Reports*
AMA	Australian Museum Archives
APSR	*American Political Science Review*
ARPA	Archaeological Resources Protection Act 1979
Arch. Rev.	*Architectural Review*
Ark. LR	*Arkansas Law Review*
ASILP	*Proceedings of the American Society of International Law*
ASLJ	*Arizona State Law Journal*
ATSIC	Aboriginal and Torres Strait Islander Commission (Aust.)
AUJILP	*American University Journal of International Law and Policy*
AULR	*American University Law Review*
AYIL	*Australian Yearbook of International Law*
BIA	Bureau of Indian Affairs (US)
BMA	Brooklyn Museum Archives
Brooklyn JIL	*Brooklyn Journal of International Law*
Buffalo LR	*Buffalo Law Review*
BULR	*Boston University Law Review*
BYIL	*British Yearbook of International Law*
CA	Court of Appeal (UK)
CAJ	*College Art Journal*

Cal. LR	*California Law Review*
CAMA	Council of Australian Museums Association
CCOR	'Continuous Cultures Ongoing Responsibilities'
CCPIA	Convention on Cultural Property Implementation Act 1983
Ch	Chancery Division (UK)
CHR	UN Commission on Human Rights
CHRWG	Working group established in accordance with Commission on Human Rights Resolution 1995/32
CHRY	*Canadian Human Rights Yearbook*
CILJ	*Cornell International Law Journal*
CJLJ	*Canadian Journal of Law and Jurisprudence*
CJTL	*Columbia Journal of Transnational Law*
CLP	*Current Legal Problems*
CLR	*Commonwealth Law Reports*
COMA	Conference of Museum Anthropologists (Aust)
Cornell LR	*Cornell Law Review*
Crim. LR	*Criminal Law Review*
CVLAJLA	*Columbia-Vanderbilt LA Journal of Law and the Arts*
CWRJIL	*Case Western Reserve Journal of International Law*
CYIL	*Canadian Yearbook of International Law*
DCMS	Department of Culture, Media and Sport (UK)
DJILP	*Denver Journal of International Law and Politics*
ECOSOC	Economic and Social Council
EJIL	*European Journal of International Law*
EPLJ	*Environmental and Planning Law Journal*
EU	European Union
exh. cat.	exhibition catalogue
F 2d	*Federal Reports (Second series)* (US)
F Supp.	*Federal Supplement* (US)
FCA	Federal Court of Australia
FCR	Federal Court Reports (Aust.)
FILJ	*Fordham International Law Journal*
FLR	*Federal Law Reports*
FO	Foreign Office (UK)
GAOR	*General Assembly Official Record*
GATT	General Agreement on Tariffs and Trade
GLJ	*Georgetown Law Journal*
GWJILE	*George Washington Journal of International Law and Economics*
GYIL	*German Yearbook of International Law*
HCA	High Court of Australia
HELR	*Harvard Environmental Law Review*
HHRJ	*Harvard Human Rights Journal*
HILJ	*Harvard International Law Journal*
HL	House of Lords

HREOC	Human Rights and Equal Opportunity Commission (Aust.)
HRJ	*Human Rights Journal*
HRQ	*Human Rights Quarterly*
IACB	Indian Arts and Crafts Board
IAIA	Institute of American Indian Arts
ICCPR	International Covenant on Civil and Political Rights
ICESCR	International Covenant on Economic, Social and Cultural Rights
ICIC	International Committee for Intellectual Cooperation
ICJ Reports	*International Court of Justice Reports of Judgments, Advisory Opinions and Orders*
ICLQ	*International and Comparative Law Quarterly*
ICOM	International Council of Museums
ICTY	International Criminal Tribunal for the former Yugoslavia
IGC	Intergovermental Committee
IIIC	International Institute of Intellectual Cooperation
IJCP	*International Journal of Cultural Property*
IJMMC	*International Journal of Museum Management and Curatorship*
ILA	International Law Association
ILC	International Law Commission
ILM	*International Legal Materials*
ILO	International Labour Organization
ILR	*International Law Reports*
IMT	International Military Tribunal, Nuremberg
IPR	*Intellectual Property Reports*
IRA	Indian Reorganization Act 1934
IRRC	*International Review of the Red Cross*
IYHR	*Israeli Yearbook on Human Rights*
IYIL	*Italian Yearbook of International Law*
JHC	*Journal of the History of Collections*
JILP	*Journal of International Law and Policy*
JRIBA	*Journal of Royal Institute of British Architects*
JYIL	*Jewish Yearbook of International Law*
LCP	*Law and Contemporary Problems*
LN	League of Nations
LNOJ	*League of Nations Official Journal*
LNTS	*League of Nations Treaty Series*
LPIB	*Law and Policy in International Business*
LQR	*Law Quarterly Review*
MGC	Museums and Galleries Commission (UK)
MGR	Military Government Regulation
Mich. LR	*Michigan Law Review*
MLR	*Modern Law Review*
MoMA	Museum of Modern Art, New York
MoPA	Museum of Primitive Art, New York

MULR	*Melbourne University Law Review*
Museums J	*Museums Journal*
n.d.	not dated
n.p.	not paginated
NAGPRA	Native American Graves Protection and Repatriation Act 1990
NAL	National Art Library (UK)
NDLR	*Notre Dame Law Review*
NGO	Non-governmental organisation
NIEO	New International Economic Order
NJIL	*Nordic Journal of International Law*
NMA	National Museum of Australia
NMAI	National Museum of the American Indian
NMAIA	National Museum of the American Indian Act 1989
NMDC	National Museum Directors Conference (UK)
NPS	National Park Service (US)
NSPA	National Stolen Property Act
NYIL	*Netherlands Yearbook of International Law*
NYUJILP	*New York University Journal of International Law and Politics*
NYURLSC	*New York University Review of Law and Social Change*
OAJ	*Oxford Art Journal*
OAS	Organization of American States
OAS Res.	Organization of American States Resolution
OASTS	Organization of American States Treaty Series
OAU	Organization of African Unity
OCULR	*Oklahoma City University Law Review*
OHCHR	Office of High Commissioner for Human Rights (UN)
OIM	International Museum Office (*Office international des musées*)
OLR	*Oregon Law Review*
Parry's CTS	*Parry's Consolidated Treaty Series*
PAU	Pan-American Union
PCIJ	Permanent Court of International Justice
PCIJ ser.A/B	*Permanent Court of International Justice, Collection of Judgments, Orders and Advisory Opinions (1931–40)*
PMCHA	Protection of Movable Cultural Heritage Act 1986
PNG	Papua New Guinea
PPNO	'Previous Possessions, New Obligations'
PRO	Public Records Office (UK)
PYIL	*Polish Yearbook of International Law*
QB	Queen's Bench
RAC	Rockefeller Archives Center
RCADI	*Recueil des cours de l'académie de droit international (The Hague)*
RdH	René d'Harnoncourt
RDI	*Revue de droit international*
RDILC	*Revue de droit international et de législation comparée*

RGDIP	*Revue générale de droit international public (Paris)*
RHD	*Revue d'histoire diplomatique*
RIAA	*UN Reports of International Arbitral Awards*
RICP	Return of Indigenous Cultural Property Program
SHR	*Scottish Historical Review*
SJILC	*Syracuse Journal of International Law and Commerce*
St Thomas LR	*St Thomas Law Review*
Stan. LR	*Stanford Law Review*
Syd. LR	*Sydney Law Review*
TGS	*Transactions of the Grotius Society*
TIAS	Trade and Other International Acts Series (US)
TLCP	*Transnational Law and Contemporary Problems*
UBCLR	*University of British Columbia Law Review*
UCDLR	*University of California Davis Law Review*
UCLJR	*University of Chicago Law Journal Roundtable*
UDHR	Universal Declaration of Human Rights
UILR	*University of Illinois Law Review*
UKTS	*United Kingdom Treaty Series*
ULR	*Uniform Law Review*
UMJLR	*University of Michigan Journal of Law and Reform*
UN	United Nations
UNCLOS	United Nations Convention on the Law of the Sea
UNESCO	United Nations Educational, Scientific and Cultural Organisation
UNGA	United Nations General Assembly
UNGA Res.	United Nations General Assembly Resolution
UNIDROIT	International Institute for the Unification of Private Law
UNSC Res.	United Nations Security Council Resolution
UNSWLJ	*University of New South Wales Law Journal*
UNTS	United Nations Treaty Series
UNWCC	United Nations War Crimes Commission
USC	*United States Code*
USTS	*United States Treaty Series*
V&A	Victoria and Albert Museum, London
WAC	World Archaeological Congress
WGHR	Working Group on Human Remains (UK)
WGIP	Working Group on Indigenous Populations
WLR	*Weekly Law Reports*
YAAA	*Annuaire des anciens auditeurs de l'academie de la Haye*
YBILC	*Yearbook of the International Law Commission*
YBUN	*United Nations Yearbook*
YJIL	*Yale Journal of International Law*

NOTE ON THE TEXT

Some important conventions, treaties and other instruments are cited in the text in abbreviated form for the sake of clarity in the detailed analysis of issues. These shortened citations are listed below with their full titles and may be compared with the Table of Instruments. The list is divided into those instruments cited alphabetically and those cited chronologically.

Alphabetical

Agreement in respect of Control of Looted Works of Art 1946   Agreement between the United States, the United Kingdom and France in respect of the Control of Looted Articles

Atlantic Charter 1941   Declaration by the united nations, Washington, 1 January 1942, Annex 1: Declaration of principles known as the Atlantic Charter delivered by the United Kingdom Prime Minister and United States President

ATSIHP Act   Aboriginal and Torres Strait Islander Heritage Protection Act 1984 (Cth)

Booty Decree   Swiss Decree of 10 December 1945 concerning Actions for the Recovery of Goods taken in Occupied Territories during the War

Committee Statute   Draft Statute of the Intergovernmental Committee concerning the Restitution or Return of Cultural Property to Their Country of Origin

Convention of San Salvador   OAS Convention on the Protection of the Archaeological, Historical and Artistic Heritage of the American Nations 1976

Draft Genocide Convention 1947   Draft Convention on the Crime of Genocide and Comments

Friendly Relations Declaration 1970   Declaration on Principles of International Law concerning Friendly Relations and Co-operation among States in Accordance with the Charter of the United Nations

Genocide Convention 1948   Convention on the Prevention and Punishment of the Crime of Genocide

IGC Statutes   Statutes of the Intergovernmental Committee for Promoting the Return of Cultural Property to its Countries of Origin or its Restitution in Case of Illicit Appropriation

ILO No.107   Convention concerning the Protection and Integration of Indigenous and Other Tribal and Semi-Tribal Populations in Independent Countries 1957

ILO No.169   Convention concerning Indigenous and Tribal Peoples in Independent Countries 1989

Law No.52   Military Government for Germany, US Zone, Law No.52 Blocking and Control of Property, 1946

Law No.59   Military Government for Germany, US Area of Control, Law No.59: Restitution of Identifiable Property, 1947

Mataatua Declaration   Declaration on Cultural and Intellectual Property Rights of Indigenous Peoples, Mataatua, 1993

Optional Protocol of ICCPR   Optional Protocol to the International Covenant on Civil and Political Rights, New York, 1966

PACE Res 1205 (1999)   Parliamentary Assembly of the Council of Europe (PACE) Resolution 1205 (1999) Looted Jewish cultural property

PAU Treaty 1935   Treaty on the Protection of Movable Property of Historic Value

Public Law 92-587 of 1974   Title II – Regulation of Importation of Pre-Columbian Monumental and Architectural Sculptures or Murals

Resolution 1205   Parliamentary Assembly of the Council of Europe (PACE) Resolution 1205 (1999) Looted Jewish cultural property

Roerich Pact 1933 (see 1935 Washington Treaty)

San José Declaration   San José Declaration: UNESCO and the Struggle against Ethnocide, 1981

Treaty of Cooperation between United States and Mexico   Treaty of Cooperation providing for the Recovery and Return of Stolen Archaeological, Historical and Cultural Properties, Mexico City, 1970

UN Charter   Charter of the United Nations, San Francisco, 1945

UNESCO Intergovernmental Committee   Intergovernmental Committee for Promoting the Return of Cultural Property to Its Countries of Origin or Its Restitution in Case of Illicit Appropriation

UNIDROIT Convention   UNIDROIT Convention on Stolen or Illegally Exported Cultural Objects, Rome, 1995

UNGA Res.96(I)   UNGA Resolution on the Crime of Genocide, UNGA Res.96(I), 1946

UNGA Res.1514(XV)   Declaration on the Granting of Independence to Colonial Countries and Peoples

UNGA Res.3201(S-VI) Declaration on the Establishment of a New International Economic Order 1974

UNGA Res.3281 (XXIX)   Charter of Economic Rights and Duties of States, 1974

Yugoslav Succession Agreement   Agreement on Succession Issues of the Former Socialist Federal Republic of Yugoslavia, 2001

Chronological

1815 Congress of Vienna   General Act of the Congress of Vienna, Paris

1863 Lieber Code   Instructions for the Government of Armies of the United States of America in the Field, General Order No.100

1874 Brussels Declaration   International Declaration concerning the Laws and Customs of War, Brussels

1878 Berlin Congress   Final Act of the Congress of Berlin for Settlement of Affairs in the East

1885 Berlin Conference   General Act of the Berlin Conference respecting the Congo

1887 Dawes Act   General Allotment Act

1899 Hague II   First Hague Peace Conference in 1899, Convention (II) with Respect to the Laws and Customs of War on Land

1907 Hague IV   Convention (IV) Respecting the Laws and Customs of War on Land Second Hague Peace Conference in 1907

1919 Treaty of St-Germain   Treaty of Peace between the Allied and Associated Powers and Austria, St Germain-en-Laye

1919 Treaty of Versailles   Treaty of Peace between the Allied and Associated Powers and Germany

1920 Treaty of Sèvres   Treaty of Peace with Turkey

1920 Treaty of Trianon   Treaty of Peace between the Allied and Associated Powers and Hungary

1932 Resolution   Resolution concerning the Protection of Historical Monuments and Works of Art of the Sixth Committee of the League Assembly

1933 OIM draft   Draft International Convention on the Repatriation of Objects of Artistic, Historical or Scientific Interest which have been Lost or Stolen or Unlawfully Alienated or Exported

1935 PAU Treaty   Treaty on the Protection of Movable Property of Historic Value, Washington

1935 Washington Treaty   Treaty on the Protection of Artistic and Scientific Institutions and Historic Monuments

1936 OIM draft   Draft International Convention for the Protection of National Historic or Artistic Treasures

1937 Cairo Conference Final Act   Final Act of the International Conference on Excavations

1938 OIM draft   International Convention for the Protection of Historic Buildings and Works of Art in Time of War

1939 draft Declaration   Draft Declaration concerning the Protection of Historic Buildings and Works of Art in Time of War (1939)

1939 OIM draft   Draft International Convention for the Protection of National Collections of Art and History

1943 Declaration of London   Declaration of the Allied Nations Against Acts of Dispossession Committed in Territories Under Enemy Occupation or Control

1945 Daes Principles and Guidelines   Principles and Guidelines for the Protection of the Heritage of Indigenous People

1946 Paris Resolution   Resolution on the Subject of Restitution attached to the Final Act and Annex of the Conference on Reparations

1946 Definition   Allied Control Council for Germany

1946 Genocide Resolution   UNGA Resolution on the Crime of Genocide, UNGA Res.96(I)

1948 Genocide Convention   Convention on the Prevention and Punishment of the Crime of Genocide

1954 Hague Convention   Convention for the Protection of Cultural Property in the Event of Armed Conflict

1954 Hague Protocol   Protocol for the Protection of Cultural Property in the Event of Armed Conflict

1956 UNESCO Recommendation   Recommendation on International Principles applicable to Archaeological Excavations

1964 UNESCO Recommendation   UNESCO Recommendation on the Means of Prohibiting and Preventing the Illicit Export, Import and Transfer of Ownership of Cultural Property

1970 Friendly Relations Declaration   Declaration on Principles of International Law concerning Friendly Relations and Co-operation among States in Accordance with the Charter of the United Nations

1970 Treaty of Cooperation between the United States and Mexico   Treaty of Cooperation providing for the Recovery and Return of Stolen Archaeological, Historical and Cultural Properties

1970 UNESCO Convention   UNESCO Convention on the Means of Prohibiting and Preventing the Illicit Export and Transfer of Ownership of Cultural Property

1972 World Heritage Convention   Convention concerning the Protection of the World Cultural and Natural Heritage

1976 Convention of San Salvador   Convention on the Protection of the Archaeological, Historical and Artistic Heritage of the American Nations

1976 UNESCO Recommendation   UNESCO Recommendation Concerning the International Exchange of Cultural Property

1978 Adelaide Conference 'Preserving Indigenous Cultures: A New Role for Museums' Adelaide Seminar recommendations

1983 Vienna Convention Vienna Convention on Succession of States in respect of State Property, Archives and Debts

1993 CAMA policy Council of Australian Museums Association (CAMA) national policy (Previous Possessions, New Obligations)

1993 Draft UN Declaration Draft UN Declaration on the Rights of Indigenous Peoples

1995 UNIDROIT Convention UNIDROIT Convention on Stolen or Illegally Exported Cultural Objects

1999 Second Hague Protocol Second Protocol to the Hague Convention for the Protection of Cultural Property in the Event of Armed Conflict

2001 UNESCO Cultural Diversity Declaration UNESCO Universal Declaration on Cultural Diversity

2002 Draft UNESCO Principles UNESCO Draft Principles relating to Cultural Objects Displaced in relation to the Second World War

INTRODUCTION

Truganini's story must stand . . . for all those that will never be written, but live in the folk memories of the descendants of the victims . . . In recent years however both sides, black and white alike, have become aware increasingly of the continuing colonial crime, the locked cupboard of our history.[1]

On 4 December 1997, the necklace and bracelet of Truganini came back to Tasmania.[2] These cultural objects were the first ever returned to Tasmanian Aboriginals by a museum anywhere in the world. The items were acquired by the Royal Albert Memorial Museum, Exeter in 1905. The museum commenced negotiations for the return with the Tasmanian Aboriginal Centre in 1994 because it was aware the objects had belonged to 'Truganini, a determined survivor of the harsh treatment endured by Tasmania's Aboriginal communities in the 19th century'.[3] For the British collector, the necklace and bracelet no doubt represented a trophy taken from Truganini, the last 'full-blooded' female Tasmanian Aboriginal.[4] For the Tasmanian Aboriginal delegation, the restitution was an assertion of their people's right to self-determination. It was also an opportunity to put asunder the popular belief that the genocidal policies of colonial authorities had been successful in Tasmania.[5]

This book considers the processes of removal and return of the cultural objects from occupied communities during colonisation. These processes are located within the broader contexts of the development of international law, the growth of museums and the altering relations between European and non-European peoples from the nineteenth to the twenty-first centuries. They are examined through the prism of Anglo-American colonialism, which has played an aggressive role in the collection and commercialisation of non-European cultural heritage. It concentrates on the significant influence exercised successively during the last two centuries by British, US and Australian governments and museums upon international law and museum policy concerning the restitution of cultural objects.

---

[1] B. Smith, *1980 Boyer Lectures: The Spectre of Truganini* (Sydney, 1980), p.10.
[2] M. Pos, Cheers ring out as Aboriginal relics find their way home, *The Hobart Mercury*, 5 December 1997, p.3.
[3] J. Legget, *Restitution and Repatriation: Guidelines for Good Practice* (London, 2000), p.19.
[4] R. Brain, *Into the Primitive Environment: Survival on the Edge of our Civilisation* (London, 1972), p.29.
[5] See Memorandum submitted by the Tasmanian Aboriginal Centre Inc., in Seventh Report of Select Committee on Culture, Media and Sport (1999–2000 HC 371), vol.3, Appendix 58.

Rationales for restitution

The return of cultural objects has been a perennial preoccupation of international law and an issue for museums since their establishment. During the last decade, public and academic interest has intensified at the international and national levels with the increased variety of claims. Despite this intensity of interest, there has been little analysis undertaken of the rationales for restitution and their relation to each other.

This book proposes a framework that delineates three rationales for restitution:

First rationale: sacred property – the principle of territoriality and the link between people, land and cultural objects.[6]

Second rationale: righting international wrongs – the reversal or amelioration of discriminatory and genocidal practices.

Third rationale: self-determination and reconciliation – amalgamation of the preceding rationales to enable self-determination and reconciliation.

Each rationale promotes the renegotiation of relations between the claimant community and museums, and redefines the role of museums generally. Furthermore, each type of claim has elicited differing responses from international law and national legal systems. This framework highlights the importance of restitution of cultural objects in ensuring the continued contribution of all peoples to the cultural heritage of all humankind, a significant purpose driving contemporary international initiatives in this area.

The link between people, territory and cultural objects is a recurring connection made in international law since the early nineteenth century. From the Congress of Vienna in 1815 to the mid twentieth century, victorious European Powers sanctioned the restitution of cultural objects to territories restored following the collapse of empires. However, this recognition of the need to return 'spoliations appertaining to those territories' following independence did not extend necessarily to the dismantling of their own empires in the late twentieth century.[7]

The first rationale exposes the connection between physical possession of people, land and cultural objects made by the occupier and the occupied during colonisation. For the occupier, its military and economic strength enabled its museums to possess the cultural objects of all peoples and territories of the empire. For the colonised peoples from whom these objects had been removed, this dispossession of cultural objects signified loss of control of land, resources and identity. Consequently, reclaiming these cultural objects became central to their assertion of autonomy from the metropolitan power. The resultant overlapping and competing interests of multiple communities in the same cultural objects (and territory) necessarily renders this rationale problematic.

---

[6] Hamilton to Elgin, 15 October 1815, cited in A. Smith, Lord Elgin and his Collection (1916) 36 *Journal of Hellenic Studies* 163 at 332.

[7] Note 15, Memoir of Lord Castlereagh [to Allied Ministers], Paris, 11 September 1815, PRO FO 92/26, 115 at 119; *British and Foreign State Papers*, vol.13, 215 at 216; and Parl. Deb., vol.32, ser.1, p.298 (1816).

However, in several ways this rationale was significantly compromised in international law with the ascendancy of the State as its exclusive subject. The principles of State succession, most international instruments sanctioning restitution of cultural objects, and various peace treaties since the First World War, all nominate the State as the subject. As will be explained, experience has shown that indigenous peoples and minorities within and across States cannot necessarily rely on national governments to protect or return their cultural heritage.

The second rationale was prompted by recognition of the harm and violence that a State can perpetrate on its own nationals, occupied peoples and their cultures. During the mid twentieth century, the international community sanctioned the restitution of those cultural objects systematically confiscated by fascist regimes as part of their discriminatory and genocidal campaign against certain groups. The Nazi campaign had been the inevitable endgame of race-based theories, which informed the assimilation policies of metropolitan powers and settler States.

Restitution between and within States became a means of reversing or ameliorating these policies and practices. Allied governments recognised that when perpetrators strove to eliminate people because of their 'race, religion, nationality, [or] ideology', they usually destroyed or removed their cultural manifestations.[8] Restitution of cultural objects to individuals or representatives of the targeted group was one way of addressing the 'eternal silence' created in the collective memory of a nation and humanity by assimilation and genocidal policies.[9] It also facilitated the rehabilitation of these groups and ensured their continued contribution to the cultural heritage of all humankind. This is an early marker of the transition within the international community from policies promoting cultural Darwinism to cultural pluralism.

In the late twentieth century, there was a reawakening to the ongoing dispossession and loss suffered by Holocaust survivors and their heirs. These claims serve to highlight that the beneficiaries of policies of violence and confiscation were not only its immediate instigators but also museums throughout the world. European and North American States and their museums have gradually looked inward at the complex histories of these objects, their collections and their collecting practices to 'right historic wrongs' – and expunge the taint of possessing objects that were removed in such circumstances.[10] Equally, it has led to a growing appreciation that restitution includes 'moral restitution that is accomplished by confronting the past honestly and internalising its lessons'.[11]

The third rationale emerged from the claims pursued by newly independent States and indigenous peoples during the decolonisation period onwards. Their efforts to

---

[8] Military Government for Germany, US Area of Control, Law No.59: Restitution of Identifiable Property, (Law No. 59), Military Government Gazette [Germany, US Zone, Issue G], No.10, November 1947; and (1948) 42(supp.) AJIL 11.

[9] M. Lachs, Address at Thirtieth Anniversary Celebration for the Protection of Cultural Property in the Event of Armed Conflict, 14 May 1984, in UNESCO, *Information on the Implementation of the Convention for the Protection of Cultural Property in the Event of Armed Conflict* (Paris, 1984), p.13.

[10] Department of Culture, Media and Sport, Press Release 84/2000, 13 April 2000.

[11] E. Bronfman to US President, 15 December 2000, in US Presidential Advisory Commission on Holocaust Assets, *Plunder and Restitution: Findings and Recommendations and Staff Report* (Washington DC, 2000).

recover cultural objects stored in metropolitan and national museums are firmly tied to the articulation of the legal right to self-determination and cultural development in international law. Indigenous peoples reject any limitation on their exercise of the right to self-determination. Included in such a right is the return of land, tangible and intangible cultural heritage. They contend that the right to self-determination is not an act, but a process involving the negotiation of political, economic, social and cultural arrangements providing autonomy within and across States.

Indigenous peoples also argue that reconciliation between indigenous and non-indigenous peoples cannot properly take place without moral restitution – the acknowledgement of policies and practices of discrimination, assimilation and genocide and their effects on individuals, peoples and cultures. These claims for restitution of cultural objects incorporate and expand upon elements of the first and second rationales. They confront foundational principles of disciplines and institutions initially established to justify European colonial and commercial expansion; principles gradually internalised and accommodated by successive States during the last two centuries. Indigenous peoples challenge the international community, States and their non-indigenous inhabitants to 'respect' peoples, narratives and laws independent of their own and existing side by side with them. Their claims for restitution of cultural heritage, nationally and internationally, are an essential component in fuelling this process of remembering by the dominant culture and of enabling their own people to exercise self-determination. This rationale has also moved restitution from a physical act of return to a process which is redefining what, why, how and where return occurs.

Parameters

During the late twentieth century, Anglo-American legal scholarship concerning the international protection and restitution of cultural objects was coloured by the ratification and implementation of instruments, like the 1970 Convention on the Means of Prohibiting and Preventing the Illicit Import, Export and Transfer of Ownership of Cultural Property (1970 UNESCO Convention).[12] Consequently, studies have been often framed within the free-trade agenda, with the interests, concerns and arguments of parties broadly divided between 'source' States and 'market' States.[13] Central tenets of this discourse have been undermined by the gradual uptake of the Convention by the major art-importing countries.

In the last few decades, an acknowledgement of and engagement with the restitution claims of indigenous peoples by settler States, like the United States, and former colonial powers, like Britain, has led to a recalibration of the debate. These developments have been reinforced by a re-emergence of the claims of Holocaust survivors and their heirs, and a reaffirmation of these States' role in past restitution and cultural reconstruction efforts. This is a role that various UN bodies like UNESCO have sought to continue throughout the intervening period. These claims

---

[12] Paris, 14 November 1970, in force 24 April 1972, 823 UNTS 231; and (1971) 10 ILM 289.
[13] See J. H. Merryman (ed.), *Thinking about the Elgin Marbles: Critical Essays on Cultural Property, Art and Law* (The Hague, 1999).

have strengthened once again the link between restitution and the right of a group to determine how its culture is preserved and developed; and the importance of ensuring such a right, for the benefit of the cultural heritage of all humankind.

These multifarious claims highlight that the protection and return of cultural objects cannot be confined to a sub-category of international law, despite the rhetoric of the restitution debate during the decolonisation era. Such a strategy served merely to neutralise these claims and ignored the collecting histories of former metropolitan museums and other colonial agents. Rather, as this book illustrates, the issue of restitution of cultural objects has 'converged and diverged' at various times with major areas of the discipline, including State succession, international humanitarian law, State responsibility, human rights and self-determination.[14] Equally, the restitution programmes of the preceding two centuries can not fit neatly into present-day legal categories which have been articulated, and in some cases codified, only in recent years.

Furthermore, I contend that the apparently disparate character of present-day claims should not serve as the basis for their treatment in isolation from each other. Indeed, it is a central contention of the proposed framework of rationales that a thread unites these claims. It is contained in the promotion by the international community of the protection of 'the cultural heritage of all humankind'.

The notion of the 'common heritage of mankind' has been a guiding purpose for the protection of cultural objects and sites in international law. However, three variant, often competing, extrapolations of this phrase have emerged since the early nineteenth century. Each interpretation conveys a distinct agenda for the preservation and development of cultural objects in international law.

The requirement that the international community should honour and protect significant objects and sites for the benefit of the arts, sciences and 'the improvement of the human race' was famously enunciated by French archaeologist Quatremère de Quincy during the pillage of Rome by Napoleonic forces in the late eighteenth century.[15] He based his plea 'not as an inhabitant of this or that nation' but 'as a member of this universal republic of arts and sciences'.[16] Like their forebears, many archaeologists and anthropologists today rail against the destruction and illicit removal of cultural objects from their context because of the damage it does to knowledge and learning.

During the course of the nineteenth century, the collecting frenzy of European empires and their settler States led to the rise of museums within the collective national imagination. By the end of that century, there was a concomitant rise in the protection of museums and their collections during armed conflict in International

---

[14] Personal communication, Vittorio Mainetti, Institut Universitaire de Hautes Etudes Internationales, Geneva, 18 February 2005 (observation concerning protection of cultural heritage in international law generally).

[15] Lettres au général Miranda sur le préjudice qu'occasionneraient aux arts et à la science le déplacement des monuments de l'art de l'Italie (1796), cited in C. de Visscher, International Protection of Works of Art and Historic Monuments, *US Documents and State Papers*, International Information and Cultural Series, No.8, June 1949, Washington, 821 at 824.

[16] Visscher, 'International Protection', 824.

Law. This protection, afforded by the international community, was grounded in their importance to the furtherance of universal learning in the arts and sciences.

From the late nineteenth century, proponents of free trade and equal access to the resources and labour of non-European peoples extended their reach to include their 'cultural resources'. Anglo-American States argued that these territories and resources were the 'common benefit of all mankind' and no group had 'a right to withhold them if they cannot or do not desire to develop them themselves'.[17] This duty became the second arm of the 'sacred trust of civilisation' which governed colonial relations during the late nineteenth and early twentieth centuries.

The notion of cultural objects as the common right of mankind is still advocated by participants in the international art trade. They argue that market forces enable such items to gravitate towards those peoples and institutions best able to ensure their preservation, accessibility and research potential. However, this gravitational pull necessarily ensures their ongoing centralisation in the former metropolitan capitals of Europe and North America, which are the current centres of the international art market.

Following decolonisation, newly independent States seeking the (re)constitution of their national cultural patrimony also defined cultural objects as cultural 'resources'. These States demanded the restitution of cultural objects that had been removed by their former colonial occupiers in order to pursue their national cultural and economic development. These interpretations of the common heritage of humankind as the common right of mankind have influenced international law for the protection and restitution of cultural objects in a manner detrimental to the interests of indigenous peoples and minorities. Indeed, indigenous peoples consider the application of the broader international law concept of 'common heritage of mankind' to their cultural heritage as a surreptitious and renewed form of colonisation.[18]

Nonetheless, indigenous peoples and other groups within and across States advocate a positive role for the international community in the protection, restitution and development of their cultures. It is suggested this role is espoused in the phrase: 'the cultural heritage of all mankind'. In the shadow of the discriminatory and genocidal policies of fascist regimes during the 1930s and 40s, the phrase was reformulated within the Convention for the Protection of Cultural Property in the Event of Armed Conflict (1954 Hague Convention) thus:

> [D]amage to cultural property belonging to any peoples whatsoever means damage to the cultural heritage of all mankind, since each people makes its contribution to the culture of the world.[19]

---

[17] J. A. Hobson, *Towards International Government* (New York, 1915), pp.138–41.

[18] See N. Roht-Arriaza, Of Seeds and Shamans: The Appropriation of Scientific and Technical Knowledge of Indigenous and Local Communities, in B. Ziff and P. Rao (eds.), *Borrowed Power: Essays on Cultural Appropriation* (New Brunswick, 1997), p.255; and J. Blake, On Defining the Cultural Heritage (2000) 49 ICLQ 61 at 69–71.

[19] Second recital, Preamble, Convention for the Protection of Cultural Property in the Event of Armed Conflict, The Hague, 14 May 1954, in force 7 August 1956, 249 UNTS 240.

This preambular recital was not simply the culmination of a century-long effort to codify the protection of cultural objects for the benefit of humanity, in the face of their possible destruction during war. Instead, its eloquent enjoinder flags the renunciation of cultural Darwinism in favour of cultural pluralism. It will be shown that this Convention is grounded firmly in related contemporary initiatives including the post-Second World War Allied restitution policy and programme, the war crimes trials, the Convention on the Prevention and Punishment of the Crime of Genocide (1948 Genocide Convention) and the international human rights framework.

The 1954 Hague Convention aims to ensure the contribution of all peoples and their cultures – not cultural objects and monuments *per se* – for the benefit of all humankind. At the close of the Second World War, the Allied restitution programme reinforced a growing awareness of the need for a people to possess cultural objects of significance to them, in order to ensure their continued contribution to the culture of the world. Indeed, this sentiment is reiterated and elaborated upon by indigenous peoples in the 1993 Draft UN Declaration on the Rights of Indigenous Peoples[20]; and the wider international community in the 2001 UNESCO Universal Declaration on Cultural Diversity.[21] The phrases, 'cultural heritage of all mankind' and 'common heritage of all mankind' are used interchangeably through the book. The latter is not intended to invoke the general principle of international law, but instead, this specific usage is contained in recent multilateral instruments covering cultural heritage.[22]

The clash of understanding cultures and their protection, as encountered by the removal of cultural objects, is further encapsulated in the tensions between the terms 'cultural heritage' and 'cultural property'.[23] The entry of an increasing number of States into the international community in the last half-century has meant that the notion of culture and its modes of expression have also widened in international law. For this reason, the term 'cultural heritage' is able to encompass a wide range of cultural manifestations from the transient, perishable and movable through to the immovable. The term 'cultural property' places emphasis on the property law aspects of cultural expressions. It reaffirms notions of 'resources', 'corporeality', thereby privileging one characteristic of the object often to the detriment of others.

The term 'cultural object' is used throughout this book. Although not value-neutral, it does evoke the primary concern of this study, that is the return of movable physical manifestations of the culture of an occupied people. The ability of a cultural object to be physically possessed and moved gives rise to the central questions of

---

[20] See second and third recitals, Preamble, draft UN Declaration on the Rights of Indigenous Peoples, approved 26 August 1994, UN Doc.E/CN.4/Sub.2/1994/56; and (1995) 34 ILM 541.

[21] Paris, 2 November 2001, UNESCO Doc.31C/44/Rev.2, Annex; (2002) 41 ILM 57.

[22] See M. Frigo, Cultural Property v. Cultural Heritage: A 'Battle of Concepts' in International Law? (2004) 86(854) IRRC 367 at 377.

[23] A. Przyborowska-Klimczak, Les notions de 'biens culturels' et de 'patrimoine culturel mondial' dans le droit international (1989–90) 18 PYIL 51; L. V. Prott and P. J. O'Keefe, 'Cultural Heritage' or 'Cultural Property'? (1992) 1 IJCP 1 307; R. W. Mastalir, A Proposal for Protecting the 'Cultural' and 'Property' Aspects of Cultural Property under International Law (1992–93) 16 FILJ 1033; and R. O'Keefe, The Meaning of 'Cultural Property' under the 1954 Hague Convention (1999) 46 *Netherlands International Law Review* 26.

removal and return. The focus is primarily, though not exclusively, on the material culture of the Asia Pacific region which experienced significant cultural losses during successive waves of European colonialism.

As explained in Part Three, the restitution claims made by indigenous peoples have emphasised the interrelation between return of land, ancestral remains, cultural objects and traditional knowledge. However, the return of skeletal remains and intangible cultural heritage is only discussed when it has bearing on the overall debate concerning the return of cultural objects in general. The repatriation of ancestral remains, in particular, involves an array of historical, political, ethical and theoretical issues which fall outside the scope of this present work.

During the nineteenth century, European colonial and commercial expansion into non-European territories was facilitated by various disciplines including international law and anthropology. These disciplines, and European colonial practices, were rationalised along scientifically sanctioned lines. Central to this rationalisation was the espousal of a unilinear progression of civilisation from the most primitive state to the most advanced (European) culture. The ascendancy of cultural Darwinism saw all peoples and their cultures placed along a trajectory that judged them in relation to Christian, European society – the 'standard of civilisation'. Under the 'sacred trust of civilisation', it became the obligation of metropolitan powers to facilitate the 'development' of non-Europeans in order to attain this 'standard'. It was assumed indigenous peoples would either vanish or be assimilated into this advanced stage of civilisation.

Public museums, especially universal survey museums (or world museums) established in various metropolitan capitals through imperial (economic and military) strength, became crucial to these processes. It has been observed that the 'basis' of such 'great national museum[s]' is 'de-contextualisation'.[24] Cultural objects gathered from every corner of the globe were centralised in museum collections, that is the 'space without place'.[25] Drained of their context, these objects became vessels for the mythologising of the dominant (imperial, national) culture. Central to such mythologising was the (Western) standard of civilisation, and the assumed inevitability of European domination.

Claims made by occupied peoples for the restitution of cultural objects housed in imperial museums are integral to their assertions of political and cultural autonomy and the reversal of the centralising practices of metropolitan powers. The entry of non-European States into the society of nations has gradually whittled away the overt manifestations of the scale of civilisation. However, the principles and practices that fuelled it have been internalised, redefined and perpetuated by these newly independent States. It is my contention that many States replicated, on a smaller scale, the methodologies of their former colonial occupiers by seeking to unify all peoples within their territorial boundaries, and within the boundaries of a national identity. Today, indigenous peoples and minorities within and across States continue

---

[24] R. Anderson, Director of the British Museum, in Seventh Report of Select Committee on Culture, Media and Sport (1999–2000 HC 371), vol.2, Q631–Q632.

[25] L. Althusser, *Montesquieu, Rousseau, Marx* (London, 1972), p.78.

to challenge these forces established for the purpose of (European) colonial and commercial expansion. Essential to their efforts is the re-contextualisation of these objects. And museums have a vital role to play in this process.

From its earliest days, museums were assigned two, often competing, roles: (i) education of the general populace; or, (ii) as a storehouse of unique and authentic objects for the purview of the connoisseur and scholar.[26] By the mid twentieth century, the second role was firmly entrenched amongst most Western museum professionals. In addition, they promoted the conception of museums as recording objectively historic processes, whilst themselves being removed from them: 'time without duration'.[27] However, by the late twentieth century the museum itself became an object of historical and critical analysis.[28] These studies, and the critical re-evaluation of related fields of anthropology, and art history and theory, have fuelled an increasing awareness of the role of these institutions and disciplines in the promotion and representation of race, difference and power within the colonial project.[29]

In the late twentieth century, these re-evaluations were refined and elaborated upon with the restitution claims of newly independent States and indigenous peoples. They have facilitated the undermining of Western perceptions of the alleged passivity of colonised peoples in the face of the arrival of Europeans and have caused reassessment of the place of cross-cultural influencing.[30] These claims, together with those of Holocaust survivors, have revealed the complexity of collecting practices and the life histories of cultural objects.[31] In addition, they have challenged the assumed physical and theoretical boundaries of museums and their purpose. The museum's role of educating the general public is increasingly being emphasised and utilised.

Each of the three parts of this book focus on a specific museum as a case study: the South Kensington Museum (now Victoria and Albert Museum), London; Museum of Modern Art and the Museum of Primitive Art, New York; and the Australian Museum, Sydney. Each institution is representative of a type of collection or museum which embodies the particular period under investigation. Unravelling the layers of meaning in archival material, contemporary texts and recent historical works inscribed in and around their collections offers rich insights into colonialism's culture and the complex role these institutions continue to play in the shifting legal,

---

[26] See D. F. Cameron, The Museum, a Temple or the Forum (1971) 14(1) *Curator* 11.

[27] Althusser, *Montesquieu*, p.78.

[28] See P. Vergo, *The New Museology* (London, 1989); I. Karp and S. Lavine (eds.), *Exhibiting Cultures: The Poetics and Politics of Museum Display* (Washington, 1991); E. Hooper-Greenhill, *Museums and the Shaping of Knowledge* (London, 1992); A. E. Coombes, *Reinventing Africa: Museums, Material Culture and Popular Imagination* (New Haven, 1994); T. Bennett, *The Birth of the Museum: History, Theory, Politics* (London, 1995); and C. Duncan, *Civilising Rituals* (London, 1995).

[29] See G. W. Stocking (ed.), *Objects and Others: Essays on Museums and Material Culture* (Madison, 1985); J. Clifford and G. E. Marcus, *Writing Culture: The Poetics and Politics of Ethnography* (Berkeley CA, 1986); J. Clifford, *The Predicament of Culture: Twentieth-Century Ethnography, Literature and Art* (Cambridge MA, 1988), pp.189ff; S. Hiller, *The Myth of Primitivism: Perspectives on Art* (London, 1991); and K. Biddick *et al.*, Aesthetics, Ethnicity and the History of Art: A Range of Critical Perspectives (1996) 78 *Art Bulletin* 594.

[30] See N. Thomas, *Entangled Objects: Exchange, National Culture and Colonialism in the Pacific* (London, 1991); and N. Thomas, *Colonialism's Culture: Culture, Anthropology, Travel* (Cambridge, 1994).

[31] See I. Kopytoff, The Cultural Biography of Things: Commodification as Process, in A. Appadurai (ed.), *The Social Life of Things: Commodities in Cultural Perspective* (Cambridge, 1986), p.64.

economic and political geography of the early twenty-first century. Two of the three collections, the V&A and MoMA, came into existence during the relevant periods and this study benefits from the historical, political and theoretical concerns driving their establishment. The Australian Museum is chosen as an exemplar of an institution and collection established during a period of intense colonial activity which is endeavouring to reinterpret its role in the present.

International law, and national laws, governing the restitution and protection of cultural objects is informed by, and in turn informs, the work of professionals, policymakers and scholars in numerous fields. To concentrate exclusively on international law pertaining to restitution would be to tell only a fraction of the story. These museum case studies serve to illustrate the intimate role museum professionals play in the development of international law in this area. Equally, the changing relations between museums and the peoples whose material cultures are represented in their collections reveal that colonised peoples are not simply passive objects of scientific study or aesthetic appreciation. Cross-cultural influences have taken place between these communities from the first point of contact until the present day.

A central theme of this work is the physical and theoretical colonisation of non-European peoples by Western colonial powers from the early nineteenth century, and its ongoing manifestations and legacies to the present day. As noted, it concentrates on the impact of the Anglo-American colonial project on the removal and return of cultural objects from the early nineteenth century onwards. This form of colonialism is significant because of the dual purpose that it purported to pursue: unfettered commercial expansion; and the 'civilising mission' to colonised peoples. As will be explained, these aims shaped significantly the fate of cultural objects of colonised peoples and their protection and restitution in international law during the preceding two centuries.

In the last decades of the twentieth century, scholars examined how the colonial relationship dictated by the interests of the imperial power and influenced by colonised peoples infected every knowledge system.[32] The scientific predilections of these knowledge systems, as defined during the nineteenth and early twentieth centuries, were essential to the perpetuation of a scale of civilisation along which all humanity's cultures were ranked. Haunted by ideas of 'sameness' and 'difference' between the colonised and coloniser, this scale was crucial to the European imaginings of non-European peoples.[33]

Imperial powers characteristically sought to centralise possession and control of colonial territories, peoples, resources and their cultural objects within the metropolitan centre. This extended to knowledge systems, formulated or redefined to facilitate European colonialism, which gradually assimilated or excluded competing modes of understanding. The imperial power's knowledge systems were (re)presented as universal and normative. A crucial and insidious component in the perpetuation of

---

[32] See E. Said, *Orientalism: Western Conceptions of the Orient*, (London, 1978); and E. Said, *Culture and Imperialism* (London, 1993).
[33] See M. Foucault, *The Order of Things: An Archaeology of the Human Sciences* (London, 1994); and M. Foucault, *The Archaeology of Knowledge* (London, 1972).

these colonial knowledge systems and methodologies has been their internalisation and replication by the colonised.[34]

The liberation movements from the mid century and the rise of international indigenous activism have fuelled an appreciation of colonialism as being neither one-dimensional nor static. It did not disappear with decolonisation, as evidenced by the latest wave of globalisation. The fate of cultural objects of non-European peoples in former imperial collections is a reminder of the ambivalent but symbiotic relationship between people who fill the roles of colonised and coloniser.

The rise of museums and imperial expansion in Europe from the nineteenth century was accompanied by an intensification of nationalism in collective communal imagining. At the metropolitan centre, nationalism was used to 'sell' the benefits of imperialism to the coloniser's own populace. At the colonial periphery, local leaders exploited it to galvanise liberation movements. Consequently, jockeying nationalisms threatened the integrity of empires. Museums and their collections played an essential role in the representation of each group's claims to nationhood. In the late twentieth century, an exponential number of critical writings on nation and nationalism showed the invention, social engineering and 'imagining' that facilitates the making of nations.[35] The power to suppress, exclude or assimilate narratives is fundamental to national cultures *and* imperialism and is one of the main connections between them.

Events during the 1990s put paid to the long-anticipated demise of nationalism and led to an acknowledgement of and engagement by the international community with the demands of indigenous peoples, minorities, displaced persons, migrants and other non-State groups. The claims of these groups within and across States and the greater mobility of people, information and capital in the twentieth-first century have disrupted existing assumptions of national imagining. However, this has also been utilised by those fuelling nationalist, populist rhetoric. As indigenous peoples and minorities negotiate their place within existing spaces – the international community, States, museums and so forth – they have challenged these physical and theoretical boundaries.

Nonetheless, the persistent influence of particular States on the protection and restitution of cultural objects in international law through the last two centuries cannot be discounted.

Overview

The book is divided into three parts. Each part broadly considers the development of the three rationales for restitution of cultural objects in international law. Furthermore, each component concentrates on the policies and practices of a particular State during a period: (1) Britain from the early nineteenth century to the inter-war

---

[34] See F. Fanon, *The Wretched of the Earth*, trans. C. Farrington (London, 1990), pp.35, 119 and 190; and H. K. Bhabha, *The Location of Culture* (London, 1994).

[35] See B. Anderson, *Imagined Communities: Reflections on the Origin and Spread of Nationalism* (rev. edn, London, 1991); E. Hobsbawm and T. Ranger, *The Invention of Tradition* (Cambridge, 1997); and F. Choay, *The Invention of the Historic Monument* (Cambridge, 2001).

period; (2) the United States from the early twentieth century to decolonisation; and (3) Australia from decolonisation to the present day. Britain and the United States have been chosen because they were the pre-eminent power during the relevant period; whilst Australia serves as an exemplar, one settler State among many including Canada, New Zealand and so forth. The country and museum case studies highlight the ongoing cross-influences from the international level to the local community level and back again.

Part One

The link between peoples, territory and cultural objects was a recurring connection made during the British age of International Law (1815–1919).[36] A practice arose in international law of returning cultural objects to territories restored to peoples following the end of foreign occupation. Part One examines the development during the nineteenth and early twentieth centuries of this first rationale for the restitution of cultural objects.

This period of escalating European colonial and commercial expansion into non-European territories fuelled the emergence of rival modes of possessing cultural objects: as a significant object (or site) or within a collection. For many peoples, the possession of an object or objects *per se* is viewed as integral to a unique collective cultural identity and usually affirms their ties to particular territory. By the early nineteenth century there evolved an alternate mode of possessing cultural objects and a collective cultural identity – the collection housed in public museums. For States and empires, the possession of cultural objects of various peoples within collections was intended to reflect a unified national identity. By their nature, such collections necessarily arose through dispossession and loss exacerbated by economic, social and political upheaval.

Whether occupation occurred within States (internal colonisation) or empires (colonisation proper) the dynamic was similar: the loss of control of land, cultural objects and identity for the occupied; and its possession by the occupier through the centralising and rationalising forces of European colonialism. Whilst the collection of cultural objects of the 'defeated' by a conqueror was not a new phenomenon, their installation within museums accessible to the general public was. In museums, these objects were drained of their original context and the circumstances of their acquisition; only to be filled with the mythologising of the coloniser. The notion of a 'scale of civilisation' was central to the mythologising of Anglo-American colonialism during this period. All peoples and their cultures became one, defined in relation to and subsumed within the occupier's culture.

In Part One, these themes are considered with reference to Britain, British imperialism and their representation at the International Exhibitions and the South Kensington Museum (renamed the Victoria and Albert Museum). Established from the profits and near the site of the Great Exhibition of 1851, the South Kensington Museum came to exemplify the collection of cultural objects and manufactures from

---

[36] W. G. Grewe, *The Epochs of International Law*, trans. and rev. M. Byers (Berlin, 2000), p.xviii.

every corner of the world to enhance British cultural and economic development. Its officials have been ambivalent about their institution's imperial origins and are often unable to resolve its competing missions of public education and as a storehouse of art works.

Chapter 1 considers the sanctioning of the restitution of cultural objects by the British delegation during the Congress of Vienna of 1815. Occurring at the same time as the British parliament approved the purchase of the Elgin collection, these two events throw into stark relief the competing modes of possessing cultural objects by national groups. Chapter 2 highlights how the disparity between these modes escalated in practice, but in theory was silenced within the walls of universal survey museums. These museums served to represent the scale of civilisation during European colonial rivalry that marred the late nineteenth century. Chapter 3 details how this silence was punctured by the ascendancy of nationalism amongst occupied peoples whose restitution claims during the post-First World War period challenged the territorial integrity of empires and imperial museum collections.

Part Two

The destruction or removal of cultural objects viewed as embodying the identity of certain groups was central to the discriminatory and genocidal policies of the Nazi and other fascist regimes during the 1930s and 40s. Equally, the victorious Allied nations affirmed the importance of the restitution of cultural objects to these victims as a means of ameliorating or reversing the effects of such acts. Part Two considers the formulation of this second rationale for the restitution in international law during the mid-twentieth century.

The policies of these regimes stemmed from the race-based theories that had also informed the colonisation of non-European peoples since the nineteenth century. However, by the mid-century, the scale of civilisation that had been espoused by International Law and anthropology was no longer sustainable. The cultural Darwinism which it represented was gradually replaced by the ascendancy of cultural pluralism, and the barbarism visited on particular groups during the Holocaust and the Second World War propelled the international community to acknowledge the contribution of all peoples to the 'cultural heritage of all (hu)mankind'.

Yet, as the twentieth century progressed, whilst the overt structures of colonialism were slowly dismantled, its underlying principles were implicitly reinforced. A stark reminder of this ongoing inequality within the international community was the retention of the cultural objects of formerly colonised peoples by metropolitan powers following decolonisation.

The cultural losses suffered by colonised peoples before and after independence were fuelled by the free-trade agenda of Anglo-American States, and by their promotion of an unfettered international art market. They maintained that the cultural objects of non-European peoples were the common right of mankind – a 'cultural resource' to be exploited and exchanged, like any other commodity. Non-European cultural objects were further de-contextualised with their inclusion in the Western art canon as 'primitive art'. Thus labelled, these objects became a foil to modern art and were mined by artists and museum officials within States who sought to develop an authentic national art movement. This agenda has shaped significantly current international legislation which governs cultural objects in a way that undermines the ability of indigenous peoples, and other non-State groups, to protect and develop their cultural heritage and identity.

In Part Two, these developments are explored with reference to the United States, its relations with Native Americans and its reflection in the work of the Museum of Modern Art and the Museum of Primitive Art, New York, from the inter-war period to the early Cold War years. Opening its doors in 1929, MoMA was driven by the perceived infallibility of capitalism and industrialisation and its goal of 'encouraging and developing the study of modern arts and the application of such arts to manu-facture and practical life'.[37] From its earliest days MoMA, the arbiter of modernism, also promoted the appreciation of cultural objects of non-European peoples, includ-ing indigenous peoples, as 'primitive art' which culminated in the establishment of MoPA.

Chapter 4 will first examine the re-evaluation of indigenous cultural objects as a cultural resource to be exploited by States in the development of a national cultural identity. In addition, the impact of the Anglo-American free-trade agenda on the ill-fated, inter-war convention for the restitution of cultural objects is explained. Chapter 5 then considers these States' implementation of the Allied restitution scheme which strove to restore the link between people and cultural objects severed during the Holocaust and the War, thereby ensuring their contribution to world culture. Chapter 6 for its part details how these lessons were compromised in the post-war period through anxieties fuelled by the Cold War and the decolonisation process. To the present day, the resultant compromises continue to bear down on the rights of indigenous peoples and minorities and their claims for the restitution of cultural objects.

Part Three

From the late twentieth century, the efforts of colonised peoples, including indigen-ous peoples, resulted in the conceptualisation of self-determination as a legal right and process encompassing economic, social and cultural development. The restitu-tion of cultural objects held in former imperial and national museums was crucial to the effective realisation of this right. Restitution, once again, became significant to ensuring cultural diversity and the continuing contribution of all peoples to the cultural heritage of humankind. Part Three examines the formulation of this third rationale for the restitution of cultural objects in international law.

As explained in the preceding Parts, the removal of the link between people, land and cultural heritage was central to colonial policies of discrimination, assimilation and genocide. In addition, adherence to cultural Darwinism had depoliticised and de-historicised the effects of these practices on colonised peoples and their cultures, which were presented as the inevitable result of the 'progression' of civilisation. By

---

[37] A. H. Barr Jr, *Painting and Sculpture in the Museum of Modern Art, 1929–1967* (New York, 1967), p.620.

the late twentieth century, 'this cult of forgetfulness' within the international community, States and museums was being exposed as untenable by indigenous peoples' organisations.[38] The articulation and resolution of claims by indigenous peoples for the restitution of cultural objects housed in metropolitan and national museums was a part of this process of remembering. In turn, 'remembering' and acknowledgement of the ongoing effects of the policies and practices of former colonial powers and settler States became integral to material and moral restitution.

For indigenous peoples, the right to self-determination 'of all peoples' and the attendant right to determine the preservation and development of their cultural identity must entail the restitution of cultural heritage (including land, ancestral remains, cultural objects and knowledge). These claims have led gradually to the reassessment of relations between indigenous peoples, States and museums. However, the ongoing resistance of certain States to indigenous demands betrays the continuing influence of the 'scale of civilisation' despite the dismantling of the overt manifestations of colonialism.

Part Three focuses on the efforts of indigenous peoples, from the 1960s to the present day, to force Australia, a settler State and former regional colonial power, to address these silences, and the need for institutions like the Australian Museum to redefine their role by renegotiating their relations with peoples whose cultures are represented in its collections. Founded in 1827 as a natural history museum, the Australian Museum became a vehicle for the colonial project and its display at the nineteenth-century International Exhibitions, at home and abroad. Its anthropologists became leading proponents of these various phases of indigenous policies, including those of assimilation, of integration and, finally, those of self-determination. Through its Aboriginal Heritage Unit, the Museum now actively supports the right of indigenous peoples to self-determination, to cultural revitalisation and to the restitution of ancestral remains and cultural heritage.

Chapter 7 opens this Part by examining the consistent failure of the international community to effectively address the restitution claims of newly independent States following decolonisation. Chapter 8 then details how during the 1980s indigenous organisations built on the campaign of new States in order to challenge the persisting 'cult of forgetfulness' and to assert their peoples' right to self-determination and redefine their relations with the international community, States and museums. Finally, Chapter 9 explains how these restitution claims of indigenous peoples form an essential part of efforts to renegotiate relations between indigenous and non-indigenous peoples at the international, national and museum levels. At a time of significant flux in international law and international relations since 1989, the restitution claims of indigenous peoples highlight the continuing vulnerability of non-State groups' efforts to determine how their culture is protected, preserved and developed.

Far from resulting in the dissolution of former metropolitan museums, present-day restitution claims have fuelled a richer understanding of these collections, colonial and collecting practices, *and* the cultures and peoples represented by these

---

[38] W. E. H. Stanner, *White Man Got No Dreaming: Essays 1938–1973* (Canberra, 1979), p.214.

cultural objects. The restitution claims of indigenous peoples challenge the international community and respective States to reaffirm and ensure the effective exercise of the right of self-determination and cultural development of all peoples, thereby ensuring their continuing contribution to the common heritage of all humankind.

Finally, a brief note concerning the use of certain terms throughout this book. The term 'indigenous peoples' is used unless groups have indicated a preference for an alternative form. Therefore, in respect of the indigenous peoples of the United States of America, the term 'Native Americans' is used to cover all tribes unless a specific tribe is referred to by name. In respect of the various indigenous communities in Australia and the Torres Strait Islands these are referred to as 'Indigenous Australians' except where a specific community is referred to by name. The words 'return' and 'restitution' are used interchangeably throughout this book unless a more technically appropriate word is applicable or a particular word is current during the period being considered.

Part One

[T]hey said, Go to, let us build us a city, and a tower, whose top may reach unto heaven; and let us make us a name, lest we be scattered abroad upon the face of the whole earth . . .

And the Lord said, Behold, the people is one, and they have all one language; and this they begin to do: and now nothing will be restrained from them, which they have imagined to do.
(Genesis XI, verses 4 and 6, King James Bible)

Figure 1.1 J. R. Smith, *Benjamin West's Joseph Banks*, April 1773.

1

The State and national culture in the early nineteenth century

[U]pon what principle deprive France of her late territorial acquisitions, and preserve to her the spoliations appertaining to those territories, which all modern conquerors have invariably respected, as inseperatable [*sic*] from the country to which they belong?[1]

[T]hese works are considered so sacred a property, that no direct or indirect means are to be allowed for their being conveyed elsewhere than where they came from.[2]

During the Congress of Vienna in 1815, the British delegation advocated the restitution of certain cultural objects to territories following the cessation of French occupation. Their efforts aimed to restore the 'sacred' link between peoples, territories and cultural objects – 'the title deeds of the countries'.[3] The possession, loss and return of cultural objects by nations and their national cultures in nineteenth-century Europe are the subject of this chapter.

Successive waves of political, economic and social revolutions during the century transformed societal relations and peoples' attachment to cultural objects from the sacred to the profane in both European international law and popular consciousness. The rise of the State as nation led to the pursuit of a national cultural identity to reinforce secularised relations between its citizenry. There was concomitant growth in public museums to house national collections of cultural objects designed to define the nation to itself and others. This phenomenon is replicated into the twentieth-first century.

The transformation of the State as nation led to two distinct and increasingly opposing modes of possessing cultural objects by national groups: as unique objects or within public collections. For national groups, the possession of a certain object (or site) was often viewed as central to its collective identity and evoked quasi-religious allusions to reliquary, prehistory and oral tradition. By contrast, the national cultural identity of most States became predicated upon the possession of national collections, which were driven by scientific, artistic or administrative concerns and were

---

[1] Note 15, Memoir of Lord Castlereagh [to Allied Ministers], Paris, 11 September 1815, PRO FO 92/26, 115 at 119; *British and Foreign State Papers* (1816), vol.13, 215 at 216; and Parl. Deb., vol.32, ser.1, p.298, (1816).
[2] Hamilton to Elgin, 15 October 1815, cited in A. Smith, Lord Elgin and his Collection (1916) 36 *Journal of Hellenic Studies* 163 at 332.
[3] Castlereagh to Allied Ministers, PRO FO 92/26, 119.

grounded in the written tradition. States, like empires, strove to centralise the cultural objects of all peoples within their territories in the museum collections of their national capitals, thereby inculcating a unique and unified national identity. Appreciation of how this dynamic formed, transformed and sustained national, cultural identities during the nineteenth century facilitates our understanding of many of the principles and parameters of restitution claims since that period.

This chapter examines how the secularisation of societal relations manifested itself in European international law through early attempts to provide protection to national groups and their cultures within States. It explains how the European powers were motivated during the 1815 Congress of Vienna to return certain cultural objects considered 'sacred' by national groups. Yet, at the same time the purchase of the Parthenon marbles by the British government signalled the notion of cultural objects as 'commodity'. Finally, it is argued that this purchase was part of a general trend, which included the Great Exhibition of 1851 and the establishment of the South Kensington Museum, to define British national identity and aid British cultural and economic development.

Protection of minorities in the nineteenth century

Present-day efforts to secure the return of cultural objects removed during colonisation are based on the assertion of group rights. Group rights in the form of minority protection gathered impetus during the nineteenth century. Early guarantees for groups within a State provided limited protection for their collective identity. The treaty-based protection afforded by the European powers to national and religious groups was grounded in liberal theory and, in a rudimentary form, pre-empted minority protection provided by the post-Second World War human rights framework.

The idea that a minority within a society possesses 'group' rights has been a political and legal concern in the West only for the last two centuries. After successive revolutions in Britain, North America and France, eighteenth-century political theorists strove to address the transfer of sovereignty from the deposed absolute monarchs to the 'nation' made up of individual citizens. Liberal theorists such as Hobbes and Locke focused on the relationship between the individual and State.[4] From Lockean theory emerged the perceived adversarial relationship between the majority and the minority created by the concept of majority rule.

The notion of group rights continued to sorely test the theoretical dynamics of the social contract between the individual and the State. By shifting the basic unit of society from the group to the individual as being the bearer of rights, eighteenth-century thinkers believed that they would effectively eliminate groups as the loci of rights. Some liberal theorists like John Stuart Mill acknowledged that individuals had bonds beyond the State and that there were inherent risks in extreme forms of

---

[4] See J. Locke, *Two Treatises on Government, Of Civil Government* (1690), ed. P. Lastlett (Reprint, Cambridge, 1960); and T. Hobbes, *Leviathan, or The Matter, form or power of common-wealth ecclesiasticall and civill* (London, 1651).

majoritarian democracy.[5] Various mechanisms were proposed to temper or avoid the possible excesses of majoritarian rule.

From at least the sixteenth century, various peace treaties concluded by European States contained provisions requiring sovereigns to guarantee certain fundamental rights to peoples who inhabited ceded territories. The protection of minorities on a supranational level was confined to bilateral treaties and was almost exclusively concerned with religious minorities.[6]

By the early nineteenth century, European States and empires had become vulnerable to the instability caused by the Revolutionary and Napoleonic campaigns, the slow disintegration of the Ottoman empire and the first manifestations of the Industrial Revolution on the continent. These forces eroded many existing communal bonds and gradually led to their reconfiguration along linguistic or ethnic lines. Although ill-disposed to accommodate these emerging communal bonds, the European Powers reinterpreted the established practice of minority protection as one method of curbing ethnic and religious unrest, pacifying demands for autonomy and securing a measure of stability in Europe. Viscount Castlereagh, the British plenipotentiary to the 1815 Congress of Vienna, realised that the stability of the existing order could not be achieved simply by the creation of large territorial agglomerations and the continual imposition of assimilatory practices.[7]

The Congress of Vienna of 1815 marked a shift to multilateral instruments with provisions protecting various minorities including national groups. The embryonic state of nationalism was reflected in the limited protection afforded national minorities generally during this period. The European Powers hoped to neutralise the threat the minority 'problem' posed by articulating treaty protections couched in liberal theory. The Final Act of the Congress in specific and isolated instances aimed to guarantee equal civil and political rights to individual members of national or religious minorities on par with other members of the State to which they had been transferred.[8] However, the guarantees were subject to the principle of State sovereignty and their compatibility with constitutional arrangements of the relevant State.[9]

These guarantees of non-discrimination identified members of the group as individuals who were to be treated as equal participants in these new or existing States. The European Powers fostered the ties the new subject (one is reluctant to say 'citizen') had with her or his State. The nexus of protection lay not in preventing assimilatory or even genocidal practices because of the possible destruction of the

---

[5] See J. S. Mill, *Considerations on Representative Government* (1861), ed. C. Shield (Reprint, New York, 1958), pp.230–31.

[6] See I. L. Claude, *National Minorities: An International Problem*, (Cambridge MA, 1955), pp.6–10; C. A. Macartney, *National States and National Minorities* (1934) (Reprint, New York, 1968), pp.157–78; and P. Thornberry, *International Law and the Rights of Minorities* (Oxford, 1991), pp.25–37.

[7] Castlereagh to Wellington, 25 October 1814, PRO FO 95/522/3 PP 154.

[8] Arts.1 and 77 of the General Act of the Congress of Vienna, Paris, 9 June 1815, *British and Foreign State Papers* (1814–1815), vol.2, p.3; Parl. Papers, vol.17, pp.335, 338 and 362 (1816); and (1815) 64 Parry's CTS 453 at 457 and 481 (1815).

[9] Intervention by the other signatories was the only remedy for non-compliance: L. Oppenheim, *International Law: A Treatise*, ed. H. Lauterpacht (3rd edn, 2 vols., London, 1920), vol.I, p.136. The guarantees proved largely ineffective in protecting minorities: Thornberry, *Minorities*, pp.32–37.

group, but in condemning practices that impeded the individual's relationship with the State. These provisions could not be interpreted as providing positive protection for the preservation and development of the group's collective identity.

Increasing public outcry over the treatment of minorities and the continued drive by the European Powers to achieve a degree of stability on the continent led to the conditional recognition of several States in Central and Eastern Europe during the second half of the century.[10] They were required to notionally embrace certain standards apparently practised by 'civilised' States before they could be accepted into the family of nations. Chapter 2 explains how in European international law entry into the society of nations was proscribed by an overarching conception of a lineal progression of civilisation upon which all cultures were placed in relation to each other. This scale of civilisation was reflected in the application of the minority treaty provisions almost exclusively to Central and Eastern European States.

Conditional recognition articulated in late nineteenth-century treaties contained essential elements which were reflected in later international agreements, that is dual minority protection and free trade guarantees. For example, Article 44 of the Final Act of the Congress of Berlin for Settlement of Affairs in the East (1878 Berlin Congress) recognising Romania provided:

(1) citizens were guaranteed civil and political rights, including individual members of minority groups on the basis of the principle of non-discrimination;
(2) religious freedom was afforded to individual members of minorities; and protection was provided to their collective identity with the guarantees extending to their organisational hierarchy and its leaders; and
(3) the newly independent State was required to ensure 'perfect equality' to the traders of 'all the Powers'.[11]

This highly qualified protection of minorities and their collective identity has survived with oscillating permutations to the present day. In turn, it impacted on international efforts to protect and restore cultural objects and adversely limited the ability of non-State groups to preserve and develop their collective cultural identity.

The rise of national cultural patrimony

Since the nineteenth century, the 'logic of possessive individualism' that defines an individual by the property she or he possesses has been assigned to national groups and nation-states.[12] Within international society, these groups are perceived as 'collective individuals', imagined to be spatially and historically defined, homogenous

---

[10] See Thornberry, *Minorities*, pp.31–32; Claude, *National Minorities*, pp.7–10; Macartney, *National States*, pp.163–175; and J. Crawford, *The Creation of States in International Law* (Oxford, 1979), pp.10–25.

[11] Berlin, 13 July 1878, *British and State Foreign Papers*, vol.69, p.749; Parl. Papers vol.83, p.679 (1878); and (1878) 153 Parry's CTS 170, 172.

[12] See C. P. Macpherson, *The Political Theory of Possessive Individualism: Hobbes to Locke*, (Oxford, 1962); M. J. Radin, Property and Personhood (1982) 34 Stan. LR 957; and R. Handler, Who Owns the Past? History, Cultural Property, and the Logic of Possessive Individualism, in B. Williams (ed.), *The Politics of Culture* (Washington, 1991), pp.63–74.

within and autonomous from other groups. Each national group strives to define itself through the possession of a unique cultural identity that is constituted by its undisputed possession of property. The history of this property was often reinterpreted to align it with the narrative of the group.

This transformation in understanding cultural objects was captured by William R. Hamilton, a member of the British delegation to Paris in 1815. In a letter to Lord Elgin, Hamilton noted that the 1815 Congress of Vienna had 'made Works of Art' a 'matter of possession, of property, not merely of taste'.[13] Furthermore, he recorded that 'all the Sovereigns in Europe' had agreed that the works were 'so sacred a property' that they were to be restored to the places from which they had been removed by the French forces.[14] In effect, Hamilton articulated two often competing ways of perceiving cultural objects: their commercial value as property; and their 'sacred' link to a particular territory and people.

This section examines how Britain was inextricably involved both at home and abroad in ordaining the fate of the 'title deeds' of other nations at the commencement of the British age of International Law. The restitution of specific cultural objects by the General Act of the Congress of Vienna highlighted the relationship between cultural objects and national cultural identity. The purchase of the Parthenon marbles by the British State reflected the increasing importance of museum collections to national cultural identity. These two events during the mid 1810s captured the inevitable clash between these two modes of possession.

Restitution and the 1815 Congress of Vienna
Most jurists up until the late eighteenth century had sanctioned the removal of cultural objects by the victor during belligerent occupation. Nonetheless, there were occasional examples of restitution. By 1815, a new premise was enunciated to denounce the French confiscation of cultural objects from occupied territories and to justify their return upon the territories' liberation following Napoleon's defeat. Restitution would no longer be dictated by the nature of the object (*res sacre*) or the circumstances of its acquisition (*praeda illicita*). The protection of certain cultural objects in peacetime and war was increasingly based on its sacredness in a secular sense to a particular territory and people.

The 1815 Congress of Vienna witnessed the earliest articulation of the first rationale for the restitution of cultural property in modern international law, that is the restoration of the 'sacred' link between people, territory and cultural objects. These events are examined as follows: (1) the pillage of cultural heritage by Revolutionary and Napoleonic forces; (2) negotiations conducted during the 1815 Congress of Vienna; (3) academic reactions to the resultant restitution; and (4) analysis of the implementation of the restitution process.

The confiscation of cultural objects from occupied territories by Revolutionary and Napoleonic forces had much in common with the colonising zeal of the European Powers in non-European territories, both in its systematic execution and in the use

---

[13] Hamilton, in Smith, 'Elgin', 332.   [14] *Ibid.*

of treaties to cede property to the conquering State. As French forces acquired territories, the commissioners, who were usually distinguished scholars, artists and scientists, systematically gathered works of art, scientific specimens and manuscripts. These items were transported to Paris to fill the Louvre, Bibliothèque Nationale and other institutions in Paris and the provinces.

These confiscations were denounced in the occupied territories and in France itself.[15] Following the plunder of Rome, renowned archaeologist Quatremère de Quincy wrote:

> It is as a member of this universal republic of the arts and sciences, and not as an inhabitant of this or that nation, that I shall discuss the concern of all parts in the preservation of the whole. What is this concern? It is a concern for civilisation, for perfecting the means of attaining happiness and pleasure, for the advancement and progress of education and reason: in a word, for the improvement of the human race. Everything that can help toward this end belongs to all peoples; no one of them has the right to appropriate it for itself, or to dispose of it arbitrarily.[16]

He contended that if his fellow citizens wished to renew their interest in antiquity they should not plunder Rome but 'exploit the ruins of Provence . . . [W]hy not restore the beautiful amphitheater at Nimes to house the ancient treasures of this Roman colony?'[17] For de Quincy, the principle of the integrity of artistic heritage *in situ* was paramount and such protection if achieved would benefit all humankind.

The encyclopedic collections of Parisian museums established during this period set the benchmark for the theoretical and concrete construction of similar institutions in other European and North American capitals. They provided enduring justifications for the centralising and universalising mentality, and the collecting practices that fed such museums, including:

(1) it was argued that the acquisition by France of these artistic, literary and scientific works ensured their preservation as part of the European cultural heritage which would otherwise have fallen into disrepair or been destroyed and be lost to future generations.[18]

---

[15] There was violent resistance to French confiscations: E. Müntz, Les annexions de collections d'art ou de bibliothèques et leur rôle dans les relations internationales (1895) 8 RHD 481–483; and R. Chamberlin, *Loot! The Heritage of Plunder* (London, 1983), pp.137ff.

[16] Lettres au général Miranda sur le préjudice qu'occasionneraient aux arts et à la science le déplacement des monuments de l'art de l'Italie (1796), cited in C. de Visscher, International Protection of Works of Art and Historic Monuments, *US Documents and State Papers*, International Information and Cultural Series, No.8, June 1949, Washington, 821 at 824. De Quincy later repudiated the contents of this letter: C. Gould, *Trophy of Conquest, the Musée Napoléon and the Creation of the Louvre* (London, 1965), pp.67–68, 121.

[17] Cited in F. H. Taylor, *The Taste of Angels: A History of Art Collecting from Rameses to Napoleon* (Boston, 1948), pp.543–44.

[18] See Gould, *Trophy*, pp.68–69; W. Treue, *Art Plunder: The Fate of Art in War and Unrest*, trans. B. Creighton (New York, 1961), p.79; and M. L. Turner, Art Confiscations in the French Revolution (1976) 4 *Proceedings of the Annual Meetings of the Western Society for French History* 274.

(2) revolutionary propaganda inculcated the idea of Paris as the beacon of European civilisation and natural home of these great works of art.[19] However, French forces gradually lost any pretence of disseminating revolutionary ideals of freedom and equality and took on the guise of a colonising force. The French Republic then turned to justifying its ambition and its attendant spoliation by alluding to ancient Rome as its imperial precedent.[20]

(3) revolutionary authorities exploited the propaganda potential of these works for the new society they hoped to build. A primary goal was the democratisation of the arts by rendering the collections accessible to the masses and the display of cultural objects from various peoples in one central location: the public museum.[21] As a visible demonstration to the populace that their sacrifices had not been for nought, the confiscated cultural objects were deposited in the Louvre only after they were triumphantly paraded from the Jardin des Plantes to the Champ de Mars.[22]

For the next two centuries, museum practitioners and government officials, resisting restitution claims for the cultural objects housed by metropolitan museums, reiterated these justifications with earnest consistency.

Following Napoleon's defeat, the Allied sovereigns directed their minds to the fate of works of art, manuscripts and archives plundered by the French armies.[23] The 1815 Congress of Vienna was the first significant effort at the European level to redistribute and restore cultural objects following the redrawing of territorial boundaries to attain some semblance of equilibrium on the continent. Castlereagh acknowledged the difficulties of achieving 'moral reconciliation' between the former occupier and newly liberated territories whilst confiscated cultural objects remain in French museums.[24] The restitution of specific cultural objects to the place 'from where they came from' was condoned to restore peace and stability to Europe by placating resentment precipitated by French plunder and not to legitimise national claims to them.[25]

The British delegation to Vienna initially gave little support to restitution claims, fearing the dismantling of national collections would hinder the reconciliation of the French people with their new sovereign.[26] Indeed, the British delegation was at pains to distance itself from allegations of being motivated by a desire to build up collections at home or acquiring items by right of conquest.[27] Nonetheless, the French fervently believed British motives were designed to denude the Louvre to embellish the British

---

[19] Villette and Hubert to Directory, n.d., cited in D. Mackay Quynn, The Art Confiscations of the Napoleonic Wars (1945) 50 AHR 437 at 439.

[20] See Visscher, 'International Protection', 824; and E. Müntz, Les Annexions de collections d'art ou de bibliothèques et leur rôle dans les relations internationales (1895) 9 RHD 375 at 377.

[21] See Taylor, *Taste*, pp.535–41; and Treue, *Art Plunder*, p.199.

[22] See Mackay Quynn, 'Art Confiscations', 439.

[23] See Treue, *Art Plunder*, pp.186–99; Gould, *Trophy*, pp.116–30; and Mackay Quynn, 'Art Confiscations', 447ff.

[24] Note 15, Castlereagh to the Allied Ministers, Parl. Deb., vol.32, ser.1, col.300 (1816).

[25] Hamilton, in Smith, 'Elgin', 332.   [26] See Treue, *Art Plunder*, p.188.

[27] See Despatch No.50, Castlereagh to 'My Lord' (Liverpool), 11 September 1815, PRO FO 92/26, 111ff.

Museum's collections.[28] Increasingly for many States, the national museum and its collections reflected the nation's conception of itself and its possessions. The escalating rivalry for the acquisition of objects for these national collections mirrored that for colonial territories.

Earlier, the French delegates had tried to have a provision inserted in the Convention of Paris of 3 July 1815 to guarantee the integrity of museums and libraries. The Allied Sovereigns and their representatives firmly rejected this proposition, arguing that it was simply a mechanism to retrospectively legalise the confiscations and thereby stifle any restitution claims.[29] However, the integrity of national collections would become a formidable consideration in the formulation of international measures for the protection and restitution of cultural objects from the late nineteenth century onwards.

By mid-1815, there was broad agreement that the French confiscations of cultural objects were contrary to contemporary rules of law and that objects could not remain in Parisian collections. Yet, there was little consensus as to what was to be done with them.[30] Castlereagh surmised only two grounds upon which the Allies could justify the return of cultural property: conquest or restitution.[31] 'Conquest' was rejected for a number of reasons. Castlereagh argued that by claiming such objects as booty, the Allies would be sanctioning a practice for which they had condemned France. Also, it would confer 'so bad and odious a title' upon the original possessors of the property. Finally, if claimed as booty then all the Allies, 'great and small', would have shared equally in the prize leading to 'division' and 'endless reclamations', thereby throwing the alliance into disarray.[32]

Castlereagh was left with the 'principle of restitution' which he readily conceded to the British Prime Minister was ill-defined and wide in application.[33] However, this was the only conceivable interpretation that could 'reconcile Policy with Justice' and promote 'conciliation and peace'.[34] By sanctioning the restitution claims, the British delegation adopted an overarching principle which stressed the territorial link between the cultural object and its place of origin – 'inseperatable [*sic*] from the country to which they belong'.[35] This is the embodiment of what I refer to as the first rationale for the restitution of cultural objects.

Crafting a 'European' settlement following Napoleon's defeat, the Allied Sovereigns sought the return of cultural objects to the European collections from which they had been removed rather than to their places of origin. This interpretation of 'the place of origin' explains several restitution outcomes following the

---

[28] See Denon to Talleyrand, 16 September 1815, cited in Mackay Quynn, 'Art Confiscations', 451; and A. Robertson to his family, 20 September 1815, cited in Taylor, *Taste*, p.575.

[29] Dispatch from Wellington to Castlereagh, 23 September 1815, PRO FO 92/28, 112–14; and Parl. Deb., vol.32, ser.1, coll.304–305 (1816).

[30] A. Alison, *Lives of Lord Castlereagh and Sir Charles Stewart the Second and Third Marquesses of Londonderry. With annals of contemporary events in which they bore a part from the original papers of the family* (3 vols., Edinburgh, 1861), vol.II, p.87.

[31] Castlereagh to Liverpool, PRO FO 92/26, 112.   [32] *Ibid.*   [33] *Ibid.*

[34] Castlereagh to Liverpool, PRO FO 92/26, 113; and Castlereagh to Allied Ministers, PRO FO 92/26, 124.

[35] Castlereagh to Allied Ministers, PRO FO 92/26, 119.

1815 Congress of Vienna. Perhaps the most celebrated anomaly was the return of St Mark's (Corinthian) horses to Venice. Although the Venetian Republic lost its autonomy to Austria, the sculpture was not returned to the Austrian capital but to the 'place of origin': Venice.[36] However, Venice was not their place of origin. They were examples of still earlier episodes of plunder and embodied the difficulties inherent in the restitution of cultural objects with complex histories.[37]

During the 1815 Congress of Vienna there was little or no recognition of the scale and effect of confiscations by Napoleonic forces on communities outside Europe. Indeed, newly emergent principles for protection and return of cultural objects were not applied to such cultural objects. This exclusion of non-European peoples from the application and protection of (European) International Law is discussed in Chapter 2.

There was little agreement amongst nineteenth-century jurists of the precedent set by the returns completed pursuant to the 1815 Congress of Vienna. Most jurists agreed that International Law relating to war did not sanction the removal of State papers, public archives, or juridical and legal records by the victorious party.[38] Such objects were judged to be essentially private property and their removal or destruction was designed to 'exasperate an Enemy Nation' by inflicting harm on civilian populations and hampering the effective administration of the State.[39]

There was no such consensus for public libraries, museums and collections of works of art largely because such institutions were still in their infancy. On balance, jurists agreed that the wanton destruction of cultural objects violated the 'modern usage of war'.[40] Nonetheless, there was no agreement that such works could not be removed as booty.[41] There were subsequent examples of restitution of archives and artworks based on the integrity of collections with a reaffirmation of the need for a territorial link.[42] In 1863, Travers Twiss referring to Castlereagh's 1815 Memoir opined that such transfers are void *ab initio* and all cultural objects removed by the occupier must be returned.[43] For Twiss, whether the war was unjust or just was irrelevant because such objects and collections were immune during war. Further,

---

[36] See Taylor, *Taste*, p.557; Treue, *Art Plunder*, p.198; and Gould, *Trophy*, p.123.

[37] See Chamberlin, *Loot!*, p.140.

[38] See H. W. Halleck, *Elements of International Law and Law of War* (Philadelphia, 1866), pp.453–55; and T. J. Lawrence, *The Principles of International Law* (London, 1895), pp.396ff.

[39] See T. Twiss, *The Law of Nations considered as Independent Political Communities on the Rights and Duties of Nations in Time of War* (Oxford, 1863), pp.128–29; H. Wheaton, *Elements of International Law*, ed. R. H. Dana Jr (8th edn, London, 1866), §347, n.5; S. Baker Bart, *Halleck's International Law or Rules Regulating the Intercourse of States in Peace and War* (London, 1878), p.103. This principle was applied to the Papal archives in 1815: E. Müntz, Les invasions de 1814–1815 et la spoliation de nos musées (1897) 105 *Nouvelle Revue* 706–07; and Mackay Quynn, 'Art Confiscations', 446.

[40] W. E. Hall, *A Treatise on International Law* (4th edn, Oxford, 1895), Pt.3, pp.438–39. See Lawrence, *Principles*, pp.197–98, 370.

[41] See Twiss, *Law of Nations*, p.129; J. L. Klüber, *Droit des gens modernes de l'Europe*, (Paris, 1874), §§253, 263, pp.362, 379; and M. de Vattel, *Le droit des gens, ou principes de la loi naturell, appliqués à la conduite et aux affaires des nations et des souverains* (1758) (Reprint, Washington DC, 1916), vol.II, p.139.

[42] Art.18 of the Treaty of Peace between Austria-Hungary and Italy, Vienna, 3 October 1866, *British and Foreign State Papers*, vol.56, p.700; and (1866) 133 Parry's CTS 209 at 215. See Visscher, 'International Protection', 829; and S. E. Nahlik, La protection internationale des biens culturels en cas de conflit armé (1967-I) 120 RCADI 62 at 87.

[43] Twiss, *Law of Nations*, p.131.

they were sacred not because of their religious affiliation but because of their value to arts and sciences of all humankind. The objects became secular reliquary which transcended national boundaries.

In later campaigns, Napoleon took the innovative step of requiring that the art works and manuscripts be ceded by treaty to give his confiscations a veil of legality.[44] Castlereagh refused to distinguish those objects removed pursuant to treaties during the restitution deliberations.[45] However, some contemporaries and jurists did find the distinction significant. British parliamentarian Samuel Romilly mused: 'It was said that these monuments of art were the fruits of unjust war; but were they not also the subject of various treaties, by which they were formally conceded to France?'[46] The argument that the cultural objects were legitimately obtained in accordance with the laws applicable at the time of acquisition has been reiterated by holding institutions through to the present day. What is usually not acknowledged is the inequality of the bargaining power of the parties to the treaty and that the laws in question were those imposed by the holding party. Scant regard was usually paid to the laws or customs of the originating community at the time of removal.

The opinion of US jurists did not necessarily accord with that of their British counterparts on this subject. Henry Wheaton did not pronounce an opinion but quoted Romilly, thereby tacitly indicating a measure of disapproval.[47] Halleck argued that 'we think the impartial judge must conclude, either that such works of Art [in the Louvre] are legitimate trophies of war, or, that the conduct of the allied powers in 1815 was in direct violation of the Laws of Nations'.[48]

Ironically, a British Court of Prize in 1813 found in favour of US interests using reasoning which mirrored de Quincy's words (and which would later be espoused by Castlereagh).[49] A collection of Italian paintings and prints had been captured by a British vessel during the war of 1812, on their passage from Italy to the United States. Alexander Croke ordered the objects to be restored to the Academy of Arts in Philadelphia because they were not the property of a particular State but 'the *property of mankind at large* . . . and that the restitution of such property to the claimants would be in conformity with the Law of Nations, as practised by all civilised countries'.[50]

Were the restitutions sanctioned by the treaty effected? Although some returns did eventuate, for various reasons the bulk of objects confiscated by the French forces

---

[44] See P. Pradier-Fodéré, *Traité de droit international public européen et américain* (9 vols., Paris, 1885–1906), vol.VII, pp.978–96.

[45] Castlereagh to Allied Ministers, PRO FO 92/26, 119.

[46] Parl. Deb., vol.32, ser.1, coll.759–760 (1816).

[47] Wheaton, *Elements*, §§346–47, pp.352–53, 356. Wheaton's position (§351, p.446) could be coloured by the bombardment of Washington by the British forces in 1814. He extracts remarks made by James Mackintosh in the House of Commons: Parl. Deb., vol.30, ser.1, coll.526–27(1814).

[48] Baker Bart, *Halleck*, §9, pp.453ff.

[49] See Twiss, *Law of Nations*, vol.II, §68, 132; and J. B. Moore, *A Digest of International Law* (8 vols., Washington, 1906), vol.VII, §1197, p.460.

[50] *The Marquis de Somerueles* case, *Stewart's Vice-Admiralty Reports*, 21 April 1813, 482 (Vice-Adm. Ct N. S. 1813) (emphasis added).

were not returned to the places from which they had been removed.[51] The 1815 Congress of Vienna did not (nor could it) restore Europe to its pre-Napoleonic past.

By the time the Allied forces descended on the Louvre, the demise of the encyclopedic collections of Paris was bemoaned by the French and the very people instrumental in instigating the returns.[52] The restitution process inflamed the French populace for whom the objects had been successfully incorporated into the public imagination and the national identity.[53] The Louvre and other collections of artistic, literary and scientific objects had been the envy of Europe for several decades because of their sheer volume and excellence.[54] The visible nature of withdrawal of the cultural objects from Paris and the reaction of the citizenry to this process naturally overshadowed the volume of objects that remained in France.[55]

Political, economic and social upheaval caused by Napoleonic conquest throughout Europe and the subsequent dismantling of the empire resulted in an exponential increase in the international antiquities and art market.[56] Although initially reticent, the English assumed the role of Europe's most enthusiastic collectors, taking full advantage of the purchasing and general collecting opportunities afforded them during this period.[57] The British Prime Minister impressed on Castlereagh that '[t]he Prince Regent [was] desirous of getting some of [the statues and pictures] for a Museum or gallery here'.[58] According to Hamilton, 'publicly' Britain could not directly negotiate the acquisition of cultural objects in French collections. However, this position 'render[ed] it the more indispensable that [Britain] should purchase (private)'.[59] To purchase was condoned but to plunder was condemned, even though both opportunities were afforded by the same circumstances: civil unrest and foreign occupation. The lack of probity of this position was little scrutinised and continues to be held in certain quarters today.

Thus great private collections were assembled in England in the early nineteenth century.[60] Also during this period, momentum gathered to render these collections more accessible to the general public. This movement towards public education occupies the remainder of this chapter: first, with the purchase of the Elgin collection on behalf of the British nation; and then, with consideration of the foundation of a museum in London which was driven by a reformist liberal agenda.

---

[51] See Mackay Quynn, 'Art Confiscations', 456; Taylor, *Taste*, pp.588–89; and Gould, *Trophy*, pp.116ff.
[52] See Dispatch (not numbered), Castlereagh to Liverpool, Paris, 21 September 1815, PRO FO 92/28, 5ff.
[53] See Anon., Considerations in the form of a letter intended to be submitted to the King of France, Paris, 1 September 1815, PRO FO 92/28, 119 at 121–22; and Taylor, *Taste*, pp.585–86.
[54] See E. Meissner, *Notes from a Doctor's Diary* (1819), cited in Treue, *Art Plunder*, p.176.
[55] For example, more than half of the objects removed from Italy remained in France: see M.-L. Blumer, Catalogue des peintures transportées d'Italie en France de 1796 à 1814, in *Bulletin de la société de l'histoire de l'art française* (Paris, 1936); and Gould, *Trophy*, p.128.
[56] See Mackay Quynn, 'Art Confiscations', 460; and Treue, *Art Plunder*, pp.180–86.
[57] See Treue, *Art Plunder*, pp.180–86; and B. B. Fredericksen (ed.), *The Index of Paintings Sold in the British Isles during the Nineteenth Century* (4 vols., Los Angeles, 1988–95).
[58] Cited in C. Vane (ed.), *Correspondences, Despatches and Other Papers of Viscount Castlereagh, Second Marquess of Londonderry* (12 vols., London, 1853), vol.X, p.453.
[59] Hamilton in Smith, 'Elgin', 322. See Parl. Deb., vol.34, ser.1, col.1027 (1816), Bankes.
[60] See Treue, *Art Plunder*, pp.180ff.

The Parthenon marbles, Greece and the British Museum

While the British delegation was sanctioning the return of cultural objects during the 1815 Congress of Vienna, British parliamentarians were considering the legitimacy of title to a collection acquired from another people subject to foreign occupation. In the current debate concerning the return of cultural objects there has been a recurring centrality and obsession by some commentators, politicians and museum professionals with Elgin and the Parthenon marbles.[61]

The Elgin debate involves a claim by Greece not against its former occupier but a third-party State, namely Britain. Many cultural objects removed during colonisation were not taken or purchased by the museums of the colonial power but by third-party States. The reach of these collectors broadened during the latter half of the nineteenth and early twentieth centuries with emerging interest in 'primitive' cultures by various disciplines including anthropology and fine arts institutions.

The Elgin debate is significant in respect of objects removed during colonisation for several reasons. First, it highlights the transformation of cultural objects to 'matter[s] of possession, of *property*, not merely taste' which thereby increases their commercial value as Hamilton informed Elgin in 1815.[62] Second, the dispute over title raises issues about the responsibility of a State to protect the cultural heritage of a minority or indigenous group within its borders. Thirdly, it focuses on the responsibility of a third-party State in respect of the importation of cultural objects removed from an occupied territory.

The 'acquisition' of the Parthenon marbles by Elgin is examined briefly, with a summary of the primary arguments raised before the Select Committee of Inquiry and House of Commons, concerning the purchase of the collection by the British State. Then, the current position of the British government and the British Museum to Greek restitution claims is noted.

Following his appointment as the British ambassador to the Court of the Sublime Porte in Constantinople in 1799, Lord Elgin obtained permission to have drawings and casts made of the Parthenon. The work was carried out mainly under the direction of his secretary, William R. Hamilton. English artists and collectors had encountered difficulties in accessing Italian sites during the Napoleonic occupation.[63] Consequently, their antiquarian efforts were redirected towards Greece which had opened up following Britain's increased sway in the Ottoman empire following its routing of French forces from Egypt.[64] Elgin, appreciating a corresponding elevation of influence at the Ottoman Court, sought broader authority for work being undertaken at his behest in Athens.

There had been public discontent in London about Elgin's activities in respect of the Parthenon whilst the work was under way and this escalated upon his return to Britain in 1806.[65] In June 1815, financial difficulties forced Elgin to present a

---

[61] See Chamberlin, *Loot!*, pp.8ff.   [62] Hamilton, in Smith, 'Elgin', 322 (emphasis added).
[63] See Treue, *Art Plunder*, pp.122ff; and Chamberlin, *Loot!*, pp.13–68.
[64] See A. Michaelis, *Ancient Marbles in Great Britain*, trans. C. A. M. Fennell (Cambridge, 1882), pp.129–30.
[65] See Michaelis, *Ancient*, pp.138–39.

petition to the House of Commons proposing that the State consider the purchase of his collection for the nation.[66] Elgin re-presented his petition to the Commons in February 1816 and a Select Committee was appointed to 'enquire whether it be expedient that the collection should be purchased on behalf of the public'.[67]

The 1816 Select Committee Inquiry report (Bankes report) found that neither the Turkish government nor the Greek populace resisted the removal of the marbles and had not actively conserved the monument. Further, the Committee determined that Elgin obtained the necessary authorisation for the removal because of his ambassadorial posting. Finally, it recommended the purchase of the collection by the State 'to improve . . . national taste for the Fine Arts'.[68] The Bankes report was debated in the House of Commons on 7 June 1816 during which Elgin's collection was finally accepted for purchase with public monies and transfer to the Trustees of the British Museum.[69]

Those who advocated the British government's purchase of the Elgin collection of Parthenon marbles did so on the following grounds. First, in his letter to the government, Elgin highlighted two significant potentialities of the collection for the British State: commodity value and its didactic value.[70] There was manifest fear in certain artistic and political circles that should the British government not agree to the purchase the collection might pass to France, her colonial and commercial rival.[71] Where France fostered the development of her public museums for the purpose of Revolutionary propaganda, the British had more utilitarian and commercial concerns.[72] The Bankes report likened the possible effects of the Parthenon sculptures to those ignited by rediscovered classical antiquities during the Italian Renaissance.[73] In effect, the collection would fuel British national economic and cultural development.

Second, one of the earliest and most enduring arguments in support of the British purchase was the salvage mentality, that is that Elgin's actions saved the marbles from pillage and almost certain destruction.[74] One parliamentarian professed reluctance that 'these sacred relics should be taken from that consecrated spot', but observed they 'were lying in their own country in a course of destruction' and national sensitivities had to be sacrificed for a higher purpose.[75]

Finally, Britain, like Napoleonic France, was not reticent in projecting its imperial ambitions through a universal survey museum befitting an imperial capital of an ever-expanding colonial empire. It conceded that the marbles removed from the

---

[66] Memorandum on the subject of the Earl of Elgin's Pursuits in Greece (1810), cited in Smith, 'Elgin', 294ff; and Michaelis, *Ancient*, pp.141–42.

[67] Parl. Deb., vol.32, ser.1, coll.823–828 (1816); and Smith, 'Elgin', 334ff. Negotiations had been suspended because of the Battle of Waterloo.

[68] Report from the House of Commons Select Committee on the Earl of Elgin's Collection, 25 March 1816, reproduced in J. Greenfield, *The Return of Cultural Treasures* (Cambridge, 1989), Appendix 2, p.437 [Report of Committee]; and Smith, 'Elgin', 341.

[69] Parl. Deb., vol.34, ser.1, coll.1027–1040 (1816). [70] Cited in Smith, 'Elgin', 324–325.

[71] Parl. Deb., vol.34, ser.1, coll.1027–1029 (1816). [72] Greenfield, Report of Committee, p.438.

[73] Greenfield, Report of Committee, p.439.

[74] Greenfield, Report of Committee, p.436, Hamilton; Michaelis, *Ancient*, pp.134, 136; and Smith, 'Elgin', 336–37.

[75] Parl. Deb., vol.34, ser.1, coll.1030–1033 (1816), Ward.

Parthenon formed part of the cultural heritage of all humankind. However, there was a presumption amongst many British parliamentarians that the legacy most naturally fell to the British nation because it more fully appreciated its potential and had the ability to preserve it for future generations.[76] If Greek claims for return were later to be characterised as nationalist, there can be little doubt that the British position was equally imbued with a sense of national pride and identity formation.

Those who took up the Greek cause for return similarly expounded several grounds against the purchase by Britain. First, the legitimacy of Elgin's title has plagued the British Museum's claim since 1816. British authorities queried whether appropriate permission was granted to Elgin; and, if so, whether he acquired the collection in the course of his employment as British ambassador, thus making it the property of the British government. Despite Elgin's protestations, the Bankes report found that he receive the necessary authorisation (*firmaun*) because of his diplomatic post.[77] Proponents of the purchase maintained that even if the work went beyond the terms of the *firmaun*, this defect was cured by the acquiescent behaviour of the Ottoman authorities and Athenians.[78] By contrast, a member of the Commons stated that he had visited Athens in 1795 and found the Greeks were clear in their intention that the marbles remain *in situ*.[79]

Second, it is generally agreed that the practice of the European Powers in their relations with the Sublime Porte meant that his sovereignty over this area was recognised and he had power to dispose of the sculptures as he saw fit.[80] However, did the Sublime Porte owe a duty to the peoples within his territories to protect and keep *in situ* their cultural heritage? Significantly, the European Powers purported to impose provisions on the Ottoman empire to protect minorities.[81] Yet, instead of protecting the cultural and religious heritage of minorities within the Ottoman empire, these States and their nationals took advantage of the unrest and resultant economic and political upheaval to reap antiquities for their private and public collections.

Third, opponents of the purchase contended that the marbles formed part of the cultural heritage of humankind and the modern Greek State was the true beneficiary of the work.[82] It was argued that the collection be held by Britain only in trust for Greece and it must upon demand undertake 'without question or negociation, to restore them, as far as can be effected, to the places from whence they were taken'.[83]

Finally, de Quincy's words were invoked when it was argued that the marbles formed part of the Acropolis and could only properly be understood in that context.[84]

---

[76] Greenfield, Report of Committee, p.453; and Parl. Deb., vol.34, ser.1, coll.1033–34 (1816), Croker.

[77] Parl. Deb., vol.32, ser.1, coll.823–28 (1816), and vol.34, ser.1, coll.1027–29 (1816).

[78] See Smith, 'Elgin', 336–37.   [79] See Smith, 'Elgin', 339.

[80] See J. Greenfield, *The Return of Cultural Treasures* (2nd edn, Cambridge, 1995), pp.77–78; and J. H. Merryman, Thinking of the Elgin Marbles (1985) 83 Mich. LR 1880 at 1892. Cf. D. N. Osman, Occupiers' Title to Cultural Property: Nineteenth Century Removal of Egyptian Artifacts (1999) 37 CJTL 969.

[81] See Thornberry, *Minorities*, pp.25–37.

[82] See C. Hitchens (ed.), *The Elgin Marbles: Should they be Returned to Greece?* (London, 1997), p.51.

[83] Parl. Deb., vol.34, ser.1, coll.1031–33 (1816), Hammersley.

[84] See Visscher, 'International Protection', 824; S. Seferiades, La question du repatriement des 'Marbres d'Elgin' considérée plus spécialement au point de vue de droit des gens (1932) 3 RDI (Paris) 52 at 73–74; and Hitchens, *Elgin Marbles*, pp.16, 50.

One parliamentarian suggested that Britain was bound to educate others about the importance of retaining the integrity of the work *in situ* because 'such works always appeared best in the places to which they were originally fitted'.[85] In 2004, the US Senate concurred with this argument when it called on the United Kingdom to return the marbles.[86] The current British government has stated that there is no legal, or 'morally or culturally . . . convincing case' for the return of the Parthenon marbles to Greece.[87] It has refused to introduce legislation enabling the British Museum to return the marbles.[88]

Similarly, universal survey museums have vigorously resisted claims for the reconstitution of cultural objects with their original site. British Museum officials argued in 1940: 'The principle of tying works of art to their places of origin is not recognised by Western Nations'.[89] In 2000, the trustees of the British Museum reaffirmed their resistance to establishing a precedent for the 'piecemeal dismemberment of collections which recognise no arbitrary boundaries of time or place'.[90] Its position was endorsed by the directors of major museums in Europe and the United States, in late 2002, who reasserted the importance of 'universal museums' that 'serve not just citizens of one nation but the people of every nation'.[91]

The mid nineteenth century saw the establishment of one of these universal survey museums: the South Kensington Museum.

Great exhibitions, South Kensington Museum and the creation of national identity

On 21 March 1850, Prince Albert delivered a speech at the Mansion House, London in which he identified himself for the first time with the Great Exhibition of 1851 and his hope that it would exemplify the unbounded potential of the age:

> Nobody who has paid any attention to the peculiar feature of our present era, will doubt for a moment that we are living at a period of most powerful transition which tends rapidly to accomplish the great end, to which, all history points – the realisation of the unity of mankind. Not unity which breaks down the limits and levels the peculiar characteristics of the different nations of the earth, but rather a unity, the result and product of those very national varieties and antagonistic qualities.
>
> Whilst formerly the greatest mental energies strove at universal knowledge, and that knowledge, was confined to few, now they are directed on specialities, and these again, even to the minutest points; but the knowledge acquired becomes at once the property of the community at large . . . The

---

[85] Parl. Deb., vol.34, ser.1, coll.1037–38 (1816), Best.

[86] US Congress, Senate, S. Con. Res.134, 108th Cong., 2nd sess. (2004).

[87] Seventh Report of Select Committee on Culture, Media and Sport (1999–2000 HC 371), vol.1, paras.148–152; and *Hansard*, HC, vol.412, coll.410–414, 29 October 2003, Morris.

[88] UNESCO Doc.CLT-2005/CONF.202/2, para.1.

[89] Cited in Greenfield, *Cultural Treasures* (2nd edn), p.66.

[90] Statement by the Trustees of the British Museum, Media Release, April 2000.

[91] International Group of Organisers of Large-Scale Exhibitions, Declaration on the Importance and Value of Universal Museums, Munich, October 2002 (2001) 57 *ICOM News* 4.

THE HAPPY FAMILY IN HYDE PARK.

Figure 1.2 John Tenniel, 'The Happy Family in Hyde Park', *Punch*, 19 July 1851.

products of all quarters of the globe are placed at our disposal, and we have only to choose which is the best and the cheapest for our purposes, and the powers of production are entrusted to stimulus of competition and capital.[92]

The words of the Prince Consort foreshadowed two competing themes that have been of recurring significance in international measures to protect and return cultural objects: cultural diversity and free trade.

This final section focuses on the first international exhibition held in London in 1851 and the consequential foundation of the South Kensington Museum (now known as the Victoria and Albert Museum). These events illustrate that Britain, like other European States during the early to mid nineteenth century, struggled to define its national cultural identity. First, it explains how a crisis of national self-confidence in parts of British society led to the Great Exhibition of 1851. And there is a discussion of the interplay between nationalism and internationalism at the international exhibitions from 1851 to the 1870s. Third, analysis is undertaken of early legislative efforts to protect British national heritage. In conclusion, the evolution of the mission of the South Kensington Museum and how the building of a collection of other peoples' cultural objects was partly triggered by the search for British national identity is considered.

Great Exhibition of 1851: nationalism v. internationalism

The Great Exhibition of 1851 was conceived as a result of growing concern among commentators, academics and bureaucrats that British manufacturing and design was inferior and desperately lagging behind that of continental Europe and the United States.[93] Although Britain had by the mid nineteenth century become the world's leading industrialised power, there was a lack of uniformity of development and distribution of its benefits.

The 1835 Report of the House of Commons Select Committee on Arts and Manufactures concluded that British products had dominated overseas markets but the Napoleonic Wars impeded their export.[94] It recommended Britain follow the example of continental Europe by establishing schools of design to educate British artists and artisans and that public taste for well-designed British products be stimulated by mounting industrial exhibitions. In his evidence before the Select Committee Gustav Waagen, the director of Berlin's Altes Museum, related a museum's educational role of improving manufacturing standards to providing 'people [with] an opportunity of seeing the most beautiful objects of art in the particular branch which they follow'.[95] Also, to encourage this exercise in judgement, Waagen argued 'the second mode of distributing knowledge among the people would be by means of public exhibitions'.[96] The Select Committee report and particularly Waagen's

---

[92] *The Times*, 22 March 1851.

[93] See P. Berlyn, *A Popular Narrative of the Origin, History, Progress and Prospects of the Great Industrial Exhibition 1851* (London, 1851), pp.7 and 12.

[94] Report of the Select Committee of Arts and Manufactures Report together with Minutes of Evidence and Appendices (1835–36 HC 1) [Select Committee]; and Second Report of the Select Committee on Arts and their Connexion with Manufacture (1836 HC), pp.ix, viii [Second Report].

[95] Select Committee, paras.81–82.   [96] Select Committee, paras.46, 81–2.

evidence provided the impetus for 'attitudinal change' that Henry Cole, the first director of the South Kensington Museum, would later exploit.[97]

In respect of the first arm of the Select Committee's recommendations, when the 1851 Great Exhibition was in its planning stages it was decided for the first time to invite all nations to take part in 'friendly competition'.[98] A primary motivator for this decision was economic and reflected Britain's efforts to seek greater access to world markets.[99] Cole spoke of the advantages that would accrue to British industry from competition with other nations and the direct benefits to London of foreign buyers and tourists visiting the metropolis.[100] The minutes of the Planning Committee reveal the organisers' struggle to balance their personal beliefs in Benthamite internationalism with the realisation that the exhibition would need to be promoted in more nationalistic and commercially beneficial terms.[101]

The Great Exhibition fostered the contradictory impulses of national competition and international cooperation. The impact of these forces was heightened because the international exhibitions were the first events where people and objects from all parts of the world were located in a single site.[102]

The overarching theme for the organisers of the Great Exhibition was pacifist internationalism.[103] It was viewed as a palliative scheme designed to address the growing popular discontent arising from the dislocation caused by industrialisation, resistance to legislative reform pertaining to free trade, and the economic downturn of the 1840s. A month prior to the opening, the *Chronicle* reported:

> The politician finds in Hyde Park a stronger bond of international
> union . . . The arid formulations of Vattel and Grotius are superseded by the
> living influences and the more substantial maxims of international reciprocity,
> and we can at length hail the exchange of a mutual chart of moral obligations,
> the value of which all communities can feel in that *common property of
> mankind* – the guaranteed liberties of unrestricted commerce.[104]

To a considerable degree, the organisers were successful in promulgating their vision of the exhibition as both a product of and cause for peace.[105] One organiser Alfred

[97] M. Goodwin, Objects, Belief and Power in Mid-Victorian England – The Origins of the Victoria and Albert Museum, in S. Pearce (ed.), *New Research in Museum Studies no.1: Objects of Knowledge*, (London, 1990) p.37.

[98] See J. A. Auerbach, *The Great Exhibition of 1851: A Nation on Display* (New Haven, 1999), p.22.

[99] P. Greenhalgh, *Ephemeral Vistas: The Expositions Universelles, Great Exhibitions and the World's Fairs 1851–1931* (Manchester, 1988), pp.10–11.

[100] *The Times*,18 October 1849; and H. Cole, Henry Cole Diaries 1848–, NAL VAA 55.CC, 29 June 1849.

[101] See C. Babbage, *The Exposition of 1851; or, the View of the Industry, the Science and the Government of England* (2nd edn, 1851) (Reprint, Farnborough, 1969), pp.41–43; Auerbach, *Great Exhibition*, p.24; and Y. Ffrench, *The Great Exhibition, 1851* (London, 1950), pp.35–37.

[102] *Chronicle*, 7 December 1850, in W. Dilke, Great Exhibition 1851. Extracts from Newspapers, 3 vols., vol.1, NAL, EX.1851.110.

[103] Cited in Auerbach, *Great Exhibition*, p.161.

[104] *Chronicle*, 7 May 1851, in Dilke, 'Newspapers', vol.2, NAL, EX.1851.111 (emphasis added).

[105] See Anon., *A Guide to the Great Exhibition; containing a description of every principal object of interest* (London, 1851), pp.11–12; and J. Tallis, *Tallis's History and Description of the Crystal Palace, and the Exhibition of the World's Industry in 1851* (3 vols., London, 1852), vol.III, p.110.

Cobden maintained the exhibition would 'break down the barriers that have separated the people of different nations and witness one universal republic; the year 1851 will be a memorable one indeed; it will witness a triumph of industry instead of a triumph of arms'.[106] Its promoters argued that the exhibition would ensure peace by reducing the potential for conflict by constructing new avenues in which nations could compete with each other and by encouraging economic, cultural and scientific ties among them.

Cobden's internationalist mission for the Great Exhibition was grounded in the philosophy of the Manchester School. The School staunchly advocated free trade and drew on the teachings of Jeremy Bentham, especially his essay 'Plan for a Universal and Perpetual Peace', in his *Principles of International Law*.[107] Bentham's plan was reflected in Henry Cole's lecture to the Royal Society of Arts 'On the International Results of the Exhibition of 1851' in which he claimed the event would lead to various practical measures which would unify humanity.[108]

Yet from their earliest origins, these exhibitions were imbued with the sense of being a continuation of war in a different setting and hence bore an extremely nationalistic character.[109] This taint was evident from the first industrial exhibition held in France in 1797, when six weeks after the display of spoils from the Italian campaigns on the Champ de Mars, a 'Temple of Industry' was erected to celebrate French produce, industry and manufacturing.[110] Prizes were awarded to those manufacturers who inflicted the most damage to English industry.[111] Tellingly, British manufacturers were vehemently opposed to the plans for the Great Exhibition until the project acquired nationalist overtones and patent reforms were guaranteed.

In the turmoil of the first industrial age, nationalism became a prominent vehicle used by governments to ensure unity among their citizens.[112] The generation of pride, the psychological naturalisation of politically determined geographic boundaries and the consolidation of different racial groups into single national units were all accomplished through relentless programmes of nationalist propaganda. The layout of the Crystal Palace, where the exhibition was located, carefully compartmentalised and choreographed Britain's relations to other States.[113] International exhibitions became a popular medium for such programmes, as was evidenced by their global proliferation.[114]

---

[106] Cited in J. Crockford, *The Journal of the Great Exhibition of 1851: Its Origins, History and Progress* (London, 1851), p.57.

[107] Jeremy Bentham, *The Works of Jeremy Bentham, published under the superintendence of his executor John Bowring*, ed. J. Bowring (11 vols., Edinburgh, 1843), vol.II, p.559.

[108] See Cole, 'Diaries', 16 September 1851, and 29 December 1861.

[109] See Auerbach, *Great Exhibition*, pp.165ff.

[110] See Berlyn, *Popular Narrative*, pp.37–38; and Greenhalgh, *Ephemeral*, p.3.

[111] See R. Brain (ed.), *Going to the Fair: Readings on the Culture of the Nineteenth-Century Exhibitions* (Cambridge, 1993), pp.22–23.

[112] See Greenhalgh, *Ephemeral*, pp.112ff.

[113] See M. Berman, *All that is Solid Melts into Air: The Experience of Modernity* (New York, 1988), pp.235–48.

[114] See Greenhalgh, *Ephemeral*, pp.112–41; and J. M. Mackenzie, *Propaganda and Empire: The Manipulation of British Public Opinion 1880–1960* (Manchester, 1984).

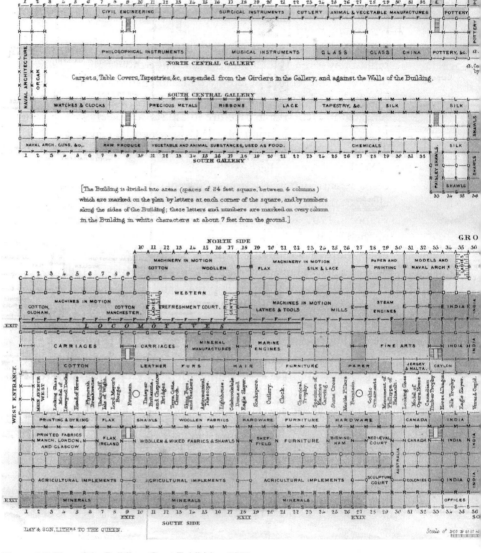

Figure 1.3 Plan of the Building. Great Exhibition 1851.

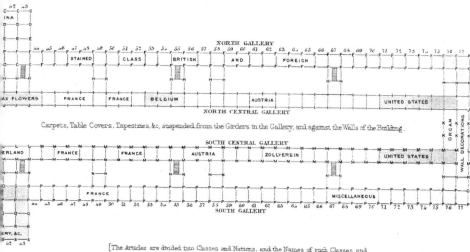

Carpets, Table Covers, Tapestries, &c. suspended from the Girders in the Gallery, and against the Walls of the Building.

[The Articles are divided into Classes and Nations, and the Names of such Classes and Nations are given on the Plan, and marked upon the iron girders of the Building.]

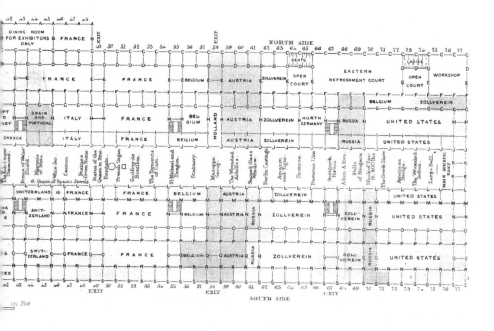

The Great Exhibitions, from 1851 to the mid 1870s, provided an opportunity for British writers and politicians to assert and reaffirm those elements they considered intrinsic to British national identity. Revolution had forced the French into national self-consciousness at an earlier date. By contrast, English nationalism as propaganda at the international exhibitions grew in inverse proportion to the decline of British colonial power. Yet, in several quarters there was a rejection of industrialisation and questioning of the very idea of progress espoused by Prince Albert in his Mansion House address. The dislocation and disruptions visited on communities by industrialisation fuelled a rise in various forms of traditionalism which pined for an imagined and idyllic past.[115] Exhibition organisers and participants were similarly motivated both by their antipathy to industrialisation and its effects on craftsmanship, as well as by their celebration of its potential.

These anomalies were replicated in institutional collecting practices in Britain where there was a willingness to gather the objects of other cultures but there was a marked trepidation in collecting and protecting local objects and sites.[116] These conflicting trends manifested themselves in the collecting practices of the South Kensington Museum and early legislative efforts to protect cultural 'property' such as the Lubbock bill.

Ancient Monuments Protection Act

In February 1873, John Lubbock introduced into the House of Commons a Bill to Provide for the Preservation of Ancient National Monuments (Lubbock bill).[117] The bill marked a significant movement in the preservation of monuments perceived as central to the British national identity. Although largely confined to monuments and sites, the ensuing parliamentary and general public deliberations and the emergent theoretical basis are equally applicable to movable cultural property. In terms reminiscent of the Elgin debate, Lubbock described the bill as a measure to impede the loss in Britain of Roman and prehistoric antiquities that were being dismantled for housing developments.[118] Resistance to Lubbock's legislative proposal was so strong that the Act was not passed until 1882 and only following significant amendments to the original bill.[119]

---

[115] See Auerbach, *Great Exhibition*, pp.170ff.

[116] See C. Saumarez Smith, National Consciousness, National Heritage and the Idea of 'Englishness', in M. Baker and B. Richardson (eds), *A Grand Design. The Art of the Victoria and Albert Museum* (London, 1999), p.275.

[117] See G. Baldwin Brown, *The Care of Ancient Monuments, An Account of the Legislative and Other Measures Adopted in European Countries for Protecting Ancient Monuments and Objects and Scenes of Natural Beauty, and for Preserving the Aspect of Historical Cities* (Cambridge, 1905), pp.152–54; C. Chippindale, The Making of the First Ancient Monuments Act, 1882, and its Administration under General Pitt-Rivers (1983) 86 *Journal of the British Archaeological Association* 1; and J. L. Sax, Is Anyone Minding Stonehenge? The Origins of Cultural Property Protection in England (1990) 78 Cal. LR 1543 at 1546.

[118] See Parl. Deb., vol.218, ser.3, col.576 (1874); vol.232, ser.3, col.1557 (1875); and vol.266, ser.3, col.885 (1882); and J. Lubbock, *Addresses, Political and Educational* (London, 1879), pp.163–66.

[119] Ancient Monuments Protection Act 1882, 45 & 46 Vict., ch.73.

There had been little legal rationale for heritage preservation legislation in common law jurisdictions prior to the Lubbock bill.[120] The bill heralded two major shifts in Anglo-American property law: first, that the protection of certain cultural property was a governmental duty; further, public ownership rights would be invoked to preserve such property even if privately owned. Parliamentary opponents vehemently resisted any erosion of private property rights.[121] Lubbock and other parliamentary proponents perceptively redirected the debate towards the bill's aim of 'no right to destruction' of monuments like Stonehenge.[122] This redefinition rendered it difficult for opponents to assert that the bill was unnecessary without exhibiting indifference to the increasing disappearance of such monuments.[123] It was not the bill's intention to acquire full public possession and control of cultural properties.[124] Instead, government would only intervene if an owner's actions were detrimental to the public interest in the property.

What was the nature of the public's interest in these cultural objects that formed the subject of the Lubbock bill? The bill implicitly ordained two distinct elements in the property. The owner retained the economic or use value in their property and when this element was taken away, she or he was entitled to full compensation.[125] However, it also recognised the monument had another element: its historic and scientific value that belonged to the nation. The nation as a collective had a pre-existing interest in certain property that had previously been considered exclusively as private property.

This conception of the dual nature of cultural heritage did not originate with Lubbock.[126] Indeed, he had invoked John Ruskin's words in parliament: 'They are not ours. They belong partly to those who built them, and partly to all the generations of mankind who are to follow us . . . [W]e have no right to obliterate . . . It belongs to all their successors.'[127] Ruskin in turn has borrowed the notion of intergenerational interest in cultural heritage from Frenchman, Abbé Grégoire. Preservation of such monuments and objects was viewed as integral to the conceptualisation of a British national cultural identity. Yet, British culture was increasingly promoted as superior to that of other (non-European) cultures along a linear progression of civilisation.[128] This view of British national cultural identity would find its expression in the collections of the newly established South Kensington Museum.

---

[120] See W. J. Davies, The Preservation of Ancient Monuments (1913) 20 JRIBA 533 at 543–44; P. J. O'Keefe and L. V. Prott, *Law and the Cultural Heritage, Volume 1: Discovery and Excavations* (London, 1984), pp.31–84; and D. Lowenthal, *The Past is a Foreign Country* (New York, 1985), pp.96–105.

[121] Parl. Deb., vol.223, ser.3, col.900 (1875), Harcourt.

[122] Parl. Deb., vol.223, ser.3, coll.901–02 (1875), Stanhope; vol.223, ser.3, coll.899–900 (1875); and vol.232, ser.3, coll.1542–43 (1877).

[123] Parl. Deb., vol.232, ser.3, col.1550 (1877), Morgan.

[124] See Lubbock, *Addresses, Political and Educational* (London, 1879) p.164.

[125] Parl. Deb., vol.223, ser.3, col.911 (1875), Dalrymple.

[126] See J. L. Sax, Heritage Preservation as a Public Duty: The Abbé Grégoire and the Origins of an Idea (1990) 88 Mich. LR 1142 at 1559; and Brown, *Ancient Monuments*, pp.73ff.

[127] Parl. Deb., vol.237, ser.3, col.1979 (1878).

[128] See Brown, *Ancient Monuments*, p.3; and T. Murray, The History, Philosophy and Sociology of Archaeology: The Case of the Ancient Monuments Protection Act (1882), in V. Pinsky *et al.*, *Critical Traditions in Contemporary Archaeology: Essays in the Philosophy, History and Socio-politics of Archaeology* (Cambridge, 1989), p.60.

Early years of the South Kensington Museum

By the 1830s, Britain had become susceptible to the continental push driving governments to make art accessible to the general public and not just to a privileged and cultivated minority.[129] If the international exhibitions were the realisation of one arm of the recommendations of the 1835 Select Committee report to improve public taste, and British design and manufacturing, the establishment of the South Kensington Museum and its adjoining school was the other arm.

When the South Kensington Museum opened in 1852, public education was a tacitly accepted but rarely stated goal of many museums.[130] By contrast, South Kensington began as a school and was readily identified as part of a broader movement to expand public education.[131] For its first director Henry Cole, the museum was not a repository for historic relics, but a way of changing people's taste by education and instruction.[132] In his first report to the House of Commons in 1854, Cole wrote:

> A museum may be a passive, dormant institution, an encyclopedia . . . or it may be an active, teaching institution, officiously useful and suggestive. The latter has emphatically been the status of this Museum from its origin.[133]

The continued resistance of the British Museum to general public access was contrasted with the South Kensington Museum where the working man was encouraged to come.[134] Cole campaigned tirelessly to achieve accessibility through such groundbreaking measures as free entry, extended hours, public lectures, guided tours and the art library.[135] Within a decade, South Kensington with its commercially driven mission aligned with public education became the most imitated and influential museum of the late nineteenth century.[136]

Following Waagen's lead, Cole promoted the reformative power of the unique and the beautiful.[137] He expanded the scope of the collections as he slowly articulated the museum's responsibility to represent the range of artistic expression encompassed by the growing British empire.[138] In essence, he suggested that the physical possession

---

[129] J. Miniham, *The Nationalization of Culture: The Development of State Subsidies to the Arts in Great Britain* (London, 1977), pp.87ff.

[130] Exhibition of the Works of Industry of All Nations 1851, *Reports by the Jurists on the Subjects in the Thirty Classes into which the Exhibitions were Divided, Presentation copy* (London, 1852), pp.691ff.

[131] A. Burton, *Vision and Accident: The Story of the Victoria and Albert Museum* (London, 1999), pp.26ff.

[132] See H. Cole, Public Galleries and Irresponsible Boards (January 1866) 251 *The Edinburgh Review* 69; Burton, *Vision*, pp.57ff and 74ff; and E. Bonython and A. Burton, *The Great Exhibitor: The Life and Work of Henry Cole* (London, 2003).

[133] *First Report of the Department of Science and Art, presented to both Houses of Parliament by command of Her Majesty* (London, 1854), Appendix G, p.228.

[134] See H. Cole, On the National Importance of Local Museums of Science and Art, *Journal of the Society of the Arts* (23 January 1874), 167–71.

[135] Burton, *Vision*, pp.74ff; and E. Bonython, *King Cole: A Picture Portrait of Sir Henry Cole, KCB 1808–1882* (London, 1982), p.14.

[136] M. Conforti, The Idealist Enterprise and the Applied Arts, in M. Baker and B. Richardson (eds.), *A Grand Design*, p.23, pp.37ff; and S. Conn, *Museums and American Intellectual Life, 1876–1926* (Chicago, 1998), p.196.

[137] See Burton, *Vision*, pp.72ff.

[138] See H. Cole, Speech at Missionary Exhibition, Manchester, on the 'Art of Savage Nations and People considered Uncivilised', *Journal of the Society of Arts* (21 January 1870) 183.

of exemplary cultural objects was a source of national wealth.[139] The origins of Britain's antiquarianism lay in the compulsion among its ruling classes to gather the material manifestations of other peoples and their cultures to reflect British imperial power.[140] This antiquarian urge is typified by the collecting practices of the museum's first curator, Charles Robinson.[141]

In the nineteenth century, collecting in most European countries was fuelled by a nationalist longing to return to the purity of folk traditions disappearing through industrialisation.[142] By contrast, Britain in the mid nineteenth century, with its strong economy and distant colonial outposts, thought more internationally.[143] Imperialism was a significant motivator for the establishment of the South Kensington Museum. The pattern of early collecting demonstrated a willingness to go on predatory expeditions, buying up works of art from other parts of the world while ignoring equivalent British cultural objects.[144] The museum's representatives travelled throughout Europe and Asia gathering items for its collections. Indeed, their collective practices were so comprehensive that Charles Yriarte noted: 'South Kensington is a mecca. England there possesses the entire art of Europe and the East, their spiritual manifestations under all forms.'[145]

The establishment of British national collections necessarily came at the cost of the removal of significant cultural objects from other national groups. Just like the Revolutionary and Napoleonic expeditions in Europe, the Middle East and North Africa had been instrumental to the creation of French collections like the Louvre. South Kensington officials were aware of escalating criticism of British museums for their acquisition of the cultural objects of other nations.[146] However, their collecting forays would increase exponentially over the ensuing decades in the pursuit of their mission of aiding British industry and representing the British empire.

Yet, in the early nineteenth century, at the same moment that British leaders were acknowledging the need to return the 'title deeds of countries', they were affirming the value of cultural objects as property and for the development of British national identity and industry. These twin forces – the 'sacred' and 'property' value of cultural objects – the promotion of cultural diversity and free trade, are perennially competing themes in successive international efforts for the protection and restitution of cultural heritage to the present day.

The next chapter examines how these forces intensified with the dissipation of the mid-century optimism for the realisation of a common humanity and perpetual

---

[139] See R. Cardoso Denis, Teaching by Example: Education and the Formation of South Kensington's Museums, in Baker and Richardson (eds.), *Grand Design*, pp.107ff.

[140] See Burton, *Vision*, pp.10ff.

[141] J. C. Robinson, Our National Art Collections and Provincial Art Museums, *Nineteenth Century* (June 1880) 988; and H. Davies, J. C. Robinson's Work at the South Kensington Museum, Part I and Part II (1998) 10 JHC 169; and 11 (1999), 95.

[142] See Murray, 'History, Philosophy'.

[143] See F. G. Kenyon, *Museums & National Life, The Romanes Lecture* (Oxford, 1927), p.9.

[144] See C. Saumarez Smith, 'National Consciousness', pp.275ff; and A. E. Coombes, Ethnography and the Formation of National and Cultural Identities, in S. Hiller (ed.), *The Myth of Primitivism: Perspectives on Art* (London, 1991), p.205.

[145] Cited in Conforti, 'Idealist Enterprise', p.33.

[146] J. C. Robinson, 'Preface', in *Notice of Works of Medieval and Renaissance Sculpture, Decorative Furniture &c., acquired in Italy, in the Early Part of the Year 1859* (London, 1860). See H. de Triqueti, The Italian Sculpture at the South Kensington Museum (1863) 1 *Fine Art Quarterly Review* 100.

peace. Instead, as the nineteenth century drew to a close, the cultural objects of non-European peoples became central to disciplines devised and modified to fuel European colonial and commercial expansion. British imperialism became the foundation of British national identity and the collections of institutions like the South Kensington Museum and British Museum played a crucial role in the projection of that national identity.

Figure 2.1 Plates from the *Catalogue of the Collection of Relics of the Late Captain James Cook RN, FRS, exhibited by Mr J. Mackrell at the Colonial and Indian Exhibition 1886.*

2

International Law, international exhibitions in the late nineteenth century

> The Indian collection is unlike any other in the world, and was made under conditions that render it impossible that any such collection can be made in the future . . . No ordinary visitor can leave the collection without carrying away some idea of the conditions under which India was won and held by great Englishmen.[1]

> What do I think of Western civilisation? I think it would be a very good idea. (Mahatma Gandhi)

As the nineteenth century progressed, the centralising drive of British imperialism strove to bring all territories and resources within its purview and possession. These very peoples, objects and places towards which the universalising character of colonialism was compelled, challenged existing European knowledge systems. Tolerance of diverse societies and cultures was replaced by cultural Darwinism, which was designed to justify and facilitate European colonial and commercial expansion. The 'scale of civilisation' formulated to promote the colonisation of non-European peoples and the removal of their cultural objects is the focus of this chapter.[2]

The preceding chapter examined the establishment of museums in various European capitals to house national collections designed to imbue the general populace with a sense of national cultural identity. During the late nineteenth century, many of these collections became repositories for the 'title deeds' of non-European peoples and their territories. For colonial powers, the removal of these cultural objects from the colonised communities to their museums symbolically reflected the transfer of sovereignty – the severance of the 'sacred' link between people, territory and cultural objects. For the populace of the metropolitan State, the display of these cultural objects at international exhibitions and national museums represented the possession of an empire and an imperial national identity.

The centralising tendencies of British museums moved beyond the physical possession of empire to a theoretical justification of it. The arrangement of the cultural objects of all peoples in relation to each other, in order to display a unilinear progression of human societal development served to propagate the idea of a scale of civilisation, that is the 'evolution' of civilisation from 'primitive' cultures to the 'advanced'

---

[1] W. Boyd Dawkins, Letter to the Editor, *Morning Post*, 4 July 1908, V&A Archives: India Museum: general, 1908–1909.

[2] S. McCalmont Hill, The Growth and Development of International Law in Africa (1900) 63 LQR 249 at 268.

(Western European) culture, with all cultures being placed along this trajectory. As International Law and museums became sites for the reformulation of relations between European and non-European peoples, they absorbed and promoted this scale of civilisation to legitimise the colonisation of non-European peoples. Both sites are fundamental to current claims by indigenous and other colonised peoples for the restitution of cultural objects. Both sites continue to struggle with the legacies of this foundational period of their histories.

This chapter details how the scale of civilisation was incorporated into International Law with its universalisation and rationalisation as a science in the late nineteenth century. Then, it explains how the possession of empire and the idea of a unilinear progression of civilisation were given three-dimensional form at the international exhibitions and South Kensington Museum. Finally, the effects of these forces on the fate of the cultural objects of 'conquered' non-Europeans is illustrated with reference to the codification of the rules of war and the display of the 'spoils of war' in British national museums.

Colonised peoples and International Law in the nineteenth century

As the Law of Nations was reformulated into International Law, and moved from naturalism to positivism, it became the science of International Law preoccupied with the commercial and colonial ambitions of European States.[3] Ironically, as International Law proclaimed its universal application it emphasised the rigidity and exclusivity of its membership. Its systematic exclusion of non-European peoples was driven in large part by the desire to control their territory and resources. The cultural objects of these communities became essential to the theories that justified colonial practices.

Whilst natural law jurists strove to include indigenous peoples within the Law of Nations, from the nineteenth century the universalisation and rationalisation of (European) International Law by positivists resulted in their exclusion from its operation. Instead, indigenous, and other colonised, peoples were confined to 'international morality'. This exclusion necessarily compromised the rights of these communities to preserve and develop their cultures. Indeed, this dichotomy between moral and legal rights and obligations remains in varying shades to date.

Spanish jurists Francisco de Vitoria and Bartolomé de las Casas, working within the natural law tradition, strove to reconcile the place of indigenous peoples, these 'exotic anomalies', within the Law of Nations during the Spanish colonisation of the Americas in the sixteenth century.[4] During the Valladolid disputation, colonists and their advocates maintained that because of their 'barbarity' evidenced by their

---

[3] A cursory look at the table of contents of the leading contemporary British texts reflects this preoccupation. See T. Twiss, *The Law of Nations considered as Independent Political Communities on the Rights and Duties of Nations in Time of Peace* (Oxford, 1861), four of twelve chapters; J. Westlake, *Chapters on the Principles of International Law* (Cambridge, 1894), three of eleven chapters; and W. E. Hall, *A Treatise on International Law* (4th edn, Oxford, 1895), Part II, Chapter 1, §26*, §26**, Chapter 2, §33*, §38*, §38**.

[4] B. Smith, *Imagining the Pacific in the Wake of the Cook Voyages* (Carlton, 1992), p.223.

cultural practices including idolatry, Indians were 'natural slaves'.[5] By contrast, Las Casas argued against the need for European tutorship of indigenous peoples and suggested the colonists' arguments were merely a device to hide their 'tyranny and injustices' perpetrated against these communities.[6] He advocated the acknowledgement of the essential humanity of all peoples, including indigenous peoples.

Vitoria postulated that the 'New World' of the Americas was an extension of the Old World and the rights afforded to its indigenous peoples should be determined by considering the legal position of the Europeans in similar circumstances.[7] His teachings served to deprive all States, including Spain, from simply taking indigenous territories and resources. However, Vitoria tempered his position by stating that indigenous peoples could lose their rights through conquest following a 'just' war fought if they resisted Christian conversion or hindered free trade. Following the Enlightenment, the Spanish jurists' theories fell into disuse as those more accommodating of colonial practices gained greater acceptance in European international law. However, Vitoria's qualification would be used to justify assimilation and free trade policies of European and settler States.

These early attempts to encompass indigenous peoples of the Americas within the Law of Nations were abandoned by Anglo-American jurists who categorically excluded these communities from the operation of International Law. The exclusion occurred with the transformation of European international law into the science of International Law. It was furthered with the privileging of the State as a subject and an understanding of a linear progression of civilisation. This scale of civilisation was reinforced with the articulation of the trusteeship doctrine.

The analysis of European colonial claims by sixteenth-century Spanish jurists involved an interplay between law and morality.[8] In Britain, this dichotomy became particularly pronounced in International Law with the writings of Jeremy Bentham and John Austin. Their work propelled the reformulation of the Law of Nations into a science, whose methodology reflected a newfound 'rationality'.[9] As a consequence, one after another, nineteenth- and early twentieth-century publicists felt obliged to show that their discipline dealt with the law and not morality.[10]

---

[5] Cited in G. C. Marks, Indigenous Peoples in International Law: The Significance of Francisco de Vitoria and Bartolomé de las Casas (1992) 13 AYIL 1 at 22.

[6] Cited in L. Hanke, *All Mankind is One: A Study of the Disputation between Bartolomé de las Casas and Juan Gines de Sepúlveda in 1550 on the Intellectual and Religious Capacity of the American Indians* (DeKalb, 1974), p.157.

[7] See F. de Vitoria, *De Indies et de jure belli relectiones*, (ed.) E. Nys (Washington DC, 1917); and J. Brown Scott (ed.), *The Spanish Origins of International Law: Lectures* (Washington, DC, 1928), pp.22 and 41.

[8] See J. S. Anaya, *Indigenous Peoples in International Law* (New York, 1996), p.23; and D. Kennedy, Primitive Legal Scholarship (1986) 27 HILJ 1 at 13–23.

[9] See W. G. Grewe, *The Epochs of International Law*, trans. and rev. M. Byers (Berlin, 2000), pp.503, 506–12; M. Koskenniemi, *From Apology to Utopia: The Structure of International Legal Argument* (Helsinki, 1989), pp. 52ff; and A. Nussbaum, *A Concise History of the Law of Nations* (rev. edn, New York, 1954), pp.79–84.

[10] Twiss, *Law of Nations*, pp.111, 121 and 139–140; Westlake, *Chapters*, pp.v–16; T. J. Lawrence, *The Principles of International Law* (London, 1895), pp.1–25; L. Oppenheim, The Science of International Law: Its Task and Method (1908) 2 AJIL 313 at 328–330; and L. Oppenheim, *International Law: A Treatise* (2nd edn, London, 1912), pp.4–5.

Positivists used this division to expunge indigenous peoples from the realm of International Law. John Westlake noted in 1894:

> [It is] the members of the international society which concern us, that of uncivilised natives international law takes no account. This is true, and it does not mean that all rights are denied to such natives, but that appreciation of their rights is left to the conscience of the state within whose recognised territorial sovereignty they are comprised.[11]

Non-European peoples were judged to be outside international society and could not seek protection from the worst excesses of colonial authorities under International Law but had to look to international morality.[12] The major principles of International Law as 'deduced' by late nineteenth- and early twentieth-century positivism ensured that the discipline was a legitimising force for colonisation rather than a guarantor of the rights of indigenous peoples. Any legal protection the Law of Nations may have afforded indigenous peoples disappeared with the extinguishment of a territory's legal personality in International Law upon colonisation, and application of the principle of State sovereignty.[13] This position was exacerbated by the universalisation of (European) International Law and the spread of European colonialism.

Positivism's interpretation of International Law formed part of the late Victorian colonial framework that included anthropology and economics and strove to exude objectivity and exclusivity. For many Anglo-American jurists, the validity of the scientific method was evidenced by the achievements of the Industrial Revolution and the scientific discoveries that drove it. Accordingly, positivists also aimed to produce 'order from chaos' by making 'International Law into a science'.[14] Lassa Oppenheim noted the irrationality of the state of nature would be replaced by positivist jurisprudence with its fixed set of principles and scheme of classification that revealed itself to the scrutiny of the expert jurist. He maintained that it required 'scientific skill to expose the real existing rules of international law, to lay bare their history and real meaning, and to criticize them in the light of reason, justice and the requirements of the age'.[15] Yet, because of their varying degrees of engagement with the colonial project, jurists were guided by an inherent subjectivity – the requirements dictated by European colonial and commercial expansion.

---

[11] Westlake, *Chapters*, p.136.

[12] See Westlake, *Chapters*, p.140; and Oppenheim, *International Law*, pp.34–35.

[13] See *Cayuga Indians (Great Britain v. United States)*, *RIAA*, vol.4, p.173 (1926); *Island of Palmas (United States v. Netherlands)*, *RIAA*, vol.2, p.831 (1946); and *Legal Status of Eastern Greenland, 1933, PCIJ, ser.A/B, No.53*, p.22.

[14] Lawrence, *Principles*, pp.93–94. See Twiss, *Law of Nations*, pp.139–40; Westlake, *Chapters*, pp.v–16; Oppenheim, *International Law*, pp.4–5; J. Lorimer, *The Institutes of the Law of Nations. A Treatise of the Jural Relations of the Separate Political Communities* (2 vols., Edinburgh, 1883–84), vol.II, pp.vii–viii; T. A. Walker, *The Science of International Law* (London, 1893); H. Wheaton, *Elements of International Law: with a Sketch of the History of the Science* (1836) (Reprint, New York, 1972), pp.38–47; and D. Sugerman, 'A Hatred of Disorder': Legal Science, Liberalism and Imperialism, in P. Fitzpatrick (ed.), *Dangerous Supplements: Resistance and Renewal in Jurisprudence* (London, 1991), p.47.

[15] Oppenheim, *International Law*, pp.328–30. See M. Schmoeckel, The Internationalist as a Scientist and Herald: Lassa Oppenheim (2000) 11 EJIL 699.

Positivists initially accepted that different normative systems of international law existed side by side throughout the world.[16] However, the escalating economic and industrial might of European and settler States combined with their colonial ambitions meant that the European international law was increasingly applied on a global scale to the gradual exclusion of any other systems of international law. Positivists rationalised this existing plurality not by applying a universal natural law, but with the explicit imposition of European international law over 'uncivilised' non-Europeans.[17]

Non-Europeans were no longer viewed as differently civilised but as 'uncivilised'. Ignoring centuries of contact between European and non-European peoples, the positivists sought to expel the non-European world from the realm of International Law by applying the distinction between civilised and non-civilised States. Henry Wheaton noted International Law's application was 'limited to the civilised and Christian peoples of Europe or those of European origin'.[18] The resultant society of nations was derived from the shared values of European (and Christian) culture. From this flowed the theory of recognition that evolved to vet the entry of other States into this society of nations. William E. Hall wrote in 1899: '[S]tates outside European civilisation must formally enter into the circle of law-governed countries. They must do something with the acquiescence of the latter . . . which amounts to an acceptance of the law in its entirety.'[19] With European norms being universalised as the standard of civilisation, they proceeded to re-admit non-European States into the society of nations, on terms beneficial to European colonial powers.[20]

As European international law was universalised and rationalised during the progress of the nineteenth century, the exclusion of non-European peoples was aligned with cultural Darwinism. With the attachment of the Darwinian conception of evolution to human societal development, tolerance of cultural pluralism was sacrificed to reinforce the idea of a unilinear progression of all humanity from the primitive, 'backward' state to the pinnacle of 'advanced' (European) civilisation. The cultural objects of non-European communities became crucial 'evidence' in the propagation of this scale of civilisation. This scale facilitated the transfer of non-European peoples, lands and resources to the spheres of influence and control of various European and settler States.

---

[16] See *The Antelope*, 23 US (10 Wheaton) 5 (1825); T. J. Lawrence, *The Principles of International Law* (4th edn, London, 1913), pp.4–5; H. Wheaton, *Elements of International Law*, ed. G. Wilson (8th edn, 1866) (Reprint, Washington DC, 1964), p.15; A. Riles, Aspiration and Control: International Legal Rhetoric and the Essentialization of Culture (1993) 106 HLR 723; and A. Anghie, Finding the Peripheries: Sovereignty and Colonialism in Nineteenth Century International Law (1999) 40 HILJ 1, 23–24.

[17] See E. Said, *Orientalism: Western Conceptions of the Orient* (London, 1995), pp.206–07; Anghie, 'Peripheries', 23–25; and Kennedy, 'Primitive', 128.

[18] Wheaton, *Elements*, p.15.   [19] Hall, *Treatise*, pp.42–43.

[20] See J. Crawford, *The Creation of States in International Law* (Oxford, 1979), pp.176–77; and Anghie, 'Peripheries', 47.

Anglo-American jurists developed a highly detailed system of classification which enabled European colonial powers to acquire 'possession' of the territories of non-European peoples. The system of classification was based on an assessment of their cultures against the standard of (European) civilisation.[21] They looked to theories developed by newly emergent disciplines, like anthropology, and the careful analysis of State practice to determine the legal status of non-European peoples.[22] However, because it was guided by practical concerns on the ground, State practice was rarely consistent or reliable.

The universalising tendency of European international law was so comprehensive that by the turn of the century 'there was only one sovereignty and one international law'.[23] The subjects of International Law narrowed to the exclusion of almost all entities except States.[24] States enjoyed exclusive sovereignty, which rendered them independent and equal, and not liable to external interference.[25] Positivists argued that International Law arose from consent between States and was not an authority outside States.[26]

As International Law yielded to the forces of European economic and colonial expansion, indigenous peoples moved from being subjects of the Law of Nations to objects of International Law; from sovereign nations to 'dependent' peoples absorbed into the sovereignty of the metropolitan State.[27] Colonised peoples, their territories and cultural objects existed in International Law as part of the metropolitan State. The principles of State sovereignty and the non-interference in the domestic acts of sovereign States meant that such peoples were unable to seek effective relief at International Law.[28] In addition, municipal courts of the colonised countries were precluded from enquiring into sovereign behaviour.[29] Nonetheless, indigenous communities from Australia, New Zealand and Canada petitioned British institutions concerning their treatment at the hands of colonial authorities.[30] They have continued to insist that their sovereignty was not extinguished with European colonisation.

---

[21] See Westlake, *Chapters*, p.145; L. Oppenheim, *International Law*, ed. H. Lauterpacht (3rd edn, London, 1920), p.286; and G. Gong, *The Standard of 'Civilization' in International Society* (Oxford, 1984).

[22] See Anghie, 'Peripheries', 45.

[23] D. Kennedy, International Law and the Nineteenth Century: History of an Illusion (1997) 17 *Quinnipiac Law Review* 99 at 127.

[24] Compare T. J. Lawrence's 1895 treatise (p.55) and his fourth edition (1913, p.54). This was a central assumption made by Bentham in the essay in which he coined the term 'International Law': M. W. Janis, Jeremy Bentham and the Fashioning of 'International Law' (1984) 78 AJIL 405 at 409.

[25] See Westlake, *Chapters*, pp.86–91; Hall, *Treatise*, pp.18–19; R. Lansing, Notes on Sovereignty in a State (1907) 1 AJIL 105 at 124; Kennedy, 'Nineteenth Century', 122–23; and B. Kingsbury, Sovereignty and Inequality (1998) 9 EJIL 599 at 605.

[26] See Twiss, *Law of Nations*, pp.111–22; and Westlake, *Chapters*, p.78.

[27] See Anghie, 'Peripheries', 34–35.

[28] See P. M. Anker, The Mandate System. Origin – Principles – Application, League of Nations, IV.A.Mandates, Geneva, 1945, 8.

[29] See Anghie, 'Peripheries', 51.

[30] See B. Attwood and A. Markus, *The Struggle for Aboriginal Rights: A Documentary History* (Sydney, 1999); A. McGrath (ed.), *Contested Ground: Australian Aborigines under the British Crown* (Sydney, 1999); J. A. Williams, *Politics of the New Zealand Maori: Protest and Cooperation* (Auckland, 1969); F. E. LaViolette, *The Struggle for Survival* (Toronto, 1961); and R. Veatch, *Canada and the League of Nations* (Toronto, 1975).

There were Anglo-American efforts to temper the behaviour of European and settler States towards colonised peoples during the nineteenth century through the application of the trusteeship doctrine.[31] Although it represented an element of humanistic thought, the nineteenth-century and early twentieth-century trusteeship doctrine emerged from the same Western philosophy that underlay the positivist construction of International Law. The objective of trusteeship was to re-educate indigenous peoples to shed their 'backward' cultures through their assimilation into the 'advanced' culture of the coloniser. The doctrine was ground in a negative conception of indigenous peoples and their cultures and became a justification for colonial oppression instead of a moderating force. In pursuing the civilising mission, colonial governments and their agents suppressed cultural practices and removed or destroyed cultural objects.

The 1837 House of Commons Select Committee on Aboriginal Tribes Report investigating the treatment of indigenous peoples in British colonies articulated the benefits of the 'civilising mission' for Britons and their subject peoples. The report acknowledged that European contact was 'a source of calamity to uncivilised nations' resulting in loss of territories, property, people and the 'debasing' of 'their character'.[32] The Committee concluded that policies which facilitated the 'spread of [European] civilisation' to non-Europeans would also assist Britons because '[s]avages are dangerous neighbours and unprofitable customers'.[33] It accentuated the moral duties of colonising States but failed to articulate any legal rights held by indigenous peoples.

The principles of trusteeship were formalised and internationalised through a series of conferences and related efforts aimed at regulating colonial penetration into Africa and the Pacific.[34] The most notable example, the 1885 Berlin Conference (General Act of Berlin 1885), aimed to quell colonial rivalry in West Africa through an agreed method of recognising colonial claims. African representatives were excluded from the conference deliberations despite its impact on the future of the people of the region. The US representative to the Conference argued that the delegates 'should aim at the voluntary consent of the natives whose country is taken possession of, in all cases where they had not provoked the aggression'.[35] However, Britain opposed any proposal to impose greater responsibility on colonising powers and argued instead for the regulation of free trade in a manner that would confer 'the advantages of civilisation on the natives'.[36]

The 1885 General Act of Berlin encapsulated the dual nature of trusteeship advocated by Anglo-American officials:

---

[31] See G. Bennett, *Aboriginal Rights in International Law* (London, 1978), pp.6–8.

[32] Cited in A. H. Snow, *The Question of Aborigines in the Law and Practice of Nations* (New York, 1921), p.10. See R. L. Barsh and J. Youngblood Henderson, *The Road: Indian Tribes and Political Liberty* (Berkeley, CA, 1980), p.86.

[33] Snow, *Question*, p.11.   [34] See Anker, 'Mandate', 8ff.

[35] Cited by Westlake, *Chapters*, p.138. See Anghie, 'Peripheries', 61ff; Bennett, *Aboriginal Rights*, p.5; Crawford, *Creation*, pp.11, 178–79; and S. E. Crowe, *The Berlin West African Conference 1884–1885* (Westport, 1970), pp.97–98.

[36] See M. F. Lindley, *The Acquisition and Government of Backward Territory in International Law: Being a Treatise on the Law and Practice Relating to Colonial Expansion* (London, 1926), pp.332–33.

first, the metropolitan power was required to 'ameliorat[e]' the 'moral and material conditions' of colonised peoples by imparting the benefits of European civilisation; and second, the metropolitan power was required to ensure the application of free trade principles in the territory and equal access to scientific expeditions.[37]

Article 6 of the Act, like the minority guarantees of the nineteenth century, provided some measure of protection for the collective cultural rights of local inhabitants.[38] And like minority guarantees, it failed to prevent mass atrocities or even improve the conditions of colonised peoples.[39]

In practice, such provisions were considered little more than declarations of moral, as opposed to legal, obligations. Nonetheless, Mark Lindley in 1926 argued that although indigenous peoples were not subjects of International Law, their rights were protected by the relevant colonial power pursuant to its obligations under general International Law.[40] However, conflicts could and often did arise between the interests of the colonised and the coloniser. And the principle of State sovereignty prevented any interference upon non-compliance of these moral obligations.

Collection and display of empire

The forces that underpinned the development of the science of International Law in the late nineteenth century also fuelled the transformation of international exhibitions into vehicles for escalating colonial rivalry.[41] The collection and display of the cultural objects of colonised peoples at the international exhibitions and South Kensington Museum were gathered to interpret, explain and justify the effects of British imperialism to its populace.

The Colonial and Indian Exhibition of 1886 was the first international exhibition devoted solely to imperial themes. Although the seeds of imperial display were present at the Great Exhibition of 1851, the British imperialist message advocated by the 1886 exhibition was far removed from its predecessor.[42] George Augustus

---

[37] Berlin, 26 February 1885, *British and Foreign State Papers*, vol.76, p.4; (1885) 165 Parry's CTS 485; (1909) 3(supp.) AJIL 7. Reaffirmed by the General Act of the Conference of Brussels relating to the African Slave Trade, 2 July 1890, *British and Foreign State Papers*, vol.82, p.55; Parl. Papers, vol.95, p.1 (1892); and (1890) 173 Parry's CTS 293; and Art.11, Convention revising the 1885 General Act of Berlin relative to the Congo, St-Germain-en-Laye, 10 September 1919, 8 LNTS 27; Cmd 477 (1919); 225 Parry's CTS 500 (1921); 15 (supp.) AJIL 314. See Snow, *Question*, pp.174–75; F. D. Lugard, *The Dual Mandate in British Tropical Africa* (Hamden, 1965); Crawford, *Creation*, p.179; and Anker, 'Mandate', 9–11.

[38] The provision also stipulated that 'religious Missions belonging to all creeds, shall not be limited or fettered in any way whatsoever'.

[39] See Anker, 'Mandate', 10, fn 1; Anghie, 'Peripheries', 63; and Lindley, *Acquisition*, pp.112–13.

[40] Lindley, *Acquisition*, pp.324–36. See Anaya, *Indigenous Peoples*, p.25; and Anker, 'Mandate'.

[41] See P. Greenhalgh, *Ephemeral Vistas: The Expositions Universelles, Great Exhibitions and the World's Fairs 1851–1931* (Manchester, 1988), pp.52ff; E. Hobsbawm, *The Age of Empire 1875–1914* (London, 1996), pp.34–83 and 142–64; and J. E. Findling and K. D. Pelle (eds.), *Historical Dictionary of World's Fairs and Expositions, 1851–1988* (New York, 1990), pp.261–301.

[42] See H. Cole, Henry Cole Diaries 1848–, NAL VAA 55.CC, 16 September 1851; J. R. Seeley, Introduction, in Colonial and Indian Exhibition 1886, *Her Majesty's Colonies, A Series of Original Papers issued under the Authority of the Royal Commission* (London, 1886), p.i; and J. Forbes Watson, *International Exhibitions* (London, 1873), pp.7–8, 10.

Sala noted: 'It [was] meant as a proclamation to all and sundry that Victoria rules an Empire . . . a just and equitable, but firm and fearless rule to the uttermost ends of the world, to the extremist limits of human civilisation'.[43] This objective was also pursued at the South Kensington Museum by its second director and organiser of the 1886 exhibition, Philip Cunliffe Owen.[44] In particular, the museum's Indian collections exemplified the complexities of British imperial policy on the Indian subcontinent and the increasing centrality of empire to the British national identity.

This section details the manner in which the possession of an empire including its peoples, cultural objects and territories became integral to British national identity. Next, there is an explanation of how the collection of the cultural objects of colonised peoples was neither objective nor random but represented the particular agendas of various colonial agents. Finally, there is an examination of the exclusion of the cultural objects of non-European peoples from the Western art canon which coincided with their exclusion from International Law.

National identity and imperial possessions
Like their French counterparts decades earlier, by the late nineteenth century the organisers of international exhibitions and museum officials in Anglo-American States harnessed the educative potential of the display of cultural objects to promote the imperial dimension of their respective national identities amongst their populace.[45] Increasingly, colonial officials advocated that possession of empire was a multilayered process, which included physical, theoretical and moral possession.

The display of the cultural objects from non-European peoples played a central role in the international exhibitions and South Kensington Museum's larger mission of national cultural self-definition. At these international exhibitions, the British State literally surrounded itself with its material and territorial acquisitions. The collection and display of cultural objects and raw materials from these territories signified British sovereignty over them. They positively prescribed the British national identity because their mere possession signified the possession of a vast colonial empire, thereby reaffirming its imperial identity. For the propagandists of imperialism, the importance of domesticating the colonies for local consumption meant stressing their 'sameness' with Britain and Britons,[46] and the economic benefits of empire.[47]

---

[43] G. A. Sala, *Illustrated London News*, 8 May 1886, cited in R. Brain, *Going to the Fair: Readings in the Culture of Nineteenth-Century Exhibitions* (Cambridge, 1993), p.172.

[44] See T. Barringer, The South Kensington Museum and the Colonial Project, in T. Barringer and T. Flynn (eds.), *Colonialism and the Object: Empire, Material Culture and the Museum* (London, 1998), p.11 at p.21.

[45] See Barringer, 'South Kensington', pp.11–27; P. Greenhalgh, Education, Entertainment and Politics: Lessons from the Great Exhibitions, in P. Vergo (ed.), *The New Museology* (London, 1989), p.74 at pp.86–89; and A. L. Lehman and B. Richardson, Preface: A Point of View, in M. Baker and B. Richardson (eds.), *A Grand Design: The Art of the Victoria and Albert Museum* (London, 1999), pp.9–14.

[46] See Seeley, 'Introduction', p.xxii; M. Foucault, *The Order of Things: An Archaeology of the Human Sciences* (London, 1994), p.xxiv; and H. Foster, The 'Primitive' Unconscious of Modern Art, or White Skin Black Masks, in H. Foster, *Recodings: Art, Spectacle, Cultural Politics* (Seattle, 1985), pp.202ff.

[47] See G. J. Mackenzie, *Propaganda and Empire: The Manipulation of British Public Opinion 1880–1960* (Manchester, 1985), pp.122–46; and T. G. August, *The Selling of Empire: British and French Imperialist Propaganda 1890–1940* (Westport, 1985).

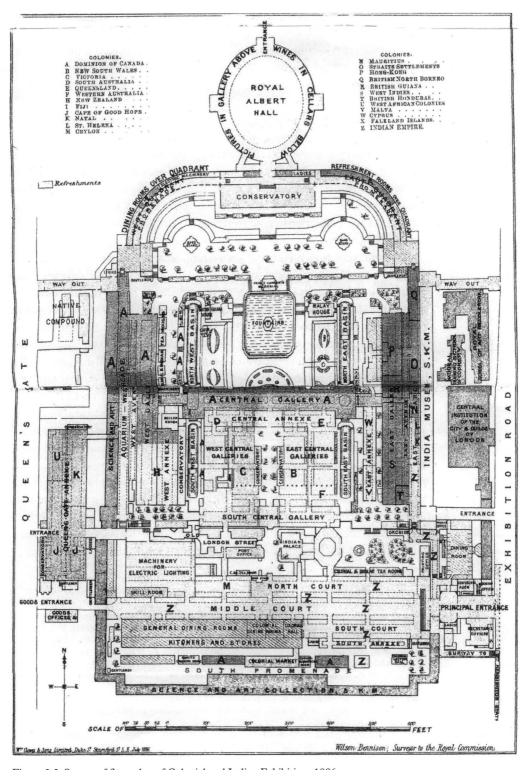

Figure 2.2 Survey of floor plan of Colonial and Indian Exhibition, 1886.

Inversely, by their difference these objects defined the margins of British identity through the grading (or even exclusion) of peoples, and the necessity of the 'civilising mission'.[48] In this setting, colonised peoples shed their own cultural identities and became British subjects; just as their sovereignty had been extinguished and their territories were absorbed into the British State under International Law.

International exhibitions and museums in the nineteenth and twentieth centuries were complicit in sustaining British rule in Asia and elsewhere. Collecting and cataloguing the cultural objects of non-European peoples was analogous to the acquisition of territory and the classification of populations necessary to maintain British supremacy in a political and economic sense.[49] Institutions maintaining close affiliations with the imperial State, such as the British Museum and the South Kensington Museum, were incapable of being confined simply to English things. These museums and their collections came to represent British national identity – an imperial identity.[50]

Thus, when the South Kensington's Architectural Courts were opened in 1873, a large part of the Eastern Court was occupied by over a hundred casts of Indian architecture and sculpture.[51] The Courts were intended to house the museum's collection of plaster casts of European monuments. However, its development coincided with an increasing popular consciousness of empire leading up to the induction of Victoria as empress of India in 1876.[52] The political significance of the casts of monuments situated in British India – excavated, reproduced and published by officers of the British army – and exhibited in Berlin and Paris could not be ignored by museum visitors. The casts were proudly displayed at the imperial centre, London as a symbol of responsible British custodianship of Indian history and culture.[53]

On the other hand, a different strategy was employed when nations, such as China and Japan, were not British imperial possessions. As Britain had to compete for advantage with other European powers, it strove to acquire these nations symbolically through the assembling of definitive representative collections.[54]

The intense colonial rivalry of the 1870s marked an exponential rise in scholarly interest in the colonies and heralded their theoretical possession. South Kensington with its Architectural Courts claimed authority over the cultural terrain of Britain's Asian empire. Moncure Conway described the Courts thus:

---

[48] See C. Clunas, The Imperial Collections: East Asian Art, in Baker and Richardson (eds.), *Grand Design*, pp.230, 231; B. Burton, International Exhibitions and National Identity (1991) 7 *Anthropology Today* 5; H. Bhabha, *The Location of Culture* (London, 1994), p.5; A. E. Coombes, Museums and the Formation of National and Cultural Identities (1988) 11 OAJ 57; and Greenhalgh, *Ephemeral*, pp.120ff.

[49] See P. Mitter and C. Clunas, The Empire of Things: The Engagement with the Orient, in Baker and Richardson (eds.), *Grand Design*, pp.221ff; and B. Anderson, *Imagined Communities: Reflections on the Origin and Spread of Nationalism* (rev. edn, London, 1991), pp.163–86.

[50] See C. Clunas, China in Britain: The Imperial Collection, in Barringer and Flynn (eds.), *Colonialism*, p.43; and Mitter and Clunas, 'Empire of Things', p.221.

[51] See Barringer, 'South Kensington', p.17.

[52] See J. Physick, *The Victoria and Albert Museum: The History of Its Building* (Oxford, 1982), pp.156–60.

[53] See M. Baker, *The Cast Courts* (London, 1982); and M. Conway, The South Kensington Museum (1875) 51 *Harper's New Monthly Magazine* 486 at 657–58.

[54] See Clunas, 'China', p.230; and A. Burton, The Image of the Curator (1985) 4 *The Victoria and Albert Museum Album* 373.

> Vista upon vista! The eye never reaches the farthest end in the past from which humanity has toiled upwards, its steps traced in victories over chaos . . . each finds himself gathering out of the dust of ages successive chapters of his own spiritual biography.[55]

Similarly, the Crystal Palace, a modern glass and steel prefabricated structure that had housed the Great Exhibition of 1851, embodied a transparency that allowed 'total surveyability'.[56] Joseph Paxton's design contained and 'tamed' peoples and things from all parts of the globe in one central location for the multitudinous gaze of the exhibition visitors.

This ordering encompassed every minutia of the British empire and its subject peoples.[57] There was a myriad of surveys that entailed the collection and ordering of physical and documentary data. For example, on the Indian subcontinent this included the Great Trigonometrical Survey (documenting the geographical and topographical operations within the boundaries of the empire), the Archaeological Survey, the Industrial Survey and the Ethnological Survey.[58] These efforts to know and order the colonial subject were also aimed at redefining and reordering their societal relations and economies to neutralise any threat to the interests of the metropolitan power.

The strategies of Europeans to possess non-European peoples, especially at the frontier, were confronted by resistance to the 'civilising mission' and lack of understanding of the 'colonial subject'.[59] Forbes Watson explained that whilst knowledge of the 'physical' attributes of a colony were important, of equal importance was 'knowledge of the character, customs, and manners, and the religious and philosophical aspirations of the various races inhabiting India, [which] supplies the means of obtaining a moral hold upon them'.[60]

Today, efforts to confront colonialism's legacies require a similar commitment. Later chapters examine how indigenous peoples have consistently emphasised that restitution of cultural heritage is a process which goes beyond the physical act of returning cultural objects to include moral restitution.

Archaeology of collection

In the late twentieth century, the restitution claims of newly independent States and indigenous peoples led to the inventorying of the vast holdings of former imperial

---

[55] See Conway, 'South Kensington Museum', 25.

[56] See J. McKean, Joseph Paxton: Crystal Palace, London 1851, in B. Dunlop and D. Hector (eds.), *Lost Masterpieces* (London, 1999), n.p.

[57] See B. Anderson, *Imagined*, pp.184–85; E. Said, *Culture and Imperialism*, (London, 1993), pp.1–72; and R. Rocher, British Orientalism in the Eighteenth Century: The Dialectics of Knowledge and Government, in C. A. Breckenridge and P. van der Veer (eds.), *Orientalism and the Postcolonial Predicament: Perspectives on South Asia* (Philadelphia, 1993), pp.215–49.

[58] See J. Forbes Watson, *On the Measures required for the Efficient Working of the India Museum and Library, with Suggestions for the Foundation, in connection with them, of an Indian Institute for Enquiry, Lecture and Teaching* (London, 1874), pp.25–26.

[59] See N. Thomas, *Colonialism's Culture: Anthropology, Travel and Government* (Cambridge, 1994), pp.11ff.

[60] Forbes Watson, *Measures*, p.41. See M. Foucault, On Governmentality (1979) 6 *Ideology and Consciousness* 5–12; and Thomas, *Colonialism*, p.41.

collections. This process has revealed that colonial engagement with non-European peoples and collection of their cultural objects was not monolithic. All collectors shaped and were shaped by the colonial project – and by colonised peoples themselves. For example, the India Museum collection, which was transferred to the South Kensington Museum in the late 1870s, was essentially an ethnographic record of British collecting of 'India'.[61]

Universal survey museums in former metropolitan capitals often display a handful of cultural objects to represent an entire culture of a people, suspended in a particular moment in time and space. It is therefore necessary to examine the agenda driving the collectors and exhibitors of these fragments of cultures. The late nineteenth- and early twentieth-century collecting practices of three agents of metropolitan power: settlers, missionaries and scientists, are guiding examples.

Although the attitudes of individual settlers varied considerably, most viewed indigenous peoples as possible sources of trade but more generally as direct competitors for limited resources on the frontier.[62] The settlers' view was reflected in the particular class of objects gathered by this group. Material evidence of perceived barbaric traits, especially weaponry, was favoured by these collectors. The displays of indigenous cultures by settler States at the international exhibitions and emerging ethnographic collections mirrored this preoccupation. Indigenous Australian objects, including a shield, collected during the Cook expedition were exhibited at the Colonial and Indian Exhibition of 1886 at the behest of the New South Wales colonial government.[63] Its official exhibition publication noted: 'The aboriginal natives have been gradually giving way before the march of European settlement'.[64] However, one commentator recorded that the colonial government had 'not found the secret of imparting the blessings without the drawbacks . . . of civilisation'.[65]

These objects represented the spoils of a conqueror and loss suffered by conquered peoples – 'the guardian gods of the defeated'.[66] For formerly colonised peoples and indigenous communities, these objects and data in museum collections are proof of the violence that occurred at the frontier and local resistance to colonialism.[67] For nineteenth-century British colonial officials, these objects aided in the perpetuation of the belief that indigenous peoples were a 'dying race' and were viewed as evidence of the necessity of the social and educative programmes for the assimilation of indigenous peoples.[68]

---

[61] See R. Desmond, *The India Museum 1801–1879* (London, 1982), p.21; and Mitter and Clunas, 'Empire of Things', pp.221ff; and J. Guy and D. Swallow (eds.), *Arts of India 1550–1900* (London, 1990), p.227.

[62] See N. Thomas, *Entangled Objects: Exchange, Material Culture and Colonialism in the Pacific* (London, 1991), pp.162ff; C. Gosden and C. Knowles, *Collecting Colonialism: Material Culture and Colonial Change* (Oxford, 2001); and H. Reynolds, *Frontier: Aborigines, Settlers and Land* (Sydney, 1987).

[63] A. L. Kaeppler, *'Artificial Curiosities': Being an Exposition of Native Manufactures Collected on the three Pacific Voyages of Captain James Cook R.N.* (exh. cat., Honolulu, 1978), p.281.

[64] Colonial and Indian Exhibition 1886, *Original Papers*, pp.139ff.   [65] Seeley, 'Introduction', p.xiii.

[66] H. K. Weihe, Licit International Trade in Cultural Objects for Art's Sake, in M. Briat and J. A. Freedberg (eds.), *Legal Aspects of International Trade in Art* (The Hague, 1996), p.57.

[67] See V. Rigg, Curators of the Colonial Idea: The Museum and the Exhibition as Agents of Bourgeois Ideology in Nineteenth Century NSW (1994) 4 *Public History Review* 188.

[68] See P. Brantlinger, Dying Races: Rationalising Genocide in the Nineteenth Century, in J. Nederveen Pieterse and B. Parekh (eds.), *Decolonisation of the Imagination: Culture, Knowledge and Power* (London, 1995), 43–55; and A. Maxwell, *Colonial Photography and Exhibitions: Representations of the 'Native', the Making of European Identities* (London, 2000), pp.7 and 133ff.

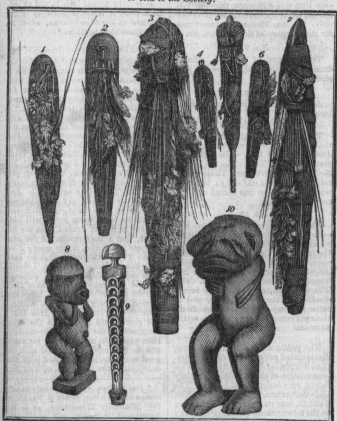

[2d Edition, Aug. 1820.

Missionary Sketches, No. III.

For the Use of the Weekly and Monthly Contributors to the
Missionary Society.

THE FAMILY IDOLS OF POMARE,

*Which he relinquished, and sent to the Missionaries at Eimeo, either to be burnt,
or sent to the Society.*

No. 1.

TERMAPOTUURA is said to be the
son of the great god ORO,* the national
protector of *Otaheite, Raiatea, Huaheine,*

* ORO. See an account of this idol, in
the Evangelical Magazine for August last.
It is a mere log of wood, now degraded
to a mean office in Pomare's kitchen,
but was formerly the occasion of bloody
wars.

OCTOBER 1818.

Taha, Borabora, and *Márua.* He is
said to have a brother named TETOI-
MATA, who is also a son of ORO.

No. 2.

The Missionaries could not learn the
name of this idol.

No. 3.

TEMEHARO, the principal god of Pomare's family. He is said to be also
one of the chief deities of the island of

Figure 2.3 Cover, *Missionary Sketches*, vol.3, no.111, October 1818.

Missionaries expressed an ambivalent attitude towards the cultural objects of colonised peoples because they were one of the primary agents for the implementation of the 'civilising mission' – the dismantling of indigenous cultures and their assimilation into the coloniser's culture.[69] They did not regard the indigenous peoples of the Asian Pacific as their equal. However, like Vitoria, they did believe in their essential humanity which made them worthy subjects of salvation through Christian conversion. The characterisation of local beliefs and customs as idolatry suited the missionary objectives because the 'idols' objectified the 'false' religion. British missionaries removed, destroyed, commissioned and purchased objects from indigenous communities, which came to signify the abandonment of indigenous beliefs. These objects were displayed in the Missionary Museum, London and eventually deposited with the British Museum.[70]

There was an inevitable tension between unstructured acquiring of diverse 'curiosities' by missionaries and settlers, and the systematic collecting undertaken by anthropologists.[71] The notion that a 'systematic' collection of objects produced or used by a particular people would be representative of their 'material culture', and a physical manifestation of their manners and customs, was the product of anthropological theory. With the rise of anthropology as a science in the late nineteenth century, cultural objects and related information from non-European communities were collected and collated in support of a linear progression of all human societal development. The resultant scale of civilisation facilitated the categorisation of peoples who became the objects of colonisation under International Law.

For Colonel A. H. Lane Fox (later Pitt Rivers) and other Victorian anthropologists, these 'primitive' cultural objects were capable of shedding light on the 'rise of European civilisation and technology'.[72] He promoted the display of objects in museums to illustrate 'successive ideas by which the minds of men in primitive condition of culture have progressed in the development of their arts from the simple to the complex, and from the homogeneous to the heterogeneous'.[73] He counselled that 'human ideas as represented by the various products of human industry' could be classified 'into genera, species, and varieties in the same manner as the products of the vegetable and animal kingdom'.[74] The Pitt Rivers collection was originally exhibited at the South Kensington Museum and it was here that he developed a method of displaying objects in his collections based on an interpretation of Darwinian theories to represent this progression of civilisation.[75]

---

[69] Thomas, *Entangled*, pp.151ff.
[70] See Thomas, *Entangled*, p.151, n.77; Kaeppler, '*Artificial Curiosities*', pp.13–14; and Mitter and Clunas, 'Empire of Things', p.223.
[71] See F. E. William, *The Collection of Curios and the Preservation of Native Culture* (Port Moresby, 1923).
[72] W. R. Chapman, Ethnology in the Museum, Ph.D thesis, University of Oxford (1981), p.48. See A. Petch, 'Man as he was and man as he is': General Pitt Rivers's collections (1998) 10 JHC 75 at 81.
[73] A. H. L. F. Pitt Rivers, *Catalogue of the Anthropological Collection lent by Colonel Lane Fox for exhibition in the Bethnal Green branch of the South Kensington Museum June 1874 Parts I and II* (Reissue, London, 1877), p.71.
[74] *Ibid.*
[75] See A. Burton, *Vision and Accident: The Story of the Victoria and Albert Museum* (London, 1999), pp.124–25; and W. R. Chapman, Arranging Ethnology: A. H. L. F. Pitt Rivers and the Typological Tradition, in G. Stocking (ed.), *Objects and Others: Essays on Museums and Material Culture* (Madison, 1985), pp.15–48. The collection was relocated to the Pitt Rivers Museum, Oxford in 1885.

Such ethnographic displays of colonised peoples and their cultural objects made empire concrete to the populace of the metropolitan centre and reaffirmed the colonising society's 'racial superiority'.[76] They 'revealed' the apparently backward state of non-European peoples which necessitated conquest by the more 'advanced' European States.[77] Indeed, it was argued that metropolitan powers would have to endure the 'burden' of coloniser until these communities were capable of ruling themselves.[78] These States would continue to perpetuate this argument well into the twentieth century.

Anthropologists prized objects that were created prior to European contact because they were perceived to embody an authentic, unsullied past.[79] Their work acquired a sense of urgency because of their fear that indigenous peoples were 'a dying race'. This perception was fuelled in part because of dramatically decreasing population numbers and the assimilation of indigenous peoples into European settler communities. The privileging of pre-contact objects by anthropologists necessarily entailed their collections representing indigenous cultures frozen in a particular moment in time. In turn, their collecting practices impacted upon indigenous cultural development through the removal of culturally significant objects and influencing indigenous manufacturing.

Universal survey collections display these objects collected by various colonial agents as though they embodied the cultural identity of a group, often misrepresenting their significance to the peoples who created them.[80] For this reason, indigenous communities include in their present-day claims for restitution of cultural heritage the right to determine how their cultures are displayed and interpreted by museums.

Displays in museums of arts and science

The penetration of European colonialism and capitalism from the late nineteenth century had the dual effect of unifying the globe and exacerbating its inequalities. The scale of civilisation perpetuated by legal positivists and anthropologists was reinforced with the universalisation of the Western art canon and the development of the dichotomy between art and ethnography, and museums of art and science.[81]

Nineteenth-century public museums, when applying taxonomies of fine and applied arts, art and ethnography, placed non-Western cultural objects (if they were classified at all) within the decorative arts and ethnography. This emphasis

---

[76] Z. Çelik, *Displaying the Orient: Architecture of Islam at Nineteenth-Century World's Fairs* (Berkeley, CA, 1992), pp.18–19.

[77] See V. G. Kiernan, *The Lords of Human Kind: European Attitudes to the Outside World in the Imperial Age* (London, 1969); P. Curtin, *The Image of Africa: British Ideas and Action 1780–1850* (Madison, 1964); B. Smith, *European Vision and the South Pacific* (New Haven, 1992); and W. Eisler and B. Smith (eds.), *Terra Australis: The Furthest Shore* (Sydney, 1988).

[78] See Brain, *Going*, pp.176–77; and Anderson, *Imagined*, pp.163–64 and 184–85.

[79] See J. Fabian, *Time and the Other: How Anthropology Makes its Object* (New York, 1983), p.xi.

[80] See R. Wagner, *The Invention of Culture* (rev. edn, Englewood Cliffs, 1975).

[81] See J. Clifford, *The Predicament of Culture: Twentieth-Century Ethnography, Literature and Art* (Cambridge, 1988), pp.189ff; J. A. Auerbach, *The Great Exhibition of 1851: A Nation on Display* (New Haven, 1999), p.101; and R. Young, *White Mythologies: Writing History and the West* (London, 1990), p.3.

Figure 2.4 Cast of the Eastern Gateway of the Great Buddhist Stupa at Sanchi, East Cast Court, South Kensington Museum, 1872.

of the utilitarian over the aesthetic, and the scientific over the artistic, reinforced the 'uncivilised' state of these peoples and their cultures in the European imagination.[82]

[82] For the 1851 Great Exhibition, Prince Albert proposed a three-tiered division encompassing 'the raw materials of industry; the manufactures made of them; and the art used to adorn them'. The entrants for the Fine Arts, Manufactures and Machinery categories were predominantly from Europe and North America while displays from the colonies fell into the Raw Materials category. See Cole, 'Diaries', 26–27 August 1850; *The Times*, 23 November 1850; and Greenhalgh, *Ephemeral*, pp.53–56.

The history of the Asian collections at the South Kensington Museum exemplified how imperial ideology assigned a subordinate yet essential role to such objects within the Western canon. The South Kensington Museum's imperial mission became overt with the relocation of the former East India Company museum to its Eastern Galleries in November 1879.[83] Under the directorship of Cunliffe Owen there emerged a distinctly ethnographic slant to the display of the cultural objects of non-European peoples.[84]

The absence of the cultural objects of peoples from Africa, and indigenous peoples of South Asia, Australia and the Americas, starkly highlighted the impact of this grading of cultures on the collecting and display practices of imperial institutions at the turn of the century. British institutions and museum practitioners viewed material culture from its Africa and Australasia colonies as 'primitive', as objects of scientific or ethnographical interest effectively outside the realm of 'Art'.[85] The assimilation and relocation policies of colonial powers, particularly between the 1870s and the 1930s, aided the most intense period of collecting of indigenous cultural objects by metropolitan and national museums. Significantly, such objects were acquired and housed almost exclusively by the British Museum rather than the South Kensington Museum. They were studied within the context of anthropology and contained in natural history museums. This practice was replicated in other European and US museums. It was not until the 1920s that art museums incorporated what was then called 'primitive art' into their collections. This transformation will be discussed more fully in Chapter 4.

This division between art and ethnography, and the allocation of non-European cultural objects to the latter category, directly impacted upon their protection in International Law from the late nineteenth century.

War and cultural objects of non-Europeans

As part of their push to rationalise their discipline into a science, positivists vigorously pursued the codification of International Law. Efforts to moderate the behaviour of 'civilised' States and their combatants during war from the mid nineteenth century meant that the first codified protection of cultural objects related to armed conflict and belligerent occupation. This final section covers the development of this area of International Law up to the Hague Conventions, to illustrate the universalisation of European international law and the exclusion of non-European peoples and their cultural heritage from its operation.

---

[83] See M. Conway, *Travels in South Kensington* (London, 1882), pp.43–44; R. Skelton, The Indian Collections: 1798 to 1978 (1978) 120 *Burlington Magazine* 297–304; and P. Mitter, *Much Maligned Monsters: A History of European Reactions to Indian Art* (Oxford, 1997), p.233.

[84] See Minute Paper, Department of Science and Art, India Office, V&A Archive: RP/1900/3175; H. Balfour, Pitt Rivers Collection to the Director, India Museum, 27 October 1900, V&A Archive: RP/1900/28353; and Baedeker, *London and its Environs* (Leipzig, 1889), pp.278–80.

[85] See Lehman and Richardson, 'Preface', pp.10ff; Clifford, *Predicament*, p.213; and A. Coombes, *Re-inventing Africa: Museums, Material Culture, Popular Imagination in Late Victorian and Edwardian England* (New Haven, 1994), pp.57–68. Cf. H. Cole, Art of Savage Nations and Peoples considered Uncivilised, *Journal of the Society of Arts* (21 January 1870), 183.

Codification of the rules of war and cultural heritage

The codification of the rules of war between 'civilised nations' during the late nineteenth and early twentieth centuries, as it pertained to the protection of cultural heritage, illustrates the developments in International Law detailed throughout this chapter, including: the universalisation of (European) International Law; the scale of civilisation and the exclusion of 'uncivilised' nations; and the privileging of European collection and classification of cultures. At each instance, International Law largely shunned non-European peoples and their cultural objects thereby significantly compromising the ability of these communities to preserve and develop their cultural heritage.

Hugo Grotius opined that the Law of Nations permitted pillage during armed conflict.[86] In the nineteenth century, Henry Wheaton summarised this position thus:

> By the ancient laws of nations, even what were called *res sacræ* were not exempt from capture and confiscation. Cicero has conveyed this idea in his . . . Fourth Oration against Verres, where he says that 'Victory made all sacred things of the Syracusans profane.'[87]

The lack of protection afforded to cultural heritage during armed conflict by the Law of Nations prior to the Enlightenment was influenced to a significant degree by the economic and colonial concerns of European States and their trading companies.[88] The practice of other normative non-European systems of international law differed from European practice. In pre-colonial Africa, Japan and under Islamic law it was prohibited to use civilian objects and sites of spiritual or cultural significance as military targets.[89] With the universalisation of European international law into International Law, there was little concession to these practices.

Following the Enlightenment there was an appreciable effort to curb the effects of war, particularly on civilian populations and cultural heritage. Such humanitarian measures were justified largely on the basis that these objects were preserved for the benefit of all humanity and should not be targeted because they were perceived to belong to this or that nation. Jean-Jacques Rousseau's reasoning that war was conducted between States and not individuals influenced Emer de Vattel to declare the inviolability of certain cultural property even during armed conflict.[90] Vattel

---

[86] See H. Grotius, *De jure belli ac pacis libri tres*, trans. F. W. Kelsey (Oxford, 1925), vol.II, pp.664–65; and H. Grotius, *De Iure Praedae Commentarius (Commentary on the Law of Prize and Booty)* (1604), trans. G. L. Williams (Oxford, 1950), vol.I, p.216.

[87] H. Wheaton, *Elements of International Law*, ed. R. H. Dana Jr (8th edn, London, 1866), pp.430–32. See J. Toman, *The Protection of Cultural Property in the Event of Armed Conflict: A Commentary on the Convention for the Protection of Cultural Property in the Event of Armed Conflict and its Protocol* (Paris, 1996), p.3; and S. E. Nahlik, La protection internationale des biens culturels en cas de conflit armé (1967-I) 120 RCADI 62 at 159ff.

[88] A. Lafiti, *Effects of War on Property being Studies in International Law and Policy* (London, 1909), pp.2–3.

[89] See A. Ndam Njoya, The African Concept, in S. Nahlik (ed.), *International Dimensions of Humanitarian Law* (Paris, 1988), p.8; S. Adachi, The Asian Concept, in Nahlik, *International*, p.16; and H. Sultan, The Islamic Concept, in Nahlik, *International*, p.38.

[90] J. J. Rousseau, *The Social Contract* (1762), trans. M. Cranston, (Harmondsworth, 1968), p.56. See D. Dudley Field, *Projet d'un code international proposé aux diplomats, aux hommes d'état, et aux jurisconsultes du droit international: Contenant en outre l'exposé du droit international actuel sur les matières les plus*

in his 1758 treatise argued that 'temples, tombs, public buildings and all works of remarkable beauty' that did not 'contribute to the enemy's strength' should be spared. To do otherwise is 'the act of a declared enemy of the human race thus wantonly to deprive men of these monuments of art and models of taste'.[91] Yet this position was open to conjecture amongst publicists until the law was codified at the turn of the century in successive Hague Conventions.[92]

By the mid century, there was a movement in International Law – 'the law of civilised nations' – to curb the worst excesses of military campaigns conducted by these States and 'civilise' or 'humanise' armed conflict.[93] The devastation inflicted on civilians and cultural heritage during the Franco-Prussian War of 1870–71 spurred the internationalists' efforts to codify (and limit) the rules of war. A growing fault line emerged amongst positivists, particularly concerning the codification of the laws of war. Some legal scholars strongly resisted any fetters being placed on a State and its methods of military engagement.[94] On the other hand, internationalists, whilst acknowledging that International Law was the law between States, argued that it was necessary to impose limits on State behaviour. Johann-Caspar Bluntschli maintained that such obligations were necessary because States, 'as members of humanity', should 'respect . . . the rights of human beings'.[95] Bluntschli became instrumental in promoting the positivist vehicle of codification to ensure the injection of 'naturalist' principles into the rules of war.[96]

However, it is important to recall that these curbs on armed conflict applied to those communities recognised as States forming part of the society of nations. Accordingly, the 1914 edition of the British Manual of Military Law made clear that these humanitarian measures only covered 'warfare between civilised nations'.[97] The operation of the rules was explicitly excluded from applying to war with 'uncivilised states and tribes' and 'their place is taken by the discretion of the commander and such rules of justice and humanity as recommend themselves in the particular circumstances of the case'.[98]

Early efforts to codify the rules of war not only excluded most non-European communities, but they also compromised the protection of the cultural heritage of such communities through the instruments' conceptualisation of culture and its manifestations specifically in European terms. For example, Article 34 of the Instructions for the Government of Armies of the United States of America in the Field (1863 Lieber Code) specifies that the property 'of museums of fine arts, or of

---

importantes (Paris, 1881), pp.536–38; Wheaton, *Elements*, pp.430–32, and footnote at pp.438–39; and J. B. Moore, *A Digest of International Law* (8 vols., Washington, 1906), vol.VII, p.198.

[91] E. de Vattel, *Le droit des gens, ou principes de la loi naturell, appliqués à la conduite et aux affaires des nations et des souverains* (1758) (Reprint, Washington DC, 1916), vol.III, p.293.

[92] See L. Oppenheim, *International Law: A Treatise* (London, 1906), vol.2, §133, n.1; and R. O'Keefe, Law, War and 'the Cultural Heritage of All Mankind', Ph.D thesis, University of Cambridge (2000), pp.98–99.

[93] See O'Keefe, 'Law, War', p.97.   [94] See O'Keefe, 'Law, War', pp.89–93.

[95] J.-C. Bluntschli, *Le droit international codifié* (Paris, 1870), p.18. See Grewe, *Epochs*, pp.494–96.

[96] See O'Keefe, 'Law, War', pp.93–96.

[97] Cited in Bennett, *Aboriginal Rights*, p.5, n.6.   [98] *Ibid.*

scientific character' enjoyed complete inviolability.[99] Article 35 expressly prohibited all 'avoidable injury' to 'classical works of art, libraries, scientific collections or precious instruments' during bombardment. Further, Article 36 provided that 'works of art, libraries, collections or instruments' belonging to the conquered nation could be removed by the conqueror; however, ownership would be determined by the terms of a peace treaty.[100] Whilst these provisions are a major step forward in the protection of cultural heritage during armed conflict in Anglo-American interpretations of International Law, they clearly reflected concepts privileged by Europeans and their settler States.

The Brussels Conference held in mid 1874 incorporated most of these developments into the first non-binding International Declaration concerning the Laws and Customs of War (1874 Brussels Declaration).[101] Article 18 strictly prohibited plunder by victorious troops, without placing any limitation on the type of objects subject to the provision. Significantly, Article 8 concerning belligerent occupation was subsequently modified to meet the request of the Ottoman delegate to cover non-Christian religious buildings (mosques, Islamic establishments, synagogues).[102]

Cultural objects (and monuments) were finally afforded some measure of codified protection during armed conflict and belligerent occupation in a series of conventions arising from the First Hague Peace Conference in 1899 (1899 Hague II),[103] and the Second Hague Conference in 1907 (1907 Hague IV).[104] The provisions of 1907 Hague IV largely reproduced those in 1899 Hague II, which in turn mirrored the 1874 Brussels Declaration. Pillage is prohibited during both armed conflict[105] and belligerent occupation.[106] The instruments replicated the narrow definition of culturally significant objects and sites found in the earlier document. Importantly, given the limited breadth of States involved in their drafting, the provisions of the

---

[99] Prepared by Francis Lieber and promulgated as General Order No.100 by President Lincoln, 24 April 1863, reproduced in D. Schindler and J. Toman (eds.), *The Laws of Armed Conflicts: A Collection of Conventions, Resolutions and Other Documents* (3rd edn, Dordrecht, 1988), Doc.1, p.8; Lorimer, *Treatise*, vol.II, Appendix No.1, pp.303ff; F. Snow, *Cases and Opinions on International Law with Note and A Syllabus* (Boston, 1893), Appendix E, pp.532–64; and P. Bordwell, *The Law of War between Belligerents: A History and Commentary* (Chicago, 1908), pp.73ff.

[100] Lorimer, *Treatise*, pp.311–12. Art. 37 refers to the obligation of the occupying forces to protect the 'religion and morality' of the 'hostile countries'.

[101] International Declaration concerning the Laws and Customs of War, Brussels, 27 August 1874, not ratified (1874–75) 148 Parry's CTS 134; *British and Foreign State Papers*, vol.65, p.118; (1907) 1(supp.) AJIL 96; P. Pradier-Fodéré, *Traité de droit international public européen et américain* (Paris, 1906), pp.465–72; Bordwell, *Law of War*, pp.101ff; Lorimer, *Treatise*, Appendix II, p.345; and Hall, *Treatise*, pp.439–40.

[102] Art.17 relating to the protection of such structures and objects during bombardment was similarly amended. These principles were reaffirmed in the Manual of the Institute of International Law, Oxford, 9 September 1880, in Lorimer, *Treatise*, pp.403ff; Pradier-Fodéré, *Traité*, p.466; and Bordwell, *Law of War*, pp.113–16.

[103] Convention (II) with Respect to the Laws and Customs of War on Land, with Annex, The Hague, 29 July 1899, UKTS 1 (1901); C 800 (1899); (1898–99) 187 Parry's CTS 429; and (1907) 1(supp.) AJIL 129.

[104] Convention (IV) Respecting the Laws and Customs of War on Land, and Annex, The Hague, 18 October 1907, UKTS 9 (1910); Cd 5030; (1907) 208 Parry's CTS 277; and (1908) 2(supp.) AJIL 90.

[105] Art.28, Regulations of 1907 Hague IV.

[106] Art.47, Regulations of 1907 Hague IV.

Hague Conventions are still in force and are generally considered to be customary international law.[107]

Article 27 of the 1907 Hague IV concerning sieges and bombardments provides protection for 'buildings dedicated to religions, art, science, or charitable purposes, [and] historic monuments'. Like the 1874 Brussels Declaration, the expression 'buildings dedicated to religions' covers the buildings of all religious persuasions, both Christian and non-Christian places of worship.[108] Article 56, on military occupation of hostile territories, makes no distinction between property belonging to private individuals, public administrations or even the State in respect of institutions dedicated to religion, the arts and sciences; historic monuments; and works of art and science.[109] The term 'institutions dedicated to religion' applies, as in the case of Article 27, to the buildings of all religions without exception.

Similar phraseology was employed in the 1919 Paris peace treaties and related negotiations to privilege the integrity of universal survey collections and trump any restitution claims by a newly independent State, as explained in Chapter 3.

Spoils of war at the South Kensington Museum

From the late nineteenth century, as 'civilised nations' were drafting treaties providing for the protection of cultural heritage during armed conflict, their national museums exponentially increased their acquisition of the cultural material of non-European peoples. This disparity was both convenient and far from being an oversight. International Law principles relating to cultural objects, if they were applied at all, were applied differently to non-European peoples.

The South Kensington Museum received cultural objects from various parts of the world which could only be (and indeed in internal memoranda were) described as 'spoils' or 'loot' and illustrate the limited practical application in the late nineteenth century of the prohibition in International Law against pillage.[110] Three cultural objects acquired as a direct result of British military campaigns in Asia serve as examples of the perspective of the coloniser, the colonised and the interplay of possession of significant objects and sovereignty.

---

[107] *Advisory Opinion on the Legal Consequences of the Construction of a Wall in the Occupied Palestinian Territory*, ICJ, 9 July 2004, No.131, para.89. At the 1899 Hague Conference, five of the twenty-seven delegates were from Afro-Asian States and at the 1907 Hague Conference, there were five out of forty-three such delegates: P. Sinha, *New Nations and the Law of Nations* (Leyden, 1967), p.25.

[108] The provision differs from 1899 Hague II with the inclusion of the words 'historic monuments'. The amendment was made at the behest of the Greek delegate and was unanimously approved. This extension of the definition reflected the growing sway of the historical preservation movement at the domestic level, more so than at the international level. See J. Scott Brown, *The Proceedings of the Hague Peace Conferences. Translation of the Official Texts* (3 vols., New York, 1921), vol.III, pp.12, 23, 353–54; and O'Keefe, 'Law, War', p.108. This protection for religious institutions forms part of customary international law: *Prosecutor v. Dario Kordić: and Mario Cerkez*, Trial Judgment, No.IT-95-14/2-T, Trial Chamber, ICTY, (26 February 2001), para.206.

[109] See Oppenheim, *International Law* (1906), pp.140, 142 and 143.

[110] See Boyd Dawkins, 'Letter', V&A Archives: India Museum: general, 1908–1909; Minute Codrington to Maclagan, 11 October 1937, V&A Archive: RP/1919–1937/4496; Board of Education Minute Paper, Director, Art Museum, 20 November 1903, V&A Archive: Indian Museum: general, 1896–1904; and Maclagan to Harcourt Smith, 27 January 1941, V&A Archive: Smith, Cecil Harcourt.

Figure 2.5 *Tippoo's Tiger*, Mysore, *c*.1790.

The display of the *Tippoo's Tiger* sculpture in London came to represent British military strength, the 'inferiority' of conquered peoples and vindication of Britain's 'civilising mission'. The Governor-General of India, on its presentation to the Directors of the East India Company, described it thus:

> This piece of mechanism represents a royal tyger in the act of devouring a prostrate European . . . The whole of this design was executed by order of Tippoo Sultan, who frequently amused himself with a sight of this emblematical triumph of the Khoudadaud [his dominions] over the English Sircar [government].[111]

Today, the *Tiger* is in the collections of the Victoria and Albert Museum (V&A). The museum displays it with other loot removed by British forces after their victorious storming of Sri Rangapattana (Seringapatam) in 1799.

After the initial pillaging of Sri Rangapattana, a Prize Committee was formed to evaluate and apportion the loot. For the British, theoretically all prize automatically

---

[111] Cited in Desmond, *India Museum*, p.766. See A. Chatterjee, *Representation of India, 1740–1840: The Creation of India in the Colonial Imagination* (Basingstoke, 1998), pp.173–94; and K. Brittlebank, Sakti and Barakat: The Power of Tipu's Tiger: An Examination of the Tiger Emblem of Tipu Sultan of Mysore (1995) 29 *Modern Asian Studies* 257.

belonged to the Crown, which redistributed it as it saw fit.[112] Objects associated with the Tipū Sultān personally, such as his robes, his ceremonial weaponry, his throne and especially the *Tiger*, acted as symbols of military conquest and the incorporation of his territories into the British empire.[113] British officials endeavoured to reserve these items for the Crown and the London officers of the East India Company.

Tippoo's Tiger progressed up the hierarchy of the East India Company and from 1808 it was displayed in its London headquarters.[114] East India House was a place of commerce with a specialist museum and library located in its peripheral quarters. The sculpture was relocated to South Kensington with the India Office collections in 1879. The *Tiger's* current installation at the Victoria and Albert Museum's Nehru Gallery of Indian Art remains intimately tied to the force which originally brought it to London – British colonialism.[115] Yet, *Tippoo's Tiger* has not been the subject of an official repatriation request.[116]

If the spoils of colonial conquest on display in London museums evoked within the minds of Britons the getting of imperial possessions, they also represented colonial subjugation for expatriates living in or visiting the metropolitan centre. The throne of Ranjit Singh provides a glimpse of the place such objects and their loss had in the collective memory of colonised peoples. In the mid-1800s, Rakhal das Haldar visited the India Office museum whilst studying in London and recorded that: 'It was painful to see the state chair of gold of the late Lion of the Punjab with a mere picture upon it . . . musical instruments without a Hindu player . . . and above all hookahs without the fume of fantastic shapes'.[117]

The throne had been made between 1820 and 1830 for Maharaja Ranjit Singh, the 'Lion of the Punjab'. He had united the Sikh community in the Punjab with Lahore as its capital and reigned from 1792 until his death in 1839. Following a struggle for succession and two Anglo-Sikh wars, the British gained control of northern India in 1849. With the British conquest, the new governor-general J. A. B. Ramsay denuded the Lahore palace of its contents, including Ranjit's throne, as prize. The throne was presented to the directors of the East India Company and was displayed in the India Museum. It passed to the South Kensington Museum with the India Office collection.

---

[112] Duke of Wellington, *Selections from the Despatches and General Orders of Field Marshall the Duke of Wellington*, ed. L. Gurwood (London, 1842), pp.102–03; R. H. Davis, *Lives of Indian Images* (Princeton, 1997), pp.51–88; and R. Gregorian, Unfit for Service: British Law and Looting in India in the Mid-Nineteenth Century (1990) 13 *South Asia* 63–64.

[113] Curzon to South Kensington Museum, 26 September 1908, V&A Archive: India Museum: general, 1908–1909.

[114] See W. Foster, *A Descriptive Catalogue of the Paintings, Statues &c, in the India Office* (3rd edn, London, 1906); M. Archer, *Tippoo's Tiger* (London, 1959); R. D. Altick, *The Shows of London* (Cambridge, 1978), p.299; and M. Archer, *The India Office Collections of Paintings and Sculpture* (London, 1986).

[115] See D. Parsons, Tipu's Tiger (1979) 1 *Antique Machines and Curiosities* 47. The Nehru Gallery was opened in 1990 from funds raised in India to establish the Nehru Trust for the purpose of preserving the V&A's Indian collections and making them more accessible to Indian citizens: National Museums Directors' Conference, *International Dimensions* (London, 2002), p.39.

[116] Personal communication: D. Swallow, Director of Collections, V&A Museum, 16 July 2003.

[117] R. Haldar, *The English Diary of an Indian Student, 1861–62* (Dacca, 1903), p.57, cited in Davis, *Lives*, p.174; and Desmond, *India Museum*, p.91.

Despite the throne's history, South Kensington authorities persistently and adamantly assured enquirers that the throne 'had nothing to do with mutiny'.[118] In October 1937, Kenneth de B. Codrington again denied it was the spoils of war but did recommend that it be returned to the Lahore museum where it 'would be received as a welcome act of grace'.[119] Several decades after the grant of Indian independence the throne became the subject of another unsuccessful repatriation claim by a regional Sikh body supported by the Indian government.[120] The throne remains in the V&A collections and was the centrepiece of its 'The Arts of the Sikh Kingdom' exhibition in 1999.[121]

Similarly, the chequered history of South Kensington's 'ownership' of the Mandalay regalia highlighted its officials' ambivalence towards the museum's imperial role and served as a prelude to the eventual restitution of such spoils. More significantly, it reflected how certain cultural objects came to symbolise the possession and dispossession of sovereignty for both the occupier and the occupied.

After the capture of Mandalay in 1885 by British troops and the incorporation of Burma into the Indian empire, the colonial government set about liquidating the Burmese regalia. The colonial authorities resolved to allow the South Kensington Museum to 'purchase, at a valuation any articles, of special interest from an artistic or archaeological point of view, which they desire to possess'.[122] Initially, museum representatives sanctioned the private sale of the regalia but reaction to this suggestion was swift and negative.[123] Whitehall noted that: '[T]he Burmese regalia . . . were the outward and visible tokens of a sovereignty which we have extinguished and . . . should be retained and placed in one of our public museums as a memento of our annexation of Burmah'.[124] It was stressed that they had a didactic value as an example of the 'indigenous art of the Burmah dynasty'; and symbolic value as regalia 'necessary to maintain state, and support the dignity, of the sovereign for the time being' which had passed to Britain with military conquest.[125] Later clarification from George Birdwood of the India Office confirmed that the museum obtained 'absolute possession in all the collections made over to South

[118] E. F. Straugh(?), memorandum entitled Collection of Indian Art – & Prof Boyd Dawkin's letter, V&A Archive: India Museum: general, 1908–1909. See Board of Education Minute Paper, 20 November 1903, V&A Archive: India Museum: general, 1896–1904.

[119] Minute Codrington to Maclagan, 11 October 1937, V&A Archive: RP/1919–1937/4496.

[120] Davis, *Lives*, p.181; and *Sunday Observer*, 24 July 1983, p.5.

[121] Since the 1990s, the V&A has actively nurtured interest and participation in the display, interpretation and conservation of Sikh cultural heritage within the diaspora in the United Kingdom as well as communities in India, at http://www.vam.ac.uk/vastatic/microsites/1162_sikhs; and NMDC, *International Dimensions* (London, 2002), p.28. The Koh-i-noor diamond was also removed by British forces during the raid and it remains part of the British regalia. It was viewed as symbolising India as the 'jewel of the British empire': Minutes of Deputation of the Royal Asiatic Society to India Museum, 12 December 1912, V&A Archive: RP/1912–1918/12/6370M.

[122] Fort William Foreign Department to HM Secretary of State of India, 18 January 1887, V&A Archive: RP/1890–1895/815.

[123] Minute Political Department: Burmese Regalia, 13 June 1890, V&A Archive: India Museum: general, 1890–1895.

[124] E. Neal(?) to A. Godley, 1 July 1890, V&A Archive: RP/1890–1895/SK 809.

[125] See Minute Political Department: Burmese Regalia, V&A Archive: India Museum: general, 1890–1895; and W. Blackstone, *Commentaries on the Laws of England* (1765–69) (4 vols., New York, 1978), vol. II, p.428.

Kensington by the India Office . . . [It] cannot even divest [itself] of them except by an act of Parliament'.[126] However, the museum did eventually return the Mandalay regalia in 1964–65 to Burma following its independence from colonial rule.

The centralising tendency of British imperialism transformed British national collections as they were filled with the cultural objects of colonised peoples from every corner of the globe. British national museums became vehicles for a distinctly imperial national identity, and their possession of the 'title deeds of the countries' symbolically represented the British empire's possession of these peoples, their territories and resources.

Despite Britain's unsurpassed economic and imperial strength during the nineteenth century, the director of the British Museum Frederick G. Kenyon reminded his fellow citizens in 1908: 'The issue at stake is not a small one. Nations are remembered less for their material development than for their contribution to the spiritual wealth of mankind.'[127] As explained in the next chapter, for metropolitan powers the development of universal survey collections containing the cultural objects of all peoples would arguably become 'their contribution to the spiritual wealth of mankind'. And even after the dismantling of empire, they continued to be haunted by their imperial national role.

However, the integrity of imperial collections would be tested in the twentieth century by the restitution claims of nationalists asserting political and cultural autonomy from the imperial centre. For colonised peoples, certain cultural objects held in these collections symbolised their loss of sovereignty and its possession by the colonial power. Accordingly, their restitution became a symbol of an autonomous identity, the cessation of colonial occupation and the resuscitation of sovereignty.

[126] G. Birdwood to J. Donnelly, 13 August 1890, V&A Archive: RP/1890–1895/5407.
[127] F. G. Kenyon, *Museums & National Life, The Romanes Lecture* (Oxford, 1927), pp.31–32.

Figure 3.1 Fragments of plaster casts of Indian architecture, Victoria and Albert Museum, *c*.1909.

3

Dismantling empires and post-First World War peace treaties

> [T]here would be no true equality between the majority and a minority, if the latter were deprived of its own institutions and were consequently compelled to renounce that which constitutes the very essence of its being as a minority.[1]

> Then you would disregard national feeling altogether? – I do not know anything about national feeling; I am a keeper of British antiquities.[2]

In the early twentieth century, the forces which brought the cultural objects of non-Europeans to imperial centres came under attack by nationalists, from Ireland to India. Their campaign to assert their independence from the imperial State was inextricably aligned with the claim to cultural autonomy – 'that which constitutes the very essence of [their] being'. Integral to these claims were efforts to reverse the centralising policies of the imperial State by requesting the restitution of cultural heritage held by their museums. This chapter focuses on the requests made for the restitution of cultural objects from imperial collections in the early twentieth century.

These requests saw rival national narratives centre on the physical and intellectual control of the cultural object. For former imperial States, the integrity of universal survey collections and the retention of the object became paramount to their national cultural identity. The assimilation of all dissenting national narratives into the imperial narrative and the suppression of alternative histories of the object were fundamental to the imperial national imagining. For newly independent States, a separate national identity necessitated restitution claims being made on imperial collections to enable the (re)constitution of their national cultural heritage. These claims challenged the status quo within International Law and metropolitan collections by demanding that their alternative voices and agenda be heard in the new international order of the inter-war period. Although there was recognition of these restitution claims within the 1919 Paris peace treaties, their lack of effective implementation reaffirmed the continued strength of the European Powers and the imperial museums that represented their interests.

The nationalists' demands reinforced existing colonial methodologies and knowledge systems laid down by the European Powers in the nineteenth century. By seeking

---

[1] *Minority Schools in Albania case (1935) PCIJ, ser.A/B, No.64*, p.17.
[2] Evidence of C. H. Read, in Celtic Ornaments found in Ireland: Copy of Reports of Committee appointed by the Lords Commissioners of Her Majesty's Treasury . . . with Evidence, Appendices and Index, C 179 (1899), [Celtic Ornaments (1899)], p.10, paras.198–201.

entry into the society of nations, these peoples implicitly accepted its underlying principles. In pursuit of autonomy, they largely internalised the standards of 'civilisation' set down in the disciplines of International Law, anthropology and the Western art canon. The entry of these communities into the international community and the acceptance of their cultural objects as 'art' did impact on these various disciplines by forcing shifts in agenda and the expansion of existing principles. But the fundamental structures that had primarily been created for the promotion of European colonial and capitalist expansion remained intact. This result can in part be explained by the fact that newly independent States were driven by the same dynamic, but on a reduced scale, as their imperial predecessors, that is the unification of all peoples within one territory and one national identity. This dynamic is examined further in Chapters 4 and 7.

This chapter explores how, despite the new international order of the inter-war period, the selective application of the minority guarantees in the 1919 Paris peace treaties perpetuated the scale of civilisation within International Law. However, the minority guarantees did recognise the centrality of cultural autonomy to any effective right to self-determination. This connection made by the peace treaties is developed further with an examination of the return and redistribution of cultural objects as part of the broader project of political and territorial reconfiguration after the First World War. Finally, consideration of claims made on British imperial collections in the early twentieth century highlights that these processes were not confined to empires dismantled by the peace treaties.

Minorities and the League of Nations

Delegations at the 1919 Paris peace conferences addressed nationalist calls by re-affirming and redefining prior International Law solutions such as the principle of self-determination, minority protection and restitution of national cultural property. Allied governments acknowledged the destabilising effect of assimilation policies by providing minority guarantees for cultural group rights. These guarantees, whilst denying non-dominant groups within a State the political right to self-determination, tried to ensure their cultural autonomy in the shadow of the dominant culture. Not all minorities in all member States of the League of Nations were afforded these cultural rights, however.

During the peace conferences, jostling incarnations of nationalism within Europe were viewed not only as a major precipitator of the First World War, threatening the territorial integrity of empires and existing States, but also as a guiding principle in the framing of the new European order.[3] Into this breach, the US President Woodrow Wilson introduced the principle of self-determination as the solution.[4] He argued that peoples should determine their own fate instead of being 'bartered about from

---

[3] See W. E. Rappard, Minorities and the League (1926) 222 *International Conciliation* 330–1; P. de Auer, The Protection of National Minorities, in ILA, *Report of the 30th Conference, 1921* (London, 1922), vol.I, pp.113–26; and G. Butler, *A Handbook to the League of Nations* (London, 1919), p.4.

[4] See H. W. V. Temperley, *History of the Peace Conference of Paris* (1920–24) (Reprint, 6 vols., Oxford, 1969), vol.VI, pp.539ff.

sovereign to sovereign, as though they were mere chattels and pawns in a game'.[5] National groups not afforded the opportunity of exercising self-determination were given treaty-based guarantees that the future League of Nations and its organs would ensure a measure of protection against the States to which they were reallocated with the redrawing of territorial boundaries.

The phenomenon articulated by Wilson was equally applicable to the fate of the cultural objects of those same peoples. Although a compromise of sorts was contained in the restitution provisions of the 1919 Paris peace treaties, they were as ineffectively implemented as the minority guarantees.

Several Allied governments, most notably Britain, vigorously campaigned against Wilson's proposal to incorporate the minority guarantees into the 1919 Covenant of the League of Nations, and bind all member States of the League.[6] Resistance to universal application was driven by fears that it would fuel secessionist movements within their own States.[7] The success of the opposition case betrayed the continued existence of a hierarchy of States, an overt scale of civilisation, within International Law and international relations. The president of the conference, Georges Clemenceau, argued that admission to the society of nations entailed an acceptance of certain principles of government dictated by, but not necessarily applicable to, Western European States which included religious tolerance and equal treatment of all citizens.[8] He stated that Allied governments had a right to impose conditions on these States because Allied military strength had secured their independence or enlarged their territories. Further, the Allied governments had a duty to the peoples affected by these redistributed boundaries and their own people to secure a lasting peace and stability.[9]

The minority guarantees had two effects on International Law: (i) they undermined the principle of State sovereignty; and (ii) reaffirmed the scale of civilisation. Despite Clemenceau's protestations that these States were not 'under the tutelage' of the major powers, the system of guarantees did impinge on their sovereignty.[10] The recognition of these States was made conditional upon their acceptance of the

---

[5] Cited in M. O. Hudson, The Protection of Minorities and Natives in Transferred Territories, in E. M. House and C. Seymour (eds.), *What Really Happened at Paris: The Story of the Peace Conference, 1918–1919 by American Delegates* (New York, 1921), p.208.

[6] See P. Thornberry, *International Law and the Rights of Minorities* (Oxford, 1991), pp.38–41; and M. Gardiner Jones, National Minorities: A Case Study in International Protection (1949) 14 LCP 599 at 605, n.30. See Wilson's Second Draft or First Paris Draft, 10 January 1919 with Comments and Suggestions by D. H. Miller, in Miller, *The Drafting of the Covenant* (2 vols., New York, 1929), vol.2, p. 65 at p. 91.

[7] See Temperley, *History*, vol.V, p.142; H. Black Calderwood, The Protection of Minorities by the League of Nations (1931) 2 *Geneva Research Information Committee Special Studies* 17–18; Auer, 'Protection', 122, 124; R. L. Buell, The Protection of Minorities, (1926) 222 *International Conciliation* 348 at 360–61; and H. Rosting, Protection of Minorities by the League of Nations (1923) 17 AJIL 641 at 646–50.

[8] Clemenceau to Paderewski, 24 June 1919, (1919), 13(supp.) AJIL 416; and *British Foreign and State Papers* (1919) vol.112, p.225.

[9] Clemenceau to Paderewski, 418. See President Wilson's speech, 31 May 1919, in Temperley, *History*, vol.V, p.130.

[10] Clemenceau to Paderewski, 419 and 421. See B. Heyking, The International Protection of Minorities: The Achilles' Heel of the League of Nations (1927) 13 TGS 31 at 35.

minority guarantees as fundamental law, which could not be altered by domestic legislation, and an external body would monitor their compliance.[11]

The increased membership of non-European States in the League of Nations and other international organisations incrementally challenged the legitimacy of the scale of civilisation but the universal application of International Law itself was not threatened. Nonetheless, the discriminatory nature of the new international order itself was exposed by the intensive, but ultimately unsuccessful, lobbying by the Japanese delegation for the insertion of a racial equality clause into the 1919 Covenant of the League of Nations.[12] Nicholas Politis noted in 1928: '[M]aterial and moral equality [between States] does not exist. As among individuals, so among nations . . .'.[13]

This inequality between States was laid bare with the selective application of minority guarantees under this new international system. The tiers of States established by the 1919 Paris peace conferences and subsequent League structures can be summarised as follows:

(1) European States and some settler States were not subject to minorities provisions;

(2) States in Central and Eastern Europe and its immediate periphery were subject to minority provisions;

(3) former colonial territories of Germany and the former Ottoman empire came under the tutelage of the first-tier States, which included minority protection; and

(4) colonial peoples were not covered by the peace treaties nor the League's 1919 Covenant.

These tiers were mirrored by the 1919 Paris peace treaty provisions covering the restitution and protection of cultural heritage.

The Allied governments, in order to defuse the destabilising potential of these minorities, guaranteed positive cultural group rights at the expense of recognising the universal application of the political right to self-determination. The minority guarantees replicated the dual protection afforded to groups in the nineteenth century:

(1) the non-discrimination component guaranteed individual members of the minority group the equal enjoyment of civil and political rights like all other citizens of the State to which they had been transferred.

---

[11] See L. Eisenmann, Rights of Minorities in Central Europe (1926) 222 *International Conciliation* 315 at 322; and C. T. Thompson, *The Peace Conference Day by Day* (New York, 1920), pp.386–387. For Legal Realists, they undermined a central principle of positivists' interpretation of International Law: J. L. Brierly, The Shortcoming of International Law (1924) 5 BYIL 14. This movement facilitated the rise of the human rights discourse in the late twentieth century to which indigenous claims for the return of cultural heritage are attached: see Chapter 9.

[12] See W. McKean, *Equality and Discrimination under International Law* (Oxford, 1983), pp.16–19; and R. J. Vincent, Racial Equality, in H. Bull and A. Watson (eds.), *The Expansion of International Society* (Oxford, 1984), p.239; N. Shimazu, *Japan, Race and Equality: The Racial Equality Proposal of 1919* (London, 1998); and B. Kingsbury, Sovereignty and Equality (1998) 9 EJIL 599 at 607.

[13] N. Politis, *The New Aspects of International Law* (Washington, 1928), p.8.

(2) national groups not afforded self-determination were placated with special group rights to education, language and allocation of State funds designed to protect their cultural identity within their new State.[14]

In the *Minority Schools in Albania* case (1935), the Permanent Court of International Justice found that both arms of the minority protections were 'interlocked', adding that both had to be realised: '[T]o ensure . . . suitable means for the preservation of their racial peculiarities, their traditions and their national characteristics'.[15] These group rights were emphatically cultural, not political, rights.[16]

The dual nature of minority guarantees made it difficult to define their ultimate purpose. On the one hand, it was assumed the guarantees were only a temporary measure and that the majority and minority would eventually tolerate each other sufficiently, or more likely the minority would effectively be assimilated, so that the guarantees would no longer be necessary.[17] Harold Temperley maintained that the provisions originated from several British policies designed to strengthen minority ties to the 'nation of which they formed a part'.[18] On the other hand, the scheme was viewed as ensuring the perpetuation of the essence of the minority's cultural identity within the State but with its members being loyal fellow-citizens.[19] Even on this more generous interpretation it is clear the Allied governments did not intend to create 'States within States' by granting national groups political autonomy.[20] Despite the lack of clarity of the nature of the political rights granted by the minority guarantees, they did provide rudimentary recognition of a right to self-determination in respect of cultural matters, for such groups.

Restitution of cultural objects and post-First World War peace treaties
The 1919 Paris peace treaty provisions relating to the restitution and redistribution of cultural objects following the dissolution of various empires and recognition of newly independent States reaffirmed the 'sacred' link between people, place and cultural heritage articulated during the 1815 Congress of Vienna. It also revisited

---

[14] See Thornberry, *Minorities*, pp.41ff; I. L. Evans, The Protection of Minorities (1923–24) 4 BYIL 95; Temperley, *History*, vol.V, pp.132–149; Hudson, 'Protection', 215–16; Heyking, 'Achilles', 35–36; C. K. Webster, *The League of Nations in Theory and Practice* (London, 1933), pp.208ff; J. Robinson, Minorities (1942) *World Organisation* 231 at 236*ff*; and C. A. Macartney, *National States and National Minorities* (Reprint, New York, 1968), pp.240ff.

[15] *Minority Schools in Albania case (1935) PCIJ, ser.A/B, No.64*, p.17.

[16] See Calderwood, 'Protection', 20–21; Heyking, 'Achilles', 33–34; Jones, 'National Minorities', 623; and Robinson, 'Minorities', 119.

[17] See Report of M. de Mello-Franco, 9 December 1925, LNOJ, 7th year (February 1926) p.141; Temperley, *History*, vol.V, p.121; Eisenmann, 'Rights', 322–24; Heyking, 'Achilles', 41–43; and R. Veatch, Minorities and the League of Nations, in Graduate Institute of International Studies and UN Library, *The League of Nations in Retrospect. Proceedings of the Symposium* (Berlin, 1983), pp.396ff.

[18] Temperley, *History*, vol.V, p.138. His argument is irreconcilable with his justification of Britain's staunch opposition to the universal application of minority protection.

[19] See A. Hobza, Questions de droit international concernant les religions (1924-IV) 5 RCADI 395; J. Rouček, *The Working of the Minorities System under the League of Nations* (Prague, 1929), pp.71–75; Robinson, 'Minorities', 242; and G. Murray, National Tolerance as an International Obligation (1930) 5 *Problems in Peace* 132–66.

[20] Buell, 'Protection', 361; and Rouček, *Working*, pp.117–22.

the ensuing rivalry between claims by predecessor States with national (imperial) collections and successor States seeking to (re)constitute their cultural patrimony.

Arguably, the various types of restitution provisions contained within the 1919 Paris peace treaties can be arranged in tiers which illustrate the perpetuation of the scale of civilisation within International Law during the inter-war period.

(1) The first tier encompassed restitution of cultural property to Western European States in response to damage and losses inflicted in violation of the rules of war.

(2) The second tier of predominantly Central and Eastern European States related to State succession to cultural property of the former Austro-Hungarian empire.

(3) The third tier covered the imposition of legislative control and equal access to archaeological sites in territories on the periphery of Europe.

(4) The fourth tier concerned the cultural objects and sites of occupied peoples not covered by the 1919 Paris peace treaties and the League's apparatus. The protection of this cultural heritage was exclusively the domain of the domestic laws of Allied colonial governments or settler States.

Western European States: restitution-in-kind for cultural loss
The restitution provisions contained in the Treaty of Peace between the Allied and Associated Powers and Germany (1919 Treaty of Versailles) set a precedent for the return of cultural objects as a remedy for deliberate cultural loss inflicted during war in contravention of International Law, even if the object being 'returned' was legally acquired by the holding State.[21] These provisions are relevant to present-day restitution claims because of the significant cultural losses visited upon occupied peoples by the military incursions of metropolitan powers. Further, the justification articulated for these provisions implicitly collapses the distinction of cultural losses being suffered during peacetime or war.

The 1919 Paris peace conference delegates were motivated by a desire to secure peace and stability by restoring communities, territories, and cultural objects and archives. The Wilsonian Fourteen Points were gradually adopted as an overarching guide for the post-war restitution process.[22] In early 1918, Wilson stated that liberated territories must be 'restored, without any attempt to limit the sovereignty which [they] enjoy with all other free nations', adding: 'Without this healing act the whole structure and validity of International Law is forever impaired.'[23] US delegate David Hunter Miller expounded that Wilson's words were not limited to physical reconstruction.[24] Instead, it would be accompanied by psychological restoration of the liberated territories, including the reconstitution of national cultural patrimonies.

---

[21] Arts.245–247, Treaty of Peace between the Allied and Associated Powers and Germany, Versailles, 28 June 1919, in force 10 January 1920, Cmd 516 (1920); *British and Foreign State Papers*, vol.112, p.1; (1919) 225 Parry's CTS 189; (1919) 13(supp.) AJIL 151 at 276; and E. Simpson (ed.), *The Spoils of War: World War II and its Aftermath: The Loss, Reappearance, and Recovery of Cultural Property*, (New York, 1997), Appendix 4, pp.280–81.

[22] See P. Mason Burnett, *Reparation at the Paris Peace Conference from the Standpoint of the American Delegation* (2 vols., New York, 1940), vol.I, pp.110ff.

[23] Burnett, *Reparation*, vol.II, p.303, Doc.454.

[24] Burnett, *Reparation*, vol.I, p.423, Doc.47.

There is little agreement amongst legal commentators of the class of the return sanctioned by the resultant Article 247. The returns prescribed by it were considered alternatively to be: restitution-in-kind, reparations or reconstitution of works of art.

The 1919 Treaty of Versailles provision originated from an initial acceptance of restitution-in-kind in recognition of the massive cultural losses suffered by France and Belgium during the First World War.[25] The French draft provision was deleted from the final treaty but Belgium successfully introduced an amended provision, Article 247, that reduced its claims for restitution from the general to the specific.[26] The provision allowed the reconstitution of specific art works that had been legally acquired by the returning States prior to the armed conflict.

Legal commentators have consistently argued that Article 247 is a seminal example of restitution-in-kind, even though the conference delegates had rejected the appearance of sanctioning such relief.[27] The British delegate expressed concern about the draft provision condoning this remedy because '[t]he bartering about of objects of art caused very bitter feeling in 1814'.[28] It is no accident that he used words that mirrored those of President Wilson's promotion of the principle of self-determination. Indeed, German commentators feared that the draft article would lead to a repetition of the Napoleonic confiscations which had occurred one hundred years before.[29] Museum officials necessarily resist this relief because it implicitly threatens the integrity of their collections with the removal of objects even regularly acquired.[30]

There was also great resistance to the 'reparations' element of the provision, with Allied governments reluctant to be seen to sanction the plunder by a victor of another State's cultural heritage. The works of art returned pursuant to Article 247 had been acquired by the German holding institutions legitimately and had not been confiscated during the First World War.[31] Therefore, Charles de Visscher argued this was a case of neither restitution nor recovery but was an acknowledgement of Belgium's 'right to compensation' for cultural losses caused by German infringement

---

[25] See J. Wilford Garner, *International Law and the World War* (2 vols., London, 1920), vol.I, pp.434ff; and C. Phillipson, *International Law and the Great War* (London, 1915), pp.159–74.

[26] See Burnett, *Reparation*, vol.I, pp.981–82 and 1009, Docs.284 and 286.

[27] See W. W. Kowalski, *Art Treasures and War: A Study on the Restitution of Looted Cultural Property pursuant to Public International Law*, ed. T. Schadla-Hall (London, 1998), p.35; A. Martin, Private Property, Rights and Interests in the Paris Peace Treaties (1947) 24 BYIL 277; and I. Vásárhelyi, *Restitution in International Law* (Budapest, 1964), pp.34ff.

[28] See Burnett, *Reparation*, vol.I, p.876, Doc.254.

[29] See O. Grautoff, Foreign Judgments on the Preservation of Monuments of Art, in P. Clemen (ed.), *Protection of Art During the War: Reports concerning the Condition of Monuments of Art at the Different Theatres of War and the German and Austrian Measures taken for their Preservation, Rescue and Research* (Leipzig, 1919), p.129; and W. Treue, *Art Plunder: The Fate of Art in War and Unrest*, trans. B. Creighton (New York, 1961), pp.222–23.

[30] See B. Leitbeger, *A Report on Tendencies Regarding Revindication and Compensations Dominant in Allied Circles* (London, 1943), cited in Kowalski, *Art Treasures*, p.71, n.117.

[31] See C. de Visscher, International Protection of Works of Art and Historic Monuments, Washington, *US Documents and State Papers*, International Information and Cultural Series, No.8, June 1949, 829–30; T. Bodkin, *Dismembered Masterpieces. A Plea for their Reconstruction by International Action* (London, 1945), pp.12–15; and D. Rigby, Cultural Reparations and a New Western Tradition (1943–44) 13 *The American Scholar* 273 at 279.

of the rules of war.[32] This interpretation was augmented by the location of the provision in the treaty and its enforcement by the Reparation Commission.

The only element on which the majority of writers reached consensus was that the provision facilitated the reconstitution of the works of art.[33] Yet, they could not agree whether the reconstitution was for the benefit of Belgian national patrimony or the cultural heritage of all humankind. Although a strong advocate of the reconstitution of dismembered works of art, Thomas Bodkin questioned the efficacy of its application in this case. He argued that the lack of security and poor conditions under which the works were kept on their return to Belgium threatened cultural objects that were part of the heritage of all mankind.[34] On the other hand, Visscher maintained the provision facilitated the reconstitution of national cultural patrimony, a purpose which rendered it consistent with the restitution provisions contained in other Paris peace treaties.[35]

The notion of the reconstitution of national cultural patrimony also imbued Article 245 of the 1919 Treaty of Versailles. This Article provided for the restitution from Germany to France of 'trophies, archives, historical souvenirs or works of art' taken from France during 'the War of 1870–71 and the World War'.[36] With the territorial restoration of Alsace-Lorraine to France, there was a similar restoration of cultural heritage with a 'sacred link' to this territory.[37] Further, there was a belief that the restoration of the cultural objects would secure a great measure of stability within Europe. Significantly, the provision endeavoured to correct a historic wrong by redistributing cultural objects which had been removed well prior to the First World War. This final rationale became a driving force behind the restitution claims of successor States upon the dissolution of the Austro-Hungarian empire.

Central and Eastern Europe: State succession and cultural property
Post-First World War peace treaties covering Central and Eastern Europe dealt with restitution of cultural property on the basis of State succession and the principles of territoriality and reciprocity. The treaty arrangements regulated the relations between predecessor and successor States following the dismantling of the Austro-Hungarian empire and the dissolution of the Hapsburg monarchy. The provisions were fuelled by the ambitions of new States to re-create, or more often create anew,

---

[32] Visscher, 'International Protection', 830; Bodkin, *Dismembered*, p.13; and UNESCO, Means of Prohibiting and Preventing the Illicit Import, Export and Transfer of Ownership of Cultural Property, Preliminary Report, 8 August 1969, UNESCO Doc.SHC/MD/3, 11. Cf. Burnett, *Reparation*, pp.127–28; B. Hollander, *The International Law of Art for Lawyers, Collectors and Artists* (London, 1959), p.32; and US Department of State, *Treaty of Versailles and After* (Washington, DC, 1947), p.443.

[33] Visscher, 'International Protection', 830; Bodkin, *Dismembered*, pp.13–15; and Rigby, 'Cultural Reparations', 279–80.

[34] Bodkin, *Dismembered*, p.14. See Visscher, 'International Protection', 830, n.31.

[35] Visscher, 'International Protection', 829.

[36] The requirements of Article 245 were fulfilled: Hollander, *International Law*, p.32.

[37] See *Plenary Commission on Reparation of Damage: Minutes* (Paris, 1919), Annex VI, p.22; and Burnett, *Reparation*, vol.II, pp.303–04, Doc.454.

a national culture which would feed the national narrative constructed to bolster the legitimacy of these States as nations and the integration of ceded territories.[38]

Notionally, the treaty provisions seemed to signal the ascendancy of the notion of national cultural patrimony and the claims of successor States. However, in practice during the inter-war period, these claims were sacrificed for the 'higher' interests of science and art represented by the universal survey collections of imperial museums. This privileging, of these museums and their collections, had been foreshadowed with the earlier codification of International Law covering the rules of war and the protection of cultural property. In addition, the limited number of returns effected by these provisions affirmed the continued strength of imperial forces even after the formal dissolution of an empire.

The Treaty of Peace between the Allied and Associated Powers and Austria of 1919 (Treaty of St-Germain) governed the redistribution of cultural property and archives between various successor States following the dissolution of the Austro-Hungarian empire.[39] Like the British empire, the Hapsburg monarchs pursued an aggressive policy of centralising cultural treasures and archives from all corners of their realm in institutions in the imperial capital, Vienna. These post-war efforts to return some items equitably to ceding States, after the collapse of the empire, are important early precedents for restitution claims made following decolonisation in the late twentieth century.

With rival national narratives to sustain, it was inevitable that conflicts arose between the predecessor State and the various successor States over claims for the same cultural objects and archives.

Austria, as the *de facto* predecessor State, resisted the dismantling of Viennese collections arguing that it should not be restricted to possessing only cultural objects of Austrian origin. Furthermore, it maintained that such cultural objects were an integral part of historic (imperial) collections forming part of its national cultural heritage.[40] Yet, the question posed by Castlereagh in 1815 became relevant: how could this predecessor State, stripped of its territorial possessions, continue to lay claim to 'the spoliations appertaining to those territories' held by imperial museums?[41] Austria replied that the integrity of existing collections should not be disturbed because they were of immense scientific and artistic value. They were, it maintained, 'the spiritual possession of all those untold thousands who lay claim . . . to culture, and . . . transcending all national boundaries'.[42]

This universalising (cultural heritage of all mankind) and objectifying (arts and sciences) of the role of museum collections strove to depoliticise the national narrative

---

[38] The elliptical nature of 'country of origin' as the basis of restitution claims troubled some jurists: Visscher, 'International Protection', 836–37.

[39] Arts.191–96 and Annex I–VI, Treaty of Peace between the Allied and Associated Powers and Austria together with Protocol and Declarations, St-Germain-en-Laye, 10 September 1919, in force 8 November 1921, UKTS No.11 (1919); Cmd 400 (1919); *British and Foreign State Papers*, vol.112, p.317; (1920) 14 (supp.) AJIL 1 at 77; and Simpson (ed.), *Spoils*, Appendix 5, pp.282–283.

[40] See Treue, *Art Plunder*, pp.223–24.

[41] Note 15, Memoir of Lord Castlereagh [to Allied Ministers], Paris, 11 September 1815, PRO FO 92/26, 115 at 119; and Parl. Deb., vol.32, ser.1, p.298, (1816).

[42] E. Leisching cited in Treue, *Art Plunder*, pp.223–24. See Burnett, *Reparation*, vol.I, p.332, Doc.705.

of the predecessor State and devalue or suppress rival claims to the cultural objects. Further, the predecessor State maintained that the collections must remain in their 'place of origin' – the imperial capital – fundamentally reaffirming the dynamics of the colonial relationship. This argument was two-pronged: (i) the more 'advanced' predecessor State was the natural guardian of this legacy for all peoples; and (ii) the superior economic and technical strength of this State meant that it was better able to care for the objects.

Conversely, the successor States charged that the same objects formed an essential part of their national cultural patrimony. For them, the peace treaty provisions facilitated the reconstitution of the national cultural heritage of communities affected by territorial changes following the dissolution of the empire.[43] Successor States refuted the suggestion that universal collections would be dismantled, by noting that their claims were modest and necessary for the administration of ceded territories.[44] These States argued the measures were a small step in righting a historic wrong, that is the reversing of the past centralising policies that had transported their cultural treasures to imperial Viennese collections.

The scheme for the redistribution of archival and historical material between predecessor and successor States under the 1919 Treaty of St-Germain favoured the principle of territoriality (Articles 192 and 193). The territorial link possibly related to a portion of, or one group of, people in the successor State, yet, the right of restitution to the cultural object was afforded to the relevant State, not to that group. This was a glaring discrepancy given the Allied governments' awareness of the detrimental and destabilising effects of assimilation policies, as evidenced by the minority guarantees.

The symbolic significance of the possession of these cultural objects for both national narratives rendered their return to ceded territories from the imperial collection particularly problematic. The 1919 Treaty of St-Germain addressed the restitution of cultural objects: in respect of specific objects (Article 195); and by a general right to negotiate (Article 196).

Article 195 (and Annexes II–IV) provided an adjudication and enforcement procedure to resolve claims by various successor States to specific manuscripts and objects. The main issue the claims brought before the Committee of Three Jurists, pursuant to the Article, was whether cultural objects purchased by a reigning Hapsburg monarch became their personal property absolutely and could therefore be removed permanently from their place of origin.[45] The claimant States argued that the objects formed part of their public domain and should revert to them upon the dissolution of the empire. Austria argued that the ceding States had no legal claim to

---

[43] See Visscher, 'International Protection', 830ff; and W. W. Kowalski, Repatriation of Cultural Property Following a Cession of Territory or Dissolution of Multinational States (2001) 6 AAL 139 at 143.
[44] See Burnett, *Reparation*, vol.I, p.336, Doc.716; and Temperley, *History*, vol.V, pp.10–11.
[45] See Allied Powers (1919–), Reparation Commission, Annex no.1141, *Belgian claims to the Triptych of Saint Ildephonse and the Treasure of the Order of the Golden Fleece, Report of the Committee of Three Jurists*, Paris, Reparation Committee 25 October 1921, Annex No.1141, pp.14, 19–21 and 51; 'O', International Arbitrations under the Treaty of St-Germain (1923–24) 4 BYIL 124 at 126 and 129; Visscher, 'International Protection', 831 at 834; Kowalski, *Art Treasures*, p.30; and Kowalski, 'Repatriation', 144.

recovery because the objects formed part of the personal property of the Hapsburg monarchy to which they had succeeded.

The Committee in all three cases found for Austria and refused to pass 'the verdict of history' on the government of the Hapsburgs. Even though the dispute was between two States, the Committee resolved the claims by reviving internal constitutional arrangements between a sovereign and its subjects. Accordingly Austria, as the designated 'predecessor' State, obtained various accoutrements of empire including imperial collections without the possession of any 'colonial' territories.[46] The Committee categorically rejected the Czechoslovak argument that it should 'right a historic wrong' by reversing the centralising policies of the Hapsburg monarchy which for centuries had removed cultural heritage from all corners of its empire.[47] It also refused to 'be guided by justice, equity and good faith', maintaining it had no authority to deviate from established juridical methods.[48] By adopting this strategy, the Committee ignored the unequal relations between the parties that had enabled the transaction to occur at all. This inequality was reaffirmed with its privileging of the law of the dominant (imperial) party.

The 1919 Treaty of St-Germain also granted successor States a general right to negotiate the restitution of cultural objects from imperial collections, which they claim as part of their national cultural patrimony, guided by the principles of territoriality and reciprocity. Article 196 recognised that 'object[s] of artistic, archaeological, scientific or historic character forming part of the [imperial] collections' could 'form part of the intellectual patrimony of the ceded districts' and 'may be returned to their districts of origin'. It also placed a freeze on the disposal of former imperial collections by the predecessor State for a period of twenty years after the dissolution of the empire; this ensured accessibility and preservation of these objects and archives for nationals of the successor States.

Despite the potentially far-reaching consequences of Article 196 for the reallocation of archives and cultural property, most scholars conceded that its application had little practical effect on the integrity of Viennese collections.[49] For example, the Italo-Austrian Treaty of 1920 amicably resolved Italian claims under Article 196 by recognising that the 'juridical and historic status of those objects was of special character' and distinguishable from the claims of other States.[50] Furthermore, Italy 'recognised the advisability of preventing, in the higher, general interest

---

[46] Cf. Art.11, Peace Treaty between Poland, Russia and the Ukraine, Riga, 18 March 1921, in force upon signature, 6 LNTS 123; and Simpson (ed.), *Spoils*, Appendix 7, pp.284–85. See Visscher, 'International Protection', 836; J. Chrzaszczewska, Un exemple de restitution. Le traité de Riga de 1921 et la patrimoine artistique de la Pologne (1932) 17–18 *Mouseion* 205; L. V. Prott and P. J. O'Keefe, *Law and the Cultural Heritage, Vol.3: Movement* (London, 1989), §1531, p.829; Kowalski, *Art Treasures*, pp.32–33; and Kowalski, 'Repatriation', 151.

[47] It found that the principle that 'a country which is an integral part of a composite State has a right, in case the State should be partitioned, to claim the property acquired with the aid of the local revenues of the said country', was not recognised in International Law nor could it be implied from the peace treaties: Visscher, 'International Protection', 832; and O, 'International Arbitration', 127.

[48] Visscher, 'International Protection', 832; and O, 'International Arbitration', 126.

[49] See Visscher, 'International Protection', 834; and Treue, *Art Plunder*, p.231.

[50] Art.4, Italo-Austrian Treaty, in Visscher, 'International Protection', 834–35. The treaty finalised Italian claims pursuant to Arts.191–96 of the Treaty of St-Germain, without recourse to adjudication.

of civilisation, the dispersion of the historic, artistic, and archaeological collections of Austria which in their entirety constitute an esthetic and historic entity, indivisible and celebrated'.[51] Yet, Austria obtained an unfettered title with no restrictions preventing it from dispersing the collections if it so wished.

The Treaty of Peace between the Allied and Associated Powers and Hungary of 1920 (Treaty of Trianon) confronted issues raised by restitution claims made by two (or more) successor States on former imperial collections.[52] Article 177 reaffirmed Hungary's right to negotiate the division of these collections on the same terms as other successor States under Article 196 of the 1919 Treaty of St-Germain.[53] Hungary persistently challenged the notion of territorial link as the trigger for selecting and returning public records and cultural objects to ceded territories. It advocated the application of the principle of nationality so that objects and archives relevant to the Hungarian people should be returned regardless of the territory of post-war Hungary.[54] In the end, the territoriality principle long contested by Hungary survived.[55] It also ceded to Austrian demands for an acceptance of the inviolability of the Viennese collections.[56]

Post-First World War restitution beyond Europe

Reflecting the increasingly universal reach of International Law, the post-First World War peace negotiations redrew territorial boundaries, relocated populations and re-allocated cultural objects within and beyond Europe. The fate of cultural objects of non-European peoples during this period starkly highlighted the unequal application of International Law principles based on the continued acceptance of the linear progression of civilisation.

Communities that had been under German colonial rule or the former Ottoman empire, for instance, were considered 'backward', incapable of withstanding the rigours of modern life. On this pretext, they were not afforded the political right of self-determination nor the right to restitution of their cultural heritage. They, their territories and their cultural objects and sites were placed under the 'trust' of the relevant mandating power. The mandate as it related to cultural objects was designed to protect the interests of the mandating power and the international community.

---

[51] Italy also agreed to 'energetically oppose' the claims of other States which if accepted would 'prejudice . . . the integrity of the Austrian collections, which must be preserved in the interests of science' (Art.9).

[52] Trianon, 4 June 1920, in force 17 December 1921, 6 LNTS 187; Cmd 896 (1920); (1921) 15(supp.) AJIL 1 at 63; and Simpson (ed.), *Spoils*, Appendix 6, pp.283–84. See Burnett, *Reparation*, vol.I, pp.333, 345–47 and 349; and Kowalski, *Art Treasures*, pp.146ff.

[53] Art.193, Treaty of St-Germain mirrored Arts.177 and 178 of the Treaty of Trianon. See Burnett, *Reparation*, vol.I, pp.346–47, Docs.740–44; Visscher, 'International Protection', 835–36; Treue, *Art Plunder*, pp.228–29; and Kowalski, 'Repatriation', 146.

[54] Burnett, *Reparation*, vol.I, pp.345–46, Doc.739.

[55] With the exception of objects specifically of Hungarian origin or character, Austria agreed to the relinquishment of a limited number of works of art to improve existing Hungarian collections of historic or artistic interest: Agreement between Austria and Hungary, Venice, 27 November 1932, 162 LNTS 396. See H. Tietze, L'accord Austro-Hongrois sur la répartition des collections de la maison des Habsbourg (1933) 23–24 *Mouseion* 92–97.

[56] See Visscher, 'International Protection', 836–37. Hungary was granted 'privileged rights' of access to collections of 'common cultural interest' (Art.4): Kowalski, *Art Treasures*, p.148.

In so doing, it contravened trust obligations owed to the people of the mandated territories.

Article 246 of the 1919 Treaty of Versailles, which sanctioned the transfer of the human remains of Sultan Mkwawa to Britain as the mandating power of East Africa, was one of two examples of restitution of non-European 'cultural property' in the 1919 Paris peace treaties.[57] Sultan Mkwawa, a tribal chief, had committed suicide while fighting the Germans in East Africa and his skull had been removed to Germany. The principle of territoriality was applied in this case for the purpose of identifying the place of origin of the remains. The remains were to be transferred to the territory's colonial successor Britain rather than to the 'place of origin'.[58]

The Treaty of Peace with Turkey of 1920 (Treaty of Sèvres) redefined relations between Turkey, successor States and mandating powers following the dismantling of the Ottoman empire.[59] The restitution provisions in this peace treaty varied from those contained in the treaties covering the dismantling of the Austro-Hungarian empire. These variations arose because the treaty arrangements did not strictly involve State succession but rather 'colonial' succession – the transfer of authority from one colonial occupier to another.[60] For example, Article 420 of the 1920 Treaty of Sèvres addressed restitution of archives and cultural property which belonged not only to the Allied Powers and their nationals but included 'companies and associations of every description controlled by such nationals'.[61] The place and conditions of return were not to be resolved by the Reparation Commission, but were 'laid down by the Governments to which they are to be restored'.[62] In addition, under Article 422 the Turkish government was required to return relevant objects to ceded territories and if they had passed into private ownership 'it would take the necessary steps by expropriation or otherwise to enable it to fulfil [this] obligation'.

The 1920 Treaty of Sèvres most starkly departed from other Paris peace treaties by requiring that mandated territories pass domestic legislation controlling archaeological sites and the export of archaeological materials (Article 421 and Annex). By the inter-war period, the intensity of past colonial rivalry had bred in the Allied Powers a determination to ensure equal access to the archaeological resources of these territories for their own museums.[63] The role of the mandating power and its

---

[57] Temperley, *History*, vol.III, pp.233–34. Art.246 also sanctioned the return to the King of the Hedjaz of the original Koran of the Caliph Othman which was in the possession of German authorities.

[58] See Kowalski, *Art Treasures*, p.31. The human remains were never located and therefore not handed over to Britain: Hollander, *International Law*, p.32; US Department of State, *Versailles*, p.523; and *The Times* (London), 13, 18 and 21 June 1988, Letters to Editor.

[59] Arts.420–25, Treaty of Peace with Turkey, Sèvres, 10 August 1920, not ratified, Cmd 964 (1920); *British and Foreign State Papers*, vol.113, p.652; and (1921) 15(supp.) AJIL 179.

[60] Arts.424–25, Treaty of Sèvres provided for the transfer of archives and records based on the principle of territoriality, with reciprocity applying only to the provision covering Wakfs, localised religious communities in areas ceded from Turkey. This class of property rights has long been recognised in Muslim countries: C. Phillipson, *Termination of War and Treaties of Peace* (London, 1916), p.319.

[61] *Ibid.*

[62] See Art.184, Treaty of St-Germain; and Art.168, Treaty of Trianon.

[63] There was a lengthy legal history of attempting to regulate the export of archaeological finds in the Ottoman territories: E. R. Chamberlin, *Preserving the Past* (London, 1979), pp.109–12; and P. J. O'Keefe and L. V. Prott, *Law and the Cultural Heritage, Vol.1: Discovery and Excavation* (London, 1983), pp.43ff, §§228–37.

relations with other powers came to the fore in the proposed scheme which regulated access and control of excavation sites and the 'equitable' division of archaeological finds.[64]

Article 421, and annex, exposed the competing interests concerning the protection of cultural objects and sites in the mandated territories. On the one hand, the mandating power had a duty to the international community to ensure free and equal access to archaeological 'resources' which would feed the universal collections of the metropolitan capitals. On the other hand, it also had a duty to the peoples of the mandated territories to protect their cultural objects and sites.

The 1920 Treaty of Sèvres was never ratified but its proposed legislative model was incorporated into the domestic laws of several States in the Middle East. The director of the British Museum George Hill was intimately involved in the redrafting of the antiquities laws for Iraq, Palestine[65] and, later, Cyprus[66] which were modelled on his reworking of the British law of treasure trove.[67] Frederick Kenyon, Hill's predecessor at the British Museum, noted in 1927 that Britain had 'every right as a nation to take pride' in providing 'for the material needs of the peoples' of mandated territories 'but [spiritual provision] ought not [to] be neglected'.[68]

Unfortunately, this was not the practice during the inter-war period. The swift reaction of British officials to any deviation from this legislative scheme affirmed that it was devised primarily to serve the interests of the mandating power and not the peoples under the mandate. By virtue of a 1922 Treaty between Great Britain and Iraq, Iraq was obliged to adopt an antiquities law based on the annex to Article 421.[69] At the end of the British Mandate in 1932, there were eleven expeditions of five different nationalities working in Iraq.[70]

In the same year, the trustees of the British Museum aired concerns about Iraqi legislation, by which it was rumoured the Baghdad Museum sought to retain 'everything of any value' and 'insist on control over expeditions, by attaching a native inspector'.[71] C. Leonard Woolley maintained that the proposed law ignored 'the interests of science' and that these antiquities were usually best conserved by Western institutions.[72] The trustees sought and got assurances that the Iraqi parliament would

---

[64] Art.421, Annex, Treaty of Sèvres, points 6 to 8. Points 1 to 5 provided the framework for the regulation of transactions of antiquities by the Department of Antiquities.

[65] Section 7, Palestine Antiquities Ordinance No.51 of 1921. See Art.21, British Mandate for Palestine, LN, LNOJ (August 1922) 3rd Year, No.8, Pt.II, pp.1007ff; G. Hill, *Treasure Trove in Law and Practice from the Earliest Time to the Present Day* (Oxford, 1936), p.270; and O'Keefe and Prott, *Discovery*, p.49, §234.

[66] Cyprus Antiquities Law 1935, ss.3 and 5. See Hill, *Treasure Trove*, p.270, nn.4 and 5; and O'Keefe and Prott, *Discovery*, p.95, §332.

[67] See Hill, *Treasure Trove*, pp.277–87. There were similar efforts by local governments in French mandated territories, for example, in Egypt, Syria and the Lebanon: LN, LNOJ, (August 1922) 3rd Year, No.8, pp.1013ff; and LN, LNOJ, (May–June 1937) 18th Year, No.5–6, p.578.

[68] F. G. Kenyon, *Museums & National Life, The Romanes Lecture* (Oxford, 1927), p.29.

[69] See Art.14, Treaty between Great Britain and Iraq, Baghdad, 10 October 1922, 35 LNTS 13. See O'Keefe and Prott, *Discovery*, p.45, §229; and Visscher, 'International Protection', 848–49.

[70] See O'Keefe and Prott, *Discovery*, pp.46–47, §231.

[71] See British Museum Trustees' Committee Minutes, Excavations in Iraq, 14 October 1933, p.5004.

[72] See C. L. Woolley, Antiquities Law, Iraq (1935) 9(33) *Antiquity* 84.

not table new antiquities legislation 'without consulting foreign archæologists'.[73] Nonetheless, the first non-British Director of Antiquities in Baghdad, Sati Al-Husri, successfully limited the rights of foreign excavators to a share of their removable finds with the passage of the Iraqi Antiquities Law No. 59 of 1936. Consequently, several foreign excavation teams left Iraq. During the same period, Lebanon and Syria experienced increased archaeological activity because of more lenient regulations.[74]

Former mandated territories employed various measures to remedy past cultural losses to reconstitute representative national collections. In August 1935, the Egyptian government advised the British Foreign Office that antiquities would only be exported on a 'system of exchange, i.e. that Egypt must have in return something which she required in the way of art, science, natural history, etc., but not necessarily antiquities'.[75] The British Museum adamantly resisted the application of the principles of payment-in-kind or reciprocity to its own institution, even though it was clearly and consistently applied in various Paris peace treaties.[76]

During the inter-war period, such tribulations of British institutions were not confined to occupied peoples in mandated territories but extended to peoples within the British empire itself.

Restitution within the British empire

Post-First World War peace treaties were silent on the protection, possession and control of the cultural objects of colonised peoples within empires not under the formal supervision of the League of Nations. Despite the absence of treaty provisions, the claims made on London's imperial collections by 'dependent' peoples within the British empire provide a practical insight into the application of the principles articulated in the 1919 Paris peace treaties.

This final section examines the question of return of cultural objects from the perspective of the Victoria and Albert Museum during the early twentieth century. First, there is consideration of the museum's involvement as an ancillary, requesting institution in a dispute over Celtic ornaments to highlight the conflicting missions of an imperial museum and a national museum. Second, there is an explanation of how its directors influenced the development of conventions for the protection and restitution of cultural objects during the inter-war period. Finally, there is an elaboration of how the museum's role as a holding institution during the dismantling of the British empire came to the fore, with the growing uncertainty over the future of its Indian collections.

---

[73] See British Museum Trustees' Committee Minutes, Excavations in Iraq, 9 December 1933, p.5094.

[74] See British Museum Trustees' Committee Minutes, Iraq Law of Antiquities, 14 July 1934, p.5095; and 13 October 1934, pp.5112–13; Hill, *Treasure Trove*, pp.270, 282; and Prott and O'Keefe, *Discovery*, pp.46–47, §231.

[75] See British Museum Trustees' Committee Minutes, Egyptian Antiquities: Proposed Alteration of the Egyptian Law, 12 October 1935, p.5212.

[76] *Ibid.* There was also resistance to Iraq's request for the restitution of the Samarra collection removed to Britain for 'safekeeping' on Churchill's orders prior to the signing of the 1922 Treaty between Great Britain and Iraq: British Museum Trustees' Committee Minutes, Excavations in Iraq, 14 October 1933, p.5004. Only a fraction of the collection was finally returned in 1935.

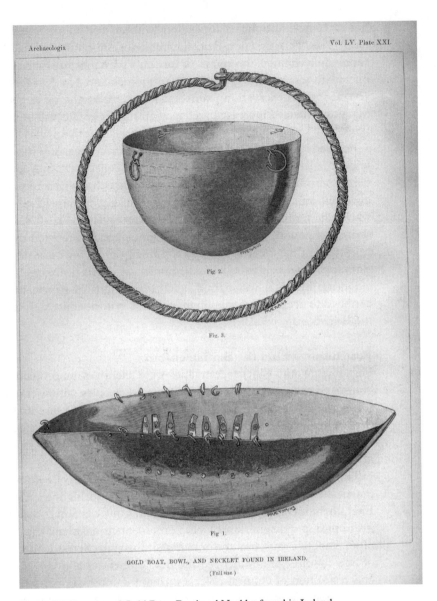

Archaeologia   Vol. LV. Plate XXI.

Fig. 2.

Fig. 3.

Fig 1.

GOLD BOAT, BOWL, AND NECKLET FOUND IN IRELAND.
(Full size.)

Figure 3.2 Drawing of Gold Boat, Bowl and Necklet found in Ireland.

All these events seriously tested the museum's mission and British national identity during the first half of the twentieth century. Understanding these processes is important for current restitution claims because many national museums in various settler States like Australia, Canada, New Zealand and the United States have experienced similar challenges from indigenous peoples in the recent past.

Celtic ornaments dilemma: imperial v. national museums
The journey of Celtic ornaments from Ireland to the British Museum at the turn of the century highlighted the growing traffic in antiquities from occupied areas to the

imperial centre. The chief players in the dispute were involved in a relationship which could be defined as internal colonisation. The British Museum represented the interests of the British empire and the Royal Irish Academy, Irish national interests.[77] The Irish claim was made in the context of increased militancy of nationalist movements within the United Kingdom and the furthest reaches of the British empire and their fervent opposition to the centralising and assimilatory practices of colonialism.

Around 1896, a hoard of Celtic ornaments was unearthed by a farm labourer in north-western Ireland.[78] The ornaments changed hands a number of times before being purchased by the British Museum in May 1897.[79] The purchase was in contravention of an established procedure whereby the British Treasury gave the Royal Irish Academy the first option of purchasing treasure trove found in Ireland.[80] The matter then became the subject of a parliamentary inquiry conducted by the 1898 Museums Committee.[81] This inquiry articulated the same competing national imaginings that would be aired during the dissolution of the Austro-Hungarian empire after the First World War.

During the 1898 Museums Committee hearings, the British Museum defined its role as both an imperial and national institution. For its museum officials, these two roles were not mutually exclusive because the British Museum's imperial role was an intrinsic element of British national identity. For its director, Edward Maunde Thompson, the British Museum represented the empire – 'It is not a London Museum, it is not an English Museum, it is a "British Museum", and as such we . . . make our collection as perfect as possible, to represent every portion of the British Empire.'[82] There was clear and deliberate delineation between being British, and being in possession of an empire; and being English, and lacking this imperial identity.

From the turn of the century, this distinction became a matter of increasing anxiety as the ties of empire loosened and London's imperial grip waned. Nationalist challenges from Ireland to India threatened the territorial integrity of the empire and claims for the return of cultural objects undermined its three-dimensional representation by imperial museums. The potential break-up of these collections made dissipating imperial strength more immediate than territorial losses.

---

[77] The Dublin Science and Art Museum was a sister institution of the South Kensington Museum. It was established with the Royal Dublin Society's collections and was incorporated under the auspices of the Department of Science and Art. The museum's fate was immersed in the campaign for Irish Home Rule and it was viewed as a device to strengthen the imperial hold over Ireland. With the creation of the Irish Free State in 1921, the museum's premises were converted into the House of Parliament and the National Museum: A. Burton, *Vision and Accident: The Story of the Victoria and Albert Museum*, (London, 1999), pp.105–06.

[78] P. Coll, 23 November 1898, in Celtic Ornaments (1899) Appendix 1, p.39.

[79] See Celtic Ornaments found in Ireland: Summary prepared by the Treasury, of Facts and Correspondence with respect to certain Celtic Ornaments found in the year 1896 at the Limavady, in the North West of Ireland, Cd 241 (1900), [Celtic Ornaments (1900)], p.A2.

[80] See A. J. Evans, On a votive deposit of the Gold Objects found on the North-West Coast of Ireland (1897) 55 *Archaeologia or Miscellaneous Tracts relating to Antiquity* 391; and (30 January 1897) 3614 *The Athenæum* 153.

[81] See Copy of Treasury Minute, 24 October 1890, V&A Archive: RP/1895–1899/15184/98; and Treasury Minute appointing the Committee, Celtic Ornaments (1899), p.iii.

[82] Celtic Ornaments (1899), p.4, para.48.

The removal of the Celtic ornaments from Ireland represented their physical and theoretical possession away from the national narrative to the dominant (occupying) culture. Charles Hercules Read, the keeper of the Department of British and Medieval Antiquities and Ethnography at the British Museum, placed heavy reliance on his 'expertise' and the potency of his physical possession of the objects to trump the Irish claim. He elevated the principle of nationality over territoriality by arguing that the ornaments had only an 'accidental relation' to Ireland and were probably manufactured by 'Ancient Britons'.[83] Read implicitly extended British national identity not only spatially but temporally, back through history. He contended that the objects were 'illustrations of British history, and could nowhere be more appropriately placed than in the British Museum, the central museum of the empire'.[84]

The centralising ethos of the imperial mind which strove to transport, display and store objects and knowledge of the colonial subject in the metropolitan centre was emphasised as evidence of London being the true guardian of this cultural legacy. Accordingly, Viscount Dillon, trustee of the British Museum, maintained that the Dublin and Edinburgh museums should yield to the British Museum's superiority as a place of learning and preservation of objects.[85] Colonel G. T. Plunkett, the director of Dublin's Science and Art Museum, rejected these assertions noting that his museum devoted more than twice as much floor space to Irish antiquities as the British Museum devoted to English, Scottish and Irish antiquities combined.[86]

Plunkett's observation had a significant political impact as well as reinforcing Dublin's educational credentials, for museums are usually able to display only a portion of their collections, the rest being held in storage. What they choose to display, and what they keep hidden, is by its nature an inherently political act. When asked whether he conceded national attachment to these ornaments, Dillon replied: 'I attach the greatest importance to it, but I look upon the people of England, Scotland and Ireland as being all members of the one nation.'[87] The display or storage of the cultural objects from these countries was essential for the development of the British imperial narrative and the suppression of rival national imaginings.

Prior to the 1898 Museums Committee inquiry, the so-called Redmond bill had been introduced to enable the British Museum to de-accession items from its collections. Museum officials strongly resisted such measures, with Maunde Thompson stating: 'I do not know where we should stop if that Act was relaxed and people were able to put in claims for all kind of things.'[88] For British Museum officials, their institution was embodied in its collections and its collecting powers reflected the strength of British empire. The Redmond bill and the Irish claim challenged this identity to the core.[89] For many, these imperial collections represented British

---

[83] Celtic Ornaments (1899), p.8, para.139.   [84] *Ibid.*
[85] Celtic Ornaments (1899), pp.24–26, paras.442, 450; and 459. Cf. Celtic Ornaments (1899), p.35, paras.618–21, Plunkett.
[86] See Celtic Ornaments (1899), p.35, para.632.   [87] Celtic Ornaments (1899), p.26, para.462.
[88] Celtic Ornaments (1899), p.4, para.90. See Celtic Ornaments (1899), p.10, para.197, Read.
[89] Celtic Ornaments (1899), p.5, paras.75–78.

national identity and if these collections were dismantled, British national identity would similarly dissolve.

For the Irish witnesses, the destiny of the objects symbolically replicated the contemporary nationalist struggle for a political, social and cultural identity separate from the British State. A national collection was fundamental to the assertion of the autonomy of their cultural identity from that of the dominant (imperial) culture. Plunkett advised that the Dublin institution was 'founded in order to supply the want of a national museum in Ireland, and . . . it was specially intended to hold the great collection of Irish antiquities'.[90]

Whilst British Museum witnesses recognised the existence of national sentiment, they strained to defuse its political potency by assimilating it within the broader imperial identity. For these officials, there was but one relevant narrative – the British imperialist narrative – with all other competing national imaginings being subsumed within it.[91] John Charles Robinson, the former keeper of the art collections at the South Kensington Museum and Her Majesty's Surveyor of Pictures, advised that with 'the Imperial sentiment [for cultural objects], the sentiment of the larger number . . . should prevail over the national sentiment of the particular country'.[92]

The travails of the ornaments also illustrated the limitations of the British treasure trove law, which was used as a template for the legislative protection of antiquities throughout the empire. The British Museum's stance undermined the operation of this law for the benefit of its own national (imperial) collection. In 1860, to acknowledge the efforts of the Royal Irish Academy to establish a national museum, the British treasury required that all treasure trove and antiquities found in Ireland pass to the Crown which in turn gave precedence to claims by the Dublin Museum.[93] The arrangement endeavoured to correct the imbalance between museums in the United Kingdom which was skewed by the British Museum's greater purchasing power. However, the attempts by the British State to bestow some measure of cultural autonomy to national groups were often thwarted by its own museum officials. Nonetheless, the British Museum eventually did return the ornaments after being ordered to do so by a British court.[94]

The Celtic Ornaments case provides an insight into the struggle between the emerging and increasingly vocal nationalists' calls within the British empire. Britain's position as an imperial power with unparalleled purchasing and collecting strength

---

[90] Celtic Ornaments (1899), p.35, para.617. See Celtic Ornaments (1899), p.37, para.634, Coffey; A. Coombes, Ethnography and the Formation of National and Cultural Identities, in S. Hiller (ed.), *The Myth of Primitivism* (London, 1991), p.205; and J. Anderson, Treasure Trove (1904) 1 *Scottish Historical Review* 74.

[91] Celtic Ornaments (1899), p.27, paras.488–89.   [92] Celtic Ornaments (1899), p.30, para.523.

[93] Celtic Ornaments (1899), p.21, para.401; and Agreement Transferring the Royal Irish Academy's Collection of Antiquities to the Science and Art Department, in Celtic Ornaments (1899), p.39, Appendix 4. Objects passed to the Dublin Museum instead of the Royal Irish Academy: Memorial of the Royal Irish Academy, in Celtic Ornaments (1899), p.40, Appendix 3.

[94] *Attorney-General* v. *Trustees of the British Museum* [1903] 2 Ch 598. See W. Martin, Treasure Trove and the British Museum (1904) 77 LQR 27; and R. Munro, The Recent Case of Treasure Trove (1903) 15 *Juridical Review* 267.

allowed it to advocate free and unimpeded transfer of cultural objects with little thought for their place within the communities of origin.[95]

The rudimentary legal protection afforded English movable cultural heritage during this period was partly explained by complacency bred of economic strength. As G. Baldwin Brown explained in 1905, Britons 'are buyers rather than sellers' with little public passion for export restrictions.[96] In 1938, Harold C. Gutteridge advised the International Museums Office that: '[T]he "phrase" *inalienable* has little or no meaning in our law so far as the property of our Museums is concerned . . . [Y]ou know we have no laws prohibiting the export of objects of artistic or historical interest'.[97]

There was equal resistance amongst sections of the Anglo-American museum fraternity to international efforts during the 1930s to promote the effective operation of foreign laws prohibiting illicit traffic. For these museum officials, the threat to their national cultural heritage came not from the illicit trade of cultural objects, but from the restitution claims made by communities whose cultures were represented in their collections.

Opposing views within the Victoria and Albert Museum

Two directors dominated the Victoria and Albert Museum during the inter-war period. Cecil Harcourt Smith (1909–1924) and Eric Maclagan (1924–1939) held very different views about the role of museums in national life. Throughout the British age of International Law there was a recurring duality in the role of museums between teaching and collection. These two views became particularly significant in the 1920s and 30s because of the very direct impact British museum officials had on the development of international legal frameworks governing cultural objects.

The views of British museum officials were increasingly coloured by restitution claims made upon metropolitan institutions in Britain and abroad. Maclagan spoke of the increasing sensitivity within the British museum establishment to such 'awkward questions' being asked of imperial collections.[98] This section considers the differing British reactions to international initiatives for the restitution of cultural objects. On the one hand, British museums became more engaged at an international level with fellow museum practitioners. On the other hand, they generally resisted any international initiatives regulating the trade and restitution of cultural objects.

---

[95] See Martin, 'Treasure Trove', 38–39. Martin notes that both government bodies incurred £3,114 in legal costs; the British Museum had paid £600 for the hoard; and the Dublin Museum's annual acquisitions budget in 1898 was £100.

[96] G. Baldwin Brown, *The Care of Ancient Monuments: An Account of the Legislative and Other Measures adopted in European Countries for protecting Ancient Monuments and Objects and Scenes of Natural Beauty and for preserving the Aspect of Historical Cities* (Cambridge, 1905), pp.66–67, §13. See Treue, *Art Plunder*, p.212; J. C. Robinson, Our Public Art Museums: A Retrospective (December 1897) *Nineteenth Century* 940 at 961. Cf. Minute Paper, 21 May 1931, V&A Archive: British Museum, 1930–1931.

[97] Gutteridge to Foundoukidis, 26 December 1938, UNESCO Archives: OIM.VI.27.III, IICI. Dossier de correspondence, office international des musées, conservation des œuvres d'art, protection de patrimoine artistique, 11–13.

[98] Maclagan to Harcourt Smith, 27 January 1941, V&A Archive: Smith, Cecil Harcourt.

Cecil Harcourt Smith was appointed director of the then recently renamed Victoria and Albert Museum (V&A) at a time when it was trying to return to its founding, educational mission.[99] He described the place of his museum within the broader governmental policy of democratising education thus:

> We have, I am glad to say, left long behind us the stupid popular fallacy that a museum is a stagnant collection of curiosities, and have come to recognise more than ever recently that such an institution is, or should be, a living and a powerful educational force.[100]

His counterpart at the British Museum Kenyon argued in 1927 that a museum 'must aim at being dynamic, not static . . . giving the attraction of novelty to old material . . . by presentation from fresh points of view'.[101] Harcourt Smith pursued these goals in numerous roles at the national and international level.

Following his retirement from the V&A, Harcourt Smith (now Purveyor of Works of Art to His Majesty the King) became intimately involved with various activities of international bodies attached to the League of Nations. From the 1930s, the International Museum Office (Office international des musées (OIM)) circulated draft conventions and declarations covering the protection and restitution of cultural heritage. Harcourt Smith had a hands-on role in the development of these draft conventions and not surprisingly the British Foreign Office requested his opinion on them.[102] The Foreign Office clearly indicated its early support for the Draft International Convention on the Repatriation of Objects of Artistic, Historical or Scientific Interest which have been Lost or Stolen or Unlawfully Alienated or Exported (1933 OIM Draft).[103]

However, the Foreign Office also sought input from various governmental bodies including the British Museum and the Board of Education (which oversaw the V&A).[104] In contrast to his predecessor, V&A director Eric Maclagan's response to the Foreign Office concerning OIM initiatives was negative and obstructive.

Eric Maclagan, described as 'the mature fruit of a long summer of civilisation',[105] envisioned the V&A's mission as a combination of an art museum and an imperial

---

[99] Harcourt Smith was Chairman of the 1908 Committee of Re-arrangement, convened to determine the fate of the museum's mission and arrangement of collections: Report of the Committee of Re-arrangement, 1908 and Minutes of the Committee of Re-arrangement, NAL, VA.1908.0001; and Anon., Reorganisation at South Kensington – I, II (1908–9) 14 *Burlington Magazine* 129.

[100] C. Harcourt Smith, The Future of Craft Museums (1916–17) 16 *Museums Journal* 152. See Burton, *Vision*, p.173; Second Report from the Select Committee on Museums of the Science and Art Department together with proceedings of the Committee, Minutes of Evidence, Appendix and Index (London, 1897), p.638, para.166, J. Donnelly; J. C. Robinson, Our National Art Collections and Provincial Art Museums (June 1880) *Nineteenth Century* 988; and Coombes, 'Ethnography', 191.

[101] Kenyon, *Museums*, p.26.

[102] He attended various OIM meetings as a Museums Association representative and a member of the Managing Committee of the OIM.

[103] See FO Minute W11597/138/98, Report of the 6th Committee's consideration of the activities of the Intellectual Organisation for Intellectual Co-operation, 13 October 1933, PRO FO 371/17386.

[104] See FO Minute W12900/138/98, Draft International Convention on the Repatriation of Objects of Artistic, Historical or Scientific Interest, 14 November 1933, PRO FO 371/17386. A FO official suggested a response be sought from the Trustees of the British Museum because they 'may begin to fear for the Elgin Marbles!'

[105] K. C., Obituary: Eric Maclagan (1951) 93 *Burlington Magazine* 358.

Figure 3.3 Entrance hall, Indian Section, Victoria and Albert Museum, 1936.

institution. For Maclagan, the V&A 'satisfie[d] communally a kind of collecting instinct of the nation' and its primary function was to 'possess and display masterpieces which can be enjoyed aesthetically by the public'.[106] In 1928, he agreed that his institution was a museum 'for connoisseurs and collectors'.[107] This trend fostered the display of objects at the V&A with an emphasis on 'masterpieces', and the creation of a reverential atmosphere.[108] The shift created a gulf between the museum's two audiences, the connoisseur and the general public.

Maclagan's perception of the role of museums impacted on his response to various draft OIM conventions. The 1933 OIM Draft was 'by no means welcome' to Maclagan and other British museum officials.[109] Their positions were in no small measure influenced by contemporary restitution claims made on museums in Britain and

---

[106] Royal Commission on National Museums and Galleries, Oral Evidence, Memorandum and Appendices to the Interim Report, (London, 1928), para.2780.

[107] Royal Commission on National Museums and Galleries, Interim Report, para.2879. See J. C. Robinson, English Art Connoisseurship and Collecting (October 1894) *Nineteenth Century* 523; Brown, *Ancient Monuments*, pp.34–41, §7; and Burton, *Vision*, pp.179–84.

[108] See Burton, *Vision*, p.184; and Royal Commission on National Museums & Galleries, Oral Evidence, Memoranda, and Appendices to the Final Report, Part II, (London, 1930), pp.81 and 88.

[109] Maclagan to Hill, 9 August 1933, V&A Archive: League of Nations, IIIC, 1925. Maclagan hoped the Foreign Office would 'raise some objection to this rather dangerous convention': Memorandum by Director, 23 July 1933, V&A Archive: League of Nations, IIIC, 1925. See Hill to Engelbach, 3 July 1933, V&A Archive: League of Nations, IIIC, 1925; and British Museum Trustees' Committee Minutes, Draft Convention for the Repatriation of Objects Lost, Stolen, or Unlawfully Alienated, 13 January 1934, pp.5030–31.

abroad. Maclagan's reply reveals that a number of contemporary events cemented his resistance to the proposed convention, including the return of a sarcophagus from the Fogg Art Museum in Boston to Spain and the effect of Soviet nationalisation policies.[110] However, he did not refer to restitution claims made on his own museum by communities within the British empire which doubtlessly also weighed on his mind.

The British Foreign Office position on the 1933 OIM Draft is instructive because the concerns it raised continued to be reiterated by consecutive British governments to explain their persistent refusal to ratify the 1970 UNESCO Convention.[111] It noted there was a lack of clarity and consistency in defining the cultural objects to be covered by the convention. Further, the non-retroactive aspects of the restitution provisions were not sufficiently stringent. In addition, the question of compensation for the bona fide purchaser was not properly addressed nor, they asserted, did it tackle funding for the processing of restitution claims.[112] Finally, it indicated a preference for the retention of informal arrangements which allowed museums to self-regulate to ensure that validity of title and any dispute were resolved on a museum-to-museum basis.[113]

The British position arguably remained entrenched to protect the last vestiges of its imperial glory – the cultural possessions collected from its colonies which continue to be housed in museums like the V&A.

V&A, the India Museum and Indian independence

The fortunes of the Indian collection have ebbed and flowed with the ever-present uncertainty of the V&A's place in British imperialism and national life. This characteristic was highlighted through a series of events in the first half of the twentieth century which included: the threatened 'loss' of the India Museum with the reorganisation of the museum's collections in 1908; the new relations between the imperial institution and the independent Indian State reflected in the Royal Academy of Art exhibition in 1948–49; and the passage of the Government of India Act 1935.

The recommendation of the 1908 Committee of Re-arrangement to absorb the Indian collections into the general collections of the V&A raised the wrath of those harbouring a dream of an India Museum befitting the capital of the British empire.[114]

---

[110] See Memorandum by Director, 23 July 1933, V&A Archive: League of Nations, IIIC, 1925. See *Princess Paley Olga* v. *Weisz* [1929] 1 KB 718; *Stroganoff-Scherbatoff* v. *Weldon*, 420 F Supp. 18 (SDNY 1976); L. V. Prott and P. J. O'Keefe, *Law and the Cultural Heritage, Volume 3: Movement*, pp.443–44, §825; and Hollander, *International Law*, pp.47–48.

[111] A. Leeper, FO to Secretary-General, LN, 25 May 1934, UNESCO Archives: OIM.IV.1927.I, 67–70. The 1934 observations concerning the convention drew heavily from the Board of Education advice that in turn mirrored Maclagan's position. The United Kingdom acceded to the 1970 UNESCO Convention in 2003.

[112] It was also feared the convention would necessitate the introduction of 'complicated and difficult' domestic legislation: Draft Memorandum, 19 January 1934; and HO Whitehall to FO, 20/34, Ref.71.622, V&A Archive: League of Nations, IIIC, 1925.

[113] See Hill to Undersecretary, FO, 16 January 1934, V&A Archive: League of Nations, IIIC, 1925.

[114] See Extracts from correspondence relating to the transfer of collections amassed by the India Office, V&A Archive: India Museum: general, 1908–1909; and Anon., Indian Collections at South Kensington (1908–09) 8 *Museums Journal* 449 at 435.

These reactions exposed the essential place of cultural objects in the narrative of colonial conquest and imperial strength, and their potency when displayed in museums like the V&A. Harcourt Smith identified these agitators as 'the Imperialist school', made up of former members of the imperial civil service who upon their return from India lobbied to preserve and display traditional Indian art and culture, as they conceived it to be, within a specialist Imperial Museum.[115]

Foremost amongst the critics of the 1908 Committee of Re-arrangement recommendation was the former Viceroy of India, George Nathaniel Curzon (1899–1905). Whilst in India, Curzon had been instrumental in the implementation of legislative and administrative measures for the restoration of Indian architectural heritage and stemming of the illicit export of cultural objects.[116] He considered such measures part of Britain's imperial trusteeship of India and crucial to reversing 'a century of British vandalism and crime'.[117] His programme was imperial, passing guardianship of the sites and objects from the local communities to the centralised government. It was also political, ignoring the layered history of these sites and their importance to more than one group. Upon his return to London, Curzon's preservation zeal was piqued with the handing down of the V&A's 1908 report.

The Imperialist school perceptively accommodated the Indian collections' role within a broader push to educate Britons about the benefits of colonial expansion and its importance to the British national identity. India and Indian cultural objects were conceived as intrinsic to British national imagining as Ireland and the Irish ornaments. In 1909, Curzon pronounced:

> [T]hat there should be in England, and, of course, in the Metropolis of this Empire, some feasible presentation of the Indian Empire . . . [O]ne of the foundation stones of the British Empire. Those of us who have had any connection with India . . . regard it as the greatest of our Imperial assets and one of the main sources both of our national duty and of national glory.[118]

Harcourt Smith refuted that it was ever the purpose of the India Museum to reflect the 'building up of Empire' nor was it the 'business of this Department and never has been to compile monuments – tangible or not'.[119] This terminology betrays the driving force of this movement: the preservation of empire. Following a persistent press campaign, parliamentary inquiry and Curzon's intervention, the imperialists

---

[115] Memorandum: On the Question of the Distribution of the India Museum, V&A Archive: India Museum: general, 1908–1909.

[116] A V&A official noted that although 'the Curzon laws' forbade illicit traffic of movable cultural property and fragments of immovables, 'the plain fact is that the present museums are full to repletion and it would be impossible to house on a museum basis all the sculptures in India, much of which is finding its way to the lime-kiln': Codrington to Maclagan, 11 October 1937, V&A Archive: India Museum: general, 1919–1937. See D. Linstrum, The Sacred Past: Lord Curzon and the Indian Monuments (1995) 11 *South Asian Studies* 1.

[117] Indian Archaeology 1899–1905: Correspondence, speeches and papers of Lord Curzon, p.421, in Curzon (George Nathaniel) Private Papers, Mss Eur F111/620–622, India Office, British Library, London.

[118] Memorandum: On the Question of the Distribution of the India Museum.

[119] Notes on 'Letter to the Editor, 4 December 1908', V&A Archives: India Museum: general, 1908–1909.

achieved partial success and the India Museum collections were left intact until the 1950s.

Indian nationalists had to counteract this preservationist drive to achieve their goals of cultural autonomy and political independence. Their agitation for independence ran in tandem with an academic campaign to elevate the status of Indian cultural objects within the Western art canon.[120] The attainment of political and cultural autonomy meant attaining the standard of civilisation set down by International Law and museums. At the conclusion of a 1909 parliamentary inquiry into the establishment of a specialist Indian museum, President Runciman 'deprecate[d] any attempt which might be made, to treat Indian art as a thing entirely by itself' and 'hope[d] it may still be possible to consider it in relation to Western art'.[121]

On 13 January 1910, a speech by George Birdwood, South Kensington's nominated expert for Indian purchases, dramatically brought into conflict old and new ways of viewing Indian cultural objects.[122] Birdwood's disparaging remarks about Indian art motivated a small group of influential writers, led by E. B. Havell, Ananda Coomaraswamy and poet Rabindranath Tagore, to found the India Society.[123] The Society promoted the merits of Indian art in Britain, as part of a wider movement for the development of an Indian national cultural movement.[124] In India, this movement was an important part of the gathering nationalist, anti-colonial movement, and closely aligned itself within other nationalist struggles, including that of the Irish.

While the nationalists challenged the exclusion of Indian art from the Western art canon, they did not challenge its central premise – the grading of the cultural objects of all peoples on a linear progression of civilisation. The eventual inclusion of Indian cultural objects within the aesthetics propounded by Western academics and arts was encapsulated in the 1948–49 exhibition of Indian art held at the Royal Academy of Arts, London.[125] The exhibition coincided with the granting of Indian independence, with Indians and their cultural objects judged to have met the necessary standard of civilisation.

Although the V&A's then director Leigh Ashton was anxious to ensure that the majority of the exhibits provided were from India, he was wary of the display's becoming a nationalist propaganda vehicle.[126] The Indian response to the exhibition plans raised one significant objection, the exclusion of all works produced after 1858. The Indian government advised that it was 'most anxious that no impression should

---

[120] See P. Mitter, The Imperial Collections: Indian Art, in M. Baker and B. Richardson (eds.), *A Grand Design: The Art of the Victoria and Albert Museum* (London, 1999), p.222 at p.227.

[121] Memorandum: On the Question of the Distribution of the India Museum.

[122] See P. Mitter, *Art and Nationalism in Colonial India 1850–1922: Occidental Orientations* (Cambridge, 1994), pp.32–33, 311–12 and 353; and T. Guha-Thakurta, *The Making of a New 'Indian' Art': Artists, Aesthetics and Nationalism in Bengal, c.1850–1920* (Cambridge, 1992).

[123] See E. B. Havell, *Indian Sculpture and Painting* (London, 1908); and Mitter, *Art and Nationalism*, pp.219–380.

[124] See India Society flyer, V&A Archive: India Museum: general, 1911.

[125] See K. de B. Codrington, Introduction, in L. Ashton (ed.), *The Art of India and Pakistan* (London, 1948), pp.3–15. Tippoo's Tiger appeared in the Royal Academy show and travelled to the Museum of Modern Art, New York in 1955, for an exhibition of Indian textiles and ornaments.

[126] See Memorandum Ashton to Part, Ministry of Education, 31 October 1945, V&A Archive: Indian Section: general, 1945–1949.

be left in the minds of the British public that India is a static country living upon the glories of its past and without any contemporary art'. It added that the exclusion of modern art 'might be misrepresented as a deliberate attempt to display India in this light'.[127] The stasis of Indian culture propagated by Britain to augment the notion of a 'backward' race had justified the British colonial presence in India. This was a misconception many formerly occupied peoples strove to debunk following decolonisation.

Earlier, the passage of the Government of India Act 1935 as part of the gradual devolution of power on the road to Indian independence created a stir within the V&A. The museum's title to the India Office collections had been relentlessly disputed from its initial acquisition by South Kensington in 1874,[128] and revisited with the 'accidental transfer' of the India Office collections with the passage of the Act.[129] Eric Maclagan was convinced that the legislation had transferred 'any rights formerly possessed by the India Office' in the collections to the Indian government, thereby opening the door to restitution requests.[130] In reply to an earlier restitution request from colonial authorities in Delhi, Maclagan defined 'the question of restoring works of art to their country of origin as a particularly thorny one'. Although he conceded that 'great examples of Indian art' should be accessible in India, he reiterated the benefits of continuing to display such 'art' in the imperial centre.[131] Indeed, Kenneth de B. Codrington, keeper of the Indian Section, argued that the museum should 'freely offer to return to India at once' the Ranjit Singh throne and the Amaravati sculptures.[132] His recommendation was not acted upon.[133]

The question of the operation of the Government of India Act 1935 re-emerged during the partition of India and the division of the former India Office collections between India and Pakistan as part of the (re)constitution of their respective national cultural patrimonies. Despite the large volume of cultural material which was transported from the subcontinent to London during British colonial occupation, Indian and Pakistani authorities have pursued only a handful of restitution claims. In turn, the massive cultural repositories of universal survey museums like the V&A have their own national identities to protect. For some Britons, the dream of a specialist museum to house the V&A's Indian collection and reaffirm the imperial past glory continued well into the late twentieth century.[134]

---

[127] G. S. Berman, Secretary to the Government of India to W. Lamb, Secretary of the Royal Academy of Arts, 16 May 1946, V&A Archive: Indian Section: general, 1945–1949.

[128] See India Office to the Board of Education, 19 August 1879, V&A Archive: India Museum: general, 1874–1886; and E. Maclagan to Irwin, 5 September 1928, V&A Archive: India Museum: general, 1919–1937.

[129] See Minute Codrington to Maclagan, 11 October 1937, V&A Archive: India Museum: general, 1919–1937.

[130] See Minute Paper, 12 October 1937, V&A Archive: RP/1919–1937/4496.

[131] See Maclagan to Irwin, 5 September 1928, V&A Archive: India Museum: general, 1919–1937.

[132] Codrington to Maclagan, 11 October 1937, V&A Archive: India Museum: general, 1919–1937. See Minute Paper Codrington to Maclagan, 17 February 1937, V&A Archive: India Museum: general, 1919–1937.

[133] However, Atul Chatterjee was appointed to the V&A's Advisory Council. This move was strongly but unsuccessfully resisted by Maclagan: Draft minute of the Advisory Council meeting, 17 November 1938, V&A Archive: RP/1938–44/5074.

[134] See R. Skelton, The Indian Collections 1798–1978 (1978) 120 *Burlington Magazine* 297 at 301–04.

The dissolution or waning of imperial power resulted in the hardening of another national imagining which strove to retain these same cultural objects within existing national collections. Former imperial States maintained that the integrity of universal survey collections was central to their national cultural identity. They artfully reinvented the importance of these collections: from national imperial collections to those forming part of the 'common heritage of all humankind'. The success of this argument during the inter-war period in staving off the restitution requests of newly independent States exposed the continuing strength of imperial methodologies even after the dissolution of empires.

However, as Maclagan witnessed during the visit of Emperor Haile Selassie to the V&A in the 1930s, the memory of cultural loss is not erased with the passage of time. He recorded: 'Naturally, I tried to steer him in the opposite direction [from the Abyssinian regalia]; and naturally he knew all about them and had in fact come to see them and weep over them.'[135]

Parts Two and Three examine the efforts of settler States like the United States and Australia to assimilate indigenous peoples and centralise their cultural objects within national collections. They too could not prevent the 'awkward questions' – the requests for cultural autonomy, and for the restitution of cultural objects from metropolitan collections.

[135] Maclagan to Harcourt Smith, 25 January 1941, V&A Archive: Smith, Cecil Harcourt.

Part Two

Whoever has emerged victorious participates to this day in the triumphal procession in which the present rulers step over those who are lying prostrate . . . According to traditional practice, the spoils are carried along in the procession . . . For without exception the cultural treasures he surveys have an origin which he cannot contemplate without horror . . . There is no document of civilisation which is not at the same time a document of barbarism.
W. Benjamin, *Illuminations* (London, 1992), p.248

Figure 4.1 University of Pennsylvania award for exhibit at the World's Columbian Exposition, Chicago, 1893.

4

Colonised peoples and the League of Nations

> Experience has shown that however valuable a world museum, in which the arts of all mankind are displayed, might be theoretically, such a museum is not practical . . . Ordinary collections, even in museums, usually reveal more of the psychology of their collector than they do of the people who originated them.[1]

> It is obvious that one studies art in art museums and not in museums of natural and social science. Thus the art of the Indian is difficult to contemplate or to study in a properly aesthetic aura, since the exhibition of ethnological collection . . . does not emphasize or dramatize examples of high artistic merit according to white standards.[2]

At the turn of the century, while colonised peoples and their lands provided cheap labour and resources to fuel European and North American industrial economies, their cultural produce fed a renewal in Western art and culture. The movement of non-European cultural objects from natural science to art museums signalled their entry into the market as a cultural 'resource' – the common right of all humankind. The control and protection of this non-renewable resource during the inter-war period is the subject of this chapter.

Both arms of the dual mandate implicitly contained in the League of Nations' mandate system, governing the administration of specific colonised peoples, reaffirmed the unilinear scale of civilisation formulated to promote European colonial and commercial interests. The trust obligations owed to indigenous communities involved a compromised application of the principle of self-determination. Colonised peoples and their cultural objects were deemed in need of tutelage to 'elevate' them 'according to white standards'. The trust obligations owed to the international community led to the strengthening of the principle of development. For States making up the society of nations, indigenous cultural objects previously reviled became a cultural resource to be mined in the creation of a unique national cultural identity.

In the preceding chapter, it was suggested that newly independent States were driven by the same motivations, but on a smaller scale, as were their imperial predecessors – the unification of all peoples within one territory and one national identity. This chapter examines how this dynamic was replicated in United States relations

[1] S. Culin, Typescript: Notes on Travel in India, General Correspondence [1.4.036], 10/1922, Brooklyn Museum Archives (BMA), pp.1–2.
[2] G. C. Valliant, *Indian Arts in North America* (New York, 1939), pp.1–2.

with Native Americans and their cultural objects as it pursued development of its national economy and national cultural identity. Just as federal government policies strove to break up Native American communities by assimilating individual members into the dominant culture, the 'elevation' of Native American cultural objects into the Western art canon had a similar result. These processes suppressed the realities of past US–Native American relations, denied the experiences of living indigenous communities and inhibited their ability to respond to current and future challenges on their own terms.

In this chapter, it is argued that the League's mandate system created a fundamental shift by internationalising the 'problem' of colonialism and by conceding that the two arms of the dual mandate were of equal importance. But the reaffirmation of separate trust obligations necessarily compromised the rights and interests of all colonised peoples and their link to their cultural objects. Next, there is an explanation of how the free trade agenda embodied in the second arm of the dual mandate significantly altered the tentative steps towards an international legislative framework for the restitution of cultural objects. Finally, the 'psychology of [US] collectors' of Native American cultural objects is examined to show how they were driven by the changing needs of the dominant national culture.

Colonised peoples, their cultural property and the League of Nations

The Covenant of the League of Nations of 1919 and the ensuing mandate system rearticulated relations between colonial peoples and metropolitan powers during the inter-war period. This new relationship was governed by efforts to balance two defining principles: the self-determination of peoples; and free trade and equal access to resources and markets. Both arms of this dual mandate impacted on the protection and control of the cultural objects and sites of colonised peoples. The United States played a crucial role in the articulation of both arms during the inter-war period.

The implications of economic and colonial rivalry to European stability and international order became painfully clear during the progress of the First World War. Consequently, there was fervent discussion about the fate of colonies and the application of self-determination to peoples generally.[3] This intensified with a growing appreciation of the swelling force of nationalism within Arab States, Africa and Asia, feeding the local calls for reform.[4] US President Woodrow Wilson warned colonial powers that: 'The rights of nations to self-determination . . . is an imperative principle of action which will be disregarded by statesmen in the future only at their own risk'.[5]

---

[3] See M. O. Hudson, The Protection of Minorities and Natives in Transferred Territories, in E. M. House and C. Seymour (eds.), *What Really Happened at Paris: The Story of the Peace Conference* (New York, 1921), p.224; S. Olivier, *The League of Nations and Primitive Peoples* (London, 1918); and E. C. Mower, *International Government*, (Boston, 1931), pp.427ff.

[4] See H. N. Brailsford, The Rise of Nationalism in the East (1927) 2 *Problems in Peace* 318–35; E. J. Hobsbawm, *Nations and Nationalism since 1780: Programme, Myth, Reality* (2nd edn, Cambridge, 1997), pp.136ff; and B. Anderson, *Imagined Communities: Reflections on the Origin and Spread of Nationalism* (rev. edn, London, 1991), pp.113ff.

[5] Cited in G. T. Morris, In Support of the Right of Self-Determination for Indigenous Peoples under International Law (1987) 29 GYIL 277 at 307.

Wilson had contemplated that self-determination should be applicable to all peoples. The victorious Allied governments while broadly agreeing that former German colonies and Turkish territories would not be returned to these defeated Powers, shied away from the universal application of self-determination. In a reaffirmation of the 'scale of civilisation' first articulated in the nineteenth century, they maintained that the inhabitants of these territories were incapable of self-governance. Instead, a definite trust was imposed which implied a right of self-determination following a period of tutelage.

President Wilson acknowledged that the rights and interests of the colonised, the coloniser and the international community were not always compatible.[6] He sought to address the imbalance of interests in the colonial relationship by arguing that: '[I]n determining all such questions of sovereignty the interests of the population concerned must have equal weight with the equitable claims of the government whose title is to be determined'.[7] The compromise reached between those pushing for annexation and those favouring some form of defined tutelage was contained in Article 22 of the 1919 Covenant of the League of Nations.[8] The mandatory power held the territory on double trust on behalf of the inhabitants of the territory, which translated into the duty of 'advanced' states to develop 'backward' territories, and the international community, to ensure its members had equal access to the territory's resources and labour.[9] The reaffirmation of the dual mandate meant there was a continuation of the internal dilemma between a trustee's duty to guard the welfare of colonised peoples and the duty to the progress of civilisation via the development of their resources. This division between the principles of self-determination and development, and their assignment to different beneficiaries, necessarily compromised the interests of colonised peoples. It impacted adversely on the ability of all colonised peoples to preserve and develop their cultural heritage.

The 1919 Covenant modified the nineteenth-century doctrine of trusteeship by articulating a 'definite trust' applicable to certain colonies. In effect, it became the duty of the mandatory power to prepare and develop the peoples of mandated territories – 'for their ultimate growth into Statehood' and the exercise of self-determination.[10] Article 22 invoked the 'sacred trust of civilisation' calling 'advanced nations' to assist 'peoples not yet able to stand by themselves under the strenuous conditions of the modern world'. The 1885 Berlin Conference had rejected the

---

[6] See M. Pomerance, The United States and Self-Determination: Perspectives on the Wilsonian Conception (1976) 70 AJIL 1.

[7] Cited in Mower, *International*, p.428; and H. W. V. Temperley (ed.), *History of the Peace Conference of Paris* (1920–24) (Reprint, 6 vols., Oxford, 1924), vol.VI, p.500.

[8] Versailles, 28 June 1919, (1919) 225 Parry's CTS 195; (1919) 13(supp.) 128. See Temperley, *History*, vol.VI, p.501; and D. H. Miller, *The Drafting of the Covenant* (2 vols., New York, 1928), vol.II, p.737, Doc.34.

[9] See L. Kastl, Colonial Administration as an International Trust (1930) 5 *Problems in Peace* 132–66; N. de Mattos Bentwich, *The Mandate System* (New York, 1930), pp.8 and 16; Royal Institute of International Affairs, *The Colonial Problem: A Report by a Study Group of Members of the Royal Institute of International Affairs* (London, 1937), p.68; and P. M. Anker, The Mandate System: Origin – Principles – Application, LN Doc.IV.A.Mandates (Geneva, 1945), 22ff.

[10] *Ibid.* See Anker, 'Mandate', 33ff.

contention that colonised peoples had a legal right against their colonial occupiers. The abject failure of the resultant dependency on moral rights to prevent the worst excesses of colonialism led the drafters of the Covenant to include a supervisory mechanism within the mandate system.[11]

The articulation of the duties owed by the mandatory powers was firmly grounded in Anglo-American notions of trusteeship.[12] The principle of trusteeship had been espoused by the US government in its dealings with Native Americans since the early nineteenth century.[13] With US military successes and westward expansion, relations between the United States and Native American tribes were legally redefined by the Supreme Court from one between independent sovereign States to one of 'pupillage'. In the words of Chief Justice Marshall in *Cherokee Nation* v. *Georgia* (1831), Native Americans: 'look to [the US] government for protection; they rely upon its kindness and its power; appeal to it for relief of their wants; and address the president as their great father'.[14] Further, the US government acknowledged that such pupillage would continue until Native Americans were 'civilised as to be able wholly to manage and care for themselves'.[15]

What effect did the principle of the sacred trust of civilisation have on the protection of the cultural heritage of colonised peoples? Select territories were allotted into three tiers of mandates ranked 'according to the stage of development of the people, the geographical situation of the territory, its economic conditions and other similar circumstances' (Article 22, 1919 Covenant). The further removed the territory was from 'centres of civilisation', and European and US economic interests, the less detailed the guidelines for control and protection of cultural objects became.

The unilinear scale of civilisation in International Law was affirmed in this layering of peoples. These tiers are analysed as follows.

- The 'A' mandates covered the former territories of the Turkish empire. The sovereignty of these States was provisionally recognised and deemed sufficiently 'developed' that they only required administrative advice from a mandatory power (Article 22(4)). The regulation of cultural heritage (specifically archaeological sites) was one area singled out as requiring 'advice and assistance'.
- The 'B' mandates applied to the former German colonies in Central Africa. They stipulated specific conditions under which the mandatory power would administer the mandated territory. This included ensuring equal opportunities to trade and equal access to resources for nationals of member States of the

---

[11] See A. McNair, Editor's Preface, in Bentwich, *Mandate*, pp.vi–vii.

[12] See A. Margalith, *The International Mandates* (Baltimore, 1930), p.26; and J. Fischer Williams, *Some Aspects of the Covenant of the League of Nations* (London, 1934), p.205.

[13] See W. F. Willoughby, *Territories and Dependencies of the United States: Their Government and Administration* (New York, 1905), p.290; T. Roosevelt, *Colonial Policies of the United States* (Garden City, 1937); Anon., American Precedents for Mandates (January 1920) *Review of Reviews* 20; and RIIA, *Colonial*, pp.245–49.

[14] 30 US (5 Pet.) 1, 17 (1831). See *Worcester* v. *Georgia*, 31 US (6 Pet.) 515 (1832); and *United States* v. *Kagama*, 118 US 375 (1886).

[15] See M. F. Lindley, *The Acquisition and Government of Backward Territory in International Law: Being a Treatise on the Law and Practice Relating to Colonial Expansion* (New York, 1926), p.331.

League. This guarantee covered cultural 'resources' such as archaeological sites (Article 22(5)).[16]

- Under the 'C' mandates, as a concession to the British Dominions, former German territories in South-West Africa and the South Pacific were administered as 'integral portions of its territory' (Article 22(6)). However, they were subject to the same conditions as the 'B' mandates.[17]
- Colonised peoples not governed by the mandate system remained under the sovereignty of their respective colonial powers with no international supervision.[18] The fate of these peoples and their cultural objects was subject to domestic legislation of their respective colonial powers or settler States.

In respect of the cultural heritage of all mandated territories, the duty of the mandatory power in practice was tipped in favour of the trust obligations owed to the international community, thereby inhibiting the ability of colonised peoples to determine how their cultures were preserved and developed.

The second arm of the so-called dual mandate articulated a 'common right of all mankind' to the resources and markets of colonial territories. J. A. Hobson maintained that: '[T]he occupier[s] of a land containing rich resources which can be developed for the benefit of mankind have no right to withhold them if they cannot or do not desire to develop them themselves'.[19] The equal treatment of all member States of the League in economic matters was considered necessary to eliminate the colonial rivalry, viewed as a significant trigger for the First World War.[20] This was a characteristically US principle with its origins in the Open Door policy.[21] Its incorporation into Article 22 of the 1919 Covenant of the league of Nations meant that concerns for the welfare of colonised peoples were balanced against the need for equitable access to their resources and labour to sustain European and North American industry. However, some commentators went as far as to accuse the United States of replacing 'political imperialism' with 'economic imperialism'.[22] With the true effect of the mandate system not being the application of self-determination to colonised peoples but the guarantee of these free trade policies.

---

[16] For discussion of colonial legislation covering cultural heritage in African States prior to independence: P. J. O'Keefe and L. V. Prott, *Law and the Cultural Heritage, Volume 1: Discovery and Excavation* (Oxford, 1984), pp.66–68, §§268–70; and L. V. Prott and P. J. O'Keefe, *Law and the Cultural Heritage, Volume 3: Movement* (London, 1989), pp.459–60, §911.

[17] The protection which 'C' mandates afforded the interests of occupied peoples in their own cultural objects was diminished because, unlike the 'B' mandates, there was no direct supervision: L. L. Ilsley, The Administration of Mandates by the British Dominions (1934) 28 APSR 287.

[18] The only universal protection afforded to all colonial peoples was Art.23(b): see H. D. Hall, *Studies in the Administration of International Law and Organization: The League Mandate System and the Problem of Dependencies* (Washington, 1948), pp.35ff; and Q. Wright, *Mandates under the League of Nations* (Chicago, 1930), pp.578–85.

[19] J. A. Hobson, *Towards International Government* (New York, 1915), pp.138–41.

[20] See RIIA, *Colonial*, pp.68ff; C. R. Buxton, *The Alternative to War* (London, 1936); Hall, *Studies*, pp.36–38; and P. B. Potter, Origin of the System of Mandates under the League of Nations (1922) 16 APSR 563 at 572.

[21] See Margalith, *International*, pp.48–49; and B. Gerig, *The Open Door and the Mandates System: A Study of the Economic Equality before and since the Establishment of the Mandate System* (London, 1929), p.199. The Open Door principle applied to 'A' and 'B' mandates.

[22] Pomerance, 'United States', 13.

The application of this principle to the 'cultural resources' of mandated territories cannot be doubted. As explained in Chapter 3, the 'A' mandate required the passage of legislation which was strictly defined to ensure equal treatment covering archaeological research and excavations to the nationals of all member States of the League of Nations.[23] This requirement was justified on the basis that these territories were 'the cradle of civilisation' (namely, Judaeo-Christian civilisation) and the preservation of its physical remnants was the duty of all humankind.[24]

These mandate provisions went beyond ensuring the preservation of 'the common heritage of mankind'. Instead, by guaranteeing equal access to archaeological excavations they privileged and promoted their redefinition as a cultural resource – the 'common right of all mankind'. The United States and Britain successfully promoted this arm of the dual mandate in response to draft conventions for the protection and restitution of cultural objects circulated during the inter-war period.

International Museum Office and restitution of cultural objects
The International Museum Office (Office international des musées (OIM)) pursued two significant international efforts to protect cultural objects between the wars. One involving the codification of the protection of cultural heritage during armed conflict is examined in Chapter 5. The other, centred on curbing the illicit traffic of cultural objects, is considered below. In summarising its achievements in the protection of cultural objects, the OIM noted: '[T]hose works which embody most completely the genius of a peoples are at the same time those in which appear most distinctly the characteristics common to all civilisations'.[25] With these OIM initiatives, as with the mandate system itself, the interests of colonised peoples in their cultural objects were compromised to accommodate the interests of the international community and States.

The OIM effort to curb illicit traffic focused exclusively on the establishment of an effective international mechanism for the restitution of cultural objects removed from States in contravention of national laws. As the convention evolved there emerged a fundamental schism between the protection of objects located in national collections and 'unknown' objects removed from archaeological sites. Inter-war negotiations privileged the restitution of cultural objects removed from museum collections, thereby elevating a Western notion of 'possessing' culturally significant items. This was invariably justified by promoting museum collections as the common heritage of all mankind and minimising 'injury' to the international art trade.

Intellectual cooperation: diversity and universality of cultures
To understand inter-war efforts to construct an international framework for the restitution of cultural objects, it is essential to describe briefly the League of Nations'

---

[23] See Anker, 'Mandate', 2, 30–31. The United States, not being a member of the League, concluded treaties with mandatory powers to secure for its citizens the same rights guaranteed to nationals of member States: see Bentwich, *Mandate*, p.14; and Temperley, *History*, vol.VI, pp.507–08.

[24] Bentwich, *Mandate*, p.43.

[25] Anon., Comparative Legislation and International Law in the field of Art and Archaeology (1940) 7–8 *Bulletin of Intellectual Co-operation* 345.

organ from which they sprang: the International Committee for Intellectual Cooperation (ICIC). The ICIC promoted the idea that peace amongst nations can be attained through a concerted effort at intellectual understanding across political boundaries. Its aims highlighted that the European ruling and intellectual elites continued to adhere to the idea of unilinear progress of civilisation and development, despite the destruction visited by the First World War.[26]

For the ICIC, the realisation of the world community necessitated the recognition and promotion of two, seemingly incompatible, principles: the diversity of national cultures and their universality.[27] Its first chairman Henri Bergson stressed that the culture of a people was incomplete in itself and could only truly be understood in context with other cultures.[28] Consequently, it was never the ambition of the ICIC to foster a uniform culture for all States. Rather, it nurtured the notion that international peace and stability depended upon countries having self-confidence and tolerance arising from knowledge of their own culture.

However, the ICIC was a predominantly European grouping and this duly affected its agenda and the formulation of its initiatives for the protection of cultural heritage.[29] The first National Committees of Intellectual Cooperation emerged in the newly independent States of Central and Eastern Europe which were forging ahead with the (re)constitution of national cultural patrimonies. Latin American States had a limited but significant impact on the work of the ICIC.[30]

Draft conventions for restitution during peacetime
By the 1920s, the OIM came under the auspices of the ICIC.[31] The importance of the OIM's work cannot be underestimated during the inter-war period in the area of the international protection of cultural objects. For the first time, there was a push to provide a comprehensive international legislative framework for the restitution of cultural objects outside the context of post-conflict reconstruction. This initiative, cut short by the Second World War, would nonetheless shape late twentieth-century measures for the control of illicit traffic of cultural objects.

The OIM itself noted in 1940 that its own formation and subsequent activities were governed by 'the internationality, the uniqueness and the universal ownership of the

---

[26] See F. S. Northedge, International Intellectual Co-operation within the League of Nations: Its Conceptual Basis and Lessons for the Present, PhD thesis, University of London (1953), p.28.

[27] Universality was the fourth principle of intellectual cooperation; and cultural diversity was tied in with the cultural rights elevated by the minority guarantees in the 1919 Paris peace treaties: see Northedge, 'International', pp.50 and 55.

[28] See Northedge, 'International', pp.13–17.

[29] In 1946, of the forty-eight National Committees, twenty-five were European, fourteen American, six Asiatic, two African and one Australasian: Northedge, 'International', p.414.

[30] States wishing to curb the European hegemony of the League were led primarily by South American States and were supported by China and India: H. Bonnet, Intellectual Co-operation (1942) *World Organization* 189 at 191–92; and J. Brown Scott, Intellectual Coöperation (1930) 24 AJIL 762.

[31] The ICIC, at the behest of France, established the International Institute of Intellectual Cooperation (IIIC) in Paris in 1925. Its Sub-committee for Arts and Letters encompassed the OIM: (1926) 6 *Monthly Summary of the League of Nations* 9–12; LN, LNOJ, Special Supplement (1926), No.44, 110; J. Destrée, Note on the Organisation of the Artistic Relations Section and the International Museum Office, 19 December 1929, LN Doc.CICI/CD/18, 4 and 7; Bonnet, 'Intellectual', 195–96; and Mower, *International*, p.501.

work of art and of the archaeological document'.[32] The distinction between 'work of art' and 'archaeological document' – or more pertinently, museum collection and archaeological site – proved crucial for the application of restitution under the 1933 OIM Draft convention. The importance of this distinction not only betrayed the scale of civilisation that had been reaffirmed by the 1919 Paris peace treaty provisions covering restitution. It also marked the ascendancy of another influence. The draft convention covering the restitution of objects, removed contrary to national laws, was gradually and significantly modified to address concerns of Anglo-American States. These States sought guarantees that the accessibility of all States to archaeological sites, deemed the common right of all mankind by the dual mandate, would be assured. Successive drafts were whittled down to accommodate this free trade agenda at the cost of their importance to the community from which they were removed.

The Resolution concerning the Protection of Historical Monuments and Works of Art approved by the Sixth Committee of the League of Nations Assembly of 1932 (1932 Resolution) articulated a number of fundamental concerns and principles covering the protection of cultural heritage during the inter-war period.[33] The overarching philosophy of the resolution was that works of art and archaeological objects were the 'heritage of mankind' and their preservation was the responsibility of 'the community of States, which are the guardians of civilisation'.[34] This concept implicitly restricts the right of national ownership by suggesting that the relevant State was not the only beneficiary of the artistic treasures in its possession.[35]

The 1932 Resolution promoted measures recognising the symbiotic relation between the mutual understanding among peoples through the appreciation of their diverse cultures and the protection of cultural objects.[36] It recommended that the League inculcate tolerance towards relics of the past whatever the civilisation or period to which they belong. This mission would be augmented with exchanges between public collections of States which 'ensur[ed] a better knowledge of the national genius of the different peoples beyond the borders within which they found expression'.[37]

A central recommendation of the 1932 Resolution was the drafting of a convention guaranteeing the integrity of national collections of States. However, it insisted that such a scheme would only apply to objects 'of unique interest to the artistic or archaeological heritage of their country' which were scheduled.[38] The possession of an object by an official act, whether by legislation or inclusion in public collection, would be the trigger for this conventional mode of restitution. Such a practice was a predominantly European (and American) activity. This qualifier became the linchpin

---

[32] See Anon., 'Comparative', 346 (see Note 25).
[33] See LN Doc.C.L.176.1932.XII, adopted by the ICIC on 23 July 1932, and approved by the Assembly of the League of Nations on 10 October 1932.
[34] Third recital, 1932 Resolution.
[35] See OIM, Annual Report of the President of the Directors' Committee of the International Museum Office, Geneva, 1 July 1932, LN Doc.ICIC/273, 2–3.
[36] Fifth and Sixth recitals, 1932 Resolution. See LN Doc. ICIC/273, 4–7.
[37] Sixth recital, 1932 Resolution; and LN Doc.ICIC/273, 6.
[38] LN Doc.ICIC/273, 7. See Recommendation 4, 1932 Resolution.

that separated the regimes covering restitution of cultural objects held by Europeans and those located in non-European territories.

There had been an exponential increase in national legislative schemes concerning cultural heritage during the early twentieth century, reflecting a growing public interest in the retention of 'the nation's artistic and historic possessions'.[39] Yet, there was little effective enforcement of national legislative controls beyond the boundaries of a State, even if the object removed was classified as inalienable or indefeasible (which implied a ban on its export).[40] The increased membership on League bodies of so-called source States spurred the campaign for an international convention for the restitution of illicitly removed cultural objects.

The passage of protective national legislation was also driven by the desire of certain States to stem the almost interminable tide of cultural loss to the United States.[41] The economic strength of the United States meant its collecting institutions had a vested interest in ensuring the continued unrestricted international trade in cultural objects. It advised the OIM in 1932 that 'objects do not disappear from public collections in this country, and there is no serious exportation of objects of artistic or historic value from private ownership in the United States', consequently there was no domestic legislation covering such acts.[42] If the United States felt secure in its ability to retain its national patrimony within its borders, the same could not be said for a significant number of States, especially after the First World War. It was this fear that drove the initial 1933 OIM Draft.

The Draft International Convention on the Repatriation of Objects of Artistic, Historical or Scientific Interest which have been Lost, or Stolen or Unlawfully Alienated or Exported (1933 OIM Draft) addressed its sole purpose in the preamble: 'insuring one another mutual assistance in the recovery of objects removed from their respective national artistic heritages'.[43] Despite the direct reference to the 1932 Resolution in its preamble, the 1933 OIM Draft mirrored significantly the concerns reflected in the restitution provisions concerning in the 1919 Paris peace treaties covering Central and Eastern Europe. This latter intellectual debt was evidenced in the description of objects to be encompassed by the proposed convention. Article 1 defined the proposed convention as being applicable to 'movable or immovable objects of an artistic, historical or scientific character'.

---

[39] See C. de Visscher, La protection des patrimoines artistiques et historiques nationaux: nécessité d'une réglementation internationale (1938) 43–44 *Mouseion* 7; C. de Visscher, Rapport de l'office international des musées a la commission internationale de coopération intellectuelle (juillet 1933) et texte du premier projet de convention internationale (1939) 1 *Art et archéologie: recueil de législation comparée et de droit international* 47ff; and C. de Visscher, International Protection of Works of Art and Historic Monuments,Washington, *US Documents and State Papers*, International Information and Cultural Series, No.8, June 1949, 821 at 856–59 (originally in (1935) 16 RDILC 32).

[40] Visscher, 'International Protection', 857.

[41] See W. Treue, *Art Plunder: The Fate of Art in War and Unrest*, trans. B. Creighton (New York, 1961), pp.212–13.

[42] L. V. Coleman, Director of the AAM to Foundoukidis, Secretary-General of OIM, 5 March 1932, UNESCO Archive: OIM.IV.27.I, p.287, IICI. Dossier de correspondence, Office international des musées, conservation des œuvres d'art, protection de patrimoine artistique, UNESCO Archives.

[43] LN Doc.CL.205.1933.XII, Annex; and Visscher, 'International Protection', Appendix B, 865–66. See OIM.IV.27.I, pp.220–86.

The only trigger necessary to attract the operation of the 1933 OIM Draft was the alienation or export of the object contrary to national legislation (Article 1). Unlike subsequent drafts, it made no distinction between objects removed from museum collections or archaeological excavations. This was reinforced by a contemporary international controversy regarding stelae removed from Tell el-Amarna, Egypt. The fragments were illicitly exported and offered for sale on the European market after the circulation of the draft.[44] The incident led the Belgian National Committee to query whether the definition of objects covered by the proposed convention covered 'fragments de monuments'.[45] Euripide Foundoukidis, of the OIM, advised that draft Article 1 covered both movables and immovables.[46] However, successive redrafts of the convention would exclude objects from archaeological excavations.

Egyptian museum officials wrote to various museums providing details of the theft and imploring them to desist from purchasing objects of uncertain provenance.[47] In reply, the trustees of the British Museum advised that it was their practice to 'refrain as far as possible from buying or accepting any figures or fragments of any kind known to have been torn from any standing monuments . . . or known to have been stolen from a public museum'.[48] Self-regulation was the preferred position of the Anglo-American museum community and this position became *de jure* in respect of cultural objects removed from archaeological sites.

Under the 1933 OIM Draft, parties were required to lend their good offices to aid in the 'restitution or repatriation' as quickly as possible of such objects located in their territory as a result of 'loss, theft, or alienation or illicit export' (Article 2). During this period, Spain instituted negotiations at the museum level between its *Museo Arqueológico Nacional* and the Fogg Art Museum, Harvard University after it learnt that the Fogg had acquired the Sahagún Tomb which had been illicitly removed from Spain.[49] The OIM publicly acknowledged the successful museum-to-museum negotiations and ensuing reciprocal exchange of objects as 'a memorable example worthy of being imitated'.[50]

In its response to the 1933 OIM Draft, the United States advised that it saw no benefit in international legislation which required its domestic courts to enforce the

---

[44] J. Capart to S. S. Pacha, Egyptian ambassador to Washington, 10 April 1933, OIM.IV.27.I, pp.172–73.

[45] J. Destrée, Belgian National Committee on Intellectual Co-operation to Foundoukidis, 27 July 1933: OIM.IV.27.I, p.171.

[46] Foundoukidis to Destrée, n.d.: OIM.IV.27.I, p.168.

[47] R. Engelbach to the Conservator, Musée du Cinquantenaire, Brussels: OIM.IV.27.I, p.177; and Engelbach to G. Hill, Director, British Museum: V&A Archive: League of Nations, IIIC, 1925.

[48] British Museum Trustees' Committee Minutes, Egyptian Antiquities: Proposed Alteration of the Egyptian Law, 12 October 1935, p.5212. The stelae were acquired by two US museums: personal communication, D. Wythe, Archivist and Manager, Special Library Collections, Brooklyn Museum, 24 January 2001.

[49] See Anon., The Spanish Government's Gifts to the Fogg Art Museum, *Harvard Alumnae Bulletin* (15 September 1933), n.p.

[50] Spain presented the Fogg Art Museum with several archaeological specimens and sculptures as a 'gift in gratitude': Anon., 'Spanish'. Visscher likened exchange to the principle of reciprocity in the restitution provision contained in the 1919 Paris peace treaties: Visscher, 'International Protection', 858–59.

laws of other States.[51] OIM officials conceded that to attract the participation of Anglo-American States drafters would have to address the foreignness of the principle of inalienability to the common law tradition.[52] Contrary to accepted wisdom, I would suggest the division between States which approved or disapproved of the 1933 OIM Draft did not necessarily fall along Civil Law/Common Law lines.[53] Instead, it is more pertinent to ascertain whether the State felt its national cultural patrimony to be under threat because of illicit traffic or whether it supported an unrestricted international art trade.

This divide was heightened by the paramount role assigned to the State in the proposed restitution framework. The 1933 OIM Draft provided that where a dispute could not be resolved diplomatically between State parties, it would be determined by an arbitral tribunal (Article 7).[54] The emphasis on the State, particularly 'national artistic heritage', became more pronounced with each successive redraft. This effectively sidelined the protection of the cultural objects of minorities or indigenous communities unless it was taken up by their relevant State. Nor was there any recourse for intra-State claims by these groups for objects removed to national collections.

The Draft International Convention for the Protection of National Historic or Artistic Treasures (1936 OIM Draft), and the subsequent amendment of draft Articles 1 and 17 occurring in the lead up to the 1937 Cairo Conference on excavations, heralded the shunning of unqualified recognition of national protective legislation.[55] This shift in emphasis marked the ascendancy of the Anglo-American free trade agenda. Further, the manner in which this accommodation was achieved meant the OIM initiative almost exclusively addressed losses from museum collections, thereby further privileging the mode of possessing cultural objects set down by European and settler States.

The definition of cultural objects covered by the 1936 OIM Draft was broadened to include 'objects of remarkable palæontological, archæological, historic or artistic interest' (Article 1(1)). This terminology picks up on that used in similar instruments proposed by American countries during the same period. Arguably, this wider definition was precipitated by the efforts of settler States to create a unified national culture through the assimilation of the cultures and histories of minorities and indigenous communities.

---

[51] See US Department of State Note, 5 April 1934: OIM.IV.27.I, pp.79–80. It also stated the proposal added nothing to existing private international law remedies.

[52] See R. Weiss to P. Lepaulle, 18 March 1933; Weiss to Lepaulle, 24(?) April 1933; and Observations of M. Giraud, Director, Legal Section, 22 June 1933, OIM.IV.1927.I, pp.234–35, 219 and 207–11.

[53] See Riddell, Canadian Advisory Officer to the Secretary-General, League of Nations, 14 May 1934 (disapproved of the 1933 OIM Draft), OIM.IV.27.I, p.73; the British Foreign Office (disapproved), pp.67–69; R. G. Casey, Commonwealth of Australia to the Secretary-General, May 1934 (approved), p.52; and Secretary of State for India, Whitehall to Secretary-General, 28 June 1934 (approved), p.48.

[54] The 1936 OIM Draft, although substantially the same as the 1933 OIM Draft, placed greater emphasis on negotiated settlements and consent of parties to arbitration (Art.11).

[55] See Draft International Convention for the Protection of National Historic or Artistic Treasures, LN Doc.C.L.34.1936.XII, Annex; and Visscher, 'International Protection', Appendix B, 866–868. For governmental responses: see OIM.IV.27.II, pp.111, 115, 117–50 and 178–80.

With the inclusion of two words: 'national' and 'treasures', the title of the 1936 OIM Draft and the preamble subtly but significantly signalled the altered focus from that of its predecessor. First, there was a gradual emphasis on the 'State' and its 'national culture' as the driving force of the 1936 OIM Draft. The 1933 OIM Draft contained unfettered sanctioning of the restitution of cultural objects removed from a claimant State in contravention of domestic legislation prohibiting alienation or export. The 1936 OIM Draft redefined its purpose as the protection of cultural objects considered by the respective State parties to be of national importance. This shift pervaded the more detailed procedural provisions.[56] Second, the operation of the convention was further narrowed to cultural objects which were considered 'treasures' and 'remarkable'.[57] The claimant State was the 'sole judge of the nature and value of such objects' (Article 1(2)).

These changes foreshadowed the latter amendment that only objects in national collections would attract the operation of the convention. This change was realised with redrafted Article 1(2) stating:

> [T]he claim, in order to be admissible, must relate to objects which, being the property of the State or of public bodies and forming part of their collections, became inalienable by virtue of the laws of the claimant State before they left the country.[58]

The redrafted Article 17 provided for the optional extension of the convention to objects in private collections. However, under the Article such objects also had to be scheduled as being 'of national concern' by an official act which excluded them from international trade prior to the illicit export.[59] These amendments were retained and extended in the 1939 redraft. The original request for 'clarification' of this provision came from States, including Britain and the United States, which had advised that the text did not 'harmonise with their municipal law'.[60] Despite these significant concessions, these States notified their intention not to participate in any related diplomatic conference.[61]

The Draft International Convention for the Protection of National Collections of Art and History (1939 OIM Draft) was prepared after the 1937 Cairo Conference

---

[56] For example, the claimant State took the place of the person(s) who had custody of the object prior to removal (Art.6(3)); the State in which the object is found was required to provide the fullest cooperation to the claimant State to facilitate the repatriation claim (Art.5); and the State should seize the object and deposit it with an appropriate museum conservator until the matter was resolved (Art.5(2)).

[57] Second recital, Preamble and Art.1(1), 1936 OIM Draft.

[58] LN Doc.C.L.34.1936.XII, Annex, Corr.2; and C. de Visscher, Nouvelle rédaction des articles 1er et 17 (1939) 1 *Art et archéologie: recueil de législation comparée et de droit international* 75.

[59] See ICIC, Report of the Committee on the Work of its Nineteenth Plenary Session, 9 August 1937, LN Doc.C.327.M.220.1937.XXII.A.1, Resolution adopted by the Plenary Commission, 17 July 1937, 24–25.

[60] A. Leeper, British Foreign Office to Secretary-General, League of Nations, 25 May 1934, OIM.IV.1927.I, pp.67–70; Report of International Committee on Intellectual Cooperation, 6 September 1937, 15 and 25, FO Minute W16679/654/98, PRO FO 371/21250; and Foundoukidis(?) to L. V. Coleman, Director, AAM, 8 June 1936, OIM.IV.27.III, pp.151–56.

[61] See S. Hawks, Secretary of the US Delegation to J. A. Avenol, Secretary-General, League of Nations, 29 April 1936: OIM.IV.27.III, pp.121–22; and H. J. Seymour, British Foreign Office to the Secretary-General, League of Nations, 24 July 1936: OIM.IV.27.III, pp.117–18.

and on the eve of the Second World War, by a drafting committee made up entirely of European jurists.[62] All of these factors influenced the further narrowing of the application of the 1939 OIM Draft and the progression to the centrality of the 'State' and its 'national culture'. The redrafted preamble stated:

> Noting the too frequent occurrence of acts prejudicial to the integrity of the artistic and historic possessions of States,
>
> And being desirous of facilitating by international mutual assistance the restitution of objects abstracted from their respective nations' collections . . .

Visscher explained that the 'new wording simply defin[ed] the concrete purpose of the Convention'.[63] It was conceded that the 'character of restitution forms the essential and also the most solid basis of the proposed convention'.[64] This purpose was specifically driven by the national concerns of State parties. The expansive operation of earlier drafts was pared down because of the lack of uniformity in national legislative schemes or agreement on the notion of its public ownership, and a desire not to impede unduly the international art trade.[65]

The type of objects covered by the convention had not been altered from the 1936 Draft. However, the ambit of cultural objects attracting the operation of the instrument was severely circumscribed in a manner previously reserved for objects in private collections. Therefore, even objects in public collections had to be scheduled by State parties prior to their illicit removal (Article 1(3)). Possession as defined by Western States, that is, 'the objects claimed were known to that administration and inventories by' the claimant States, was the key to restitution.[66] The redrafted and significantly narrower Article 1 did not address (and by its operation specifically excluded) objects removed clandestinely from archaeological sites.

This tightening of the Convention's application incorporated several other concessions to the United States and Britain. First, the drafting committee accepted that inalienability was not recognised by all States and the convention as drafted would severely undermine the international art trade.[67] The 1939 OIM Draft required that the act triggering its operation be contrary to the property rights 'under the criminal law of the claimant State' (Article 2(1)).[68] Second, the Committee acknowledged the OIM's efforts to promote the universal appreciation of all cultures through the regulation of international art exhibitions and exchanges (Article 2(2)). The provision gave a 'legitimate owner' whose objects were overseas for an exhibition or repair the same rights he or she would have in their own State.[69] Thirdly, the 1939 OIM Draft explicitly provided for non-retroactivity (Article 2(3)).[70] Finally, it reaffirmed

---

[62] Visscher, 'International Protection', Appendix B, 869–871; and C. de Visscher, Le projet définitif établi en 1939 en vue de la conférence diplomatique (1939) 1 *Art et archéologie: recueil de législation comparée et de droit international* 78–79.

[63] Visscher, 'Projet', 93.   [64] LN Doc.C.327.M.220.1937.XII, 69.

[65] Visscher, 'Projet', 89, 91.

[66] LN Doc.C.327.M.220.1937.XII, 69; and FO Minute W16679/654/98, PRO FO 371/21250.

[67] See Visscher, 'Projet', 89.   [68] Visscher, 'Projet', 93, 95.

[69] *Ibid.* By late 1936, the OIM had circulated to the various member States for comment a draft Recommendation regarding International Art Exhibitions, LN Doc.C.L.207.1936.XII, Annex.

[70] E. Foundoukidis to U. Aloisi, 15 March 1935: OIM.IV.27.II, pp.104–05.

the precedence of 'diplomatic channels' as the first avenue for resolving disputes under the instrument (Article 4(1)).[71] This provision was influenced to a significant degree by 'the daily experience of museums'; the preferred Anglo-American position of museum-to-museum negotiations (instead of judicial avenues contained in the original 1933 OIM Draft); and the outcome of the 1937 Cairo Conference.[72]

During the inter-war period, the promotion of free trade and equal access to cultural resources was most pronounced in the international regulation of archaeological sites, which reinforced the principles set down by the mandate system. The promotion of 'international custodianship' of archaeological sites was largely motivated by efforts of museums in metropolitan centres to access objects in mandated and colonial territories according to standards dictated by them.

The regulation of excavations was raised early in the OIM's work and repeatedly broached by non-European States in response to inter-war draft OIM conventions. Early OIM drafts were intended to cover illicit traffic of cultural objects, regardless of where they had been located. The tension created by the twin aims of curbing the illicit export of national cultural heritage and the need to facilitate the international art trade resulted in significant amendment to draft Article 1. The futility of such a system for protection and restitution of cultural objects located in non-European States was articulated by the Iraqi delegation. It argued that in States 'where illegal and secret excavations . . . [are] extremely difficult to control . . . It follows that stolen objects cannot be always known and therefore [are] not registered by the authority concerned'.[73] It maintained that the trigger for the Convention should be the lack of appropriate 'exportation certification'.[74] In response, it was argued that the inclusion of objects removed from clandestine excavations would 'compromise' the proposed OIM draft convention because such objects, by their nature, could not satisfy the requirement of 'prior possession . . . the indispensable condition of the [restitution] claim'.[75]

The Final Act of the International Conference on Excavations (1937 Cairo Conference Final Act) enunciated recommendations complementing and even extending the obligations of the 1936 OIM Draft.[76] The 1937 Cairo Conference Final Act, which preceded the 1939 OIM Draft, reflected the ascendancy of the notion of the common right of all humankind to archaeological sites and cultural objects contained there, in much the same way as the mandate system guaranteed the free trade and equal access to these cultural resources.

European and North American archaeological congresses and learned societies promoted the universal and educative role of public collections to all peoples and

---

[71] This was tempered by a number of qualifiers: 'The country to which the claim is addressed shall, at the earliest possible date and in conformity with its legislation, take all necessary steps to locate the object, prevent its export or its acquisition by its collections and induce the holder to surrender it voluntarily' (Art.4(2)).

[72] Visscher, 'Projet', 99.

[73] Iraqi delegation to Secretary-General, League of Nations, 21 May 1936, OIM.IV.27.II, pp.162–63.

[74] OIM.IV.27.II, pp.162–63.   [75] LN Doc.C.327.M.220.1937.XII, 69.

[76] See E. Foundoukidis and OIM, *Final Act of the International Conference on Excavations* (Paris, 1937); LN Doc.C.L.191.1937.XII; LN Doc.C.327.M.220.1937.XII, 68–70, and Appendix 2, 84–89; and (1937) 39–40 *Mouseion* 251–55.

the need to 'conciliate the interests of the State on the soil of which excavations are undertaken with the requirements of international collaboration'.[77] To dissuade illicit activities and assist museums in the pursuit of their 'scientific and educational mission', States were recommended to provide means of legally acquiring such objects, including the equitable division of archaeological finds, the disposition of duplicates, the relaxation of export controls to encourage exchange, de-accession and depositing in foreign museums, the waiver of the right of restitution, and free trade in objects not subject to export controls.[78] All these measures reaffirmed the Anglo-American position that such cultural objects were a 'resource' forming the common right of all humankind.

Unlike the OIM drafts, which sought to facilitate the restitution of national cultural objects removed contrary to the national export controls, the 1937 Cairo Conference Final Act laid down principles to establish uniformity amongst domestic legal systems.[79] Later OIM drafts gradually restricted the breadth of cultural objects covered by the convention in a manner that *implicitly* dictated the type of national regulation of cultural property that would attract the operation of the instrument. It privileged domestic legislation which reaffirmed Western models of possessing cultural objects significant to a State. The 1937 Cairo Conference *explicitly* recommended the need to legislate and the type of laws to be passed in order to attract the 'possibility' of a negotiated return.

The 1937 Cairo Conference Final Act addressed the protection and distribution of 'cultural resources' with a greater emphasis on its accessibility to all States. This concession was telling given that cultural objects are a non-renewable resource. The ascendancy of the notion of the common right of mankind in respect of archaeological sites was evident in the recommendations for the repression of clandestine excavations. The primary recommendation, which required that museums adopt a non-binding, self-regulating approach to acquisition policy, was one broadly espoused by metropolitan institutions. It stated: '[T]he museums should . . . satisfy themselves that nothing in its intrinsic character or the circumstances in which it is offered . . . warrants the belief that the object is the result of clandestine excavation or any other illicit operation'.[80] Foundoukidis noted that these recommendations were significant because 'they complete legal clauses that figure in the [1936 OIM Draft]'.[81]

The restitution scheme contained within the OIM draft provided legal avenues for enforcement. In contrast, the 1937 Cairo Conference 'preferred to seek a moral agreement among the museums . . . [that] would obtain a more immediate

---

[77] Foundoukidis and OIM, *Final Act*, p.3.
[78] Section II, Recommendation 13(b) and (c); and Section III, Recommendations 18, 21 and 22, Section II, of the 1937 Cairo Conference Final Act.
[79] The principles covered the protection and preservation of archaeological property; uniform definition of the 'antique object'; uniform concept of the ownership of the archaeological subsoil; standardising the regulation of the trade in antiquities in the 'higher interest of a common heritage'; and the introduction of legislative provisions on the system of archaeological excavations in countries where they did not exist.
[80] Recommendation 15, Section III of the Cairo Final Act.
[81] Foundoukidis and OIM, *Final Act*, p.3.

result . . . than by seeking to secure engagements of a legal character'.[82] A museum that was offered an object it suspected was illicitly exported was required to notify the relevant authorities and facilitate its repatriation to its 'country of origin'.[83] The inadequacy of solely relying on a moral right and the goodwill of museum staff is described in Chapter 3.

Another significant by-product of the 1937 Cairo Conference was the *Manual on the Technique of Archæological Excavations* (1940).[84] The Manual gave pointers to archaeologists in their dealings with 'native' peoples.

(1) Care should be taken not to do anything which would clash with 'native' usage and persons in authority.

(2) The sacred nature of some objects may mean that the archaeologists' work is viewed as sacrilege, therefore, natives should be 'educate[d]' that their work was a 'respectful study of their history and of their own past'.

(3) There was recognition that 'native' peoples could provide invaluable additional information concerning the objects being excavated.

(4) The development of the relationship between 'native' peoples and the excavators would assist in the preservation and security of the site. To facilitate this later goal, archaeologists would need to 'educate' locals that 'these tokens of the past . . . are entitled to the same reverent respect as their own beliefs and traditions'.[85]

Importantly, the manual conceded that archaeologists' work in pursuing 'a valuable document for science' also 'involved to a certain extent the destruction or removal of these historic records'.[86] This anomaly was evident in US government efforts to fulfil its trust obligations to Native Americans and their cultural heritage during this period.

United States and Native Americans: assimilation to Indian New Deal

During inter-war treaty negotiations, the US conceptualisation of cultural objects as cultural resources was extended to include its own cultural patrimony and that of Native Americans. This final section focuses on how the relationship between the US government and Native Americans reflected and influenced the changing modalities of Anglo-American colonialism from the late nineteenth century. Further, whilst the US government acknowledged that it owed a duty to Native Americans, this duty was largely defined by the dominant culture and not by Native Americans themselves.

First, there is an examination of the assimilation policies to suppress and replace the Native American cultures with that of Euro-American culture as part of a push to maximise the availability of land for US settlement and industry. Then, there will be an explanation of how these policies were replaced in the early twentieth century with the redefinition of Native American objects as 'primitive art', a resource to

---

[82] Foundoukidis and OIM, *Final Act*, p.5.
[83] Foundoukidis and OIM, *Final Act*, Section III, Recommendations 16 and 17.
[84] OIM, *Manual on the Technique of Archæological Excavations*, (Paris, 1940), p.9.
[85] OIM, *Manual*, pp.10–11.   [86] *Ibid.*

be exploited in the search for an 'authentic' US art movement. Each phase deeply affected legislative protection of Native American cultural objects and practices in a manner largely prescribed by non-indigenous officials' perception of indigenous peoples' needs and the dominant culture's own agenda.

Assimilation and the salvage mentality

This first phase – covering the 'golden age' of museum collecting from the 1870s to 1920s – coincided with the rapid westward expansion of US settlements. The period was marked by the aggressive implementation of assimilation policies upon Native Americans by the US government. This, in turn, led anthropologists and museums to adopt a 'salvage mentality' towards Native American cultures and cultural objects.

During the nineteenth century, a series of US Supreme Court decisions wound back US recognition of the sovereignty of Native American nations. The Bureau of Indian Affairs (BIA) was established in 1834 as a quasi-domestic foreign office within the War Department. By 1849, as the BIA took on the role of guardian to defeated tribes, it was transferred to the Department of the Interior. Native Americans driven from their traditional lands during this period suffered the loss of their own existing economic, political, social and cultural structures.

In response, the US government entered into agreements with the tribes to establish reservations for these communities to be 'protected' while being 'trained' to cope with their changed circumstances.[87] By 1871, the US government abandoned the treaty-making system, which signalled the complete usurpation of Native American sovereignty in International Law and the assumption of the role of trustee by the federal government.[88] Although this trusteeship phase was assumed to be temporary, there was constant disagreement on the method of its termination.

Through the nineteenth and early twentieth centuries, the dominant policy aimed at terminating trusteeship was assimilation through detribalisation. The General Allotment Act of 1887 (1887 Dawes Act) aimed to facilitate the demise of the reservation system by allotting portions of tribally owned land to individual Native Americans, with the 'surplus' being opened up to non-indigenous settlement.[89] This form of assimilation was justified on the basis that development of the lands and resources was necessary for the progress of civilisation generally. A contemporary report noted: '[W]e have securely paved the way for the extermination of the Indian races . . . [T]his attempt to manufacture him into a white man by act of Congress . . . [is] the most unjustifiable'.[90] Assimilationists considered it desirable to end the tribe as a separate political and cultural unit. In effect, Native Americans as 'groups' were to be

---

[87] See W. A. Brophy and S. D. Aberle, *The Indian. America's Unfinished Business: Report of the Commission on the Rights, Liberties and Responsibilities of the American Indian* (Norman, 1966), pp.13ff; and F. S. Cohen, *F S Cohen's Handbook of Federal Indian Law*, ed. R. Strickland (Charlottesville, 1982), pp.98ff.

[88] See Cohen, *Handbook*, pp.105ff; H. Fritz, *The Movement for Indian Assimilation 1860–1890* (Philadelphia, 1963); and W. E. Washburn, *Red Man's Land/White Man's Law: The Past and Present Status of the American Indian* (2nd edn, Norman, 1995), pp.73ff.

[89] 24 Stat. 388 (1887). Reproduced in F. P. Prucha (ed.), *Documents of United States Indian Policy* (2nd edn, Lincoln, 1975), pp.171–74.

[90] US Congress, House, Minority Report of the House Committee on Indian Affairs, House Report (Rpt.) no.1576, 7–10, 46th Cong., 2nd sess., serial 1938 (1887), cited in Morris, 'Support', 301, n.97.

dismantled and their individual members 'civilised' by their assimilation into US society.

Archaeologists and anthropologists were intimately involved on various levels in this phase of the 'civilising mission' of Native Americans by US authorities. On a practical level, they assisted in the administration of the 1887 Dawes Act which in turn facilitated the most intense period of collecting of Native American cultural objects.[91] There was an acute perception amongst anthropologists that indigenous cultures were declining and threatened with extinction because of not only warfare and disease but also assimilation and acculturation policies. They strove to 'salvage' these cultures through the collection of objects and data before Native Americans 'vanished'.[92]

For many anthropologists, the removal of sacred objects from the tribe and their placement in museum collections facilitated the assimilation of indigenous individuals into the dominant settler culture through the severance of ties to their communities and existing way of life.[93] Indigenous peoples challenged and continue to challenge the assumption that they voluntarily relinquished such objects.[94] Also, they argue that it is incorrect to presume an intention to relinquish custodianship permanently.

Like its European counterpart, from its inception American anthropology promoted its practical application to the expansionist policies of the dominant culture. Contemporary anthropological theories strove to 'demonstrate' the inferiority of Native Americans and the 'inevitable' extinction of Native Americans to justify the 'civilising mission' and confiscation of tribal territories.[95] For the US anthropological establishment, the 1893 World's Columbian Exposition became an ideal opportunity to 'educate' the general public of this 'self-evident' linear progression of civilisation. Cultural objects from all periods and peoples were arranged in series, with Native American objects placed at an early stage of development leading to the Euro-American manufactures at the end.[96]

[91] See R. Niezen, *Spirit Wars: Native North American Religions in the Age of Nation Building* (Berkeley, 2000), 161ff; and C. M. Hinsley, *The Smithsonian and the American Indian: Making a Moral Anthropology in Victorian America* (Washington, 1994).

[92] See S. Culin cited in D. Fane, The Language of Things: Stewart Culin as Collector, in D. Fane, I. Jacknis and I. M. Breen, *Objects of Myth and Memory: American Indian Art at The Brooklyn Museum* (exh. cat., New York, 1991), p.13 at p.20; Fane, 'Language', 21; and R. W. Rydell, *All the World's a Fair: Visions of Empire at American International Expositions, 1879–1916* (Chicago, 1984), pp.23–24.

[93] Peabody Museum, *Annual Report* (Cambridge, MA, 1890), p.91, also cited in Niezen, *Spirit*, p.178.

[94] For example, Onondaga tribe's unsuccessful proceedings against the New York State Museum: *Onondaga Nation v. Thatcher*, 26 Misc. 428, 433–34, 61 NYS 1027 (NY Sup. Ct 1899); affd 53 AD 561, 65 NYS 2d 1014 (NY App. Div. 1900); affd 169 NY 584, 62 NE 1098 (1901); appeal dismissed on other grounds 189 US 306 (1903); G. Abrams, The Case for Wampum: Repatriation from the Museum of the American Indian to the Six Nations Confederacy, in F. Kaplan (ed.), *Museums and the Making of 'Ourselves': The Role of Objects in National Identity* (London, 1994), p.351; and S. Platzman, Objects of Controversy (1992) 41 AULR 517. See L. M. Breen, The Osage of Oklahoma, in Fane *et al.*, *Objects*, p.281.

[95] R. H. McLaughlin, The Antiquities Act of 1906: Politics and the Framing of an American Anthropology and Archaeology (1998) 23 OCULR 61 at 63.

[96] See Rydell, *Visions*, pp.45–46; C. M. Hinsley, The World as Marketplace: Commodification of the Exotic at the World's Columbian Exposition, Chicago, 1893, in I. Karp and S. D. Lavine (eds.), *Exhibiting Cultures: The Poetics and Politics of Museum Displays* (Washington, 1991), p.344; W. J. Rushing,

Figure 4.2 University of Pennsylvania exhibit at the World's Columbian Exposition, Chicago, 1893.

The assimilation of indigenous peoples and their cultures into this unilinear progression of civilisation, defined by the dominant culture, was reinforced with the passage of the Antiquities Act of 1906.[97] At the turn of the century, there was a growing awareness of the impact of assimilation on indigenous cultural production, the exponential tourist market, local museums and overseas collectors and, consequently, awareness of the depletion of Native American 'archaeological' sites.[98] The House of Representatives' Committee on Public Lands recognised the threat of uncontrolled excavation of these sites. In 1906, the Committee pointed out that 'practically every civilised government in the world had enacted laws for the preservation of the remains of the historic past, and had provided that excavations and explorations shall be conducted in some systematic and practical way'.[99] The Antiquities Act is significant because the 1939 OIM Draft and the 1937 Cairo Conference Final Act accommodated many of its preoccupations.

The Antiquities Act of 1906 made looting of Native American sites on federal land a criminal offence and formally entrusted their excavation to scientists. It empowered the President to designate key archaeological sites and 'other objects of historic or scientific interest' on land owned or controlled by the US government, as national monuments. Section 3 provides:

Native American Art and the New York Avant-Garde (Austin, 1995), pp.6–7; I. Jacknis, The Road to Beauty: Stewart Culin's American Indian Exhibitions at The Brooklyn Museum, in Fane *et al.*, *Objects*, p.29; and D. Fane, New Questions for 'Old Things': The Brooklyn Museum's Zuni Collection, in J. C. Berlo (ed.), *The Early Years of Native American Art History* (London, 1992), p.62.

[97] Pub.L. 59–209, 34 Stat. 225 (1906), codified at 16 USC §§431–33 (2000).

[98] See S. Culin, The Road to Beauty (1927) 14 *The Brooklyn Museum Quarterly* 41 at 49; and S. Culin to E. Mindt, 9 November 1925, General Correspondence [1.4.022], 1926/11, BMA. See D. Hurst Thomas, *Skull Wars: Kennewick Man, Archaeology and the Battle for Native American Identity* (New York, 2000), pp.140ff; and C. M. Hinsley, Collecting Cultures and Cultures of Collecting: The Lure of the American Southwest 1880–1915 (1992) 16 *Museum Anthropology* 12.

[99] Cited in A. Trachtenberg, *The Incorporation of America: Culture and Society in the Gilded Age* (New York, 1982), p.36; and Thomas, *Skull*, p.141.

That the examinations, excavations, and gatherings, subject to such rules and regulations are undertaken for the benefit of reputable museums, universities, colleges, or other recognised scientific or educational institutions, with a view to increasing the knowledge of such objects, and that the gathering shall be made for the permanent preservation in public museums.[100]

The Antiquities Act of 1906 legally transferred Native American sites and objects to the US public trust. It was developed without Native American involvement and with no suggestion that they might have legitimate affiliations with these sites and objects. As explained in Chapter 9, for Native Americans these are not archaeological sites and artefacts of the past but ancestral graves and religious objects of living cultures.

By the late nineteenth century, there were invariably more examples of these artefacts in the museums than in the communities from which they originated.[101] Museum practitioners augmented the myth of the 'vanishing Indian' by displaying indigenous cultural materials as 'anonymous' and 'timeless representations', even though they often knew when and by whom they were created.[102] The collections of many natural history museums were established between 1870 and the 1920s when indigenous population numbers and their social structures were in decline. Objects and information collected during this time were promoted as 'authentic' indigenous arts and crafts, unsullied by external influences.[103]

When indigenous population numbers began to increase in the early twentieth century, anthropological collecting began to fall away because of the influence of Boasian theory.[104] Franz Boas argued that: '[a]ny array of objects is always only an exceedingly fragmentary presentation of the true life of a people . . . For this reason, any attempt to present ethnological data by systematic classification of specimens will not only be artificial, but will be entirely misleading'.[105] He pressed for an overturning of prior definitions of 'civilisation' as a singular entity and the comparison of cultures in relation to each other. Boasian anthropology would inevitably face

---

[100] Congress asked the Smithsonian Institution to identify America's most important archaeological sites and to issue permits to professional archaeologists properly qualified to work on them. Reg.17, Uniform Rules and Regulations. Prescribed by the Secretaries of the Interior, Agriculture and War to carry out the provisions of the 'Act of Preservation of American Antiquities', Approved 8 June 1906 (34 Stat.225). See R. F. Lee, The Antiquities Act (2000) 42 *Journal of the Southwest* 1, and at http://www.cr.nps.gov/aad/pubs/lee/lee_fpm.htm.

[101] See J. C. Berlo, *The Early Years of Native American Art History: The Politics of Scholarship and Collecting* (Seattle, 1992), p.3.

[102] Rushing, *Native*, p.11; and Jacknis, 'Road', 32.

[103] See Fane, 'New Questions'; J. King, Tradition in Native American Art, in E. Wade (ed.), *The Arts of the North American Indian: Native Traditions in Evolution* (New York, 1986), p.65 at p.70; and D. Lowenthal, *The Past is a Foreign Country* (Cambridge, 1985), p.405.

[104] See G. W. Stocking, Philanthropy and Vanishing Cultures: Rockefeller Funding and the End of the Museum Era in Anglo-American Anthropology, in G. W. Stocking (ed.), *Objects and Others: Essays on Museums and Material Culture* (Madison, 1985), p.112.

[105] F. Boas, Some Principles of Museum Administration (1907) 25 *Science* 921 at 928. See F. Boas, *Race, Language and Culture*, (Chicago, 1982), pp.243–59, 270–80, 628–38; and V. A. Pinsky, Archaeology, Politics and Boundary-Formation: The Boas Censure (1919) and the Development of American Archaeology during the Inter-war Years, in J. E. Reyman (ed.) *Rediscovering Our Past: Essays on the History of American Archaeology* (Aldershot, 1992), p.161.

confrontations with racial evolutionists during the inter-war period.[106] This shifting mindset infused Indian New Deal policies. Chapters 5 and 6 detail how this facilitated the undermining of the scale of civilisation in International Law through an increasing appreciation of the contribution of all peoples to the 'cultural heritage of all mankind'.

Being modern, being primitive: search for US cultural identity

By the inter-war period, US museum officials and policymakers viewed Native American cultural objects as a 'cultural resource' for indigenous communities themselves and the nation as a whole. For Native Americans, the Indian New Deal policies promoted this resource as essential to aiding cultural renewal to make their communities economically self-sufficient. For the US nation, this resource was taken up by local avant-garde artists to feed the creation of an authentic local modern art movement. In both instances, the 'elevation' of these cultural objects from ethnographic specimens to art necessarily de-historicised and depoliticised the context of their removal from the communities of origin and the relationship between Native Americans and US society generally.

In the early twentieth century, increasing indigenous population numbers made it clear that Native Americans were not 'vanishing'; and organised resistance by these communities to the policies and practices of the dominant culture gradually led to a rethink of assimilation. In 1922, the US Secretary of the Interior flagged escalated measures to acquire the land and resource titles from Native Americans, which reached its height in the Bursum bill.[107] Linked with this bill were the initiatives of the Indian Commissioner to criminalise certain Native American religious practices.[108] Native American tribal leaders gathered to successfully oppose this renewed legislative onslaught.[109]

Opposition to the Bursum bill also exacerbated a struggle amongst lobbyists, between those promoting the assimilation process and its opponents. The Indian Rights Association included former BIA educators who advocated escalation in the assimilationist policies through mainstream education, suppression of native religious practices and individual allotment of communal Indian lands of the federal government.[110] They promoted Native American arts and crafts revival amongst

---

[106] See McLaughlin, 'Antiquities', 86ff; S. Conn, *Museums and American Intellectual Life, 1876–1926* (Chicago, 1998), pp.107–8; and I. Jacknis, Franz Boas and Exhibits: On the Limitations of the Museum Method of Anthropology, in Stocking (ed.), *Objects*, p.75.

[107] See Thomas, *Skull*, p.187; and D. E. Wilkins, *American Indian Sovereignty and the US Supreme Court: The Masking of Justice* (Austin, 1997), p.13, n.37. Compare decision of the US Supreme Court in *United States* v. *Joseph*, 94 US 616 (1876) which defined the Pueblo as 'civilised'; and a 1913 decision defining them as being in a 'primitive' state and effectively sanctioning Congressional paternalistic policies: *United States* v. *Sandoval*, 231 US 28 (1913).

[108] See J. Collier, *From Every Zenith: A Memoir and Some Essays on Life and Thought* (Denver, 1963), pp.128 and 136; and J. Collier, The United States Indian, in J. B. Gittler (ed.), *Understanding Minority Groups* (New York, 1956), p.33 at p.40.

[109] See V. Deloria Jr and C. Lytle, *The Nations Within: The Past and Future of American Indian Sovereignty* (New York, 1984); and K. Philp, *Termination Revisited: American Indians on the Trail to Self-Determination, 1933–1953* (Lincoln, 1999).

[110] See Welsh to Woods, 16 January 1925; Goss to Young, 27 July 1948; Sniffen to Chorley, 5 May 1925; and Document entitled, 'National Information Bureau Inc., Indian Rights Association, July

native communities as a means of 'uplifting' Indian peoples from their 'backward' state to civilisation.[111]

The Association's influence in Washington slowly gave way to the likes of the American Indian Defence Association.[112] This group opposed assimilation policies and encouraged the revival of 'high-quality', 'traditional' arts and crafts as a means of insulating Native Americans from the dominant culture.[113] The artists and anthropologists of the Santa Fe and Taos art colonies formed the core of this 'preservationist' arm and had three motivators.

(1) Indigenous arts and crafts would be repackaged and Native Americans and the US public re-educated to enable indigenous communities to become economically self-sufficient. This development is considered in Chapter 5.

(2) It was a reaction against industrialisation and a search for authentic modes of production.[114] Holger Cahill noted that popular opinion of the Native American as a 'strange, ferocious creature' was slowly giving way to 'a comparatively peaceful, industrious figure'.[115] He compared the Native American culture favourably with Western cultures and signalled 'the birth of a new art in America'.[116] Such reasoning denied the effects of Indian policy on contemporary indigenous communities.

(3) The search for a 'genuine' US art movement led artists and critics to turn to Native American cultures in the same way that Central and Eastern European States looked to the work of peasants in the folk art revivals.[117]

US policymakers and museum practitioners drew on Native American arts and crafts in the museums of New York, London, Paris and so forth – as a resource which could be mined by the avant-garde and by theorists searching for an authentic American art movement. Marsden Hartley argued in 1920: 'Our soil is as beautiful and as distinguished as any in the world. We must therefore be the discoverers of our own wealth as an esthetic factor, and it is the redman that offers us the way to go.'[118]

27, 1948', in Folder 646, Box 65, Series III.2E, RG 2, Rockefeller Foundation Archives, Rockefeller Archives Center, Sleepy Hollow, New York (RAC).

[111] Sniffen to N. Rockefeller, 9 February 1924, Folder 646, Box 65, Series III.2E, RG 2, Rockefeller Foundation Archives, RAC.

[112] See L. Kelly, *The Assault on Assimilation: John Collier and the Origins of Indian Policy Reform* (Albuquerque, 1983), pp.213–54; and K. Philp, *John Collier's Crusade for Indian Reform 1920–1954* (Tucson, 1977), pp.26–54.

[113] See J. J. Brody, *Indian Painters & White Patrons* (Albuquerque, 1971), pp.57ff; Rushing, *Native*, pp.13–41; and M. Mullin, The Patronage of Difference: Making Indian Art as Art, Not Ethnology (1992) 7 *Cultural Anthropology* 395.

[114] See J. Collier, *The Indians of the Americas* (New York, 1947); and J. Collier, The Red Atlantis (1922) 2 *Survey Graphic* 15 at 63 and 66.

[115] E. H. Cahill, America Has its Primitives (1920) 75 *International Studio* 80 at 82–83.

[116] Cahill, 'America', 80–81.

[117] See H. J. Spinden, Fine Art and the First Americans, in J. Sloan and O. La Farge (eds.), *Introduction to American Indian Art to Accompany the First Exhibition of American Indian Art Selected Entirely with Consideration to Esthetic Value* (1931) (Reprint, Glorieta, 1970), p.69; Brody, *Indian*, pp.60ff; Collier, *Zenith*, pp.199, 201, 203 and 214; and J. Pring, Reminiscences of Holger Cahill (1957), Holger Cahill Papers, Archives of American Art, Smithsonian Institution, Washington DC, [AAA: 5285;189].

[118] M. Hartley, Red Man Ceremonials: An American Plea for American Esthetics (1920) 9 *Art and Archaeology: The Arts throughout the Ages* 7 at 14.

The transition of Native American cultural objects from artefact to art was recognition of their value not only aesthetically but also as a vehicle for political nationalism.

The Institute of Government Research report (Meriam Report) (1928) criticised the paternalistic administration of Indian policy that did not support Indian self-sufficiency.[119] It found the 1887 Dawes Act was little more than a means of removing Native Americans from their land.[120] Its recommendation that federal Indian policy be directed towards pluralism rather than assimilation became a central tenet of the Indian New Deal under the Roosevelt administration.

The report stated 'Indian rights' went beyond property rights to include economic, social and cultural rights which encourage Native Americans to preserve and develop their cultural identity. It acknowledged that '[t]he Indians have much to contribute to the dominant civilisation, and the effort should be made to secure this contribution . . . [and] stimulat[e] a proper race pride and self-respect'.[121] Its central recommendation was that the BIA must consider the 'desire' of each individual Native American either to 'merge' with the dominant culture or 'remain an Indian'.[122] This emphasis on assisting the individual members of indigenous groups pre-empted the United States promotion of human rights over any recognition of groups' rights in the post-1945 era.

The Meriam report sanctioned the preservationists' work which nurtured the market for 'traditional' cultural objects, thereby obscuring the dynamics of Native American societies and inhibiting their ability to adapt to changing circumstances. As noted, economic self-reliance of Native Americans through education and training became the foundation of the Indian New Deal under the Roosevelt administration. In 1933, President Franklin D. Roosevelt appointed John Collier as Commissioner of Indian Affairs. His administration accelerated the reforms that were commenced with the Meriam Report; he was instrumental in the passage of the Indian Reorganization Act of 1934 (IRA) and subsequent collateral legislation such as the Indian Arts and Crafts Board Act of 1935.[123]

The IRA of 1934 marked the end of the allotment period and according to Collier, it 'abolished the Indian Bureau's power to suppress or interfere with Indian freedom of religion, speech and association'.[124] The IRA recognised the importance of Indian communal life as an agency for preserving and encouraging Native Americans to determine how their cultures and economies were maintained and developed.[125]

---

[119] L. Meriam, *The Problem of Indian Administration* (Baltimore, 1928). See Collier, *Zenith*, pp.136–47; Philp, *Collier's Crusade*, pp.113ff; and Collier, *Indians*, pp.261ff.

[120] See Cohen, *Handbook*, pp.144ff.

[121] Meriam, *Indian Administration*, pp.21–22, 86–89; and Prucha, *Documents*, pp.219–21, Doc.136.

[122] *Ibid.*

[123] 74 Pub.L. 35, 49 Stat. 891 (1935), codified at 25 USC §§305 *et seq* (2000); and Prucha, *Documents*, pp.228–29, Doc.140.

[124] Collier, *Zenith*, p.193. 73 Pub. L. No.383, 48 Stat. 985 (1934), codified at 25 USC §§461 *et seq* (2000); Prucha, *Documents*, pp.222–25, Doc.138; and Cohen, *Handbook*, pp.147ff. See Collier, *Zenith*, pp.169ff; and C. Klukhohn and R. Hackenberg, Social Science Principles and the Indian Reorganization Act, in W. Kelly (ed.), *Indian Affairs and the Indian Reorganization Act, The Twenty Year Record* (Tucson, 1954), pp.29–30.

[125] See Brophy and Aberle, *The Indian*, p.20.

To augment this policy, the Indian Arts and Crafts Board (IACB) was established in mid August 1935 to encourage the revival of indigenous arts and crafts and improve the economic status of Native Americans. The IACB was authorised to engage market contracts, aid in securing financial support for production and sale of Indian products, and create government trademarks for those products. The IACB's aim, according to Collier, was 'primarily to increase income to the Indian from the sale of his arts and crafts products'.[126] As explored in Chapter 5, for Collier the only person capable of realising the IACB's aims was René d'Harnoncourt.

The fine art museums of national capitals were potentially more successful in suppressing a cultural object's life history than the 'world museums' of former imperial centres. In Chapter 3, I suggested that colonised peoples pursuing independence co-opted the standard of civilisation dictated by International Law and promoted their cultural objects as worthy of inclusion in the Western art canon. Within settler States a similar phenomenon occurred in respect of the cultural material of indigenous peoples. This transformation had a two-fold purpose: first, aiding the establishment of a unique national cultural identity; and second, enabling this national narrative to have its beginnings in the 'timeless' past. Within the free market policies pursued by the US government, the transfer of Native American cultural objects from natural history museums to art galleries had a third result. Its categorisation as 'Art' elevated its commodity-value and suppressed historic–political implications of its possession by the dominant culture.[127]

In the twenty-five years prior to the groundbreaking 1941 Museum of Modern Art (MoMA) exhibition 'Indian Art of the United States', the history of marketing Native American art and artists was aligned with the movement to 'elevate' their cultural objects from natural science into fine art museums.[128] This movement was part of a wider campaign encompassing every level of the art world including museum exhibitions, the avant-garde and general public interest,[129] and articles and books on the cultural objects of North America, Africa and Oceania.[130] The 'Exposition of Indian Tribal Arts', held at the Grand Central Art Galleries in New York in 1931, was touted as the 'first exhibition of American Indian art selected entirely with consideration to esthetic value'.[131] According to the organisers, museums were primarily at fault for the emphasis on scientific knowledge at the expense of aesthetic excellence. One commentator noted that the 'aim is to present Indian art as *art*' and

---

[126] Collier, *Zenith*, p.194.

[127] See Rushing, *Native*, p.12; Berlo, *Early Years*, p.8; and M. Cohodas, Washoe Innovators and their Patrons, in E. Wade (ed.), *The Arts of the North American Indian* (New York, 1986), pp.203–20.

[128] See J. Clifford, *The Predicament of Culture: Twentieth-Century Ethnography, Literature, and Art* (Cambridge, MA, 1988), pp.187–252.

[129] See W. J. Rushing, Marketing the Affinity of the Primitive and the Modern: René d'Harnoncourt and 'Indian Art of the United States', in Berlo, *Early Years*, pp.191–95.

[130] The 1926 edition of Helen Gardner's classic art history survey devoted a chapter to 'aboriginal American art' and the 1936 edition had a Native American motif on its front cover: *Art Through the Ages: An Introduction to Its History & Significance* (New York, 1926 and 1936). Cf. Robert Goldwater's *Primitivism in Modern Art* (New York, 1938) which dealt exclusively with African and Oceanic cultural objects as they related to modern art.

[131] Sloan and Farge (eds.), *Introduction*; and Anon., Indian Tribal Arts (1931) 22 *The American Magazine of Art* 303 at 304. Cf. Culin's Rainbow Room (1925–29), Brooklyn Museum, in Jacknis, 'Road', p.40.

Figure 4.3 The Rainbow House, Gallery of Ethnology, The Brooklyn Museum, 1930.

facilitate its appreciation in the same way as 'the primitive and folk art of every other race and country'.[132] Reviewers argued that US artists should 'use' Native American material culture in the same way that the European avant-garde was inspired by African sculpture.[133]

Effectively, Native American objects became a cultural resource appropriated by modern artists and museum officials under the pretext of searching for an 'authentic' national cultural identity. This call intensified during the 1930s and peaked with the 1941 MoMA exhibition. In the foreword to the MoMA exhibition catalogue, Eleanor Roosevelt noted: 'At this time, when America is reviewing its cultural resources . . . In appraising the Indian's past and present achievements, we realise . . . that his heritage constitutes part of the artistic and spiritual wealth of this country'.[134]

The Museum of Modern Art in New York opened its doors in 1929 to collect and display contemporary avant-garde works deliberately overlooked by more traditional museums like the Metropolitan Museum of Modern Art. From its earliest years, MoMA promoted the elevation of indigenous and non-European cultural objects as works of art in themselves (Primitive Art) and as a rich resource for inspiring US

[132] J. Sloan, Prospectus, New York, Exposition of Indian Tribal Arts Inc., in Records of the Department of the Arts of Africa, the Pacific Islands and the Americas, Extra-Museum activities, Exposition of Indian Tribal Arts (file #134), Spinden, Herbert J., 10/1930–1/1935, BMA. Cf. R. d'Harnoncourt, 'Indian Arts of the Americas', November 1943, in The Museum of Modern Art Archives, NY: René d'Harnoncourt Papers [AAA: 2919; 290 at 295–96].

[133] See E. Alden Jewell, The American Indian Exhibition: A Tradition Lives On, *New York Times*, 6 December 1931, p.18.

[134] E. Roosevelt, Foreword, in F. H. Douglas and R. d'Harnoncourt, *Indian Art of the United States* (exh. cat., New York, 1941), p.8.

artists to create a home-grown art movement. In 1967 MoMA's first director, Alfred H. Barr Jr, proudly recalled that the museum hosted seven exhibitions of 'primitive and pre-Columbian art' between 1933 and 1954, when such objects 'rarely appeared in art museums [but were almost] as deeply involved in the taste and esthetics of our century as . . . abstract art'.[135] As Barr's seminal diagram 'The Tree of Modern Art' endeavoured to illustrate, these cultural resources created by 'primitive artists' were essential to the development of modern art and its narrative.[136] By placing these works at the commencement of the story of modern art, he would affirm his belief in their status as one of its sources. Like any other resource, it required 'civilised taste' to discover, develop and exploit them.[137]

Objects and practices once denigrated and targeted for destruction so as to facilitate European colonial expansion and economic development were transferred from the natural science to the art museums. And where the assimilation of indigenous individuals into the dominant culture diffused the 'threat' posed by Native American groups, the inclusion of their cultural objects into the national cultural identity had a similar effect.

Barr's successor as MoMA director, D'Harnoncourt, railed against the description of 'Primitive Art' and its placement of Native American cultural objects in the primordial past, implicitly reaffirming the 'backwardness' of the communities from which they originated.[138] Indeed, this process effectively suppressed the past histories of conflict and loss following European settlement. In turn, it enabled the dominant culture to posit its own national narratives with prehistoric origins.

In the face of genocidal practices perpetrated during the Second World War, this suppression of national collective memory and its effect on Native Americans and their living cultures could not be sustained. Eleanor Roosevelt ended her foreword to the 1941 exhibition catalogue with these words: '[T]he Indian people of today have a contribution to make toward the America of the future'.[139] The shift from assimilating indigenous peoples into one linear progression of (European) civilisation to the appreciation of their contribution to national and international culture is embodied in the words: 'the cultural heritage of all mankind'. The evolution of this phrase in the post-1945 context is examined in the following chapter.

---

[135] K. Kuh, Alfred Barr: Modern Art's Durable Crusader, *Saturday Review*, 30 September 1967, p.51. See A. Blackburn, Present Status and Future Direction of the Museum of Modern Art, 1933, in: The Museum of Modern Art Archives, NY: Alfred H. Barr, Jr Papers, 9A.8.

[136] A. H. Barr Jr, The Museum Collection Gallery I: Modern Primitives, Artists of the People (November 1941) *Bulletin of the Museum of Modern Art* 6–9: MoMA Archives, NY: AHB, 17.9A.

[137] A. H. Barr Jr, Letter to the Editor, *New York Times*, 29 March 1931.

[138] Douglas and d'Harnoncourt, *Indian Art*, p.12.

[139] Roosevelt, 'Foreword', in Douglas and d'Harnoncourt, p.8.

Figure 5.1 MoMA entrance during the exhibition 'Indian Art of the United States', The Museum of Modern Art, New York, 22 January–27 April 1941.

5

Restitution in the mid twentieth century

Nations have memories, too. And those memories are almost unfailingly self-serving. If there is to be a correction in memory here, let it be our own. First, let's remember what it means to send people to war . . . War is mostly violence – economic, emotional, physical – against civilians.[1]

For four centuries the Indians of the United States were exposed to the onslaught of the white invader, and military conquest was followed everywhere by civilian domination . . . Indian tradition was seen as an obstacle to progress and every available means was employed to destroy it thoroughly and forever.[2]

The systematic campaign of discrimination and violence against particular groups during the 1930s and 40s also targeted their cultural heritage. The perpetrators used 'every available means' to expunge the group's existence 'thoroughly and forever' from the collective memory of future generations – to create an 'eternal silence'.[3] Post-Second World War restitution efforts to reverse these processes and international legislative initiatives to prevent their repetition are the subjects of this chapter.

Central to the post-war restitution and prevention push was the recalibration of the phrase – 'cultural heritage of all mankind' – the focus of the Convention for the Protection of Cultural Property in the Event of Armed Conflict (1954 Hague Convention). The phrase as it is used in this Convention arose from the experiences of the post-war restitution programme, the Nuremberg trials and the Convention on the Prevention and Punishment of the Crime of Genocide (1948 Genocide Convention). It embodies the gradual but decisive shift from cultural Darwinism that dominated colonial methodologies until the inter-war period and strove to 'civilise' all peoples into acceptance of a 'superior' (European) culture, towards cultural pluralism, signalled by the rejection of a unilinear progression of civilisation with the affirmation of the contribution of all peoples and their cultures to humanity.

This chapter explains how the re-evaluation of the contribution of indigenous peoples and their cultures by the United States and other American countries in the 1930s and 40s acted as a foil to the rising spectre of fascism and its attendant

---

[1] T. Wolff, War and Memory, *New York Times*, 28 April 2001.
[2] F. H. Douglas and R. d'Harnoncourt, *Indian Art of the United States* (exh. cat., New York, 1941), p.9.
[3] M. Lachs, Address at Thirtieth Anniversary Celebration for the Protection of Cultural Property in the Event of Armed Conflict, in UNESCO, *Information on the Implementation of the Convention for the Protection of Cultural Property in the Event of Armed Conflict* (Paris, 1984), p.13.

genocidal policies. By pursuing 'a correction in memory', these States acknowledged that the disappearance of a group and its cultural manifestations was not inevitable because of some inherent inferiority. Rather, it was part of calculated policies by the dominant culture and its governmental apparatus which included the systematic removal and destruction of their cultural manifestations. In the popular imagination, indigenous cultures moved out of the immemorial past and became living examples of cultural vitality in the face of adversity.

This reassessment process by American States was circumscribed not by indigenous peoples but by the dominant culture. The limitations of these 'corrections in memory' were exposed by the application of a large-scale restitution programme for the reconstruction of post-war Europe and its non-application in the decolonisation process. Native Americans would wait a further half-century before the restitution of their cultural objects held in national museums was addressed by the United States.

As this argument unfolds, there is an examination of the place of indigenous peoples and their cultural objects within American national imagining and within International Law during the mid century. Second, there is an outlining of how Pan-Americanism impacted upon International Law for the protection of cultural heritage. Next, there is explanation of how this development and the lessons of the post-Second World War Allied restitution programme shaped awareness within the international community of the contribution of all peoples to the 'cultural heritage of mankind'. Finally, the significant shift in US policy towards Native American cultures driven by an acknowledgement of their significance to US national identity and the cultural and economic development of these communities is detailed.

Indigenous peoples, American identities and UN trusteeship

During the mid twentieth century, US and Latin American policies concerning indigenous peoples converged with their reassessment of the place of these communities and their cultural objects within their national narratives. This movement was fuelled by efforts to make the world anew according to the experiences and needs of the Americas. These States actively supported the efforts of colonised peoples to seek independence after the Second World War. Yet, this support for the right of self-determination did not extend to indigenous peoples within their own borders. This distinction had profound implications for indigenous peoples and their cultural heritage in the post-war context.

A groundswell of Pan-Americanism swept Latin American States in the late nineteenth and early twentieth centuries. This movement led to efforts to formulate a uniquely American identity that infected a broad swathe of disciplines. Efforts included the promotion of an American international law and a hemispheric cultural identity shaped by its indigenous heritage and colonial experience. Chilean jurist Alejandro Alvarez maintained that International Law had been formulated by the European Powers during the nineteenth century to promote their national interests and agitated for its 'Americanising' to address the practices and concerns of the

'New World'.[4] Despite the recognition of the contribution of indigenous peoples and their cultures during the 1930s and 40s, there was no deviation from the pursuit of a unified national cultural identity.

At the First Inter-American Conference on Indian Life in 1940, the United States and Mexico drew up the basic policy of the newly established Inter-American Indian Institute. It declared: 'the democratic intentions of the Pan-American nations towards their Indians, and insisted that cultural pluralism, in the place of coerced conformity, must be the guiding principle in the dealings of governments with Indians'.[5] Such was the tentative nature of these changes that the liberal individualist orientation which *indigenismo* had displaced re-emerged in the United States and international fora like the United Nations, following the Second World War. This, in turn, delayed the restitution of cultural objects to indigenous communities.

Non-European States, particularly former colonies participating in the drafting of the UN Charter (1945), were naturally interested in the fate of all colonial territories. Colonised peoples who had been called to fight for freedom by the Allied Powers during the war expected the same freedoms when they returned home. The war had also shattered the relationship between European metropolitan powers and their Asian and African colonies, and local nationalist leaders quickly filled the resultant vacuum.

The non-European States made effective use of several Allied and UN declarations as ideological instruments in their efforts to accelerate the decolonisation process.[6] The Atlantic Charter (1941), a US–British declaration of principles, included the support of the right of peoples to choose their own form of government.[7] Britain maintained that the Charter referred only to Nazi and Fascist occupied areas.[8] The United States, however, held that it applied to the whole world, including all colonised territories.[9] In May 1942, US Vice-President Henry Wallace argued: 'Older nations will have the privilege to help younger nations to get started on the path to industrialisation, but there must be neither military nor economic imperialism. The methods of the nineteenth century will not work in the people's century.'[10] After the war, Chapter XI of the UN Charter (Declaration regarding Non-Self-Governing Territories) obliged administering States 'to ensure, with due

[4] A. Alvarez, The New International Law (1929) 15 TGS 35 at 38–44, 47.

[5] J. Collier, *From Every Zenith: A Memoir and Some Essays on Life and Thought* (Denver, 1963), pp.310–11.

[6] See Y. El-Ayouty, *The United Nations and Decolonization: The Role of Afro-Asia* (The Hague, 1971), pp.3–28.

[7] Declaration by the united nations, Washington, 1 January 1942, annex 1: Declaration of principles known as the Atlantic Charter delivered by the United Kingdom Prime Minister and United States President, 14 August 1941, 204 LNTS 231; and (1941) 35 (supp.) AJIL 191.

[8] See H. Kellock, Colonies after the War (1943) 1 *Editorial Research Papers* 287 at 296; A. Creech Jones and R. Hinden, *Colonies and International Conscience: Report of the Fabian Colonial Bureau* (London, 1945), p.3; and G. Thullen, *Problems of the Trusteeship System: A Study of Political Behaviour in the United Nations* (Geneva, 1964), p.28.

[9] See US Congress, Senate, Sub-Committee on the United Nations Charter, The United Nations and Dependent Territories, 84th Cong., 1st sess. (1955), 2.

[10] United Nations Conference on Food and Agriculture, Cmd 6451 (1943), cited in Fabian Society, *International Action and the Colonies: Report of a Committee of the Fabian Colonial Bureau* (London, 1943), pp.17–18.

respect for the culture of the peoples concerned, their political, economic, social and educational advancement, their just treatment and their protection against abuses' (Article 73(b)).

The rights and interests of colonised peoples were no longer simply the domestic concern of the relevant metropolitan power. No longer would their interests be subordinated to the interests of other States in their labour and resources. For the first time in an international instrument there was recognition of the supremacy of the interests of local peoples.[11]

The concept of trusteeship over colonial peoples was central to the scale of civil-isation perpetuated by International Law. Its proposed inclusion in the 1945 UN Charter triggered a heated debate between anti-colonial and colonial States about the role of the 'civilising mission' within this sacred trust. Iraq had objected to the phrase 'peoples not yet able to stand by themselves' and the reference to 'the sacred trust of civilisation' in draft Article 73.[12] It argued that the war had revealed that few countries were capable of military or economic self-sufficiency and many colonised peoples had a long heritage of civilisation. Iraq also maintained that colonial practices had suppressed local cultures thereby weakening 'the basis for autonomous devel-opment and ultimate self-government'.[13] Consequently, Article 73(b) of the UN Charter would provide for progressive development of free political and cultural institutions of colonised peoples.

By the 1950s, Belgium rejected international interference in its colonial policies and sought to reintroduce the words 'of civilisation' into Article 73. It argued the sacred trust was exercised by 'States which enjoy a superior civilisation' in relation to 'populations of inferior civilisation which they administer' and must 'assume the responsibility of introducing them to civilisation'.[14] Ironically, the remainder of the Belgian argument disturbed its opponents most. It contended that the application of Article 73 only to colonies and protectorates was arbitrary and discriminatory. Belgium pressed for the extension of the sacred trust to indigenous peoples in North and Latin American republics and newly independent States in Asia.[15] It suggested 'primitive' communities living within States, subject to internal colonisation, were more likely to be targeted by assimilation policies and also needed protection under the 1945 UN Charter.[16]

African, Asian and American States strongly opposed this reinterpretation of Article 73. They declared it a covert attempt by former metropolitan powers to promote instability by continuing to interfere in their internal affairs and

---

[11] See A Commentary on the Charter of the United Nations signed at San Francisco on 26th June, 1945, Cmd 6666 (1945), para.58; US Congress, Senate, 84th Cong., 1st sess., (1955), 6; G. M. Charles, *Independence of Africa* (New York, 1960), p.xii; and El-Ayouty, *Colonization*, p.45.

[12] R. B. Russell and J. E. Munther, *A History of the United Nations Charter: The Role of the United States, 1940–1945* (Washington DC, 1958), p.816.

[13] El-Ayouty, *Colonization*, p.25.

[14] UN Doc.A/C.4/SR.253 (1952), paras.14–30, Ryckmans (Belgium).

[15] UN Doc.A/C.4/SR.419 (1954), para.25, Ryckmans (Belgium).

[16] Ad Hoc Committee on Factors (Non-Self-Governing Territories), Replies of Governments, 8 May 1953, UN Doc.A/AC.67/2, para.27. See G. Bennett, *Aboriginal Rights in International Law* (London, 1978), pp.12–13.

'convert the whole world into a vast colonial system'.[17] This apprehended threat to the sovereignty of newly independent States secured the eventual rejection of the Belgian thesis and the restricted application of the right of self-determination in the late twentieth century.[18] They denied the assertion that colonialism, as practised by the former European colonial powers, was replicated by newly independent States. Ecuador maintained that its indigenous communities were 'the very root and origin of the nation'.[19] Iraq noted: '[C]olonialism must give place to self-government . . . *People of one language, culture and thought* could not submit forever to domination and division by a different culture'.[20] For indigenous peoples and minorities, however, the assimilationist forces of imperialism were replaced by those of nationalism.

Legal protection of cultural heritage during armed conflict at the mid century

The development of the international and regional legal protection of cultural objects and sites during armed conflict in the mid twentieth century most starkly revealed the shift from a rationale of 'common right of mankind' to 'the cultural heritage of mankind'. There was a movement from the Anglo-American reduction of all cultural objects into a 'resource' to an appreciation of their importance to the continued viability of groups and their contribution to the cultural life of the nation and humanity.

Up until the inter-war period, International Law governing the protection of cultural objects during armed conflict was defined by European and North American jurists, contemplating Western conflicts and protecting, primarily, Western cultural objects and monuments. However, by the first half of the twentieth century the campaign to 'Americanise' International Law impacted on this branch of the discipline. These efforts can be contrasted with tandem 'Old World' initiatives by the League of Nations. It is suggested that the rationale's recalibration with the 1954 Hague Convention reflected the earlier work of American States. Yet, as explained in Chapter 6, the convention is also influenced by the post-war, Allied restitution programme.

1935 PAU Treaty and 1935 Washington Treaty

As part of its agenda to formulate an American international law, the Pan-American Union (PAU) promoted its own conventions as well as seeking to shape the International Museum Office (OIM) initiatives. The PAU treaties, forerunners of international agreements in their respective areas, included:

- The Treaty on the Protection of Movable Property of Historic Value (1935 PAU Treaty) which promoted mutual recognition of export restrictions between State parties and restitution procedures in cases of illicit export;[21] and

---

[17] UN Doc.A/C.4/257, para.5, Apunte (Ecuador).
[18] See R. L. Barsh, Indigenous North America and Contemporary International Law (1983) 62 OLR 73 at 84–90.
[19] UN Doc.A/C.4/257, para.5, Apunte (Ecuador).
[20] UN Doc.A/C.4/257, para.11, Khalidy (Iraq) (emphasis added).
[21] Washington DC, 15 April 1935, in force 17 July 1936, OASTS No.28, and M. Hudson, *International Legislation: A Collection of the Texts of Multipartite International Instruments of General Interest* (9 vols., Washington, 1919–1950) (1935–37), p.59.

- The Roerich Pact (1933) and the Treaty on the Protection of Artistic and Scientific Institutions and Historic Monuments (1935) (1935 Washington Treaty) which provided protection for monuments in peace- and wartime.[22]

The differences between the schemes of the PAU (an American organisation) and the OIM (largely a European concern) reflected divergent notions of what constituted the cultural patrimony of these States and how it should be protected.

The PAU pursued one overarching aim in its work in this area: the expansion of international legislative protection to cultural heritage, viewed as essential to the national narratives of American States. For example, the 1935 PAU Treaty covered a broad range of movable objects from the pre-Columbian, the colonial, the liberation and republican periods and others found within collections, libraries and archives (Article 1). Following the intervention of Latin American States, the OIM broadened the definition of cultural objects to those of 'remarkable palæolontological, archæological, historic or artistic interest' in its 1936 OIM Draft convention.[23]

Even though both initiatives aimed to provide a restitutory procedure, there were marked differences between the 1935 PAU Treaty and the 1939 OIM Draft convention. The 1939 OIM Draft narrowly defined the cultural objects and acts of removal which would have triggered its operation. These qualifiers reflected the increasing influence of the Anglo-American free trade agenda. In contrast, the 1935 PAU Treaty is a response to the anxiety of American States about cultural losses occasioned by the purchasing power of the US market.[24] The restitution obligations on State parties to this instrument were largely proactive, whilst the OIM proposal was reactive. For example, the 1935 PAU Treaty required State parties to legislate to limit title to cultural objects within its ambit to usufruct, that is its right to possess and use (Article 4). Permits for exportation were only to be granted if similar objects of the same value remained in the country (Articles 2 and 3). Finally, customs officials of State parties were required to ensure that the importer had the necessary authorisation. Otherwise, they were required to seize the object and return it to the government of the 'country of origin' (Article 5).[25]

The Roerich Pact was originally a European initiative that was ignored by the OIM and fervently taken up by American States. President Franklin D. Roosevelt

---

[22] Washington DC, 15 April 1935, in force 26 August 1935, 167 LNTS 289; USTS 899; (1936) 30(supp.) AJIL 195–98; and Hudson, *International Legislation* (1935–37), p.56. The Roerich Pact was drafted by George Chklaver. Chklaver and Nicholas Roerich submitted it to the League of Nations in 1930: LN, LNOJ, 11th Year, No.11, (November 1930), 1431; and G. Chklaver, Projet d'une convention pour la protection des institutions et monuments consacrés aux arts et aux sciences (1930) 6 RDI 589. The Pact was not favourably received by the League.

[23] Draft International Convention for the Protection of National Historic or Artistic Treasures (1936), LN Doc.C.L.34.1936.XII, Annex. See F. C. Najera, Mexican Legation to Secretary-General, League of Nations, 21 February 1934; and Anon., Protection of Movable Monuments (February 1935) *The Bulletin of the Pan-American Union* 92, UNESCO Archives: OIM.IV.27.I, pp.89ff; and OIM.IV.27.II, p.116, Dossier de correspondence, office international des musées, conservation des œuvres d'art, protection de patrimoine artistique.

[24] For this reason it is suggested that the 1935 PAU Treaty bore greater affinity with the 1933 OIM Draft than the 1939 redraft. The United States was not a signatory to the 1935 PAU Treaty.

[25] See L. V. Prott and P. J. O'Keefe, *Law and the Cultural Heritage, Volume 3: Movement* (London, 1989), p.688, §1336.

described the subsequent treaty, signed in Washington on the same day as the 1935 PAU Treaty, as an 'expression' of the 'doctrine of continental responsibility and continental solidarity'.[26] Although the treaty was always conceived to protect immovable cultural heritage, it is significant to the development of international protection of cultural objects for several reasons.

First, by implementing the Roerich Pact, the treaty promoted the notion that certain cultural property is the common heritage of all humankind and must be afforded international protection. The preamble of the Pact stipulated:

> Whereas their high offices impart on them the sacred obligation to promote the moral welfare of their respective Nations, and the advancement of Arts and Science in the common interest of humanity.
>
> Whereas the Institutions dedicated to the education of youth, to Arts and Science, constitute a common treasure of all the Nations of the World.[27]

This dual purpose pursued by the International Committee for Intellectual Cooperation (ICIC) during the inter-war period – diversity and universality of cultures – was reaffirmed by US Secretary of Agriculture Henry A. Wallace in the American context. He related the aims of the Roerich Pact to the philosophy of the New Deal generally which 'replace[d] the outworn competitive spirit so far as possible with the cooperative ideal'.[28] As the war approached, this dual purpose was resolved as the universal importance of all cultures. The 1935 Washington Treaty reaffirmed its exclusive application to 'historic monuments, museums, scientific, artistic, educational and cultural institutions' (Article 1). This was tempered by reference in the preamble to 'the cultural treasures of peoples'.

Second, the preamble of the Roerich Pact reaffirmed the international treaty guarantees of equal access for archaeological expeditions to colonial territories.[29] This was a concession to the Anglo-American free trade agenda in respect of cultural objects during this period. Although this purpose was not specifically reiterated in the 1935 Washington Treaty, the treaty's intent was to give the Roerich Pact conventional form.

1938 OIM Draft Convention and 1939 Draft Declaration

Despite their common origin, the 1935 Washington Treaty and the preliminary Draft International Convention for the Protection of Historic Buildings and Works

---

[26] See US Congress, Senate, Report of the Committee on Foreign Relations, Artistic and Scientific Institutions and Historic Monuments, Senate Executive Report No.11, 74th Cong., 1st sess., (1935), 2.

[27] Second and third recitals, Preamble, Roerich Pact, in Seventh International Conference of American States, *Minutes and Antecedents with General Index* (Montevideo, 1933), n.p., Roerich Museum Archives, New York. See *Nederlandsche Oudheidkundige Bond*, La protection des monuments et objets historiques contre les destructions de la guerre, 1918 (1919) 26 RGDIP 329 at 331–6.

[28] Roerich Museum, *Proceedings Third International Convention for the Roerich Pact and Banner of Peace, 17 and 18 November 1933, Washington DC* (2 vols., New York, 1934), vol.II, pp.26–27.

[29] Sixth recital, Roerich Pact, refers to the General Act of the Conference of Berlin respecting the Congo, 26 February 1885 and Art.11, Treaty of St-Germain, 10 September 1919.

of Art in Time of War (1938 OIM Draft) were considered rival instruments.[30] The former instrument yielded greater input from the so-called New World. The 1938 OIM Draft was viewed not only as part of the apparatus of the League of Nations but as largely reflecting the preoccupations of the Old World.[31] Not until the late 1930s in reaction to European circumstances, including the Spanish Civil War and impending continental conflict, did the OIM call a Committee of Experts to consider a preliminary draft convention for the protection of cultural property during armed conflict.[32]

The rationale of the draft convention adopted a similar stance to the Roerich Pact:

> Whereas the preservation of artistic treasures is a concern of the community of States and it is important that such treasures should receive international protection;
>
> Being convinced that the destruction of a masterpiece, whatever nation may have produced it, is a spiritual impoverishment for the entire international community.[33]

In 1938, the director of the International Institute of International Cooperation (IIIC) reported that '[t]he countries possessing artistic treasures are merely their custodians and remain accountable for them to the international community'.[34] By 1940, with the rising spectre of massive and systematically targeted cultural losses the OIM elaborated further: 'any injury to these treasures . . . constitutes a loss to mankind as a whole, to the present and to future generations'.[35]

The protection of all cultures, not just those deemed of national or universal importance, led the IIIC to extend the operation of the 1938 OIM Draft to internal disturbances (Article 10).[36] Significantly, the international community was prepared to override State sovereignty to protect cultural objects, because it recognised that groups within State boundaries did not necessarily agree upon the value of cultural objects and their preservation. The threat of the State to its own peoples and their cultural objects became more pronounced as the war progressed.

Bolivian advocacy for the need to protect museum collections threatened by the Spanish Civil War and the wider European conflict exposed the continuing link

---

[30] See LN, LNOJ, 19th Year, No.11, (November 1938), 937; (1939) 20 RDILC 608; and C. de Visscher, *International Protection of Works of Art and Historic Monuments,* Washington, US Documents and State Papers, International Information and Cultural Series, No.8, June 1949, 829 at 861–865.

[31] FO Minute W7682/816/98, Randall notes of conversation with Blackford. See Markham, Museums Association to Butler, 5 May 1939, PRO FO 371/24037 (supported the Pact).

[32] The Draft Declaration was prepared by the OIM and submitted to the Council and Assembly of the League of Nations in late 1938. The diplomatic conference was never held because of the outbreak of the war. Instead, OIM prepared a declaration outlining ten principles for the protection of cultural heritage during armed conflict: Visscher, 'International Protection', Appendix A, 859–860. See LN, LNOJ, 18th Year, No.12 (December 1937), 1047; LN, LNOJ, 19th Year, No.11 (November 1938), 936–41; and LN, LNOJ, 20th Year, No.1 (January 1939), 8.

[33] Second and third recitals, Preamble, 1938 OIM Draft.

[34] LN, LNOJ, 19th Year, No.11 (November 1938), 961.

[35] Anon., Comparative Legislation and International Law in the field of Art and Archaeology (1940) 7–8 *Bulletin of Intellectual Co-operation* 345.

[36] See LN Doc.C.327M.220.1937.XXII.A.2, para.9(b).

between coloniser and colonised even after formal independence.[37] Former colonies had a direct stake in preserving their cultural patrimony, stored in former imperial collections in European capitals. A proposal for a convention binding signatories 'to treat as null and void all sales of works of art from national collections carried out during civil disturbance' was rejected.[38] However, its underlying rationale was taken up by the Declaration of the Allied Nations against Acts of Dispossession Committed in Territories Under Enemy Occupation or Control (1943 Declaration of London) that heralded the Allied governments' restitution programme.

1954 Hague Convention
The momentum created by the 1938 OIM Draft was revived in earnest by the United Nations Educational, Scientific and Cultural Organisation (UNESCO) in the post-war period. The result was the Convention for the Protection of Cultural Property in the Event of Armed Conflict (1954 Hague Convention).[39] The preliminary UNESCO draft conceded the initiative's link explicitly to the 1935 Washington Treaty; and implicitly to the ill-fated 1938 OIM Draft by reproducing its first two preambular recitals.[40] The preamble reads in part:

> [T]hat damage to cultural property belonging to any people whatsoever means damage to the cultural heritage of all mankind, since each people makes its contribution to the culture of the world.
> Considering that the preservation of the cultural heritage is of great importance for all peoples of the world and that it is important that this heritage should receive international protection.[41]

In the wake of the atrocities of the 1930s and 40s and various international humanitarian instruments drafted in the intervening period, the 1954 Hague Convention aimed to ensure the contribution of all peoples and their cultures – not cultural objects *per se* – for the benefit of all humankind.

This interpretation is reinforced by the 1954 Hague Convention's application during international and internal armed conflicts (Article 19). This protection was augmented by Article 53 of the 1977 Protocol Additional I and Article 16 of the 1977 Protocol Additional II of the 1949 Geneva Convention.[42] Both Protocols refer

---

[37] FO Minute UK delegation to the Sixth Committee, ICIC, W14374, 26 October 1936, PRO FO 371/20470.

[38] See FO Minute W13511/654/98, Sert to Eden, 1 July 1937, PRO FO 371/21249. For British rejection of proposal: FO Minute W13511/654/98 PRO FO 371/21249.

[39] The Hague, 14 May 1954, in force 7 August 1956, 249 UNTS 240. See J. Toman, *The Protection of Cultural Property in the Event of Armed Conflict: Commentary on the Convention for the Protection of Cultural Property in the Event of Armed Conflict and its Protocol* (Paris, 1996).

[40] UNESCO, Circular Letter regarding Draft Convention for the Protection of Cultural Property in the Event of Armed Conflict, 5 February 1953, UNESCO Doc.CL/717.

[41] Second and third recitals, Preamble, 1954 Hague Convention.

[42] Protocol Additional I to the Geneva Convention of 12 August 1949, and relating to the Protection of Victims of International Armed Conflict, Geneva, 8 June 1977, in force 7 December 1979; and Protocol Additional II to the Geneva Convention of 12 August 1949, and relating to the Protection of Victims of Non-International Armed Conflict, Geneva, 8 June 1977, in force 7 December 1978, 1125 UNTS 3 and 609.

to the 'cultural or spiritual heritage of peoples'. A proposed reference, during their drafting, to the 'heritage of a country' was rejected because it was acknowledged that 'problems of intolerance could arise with respect to religions which do not belong to the country concerned, and with respect to places where such religions are practised'.[43]

John Henry Merryman maintains that the 1954 Hague Convention preamble has profound implications for law and policy covering the international art trade and restitution of cultural objects.[44] Whilst I agree with his assessment of the importance of the preamble, I disagree with his understanding of its essence. Anglo-American legal scholars have made much of the distinctive purposes of the 1954 Hague Convention and the 1970 UNESCO Convention. Namely, the former is conceived for general protection of cultural objects in the face of its possible destruction during armed conflict, the latter being a compromise achieved between 'market' and 'source' States in the regulation of the illicit trade of cultural objects generally.[45]

The 1954 Hague Convention has been seized on by so-called 'cultural internationalists' as a barometer of the ideal that an international instrument regulating cultural property should strive to achieve. Merryman traces its development from the 1863 Lieber Code (Instructions for the Government of Armies of the United States of America in the Field), the 1874 Brussels Declaration, the 1899 and 1907 Hague Conventions (II and IV), the Roerich Pact and the 1938 OIM Draft. It is suggested that this genealogy, so fundamental to his argument, is only part of the narrative. He overlooks the significant shift that occurred in the inter-war period in the interpretation of the phrase – 'the cultural heritage of mankind'. His position is essentially a reiteration of the Anglo-American position – the common right of all mankind – aimed at resisting impediments to the international art trade.

The phrase 'the cultural heritage of all mankind' within the context of the 1954 Hague Convention cannot and should not be interpreted without its enjoinder – 'each people makes its contribution to the culture of the world'. The Convention was a response to the destruction from the Second World War, caused by belligerents, to the enemy and their own people. It reflects a common thread amongst contemporary documents, including those related to the Allied restitution policy and programme, the war crimes trials, the 1948 Genocide Convention and various human rights covenants: the notion of cultural pluralism and the contribution of every people and their culture to humankind.

These developments affirmed that the destruction of a group and/or their culture is an affront to all peoples. The restitution of cultural objects became an essential part of ensuring the continuation of their contribution. Therefore, the 1954 Hague Convention's purpose is complementary to, rather than distinct from, the 1970 UNESCO Convention.

---

[43] Y. Sandoz, S. Swinarksi and B. Zimmerman (eds.), *Commentary on the Additional Protocols of 8 June 1977 to the Geneva Conventions of 12 August 1949* (Geneva, 1987), p.640.

[44] J. H. Merryman, Two Ways of Thinking about Cultural Property (1986) 80 AJIL 831 at 833.

[45] See UNESCO, Means of Prohibiting and Preventing the Illicit Import, Export and Transfer of Ownership of Cultural Property: Preliminary Report, 8 August 1969, UNESCO Doc.SHC/MD/3 para.10, 2–3; and Prott and O'Keefe, *Movement*, pp.729–30, §1407.

Restitution following the Second World War

The post-Second World War restitution framework and its invocation in subsequent international legislation reaffirmed the significance of the return of cultural objects in the reconstruction process following the end of occupation. Nonetheless, the scale and complexity of its operation, whilst of continuing benefit to present-day claims, stands as a stark reminder of the silence surrounding the return of cultural objects which accompanied that other major cessation of occupation of the mid century: decolonisation. This silence was broken in the late twentieth century by newly independent States who referred to principles established during the post-war, Allied restitution programme in support of their claims against former metropolitan powers.

The Allied restitution programme articulated a number of significant principles of direct relevance to present-day restitution claims. Yet, even more fundamental was the Allied governments' acceptance that restitution of cultural objects to a group was necessary to ensure their continuing contribution to the cultural heritage of all mankind. Cultural objects were removed or destroyed by the Nazi regime because of their or their owner's affiliation with a particular group. The Allied programme acknowledged this motivation and strove to reverse or ameliorate such discriminatory and genocidal policies. However, with the onset of the Cold War, the United States and its allies strenuously opposed any effective international recognition of group rights or minority protection. This stance stymied restitution claims following decolonisation.

1943 Declaration of London

During the Second World War, the Allies prospectively announced their intent to restore cultural property and define the programme's foundational principles without waiting to do so in a reactive fashion in peace treaties, as happened after the First World War. This move emphasised a fundamental shift in the rationale between the respective restitution programmes. The post-First World War framework grappled with State succession to imperial collections following the cessation of occupation with the dissolution of empires. The post-Second World War programme served to reverse or ameliorate the genocidal policies of States towards occupied peoples and their *own* nationals, thereby enunciating and implementing the second rationale for restitution in International Law.

The first distinct announcement by the Allies, later cited in numerous documents of the decolonisation period, was the 1943 Declaration of London.[46] The declaration provided a general interpretation clause to cover the investigation of all claims for the restitution of looted cultural property, including:

---

[46] (1943) 8 *Department of State Bulletin* 21; and W. W. Kowalski, *Art Treasures and War: A Study on the Restitution of Looted Cultural Property pursuant to Public International Law*, ed. T. Schadla-Hall (London, 1998), Annex 3, pp.93–94; and E. Simpson (ed.), *The Spoils of War. World War II and Its Aftermath: The Loss, Reappearance and Recovery of Cultural Property* (New York, 1997), Appendix 9, p.287.

(1) it extended existing norms of International Law beyond the territorial boundaries of the former occupier, by putting neutral countries on notice that profiteering from these unlawful acts would not be tolerated; and

(2) it made clear that Allied governments would not necessarily accept as valid, transactions undertaken during the relevant period even if 'apparently legal in form, even when they purport to be voluntarily effected'. It recognised: (i) the inequality of power between the parties to the transaction; and (ii) use of the law to affirm this inequality of power and the legality of ensuing transactions. Included in the latter was the warning that the usual protection afforded to a bona fide purchaser may not be applicable.

The principles contained within the 1943 Declaration of London were elaborated gradually with their implementation following the defeat of the Axis forces.

The restitution of cultural objects after the Second World War is examined as follows: (1) external restitution from Germany and Axis territories; (2) restitution-in-kind; (3) restitution from neutral States; (4) internal restitution and the claims of Holocaust survivors and their heirs today; (5) State succession; and (6) the Protocol for the Protection of Cultural Property in the Event of Armed Conflict (1954 Hague Protocol).

External restitution

The 1946 Definition of the Term 'Restitution' covering the entire German territory and adopted by the Allied Control Council for Germany (1946 Definition),[47] drew heavily from the Resolution on the Subject of Restitution attached to the Final Act and Annex of the Paris Conference on Reparations (1946 Paris Resolution).[48] The most pertinent principles for present purposes are summarised as follows.

The 1943 Declaration of London and subsequent regulations of the occupied zones made clear that restitution was triggered by the violation of the norms of international law.[49] Also, the post-Second World War restitution programme reaffirmed the application of the territoriality principle that was applied in the 1815 Congress of Vienna and the 1919 Paris peace treaties. Therefore, the State claiming restitution did not need to show that the object was owned by a national; rather, it was sufficient that it was simply removed from its territory.[50] Accordingly, any legal proceedings were completed with the handing over of the object to the government

---

[47] Definition of the Term 'Restitution', 22 January 1946, Press Handout No.151, PR Branch, C.C.G. (BE), Berlin; and Kowalski, *Art Treasures*, Annex 5, p.106. No uniform agreement governing all four zones of military occupied Germany was reached on the principles governing restitution.

[48] Paris, 14 January 1946, Annex 1: Resolution on Subject of Restitution (1946) 40 (supp.) AJIL 117; reproduced in J. Howard, *The Paris Agreement on Reparations from Germany* (Washington, 1946), p.19; and Kowalski, *Art Treasures*, Annex 4, pp.95–105.

[49] See Kowalski, *Art Treasures*, p.48; and I. Vásárhelyi, *Restitution in International Law*, (Budapest, 1964), pp.87ff. Cf. E. Langen and E. Sauer, *Die Restitution im internationalen Recht* (Dusseldorf, 1949), pp.11ff.

[50] 1943 Declaration of London; 1946 Definition, point 2; and Title 18: Monuments, Fine Arts and Archives (MGR 18) MGR 18–106, and 110, Office of the Military Government for Germany, US Military Government Regulations, in Kowalski, *Art Treasures*, Annex 10, pp.153–60.

of the claimant State.[51] That State and its domestic laws governed the subsequent location of the recovered object. The Allied governments' continued adherence to the territoriality principle and privileging of the claimant State was irreconcilable with their awareness of the discriminatory and genocidal policies of the Nazi regime against its own citizens.[52] However, the restitution schemes in neutral States did permit individual claimants to pursue a claim directly against the present possessor of their property in enemy territory.[53] This allowance for non-State actors in restitution claims is an important precedent for present-day claimants confronting an uncooperative State.

Under the 1946 Paris Resolution, restitution was confined to identifiable objects that existed prior to occupation and were removed with or without payment, or were produced during occupation and removed by force.[54] The requirement that the property subject to restitution be identical to that removed during the occupation was difficult to fulfil in the aftermath of Nazi policies, aimed at the destruction and dislocation of cultural objects, archives and their owners.[55] In recognition of this problem, the military governments for Germany simultaneously pronounced regulations blocking transactions of cultural objects to assist in the location and identification of all looted objects.[56] Until these surveys were completed, persons protecting or controlling art collections were required to preserve and supervise objects remaining in their possession and to notify the appropriate German authorities of certain objects. Furthermore, German possessors of looted objects were required to declare them to Allied authorities.[57]

The multifaceted forms of Nazi confiscations and the nature of the regime led the US Military Government for Germany to sanction a wide interpretation of 'force'.[58] It reflected a recognition of the discriminatory nature of laws which had validated the confiscation of cultural objects from particular groups. Therefore, each transaction was to be judged on a case-by-case basis in the light of the 1943 Declaration of London and subsequent resolutions and declarations. The possessor of the property

---

[51] MGR 18–101, 106, 110 and 445.3, in Kowalski, *Art Treasures*, Annex 10, pp.153–60 and 158–59.

[52] During 1947 and 1948, the United States returned looted property only to the owners and not the countries of origin (Soviet zone) when the owners had fled the country for religious, racial or ideological reasons: M. Kurtz, The End of the War and the Occupation of Germany, 1944–52, Laws and Conventions Enacted to Counter German Appropriations: The Allied Control Council, in Simpson (ed.), *Spoils*, p.116.

[53] See A. Martin, Private Property, Rights and Interests in the Paris Peace Treaties (1947) 24 BYIL 274 at 282.

[54] 1946 Paris Resolution, Annex, para.(b).

[55] 1946 Paris Resolution, Annex, para.(b); 1946 Definition, point 2; and US regulations, MGR 18–106, 110, 445.3. See Vásárhelyi, *Restitution*, p.101; and Kowalski, *Art Treasures*, pp.50–51.

[56] MGR 18–400 to 401.6. Military Government for Germany, US Zone. Law No.52 Blocking and Control of Property, *Military Government Gazette* [Germany, US Zone, Issue A], 1 June 1946, 24 (Law No.52). See Kowalski, *Art Treasures*, Annex 7, pp.108–09 (reproduces the British Zone Law).

[57] 1946 Paris Resolution, Annex, para.(g).

[58] Title 19: Restitution, Berlin, 1946, MGR 19–100(2a); Office of Military Government for Germany, US Military Government Regulations; Office of Military Government, US Property Division, Reparation and Restitution Branch, Memorandum on Restitution as Affected by Reparations, Force and the German Minimum Economy, 15 October 1946; Office of Military Government, US Property Division, Reparation and Restitution Branch, Memorandum on Procedure of Restitution, 23 June 1948. See Kowalski, *Art Treasures*, pp.52–54; and Vásárhelyi, *Restitution*, pp.105–08.

bore the burden of proof that this was a 'normal' transaction. The only transaction at issue was the one which located the cultural object in the occupier's territory. All documentation validating the possessor's title signed in a territory occupied at that time was disregarded and payment was not sufficient to overcome this burden. The wider commercial relationship existing between the seller and the buyer before and during the occupation was subject to scrutiny. In practical terms, there was effective removal of the protection of the bona fide purchaser, a defence usually recognised in international law concerning cultural property.[59]

Although restitution claims may become time-barred in private law, there are consistent examples since 1815 showing that this is not necessarily the case in public international law. The Second World War restitution programme recognised that the process does not have a time limit.[60] The confiscation of the property was part of the discriminatory, persecutory or genocidal acts, and restitution marked the cessation of an ongoing international wrong. Even in private law, recent US case law involving the restitution of cultural objects removed during the Nazi regime or during the US military occupation of Germany takes a generous approach towards time limits.[61] The US State Department assumed the role for post-war recovery of cultural objects that were looted and found their way to the United States.[62] In 1982, the department reaffirmed that: 'The United States considers that on grounds of principle, good foreign relations, and concern for the preservation of the cultural heritage of mankind, it should render assistance in these situations.'[63]

Restitution-in-kind

If restitution is the cessation or reversal of a wrongful act, then restitution-in-kind (and its limitations) reinforced the importance of return of cultural objects for the rehabilitation of the persecuted group. The Allied resolutions sanctioned a generalised programme of restitution-in-kind. The ambit of this relief gradually narrowed with subsequent peace treaties and the regulations of the military governments of Germany. The 1946 Paris Resolution stipulated that objects of an artistic, historic, scientific, education or religious character which had been looted by occupier and

---

[59] See W. Wengler, Conflicts of Laws, Problems relating to Restitution of Property in Germany (1962) 11 ICLQ 1131 at 1133.

[60] See A. R. Hall, The Recovery of Cultural Objects Dispersed During World War II (1951) 25(635) *Department of State Bulletin* 339; L. V. Prott, Principles for the Resolution of Disputes Concerning Cultural Heritage Displaced during the Second World War, UNESCO Doc.CLT-99/CONF.203/2, Annex I; and Kowalski, *Art Treasures*, p.57.

[61] See *Kunstsammlungen zu Weimar* v. *Elicofon*, 536 F Supp. 829 (EDNY 1981), affd 678 F 2d 1150 (2nd Cir. 1982); (1973) 12 ILM 1163; (1981) 20 ILM 112; (1982) 21 ILM 773; *Menzel* v. *List*, 267 NYS 2d 804 (S. Ct 1966) modified 279 NYS 2d 608 (NY App. Div. 1967) revd 24 NY 2d 91 (NY 1969); *DeWeerth* v. *Baldinger*, 658 F Supp. 688 (SDNY 1987); and *Republic of Austria* v. *Altmann*, 372 F 3d 1246 (9th Cir. 2003); 539 US 987 (2004), 124 S. Ct. 46.

[62] See A. R. Hall, Return of Looted Objects of Art to Countries of Origin (1947) 16 (399) *Department of State Bulletin*, 358; and A. R. Hall, The US Program for the Return of Historic Objects to Countries of Origin, 1944–54 (1954) 31(797) *Department of State Bulletin* 493.

[63] US Code Cong. & Adm. News 4100 [1982], cited in E. Maurer, The Role of the State Department regarding National and Private Claims for the Restitution of Stolen Cultural Property, in Simpson (ed.), *Spoils*, p.143, n.2.

could not be restored would, where possible, be replaced by equivalent objects.[64] Likewise, the 1947 peace treaties (with Italy, Hungary and Bulgaria) provided for restitution-in-kind where actual restitution was not possible, and individual artistic, historical or archaeological objects of the same kind and approximate value were available.[65] Two provisos were imposed. First, equivalents could only be sought of objects forming part of the claimant State's cultural heritage. Second, the obligation was only to be adhered to if an object of equivalent value could be found.

The US Military Government for Germany declined to apply restitution-in-kind within its zone, declaring it could not condone an extensive replacement programme if it 'could only be accomplished at the expense of . . . the cultural heritage of the German people'.[66] The US State Department added that it was US policy to 'respect [the] artistic and historic property of all nations'.[67] The limitations placed on the application of restitution-in-kind reaffirm the crux of the 1954 Hague Convention preamble. Any depletion in the cultural patrimony of a people would impede or diminish their contribution to the cultural heritage of mankind.

Restitution-in-kind was defined to benefit the persecuted group rather than extracting reparations or retribution from the offending State. US museum officials had reacted badly to these provisions, stating: '[T]o *use* treasures *as* reparations is contrary to the principles of international law . . . and makes the United Nations no better than the Nazis'.[68] They were reluctant to be seen to be sanctioning the transfer of cultural objects as reparations. Indeed, the subsequent 1954 Hague Protocol prohibits the use of cultural objects as reparations.

[64] 1946 Paris Resolution, Annex, para.(d); 1946 Definition, para.3; Directive regulating the Procedural Details of Restitution-in-kind pronounced by the Allied Control Authority, 25 February 1947, Doc.CORC/M/46/34, and Kowalski, *Art Treasures*, Annex 6, p.107; MRG 18-116; and Study Group of the Council of Foreign Relations, A Memorandum on the Restitution or Indemnification of Property Seized, Damaged, or Destroyed during World War II, in *The Postwar Settlement of Property Rights*, (New York, 1945), p.1.

[65] Treaties of Peace with Italy (Art.75(9)), Bulgaria (Art.22(3)) and Hungary (Art.24(3)), Paris, 10 February 1947, 49 UNTS 3 at 129; Cmd 7022 (1947), p.117; and (1948) 42(supp.) AJIL 47. See Martin, 'Private', 277; B. Hollander, *The International Law of Art for Lawyers, Collectors and Artists*, (London, 1959), pp.43–45; Kowalski, *Art Treasures*, pp.70–72; and Vásárhelyi, *Restitution*, pp.96–101.

[66] Directive of the Commander-in-Chief, US Forces of Occupation, regarding the Military Government of Germany, JCS 1779, 11 July 1947, (1947) 17 *Department of State Bulletin* 190. See Roberts Commission, Resolution of the American Commission for the Protection and Salvage of Artistic and Historic Monuments in War Areas, 20 June 1946, (1951) 11 CAJ 34.

[67] Anon., US Seeks to Replace Cultural Property Displaced during World War II (1951) 25(635) *Department of State Bulletin* 345.

[68] R. F. Howard, US Military Government for Germany to T. L. Parker, American Federation of Art, 20 August 1947, The Museum of Modern Art, NY: Alfred H. Barr, Jr Papers [AAA: 2173;433] (original emphasis). There was a similar reaction from museum officials to the removal of 202 paintings from the Kaiser Friedrich Museum, Berlin to the United States for a touring exhibition. The Monument, Fine Arts and Archives officers' Wiesbaden Manifesto reminded the US government that it had rejected the defences of Nazi officers, that the looting of the regime had been done on the pretext of 'protective custody'. They added: '[N]o historical grievance will rankle so long, or be the cause of so much justified bitterness, as the removal, for any reason, of a part of the heritage of any nation, even if that heritage may be interpreted as a prize of war': W. I. Farmer, Custody and Controversy at the Wiesbaden Collecting Point, in Simpson (ed.), *Spoils*, p.131 at p.133. See Anon., Removal of German art objects to the United States (1945) 13(327) *Department of State Bulletin* 499; US Congress, House, Committee on Armed Services, Temporary Retention in the US of Certain German Paintings, 80th Cong., 2nd sess., S. Hrg (1948), 25.

Returns from neutral States

The post-Second World War restitution scheme foreshadowed by the 1943 Declaration of London was extraordinary because it included neutral States. Furthermore, these States were required to pass domestic legislation to facilitate restitutory relief for victims of the fascist regimes.[69] The Swiss Decree of 10 December 1945 concerning Actions for the Recovery of Goods taken in Occupied Territories during the War (Booty Decree) provided that:

(1) a person in occupied territory who was dispossessed of objects by an occupying power contrary to international law and using violence, confiscation or similar methods, could recover them from the present possessor if they were in Switzerland (Section 1);

(2) where restitution was ordered, a bona fide possessor had a right to be repaid the purchase price from the person from whom it was acquired;

(3) when the bad faith transferor was insolvent or could not be sued in Switzerland, the bona fide purchaser could recover from the Swiss Confederation (Section 4).[70]

In addition, under the Agreement in respect of the Control of Looted Works of Art (1946), liberated States would provide neutral States with inventories of looted objects not found in Germany or Austria.[71] Neutral States were required to distribute the lists widely, search for these objects in their territories, prevent their export, and their citizens were required to report the location of any listed object.[72]

These laws were so far-reaching in terms of State responsibility that it was suggested they represent a new principle of international law.[73] The 1954 Hague Protocol, however, does not extend such responsibilities to neutral States but restricts them to belligerent occupiers that are State parties.

Internal restitution

The principles laid down by Allied military governments to effect internal restitution most starkly capture the essence of the second rationale of restitution in international law, that is the amelioration or reversal of the effect of internationally wrongful acts, namely discrimination, persecution and genocide. The legacy of these principles guides present-day responses by several governments, including the United States and United Kingdom in addressing the claims of Holocaust survivors and their heirs during the last decade.

---

[69] See Kowalski, *Art Treasures*, pp.62–64; Prott and O'Keefe, *Movement*, pp.807ff, §1507; Vásárhelyi, *Restitution*, pp.117ff; and Martin, 'Private', 279ff.

[70] See *Rosenberg* v. *Fischer*, (1949) JdT 1946 I 25, Note, 1949; and Prott and O'Keefe, *Movement*, pp.808–09, §1508. The equivalent Swedish law, Looted Objects Law of 29 June 1945, allowed Swedish citizens who were unclear of the origin of an object to sue the State Treasury for the purchase price.

[71] Agreement between the United States, the United Kingdom and France in respect of the Control of Looted Works of Art, 8 July 1946, (1951) 25 *Department of State Bulletin* 340.

[72] See N. Robinson, *Reparations and Restitution in International Law* (1949) 1 JYIL 186 at 203.

[73] See Martin, 'Private', 280; Vásárhelyi, *Restitution*, pp.115–16; and Kowalski, *Art Treasures*, p.63.

The post-war restitution programme created the legal basis for the restitution of cultural objects confiscated from individuals within German territory.[74] The precedent is important because it moves restitution of cultural objects beyond State actors to include individuals and non-State groups by amalgamating two areas of international law, namely minority protection and restitution of cultural property.

The US Zone, Law No.59: Restitution of Identifiable Property provided for 'speedy restitution of identifiable [tangible and intangible] property' which had been removed from its owner during the Nazi incumbency because of 'race, religion, nationality, ideology or political opposition to National Socialism'.[75] A presumption was made in favour of the claimant that any transaction during the relevant period constituted confiscation, if he or she was: (i) directly persecuted because of these grounds; or (ii) belonged to a group of persons who because of these grounds 'was to be eliminated in its entirety from the cultural and economic life of Germany by measures taken by the State or the NSDAP' (Article 3(1), Part 2). These transactions were clearly within the realm of private law.[76] The Allied restitution programme was effectively an act of humanitarian intervention by the international community in the domestic activities of a State.[77] The confiscations were viewed as an integral part of a genocidal campaign and a matter of international concern.

Allied governments recognised that the law itself had been used as a tool in oppression of groups by the Nazi regime. Law No.59 set down that it was not permissible 'to plead that an act was not wrongful or *contra bonos mores* because it conformed with a prevailing ideology concerning discrimination against individuals on account of their race, religion, nationality, ideology or their political opposition to National Socialism' (Article 2(2), Part 2). Museum officials today in response to current restitution claims often argue that the objects were legally acquired according to laws in force at the time. As detailed in Chapters 2 and 3, however, these laws were part of a general apparatus that perpetuated the scale of civilisation essential to European colonialism. They must be similarly scrutinised within the broader context of institutionalised, discriminatory and genocidal policies of colonial powers.

Jewish organisations successfully argued that property should not be returned to States which persecuted or continued to persecute affected minorities.[78]

---

[74] See E. J. Cohn, A Novel Chapter in the Relations between Common Law and Civil Law (1955) 4 ICLQ 493; Kowalski, *Art Treasures*, pp.58–59; Prott and O'Keefe, *Movement*, pp.806–07, §1506; and N. de Mattos Bentwich, International Aspects of Restitution and Compensation for Victims of the Nazis (1955–56) 32 BYIL 204. The armistice treaties with Italy, Bulgaria, Hungary and Romania did not contain specific provisions for internal restitution but they were required to repeal discriminatory legislation. The subsequent 1947 Paris peace treaties with Hungary (Art.27(1)) and Romania (Art.25(1)) sanctioned internal restitution.

[75] Art.1, Military Government for Germany, US Area of Control, Law No.59: Restitution of Identifiable Property, *Military Government Gazette* [Germany, US Zone, Issue G], No.10, November 1947; and (1948) 42(supp.) AJIL 11; and Kowalski, *Art Treasures*, Annex 9, p.115. See D. Hirst, *Report of the Spoliation Advisory Panel in respect of a Painting now in the Possession of Glasgow City Council,* (London, 2004), para.8.

[76] See Prott, 'Principles', 226. State sovereignty was also overridden by Law No.59 which guaranteed that the international principle of restitution asserted by the Allies would not be negated by conflicting provisions in national law including protection of bona fide purchasers. See Kowalski, *Art Treasures*, pp.58–59; and Prott and O'Keefe, *Movement*, p.407, §759.

[77] Bentwich, 'International Aspects', 205.

[78] See M. J. Kurtz, *Nazi Contraband: American Policy on the Return of European Cultural Treasures, 1945–1955* (New York, 1985), pp.198ff.

Accordingly, a crucial element of internal restitution was the explicit statement that property confiscated in these circumstances was to be returned to its previous owner or his or her legal heir, or successor organisations, representing missing or deceased persons.[79] These organisations were required to use the property to provide 'relief and rehabilitation for surviving members of such groups, organizations and communities'.[80] Debate quickly arose whether this obligation was confined to communities within the State or extended to communities which had established themselves in third countries.

From the late 1980s, the collapse of the Communist bloc in Central and Eastern Europe and greater accessibility to official archives in the Western States facilitated the re-emergence of the claims for the restitution of cultural objects confiscated by the Nazi regime. It became clear that museums, the world over, have 'benefited' from the dislocation and destruction perpetrated during the mid-century.[81] In December 2002, a UNESCO committee of experts finalised Draft Principles relating to Cultural Objects Displaced in relation to the Second World War.[82] As at February 2005, the principles were being deliberated by UNESCO Member States. The principles were developed in response to resurgent interest in Holocaust claims but, however, their application is more restrictive than the post-war schemes. They cover objects lost or removed from a territory subjected to hostilities or occupation *during* the war (Principle 2).

States in which the object is located are obliged to return it (or prohibit its export until its return) to the competent authorities of the territory from which it was removed (Principle 3). Importantly, the State from which the object was removed and has been returned to must exercise due diligence to identify and locate the person, entity or their successor who was entitled to it at the time of removal or loss 'in accordance with the laws of the recipient State' (Principle 7).

The State responsible for the loss or removal during the war must locate and return the object to the competent authorities of the relevant territory.[83] This obligation extends to indemnification of a bona fide purchaser (Principle 4). Restitution-in-kind is permitted where the object has been destroyed. However, no State is required to relinquish a cultural object 'having a closer cultural link to [it] than to the requesting

---

[79] Arts.7–13, Part 3, Law No.59. See Convention on the Settlement of Matters Arising out of the War and the Occupation, Bonn, 25 May 1952, Cmnd 656 (1959), p.3; Bentwich, 'International', 207 and 211; and Kowalski, *Art Treasures*, pp.59–60. See Art.144, Treaty of Peace with Turkey, Sèvres, 10 August 1920, not ratified, Cmd 964 (1920); and (1921) 15 (supp.) AJIL 179.

[80] The 1947 Paris peace treaties with Romania and Hungary specified that it related to groups within the respective States.

[81] See US Department of State and United States Holocaust Memorial Museum, *Washington Conference on Holocaust-Era Assets in the United States* (Washington DC, 1998); Seventh Report of Select Committee on Culture, Media and Sport (1999–2000 HC 371), vol.1, paras.167ff; L. Nicholas, *The Rape of Europa: The Fate of Europe's Treasures in the Third Reich and the Second World War* (London, 1995); and H. Feliciano, *The Lost Museum: The Nazi Conspiracy to Steal the World's Greatest Works of Art* (New York, 1997).

[82] UNESCO, Expert Meeting on the Settlement of Disputes relating to Cultural Objects Displaced in relation to the Second World War, 24 February 2003, UNESCO Doc.CLT-2002/CONF/602/3. The principles rely on those enunciated by Prott, 'Principles'; Articles on Responsibility of States for Internationally Wrongful Acts, UNGA Res.58/83, 12 December 2001; and the 1954 Hague Protocol.

[83] Together with all relevant scientific and technical documentation to facilitate conservation and restoration: Principle 11, UNESCO Doc.CLT-2002/CONF/602/3, 11.

State' (Principle 9). Finally, where an object has been destroyed and an appropriate substitute cannot be found, the responsible State must provide compensation, 'either monetary . . . or by contributing to the cultural development' of the relevant territory (Principle 10). These alternate forms of relief are afforded to the territory from which the object was removed and not the persecuted individual, entity or their successor.

In 2000, the US Presidential Advisory Commission on Holocaust Assets concluded that restitution involved material and moral restitution. It noted that the latter could only be achieved: 'by confronting the past honestly and internalizing its lessons'.[84] As explained in Chapter 8, the claims of Holocaust survivors and their heirs have occurred at a time of increased activism on the international stage by indigenous communities.[85] These respective campaigns for restitution of cultural objects have significant parallels: the systematic suppression and destruction of particular groups and their cultural manifestations, justified by racialised, scientific theories; the 'legalisation' of such acts within the domestic legal system; and the present-day theoretical and practical initiatives to reverse or ameliorate the effects of discriminatory and genocidal acts.

During the 1930s and 40s, the United States tried to confront its own discriminatory and genocidal policies towards Native Americans. Its efforts and those of other settler States is 'an open-ended process' resisted continually by the dominant culture to this day. They are particularly averse to recognising the right of indigenous peoples to restitution of cultural heritage in international law.

State succession and the Second World War
In respect of the post-Second World War restitution programme, the principles and implementation of returns related to violations of international humanitarian law are more useful to post-colonial restitution claims than those concerning State succession.[86] Nonetheless, the 1947 Treaty of Peace with Italy is instructive for two reasons: (i) the reaffirmation of the territoriality principle; and (ii) the requirement that a European State restore cultural property to a non-European State following succession.[87]

Article 37 of the Treaty of Peace required that Italy return to Ethiopia all 'works of art, religious objects, archives and objects of historical value' belonging to that State or its nations but removed since its occupation. Article 12(3) provided for restitution-in-kind by Italy if it is unable to return certain objects. The treaty is of

---

[84] E. Bronfman to US President, 15 December 2000, in US Presidential Advisory Commission on Holocaust Assets, *Plunder and Restitution: Findings and Recommendations of the Presidential Advisory Commission on Holocaust Assets in the United States and Staff Report* (Washington DC, 2000).

[85] See ILA, Report of the Cultural Heritage Law Committee, (London, 2004), p.3.

[86] See C. G. Fitzmaurice, The Juridical Clauses of the Peace Treaties (1948-II) 81 RCADI 327; Kowalski, *Art Treasures*, pp.41–42; and W. W. Kowalski, Repatriation of Cultural Property Following a Cession of Territory or Dissolution of Multinational States (2001) 6 AAL 139 at 153.

[87] Ethiopia viewed the Italian confiscations as a breach of international law: Imperial Ethiopian Legation to UNWCC, 12 August and 8 October 1947, Docs.A55 and A56, box 5, reel 34, PAG 3/1.0.0, United Nations War Crimes Commission 1943–1949, Predecessor Archives Group, United Nations Archives, New York. Italy signed further agreements in 1956 and 1997 to restore cultural property to Ethiopia. The Axum Obelisk removed in 1937 was returned in 2003.

limited application because of the Allies' failure to enforce its provisions, a reluctance no doubt coloured by Ethiopian booty removed in the nineteenth century and held in their own museums.[88]

1954 Hague Protocol
The Protocol for the Protection of Cultural Property in the Event of Armed Conflict (1954 Hague Protocol) modified and codified the developments achieved in the restitution of cultural property following the Second World War.[89] The UNESCO Draft International Protocol drew heavily from the 1943 Declaration of London.[90] Given the leading role of the United States and the United Kingdom in the post-war restitution programme, it is difficult to fathom their strenuous opposition to the inclusion of restitutory relief in the 1954 Hague Convention. These States successfully had the restitution provision extricated from the 1954 Hague Convention and it became a Protocol, enabling States to sign it independently of the Convention.[91] This division of the restitutory relief from the protection of cultural heritage during armed conflict runs contrary to international practice applied since the 1815 Congress of Vienna.

Under the 1954 Hague Protocol, a State party must prevent the export of cultural objects from territory it occupies during armed conflict (Article 1).[92] Each State party must take into custody cultural objects imported into its territory, either directly or indirectly, from any occupied territory immediately upon importation or at the request of the authorities of the occupied territory (Article 2).[93] Following cessation of hostilities, a State party must return all cultural objects removed in contravention of the Protocol to the competent authorities of the territories it formerly occupied. Such objects cannot be retained as war reparations (Article 3). There is no time limit for lodging a claim for the return of such cultural objects.[94]

A State party which fails to prevent the export of cultural objects is obliged to pay an indemnity to bona fide purchasers of objects which must subsequently be returned (Articles 1 and 4). This provision is more limited than the post-1945 restitution

---

[88] See R. Pankhurst, The Case of Ethiopia (1986) 38 *Museum* 58 at 60; J. Greenfield, *The Return of Cultural Treasures* (2nd edn, Cambridge, 1996), pp.192 and 266; and Prott and O'Keefe, *Movement*, p.830, §1532.

[89] The Hague, 14 May 1954, in force 7 August 1956, 249 UNTS 358. See L. V. Prott, The Protocol to the Convention for the Protection of Cultural Property in the Event of Armed Conflict (The Hague Convention) 1954, in M. Briat and J. A. Freedberg (eds.), *Legal Aspects of International Trade in Art* (Paris, 1996), pp.163–73.

[90] UNESCO Doc.CL/717, Annex 4, 46–47; and UNESCO Doc.7C/PRG/7, Annex.

[91] *Intergovernmental Conference on the Protection of Cultural Property in the Event of Armed Conflict – The Hague, 1954: Records of the Conference* (The Hague, 1961), paras.1645–90 and 1750–56. The United States and United Kingdom have not ratified either the 1954 Hague Convention or Protocol. Australia ratified the Convention on 19 September 1984 (with reservations) but has yet to ratify the Protocol.

[92] Excavations are more fully covered by Art.32, UNESCO Recommendation on International Principles applicable to Archaeological Excavations, New Delhi, 5 December 1956; and Art.9, Second Protocol to the Hague Convention for the Protection of Cultural Property in the Event of Armed Conflict, The Hague, 26 March 1999, in force 9 March 2004, (1999) 38 ILM 769.

[93] See *Records of the Conference*, para.1673, 256.

[94] See UNESCO Doc.CL/717, Annex IV, 47; S. E. Nahlik, La protection internationale des biens culturels en case de conflit armé (1967-II) 120 RCADI 61 at 147; and Prott, 'Protocol', 167.

scheme because it does not extend to neutral third party States.[95] Cultural objects deposited in the territory of a State party for the purpose of safekeeping during armed conflict must be returned to the depositing State at the close of hostilities (Article 5).[96]

The 1954 Hague Protocol is of limited application to restitution claims by indigenous communities and minorities because: (i) the instrument privileges State claimants; (ii) the inclusion of a colonial clause leaves the administering State to determine whether it shall apply to colonial territories (Article 12 and 13); and (iii) it does not apply to internal conflicts.[97] Despite these limitations, by codifying principles derived from the post-war restitution programme, it can be an important tool for future restitution schemes.

Native American cultures in the mid twentieth century

Whilst the US government and museum fraternity roundly condemned the direct, 'public' acquisition of objects, US collectors and museums took advantage of the unrest and dislocation visited by the Second World War to 'privately' purchase objects which came on the market.[98] US collectors' reticence in appreciating the aesthetic value of indigenous arts from the Americas prior to the conflict had meant that the best collections were located in Europe.[99] The war in Europe enabled the United States to reclaim its cultural inheritance during a period of heightened public and governmental accord concerning the centrality of Native American objects to the national culture.

This final section focuses on the 'return' of Native American cultural objects to the US national imagining during the 1930s and 40s. There was a cognisance of both the significance of living indigenous cultures and cultural objects to the pursuit of an authentic national and hemispheric cultural identity, and efforts to afford Native Americans a measure of self-determination through cultural renewal. These processes involved an acknowledgement of the destructive policies of the past US administrations towards Native Americans and their cultures. This reassessment pre-empted and fuelled an awareness of the importance of all peoples and their cultural

---

[95] See *Records of the Conference*, paras.1630 and 1637.

[96] See UNESCO Doc.CBC/DR/157. Art.9 enables States at the time of signing, ratifying or accession to the instrument to stipulate whether they wish not to be bound by Section 1 (Arts.1 to 4) or Section 2 (Art.5). This paragraph was proposed by Poland: *Records of the Conference*, paras.1644, 1663–70; and UNESCO Doc.CBC/DR/157. See Polish–Canadian case: J. G. Castel, Polish Treasures in Canada – 1940–1960: A Case History (1974) 68 ASILP 121; S. A. Williams, The Polish Art Treasures in Canada: 1940–60 (1977) 15 CYIL 292; and S. E. Nahlik, The Case of the Displaced Art Treasures (1980) 23 GYIL 255.

[97] The *travaux* noted that: 'Where property has changed hands on the national territory and has not been exported, the case is one for the national legislation alone': UNESCO Doc.CL/717, Annex iV, 47. Compare with Art.19, 1954 Hague Convention, and Ch.5, 1999 Second Hague Protocol. Cf. Prott, 'Protocol', 170.

[98] Alaskan authorities requested assistance from the US Military Government for Germany for the return to Alaska of 'certain primitive art specimens from Alaska believed to be in Germany': L. D. Clay, US Deputy Military Governor for Germany to E. Gruening, Governor of Alaska, 17 November 1945, MoMA Archives, NY: RdH [AAA: 2925].

[99] Interview with D. C. Miller, 24 June 1957, Holger Cahill Papers, Archives of American Art, Smithsonian Institution, Washington DC [AAA: 5285; 592 at 620].

contribution in the face of the genocidal policies of fascist regimes during the 1930s and 40s. A thematic thread can be drawn from the Indian New Deal policies, Allied reactions to the devastation of the War and ensuing reforms in international law. The survival of indigenous peoples in the face of past adversity was held up as a beacon to all humanity at a moment when European civilisation felt itself under threat.

Indigenous peoples and American national identities

During the inter-war period, the United States isolated itself from the woes of Europe and sought engagement with its Latin American neighbours. This redirection profoundly affected US Indian policy and public perceptions of Native American cultures. Indian New Dealers' promotion of Native American cultural objects centred on educating the general public about living cultures that needed to be nurtured for the good of indigenous communities, the US nation and civilisation generally.[100]

For many during this period, indigenous peoples of both continents represented the possibility of a new hemispheric identity independent of Europe. Mexican muralist Diego Rivera articulated the hope thus: 'Your antiques are not found in Rome. They are to be found in Mexico.'[101] René d'Harnoncourt extended the goals of the endeavour by concluding: 'We are creating in this New World for the Americas the promise of a New World for mankind.'[102] US artists, art critics and policymakers looked to replicate the resurgent Mexican cultural vitality that was attributed to the incorporation of the cultural heritages of its indigenous inhabitants.[103]

With the American Federation of Arts, d'Harnoncourt organised the 'Mexican Arts and Crafts' exhibition that opened at the Metropolitan Museum of Art, New York in 1930.[104] He was cognisant of the devastating effects of assimilation policies on indigenous populations. He would later write: 'By imposing on them one religion, one language and one code of ethics and social forms, and by breaking up all their material manifestations . . . the Spaniards succeeded in the complete destruction of the different nations'.[105] This Mexican ideal reached its zenith with the 1940 MoMA exhibition 'Twenty Centuries of Mexican Art' which recapitulated the chronology of the progressive layers of cultural influences which had led to the contemporary renaissance in its art scene.[106] This chronology, which accorded indigenous objects

[100] See R. d'Harnoncourt, Indian Arts and Craft and their Place in the Modern World, 1940, The Museum of Modern Art Archives, NY: René d'Harnoncourt Papers [AAA: 2919;161ff].

[101] D. Rivera cited in T. Smith, *Making the Modern: Industry, Art and Design in America* (Chicago, 1993), p.212. See H. J. Spinden, Indian Art on its Merits (1931) 3 *Parnassus* 12; and F. A. Whiting Jr, The New World Is Still New (1939) 32 *Magazine of Art* 613.

[102] R. d'Harnoncourt, Notes for specialised talk entitled Art of Latin America, Cleveland, 14 June 1943, MoMA Archives, NY: RdH [AAA: 2919;303–304].

[103] See O. Baddeley and V. Fraser, *Drawing the Line: Art and Cultural Identity in Contemporary Latin America* (London, 1989), 79–98. Cf. S. Errington, *The Death of Authentic Primitive Art and Other Tales of Progress* (Berkeley, 1998), pp.161–87.

[104] See R. d'Harnoncourt, *Mexican Arts*, (New York, 1930), p.xi; Anon., The Loan Exhibition of Mexican Arts (1930) 25 *Bulletin of the Metropolitan Museum of Art* 210; and R. d'Harnoncourt, Exhibition of Mexican Arts (1931) 4 *The Carnegie Magazine* 227.

[105] R. d'Harnoncourt, A Mexican Interpretation of Mexico, MoMA Archives, NY: RdH [AAA: 3831;155ff].

[106] MoMA, *Twenty Centuries of Mexican Art* (exh. cat., New York, 1940).

a prominent place, replicated the layered definition of cultural property in various American instruments for the protection of cultural heritage.[107]

D'Harnoncourt acknowledged in the 1930 exhibition catalogue that 'political independence . . . did not immediately liberate cultural tendencies'. But, he argued, Mexican intellectuals after 1910 were the first to promote the 'heretical' idea that their country nurture a 'unique' national culture which might 'be of value to the world'.[108] The draft foreword to the 1940 exhibition catalogue noted:

> Americans have until recently felt a certain condescension toward Mexico . . .
> But have these political and technological achievements produced a
> civilisation culturally superior to that of Mexico? With regret we must admit
> that they have not . . . Mexican culture as it is expressed in its art
> seems . . . far more deeply rooted among the people than does ours.[109]

For US artists the lesson was clear: to create an original, indigenous national art, not indebted to Europe, they had to look, as the Mexicans did, to the arts and crafts of their indigenous inhabitants. The recalibration was mirrored in a significant amendment to MoMA's 'famous torpedo' that illustrated the museum's progressing collection policy.[110]

This re-evaluation came at a price for indigenous communities and some American States. The promotion of Mexican cultural heritage in the United States led to the haemorrhaging of objects to the US market and fuelled efforts to formulate a hemispheric treaty to control their illicit traffic. By the late 1930s, this market was so voracious that the National University of Mexico was required to request loans from US institutions for the 1940 MoMA exhibition,[111] whilst villagers in the state of Oaxaca demonstrated against the removal of objects from the local museum for the MoMA show and local State authorities called police into the fray to force their return.[112]

The 1940 MoMA exhibition was part of a broader propaganda campaign articulated in the *New Yorker* review: 'Despite invasions, oppression, and exploitation, [Mexican] art that is the purest expression of a people's soul remains very much as it always was . . . There ought to be a lesson in that for some of those overwrought

---

[107] For example, 1935 PAU Treaty, p.134; and the 1976 Convention on the Protection of the Archaeological, Historical and Artistic Heritage of the American Nations (1976 Convention of San Salvador), p.192.

[108] D'Harnoncourt, *Mexican Arts*, pp.xi–xiii. See R. d'Harnoncourt, Four Hundred Years of Mexican Art (1932) 33 *Art and Archaeology* 71.

[109] Document entitled 'Preface', Folder 1354, Box 138, Series III 4L, RG4 NAR Personal Projects, Rockefeller Family Archives, Rockefeller Archives Center, Sleepy Hollow, New York (RAC). See Foreword, in MoMA, *Twenty Centuries*, p.11.

[110] See Minutes from 63rd Advisory Committee Meeting of MoMA, Folder 1256, Box 128, III 4L, RG4 NAR Personal Projects, RAC; and K. Varnedoe, The Evolving Torpedo: Changing Ideas of the Collections of Painting and Sculpture of the Museum of Modern Art, in J. Elderfield (ed.), *The Museum of Modern Art at Mid-Century: Continuity and Change* (New York, 1995), pp.12–73.

[111] Rio to N. Rockefeller, 5 January 1940, Folder 1354, Box 138, III 4L, RG4 NAR Personal Projects, Rockefeller Family Archives, RAC.

[112] See Wheeler to N. Rockefeller, 12 March 1940, Folder 1354, Box 138, III 4L, RG4 NAR Personal Projects, Rockefeller Family Archives, RAC.

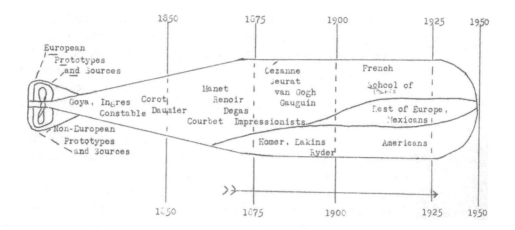

In the past nine years the torpedo has moved a little farther and the Committee would sketch it today in the following form:

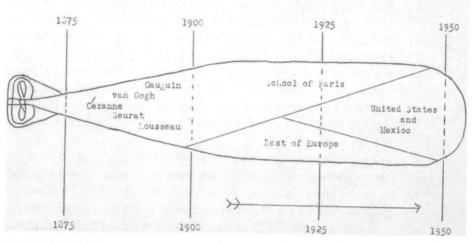

Figure 5.2 MoMA torpedo, 1933–1946, in Nelson A Rockefeller Personal Objects folders, Rockefeller Archives Center, New York.

totalitarians overseas.'[113] But the lesson, some argued, should not be confined to totalitarian regimes. One 1940 MoMA publication proffered: '[O]ur sense of history, our conviction that America is great in terms of her past and her peoples, can be strengthened and vitalised by more knowledge of the continent's first inhabitants'.[114]

[113] Anon., The Art Galleries: Mexicans, Americans, Italians and Dutch, *New Yorker*, 25 May 1940.
[114] Anon., Museums in these Times (December 1940) *Junior Council Magazine* (MoMA) n.p., in The Museum of Modern Art Archives, NY: Department of Public Information, I [12; 241].

The Indian Arts and Crafts Board (IACB) under d'Harnoncourt's leadership greatly aided this reinterpretation of the place of indigenous communities and their cultures within US society. Although largely led by non-indigenous peoples, the IACB's work was a significant precursor to the defining of cultural heritage as a 'resource' by newly independent States in the late twentieth century, a resource that indeed was the 'common heritage of mankind' and essential for the cultural self-determination and development of their peoples.

John Collier and René d'Harnoncourt, in pursuing the Indian New Deal policy of cultural pluralism and economic development of Native American communities, launched a two-pronged education campaign. First, indigenous arts and crafts education facilitated cultural renewal as part of an Indian New Deal campaign of internal self-determination.[115] Second, there was a focus on the education of the general public about the 'major contribution' of Native Americans and their culture to US society and civilisation generally. Both arms were defined by the dominant culture within the context of the national market economy.[116]

Native American cultural and economic independence

Established federal education policies pertaining to Native Americans had become highly contentious during the inter-war period because of increasing challenges to assimilation. Collier maintained that the Bureau of Indian Affairs (BIA) needed to decrease the paternalism of its work in order to elevate civil rights and modern business practices within Native American communities.[117] He argued that these changes would encourage Native Americans 'to develop their own patterns not as segregated minorities but as noble elements in our common life'.[118] Cultural pluralism was sanctioned within the defined parameters of the dominant national culture and economy.

The establishment of a local collection in Santa Fe, to make indigenous cultural objects more accessible to the communities themselves and alleviate losses to large museums and private collections, was an early initiative. The Laboratory of Anthropology collection aimed to 'familiarise Indian pupils with the finest examples of their own ancestral arts'.[119] This restitution of cultural objects to indigenous communities was designed 'to foster, encourage, and promote the arts and industries, and the spiritual, social, economic and physical welfare of the aboriginal American races' – in a

---

[115] See R. d'Harnoncourt, Indian Arts and Crafts and their Place in the Modern World, in O. La Farge (ed.), *The Changing Indian* (Norman, 1942), p.144. D'Harnoncourt believed that the only method possible in dealing with Indian arts and crafts was to work with each tribe as a separate entity: R. F. Schrader, *The Indian Arts and Crafts Board: An Aspect of New Deal Indian Policy* (Albuquerque, 1983), p.129.

[116] See W. J. Rushing, Marketing the Affinity of the Primitive and the Modern: René d'Harnoncourt and 'Indian Art of the United States', in J. C. Berlo (ed.), *The Early Years of Native American Art History: The Politics of Scholarship and Collecting* (Seattle, 1992), pp.198–200.

[117] K. R. Philp, *John Collier's Crusade for Indian Reform 1920–1954* (Tucson, 1977), p.118.

[118] *Ibid.*

[119] Report, Curator to Director, 1 January 1930, in 234D Laboratory of Anthropology at Santa Fe, Report, Folder 5, Box 1, Series 234, RG 1.1, Rockefeller Foundation Archives, RAC. The Laboratory obtained objects confiscated by federal authorities pursuant to the Antiquities Act of 1906: Nusbaum to Packard, 17 May 1933, Folder 174, Box 17, Series III.2E, RG 2, Rockefeller Foundation Archives, RAC.

manner defined by the dominant society.[120] Ownership of the objects and their usage was vested in non-indigenous hands.[121] Further, its usage was clearly prescribed to 'guard against decadence', thereby inhibiting the development of indigenous cultural production.[122]

However, René d'Hanoncourt as General Manager of the IACB from 1936 to 1944 shared the Indian New Deal visions of promoting indigenous arts and crafts to stimulate cultural renewal and facilitate economic self-sufficiency in the manner determined by the communities themselves. He believed the indigenous communities gave the 'craftsmen an irreplaceable sympathetic background and safeguard[ed] Indian production from the dangers of losing its most valuable asset, its Indian identity'.[123] He argued that the Indian New Deal:

> permitted the Indians to maintain again openly their cultural heritage, and governmental agencies joined with Indian leaders in their efforts to blend native concepts with modern achievements so that the tribes could live in modern society without losing their personality.[124]

It discouraged Native American cultural isolation and stagnation, and recognised that a people aware of their cultural heritage could thrive.

D'Harnoncourt reacted against the promotion by some US policymakers and artists of the preservation of what they perceived to be the traditional elements of indigenous cultures unaffected by white contact.[125] Through his work with indigenous communities in Mexico and the United States, he knew these were living cultures that were always responding to foreign influences. D'Harnoncourt argued that such influences should be made available to these communities if they wished to incorporate them into their cultural production.[126] And the choices were to be made by Native Americans and not outsiders.[127] As shown in Chapter 9, these principles have been reinforced by the Native American civil rights campaign in the late twentieth century.

IACB exhibitions from San Francisco to New York

D'Harnoncourt mounted several seminal exhibitions to educate the US public about the living cultures of Native Americans and their contribution to the nation and

---

[120] Preliminary Statement of Executive Committee to Board of Trustees, November 1927, Folder 643, Box 65, Series III.2E, RG 2, Rockefeller Foundation Archives, RAC.

[121] By agreement dated October 1929, the collections of the Indian Arts Fund were transferred into the custody of the museum of the Laboratory of Anthropology: Report of Curator to Director, 1 January 1930.

[122] Mekeel, Laboratory of Anthropology to Keppel, Carnegie Corporation, 27 January 1939, Folder 10, Box 1, Series 234, RG 1.1, Rockefeller Foundation Archives, RAC.

[123] D'Harnoncourt, 'Indian', 146; and Schrader, *Indian Arts*, pp.142–146.

[124] R. d'Harnoncourt, Document entitled 'Foreword', MoMA Archives, NY: RdH [AAA: 2922; 607ff].

[125] See d'Harnoncourt, 'Indian', 153.

[126] See R. d'Harnoncourt, Notes for specialised talk entitled Art of Latin America, Cleveland, 14 June 1943, MoMA Archives, NY: RdH [AAA: 2919; 303–304]; and A. Marriott and C. K. Rachlin, Ethnohistory of the Indian Arts and Crafts Board of the Department of the Interior, Draft 2, n.d., MoMA Archives, NY: RdH [AAA: 3830; 1018at 1023].

[127] D'Harnoncourt, 'Indian', 154.

humanity generally. This campaign was largely conducted within the context of the US market economy, with consumers being educated about the 'quality' and 'usefulness' of Native American crafts.[128] He felt that this market was the only means of successfully allowing Native Americans to develop their arts and crafts whilst achieving economic self-sufficiency.[129] The Native American artist's New Deal was realised in part by the San Francisco Golden Gate International Exposition and the 1941 MoMA exhibition.

The IACB's 1939 exhibition, 'Indian Arts in the United States and Alaska', at the Golden Gate International Exposition at San Francisco (1939 International Exposition) aimed to show that Native American arts and crafts merited appreciation both aesthetically and for their saleability.[130] A selective gift shop was assembled in the sales area and individual Native Americans demonstrated their skills to the general public.[131] Liberated from the ahistorical and depoliticised representations of a 'vanishing race' depicted in most US museums, the 1939 International Exposition evidenced the resilience of indigenous peoples who had a vital contribution to make to the nation's future. The IACB exhibition was the first time the US government gave Native Americans a central position at an international exhibition.[132] D'Harnoncourt argued that if the US public became aware of the achievements of Native Americans, 'they would become a real contribution to our contemporary life and would thus give the Indian his deserved place in the contemporary world'.[133]

The 1939 International Exposition was so successful that plans were made for a show on the east coast in early 1941.[134] The 'Indian Art of the United States' exhibition, devoted solely to Native American objects in the pantheon of modern art, MoMA, was organised by d'Harnoncourt under the auspices of the IACB.[135] One reviewer wrote that MoMA had succeeded in placing Native American cultural objects 'among the American fine arts'.[136] However, despite the promulgation of cultural pluralism, the worth of cultures was still judged by arbiters and institutions of the dominant culture.[137]

---

[128] See Schrader, *Indian Arts*, p.144; and d'Harnoncourt, 'Indian', 146–47.

[129] See R. d'Harnoncourt(?), Final Draft: Memorandum on a proposed plan for the study and promotion of the native arts and crafts of the two Americas, MoMA Archives, NY: RdH [AAA: 2921; 268–77]; and Joint Committee on Latin American Studies Outline of a Short Report on Conference on Studies in Latin American Art, 1945, MoMA Archives, NY: RdH [AAA: 2922; 1003ff].

[130] See R. d'Harnoncourt, North American Indian Arts (1939) 32 *Magazine of Art* 164–67. See Schrader, *Indian Arts*, pp.163ff; Rushing, 'Marketing', 200–06; and W. J. Rushing, *Native American Art and the New York Avant-Garde: A History of Cultural Primitivism* (Austin, 1995), pp.104ff.

[131] See d'Harnoncourt, 'North', 167. There were 1,250,000 visitors and sales of Indian arts and crafts rose by almost 25 per cent in the year of the exhibition: Schrader, *Indian Arts*, pp.184 and 195.

[132] D'Harnoncourt to Rutherford, 2 December 1938, cited in Schrader, *Indian Arts*, p.184.

[133] D'Harnoncourt, 'North', 164.

[134] D'Harnoncourt to Barr, 25 September 1939, cited in Schrader, *Indian Arts*, p.194.

[135] See Rushing, *Native*, p.104; Rushing, 'Marketing', 191–236; and A. Jonaitis, Creations of Mystics and Philosophers: The White Man's Perceptions of Northwest Coast Indian Art from the 1930s to the Present (1981) 5 AICRJ 4.

[136] Anon., 20,000 Years of Indian Art Assembled for New York Show, *Newsweek*, 17 February 1941, pp.57–58.

[137] D'Harnoncourt acknowledged that the authoritative force of MoMA's institutional credibility augmented his aims: R. d'Harnoncourt, Suggestions for Future Activities of the Indian Arts and Crafts Board, 21 September 1939, cited in Rushing, *Native*, p.106.

Figure 5.3 Fred Kabotie (Hopi), artist and Eleanor Roosevelt at the 'Indian Art of the United States', The Museum of Modern Art, New York, 22 January–27 April 1941.

Unlike prior MoMA exhibitions of non-European peoples, this exhibition was extraordinary because of d'Harnoncourt's avowed aim to represent living and vibrant cultures – not timeless anthropological specimens. This purpose was reflected in the exhibition's layout:

(1) the 'great Indian traditions of the past, including mound builder materials, Bering Strait culture and other Indian civilisations now dead' were shown only as 'art for art's sake';[138]

(2) the 'Living Traditions' section included historic materials considered part of the art of living indigenous cultures. D'Harnoncourt strove to indicate 'the place of each specimen in its native civilisation' emphasising aspects beyond 'an art-for-art's sake display'[139]; and

(3) in the 'Indian Art for Modern Living' section, contemporary art objects were arranged to show the potential contribution of Native arts and crafts to modern decorative arts, with the displays being 'very contemporary and Fifth Avenue in the best sense of the word'.[140]

---

[138] D'Harnoncourt to Douglas, 30 September 1939, cited in Rushing, *Native*, p.108. See Douglas and d'Harnoncourt, *Indian Art*, pp.49ff.

[139] D'Harnoncourt to G. Heye, 9 October 1940, cited in Rushing, *Native*, p.108. See R. d'Harnoncourt, Living Arts of the Indians (1941) 34 *Magazine of Art* 72; Douglas and d'Harnoncourt, *Indian Art*, pp.115ff; and M. A. Staniszewski, *The Power of Display: A History of Exhibition Installations at the Museum of Modern Art* (Cambridge MA, 1998), pp.87ff.

[140] D'Harnoncourt to Barr, 8 November 1939, cited in Rushing, *Native*, p.108. See Douglas and d'Harnoncourt, *Indian Art*, pp.197ff. Among the individual artists represented in this section were Fred Kabotie, Oscar Howe (Dakota), Harrison Begay (Navajo) and Monroe Tsatoke (Kiowa).

The propaganda potential of the exhibition was not lost on d'Harnoncourt who was sensitive to the intensive search for a national cultural identity. He claimed Native American art solely for the United States and this was reflected in the show's title: 'Indian Art of the United States'. Oliver La Farge commented that aspects of Indian civilisation could 'stand comparison with skyscrapers or the present apex of white civilisation in Europe'.[141]

Nonetheless, for d'Harnoncourt the diversity of Native American cultures had to be promoted for the benefit of US national cultural identity and the communities themselves. He showed a marked preference for the term 'folk art' over 'primitive art', because Native American cultures were 'always an inextricable part of all social, economic and ceremonial activities of a given society'.[142]

The extrication of indigenous cultures from a romanticised past enabled their rehabilitation as examples of the resilience and adaptability of Americans in the face of global conflict. The Museum of Modern Art found that the Indian New Deal fitted its role 'as a living museum, not a collection of curious and interesting objects [but] woven into the very warp and woof of our democracy'.[143] Roosevelt added during the 1939 opening of the MoMA's new premises: 'The arts cannot thrive except where men are free to be themselves and to be in charge of the discipline of their own energies and ardors.'[144] The purpose of the 1941 MoMA exhibition according to its organisers was to show: '[t]hat Indian art, like any other living art, had never been static. It grew with the cultural development of the various Indian groups, has been able to adopt and absorb many foreign elements from neighbors.'[145] For d'Harnoncourt, cultural freedom was essential to any group's cultural development and the realisation of cultural pluralism.

For the organisers of the 1941 MoMA exhibition, this reassessment of indigenous cultural objects within the national narrative was accompanied by an acknowledgement of the devastation caused by prior US Indian policies, a purpose incorporated in the exhibition catalogue's front cover: a shield design with a bear charging into a barrage of bullets. Reviewer Jean Charlot noted: '[O]ur pride in the æsthetic achievements of the Indian . . . should be tinged with introspective compunction: some of the objects now on exhibit were "collected" by our War Department, presumably as spoils'.[146] The exhibition catalogue argued that past US Indian policies were 'not merely a violation of intrinsic human rights but were actually destroying values which could never be replaced, values [that] are a source of strength for future generations'.[147] For d'Harnoncourt and the IACB, the MoMA exhibition was a means of ameliorating or reversing the effects of these policies.

During the 1930s and 40s, the 'correction in [US collective] memory' of its treatment of Native Americans and the reassessment of their cultures occurred against

---

[141] O. La Farge, The Indian as Artist, *New York Times*, 26 January 1941, p.9.

[142] Douglas and d'Harnoncourt, *Indian Art*, p.12. See R. d'Harnoncourt, All-American Art (1 January 1941) *Art Digest* 15 at 17; and R. d'Harnoncourt, Naïve Painting, MoMA Archives, NY: RdH [AAA: 2919; 212].

[143] F. D. Roosevelt, Radio Speech Attendant upon the Dedication of the New Building of the Museum of Modern Art, New York City, 10 May 1939, *New York Times*, 11 May 1939, p.29.

[144] *Ibid.*   [145] D'Harnoncourt, 'Living Arts', 72.

[146] See J. Charlot, All-American, *The Nation*, 8 February 1941, p.165.

[147] Douglas and d'Harnoncourt, *Indian Art*, p.9.

Figure 5.4 Painted Shield Cover, Kiowa, Oklahoma, reproduced on original cover of exhibition catalogue, *Indian Art of the United States*, Museum of Modern Art, New York, 1941.

the growing shadow cast by the genocidal practices of fascist regimes. Having worked with American indigenous communities, d'Harnoncourt could write candidly: 'To rob a people of tradition is to rob it of inborn strength and identity. To rob a people of opportunity to grow through invention or through acquisition of values from other races is to rob it of its future.'[148] The United States has repeatedly affirmed that the restitution of cultural objects to their community of origin is an essential element in ensuring its continued contribution to 'the cultural heritage of all mankind'.

[148] Douglas and d'Harnoncourt, *Indian Art*, p.10. See Rushing, *Native*, p.115, n.105 (regarding authorship of catalogue).

Yet similar concessions concerning restitution were not made to Native Americans within its own borders. They, unlike other occupied peoples, were not afforded the right of self-determination or the return of their cultural objects from metropolitan museums until the end of the twentieth century. To this day, these rights are not guaranteed by international law but are prescribed by US domestic legislation and its national agenda.

In the following chapter, it is suggested that the United States' championing of individual rights over group rights occasioned this discrepancy. Cold War tensions resulted in cultural pluralism fading into cultural integration, and the categorisation of formerly sovereign Native American nations as but one of 'our country's minority groups'.[149] However, Native Americans would no longer be silenced. They built on the momentum of the Indian New Deal to chart their own course towards self-determination,[150] development and cultural renewal in the second half of the twentieth century, and the restitution of cultural objects would be at the forefront of their claims.

---

[149] Anon., 'Museums'.

[150] See R. A. Nelson and J. F. Sheley, Bureau of Indian Affairs Influence on Indian Self-Determination, in V. Deloria Jr (ed.), *American Indian Policy in the Twentieth Century* (Norman, 1985), pp.177ff.

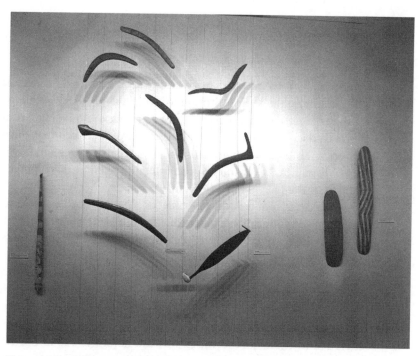

Figure 6.1 Installation view of Indigenous Australian artefacts at the exhibition 'Art of the South Seas', The Museum of Modern Art, New York, 29 January – 19 May 1946.

6

Genocide, human rights and colonised peoples during the Cold War

> None of us know enough about the other fellow's life to have a right to wipe it out. We are not gods to make other men in our own image.[1]

> In it, history evaporates . . . Nothing is produced, nothing is chosen: all one has to do is to possess these new objects from which all soiling trace of origin or choice has been removed.[2]

Immediately after the Second World War, the United States and Britain accepted the premise that the restitution of cultural property is an integral component of the reconstruction process and of ensuring the ongoing cultural contribution of formerly occupied peoples. From the mid-twentieth century, the formal apparatus of European colonial occupation of non-European peoples and territories was gradually being dismantled. Contrary to consistent international law practice of the preceding century and a half, the post-colonial reconstruction process did not encompass the large-scale restitution of cultural objects. The central reasons for the failure to address the return of cultural objects during decolonisation is the subject of this chapter.

The failure to extend principles developed during the post-Second World War restitution programme to formerly colonised peoples and indigenous communities was indicative of a succession of compromises forged as a consequence of the Cold War and fears of secessionist movements. The lessons learnt in the aftermath of the Second World War contributed to major developments in international law, but these developments were significantly constricted by contemporary international relations. Included in these compromises was the failure to retain the cultural components within the definition of genocide; and the repeated failure to provide positive protection for minorities in international human rights instruments. These compromises continue to hinder the ability of indigenous communities and minorities to preserve, protect and develop their cultural identity – their contribution to the culture of the world. With the end of the Cold War, little constructive reconsideration of these concessions has been brought.

This chapter shows how the United States and other settler States actively campaigned for and attained these compromises at the international level. There is also an examination of the translation of such policies into the domestic sphere by the United States. The United States co-opted the rhetoric of decolonisation to justify the

[1] F. S. Cohen, Americanizing the White Man (1952) 21 *The American Scholar* 177 at 191.
[2] R. Barthes, Myth Today, in R. Barthes, *Mythologies*, trans. A. Lavers (London, 1993), p.151.

severance of its obligations to the occupied peoples within its own borders: Native Americans. In an attempted renunciation of the history of US–Native American relations, these communities became minorities within this nation-state. Integration policies allowed individual members of minorities cultural freedom as long as it did not disrupt national unity. The State condoned loyalty only unto itself and actively discouraged the preservation and development of indigenous cultures and group identity. Once again the cultural objects of these communities were collected and displayed by the dominant culture as primitive art – 'from which all soiling trace of origin . . . has been removed'.

However, indigenous peoples and minorities organised civil rights movements in the coming decades which challenged these policies.

Genocide and cultural heritage

In the aftermath of the Second World War there was a clear understanding that the removal and destruction of the cultural objects of a group was intrinsic to genocidal policy, and that such acts directly and adversely affected the contribution of targeted groups to the cultural heritage of humankind. The Allied governments recognised the importance of returning cultural objects to reverse and ameliorate the impact of such policies. I have called this the second rationale for the restitution in international law.

The extrication of the cultural elements from the definition of genocide during negotiations for the Convention on the Prevention and Punishment of The Crime of Genocide (1948 Genocide Convention), as a concession to metropolitan powers and settler States, interrupted this important lesson. It also compromised the role of restitution of cultural property as part of the reconstruction process following the cessation of such acts.

The fate of the cultural elements of genocide is considered over three periods in the last half-century or so:

(1) the first period from the close of the Second World War to the Nuremberg indictment and the work of various legal bodies and academics in the articulation of the international crime of genocide. This period is marked by the recognition of the integral nature of the cultural component of this crime and the role of restitution of cultural property in its reversal;

(2) the second period considers the negotiations for the Genocide Convention and the colonial and Cold War machinations which led to the exclusion of cultural genocide from the final draft treaty and the concomitant alienation of restitutory relief; and

(3) the third and final period covers the work of indigenous groups and UN bodies in re-examining colonial policies and the push for the recognition of the effects of 'ethnocide'.

This last period has led to an increased appreciation of the devastation wrought by assimilation and related policies on the preservation and development of indigenous cultures and of other occupied peoples.

Nonetheless, the continuing division of cultural genocide from genocide proper during this last phase is misguided. It serves only to perpetuate a distinction first made by the very States that were implementing assimilation and integration policies. In so doing, it detracts from the importance of cultural policy, particularly the destruction or removal of cultural objects, in the genocidal process.

UNWCC, Lemkin and Nuremberg trials

The articulation of the crime of genocide in the mid-twentieth century grew from the convergence of two areas of international law: protection of minorities and international humanitarian law. International bodies like the United Nations War Crimes Commission (UNWCC) and legal scholars like Raphaël Lemkin fuelled this work.[3]

From the early nineteenth century, the European Powers had provided qualified protection to certain minority groups within Europe. The UNWCC's earliest response to genocide was the rearticulation of the 'denationalisation of inhabitants of occupied territory' which evolved from this tradition.[4] Committee III (Legal) of the UNWCC defined 'denationalisation' as a crime driven by policies adopted by an occupying power for the purpose of 'disrupting and disintegrating the national conscience, spiritual life and national individuality'.[5] The committee agreed that such policies usually had the aim of 'killing the soul of the nation' through the twin actions of: the destruction of the national identity of the occupied or oppressed group; and the imposition of the national identity of the occupier or oppressor through assimilatory policies. Also, it was committed not against individuals but against the group; and perpetrated by the abuse of power possessed by the *de facto* occupying power.[6]

Following public outcry and intervention from the British section of the World Jewish Congress, the UNWCC's work broadened to include crimes committed against peoples simply because of their 'race, nationality, religious or political belief . . . irrespective of where they have been committed'.[7] The Commission no longer differentiated between crimes perpetrated by the Axis Powers against occupied peoples or its own people. This blow to the former impenetrability of State sovereignty was crucial because such atrocities are often perpetrated by governments, against their

---

[3] See PAG-3/Rev.1, 1987, United Nations War Crimes Commission 1943–1949, Predecessor Archives Group, United Nations Archives, New York, pp.i–ii; UNWCC, *History of the United Nations War Crimes Commission and the Development of the Laws of War* (London, 1948); M. E. Bathurst, The United Nations War Crimes Commission (1945) 39 AJIL565; and E. Schwelb, Legal Aspects of the Work of the United Nations War Crimes Commission, 29 January 1947, box 5, reel 34, PAG-3/1.0.2, UNWCC.

[4] See Notes of Committee III meeting, 9 October 1945, box 5, reel 34, PAG-3/1.0.2, UNWCC. Denationalisation had been enumerated by the Commission on the Responsibility of the Authors of the War and on Enforcement of Penalties, Violation of the Laws and Customs of War: Reports of Majority and Dissenting Reports of American and Japanese Members of the Commission of Responsibilities, Conference of Paris, 1919, (1920) 14 AJIL 95 at 114.

[5] Report Sub-Committee, 2 December 1942, C.1, and Preliminary Report Chairman of Committee III, 28 September 1945, C.148, 2, box 6, reel 34, PAG-3/1.1.0, UNWCC.

[6] See Criminality of Attempts to Denationalise the Inhabitants of Occupied Territory, 4 October 1945, C.149, para.6, box 6, reel 34, PAG-3/1.1.0, UNWCC.

[7] See Memorandum on the Present Position of the United Nations War Crimes Commission, the Work Already Done, and its Future Tasks, B. Ečer, 8 February 1945, C.76, 11; and Reports on Special Classes of Axis War Crimes, Note by the Secretary-General on the History of the Question, Origin of the Idea, 29 January 1945, C.72, 4–5, box 6, reel 34, PAG-3/1.1.0, UNWCC.

own inhabitants. Indeed, minority protection operates on this basic assumption: the protection of the non-dominant group against adverse policies and acts of the dominant group including the confiscation of their cultural objects. This rationale converged with the Allied restitution programme covering internal restitution, that is the return of cultural objects within a State.

The second area of international law that facilitated the development of the crime of genocide, and directly overlapped with the post-war restitution process, was international humanitarian law.[8] In its early meetings, the UNWCC cooperated closely with the Vaucher Committee, the British governmental body established for the protection and restitution of cultural property and its US equivalent, the Roberts Commission. The UNWCC observed that the Vaucher Committee's objective, 'though different, was supplementary' to its own.[9]

The UNWCC maintained that 'denationalisation' was not legal, even if it was not specifically enumerated in the various Hague Conventions.[10] It pointed to the preamble of the 1907 Hague IV Convention which stipulates that if an act is not covered by the Convention, it must be considered in the light of principles derived from 'the laws of humanity and dictated by public conscience'.[11] It also found that the acts of Axis forces fell under the existing heading of war crimes, including pillage and confiscation of property.[12]

Consequently, Committee III pronounced an expanded interpretation of Article 56 of the 1907 Hague IV Convention.[13] It suggested that the 'rationale' for this provision was the protection of spiritual values and intellectual life related to such institutions and objects.[14] Furthermore, the deliberate removal or destruction of cultural objects from the group is a fundamental component of this international crime.[15] At varying times European colonial powers and their settler States employed these measures under the guise of the 'civilising mission' and accompanying assimilation policy. When these provisions were interpreted in the spirit of the preamble

---

[8] See Commission on the Responsibility of the Authors of the War and on Enforcement of Penalties, pp.114–15, points 13, 14, 18 and 20 on the 1919 List; and H. Lauterpacht *et al.*, List suggested in the Course of the Proceedings of the A. McNair Commission, box 1, reel 33, PAG-3/1.0.0, UNWCC.

[9] Minutes of 51st meeting of UNWCC, 7 March 1945, box 1, reel 33, PAG-3/1.0.0, UNWCC. UNWCC viewed criminal prosecutions as its role and restitution of cultural objects as being adequately conducted by other bodies: Minutes of 68th meeting of UNWCC, 4 July 1945, 1/33/PAG-3/1.0.0, UNWCC.

[10] Report of Sub-Committee, C.148, 28 September 1945, 2–3, 6/34/PAG-3/1.1.0.

[11] Sixth to eighth recitals, Preamble, Convention (IV) Respecting the Laws and Customs of War on Land, and Annex, The Hague, 18 October 1907, Cd 5030; (1907) 208 Parry's CTS 277; and (1908) 2(supp.) AJIL 90; and B. Ečer, Scope of the Retributive Action of the United Nations according to their Official Declarations, III/4, 27 April 1944, 6, box 9, reel 36, PAG-3/1.1.3, UNWCC.

[12] See 'Criminality', C.149, 4 October 1945, para.6, 6/34/PAG-3/1.1.0.

[13] See E. Schwelb, Note on the Criminality of 'Attempts to Denationalise the Inhabitants of Occupied Territory', III/15, 10 September 1945, para.11; and Draft Report Committee III on the Criminality of 'Attempts to Denationalise the Inhabitants of Occupied Territory', III/17, 24 September 1945, paras.8 and 9, box 9, reel 36, PAG-3/1.1.3, UNWCC.

[14] 'Criminality', C.149, 4 October 1945, para.8, 6/34/PAG-3/1.1.0.

[15] It also included the deportation of children to the occupier's State to educate them; the interference in occupied people's religious traditions; removal of national symbols and names; compulsory or automatic granting of citizenship of the occupier; and colonisation of the occupied territory by nationals of the occupier: III/17, 24 September 1945, para.6, 9/36/PAG-3/1.1.3.

of the 1907 Hague IV Convention, Committee III unanimously agreed that 'denationalisation' was forbidden by international law.[16]

By late 1945, Committee III started debating the replacement of 'denationalisation' with a crime defined by Raphaël Lemkin as 'genocide'.[17] Lemkin had rejected terms like 'denationalisation' because they failed to convey the totality of genocidal projects which covered multiple fields including political, social, cultural, economic, biological, physical and so forth.[18] He described the cultural aspect of genocide as the deprivation of 'existing cultural and artistic values' including the destruction of monuments and the removal of cultural objects and materials from libraries, archives, museums and galleries.[19] The 1943 Declaration of London proclaiming the Allied restitution programme and principles laid down for internal restitution encompassed many of Lemkin's concerns. He maintained that any proposal needed to cover acts by governments against their own citizens and should be applied during both war and peacetime.[20]

Lemkin affirmed that: 'Genocide is directed against the national group as an entity, and the actions involved are directed against individuals, not in their individual capacity, but as members of the national group.'[21] In effect, his definition was directed towards the group rights aspects of earlier provisions protecting minorities. The destruction of collective identity is the fundamental driving force of genocidal activities. It is the essence of the group as a group which perpetrators of genocide seek to destroy. The concessions made during the negotiations for the 1948 Genocide Convention sacrificed recognition of this essential element of the crime.

Following the inclusion of genocide as a count in the indictment against major German war criminals,[22] Lemkin rationalised its criminalisation thus:

> World culture is only as strong and vital as the spiritual forces which are brought to it by various contributing peoples. If these peoples are annihilated, their cultural heritage is also destroyed. The destruction of a people by genocide results in an immediate, irretrievable loss to world culture.[23]

This reasoning figures in the preamble of the 1954 Hague Convention and 1946 UN General Assembly Resolution on the Crime of Genocide (UNGA Res.96(I)). The legal condemnation of genocide by the various post-war military tribunals provoked interest within the United Nations.[24] Yet during the drafting of the 1948 Genocide

---

[16] III/17, 24 September 1945, para.8, 9/36/PAG-3/1.1.3.
[17] See R. Lemkin, *Axis Rule in Occupied Europe: Laws of Occupation, Analysis of Government, Proposals for Redress* (Washington, 1944).
[18] See Lemkin, *Axis*, p.80.   [19] Lemkin, *Axis*, p.84.
[20] See R. Lemkin, Genocide: A New International Crime Punishment and Prevention (1946) 17 *Revue Internationale de Droit Pénal* 360 at 364.
[21] Lemkin, *Axis*, p.79.
[22] Indictment presented to the International Military Tribunal sitting at Berlin on 18 October 1945, Cmd 6696 (1945). See Notes of meeting of Committee III, 9 October 1945, 5/34/PAG-3/1.0.2, UNWCC.
[23] Lemkin, 'Genocide', 364.
[24] See IMT, *Trial of the Major War Criminals before the International Military Tribunal, Nuremberg, November 14, 1945–October 1, 1946* (42 vols., Nuremberg, 1947–1949), I:406 and XX:1; and UNWCC, *Law Reports of Trials of War Criminals* (15 vols., London, 1947–49), vol.VI: 48; vol.VII: 7–9 and 24–26; vol.XIII: 2, 3, 5, 112; and vol.XIV: 122–23. See W. A. Schabas, *Genocide in International Law* (Cambridge, 2000), pp.47–50.

Convention, certain States pressed for a definition that excluded its cultural elements, because of their aversion to international scrutiny of their domestic policies concerning indigenous peoples within their territory.

1948 Genocide Convention

The Convention on the Prevention and Punishment of the Crime of Genocide (1948 Genocide Convention) was born out of the horrors of the Second World War; but was eventually betrayed by anxieties surrounding the Cold War and the colonial question.[25] By focusing exclusively on the physical and biological elements of genocide, the conceptualisation of the crime fundamentally altered. There was a shunning of the cultural pluralism and an implicit recapitulation of the racialised theories of the early twentieth century.

The cultural elements that defined the group as a group, and made them a target of genocidal policies, was left by the wayside. Delegates ignored a central theoretical foundation of the crime – the deprivation of the contribution of the group to world culture. This rationale was included in the 1946 UNGA Genocide Resolution and the 1954 Hague Convention. Its exclusion from the 1948 Genocide Convention ignores the importance of the alienation of cultural objects in genocidal policies. By extension, it weakens the applicability of restitutory relief to reverse or ameliorate the effects of such acts.

At its first session, the United Nations General Assembly included on its agenda an item entitled Resolution on the Crime of Genocide, which was adopted unanimously and without debate on 11 December 1946 (UNGA Res.96(I)).[26] It became the basis for UN action on the criminalisation of genocide. Subsequent discussions concerning the parameters of genocide have been constricted by its terms.

UNGA Res.96(I) pre-empted the rationale of the 1954 Hague Convention. Its preamble notes that such acts 'shocked the conscience of mankind [and] result[ed] in great losses to humanity in the form of cultural and other contributions represented by these groups'.[27] The phrase recalled the international humanitarian law origins of the proposed convention and the rationale propagated by Lemkin.

Yet, the Resolution went on to define genocide narrowly as 'a denial of the right to existence of entire human groups, as homicide is the denial of the right to live of individual human beings'.[28] Subsequent negotiations emphasised physical and biological genocide and eventually subsumed the cultural element. This compromise is evident in the preamble of the 1948 Genocide Convention, which retains the words: 'resulted in great losses to humanity'. The remainder of the phrase – 'in the form of cultural and other contributions represented by these groups' – was deleted.

The preamble of the draft Genocide Convention prepared by the UN Secretariat in June 1947 reiterated the sentiment of UNGA Res.96(I). That is, genocide 'inflicts

---

[25] 9 December 1948, in force 12 January 1951, UNGA Res.260A(III), 78 UNTS 277. See ECOSOC, *Prevention and Punishment of Genocide: Historical Summary*, 26 January 1948, UN Doc.E/621; Schabas, *Genocide*, pp.51–102, 178–205; P. Thornberry, *International Law and the Rights of Minorities* (Oxford, 1991), pp.57ff; and J. Robinson, *The Genocide Convention: A Commentary* (New York, 1960).

[26] YBUN 1946–47, p.255.   [27] First recital, Preamble, UNGA Res.96(I).   [28] *Ibid.*

irreparable loss on humanity by depriving it of the cultural and other contributions of the group'.[29] The Secretariat defined the purpose of the 1948 Genocide Convention as the 'prevention of the destruction of racial, national, linguistic, religious or political groups of human beings'.[30] Similar terminology was used to describe persons targeted by Nazi confiscation policies and entitled to internal restitution of cultural objects following the Second World War.[31]

Importantly, the Secretariat draft definition of genocide included the phrase: 'for the purpose of destroying them in whole or in part, or of preventing their preservation or development'.[32] These words flagged the minority protection origins of the 1948 Genocide Convention, in particular those contained in the second arm of the minority guarantee that places a positive obligation on a State.[33] The deletion of these words during the treaty negotiations substantially diminished the Convention's ability to realise its mandate of preventing genocide.

The draft then went on to categorise acts constituting genocide in three parts: physical; biological; and cultural. Unlike the UNWCC, the Secretariat did list acts that constituted the cultural element of its genocide definition, including 'destruction or dispersion of documents or objects of historical, artistic or religious interest and of religious accessories'.[34] Of the legal experts consulted by the Secretariat, only Lemkin supported the inclusion of 'cultural genocide.' He argued:

> [A] group's right to existence was justified not only from the moral point of view, but also from the point of view of the value of the contribution made by such a group to civilisation generally. If the diversity of cultures were destroyed, it would be as disastrous for civilisation as the physical destruction of nations.[35]

The Secretariat implicitly discouraged the inclusion of the cultural elements of genocide. It counselled for an adherence to the 'literal definition' of the UNGA Res.96(I). Otherwise, it warned, genocide would be 'expanded indefinitely to include the law of war, the right of peoples to self-determination, the protection of minorities, the respect of human rights, etc'.[36] This became the linchpin of the argument for those who opposed the extension of genocide to include cultural elements. The ensuing failure of the 1948 Genocide Convention to place itself within the context of the areas of international law listed by the Secretariat, many of which are its originating sources, weakens the jurisprudential basis of the final document.

---

[29] Draft Preamble, Secretariat draft, in Committee on the Progressive Development of International Law and its Codification, Draft Convention for the Prevention and Punishment of Genocide prepared by the Secretariat, 6 June 1947, UN Doc.A/AC.10/42, 1.

[30] Art.1(1), Secretariat draft.

[31] See also Art.6(c), Charter of the International Military Tribunal, in Agreement by United Kingdom, United States, France and USSR for the Prosecution and Punishment of the Major War Criminals of the European Axis, Cmd 6668 (1945), p.5.

[32] Art.1(2), Secretariat draft.

[33] The Secretariat specifically excluded the definition of the forced assimilation of a group as genocide, unless carried out by flagrantly immoderate methods: UN Secretary-General, Draft Convention on the Crime of Genocide and Comments, 26 June 1947, UN Doc.E/447, 25.

[34] Art.3(e), Secretariat draft.   [35] See UN Doc.E/447 at 27.   [36] UN Doc.E/447 at 16.

After the Secretariat draft was deliberated upon by the committee of legal experts, it passed through various stages in the UN system.[37] As it progressed within the United Nations, the division between the camps for and against the inclusion of cultural elements became more pronounced.

The main arguments advanced for inclusion of a provision covering cultural genocide were:[38]

(1) Genocide deprived humanity of the cultural and other contributions of the group;

(2) Cultural genocide cannot be separated from physical or biological genocide because:

    (i) historical examples show that physical genocide was often preceded or accompanied by cultural genocide, which when left unpunished culminated in the physical destruction of the group;

    (ii) a group could be deprived of its existence not only through the mass destruction of its members but also through the destruction of its specific collective traits; and

    (iii) physical and cultural genocide have the same motivating force: the destruction of the group;

(3) Conventions espousing the rights of individuals or minorities did not criminalise the behaviour, and do not provide measures for the prevention or punishment of such acts.

On the other hand, opponents for the inclusion of the cultural elements of genocide argued:

(1) That one could not equate the acts which resulted in the extermination of minorities in crematoria during the last war with the 'closing of libraries'.[39] They maintained it was the exceptionally horrifying aspects of 'physical' genocide that had shocked the conscience of humankind;

(2) The notion of cultural genocide was too vague to be criminalised and was best left to the protection of human rights and minorities;

(3) Several States feared that the proposed Genocide Convention would become a tool of political propaganda aimed at their assimilation policies to 'civilise' indigenous inhabitants and create a unified national identity;

---

[37] Ad Hoc Committee on Genocide agreed to retain 'cultural genocide' but as a separate provision and narrowly defined: K. Azkoul, Report of the Committee and Draft Convention drawn up by the Committee, 24 May 1948, UN Doc.E/794, 17. Next, the Sixth (Legal) Committee deliberations were confined to the question of whether the Convention would include cultural genocide and the details of any such provision were not fully considered. The Committee voted against its inclusion: UN Doc.A/C.6/SR.83 at item 30, 206. Then, in the Economic and Social Council: UN Doc.E/SR.218 and 219; and J. Spiropoulos, Genocide: Draft Convention and Report of the Economic and Social Council, Report of the Sixth Committee, 3 December 1948, UN Doc.A/760, and finally, the UN General Assembly: UN Doc.A/PV.178 and 179.

[38] UN Doc.E/CN.4/Sub.2/416, para.447, 124–25.

[39] UN Doc.A/C.6/SR.83, item 30, 199 (Denmark), (Sixth Comm.).

(4) Finally, the inclusion of cultural genocide might hinder many countries from becoming parties to the proposed Genocide Convention and jeopardise its success.

The treaty negotiations were clearly coloured by the hardening of East–West alignments with the escalation of the Cold War. Soviet bloc countries baited the United States and its allies over their treatment of indigenous inhabitants. The Soviet bloc States' treatment of their minorities at the very moment they were lauding the need for minority protection on the international stage must not be overlooked.[40]

Yet, the more important dynamic during the negotiations was the emerging question of decolonisation and the opposition of formerly colonised peoples to the assimilation policies of metropolitan powers. On the other hand, many settler States with indigenous peoples vehemently opposed the inclusion of cultural genocide. They were concerned that what they considered legitimate nation-building policies, particularly towards indigenous communities, would be held up to scrutiny. It was at this level that inclusion of cultural elements of genocide was lost.

Hersch Lauterpacht's opposition to the crime of genocide captured the intrinsic flaw of the 1948 Genocide Convention as a whole. He said: '[I]f one emphasises too much that it is a crime to kill a whole people, it may weaken the conviction that it is already a crime to kill one individual'.[41] The question of genocide, its prevention and punishment cannot and should not be one of loss of human life. By concentrating only on the physical and biological aspects of genocide, the 1948 Genocide Convention fails to fully comprehend the primary motivator of genocidal acts – the elimination of *difference*. It is this difference, of the minority group, which is so reviled by the perpetrators of genocidal policies.

Following the adoption of the 1948 Genocide Convention by the General Assembly, its president H. V. Evatt stated: '[The] wholesale or partial destruction of religious, racial and national groups had long shocked the conscience of mankind . . . The Convention on Genocide protected the fundamental right of a human group to exist as a *group*.'[42] However, the 1948 Genocide Convention fails to protect those very elements which define the group as a group. It fails to acknowledge the multifaceted nature of genocidal programmes and that all such acts adversely impact on a people's contribution to the cultural heritage of humankind.[43] It fails to recognise that individual members of a group can continue to live even after the group has disappeared – following the effective intervention of a dominant group.[44] As the

---

[40] See T. Martin, *The Affirmative Action Empire: Nations and Nationalism in the Soviet Union, 1923–1939* (Ithaca, 2001).

[41] E. Schwelb to J. Humphrey, Director, Division of Human Rights, 19 June 1947, box 26, reel 41, PAG-3/1.3, UNWCC.

[42] See UN Doc.A/PV.179, 851–2 (emphasis added). See Art.7(2)(g), Statute of the International Criminal Court, Rome, 17 July 1998, in force 1 July 2002, UN Doc.A/CONF.183/9, and 2187 UNTS 3.

[43] See Sub-Commission on Prevention of Discrimination and Protection of Minorities, Contribution of the Convention of Prevention and Punishment of Genocide to the Prevention of Discrimination of the Protection of Minorities, 7 December 1949, UN Doc.E/CN.4/Sub.2/80, para.38, 14.

[44] Cf. *Prosecutor v. Radislav Krstić*, Trial Judgment, No.IT-98-33-T, Trial Chamber I, ICTY, (2 August 2001), para.574.

International Criminal Tribunal for the former Yugoslavia recently observed, the international community has declined every opportunity since 1948 to extend the definition of genocide to include acts covering cultural elements.[45]

Colonialism and ethnocide

In the late twentieth century, through the work of UN bodies and NGOs there was renewed interest in the effects of the cultural elements of genocide, within examinations of colonial policies. Special Rapporteur, Nicodème Ruhashyankiko noted that policies such as assimilation, integration and cultural absorption were often foisted onto the cultural structures and cultures of indigenous communities by the dominant settler culture.[46] Later, Special Rapporteur Ben Whitaker made clear that discussion of genocide had spread from its initial preoccupation with European examples, particularly the Holocaust, to international examples implicating colonialism.[47]

Various indigenous organisations have sought to reinvigorate the notion of genocide deleted from the initial 1947 UN Secretariat Draft, contained in the words: 'preventing their preservation or development'. From the first session of the UN Working Group on Indigenous Populations (WGIP), indigenous representatives emphasised the importance of the 1948 Genocide Convention in understanding the current circumstances of indigenous peoples.[48] WGIP chair Erica-Irene Daes noted that beyond physical genocide there was a need to recognise the cultural aspects of ethnocide and the right to cultural development,[49] and that a group has a right to enjoy, develop and transmit its own culture and its own language.[50]

The preamble of the Draft UN Declaration on the Rights of Indigenous Peoples (1993 Draft UN Declaration) expands on the rationale enunciated by Lemkin a half-century ago, by affirming: '[T]hat all peoples contribute to the diversity and richness of civilisations and cultures, which constitute the common heritage of humankind'.[51] However, the draft Declaration contains two provisions covering genocide. The provision against genocide proper covers the same parameters as the 1948 Genocide Convention (Article 6). The other encompasses a prohibition against ethnocide and

---

[45] *Krstić*, Trial Judgment, para.576. However, the ICTY stated that such acts could establish the necessary intent to commit genocide. See, however, dissenting opinion of Judge Mohamed Shahabuddeen in *Prosecutor v. Radislav Krstić*, Appeals Judgment, Case No.IT-98-33-A, (19 April 2004), para.50.

[46] N. Ruhashyankiko, Study of the Question of the Prevention and Punishment of the Crime of Genocide, 4 July 1978, UN Doc.E/CN.4/Sub.2/416, paras.459 and 461, 128. He made no recommendation regarding the revision of the existing convention to include cultural genocide.

[47] B. Whitaker, Review of Further Developments in Fields with which the Sub-Commission has been concerned: Revised and Updated Report on the Question of the Prevention and Punishment of the Crime of Genocide, 2 July 1985, UN Doc.E/CN.4/Sub.2/1985/6, paras.18ff and 33.

[48] It also referred to the definition of 'ethnocide' in the San José Declaration, 1981, in J. R. Martínez Cobo, Study of the Problem of Discrimination against Indigenous Populations, Final Report (Supp. Pt), 16 May 1982, UN Doc.E/CN.4/Sub.2/1982/2/Add.1, Annex 6.

[49] See UN Doc.E/CN.4/Sub.2/SR.659, 64, Daes; UN Doc.E/CN.4/Sub.2/SR.672, 75, Daes; and E.-I. Daes, Protection of Minorities under the International Bill of Human Rights and the Genocide Convention, in *Xenion: Festschrift für Pan J Zepos anlasslich seines 65*, II (Athens, 1973), p.35 at pp.82ff.

[50] E.-I. Daes, Study on the Protection of the Cultural and Intellectual Property of Indigenous Peoples, 28 July 1993, UN Doc.E/CN.4/Sub.2/1993/28, para.2.

[51] Approved 26 August 1994, UN Doc.E/CN.4/Sub.2/1994/56, and (1995) 34 ILM 541.

cultural genocide (Article 7).[52] The ambit of this provision is much wider than mid-twentieth-century articulations of cultural genocide. For example, the draft defines cultural diversity as both a collective and individual right and prohibits assimilation or integration policies. The right to restitution of cultural objects is dealt with independently of these provisions (Article 12).

The reaffirmation of the division between physical and biological genocide and cultural genocide splinters the original rationale of the 1948 Genocide Convention, that is the need to protect groups as a collective because of their unique contribution to humankind generally. Ironically, these critiques of colonialism have reaffirmed the division originally espoused by the very States whose assimilation policies they condemn.

The 1948 Genocide Convention preamble itself acknowledges that genocide occurred 'at all periods of history'. And as events of recent decades demonstrated, it continues to be perpetrated worldwide. However, the compromises imposed on the 1948 Genocide Convention and the international human rights framework largely precluded restitutory relief for such peoples. Yet, this form of relief was recognised and implemented by the Allies at the end of the Second World War.

Human rights and group rights during the Cold War

A primary argument for certain States' opposition to the inclusion of the cultural component in the 1948 Genocide Convention was that it was more properly dealt with under the protection of minorities and human rights. Yet, concessions extracted by these States in respect of international human rights instruments resulted in a failure to sanction a positive obligation owed by States to minorities for the preservation and development of their cultures.

The United States, and its Allies, promoted the recognition of individual human rights and the contribution of the individual, as opposed to a people, to the cultural heritage of humankind. The privileging of the individual within the human rights discourse in the post-1945 period had the same effect as the collection and display of non-European cultural objects in museums in metropolitan capitals. People and their cultural objects became depoliticised and de-historicised – 'all soiling trace of origin or choice has been removed', thereby enabling the dominant culture to define their role and place within the State. This mindset necessarily negated the contemplation of the return of cultural objects to formerly colonised and indigenous peoples by these States.

In this section, there is an examination of how the protection afforded minorities during the inter-war years was pared down to the principle of non-discrimination in the early years of the United Nations. Next, there is an explanation of how this concession was extracted at the behest of settler States pursuing integration policies at home. Integration provided individual members of a group cultural freedom as long as exercise of that freedom did not disrupt national unity. Finally, there is

---

[52] See L.-E. Chávez, Report of the Working Group Established in Accordance with Commission on Human Rights Resolution 1995/32, Eighth Session, 6 January 2003, UN Doc.E/CN.4/2003/92, paras.51–61 and Annex, 23–26.

consideration of the minority protection provision in the International Covenant on Civil and Political Rights (ICCPR).

Minorities and the principle of non-discrimination

With the hardening of the Cold War divisions and independence movements in Asia and Africa, the United States and its allies stymied any effort to revive a broad protection of group rights. Instead, they privileged individual human rights and non-discrimination as the means of protecting the rights of minorities and indigenous peoples. The 1945 UN Charter of the UN and the Universal Declaration of Human Rights (UDHR) bear the legacy of this preoccupation.

The League of Nations afforded certain minorities international guarantees for the equal treatment of individual members of the group (non-discrimination); and for the preservation and development of the cultural characteristics of the group (group rights).[53] Under the League's successor, the United Nations, the protection of minorities fell within the human rights framework and specifically the principle of non-discrimination.[54] The preamble of the 1945 UN Charter states that the peoples of the United Nations are determined 'to reaffirm faith in fundamental human rights, in the dignity and worth of the human person, in the equal rights of men and women'.[55] There is no mention of the second arm of the inter-war minority guarantees. So-called 'countries of immigration', led by the United States and Latin American States, reiterated concerns aired in opposition to the universalisation of minority guarantees during the inter-war period. They argued that such group rights would threaten their national unity and the stability of existing economic, social and political structures.[56]

Similarly, any proposals to reaffirm minority protection afforded under the League of Nations in the UDHR were repelled resoundingly by the United States and its Allies.[57] This rejection of a positive obligation on States to facilitate peoples in the preservation and development of their cultures necessarily undermines their claims for the return of cultural objects.

---

[53] *Minority Schools in Albania case*, (1935) PCIJ, ser.A/B, No.64, p.17.

[54] A Commentary on the Charter of the United Nations, Cmd 6666 (1945), paras.49 and 90; A Commentary on the Dumbarton Oaks Proposals for the Establishment of a General International Organisation, Cmd 6571 (1944), para.47; and Atlantic Charter, 14 August 1941, 204 LNTS 231; and (1941) 35(supp.) AJIL 191. See H. Hannum, *Autonomy, Sovereignty and Self-Determination: The Accommodation of Conflicting Rights* (Philadelphia, 1990), pp.50ff.

[55] San Francisco, 26 June 1945, in force 24 October 1945, 59 Stat.1031; T.S.993; and (1945) 39(supp.) AJIL 190. Art.1(3) lists the promotion and encouragement of respect for human rights and fundamental freedoms for all 'without distinction as to race, sex, language, or religion' as a purpose of the organisation. The same purpose is ascribed to the General Assembly (Art.13), ECOSOC (Art.55), the trusteeship system (Art.76), and UNESCO, see p.183 below.

[56] See J. Robinson, From the Protection of Minorities to the Promotion of Human Rights (1949) 1 JYIL 115 at 130; Thornberry, *Minorities*, p.122; and I. L. Claude, *National Minorities: An International Problem* (Cambridge, MA, 1955), p.167. See Art.24, American Convention on Human Rights, 22 November 1969, in force 18 July 1978, OASTS No.36, 1144 UNTS 123; and Art.2, American Declaration on the Rights and Duties of Man, adopted by the Ninth International Conference of American States, 2 May 1948, OAS Res.30; (1949) 43(supp.) AJIL 133.

[57] UNGA Res.217A(III), 10 December 1948, UN Doc.A/810, 71; and (1949) 43(supp.) AJIL 127.

The question of an international bill of human rights preoccupied many politicians, jurists and legal academics towards the close of the Second World War. Pre-eminent among these was Lauterpacht's *An International Bill of the Rights of Man* (1945).[58] Building on the lessons of the League's minority guarantees, his proposal of universal applicability carried a dual responsibility to minorities: non-discrimination[59]; and a positive obligation on a State pertaining to their cultural requirements.[60] The second arm recognised the right of minorities:

> [T]o establish and maintain, out of an equitable proportion of the available public funds, their schools and cultural and religious institutions and to use their own language before the courts and other institutions and organs of the State.[61]

Lauterpacht noted that denial of such a right posed a danger to international peace and its recognition would curb assimilation policies by States.[62]

The UN Sub-Commission on the Prevention of Discrimination and Protection of Minorities, and the Secretary-General of the United Nations rearticulated this two-pronged minority protection.[63] They distinguished between:

- non-discrimination provisions that promote equality by a negative, prohibitory mode through the suppression of unequal treatment. These provisions are required only for the period that discrimination against ethnic or religious groups exists; and

- a regime for the *protection of minorities* confronting the problem in a direct, positive manner, by requiring the establishment of educational and cultural institutions for non-dominant groups. It implied a permanent set of arrangements to protect the culture, language and religion of the minority.[64]

Any effort to include a minority protection provision in the UDHR proved fruitless.

The UN General Assembly adopted the UDHR the day after the 1948 Genocide Convention. It does not include positive protection for minorities but does provide for the principle of non-discrimination.[65] Nonetheless, it arguably assists a

---

[58] H. Lauterpacht, *An International Bill of the Rights of Man* (New York, 1945). See H. Lauterpacht, International Protection of Human Rights (1947-I) 70 RCADI 1.

[59] Art.7, Lauterpacht, *International*, p.115.

[60] Art.12, Lauterpacht, *International*, p.152. He argued that the combined effect of both Articles would provide the protection within an international human rights framework similar to that afforded in the Minorities Treaties and under the auspices of the League of Nations.

[61] Lauterpacht, *International*, p.151.   [62] See Lauterpacht, *International*, p.153.

[63] Memorandum Division of Human Rights, UN Secretariat to the Sub-Commission: 'Definition of the Expressions "Prevention of Discrimination" and "Protection of Minorities"', 29 October 1947, UN Doc.E/CN.4/Sub.2/8.

[64] See Thornberry, *Minorities*, p.126; F. Capotorti, The Protection of Minorities under Multilateral Agreements on Human Rights (1976) 2 IYIL 3; and F. Capotorti, Study of the Rights of Persons Belonging to Ethnic, Religious and Linguistic Minorities, 20 June 1977, UN Doc.E/CN.4/Sub.2/384/Add.5, paras.29ff.

[65] Arts.2 and 7, UDHR. See H. Lauterpacht, *International Law and Human Rights* (London, 1950), pp.354ff. The Division on Human Rights prepared a draft article almost identical to Lauterpacht's Art.12. However, it was dropped from the UDHR. See E. St Lot, Draft International Declaration of Human Rights, Report of the Third Committee, 7 December 1948, UN Doc.A/777; and Claude, *Minorities*, pp.158ff.

group to preserve and develop its cultural identity by guaranteeing related rights and freedoms, including freedom of religion and the right to association.[66] For Lauterpacht, however, it was a 'sign of the political and moral retrogression in international relations' that minorities obtained less protection under the United Nations in a non-binding declaration than they did under its predecessor, the League of Nations.[67]

Several States had proposed an amendment which added the group rights of minorities when the Third (Humanitarian and Social Affairs) Committee of the UN General Assembly considered the draft UDHR.[68] The ensuing debate over its inclusion, which was eventually lost, replicated many of the arguments raised during the 1948 Genocide Convention deliberations. It also reflected the increasing overlap of minority and indigenous issues within the United Nations.

Soviet bloc States, whilst generally supporting the inclusion of a minority guarantee, used the occasion to attack Western States' treatment of minorities and indigenous communities.[69] They argued that the assimilation and integration policies of settler States and metropolitan powers were antithetical to the right of minorities and indigenous communities to maintain and develop their cultures.

American States stated that the minority question was not of a universal character but a uniquely European concern. Therefore, it should not be included in the UDHR.[70] They maintained that such guarantees would hinder national unity and integration policies. US representative Eleanor Roosevelt suggested 'the best solution for the problem of minorities was to encourage respect for human rights'.[71] For Roosevelt, the right to cultural freedom was predicated on the individual right holder rather than the collective nature of cultural identity and development.[72]

For States with secessionist movements, the protection of individual human rights was eminently preferable to the resuscitation of minority guarantees.[73] Lauterpacht answered their arguments thus: 'The cultural . . . unity of the national State at the expense of its minorities is not an ideal entitled to respect so absolute as to sanction the denial of equality thus conceived'.[74] The efforts of settler States to deflect scrutiny

---

[66] Including the right to freedom of thought, conscience and religion (Art.18); the right to freedom of opinion and expression (Art.19); the right to peaceful assembly and association (Art.20); the right to education which shall 'promote understanding, tolerance and friendship among all nations, racial or religious groups' (Art.26); and the right to freely participate in the cultural life of the community (Art.27).

[67] Lauterpacht, *Human Rights*, p.353.

[68] See UN Doc.A/C.3/307/Rev.2, 45–46. For the Third Committee's discussion of the declaration: UN Doc.A/C.3/SR.161–63, 717–40; and Claude, *Minorities*, pp.157–60 and 163.

[69] See UN Doc.A/C.3/SR.162, 727–28. These States, over the protestation of Anglo-American States, successfully included a provision to explicitly apply the UDHR to all persons belonging to Trust and Non-Self-Governing Territories: UN Doc.A/C.3/SR.163, 741. Britain and the United States argued that the principle of non-discrimination should apply to all people including those 'behind the "iron curtain"': UN Doc.A/C.3/SR.163, 744.

[70] UN Doc.A/C.3/SR.161, 721 and 726.   [71] *Ibid.*

[72] See UN Doc.A/C.3/SR.150, 619–20. See Arts.22 and 27, UDHR. Cf. American Anthropological Association, Statement on Human Rights (1947) 49 *American Anthropologist* 539.

[73] See UN Doc.A/C.3/SR.162, 723.

[74] Lauterpacht, *Human Rights*, pp.352–53. See D. Wippman (ed.), *International Law and Ethnic Conflict* (Ithaca, 1998), pp.13–16.

of their treatment of indigenous peoples by quarantining minority protection within the non-discrimination rubric ultimately proved unsuccessful.[75]

In an early UN study of States' measures for the protection of minorities, the United States referred to the Indian Reorganization Act of 1934 (IRA) as governing its treatment of Native Americans.[76] Yet, within a decade, the Indian New Deal was dismantled to facilitate the integration of the Native Americans into the general population. Special Rapporteur on Racial Discrimination Hernán Santa Cruz described this fundamental shift in US policy away from the cultural pluralism of the inter-war years, towards the early Cold War integrationist policies in his 1971 report.[77] He defined integration thus:

> [A] process by which diverse elements are combined into a unity while retaining their basic identity. There is no insistence upon uniformity or elimination of all differences, other than those differences of each component part which would disturb or inhibit the total unity.[78]

These policies aimed to guarantee the 'same rights, opportunities and responsibilities to all citizens'.[79] Unlike assimilation, integration did not pursue the deliberate extinguishment of indigenous cultural practices but it often had the same result. By stressing 'sameness', through equality and non-discrimination, it obliterated difference.

Integration, favoured by most American and settler States, infused the first international instrument covering indigenous peoples. The International Labour Organisation Convention (ILO No.107 of 1957) concerning the Protection and Integration of Indigenous and Other Tribal and Semi-Tribal Populations in Independent Countries provided international standards for the integration of indigenous and tribal communities into the national community in order to 'improve' their living standards.[80] The rights of indigenous communities to retain their own customs and institutions were protected where these are not incompatible with the national legal system or the objectives of the integration programme. ILO No. 107 was condemned by indigenous groups and found little favour with States.[81]

Article 27 of the ICCPR

During negotiations for the 1948 Genocide Convention, several States observed that the integration and assimilation policies of many contemporary governments could

---

[75] See H. Santa Cruz, *Special Study on Racial Discrimination in the Political, Economic, Social and Cultural Spheres*, 1971, UN Doc.E/CN.4/Sub.2/307/Rev.1, paras.27ff.

[76] See UN Doc.E/CN.4/Sub.2/L.45.

[77] See UN Doc.E/CN.4/Sub.2/307/Rev.1, paras.473–75, 492 and 531.

[78] UN Doc.E/CN.4/Sub.2/307/Rev.1, para.373.   [79] UN Doc.E/CN.4/Sub.2/307/Rev.1, para.374.

[80] 26 June 1957, in force 2 June 1959, and Recommendation No.104, 328 UNTS 247; and ILO, *Conventions and Recommendations Adopted by the International Labour Conference, 1919–66* (Geneva, 1966), pp.901 and 909. See G. Bennett, *Aboriginal Rights in International Law* (London, 1978), pp.16–48; and Thornberry, *Minorities*, p.339.

[81] At the First Congress of Indian Movements in South America, the Indian Council of South America declared its belief that the ILO 107 legalised the colonial oppression of the Indian peoples and would result in the total destruction of Indian cultures: UN Doc.E/CN.4/Sub.2/476/Add.5, Annex 5, para.2.

be just as effective in eliminating groups. Although sparing the individual members, their identity or difference was expunged when they assumed the culture of the dominant group. The first provision for the protection of minorities of universal application was finally realised with Article 27 of the United Nations' International Covenant on Civil and Political Rights (ICCPR).[82]

Unlike the UDHR, the ICCPR includes the right to self-determination and a (limited) minority protection provision.[83] These additions reflected the altered agenda within the United Nations from 1948 to 1966, driven by the increasing number of newly independent States during decolonisation. Article 27 of the ICCPR had its genesis in the UNGA Resolution on the Fate of Minorities adopted on the same day as the UDHR.[84] Article 27 reads:

> In those States in which ethnic, religious or linguistic minorities exist, persons belonging to such minorities shall not be denied the right, in community with other members of their group, to enjoy their own culture, to profess and practise their own religion, or to use their own language.

For this provision to effectively allow groups to enjoy their culture it must enable them to pursue the restitution of cultural objects and prevent future culture losses. Unfortunately, Article 27 ICCPR is couched in language so restrictive that it impedes rather than assists such claims.

American States voted for the draft Article on the understanding that they 'did not recognise the existence of minorities on the American continent'.[85] As in 1948, they maintained that neither indigenous inhabitants nor migrants could justifiably claim to have minority status for this would disrupt their national unity.[86] Mexico, however, advocated that the provision should acknowledge the need for the elevation of the economic and social standards of minorities without prejudicing their individual cultural heritage.[87] That a State can itself determine whether or not a group comes within Article 27 ICCPR would negate its very purpose: the protection of that group

---

[82] 16 December 1966, in force 23 March 1976, UNGA Res.2200A(XXI), 21 UN GAOR Supp.(No.16), p.52, UN Doc.A/6316 (1966), 999 UNTS 171, and (1967) 6 ILM368. See V. Pechota, The Development of the Covenant on Civil and Political Rights, in L. Henkin (ed.), *The International Bill of Rights: The Covenant on Civil and Political Rights* (New York, 1981), pp.32ff; and Claude, *Minorities*, pp.160–63.

[83] The UDHR defined civil and political rights *and* economic, social and cultural rights as being indispensable to human dignity, realisable through national effort and international cooperation. Yet, Western States preferred to have the rights dealt with within separate instruments. The United States advised it would not accept a Covenant which included economic, social and cultural rights because it exceeded the US Constitution and was unenforceable in its domestic courts: Perchota, 'Development', p.42.

[84] UNGA Res.217C(III), 10 December 1948, UN Doc.A/810. See UN Doc.A/PV.180–81; UN Doc.E/CN.4/Sub.2/112; and M. J. Bossuyt, *Guide to the 'Travaux Préparatoires' of the International Covenant on Civil and Political Rights* (Dordrecht, 1987), pp.493–98.

[85] See UN Doc.A/C.3/SR.1103, paras.8–14. The position supported by Latin American States, certain African States and Australia represented the clearest view of Art.27 as 'pertain[ing] only to certain regions of the world': UN Doc.A/C.3/SR.1104, para.23.

[86] UN Doc.A/C.3/SR.1103, paras.8–14 and 18–23. The explicit duty of loyalty of the individual to the State to which he or she belongs was not incorporated into the provision: UN Doc. E/CN.4/Sub.2/38, 4; and UN Doc.E/CN.4/Sub.2/SR.676, 118.

[87] UN Doc.A/C.3/SR.1104, paras.2–3.

within a State.[88] Whilst it is valid to suggest that the ever-changing nature of groups makes it extremely difficult to formulate criteria for their recognition,[89] nonetheless the lack of criteria weakens the legitimate claims of minorities and indigenous communities and the effectiveness of Article 27 ICCPR.

The inclusion of the minority protection within the international human rights framework reinforced the assumption that the right holder is an individual and *not* a group.[90] The Sub-commission expressed preference for the phrase 'persons belonging to minorities' over the term 'minorities' alone, because individuals, unlike minorities, are a recognised subject of international law. Furthermore, the complaint mechanism contained in the Optional Protocol to the International Covenant on Civil and Political Rights provides standing to States or individuals but not to 'communities'.[91] The concession to the collective aspect of minority rights came with the words 'in community with other members of their group'. This compromise reflects the ambivalence between the individual and collective characteristics of the minority protection provided by Article 27 ICCPR. The right of enjoyment of culture, practice of religion, or use of language can only be realised meaningfully when exercised 'in a community', that is as a group.[92]

The right contained in Article 27 is negatively conferred, with the addition of the words 'shall not be denied the right'.[93] Special Rapporteur Francesco Capotorti rejected this narrow reading of the obligations enunciated in Article 27. He affirmed that the principles of non-discrimination and protection of minorities were

---

[88] See J. Crawford, The Rights of Peoples: 'Peoples' or 'Governments'?, in J. Crawford (ed.), *The Rights of Peoples* (Oxford, 1988), p.55; A. Anghie, Human Rights and Cultural Identity: New Hope for Ethnic Peace? (1992) 33 HILJ 339; T. Makkonen, *Identity, Difference and Otherness: The Concepts of 'People', 'Indigenous People' and 'Minority' in International Law* (Helsinki, 2000), p.83; and J. Crawford, The Right of Self-Determination in International Law, in P. Alston (ed.), *Peoples' Rights* (Oxford, 2001), pp.23–24.

[89] See F. Ermacora, The Protection of Minorities before the UN (1983-IV) 182 RCADI 251 at 299; and UN Doc.E/CN.4/Sub.2/384/Add.2, para.124; F. Capotorti, Study on the Rights of Persons Belonging to Ethnic, Religious and Linguistic Minorities, 28 June 1977, UN Doc.E/CN.4/Sub.2/384/Add.5, para.59; Declaration on the Rights of Persons Belonging to National or Ethnic, Religious and Linguistic Minorities, UNGA Res.47/135 (1995), 18 December 1992, UN Doc.A/Res/47/135; (1993) 32 ILM 911; and P. Leuprecht, Minority Rights Revisited: New Glimpses of an Old Issue, in Alston (ed.), *Peoples*, p.111.

[90] See UN Doc.E/CN.4/Sub.2/384/Add.2, paras.125ff; Human Rights Committee, General Comment No.23, UN Doc.HRI/GEN/1/Rev.1 at 38 (1994), para.1; Daes, 'Protection', 62; Wippman, *International Law*, pp.13–15; D. Makinson, Rights of Peoples: Point of View of a Logician, in Crawford (ed.), *Rights*, pp.69–72; and Ermacora, 'Protection', 308–09.

[91] Optional Protocol to the International Covenant on Civil and Political Rights, UNGA Res.2200A(XXI), 16 December 1966, in force 23 March 1976, 21 UN GAOR Supp.(No.16), p.59; UN Doc.A/6316 (1966); 999 UNTS 302; and (1967) 6 ILM 368. See *Lovelace* v. *Canada*, No.24/1977, UN Doc.A/36/40, p.166 (1981) (Human Rights Committee). Cf. E. Evatt, Individual communications under the Optional Protocol to the International Covenant on Civil and Political Rights, in S. Pritchard (ed.), *Indigenous Peoples, the United Nations and Human Rights* (Sydney, 1998), p.113.

[92] See *Kitok* v. *Sweden*, No.197/1985, UN Doc.A/43/40, p.221 (1988) (Human Rights Committee); *Lubicon Lake Band (Bernard Ominayak)* v. *Canada*, No.167/1984, UN Doc.A/45/40, Pt.2, p.1 (1990) (Human Rights Committee); and *Länsman* v. *Finland*, No.511/1922, UN Doc.CCPR/52/D/511/1992, and No.671/1995, UN Doc.CCPR/C/58/D/671/1995.

[93] See UN Doc.E/447, para.55; UN Doc.E/CN.4/Sub.2/351, 13-14; UN Doc.E/CN.4/Sub.2/SR.647, 158; UN Doc.E/CN.4/Sub.2/384/Add.2, paras.130ff; Crawford, 'Right', 23; J. Robinson, International Protection of Minorities: A Global View (1971) 1 IYHR 61 at 89; Claude, *Minorities*, pp.165ff; Ermacora, 'Protection', 275; Thornberry, *Minorities*, p.179; and J. W. Bruegel, A Neglected Field: Protection of Minorities (1971) 4 HRJ 413 at 436–37.

distinctive. He added that the protection of minorities, even if it was contained in the ICCPR, resembled the 'economic and social' rights that require a State to act proactively on behalf of the rights holders.[94]

Special Rapporteur Capotorti recognised the importance of cultural development for newly independent States following decolonisation. He also acknowledged the effects of past assimilation policies of former colonial powers and the importance of cultural development for economic and social development.[95] Nonetheless, Capotorti categorically denounced assimilationist policies by all States and reaffirmed their responsibility to encourage and assist the cultural development of minorities.[96] This positive interpretation of minority protection was reaffirmed in the 1966 UNESCO Declaration of the Principles of Cultural Co-operation.[97] Article 1 states:

> (1) Each culture has a dignity and value which must be respected and preserved.
> (2) Each people has a right and duty to develop its culture.
> (3) In their rich variety and diversity and in the reciprocal influence they exert on one another, all cultures form part of the common heritage belonging to all mankind.

The UN Human Rights Committee has stated that the right enunciated in Article 27 ICCPR 'is directed to ensur[ing] the survival and continued development of the cultural, religious and social identity of the minorities concerned . . . State parties, therefore, have an obligation to ensure that the exercise of these rights is fully protected'.[98] Despite the pall of Cold War politics over the United States, René d'Harnoncourt adhered to these aims in his work with indigenous peoples and their cultures.

United States, indigenous peoples and the Cold War
These compromises in international law, which were extracted because of Cold War politicking and the insecurities fuelled by decolonisation, affected indigenous peoples within and across States. The final part of this chapter explains how the US position during negotiation for the 1948 Genocide Convention and UDHR translated into its domestic and regional policy covering indigenous peoples and their cultural objects. It examines how the US federal government aimed to terminate its trustee relationship with Native Americans through integration. There is a detailing

---

[94] UN Doc.E/CN.4/Sub.2/384/Add.2, paras.130–36, 160–61; and UN Doc.E/CN.4/Sub.2/384/Add.5, paras.24–30. See General Comment No.23, paras.6.1 and 6.2.

[95] F. Capotorti, Study on the Rights of Persons Belonging to Ethnic, Religious and Linguistic Minorities, 9 June 1977, UN Doc.E/CN.4/Sub.2/384/Add.4, para.12.

[96] UN Doc.E/CN.4/Sub.2/384/Add.5, paras.22–23, 34, 39 and 41.

[97] Adopted 4 November 1966, UNESCO Doc.14C/Resolutions, and UNESCO, *Cultural Rights as Human Rights* (Paris, 1970), p.123. See Seminar on the Multinational Society, Ljubljana, 8–15 June 1965, UN Doc.ST/TAO/HR/23; Seminar on the Promotion and Protection of the Human Rights of National, Ethnic, and other Minorities, Ohrid, 1974, UN Doc.ST/TAO/HR/49, paras.29–36; Arts.2, 13, 15 and 19, Universal Declaration of the Rights of Peoples (1976), cited in Crawford (ed.), *Rights*, p.187; and Arts.22(1) and (2), African Charter on Human and Peoples' Rights adopted 27 June 1981, in force 21 October 1986, OAU Doc.CAB/LEG/67/3, rev.5, 1520 UNTS 217, and (1982) 21 ILM 58.

[98] General Comment No.23, para.9.

of how, after 1945, d'Harnoncourt facilitated programmes of cultural preservation, development and exchange in his various roles with MoMA, regional organisations and UNESCO. In addition, there is an explanation of how the collection, display and interpretation of the cultural objects of non-European peoples were defined once again as 'primitive art'. Finally, how the US free trade agenda pertaining to cultural objects was tempered by the demands of its American neighbours is detailed.

Dismantling the Indian New Deal

During the 1940s and 50s, US administrations employed rhetoric applicable to the decolonisation process when describing domestic policies covering Native Americans.[99] Yet unlike formerly colonised peoples, Native Americans were not afforded the right of self-determination; nor did their territories cease to be occupied by the metropolitan power. Indeed, the introduction of integration policies meant that the reverse was true.

The dismantling of the Indian New Deal and the termination policy reached its apex with the Eisenhower administrations.[100] Public Law 280 of 15 August 1953 was designed to bring tribal lands under the criminal and civil jurisdiction of various States.[101] Eisenhower allowed the passage of the Act, despite its failure to provide for consent from or consultation with tribes. He argued that its purpose represented a significant step towards the realisation of complete political equality for Native Americans.[102] Former Indian Commissioner John Collier concluded that the administration's 'prepossession seems to be, merely, that cultural and social distinctiveness is offensive, and is contrary to the American way'.[103] He described the legislation as pushing Native Americans to 'a kind of social, cultural, and spiritual self-genocide'.[104]

Two weeks before, the Senate had passed the House Concurrent Resolution No.108 with the declared purpose of making Native Americans: '[S]ubject to the same laws and entitled to the same privileges and responsibilities as are applicable to other citizens of the United States, to end their status as wards of the United

---

[99] UN Doc.E/CN.4/Sub.2/307/Rev.1, para.531.

[100] See G. D. Taylor, *The New Deal and American Indian Tribalism: The Administration of the Indian Reorganization Act, 1934–45* (Lincoln, 1980), pp.139ff; F. S. Cohen, *F S Cohen's Handbook of Federal Indian Law*, ed. R. Strickland (Charlottesville, 1982), pp.152–58; D. L. Fixico, *Termination and Relocation: Federal Indian Policy, 1945–1960* (Albuquerque, 1986); W. Brophy and S. Aberle, *The Indian. America's Unfinished Business: Report of the Commission of the Rights, Liberties and Responsibilities of the American Indian* (Norman, 1966), pp.21ff; R. F. Schrader, *The Indian Arts and Crafts Board: An Aspect of New Deal Indian Policy* (Albuquerque, 1983), pp.286ff; W. E. Washburn, *Red Man's Land/White Man's Law: The Past and Present Status of the American Indian* (2nd edn, Norman, 1995), pp.83ff; and K. R. Philp, *John Collier's Crusade for Indian Reform 1920–1954* (Tucson, 1977), p.225.

[101] 15 August 1953, Ch.505, 67 Stat.588, codified at 18 USCS §1162 (2002). See Cohen, *Handbook*, pp.175–77.

[102] See Commissioner of Indian Affairs, *Annual Report, 1954* (Washington, 1955), pp.243–44; and Washburn, *Red*, p.87.

[103] J. Collier, The United States Indian, in J. B. Gittler (ed.), *Understanding Minority Groups* (New York, 1956), p.33 at p.50. See S. Tyler, *Indian Affairs: A Study of Changes in Policy of the United States towards Indians* (Provo, 1964), p.98 regarding the resistance of the National Congress of American Indians to termination legislation.

[104] Collier, 'Indian', 51. See J. Collier, *From Every Zenith: A Memoir and Some Essays on Life and Thought* (Denver, 1963), pp.371ff; and Philp, *Collier's*, p.232.

States'.[105] The future Indian Commissioner, Glenn L. Emmons, in response to the Resolution, stated: 'The Indian people are the finest minority group we have in America and given an opportunity, they can make their own way.'[106]

By 'liberating' Native Americans (and itself) from the trust relationship, the US government redefined these communities as minorities It effectively denied their status as a 'conquered' people and absolved the US government of any obligations arising from such occupation. Like any other minority, they were not afforded group rights. Rather, Native American individuals were to pursue economic and cultural development offered by the 'cultural freedom' and 'democracy' provided by the United States. The contribution of the group to national and world culture was replaced by the individual's contribution. Unlike the 'liberated' peoples of Europe after the Second World War, Native Americans were not afforded the restitution of their cultural objects housed in national museums and private collections. Instead, these communities would wait another half-century before the US government addressed such claims.

The Indian Arts and Crafts Board (IACB) felt the full brunt of the economic shortages precipitated by the Second World War and the Congressional backlash against the promotion of cultural pluralism. By 1951, despite the ascendancy of termination policies, the fortunes of the Board improved.[107] The IACB lobbied for the establishment of the Institute of American Indian Arts (IAIA), in Santa Fe, which reflected the US preoccupation with individualism, democracy and modernism during the 1950s and 60s.[108] The Institute was promoted as the embodiment of the United States' leadership in addressing racial discrimination. The IAIA's Basic Statement of Purpose provided: 'A key aim is to present to people of the world – in Asia, Africa, Europe, and South America – an American educational program which particularly exemplifies respect for a unique cultural minority.'[109]

At the peak of the Cold War, René d'Harnoncourt and MoMA marketed Native American cultural objects as an example of contemporary American art.[110] In contrast to the inter-war years, emphasis was placed on the contribution of individual

[105] H R Con. Res. 108, 83rd Cong., 1st sess., 67 Stat.B132 (1953), in W. E. Washburn (ed.), *The Indian and the White Man* (Garden City, NY, 1964), pp.397–98.

[106] US Congress, Senate, Subcommittee on Indian Affairs, Hearings before the Subcommittee on Indian Affairs of the Committee on Interior and Insular Affairs . . . on Bills pertaining to Federal Indian Policy, Washington, 85th Cong., 1st sess. (1957), 164; and Washburn, *Red*, p.89.

[107] See Schrader, *Indian Arts*, pp.286, 293. D'Harnoncourt resigned as general manager of the IACB in 1944 to take up various posts at MoMA. He continued to guide the IACB as a board member and subsequently its chair.

[108] See J. L. Gritton, *The Institute of American Indian Arts: Modernism and US Indian Policy* (Albuquerque, 2000), pp.65ff; W. Garmhausen, *History of Indian Arts Education in Santa Fe: The Institute of American Indian Arts with Historical Background 1890–1962* (Santa Fe, 1988), pp.62ff; F. Dockstader, *Directions in Indian Art, in Proceedings of a Conference held at the University of Arizona, 20–21 March 1959* (Tucson, 1959), p.13; M. Archuleta and R. Strickland (eds.), *Shared Visions: Native American Painters and Sculptors in the Twentieth Century* (Phoenix, 1992), pp.74ff; and The Museum of Modern Art Archives, NY: René d'Harnoncourt Papers [AAA: 2921; 263].

[109] Gritton, *Institute*, p.3.

[110] Gritton, *Institute*, p.4. In 1951, MoMA had only one example of modern Indian painting in its permanent collections: D. Dunn to R. d'Harnoncourt, 17 December 1951, MoMA Archives, NY: RdH [AAA: 2925].

Native American artists, not indigenous communities.[111] In a 1948 speech, René d'Harnoncourt noted:

> [T]he dilemma of our time . . . can be solved only by an order which reconciles the freedom of the individual with the welfare of society and replaces yesterday's image of one unified civilisation by a pattern in which many elements . . . [form a] society enriched . . . by the full development of the individual for the sake of the whole.[112]

He suggested democracies represented such societies and modern art was its 'foremost symbol'.[113] MoMA's detractors likened its promotion of modernist individualism to the 'civilising mission' spread by missionaries to facilitate European settlement of indigenous lands. They argued that Native American cultural objects were incorporated into the modernist chronology of art propagated by MoMA, and that the IAIA aided these pseudo-colonial methodologies by its refusal to engage in equitable cultural dialogue.[114]

Relations between Native Americans and US society during the mid-century were more problematic than a simple replication of past Anglo-American colonial policies. The spark lit by the Indian New Deal – where Native American communities determined how their cultures were portrayed, preserved and developed – could not be dimmed by termination policies.[115] D'Harnoncourt's core message during the 1950s changed little from that which he had espoused a decade earlier. He reaffirmed that indigenous arts and crafts provided Native Americans with 'a living for some, a means of rehabilitation for others, a source of pride and status for all'.[116] Native American artists like Lloyd 'Kiva' New and Charles Loloma promoted the IAIA as a vehicle for re-educating the public perception of indigenous arts and crafts, from traditional, static and timeless to dynamic and evolving cultural forms responding to the present circumstances.[117]

More importantly, regressive federal policies precipitated a groundswell in Indian nationalism and pan-Indianism that fuelled the Native American Civil Rights

---

[111] See J. J. Brody, *Indian Painters & White Patrons* (Albuquerque, 1971), pp.189ff.

[112] R. d'Harnoncourt, Challenge and Promise: Modern Art and Modern Society (1948) 41 *Magazine of Art* 250 at 252.

[113] *Ibid.* See M. Kimmelman, Revisiting the Revisionists: The Modern, Its Critics and the Cold War, in J. Elderfield (ed.), *The Museum of Modern Art at Mid-Century: At Home and Abroad* (New York, 1994), pp.38ff; H. M. Franc, The Early Years of the International Program and Council, in Elderfield (ed.), *Home*, pp.10ff; and F. Stonor Saunders, *Who Paid the Piper? The CIA and the Cultural Cold War* (London, 1999).

[114] See Gritton, *Institute*, pp.152–53, 155; A. L. LaRiviere, New Art by the Oldest Americans (1973) 65 *Westways* 23; and D. Fisher, Rockefeller Philanthropy and the Rise of Social Anthropology (1986) 2 *Anthropology Today* 5–8.

[115] See P. J. Deloria, *Playing Indian* (New Haven, 1998), p.146; Philp, *Collier's*, p.244; Taylor, *New Deal*, p.150; S. O'Brien, Federal Indian Policies and the International Protection of Human Rights, in V. Deloria Jr (ed.), *American Indian Policy in the Twentieth Century* (Norman, 1985), pp.35ff; and S. O'Brien, Tribes and Indians: With Whom Does the United States Maintain a Relationship? (1991) 66 NDLR 1461.

[116] See R. d'Harnoncourt, Speech entitled 'American Indian Arts and Crafts in the Mid-Century (1958–59)', MoMA Archives, NY: RdH [AAA: 2924; 1403ff].

[117] See Gritton, *Institute*, pp.7–39 and 42ff.

movement and indigenous participation in international fora.[118] They sought and gradually realised the right to (internal) self-determination, and the preservation and development of their cultures, including the restitution of cultural objects and ancestral remains.

Early years of UNESCO and d'Harnoncourt's vision

From its earliest years, UNESCO engaged in the question of the preservation and development of indigenous cultures. Its initial responses were influenced significantly by d'Harnoncourt and his experience in the American context. He always endeavoured to balance the (sometimes opposing) goals of cultural preservation, development and exchange. He conceded that cultural exchange was not necessarily voluntary, especially for occupied peoples.

René d'Harnoncourt, in his multiple roles with MoMA, the US federal government and private institutions, strove to remedy the destructive effects of colonisation and assimilation on indigenous communities of the Americas.[119] After the Second World War, his influence extended beyond the Western hemisphere when he assisted in setting up UNESCO.[120] UNESCO absorbed the functions of the League of Nations International Committee for Intellectual Cooperation, but adopted a more global outlook than its predecessor. A preparatory document for the 1946 London Conference noted: 'In the human family, each country and region has its own characteristics and its own distinct values, and *each makes its distinctive contribution to the common treasure of culture.*'[121]

Following his appointment as senior counsellor to UNESCO, d'Harnoncourt nurtured policies to 'preserve' and 'stimulate' indigenous cultures, the themes that had preoccupied him for decades.[122] The UNESCO policy devised for non-industrialised peoples strongly echoed the Indian New Deal but also betrayed the influence of the Cold War environment. The policy suggested that to guard against the 'fossilisation' of indigenous arts and crafts the indigenous artist should 'apply his [*sic*] own creative talent' to 'the enrichment of the world and for his own satisfaction and economic benefit'.[123] Like its parent body, one of UNESCO's purposes is the promotion among

---

[118] See Indian Civil Rights Act of 1968, Pub. L. No. 90–284; 82 Stat. 73, Title II – Rights of Indians, codified at 25 USC §§1302 *et seq* (2002); V. Deloria, *Custer Died for Your Sins: An Indian Manifesto* (New York, 1969); J. Chaudhuri, American Indian Policy: An Overview, in Deloria (ed.), *American*, pp.29–32; and Cohen, *Handbook*, pp.180ff.

[119] See MoMA Archives, NY: RdH [AAA: 2922; 544–45]; Schrader, *Indian Arts*, p.289; and R. Lynes, *Good Old Modern: An Intimate Portrait of The Museum of Modern Art* (New York, 1973), p.271.

[120] See Huxley to d'Harnoncourt, 12 June 1946, Folder 1323, Box 135, Series III.4L, RG 4 NAR Personal Projects, Rockefeller Family Archives, Rockefeller Archives Centre, Sleepy Hollow, New York (RAC); and M. Wheeler, in MoMA, *René d'Harnoncourt 1901–1968: A Tribute* (New York, 1968), n.p.

[121] UNESCO Doc.UNESCO/Lond/9, 2 (emphasis added).

[122] D'Harnoncourt to A. Brandebury, Alaskan Arts and Crafts Inc., 28 June 1946, MoMA Archives, NY: RdH [AAA: 2925]. See C. A. Thomson, Office of International Information and Cultural Affairs, US Department of State to A. H. Barr Jr, 8 July 1946, The Museum of Modern Art Archives, New York: Alfred H. Barr Jr, Papers [AAA: 2181; 521ff].

[123] UNESCO Doc.UNESCO/Lond/9, 9–10. See J. Huxley, *Memories II*, (New York, 1973), p.177.

nations, through culture, of the non-discriminatory application of human rights and fundamental freedoms.[124]

Another of UNESCO's purposes was the promotion of cultural exchange.[125] The United States has consistently insisted on the insertion of provisions reflecting this goal in international agreements covering cultural heritage. The aim of cultural exchange also overlapped with its traditional free trade agenda in the field.

The promotion of the free flow of ideas, images and objects unimpeded by national, cultural, economic or social boundaries had been part of d'Harnoncourt's *raison d'être* since the inter-war period. In a 1963 speech, he noted that the international art trade had 'always been a basic factor in the development of civilisation'. However, he maintained that a distinction had to be made by museums between 'the natural and inevitable flow of cultural values from country to country, and the systematic encouragement of such flow as a matter of national or international policy'.[126] US economic strength meant that the cultural exchange of cultural objects was disproportionately in its favour. This flow of cultural material into the United States was particularly acute from the Pacific and the Americas.

The US armed forces' engagement in the Pacific theatre of war opened up this region to the domestic public's imagination. The volume of cultural objects collected from Pacific communities by the military was breathtaking to US museum officials.[127] These activities highlight that large-scale cultural losses experienced by Pacific peoples were not quarantined to the colonial period. The 'cross-fertilisation' of cultures and resultant cultural renewal was a central theme of a 1946 MoMA exhibition entitled 'Arts of the South Seas'.[128] The exhibition designed by d'Harnoncourt was significant for two reasons.

First, the cultural objects were arranged on the premise that 'a work of art can best be appreciated in the context of its own civilisation'.[129] This reasoning represented the triumph of Boasian anthropological theory.[130] Boasian disciple Alfred L. Kroeber noted that: 'Anthropologists now agree that each culture must be examined in terms of its own structures and values instead of being rated by the standards

---

[124] Final Act of the United Nations Conference for the Establishment of an Educational, Scientific and Cultural Organisation, Cmd 6711 (1946), p.5.

[125] Art.1(2)(c), Constitution of UNESCO, London, 16 November 1945, in force 4 November 1946, 4 UNTS 275, and Cmd 6711 (1945); and UNESCO Recommendation Concerning the International Exchange of Cultural Property, Nairobi, 26 November 1976, in UNESCO, *Conventions and Recommendations of UNESCO concerning the Protection of the Cultural Heritage* (Paris, 1983), p.181.

[126] R. d'Harnoncourt, The Art Museum's Role in International Cultural Exchange, 1963, MoMA Archives, NY: RdH [AAA: 2924; 414].

[127] See E. Douglas to R. d'Harnoncourt, 28 April 1949, MoMA Archives, NY: RdH [AAA: 2921; 364].

[128] R. Linton and P. S. Wingert, *Arts of the South Seas*, (exh. cat., New York, 1946), p.7; and M. A. Staniszewski, *The Power of Display: A History of Exhibition Installations at the Museum of Modern Art* (Cambridge MA, 1998), pp.110ff.

[129] See Linton and Wingert, *Arts*, p.8.

[130] See F. Boas, *Race, Language, and Culture* (1910) (Reprint, New York, 1940); G. W. Stocking Jr, Philanthropoids and Vanishing Cultures: Rockefeller Funding and the End of the Museum Era in Anglo-American Anthropology, in G. W. Stocking Jr (ed.), *Objects and Others: Essays on Museums and Material Culture* (Madison, 1985), pp.112–24; and G. W. Stocking Jr, Ideas and Institutions in American Anthropology: Thoughts toward a History of the Interwar Years, in G. W. Stocking Jr (ed.), *Selected Papers from the American Anthropologists* (Washington DC, 1976), pp.1–53.

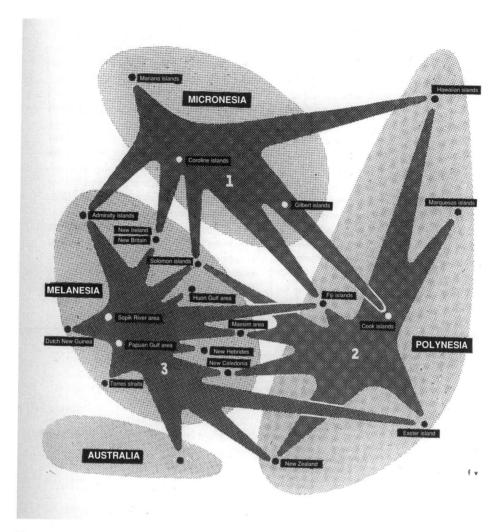

Figure 6.2 René d'Harnoncourt, 'Chart of Affinities', reproduced in exhibition catalogue, *Arts of the South Seas*, The Museum of Modern Art, New York, 1946.

of some other civilisation exalted as absolute.'[131] Although cultural Darwinism was debunked in the post-war period, racialised thinking most definitely was not. Despite the pronouncement of the 'equality of cultures', cultural objects of non-European peoples continued to be displayed and interpreted in accordance with the Western aesthetic. The MoMA catalogue conceded that 'appreciation' of the cultural objects of others 'is always connected with the group's own preoccupations'.[132]

During this period, indigenous peoples and their cultural objects were treated alike: individualised and equalised. One reviewer noted: 'the spectator can usually only make a dim guess at the nature and uses of the things displayed . . . The sad

[131] A. L. Kroeber, *The Nature of Culture*, (Chicago, 1952), p.139.
[132] Linton and Wingert, *Arts*, p.7.

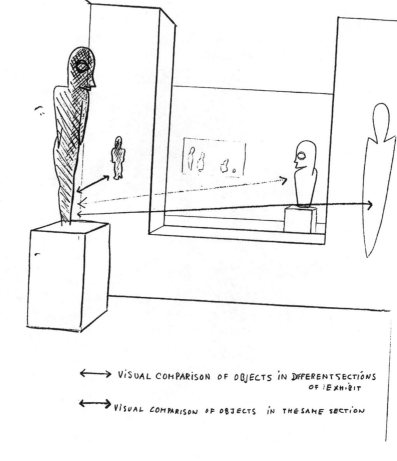

→ VISUAL COMPARISON OF OBJECTS IN DIFFERENT SECTIONS OF EXHIBIT

→ VISUAL COMPARISON OF OBJECTS IN THE SAME SECTION

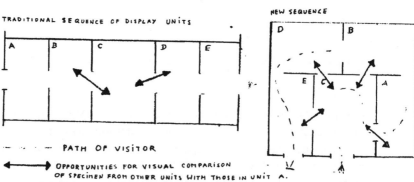

Figure 6.3 (a) and (b) René d'Harnoncourt, preparatory sketches for the exhibition 'Arts of the South Seas', The Museum of Modern Art, New York, 29 January – 19 May 1946, in Rockefeller Foundation folders, Rockefeller Archives Center, New York.

Figure 6.4 Installation view of the exhibition 'Art of the South Seas', The Museum of Modern Art, New York, 1946.

truth is that a large proportion of the objects shown were collected with no information of their use'.[133] The MoMA catalogue did not emphasis 'historic process', relying instead 'on the character of the objects themselves'.[134] Like the members of a minority group, these objects were de-contextualised and their possession by the dominant culture presented as a neutral act.

The second theme of the 'Arts of the South Seas' exhibition was the growing appreciation of migration on cross-cultural influencing of artistic styles and thinking. D'Harnoncourt's innovative exhibition layout provided a visual representation of the benefits of voluntary cultural exchange. He departed from traditional displays that guided the visitor through a preconceived linear progression of cultural development.[135] Instead, he strove to develop vistas that conveyed interrelations and cross-fertilisation between cultures in a region.[136]

This contrast is most striking when one compares images of displays of Indigenous Australian objects during the great exhibitions and the 1946 MoMA exhibition. They capture the shift from the imperial storehouse of objects 'captured' from every corner of the globe, to the austere clinical display within the walls of the museum of 'Modern Art', where the display itself becomes a work of art. However, in both exhibitions,

[133] G. Bateson, Exhibition Review: Art of the South Seas (June 1946) 28 *The Art Bulletin* 119 at 121.
[134] Linton and Wingert, *Arts*, p.9.
[135] R. d'Harnoncourt, 'New Display'; and D'Harnoncourt to Stevens, Rockefeller Foundation, 7 December 1945, Folder 2981, Box 250, Series 200, RG1.1, Rockefeller Foundation Archives, RAC.
[136] Anon., Art of the South Seas (May 1946) *The Architectural FORUM* 97.

the object is removed from its original context – 'history evaporate[ed]'.[137] It has become a potent vessel for the mythologising of the dominant culture.

D'Harnoncourt was fully aware of the power wielded with the possession, display and interpretation of cultural objects:

> It seems reasonable to assume . . . that the importation of art from conquered lands often served as a demonstration of the victors' military and political power; and that the exportation of works of art to foreign countries was often used as a means of increasing national prestige.[138]

He was cognisant of the divide between voluntary and involuntary 'cultural exchange'.[139] He championed cultural pluralism and viewed voluntary cultural exchange as an essential element of every culture's development. For these reasons, he rejected, in equal measure, assimilationist policies and revivalist programmes that froze Native American cultural production in an idealised past. Instead, he advocated the right of indigenous peoples to adopt non-traditional production methods to assist their cultural and economic development.[140]

Museum of Primitive Art and trade in cultural objects

Decolonisation brought with it the replication of colonial tropes in respect of the cultural resources of indigenous communities and newly independent States, including the (re)presentation of non-European cultural objects as 'primitive art' by museums in former metropolitan capitals; and the reinvigorated promotion of the unrestricted traffic in non-European cultural objects. Both attempts to regress to pre-war knowledge systems and methodologies proved unsuccessful. Replication of colonial practices of the pre-war period and the ever-increasing collection and display of non-European cultural objects came under concerted attack, domestically and internationally.

It is no coincidence that at a time when the United States was administering various Pacific territories and pursuing an integration policy towards Native Americans, there was an institutionalisation of primitive art on US soil and an exponential increase in the US market for non-European cultural objects. MoMA had mounted several important exhibitions of primitive and folk art during the 1930s and 40s.[141] However, the Museum of Primitive Art (MoPA), established to house Nelson A. Rockefeller's burgeoning personal collection of primitive art, did not open its doors until February 1957.[142] The charter of the Museum of Indigenous Art (as it was

---

[137] Barthes, 'Myth Today', in Barthes, *Mythologies*, p. 51.
[138] D'Harnoncourt, 'Cultural Exchange', 8 (original emphasis).
[139] D'Harnoncourt, 'Cultural Exchange', 9.
[140] D'Harnoncourt, American Indian Arts and Crafts at Mid-Century, MoMA Archives, NY: RdH [AAA: 2924;140 at 152].
[141] See Staniszewski, *Power*, pp.59ff.
[142] Rockefeller was MoPA's president, d'Harnoncourt was vice-president and Robert Goldwater was the first director. Originally called the Museum of Indigenous Art, MoPA underwent a name change at Goldwater's behest: Minutes Annual Meeting of the Members of the Museum of Indigenous Art, 12 June 1956, Folder 1679, Box 165, Series III 4L, RG4 NAR Personal Projects, Rockefeller Family Archives, RAC.

then) stated: '[It] will be not only to contribute to the public's enjoyment of the arts by revealing the artistic excellence of objects usually presented in scientific terms only, but also . . . to the sympathetic understanding and appreciation of civilisations other than our own'.[143]

In contrast to d'Harnoncourt's MoMA exhibitions, which emphasised the living cultures of indigenous peoples, MoPA's director Robert Goldwater reverted to the modernist mode of placing non-European objects in a static, de-contextualised past. One conservative reviewer expounded on:

> [T]his blanket otherness of spirit which is domesticated here . . . Regardless of their time and place of origin or of their disparate levels of intensity, they are all dissolved into a spectacle of the 'primitive', transformed into a coefficient of our current interests . . . It equalizes what might better have remained an unequal experience.[144]

Goldwater did little to refute such criticism, stating: 'Primitive art, like primitive society, should be static; the idea that it may be developing or evolving (or that the peoples themselves may be changing) does not fit in with the notion of a simple, immemorial primitiveness.'[145] In addition, there was a return to the rhetoric of 'dying' cultures whose traditions were 'rapidly disappearing' because of modernisation and industrialisation.[146]

Unlike the success of d'Harnoncourt's MoMA exhibitions, the MoPA agenda failed to ignite the public's imagination.[147] Within two years, doubts had begun to emerge about its viability.[148] The eventual transfer of the collection to the Metropolitan Museum of Art, New York in the late 1960s and early 70s was marred by a controversial repatriation claim made by the Guatemalan government.[149] This claim served as a wake-up call to both individual and institutional collectors.

By the 1960s, Rockefeller conceded to *Newsweek* that collecting cultural objects had become more complex than during the 1930s because of the passage of national laws restricting exports. He added: 'You can't get pieces out, but they come out'.[150] Not long before, MoPA was advised by the US State Department of a diplomatic note from the Guatemalan embassy inquiring about the provenance of a Mayan stela in

---

[143] Charter of the Museum of Indigenous Art, 17 December 1954, Folder 1651, Box 162, Series III 4L, RG4 NAR Personal Projects, Rockefeller Family Archives, RAC.

[144] H. Kramer, Month in Review (May 1957) *Arts* 42 at 45, Folder 1692, Box 166, Series III 4L, RG4 NAR Personal Projects, Rockefeller Family Archives, RAC.

[145] R. Goldwater, *Primitivism in Modern Art* (1938) (Enlarged edn, Cambridge, 1986), p.266.

[146] Bateson, 'Exhibition'; and Rockefeller to Clarke, Chairman, MoMA Board of Trustees, 16 December 1942, Folder 1642, Box 161, Series III 4L, RG4 NAR Personal Projects, Rockefeller Family Archives, RAC.

[147] MoPA Memo Kurtz to Boyer, 6 June 1961, Folder 1642, Box 161, Series III 4L, RG4 NAR Personal Projects, Rockefeller Family Archives, RAC.

[148] Interview R. Goldwater, Director, Museum of Primitive Art, 8 January 1959, Folder 184, Box 21, Series 200, RG2 1959, Rockefeller Foundation Archives, RAC.

[149] Nigeria also made a restitution claim on MoPA: Folder 1652, Box 162, Series III 4L, RG4 NAR Personal Projects, Rockefeller Family Archives, RAC; and the Museum of Mankind, London: E. Epo, Nigeria (1979) 31 *Museum* 18.

[150] Anon., Rocky Road to Art, *Newsweek*, 18 July 1966, p.90.

its collections.[151] Guatemala did not allege the museum was involved in the removal of the stela, nor did it dispute its title. Instead it requested the object's voluntary return because 'no institution that calls itself a museum can accept . . . works that have been obtained by looting or theft'.[152]

Guatemala relied upon the Treaty on the Protection of Movable Property of Historic Value (1935 PAU Treaty) as the basis for the return of stelae from both the Brooklyn Museum and MoPA.[153] Rockefeller was advised that the laws cited by Guatemala were unenforceable in the United States and there was 'no legal obligation to return the stelae'.[154] New York museum officials cautioned against return because 'voluntary action would foster a raft of similar claims relating to objects in collections throughout the country'.[155] The stelae were eventually returned, not through the operation of the treaty but following diplomatic and public pressure.

There was growing awareness in the US public and legal community of the impact of illicit traffic feeding Western, mainly US, art markets.[156] The chair of the American Society of International Law panel on the international art trade wrote to Rockefeller: 'It is plain to me now that the Pre-Columbian art of Latin America is in deep trouble . . . Unless something is done quickly, what is now left in the field will be gone.'[157] In March 1970, Rockefeller formally advised the Guatemalan President, Mendez Montenegro of his intention to return the stelae noting: 'I do not believe that we can or should condone destruction of great historical monuments for the purposes of trade.'[158]

The *Wall Street Journal* coverage of the restitution echoed the words of Quatremère de Quincy 150 years before. It noted in part: 'Even pieces looters do save lose almost all historical value because they have been yanked out of their archaeological context . . . "These pieces are like men without souls," says one archaeologist.'[159]

---

[151] See File Guatemalan Mayan Stela 1966–70, Folder 1654, Box 163, Series III 4L, RG4 NAR Personal Projects, Rockefeller Family Archives, RAC.

[152] Memo Empson to Rockefeller, 8 March 1967, Folder 1654, Box 163, RG III 4L, NAR Personal Projects, Rockefeller Family Archives, RAC. See K. Meyer, *The Plundered Past: The Traffic in Art Treasures* (New York, 1973), pp.26–27.

[153] See Memo Maginnes to Rockefeller, 30 September 1969, Folder 1654, Box 163, Series III 4L, RG4 NAR Personal Projects, Rockefeller Family Archives, RAC.

[154] Empson to Rockefeller.

[155] *Ibid.* Goldwater notified the US State Department that the MoPA was the bona fide purchaser and would not voluntarily return the object to the Guatemalan government. But it would resell it to the Guatemalan government: Goldwater to Killaran, Chief, Guatemalan Affairs, Department of State, 22 March 1967, Folder 1654, Box 163, Series III 4L, RG4 NAR Personal Projects, Rockefeller Family Archives, RAC.

[156] See C. Coggins, Illicit Traffic in Pre-Columbian Antiquities (1969) 29 *Art Journal* 94; and Meyer, *Plundered*.

[157] Rogers to Rockefeller, 6 December 1969, Folder 1654, Box 163, RG III 4L, NAR, RAC.

[158] Rockefeller to Mendez, 16 March 1970; and Mendez to Rockefeller, 5 May 1970, Folder 1654, Box 163, Series III 4L, RG4 NAR Personal Projects, Rockefeller Family Archives, RAC. The Mexican authorities agreed to the long term loan of the stela to the Metropolitan Museum, New York: S. Williams, *The International and National Protection of Movable Cultural Property* (Dobbs Ferry, 1978), pp.131–32.

[159] B. Carley, Stolen Treasure: Archaeological Items are Smuggled Widely as Prices Soar, *Wall Street Journal*, 2 June 1970, pp.1 and 25.

Illicit trade and restitution in the Americas

By the late 1960s, pressure within and outside the United States was such that it could no longer ignore the role of the US art market in the illicit traffic of objects from Central and South America. The US support of an unrestricted international art trade was gradually tempered by a series of bilateral agreements with Latin American States. However, the United States remained reluctant to obligate itself in a multilateral fashion.

As explained in Chapter 4, the international regulation of archaeological excavations became synonymous with the efforts of non-European States to curb illicit traffic of cultural objects from their territories. Immediately after the Second World War, UNESCO, with the assistance of the International Council of Museums (successor to the OIM), took up the momentum of the 1937 Cairo Conference (Final Act).[160]

The preamble of the Recommendation on International Principles applicable to Archaeological Excavations (1956 UNESCO Recommendation) notes that while States are concerned with archaeological sites and objects on their territory, the whole international community also held a concomitant interest.[161] It sanctions measures that encourage cultural exchange between States (Article 23). However, archaeological finds are to be assigned primarily to enable the country in which the excavation is located to have collections that are 'fully representative of [its] civilisation, history, art and architecture' (Article 23(b)). States should facilitate restitution requests where objects have been removed from a clandestine excavation and/or illicitly exported from the country of origin (Article 31).[162] The 1956 UNESCO Recommendation also encourages States to enter bilateral agreements to achieve its aims (Article 33).

The Treaty of Cooperation providing for the Recovery and Return of Stolen Archaeological, Historical and Cultural Properties (1970 Treaty of Cooperation between the United States of America and Mexico) was designed to balance the competing interests of the country of origin, the international art trade and archaeologists.[163] Cultural objects covered by the treaty echoed inter-war regional agreements. All objects had to be the property of the government or its instrumentalities and of 'outstanding importance to the national patrimony'.[164]

---

[160] ICOM was established at the Second UNESCO General Conference held in Mexico City in 1947.

[161] New Delhi, 5 December 1956, in UNESCO, *Conventions*, p.101. See Williams, *International*, pp.174–75; and P. J. O'Keefe and L. V. Prott, *Law and the Cultural Heritage, Volume 1: Discovery and Excavation* (London, 1984), pp.75–78.

[162] There was a proviso that restitution is only facilitated where the object will be returned to a public museum and other requirements concerning cultural exchange are met. Article 30 encourages museums similarly to facilitate restitution requests and pursue an ethical acquisition policy.

[163] Mexico City, 17 July 1970, in force 24 March 1971, 791 UNTS 313; (1971) 22 USTS 494; and (1970) 9 ILM 1028. See L. V. Prott and P. J. O'Keefe, *Law and the Cultural Heritage, Volume 3: Movement* (London, 1989), pp.668–72, §§1304–09; J. J. Fishman and S. Metzger, Protecting America's Cultural and Historical Patrimony (1976) 4 SJILC 57; J. B. Seabrook, Legal Approaches to the Trade in Stolen Antiquities (1974) 2 SJILC 51; and J. Greenfield, *The Return of Cultural Treasures* (Cambridge, 1989), pp.189–93.

[164] See Williams, *International*, pp.132–33; and M. A. Gonzalez, New Legal Tools to Curb the Illicit Traffic in Pre-Columbian Antiquities (1973) 12 CJTL 316.

At the United States' behest, the treaty recognised that exchange of cultural objects facilitated a mutual appreciation of the patrimony of each State. It was hoped this provision, together with the regulation of archaeological excavations, would dampen illicit traffic into the United States.[165] Ironically, the 'tastemaking' power of the US institutions like MoMA and MoPA, through public exhibitions and their collecting practices, created markets where previously none existed.[166]

The 1970 Treaty of Cooperation satisfied the Mexican requirement for a mechanism facilitating the recovery of cultural objects in particular circumstances (Article 3).[167] It also eased the introduction of US domestic legislation facilitating return of illicitly removed Pre-Columbian objects. The US Senate passed Public Law 92–587 of 1974 (Title II: Regulation of Importation) which provided for return of illicitly removed Pre-Columbian cultural objects imported into the United States and the criminal prosecution of those involved in the importation.[168] The law does not operate retrospectively. However, it signalled US recognition that measures to curb illicit trade would only be effective when importing States also enacted domestic legislation controlling the flow of such objects onto their territory.[169] A US delegate to the 1970 UNESCO Convention negotiations admitted this shift in his State's previous free trade position.[170] US concessions to restrict the trade of cultural objects were done in a piecemeal fashion through bilateral agreements, thereby studiously avoiding multilateral agreements. Even when the United States finally ratified the 1970 UNESCO Convention, it reaffirmed its preference for bilateral arrangements.[171]

The 1976 OAS Convention on the Protection of the Archaeological, Historical and Artistic Heritage of the American Nations (1976 Convention of San Salvador) recognised that escalating illicit traffic of cultural objects had 'damaged and reduced the archaeological, historical, and artistic wealth, through which the national character of their peoples is expressed'. Furthermore, there is a 'basic obligation' to preserve such a 'legacy of cultural heritage' for future generations.[172] Although not retrospective in operation, the treaty obligates State parties to undertake 'whatever measures it may consider effective' to effect restitution (Article 10). The restitution mechanism strongly resembles the provisions of the 1970 Treaty of Cooperation (Articles 11 to 14). The treaty also encourages cultural exchange (Article 15). Accordingly, it provides that objects loaned to the museums, exhibitions or scientific

---

[165] See W. D. Rogers, The Legal Response to the Illicit Movement of Cultural Property (1973) 5 LPIB 936 at 948; and Williams, *International*, p.133.

[166] See A. H. Barr, 'Tastemaking' Mr Barr of the Museum of Modern Art Files a General Demurrer, *New York Times*, 25 September 1960.

[167] Although the treaty was invoked infrequently by Mexico, it has only once formally requested US assistance with a return request: Gonzalez, 'New', 322, n.27; and Prott and O'Keefe, *Movement*, p.670, §1307.

[168] Title II – Regulation of Importation of Pre-Columbian Monumental and Architectural Sculpture and Murals of 1972, Pub. L. No. 92–587, 86 Stat. 1297, codified at 19 USCS §§2091 *et seq* (2000). See Prott and O'Keefe, *Movement*, p.598, §1134; and P. M. Bator, An Essay on the International Trade in Art (1982) 34 Stan. LR275 at 333–35.

[169] See Williams, *International*, p.134.

[170] M. Feldman, in L. D. DuBoff *et al.*, Proceedings of the Panel on the US Enabling Legislation of the UNESCO Convention on the Means of Prohibiting and Preventing the Illicit Import, Export and Transfer of Ownership of Cultural Property (1976) 4 SJILC 97 at 133.

[171] See p. 243 Chapter 8 below.

[172] Second and third recitals, Preamble, OAS GA Res.210 (VI-0/76), 16 June 1976, OASTS No.47, and (1976) 15 ILM 1350.

institutions of another State party shall not be subject to 'seizure as a result of public or private lawsuits' (Article 16).

The United States resisted the OAS initiative by arguing that the illicit art trade was a global phenomenon that could only be controlled by an international regime, like the 1970 UNESCO Convention.[173] The statement was made when the United States was not yet party to the 1970 UNESCO Convention. The US Assistant Secretary for Inter-American Affairs, Terence A. Todman, argued that there was a 'need to liberalize export controls to allow for greater movement' of cultural objects in ways that did not threaten national cultural patrimonies. He added that: 'Art treasures, from whatever era or cultural form, are the heritage of mankind and should be shared with all those who appreciate them.'[174] However, the effectiveness of the Convention is diminished because the United States, the only major importing State in the region, is not party to it.

Since the late nineteenth century, concessions for the international art trade during the drafting of international instruments seriously undermine the interests of indigenous peoples and minority groups. This lobby's continued clout is evidenced with the current campaign in the United States to have Article XX(f), the cultural exception clause, removed from the 1947 General Agreement on Tariffs and Trade (GATT). This provision makes an exception for export controls which are 'imposed for the protection of national treasures of artistic, historic or archaeological value'.[175] The campaign has proved unsuccessful to date.[176]

With the uncertainties and insecurities created by the Cold War and decolonisation, the United States domestically and internationally pursued an agenda which affirmed the diversity of cultures whilst emphasising the equality of individuals. In January 1955, MoMA opened its photography exhibition entitled 'The Family of Man' which would journey to sixty-eight countries during the next decade.[177] Edward Steichen, the show's originator, had initially intended to depict a national exhibition around the themes of Human Relations and Human Rights.[178] What evolved was a display of the diversity of human cultures which, at its core, followed the human life cycle – thereby emphasising the sameness of individual experience.[179] Roland Barthes responded to the Paris exhibition thus:

> We are held back at the surface of an identity, prevented precisely by
> sentimentality from penetrating into the ulterior zone of human behaviour
> where historical alienation introduces some 'differences' which we shall here
> quite simply call 'injustices'.[180]

[173] OEA/Ser.J/II.18; CIECC/doc.12 (1975), 9.
[174] See Note T. A. Todman to R. Silva, Chairman, OAS Permanent Council, in *Digest of United States Practice in International Law 1977* (New York, 1964), pp.880–81.
[175] 30 October 1947, provisionally approved 1 January 1948, 61 Stat.A-11; TIAS 1700; and 55 UNTS 194.
[176] P. J. Boylan, Culture and World Trade (2002) 55 *ICOM News* 4.
[177] See J. Szarkowski, 'The Family of Man', in J. Elderfield (ed.), *The Museum of Modern Art at Mid-Century: Art Home and Abroad* (New York, 1994), p.12.
[178] Staniszewski, *Power*, p.33.
[179] MoMA, *The Family of Man* (exh. cat., New York, 1955).
[180] R. Barthes, The Great Family of Man, in Barthes, *Mythologies*, p.101.

The efforts of Western States to impose a similar framework on international law and the display and interpretation of the cultural objects of non-European peoples during the 1940s, 50s and 60s would also be challenged.

As explained in Part Three, in the late twentieth century, newly independent States and indigenous peoples would remind both the Western and Eastern blocs that differences continued to exist and had to be addressed. Their claims built upon the foundations set by d'Harnoncourt and other Indian New Dealers who had worked in collaboration with indigenous peoples in the pursuit of cultural pluralism and the preservation and development of indigenous cultures. They would also work from the principles articulated and implemented by the United States and other Allied governments in the post-Second World War restitution programme. The US government efforts during the 1990s to facilitate the return of cultural objects to Native American communities and Holocaust survivors reaffirm that country's commitment to the restitution of cultural objects removed pursuant to genocidal and discriminatory policies.

Part Three

What may have well begun as a simple forgetting of other possible views turned into habit and over time into something like a cult of forgetfulness practised on a national scale. We have been able for so long to disremember the Aborigines that we are now hard put to keep them in mind even when we most want to do so.

W. E. H. Stanner, *White Man Got No Dreaming: Essays 1938–1973*, (Canberra, 1979), p.214.

Figure 7.1 Ethnological Court at the Garden Palace Exhibition, Sydney, 1879–80.

7

Decolonisation without restitution

> The return of a work of art or record to the country which created it enables a
> people to recover part of its memory and identity, and proves that the long
> dialogue between civilisations which shapes the history of the world is still
> continuing in an atmosphere of mutual respect between nations.[1]

By the mid 1960s, the silence that surrounded the fate of cultural objects removed
from colonial territories to museums in metropolitan centres was slowly being broken. Formerly colonised peoples firmly tied their right to self-determination and
pursuit of cultural development to the restitution of cultural objects removed during
colonial occupation. This chapter investigates the campaign pursued by these States,
in various international fora during the 1960s and 70s, for the restitution of cultural
objects from imperial collections.

This campaign by newly independent States extended restitution beyond the physical act of return of objects, to include the transfer of knowledge and resources ensuring an equitable exchange between cultures. However, the mechanisms invoked by
these States in the United Nations and UNESCO proved largely ineffectual in achieving the restitution of cultural objects removed during colonial occupation prior to
1970. This was the result of the continuing sway held by former metropolitan powers
and their methodologies and knowledge systems.

By the late twentieth century, newly independent States internalised the dynamic
of their colonial predecessors, on a lesser scale, to unify all peoples within one territory and one national identity. They inherited territorial boundaries defined by the
former colonial powers. They strove to establish national museums to house and
represent a national identity circumscribed by these boundaries. The campaign for
restitution of cultural objects from imperial collections was deployed by these governments to enable the (re)constitution of a national cultural patrimony. It was used
as a political tool to galvanise diverse communities behind a unified national identity.
The national cultures which newly independent States sought to (re)constitute were
'cultures without memory'. These States co-opted the cultural objects of indigenous peoples and minorities within their borders to manufacture a national collective
memory in a manner akin to settler States. Cultural objects became a 'resource' to be
reclaimed from the State's colonial predecessor in the pursuit of national economic
and cultural development. For indigenous peoples and minorities, decolonisation

---

[1] A.-M. M'Bow, A Plea for the Return of an Irreplaceable Heritage to those Who Created It: An Appeal
by the Director-General of UNESCO (1979) 31 *Museum* 58.

was an incomplete process that merely replaced one occupier, the former metropolitan power, with another, the newly independent nation-state.

This chapter explains how these processes manifest themselves during decolonisation with the qualified exercise of the right to self-determination and the silence concerning State succession to cultural objects. Then, there is an examination of the replication of these compromises with the failure of the 1970 UNESCO Convention to address the return of cultural property removed during colonial occupation and the privileging of the State claimant. Next, it is detailed how the UNESCO Intergovernmental Committee, established to address this gap within the 1970 UNESCO Convention, replicated its shortcomings. Finally, the way in which these international initiatives and escalating pressure from newly independent States and indigenous peoples forced changes in the policies and practices of Australian museums is considered.

Decolonisation and self-determination

The second wave of dissolution of empires in the twentieth century altered the complexion of the debate concerning restitution of cultural objects. These changes included:

(1) the articulation of the right to self-determination as inextricably tied to cultural development;
(2) the limited circumstances in which the international community tolerated the exercise of this right; and
(3) the failure to address the question of State succession to cultural property which was challenged by the New International Economic Order (NIEO).

The right to self-determination as recognised by international law during decolonisation privileged the recognition of States defined by territorial boundaries drawn by former colonial powers, to the detriment of indigenous peoples and minorities. This compromise had a profound effect on the claims of these peoples for the return of their cultural heritage from imperial museums.

The inconsistent and narrow circumstances in which the principle of self-determination was applied in the inter-war period meant it was not a rule of international law at the time of the drafting of the 1945 UN Charter.[2] However, successive United Nations General Assembly (UNGA) Resolutions and State practice since 1945 have sufficiently refined the definition of self-determination and its application that it is now generally accepted as a basic principle of international law.[3] The 1960

---

[2] Arts.1(2), 55, 73 and 76(b), Charter of the United Nations, San Francisco, 26 June 1945, in force 24 October 1945, UNCIO XV, 335; amendments by General Assembly Resolutions in UNTS 557, 143/638, 308/892, 119. See Report of the International Committee of Jurists, *Opinion upon the Legal Aspects of the Aalands Islands Question*, LNOJ,SS, (October 1920), No.3, 5; and C. Eagleton, *Self-Determination and the United Nations* (1957) 47 AJIL 88.

[3] See UNGA Res.1514(XV), 14 December 1960; 1541(XV), Annex, 15 December 1960, 15 UN GAOR Supp.(No.16), UN Doc.A/4684, and I. Brownlie, *Basic Documents in International Law* (4th edn, Oxford, 1995), p.307; 2105(XX); 2200A(XXI); 2625(XXV), Annex, 24 October 1970, 25 UN GAOR Supp.(No.28), UN Doc.A/5217. See J. Crawford, *The Creation of States in International Law*

UNGA Resolution entitled the Declaration on the Granting of Independence to Colonial Countries and Peoples (UNGA Res.1514(XV)) stipulated in part:

> All peoples have the right to self-determination; by virtue of that right they freely determine their political status and freely pursue their economic, social and cultural development.[4]

This link between self-determination and collective cultural identity has been made since the League of Nations' minority guarantees and mandates.

Whilst UNGA Res.1514(XV) works from principles developed during the inter-war period, it is distinguishable in three important respects. First, the legal right to self-determination is universal (though not in application). Second, peoples not able to exercise the right of self-determination were not afforded effective international protection for the preservation and development of their collective cultural identity.[5] Third, the international community recognised the supremacy of colonised peoples' right to self-determination and the right to cultural development. Following decolonisation, newly independent States and indigenous peoples promoted the integral nature of cultural preservation and development to the right to self-determination. Furthermore, they argued that the restitution of cultural objects held by former imperial collections was, by extension, imperative to such a right.

Despite the pronouncement of the right to self-determination attaching to 'all peoples', during the 1960s, 70s and 80s the international community would tolerate the exercise of the right only in certain circumstances. Successive post-war international initiatives for the protection and restitution of cultural objects refer exclusively to the State claimant. The limitations in international law on the ability of peoples to attain statehood impacted directly on their ability to preserve and develop their cultural identity. These groups could rely on only the rights afforded individual members under the international human rights framework, or the benevolence of the relevant State to provide a measure of protection for their collective identity.

The prevailing State practice under the 1945 UN Charter, during decolonisation, severely restricted the right of peoples to self-determination in two important respects:

(1) self-determination is limited to the colonial relations in place at the end of the Second World War.[6] Upon independence, the new State succeeded to the boundaries drawn up by former colonial powers pursuant to their own interests.

(Oxford, 1979), pp.89–97; J. Crawford, The Right to Self-Determination in International Law: Its Development and Future, in P. Alston (ed.), *Peoples' Rights* (Oxford, 2001), p.7 at 15ff; H. Hannum, *Autonomy, Sovereignty and Self-Determination: The Accommodation of Conflicting Rights* (Philadelphia, 1990), pp.33ff; and A. Cassese, Political Self-Determination – Old Concepts and New Developments, in A. Cassese (ed.), *UN Law/Fundamental Rights* (Sijthoff and Noordhoff, 1979), pp.137–65.

[4] See Common Art.1 of the International Covenant on Civil and Political Rights, 16 December 1966, in force 23 March 1976, UNGA Res.2200A(XXI), 999 UNTS 171, and (1967) 6 ILM 368; and International Covenant on Economic, Social and Cultural Rights, in force 3 January 1976, 993 UNTS 360; *Namibia Opinion, ICJ Reports 1971*, pp.16, 31; and *Western Sahara ICJ Reports 1975*, pp.12, 31–33.

[5] Cf. T. Makkonen, *Identity, Difference and Otherness: The Concepts of 'People', 'Indigenous People' and 'Minority' in International Law* (Helsinki, 2000), pp.83–84 (suggests Art.27, ICCPR fulfils this role).

[6] See Crawford, *Creation*, pp.94 and 359–60; and Crawford, 'Right', 20.

This was the case even if it resulted in the division of an ethnic group between a number of States or, alternatively, the inclusion of two or more groups within a State[7]; and

(2) in deference to the fears of newly independent and settler States of secessionist movements, self-determination was only available 'in respect to territory which is geographically separate and is distinct ethnically and/or culturally from the country administrating it',[8] and the international law principles of State sovereignty and territorial integrity were reaffirmed.[9]

The right to self-determination did not extend to indigenous peoples and minorities within existing States. These limitations on exercise of the right to self-determination and cultural development had far-reaching consequences on the ability of these groups to seek restitution and protect their cultural heritage during this period.

Decolonisation and State succession to cultural property

There has been a consistent practice in (European) international law to address the State succession to cultural property and archives following territorial reconfiguration since at least 1815. Yet during decolonisation, treaties concluded between colonial powers and their former subjects, with rare exception, were silent on this topic.[10] This oversight was reaffirmed by the 1983 Vienna Convention on Succession of States in respect of State Property, Archives and Debts (1983 Vienna Convention).[11] This omission reflected the continuing influence wielded by former metropolitan powers and museums representing their interests. In 1968, the International Law Commission (ILC) charged Special Rapporteur, Mohammed Bedjaoui with investigating and preparing draft articles on State succession to public property, with particular reference to decolonisation.[12] The ILC noted that State succession in the colonial context was unique because it exhibited aspects of 'continuity and rupture'.[13] Bedjaoui's work led to the 1983 Vienna Convention.

---

[7] See T. Franck, Postmodern Tribalism and the Right to Secession, in C. Brölmann, R. Lebefer and M. Zieck (eds.), *Peoples and Minorities in International Law* (Boston, 1993), p.3 at p.9.

[8] See UNGA Res.1541(XV), Principle 4.

[9] See UNGA Res.1514(XV), para.6; 2131(XX), 21 December 1965; 2625(XXV); *Namibia Opinion, ICJ Reports 1971*, p.16 at p.31; and *Western Sahara ICJ Report 1975*, p.12.

[10] See M. Bedjaoui, Third Report on the Succession of States in Respect of Matters other than Treaties, 24 March 1970, UN Doc.A/CN.4/226, 67; and M. Bedjaoui, Eleventh Report on Succession of States in respect of Matters Other Than Treaties: Succession to State Archives, 18 May 1979, UN Doc.A/CN.4/322, 32–53 and Add.1, paras.2 and 4.

[11] Vienna, 7 April 1983, not in force, UN Doc.A./CONF.117/4; and (1983) 22 ILM 306. As at 2004, only six states signed and five have ratified the Convention. Nonetheless, the Convention was a reference for the Agreement on Succession Issues and Annexes A to G, 29 June 2001 (2002) 41 ILM 3. See C. Stahn, The Agreement on Succession Issues of the Former Socialist Federal Republic of Yugoslavia (2002) 96 AJIL 376 at 383.

[12] Report of the International Law Commission on the work of its thirty-third session, 28 January 1983, UN Doc.A/CONF. 117/4, paras.13–61.

[13] UN Doc.A/7209/Rev.1, para.64. See First recital, Preamble, 1983 Vienna Convention. Provisions were incorporated into the final treaty to cover decolonisation, even though this process was almost completed, because 'the effects of decolonisation including, in particular, problems of succession to State property, remain for years after political independence is achieved': UN Doc.A/36/10, 74.

Bedjaoui's recommendation that 'works of art', not State property, be excluded from the draft Convention was accepted and is reflected in its final form.[14] This excision is extremely problematic, especially for many non-European cultures for which such objects occupy a role similar to archives in Western cultures.[15] The ILC proposed that title to these materials be determined not by the principles of State succession but by the specialist UNESCO Committee for 'return and restitution'.[16] As explained below, this Committee has had limited effect in resolving the claims for restitution of cultural objects removed prior to decolonisation. However, the principles articulated by Bedjaoui, in respect of State property and archives, can be extrapolated to include 'works of art, museums and public libraries'.[17]

Only after the Second World War did the international community recognise categorically the primacy of the right of colonised peoples to the preservation and development of their cultural identity over the right of the international community to unfettered access to these cultural 'resources'. Bedjaoui found that the 1970 Declaration on Principles of International Law Concerning Friendly Relations and Co-operation among States made clear that every non-self-governing territory has a legal status independent of the administrating State that is regulated and protected by international law.[18] Further, he noted the administrating State could not 'improperly dispos[e] of property which should revert to [the successor State] or by arrogating to itself, directly or indirectly, its resources of any kind'.[19] Arguably, if the obligation of the administrating State was to prepare colonised peoples to exercise the right of self-determination and pursue their cultural development, the protection of their cultural heritage was an integral component of this duty. The promulgation by various administrating States of domestic legislative frameworks, which regulated the export of cultural objects from these territories, reflected their cognisance of this obligation. However, the passage of protective legislation was one thing; its effective implementation by an administrating State was another matter entirely.

The unequal nature of the colonial relationship, and the disruption it visited on indigenous communities in particular, necessarily meant the relevant metropolitan power, its nationals and third parties had greater access to their cultural objects. Bedjaoui noted that experience had shown that this threat become pronounced as independence loomed, with movable property of significant 'patrimonial content' being most vulnerable.[20] He found that transfer of cultural objects in the colonial

---

[14] See UN Doc.A/CN.4/322, paras.40ff; UN Doc.A/C.6/34/SR.47, para.31, Crick (Australia); and UN Doc.A/CONF.117/4, 51.

[15] UN Doc.A/C.6/34/SR.49, para.49, Sanyaolu (Nigeria); and M. Bedjaoui, Thirteenth Report on Succession of States in Respect of Rights and Duties Resulting from Sources Other Than Treaties, 5 June 1981, UN Doc.A/CN.4/345/Add.2, paras.227–236.

[16] See UN Doc.A/CONF.117/4, 51 and 65.

[17] See M. Bedjaoui, Fifth Report on the Succession of States in Respect of Matters Other Than Treaties, International Law Commission, United Nations, 4 April 1972, UN Doc.A/CN.4/259, para.12, 6; Third Report on Succession of States in Respect of Matters Other Than Treaties, UN Doc.A/CN.4/226, 68–71; and UN Doc.A/CN.4/322, 12–13.

[18] See UNGA Res.2625(XXV), Annex; and UN Doc.A/CN.4/292, paras.125–28.

[19] UN Doc.A/CN.4/292, para.127.

[20] UN Doc.A/CN.4/292, para.135. See J. Specht, The Australian Museum and the Return of Artefacts to Pacific Island Countries (1979) 31 *Museum* 28.

context was rarely 'in accordance with the canons of justice, morality and law'.[21] Bedjaoui's exclusion of cultural objects from his report despite his acknowledgement of the cultural losses fuelled by colonial occupation is inexplicable. The 1970 UNESCO Convention offers little recourse for peoples who have suffered cultural losses prior to its operation.

Silence concerning the return of cultural objects and archives during decolonisation was in marked contrast to the extensive restitution programme implemented following the defeat of Axis forces during the Second World War. Despite its exclusion of cultural objects, the 1983 Vienna Convention reflects and modifies principles developed by Allied restitution programmes to the principles of State succession.[22]

Upon succeeding to the territory of the predecessor State, the successor State succeeds to the public property of that State (as distinct from property belonging to its nationals or inhabitants), wherever it may be situated.[23] Since at least 1815, European treaties governing territorial redistribution provided a general right to negotiate restitution or a specific right to the return of certain cultural objects from predecessor to successor States. In contrast, the inclusion of such a clause during decolonisation, particularly by Anglo-American States, was sparse.[24]

The 1983 Vienna Convention lays down the following principles concerning State succession to movable State property located in the predecessor State. First, movable State property linked with the ceding territory passes to the newly independent State (Article 15(e)).[25] Second, where a newly independent State contributed to the creation of movable property of the predecessor State, the property passes to the successor State 'in proportion to the contribution of the dependent territory' (Article 15(f)). For the ILC, this latter provision was a 'concrete application of the concept of equity' forming part of 'a rule of positive international law which is designed to preserve, inter alia, the patrimony and the historical and cultural heritage' of the occupied people.[26]

The ILC acknowledged that State succession in the context of decolonisation would also involve relations between the new State and third-party States, and their nationals.[27] This is relevant to succession to cultural objects because of the insistence by Anglo-American States since the nineteenth century on free and equal access to the cultural resources of colonial territories. The ILC argued that formerly occupied

---

[21] UN Doc.A/CN.4/292, para.136. See M. Bedjaoui, Fourth Report on the Succession of States in Respect of Matters Other Than Treaties, International Law Commission, UN Doc.A/CN.4/247 and Add.1.

[22] UN Doc.A/CONF.117/4, 37.

[23] UN Doc.A/CN.4/226, 78–91 and 96–108; UN Doc.A/CN.4/267, 107–13; and M. Bedjaoui, Seventh Report on the Succession of States in Respect of Matters Other Than Treaties, International Law Commission, 3 July 1974, UN Doc.A/CN.4/282, paras.95–96 and 102–04. See *Temple of Preah Vihear (Cambodia v. Thailand), Merits, Judgment ICJ Reports 1962*, p.6 at pp.11, 37.

[24] See UN Doc.A/CN.4/322, 32–53; and M. Simpson, *Museums and Repatriation: An Account of Contested Items in Museum Collections in the UK, with Comparative Material from Other Countries* (2nd edn, London, 1997), pp.57ff.

[25] Art.28 (1)(a)–(c), 1983 Vienna Convention (regarding archives).

[26] UN Doc.A/CONF.117/4, 38 and 42. See Art.3(2), Annex A, 2001, Yugoslav Succession Agreement.

[27] See UN Doc.A/CN.4/226, 108–17; UN Doc.A/CN.4/267, 113–15; UN Doc.A/CN.4/282, paras.97–98 and 114; and UN Doc.A/CN.4/292, 78–79 and 206.

peoples should not be 'obliged to suffer' the continued losses resulting from colonial occupation. It suggested that 'special rules for cases in which third States had profited from the colonial occupation' needed to be drafted.[28] This rationale, championed by newly independent States, led them to invoke the 1943 Declaration of London in support of their restitution claims. Reflecting provisions included in peace treaties following both World Wars,[29] Article 28(4) of the 1983 Vienna Convention provides:

> The predecessor State shall co-operate with the successor State in efforts to recover any archives which, having belonged to the territory to which the succession of States relates, were dispersed during the period of dependence.[30]

Some metropolitan powers, like Australia have assisted their former colonial territories and indigenous peoples to recover cultural objects from third party States.

The non-consensual, licit and illicit, transfer of cultural objects from the colonial territory to third parties is in contravention of the metropolitan powers' international obligations.[31] Therefore, at the very least it should be required to conform to the obligation prescribed by Article 28(4). However, the relief arising from breaches of State responsibility, including restitution and compensation has to date been successfully resisted by former metropolitan powers.[32]

Colonial policies, like assimilation and the relocation of communities, mean that there may be multiple successors to imperial collections.[33] Under the 1983 Vienna Convention archives are to be divided equitably between successor States except those linked to the territory of a particular successor State or necessary for its administration (Article 31(2)).[34] In keeping with the principle of reciprocity, each successor State is required to provide copies or exchange of such archives to other successor States (Article 31(5)). The application of this principle to cultural objects is usually limited because of the importance placed by claimants on possession of the original object. Nonetheless, the right to copies and casts where restitution is refused could be beneficial for the cultural development and renewal of that State. However, the exercise of this option should not prejudice the claim for restitution of the

---

[28] UN Doc.A/7209/Rev.1, para.67.

[29] See Art.422, Treaty of Peace with Turkey, Sèvres, 10 August 1920, not ratified, Cmd 964 (1920); *British and Foreign State Papers*, vol.113, p.652; (1921) 15(supp.) AJIL 179; and Art.1, Armistice Treaty between Italy and Yugoslavia, Rome, 23 December 1950, in force as from signature, 171 UNTS 293.

[30] See UN Doc.A/CN.4/322/Add.1, paras.24–25; and UN Doc.A/CONF.117/4, 62–64.

[31] See L. V. Prott and P. J. O'Keefe, *Law and the Cultural Heritage, Volume 3: Movement* (London, 1989), pp.831–32, §1533; and R. Fraoua, *Le trafic illicite des biens culturels et leur restitution*, (Fribourg, 1985), p.170.

[32] UN Doc.A/36/10, 328–36. Cf. Art.3(3), Annex, 2001 Yugoslav Succession Agreement. It is unclear whether the provision applies to property of 'great importance to the cultural heritage' of the aggrieved State, cf. Stahn, 'Agreement', 388–89. Stahn notes this provision marries two areas of international law, State succession and State responsibility, for acts committed during armed conflict contrary to international humanitarian law.

[33] For example, the division of the India Office library following Indian partition: UN Docs.A/CN.4/226, 92; and A/CN.4/267, 147–49.

[34] See UNESCO, Report of the Director-General on the Study Regarding Problems Involved in the Transfer of Documents from Archives in the Territory of Certain Countries to the Country of Their Origin, 25 August 1978, UNESCO Doc.20C/102, para.25.

original. Alternatively, the question of ownership may be replaced by recognition of mutual rights and obligations. Under the 2001 Agreement on Succession Issues of the Former Socialist Federal Republic of Yugoslavia (Yugoslav Succession Agreement), successor States are required to take 'necessary measures to prevent loss, damage or destruction to State archives . . . property and assets [in which] one or more of the successor States have an interest' (Article 2).

Although the 1983 Vienna Convention did not address rights and duties of States following independence, the Special Rapporteur's report broached these concerns by engaging the tenets of the NIEO.[35] During the 1960s and 70s, newly independent States agitated for the widening of self-determination beyond a political act that was extinguished upon independence.[36] Instead, they maintained that self-determination was an ongoing process in which they endeavoured to attain *de jure* and *de facto* equality with other States. This process included 'the right of every independent people to regain, enjoy and enrich their cultural heritage'.[37]

Bedjaoui advocated a new international order that entailed a new international cultural order.[38] In 1976, the UN Secretary-General noted that:

> [R]ecognition of cultural identity . . . is an essential factor in independence and national development. Every State should [study] its national culture, focusing attention on its individual values . . . [T]o protect its authenticity from the risks of uprooting or levelling as well as from the new forms of colonialism, and to participate, with equal right and dignity, in the work of international cultural co-operation.[39]

The following initiatives were considered essential to a people's cultural development and exercise of the right to self-determination:

(i) restitution of cultural objects removed prior to independence;
(ii) technical and financial assistance for the preservation and development of their cultures and their physical manifestations; and
(iii) regulation of the illicit export, import and transfer of cultural objects.[40]

---

[35] See M. Bedjaoui, First Report on Succession of States in Respect of Rights and Duties Resulting from Sources Other Than Treaties, 5 April 1968, UN Doc.A/CN.4/204, 32, para.73; and UN Doc.A/CN.4/322, paras.46–56.

[36] See Declaration on the Establishment of a New International Economic Order, UNGA Res.3201 (S-VI), 1 May 1974; (1974) 13 ILM 715; and (1974) 68 AJIL798; and M. Bedjaoui, *Towards a New International Economic Order* (New York, 1979).

[37] A. Cristescu, The Historical and Current Development of the Right to Self-Determination on the basis of the Charter of the United Nations and Other Instruments adopted by United Nations Organs, with particular reference to the Promotion and Protection of Human Rights and Fundamental Freedoms, Preliminary Report, 24 June 1975, UN Doc.E/CN.4/Sub.2/L.625, para.17, and paras.160–64; and Final Report, UN Doc.E/CN.4/Sub.2/404, 641–77. See UNGA Resolution on Preservation and Further Development of Cultural Values, UNGA Res.3148 (XXVIII), 14 December 1973.

[38] See UN Doc.A/CN.4/322, para.46. He termed this the 'right to a collective "cultural memory"'.

[39] Preservation and Further Development of Cultural Values, Note by the Secretary-General, 24 August 1976, UN Doc.A/31/111, para.66. See UNESCO, *Moving towards Change: Some Thoughts on the New International Economic Order* (Paris, 1976), pp.25–26.

[40] See UN Doc.A/31/111, paras.57–64; and UN Doc.A/33/157, paras.56ff.

The restitution of cultural objects from imperial collections to facilitate the (re)constitution of the national cultural heritage was viewed as crucial to assertion of cultural autonomy.[41] Accordingly, cultural objects became a cultural resource, mined by these States to develop a national cultural identity. NIEO proponents argued that these objects were part of the 'common heritage of mankind' necessitating its exploitation by the country of origin. For newly independent States in Asia and Africa, the process of decolonisation included the recovery of archives and cultural objects as 'instruments of their development and as an expression of their cultural heritage'.[42] UN organs, including UNESCO, made several non-binding pronouncements that all States should assist emerging nations in their efforts to reconstitute their heritage.[43] Yet, unlike the first wave of empire collapses after the First World War, there was no treaty-based provision for the restitution of cultural objects upon decolonisation.

Despite Bedjaoui's specific exclusion of cultural objects, it was nevertheless argued that his work 'supplemented the efforts made by the United Nations and UNESCO to preserve the rights of peoples to conserve and recover their historical and cultural heritage'.[44] This position was implicitly recognised in Article 28(7) which states that agreements between predecessor and newly independent States 'shall not infringe the right of the peoples of those States to development, to information about their history, and to their cultural heritage'.[45] Nonetheless, the 1983 Vienna Convention is wholly unsatisfactory in resolving the claims for restitution of cultural objects removed prior to decolonisation. And later in this chapter it is argued that the special UNESCO Committee established to address such claims has met with limited success. However, the lasting legacy of the campaign by newly independent States was the adoption of an understanding of restitution beyond the physical act of returning an object.

Like other States before them, these newly independent States strove to acquire collections that articulated a national narrative befitting their statehood and co-opted Western modes of preserving, housing and displaying their cultures within museums. By seeking to (re)constitute their national cultural heritage, they found significant gaps in their collections occasioned by previous and ongoing cultural losses. Furthermore, limited resources meant these States were constricted in their ability to build facilities, train requisite staff or implement effective customs procedures to prevent the illicit export of cultural material.[46] They argued that their former metropolitan power had an ongoing obligation to provide such financial and technical assistance. These States maintained that underdevelopment nurtured by colonial occupation, which led to cultural losses, did not simply cease or change with the grant of independence. The consequences of these losses, both past and present, were identical: the

---

[41] See UN Doc.A/CN.4/322, para.48; and Art.16(1), Charter of Economic Rights and Duties of States, UNGA Res.3281 (XXIX), 12 December 1974; (1975) 14 ILM 251; and (1975) 69 AJIL 484.
[42] UN Doc.A/CN.4/322/Add.2, para.3.   [43] UN Doc.A/CN.4/322, paras.40ff.
[44] UN Doc.A/C.6/34/SR.44, para.14.
[45] See Art.31(4), 1983 Vienna Convention (covering multiple successor States). Bedjaoui opined that this provision articulated a peremptory rule of international law: UN Doc.A/CN.4/345/Add.3, para.270.
[46] See UN Doc.A/CN.4/322, paras.49–53.

items found their way to the museums and private collections of former metropolitan capitals.

This extension of the return of cultural objects beyond the physical act not only takes it beyond the realm of State succession. The notion of return as process can be read in one of two ways: a continuing obligation by the former metropolitan power; or an obligation to address ongoing injury caused by international wrongful acts. This latter characterisation, and the restitution and compensation it entails, has been strongly resisted by former colonial powers.

After the First World War source States strove to protect their national cultural heritage with the formulation of a convention to curb illicit export and enable restitution of cultural property. Upon independence, Asian and African States became similarly alarmed at the escalating flow of cultural objects from their territory onto the international art market.[47] The international legislative framework initially proposed during the 1930s was finally realised during the second wave of dismantling of empires: the 1970 UNESCO Convention.

Restitution and the 1970 UNESCO Convention

Following decolonisation, newly independent States inherited not only old colonial boundaries, but also policies and practices that profoundly moulded the way they imagined their dominion. These States looked to the museums, filled with cultural objects, to aid the creation of a cohesive national identity. The intensely political act of building a national collection rendered these States acutely conscious of the cultural losses suffered during colonisation and following independence.

In 1960 the campaign for an international instrument enabling the restitution of cultural objects to their country of origin, suspended because of the war, was put back on the international agenda by Mexico and Peru. Like the limitations placed on the exercise of the right to self-determination, the resultant 1970 UNESCO Convention compromised the rights of all peoples to their cultural heritage by accommodating the interests of former metropolitan powers and newly independent States.

Newly independent States did not seek to differentiate between objects removed before or after independence. However, the continuing influence of former metropolitan powers and their museums became clear with the continual deferral of the restitution of objects removed during colonial occupation. The preparatory documents for both the 1964 UNESCO Recommendation on the Means of Prohibiting and Preventing the Illicit Export, Import, and Transfer of Ownership of Cultural Property[48] and the 1970 UNESCO Convention[49] revisited several themes

---

[47] From 1940 to 1970 there was an exponential rise in national legislation for the protection of national cultural heritage in Africa, Asia Pacific, South America and the Middle East: B. Burnham, *The Protection of Cultural Property: A Handbook on National Legislations* (Paris, 1974).

[48] Recommendation on the Means of Prohibiting and Preventing the Illicit Export, Import and Transfer of Ownership of Cultural Property, Paris, 19 November 1964, in *Conventions and Recommendations of UNESCO concerning the Protection of the Cultural Heritage* (Paris, 1983), p.137.

[49] Paris, 14 November 1970, in force 24 April 1972, 823 UNTS 231, and (1971) 10 ILM 289. See J. B. Gordon, The UNESCO Convention on the Illicit Movement of Art Treasures (1971) 12 HILJ

that infused the inter-war International Museum Office (OIM) draft conventions. These included non-retroactivity, the distinction between objects located in museums and archaeological sites, the central role of the State, and tensions between the 'national cultural heritage' and the 'common heritage of all mankind'.

Non-retroactivity

The 1970 UNESCO Convention allows for the restitution of the cultural objects exported or transferred in contravention of the laws of the country of origin, after it came into force. Its non-retroactive application can be assumed from customary international law, Article 28 of the 1969 Vienna Convention on the Law of Treaties and *travaux préparatoires* of the 1970 UNESCO Convention itself.[50] It is a measure of the anxiety of former metropolitan powers and the perceived vulnerability of their museums that they insisted on the inclusion of a provision confirming non-retroactivity in the 1970 UNESCO Convention.[51] Whilst no explicit provision was included in the treaty, Article 15 encourages States to enter bilateral negotiations to resolve claims for cultural objects removed prior to its operation. The *travaux* indicated that the need to maintain the integrity of the collections for 'scientific purposes' is an important consideration in any such negotiations.[52]

In response to draft Article 11 (adopted as Article 15), the Chinese government suggested the following amendment:

> [A] State Party which, when the Convention comes into force, is in possession of an important cultural property, illicitly acquired, and inalienable to, and inseparable from, the history and civilisation of another State, shall, in the interest of international goodwill, endeavour to restitute the same to the latter.[53]

Even this highly qualified acknowledgement of the cultural losses suffered by communities prior to the operation of the convention was rejected.[54] However, a draft provision obliging State Parties to provide blanket recognition of ownership vested

537; H. Nieciówna, Sovereign Rights to Cultural Property (1971) 4 PYIL 239; S. Williams, *The International and National Protection of Movable Cultural Property* (Dobbs Ferry, 1978), pp.178–91; Prott and O'Keefe, *Movement*, pp.726ff, §§1401ff; G. Carducci, *La restitution internationale des biens culturels et des objets d'art volés ou illicitement exportés* (Paris, 1997), p.311; and P. J. O'Keefe, *Commentary on the UNESCO 1970 Convention on Illicit Traffic* (Leicester, 2000).

[50] Vienna, 23 May 1969, in force 27 January 1980, 1155 UNTS 331; (1969) 8 ILM 679; UNESCO Doc.78EX/9, Annex, para.51, 8; and Report of the Special Committee of Governmental Experts to examine the Draft Convention on the means of Prohibiting and Preventing the Illicit Import, Export and Transfer of Ownership of Cultural Property, UNESCO Doc.16C/17, 13 July 1970, Annex 2, paras.18 and 29; and (1970) 9 ILM 1038.

[51] For example, UNESCO, Final Report for Special Committee of Governmental Experts, 21 March 1964, UNESCO Doc.CUA/123/Add.1, Annex 1, 22–23 (UK) (regarding the 1964 Recommendation); and UNESCO, Means of Prohibiting and Preventing the Illicit Import, Export and Transfer of Ownership of Cultural Property: Replies to Draft Convention, UNESCO Docs.SHC/MD/5, Annex 1, 22 (USA).

[52] See UNESCO, Means of Prohibiting and Preventing the Illicit Import, Export and Transfer of Ownership of Cultural Property: Preliminary Report, 8 August 1969, UNESCO Doc.SHC/MD/3, paras.12–13 and 80; and UNESCO Doc.SHC/MD/5.

[53] UNESCO Doc.SHC/MD/5, Annex 1, 4.   [54] UNESCO Doc.SHC/MD/5, Annex 2, 10.

in a State, or its nationals, of cultural objects acquired prior to the 1970 UNESCO Convention's operation was also deleted.[55] A State Party may temper this non-retroactivity by passing implementing legislation that prohibits the importation of cultural objects exported illegally from another State at any time, not just after the 1970 Convention came into operation.[56]

Museums and archaeological sites

Market States successfully resuscitated the differentiated protection of cultural objects located in museums and archaeological sites, which marked inter-war efforts to regulate the illicit trade.[57] This move reflected the continued sanctioning of Western modes of possessing cultural heritage and the unfettered international trade in cultural objects. The division was manifested clearly in Articles 7(b) and 9 of the 1970 UNESCO Convention. Inserted at the behest of the United States, the application of these provisions was further narrowed by US implementing legislation.

Like the earlier OIM drafts, the 1970 UNESCO Convention was driven by the escalating cultural losses experienced by source States through clandestine excavations. Yet, fundamental shifts in the intervening forty years fuelled the realisation of the Convention, including: the proportion of source States in the international community which increased substantially with decolonisation; the gradual US recognition of its role in the illicit antiquities trade and its impact on the cultural heritage of neighbouring States; and the finalisation of other multilateral agreements for the protection of archaeological objects and sites.[58]

Despite its limitations, the 1970 UNESCO Convention does extend protection to objects removed from archaeological sites (Article 1(c)). It recognises the 'indefeasible' right of each State Party to nominate certain cultural property as 'inalienable', that it cannot be exported (Article 13(d)). It also incorporates Iraq's 1936 proposal that cultural objects removed without an export certificate be defined as illicit (Articles 3 and 6(b)). In addition, the Convention acknowledges the role of museums in curbing the illicit traffic of cultural objects (Article 7(a)).[59]

1943 Declaration of London and colonialism

Although the 1970 UNESCO Convention excludes claims for the restitution of cultural objects removed prior to decolonisation, newly independent States were able to negotiate the inclusion of two provisions inspired by the 1943 Declaration of London. Articles 11 and 12 are pertinent to the question of what constitutes 'illicit' removal of cultural objects by an occupying State.[60] As the declaration was invoked in the *travaux*, these provisions arguably encompass: the broad notion of

---

[55] See Draft Art.4(f), UNESCO Doc.SHC/MD/3, Annex, 2; Mexico, UNESCO Doc.SHC/MD/5, Annex 1, 14; Hungary, 9; Iraq, 10; Italy, 11; and USSR, 19.

[56] O'Keefe, *Commentary*, pp.15–17. [57] See UNESCO Doc.16C/17, Annex 2, para.19.

[58] See 1956 UNESCO Recommendation; and European Convention on the Protection of the Archaeological Heritage, London, 6 May 1969, in force 20 November 1970, 788 UNTS 228; ETS No.66 (replaced by European Convention on the Protection of the Archaeological Heritage (Revised), Valetta, 16 January 1992, ETS No.143).

[59] See J. Nafziger, Article 7(a) of the UNESCO Convention, in L. D. DuBoff (ed.), *Art Law: Domestic and International* (South Hackensack, 1975), p.387.

[60] Draft Arts.8 and 9, UNESCO Doc.SHC/MD/3, 9.

involuntary transfers – 'apparently legal in form, even when they purport to be voluntarily effected'; and neutral States and their nationals profiteering from such unlawful acts.

Article 11 reaffirms obligations contained in the 1954 Hague Convention and Protocol, which are more detailed in scope.[61] It states: 'The export and transfer of ownership of cultural property under compulsion arising directly or indirectly from the occupation of a country by a foreign power shall be regarded as illicit.' Iraq's effort to enable retrospective application of the provision with the inclusion of the words: 'including any such action in the past', was defeated.[62]

Article 12 provides that State Parties will 'take all appropriate measures to prohibit and prevent' the illicit transfer of cultural property 'within the territories for the international relations for which they are responsible'. The *travaux* defined such territories as 'colonies, or extra-metropolitan territories, of federated States within a federation of States'.[63] Arguably, the provision does not extend to indigenous peoples or minorities unless they enjoy a degree of autonomy within the State Party.[64] Importantly, however, as explained in Chapters 8 and 9, several States have passed legislation to protect the cultural objects of certain communities, particularly indigenous peoples within their territory.

The effectiveness of Articles 11 and 12 is compromised because of the State-centric nature of the 1970 UNESCO Convention. Peoples within the territory of State parties depend upon it to enforce the Convention on their behalf.[65] If non-retroactive application represents the continuing strength of imperial imagining, then the 1970 UNESCO Convention's privileging of the State reflects the lingering influence of positivism in international law and the assimilatory tendencies of newly independent and settler States as they pursue a national imagining.

State-centric

The most striking aspect of the final form of the 1970 UNESCO Convention is what sets it apart from the 1954 Hague Convention. The 'State' and its 'national' culture, laws, institutions and enforcement regimes permeate every aspect of the 1970 instrument to a degree not matched by the 1954 Convention. This characteristic was driven by the same influences which constrained the application of the right to self-determination during decolonisation. Under the 1970 UNESCO Convention, the State defines which cultural objects are to be protected and implements the measures for their protection.[66] The trigger for control and enforcement procedures is the removal of the cultural objects from a State's territory.[67]

---

[61] Arts.4 and 19 of the Convention for the Protection of Cultural Property in the Event of Armed Conflict, The Hague, 14 May 1954, in force 7 August 1956, 249 UNTS 240; and Art.1 of the Protocol for the Protection of Cultural Property in the Event of Armed Conflict, 14 May 1954, in force 7 August 1956, 249 UNTS 358.

[62] UNESCO Doc.SHC/MD/5, Annex 1, 10.   [63] UNESCO Doc.SHC/MD/3, para.67.

[64] Cf. O'Keefe, *Commentary*, pp.83–84.

[65] This limitation was implicitly recognised in Iraq's unsuccessful redrafting of Art.4(c) to include 'with the consent of the national competent authorities with full sovereignty of the country of origin of such property': UNESCO Doc.SHC/MD/5, Annex 1, 10.

[66] See Arts.1, 5 and 14, 1970 UNESCO Convention. Art.12 is arguably a concession.

[67] See Arts.3, 5(a), and 6, 1970 UNESCO Convention; and UNESCO Doc.SHC/MD/3, paras.10–13.

This emphasis on the State and its national culture reflects a significant shift in the ongoing and evolving debate as to which community should have custody of certain cultural objects. During this period, the debate oscillated between opposing interpretations (and appropriations) of the notion of the 'common heritage of mankind'.[68] On the one hand, newly independent States stressed that the international community was required to distribute equitably all resources and assist peoples to preserve and develop their cultures. This obligation entailed the transfer of the cultural 'resources' (or property) held in the former imperial collections to their countries of origin. On the other hand, former metropolitan powers and market States argued against the break-up of existing collections, as they had done during the inter-war period. They maintained that the collections of universal survey museums represented the 'genius of all mankind', and these institutions alone were equipped to protect and preserve it for all peoples. Both arguments are necessarily the product of competing national narratives. However, in contrast to the inter-war period, the 1970 UNESCO Convention clearly marked a shift in favour of the position advocated by newly independent States.

The dichotomy between cultural nationalism and cultural internationalism is overly simplistic.[69] It avoids the fundamental purpose promoted by the 1954 Hague Convention – each people's contribution to the culture of the world.[70] The State-centric approach of the 1970 UNESCO Convention significantly impairs its ability to fulfil this principle.[71] Yet, the *travaux* had defined the Convention's purpose as controlling the illicit transfer of the cultural heritage of 'peoples'. The preamble of the preliminary draft had provided that:

> [U]nder Article 27 of the Universal Declaration of Human Rights everyone has the right freely to participate in the cultural life of the community . . . which means that it is incumbent upon States to protect the cultural property existing within their territory against the dangers from the illicit export and transfer of such property.[72]

The United States opposed this interpretation of Article 27 and successfully negotiated its deletion from the final text.[73] However, during the 1990s, the UN Committee on Economic, Social and Cultural Rights confirmed that Article 15(1)(a) of the International Covenant on Economic, Social and Cultural Rights (ICESCR),

---

[68] See Williams, *International*, pp.52ff; A. Strati, Deep Seabed Cultural Property and the Common Heritage of Mankind (1991) 40 ICLQ 859; K. Baslar, *The Concept of the Common Heritage of Mankind in International Law* (The Hague, 1998), pp.296–303; R. W. Mastalir, A Proposal for Protecting the 'Cultural' and 'Property' Aspects of Cultural Property under International Law (1992–3) 16 FILJ 1033 at 1042; and J. Nafziger, Comments on the Relevance of Law and Culture to Cultural Property Law (1983) 10 SJILC 323.

[69] See UNESCO Doc.CUA/123/Add.1, Annex 1, 23 (USA); J. H. Merryman, International Art Law: From Cultural Nationalism to a Common Cultural Heritage (1983) 15 NYUJILP 757; J. H. Merryman, Two Ways of Thinking About Cultural Property (1986) 80 AJIL 831; Mastalir, 'Proposal', 1058–63; and A. Sljivic, Why do you think it's you? An exposition of the jurisprudence underlying the debate between cultural nationalism and cultural internationalism (1997–1998) 31 GWJILE 393.

[70] See UNESCO, The Cultural Heritage of Mankind: A Shared Responsibility, UNESCO Doc.CLT-82/WS/27 (Paris, 1982).

[71] First recital, Preamble, 1970 UNESCO Convention reaffirmed the provisions of the 1966 UNESCO Declaration of the Principles of Cultural Co-operation.

[72] UNESCO Doc.SHC/MD/3, paras.9 and 10.   [73] UNESCO Doc.SHC/MD/5, Annex 1, 22.

which translated this right into treaty form, encompasses a positive duty to protect such heritage from theft and deliberate destruction.[74]

By the late 1970s, indigenous civil rights movements in settler States escalated their challenge to the façade of uniform national concerns and interests within States. For indigenous peoples, decolonisation was the replacement of an overseas occupier with a domestic one. The shift in emphasis to the newly independent States and their national museums was merely part of the return journey for these objects. Their claims for autonomy and restitution of cultural objects would be made against the respective museums of former metropolitan powers and settler States.

Restitution and the UNESCO Intergovernmental Committee

Lyndel V. Prott and Patrick J. O'Keefe note that the deliberations for the 1970 UNESCO Convention put former colonial powers and settler States on notice that national and international laws, relied upon to assert their title to the cultural objects of non-European peoples, were being challenged outright.[75] In 1978, UNESCO established the Intergovernmental Committee for Promoting the Return of Cultural Property to its Countries of Origin or its Restitution in case of Illicit Appropriation (Committee) to facilitate the resolution of restitution claims for objects removed prior to the operation of the Convention.

NIEO proponents, who promoted the restoration of cultural resources to their countries of origin to assist their cultural development, drove the creation of the Committee. The Committee replicates the preoccupations and deficiencies of the 1970 UNESCO Convention. The working methods of the Committee are considered below and its work to date is assessed in Chapter 8.

Restitution and decolonisation

In 1973, the impetus to resolve the status of cultural objects removed during colonial occupation regained momentum with the Third Congress of the International Association of Art Critics in Kinshasa-N'Sele and the Fourth Conference of Non-Aligned Countries in Algiers 1973.[76] These conferences focused on the ongoing effects of colonisation on the cultural heritage of formerly occupied States and the need to remedy the depletion of cultural 'resources' through restitution. The Political Declaration of the Algiers conference stated:

> It is also a question of establishing a genuine independence by eliminating
> foreign monopolies and assuming control over their national resources and
> exploiting them for the benefit of their peoples. The peoples of the
> non-aligned countries wish to safeguard their own personality, to revive and
> enrich their cultural heritage.[77]

---

[74] See UN Docs.E/1991/23, para.79; E/1992/23, paras.310, 312; E/1993/22, para.186; and E/1995/22, para.136.

[75] See Prott and O'Keefe, *Movement*, p.813, §1514.

[76] Resolution of the Fourth Conference of Non-Aligned Countries, Algiers, 1973, UNGA Doc.A/9199, 2. See Resolution of the Fifth Conference of Non-aligned Countries, Colombo, 1976, UNGA Doc.A/31/1976, Annex VI.

[77] UN Doc.A/9199, 2; and UN Doc.A/9330 and Corr.1, para.18.

In response to these conferences a draft UN General Assembly Resolution, prepared by Zaire, read in part:

1. Affirms that the prompt restitution to a developing country of its works of art, monuments and museum pieces by a developing country, without charge, is calculated to strengthen international co-operation inasmuch as it constitutes just reparation for damage done;
2. Recognises the special obligations in this connexion of those countries which had access to such objects only as a result of colonial occupation.[78]

The resultant UNGA Resolution 3187(XXVIII) of 1973 entitled 'Restitution of Works of Art to Countries [which are] Victims of Expropriation', made specific reference in its preamble to UNGA Res.1514(XV).[79] The equivalent Resolution 3.428 of the UNESCO General Conference also drew attention to the 1943 Declaration of London.[80]

UNGA Res.3187(XXVIII) on 'Restitution of Works of Art' invited the Director-General of UNESCO to prepare a report investigating the most suitable methods to facilitate the resolution of these restitution claims.[81] In 1976, a committee of experts was convened by UNESCO to examine and report on probable technical and legal problems, and the most suitable ways and means of facilitating restitution and the fostering of bilateral arrangements for this purpose. The resultant Venice Report recommended that because of the complexity and variety of restitution claims, a body should be established 'by international instrument'.[82] To help implement the findings of the Venice Report, UNESCO requested ICOM to prepare a study on the principles, conditions and means for the restitution or return of cultural property with a view to reconstituting dispersed heritages.[83] Following the completion of the ICOM Study, the Director-General convened a Committee of Experts at Dakar in 1978 to advise on the establishment of the body. The Dakar Report adopted the bulk of the proposals in the ICOM Study and drafted the statute for the proposed body.[84]

---

[78] UN Doc.A/9199, 3–4; and UN Doc.A/BUR/28/SR.216.

[79] UNGA Res.3187(XXVIII), 18 December 1973, 28 UN GAOR Supp.(No.30), 9, UN Doc.A/9030; and UNGA Res.3391(XXX), 19 November 1975. There have been successive UNGA Resolutions and Reports of the Secretary-General to the General Assembly on the work of the UN and UNESCO on this topic to date.

[80] Res.3.428 adopted by the General Conference of UNESCO at its eighteenth session in UNESCO, Committee of Experts to Study the Question of the Restitution of Works of Art, Venice, 23 March 1976, UNESCO Doc.SHC-76/CONF.615/3, Annex 1.

[81] See Anon., A Brief History of the Creation by UNESCO of an Intergovernmental Committee for Promoting the Return of Cultural Property to its Countries of Origin or its Restitution in Case of Illicit Appropriation (1979) 31 *Museum* 59.

[82] UNESCO, Committee of Experts to Study the Question of the Restitution of Works of Art, Venice, Final Report, 21 April 1976, UNESCO Doc.SHC-76/CONF.615/5, para.25–26, 5.

[83] ICOM, Study on the Principles, Conditions and Means for the Restitution or Return of Cultural Property in View of Reconstituting Dispersed Heritages, UNESCO Doc.CC-78/CONF.609/3, Annex 1, and (1979) 31 *Museum* 62.

[84] UNESCO, General Conference 20th session, Proposals of the Director-General with a view to the Establishment of an Intergovernmental Committee entrusted with the Task of Seeking Ways and Means of Facilitating Bilateral Negotiations for the Restitution or Return of Cultural Property to the

Working methods of the UNESCO Intergovernmental Committee

The UNESCO Intergovernmental Committee's establishment was driven by a desire to complete the decolonisation process in respect of the cultural 'property' of formerly colonised peoples. Zaire suggested that 'commonsense, justice and equity' required developed countries, that had considered 'it was quite normal' to recover their cultural objects that had been confiscated by the Nazi regime, 'to restore to the developing countries their works of art'.[85] Indeed, the ILC had alluded to the Committee when excluding 'works of art' from the operation of the 1983 Vienna Convention. UN and UNESCO resolutions on restitution of cultural heritage initially emphasised the reconstitution of national cultural heritage through the restitution of cultural objects removed during colonisation and housed in former imperial museums. By the close of the decade, emphasis had shifted to curbing the illicit traffic of cultural objects generally and attainment of the broader cultural development goals by new States.[86] A similar shift occurred in the work of the Committee. It highlights that the processes and inequalities which facilitate the involuntary removal of cultural objects from occupied communities onto the international art market and into museums continue after decolonisation.

Despite the rhetoric of certain museum officials and art dealers in holding States, the Venice and Dakar Reports did not advocate wholesale repatriation of collections from metropolitan centres.[87] Indeed, this reflected the position of most requesting States which reiterated their need for representative collections.[88] Priority is given to objects of 'ethnographic, historical or religious importance which are of significance for the identity' of the requesting State and that 'only take on their full and true meaning' when they are in 'their original context'.[89] This qualification is more restrictive than the requirement under the 1970 UNESCO Convention (Article 13(d)). It is reminiscent of the qualifications placed on later OIM drafts during the inter-war period at the behest of Anglo-American countries.

The increasing numbers of non-European States in the United Nations and UNESCO led to a concerted challenge to the accepted Western conceptions of 'cultural property'. The wider range of cultural objects covered by the 1970 UNESCO Convention compared to preceding OIM drafts reflected the concerns of these newly independent States. The Intergovernmental Committee Statute's definition of the

---

Countries Having Lost such Property as a Result of Colonial or Foreign Occupation, Final Report, Dakar, 29 September 1978, UNESCO Doc.20C/86, Annex 2, [Dakar Final Report]; UNESCO, Committee of Experts on the Establishment of an Intergovernmental Committee concerning the Restitution or Return of Cultural Property, Dakar, Secretariat Papers, 16 February 1978, UNESCO Doc.CC-78/CONF.609/6 [Dakar Report]; and Annex 1, Draft Statute of the Intergovernmental Committee concerning the Restitution or Return of Cultural Property to Their Country of Origin [Committee Statute].

[85] UN Doc.A/PV.2355, para.241.

[86] See D. N. Thomason, Rolling Back History: The United Nations General Assembly and the Right to Cultural Property (1990) 22 CWRJIL 47 at 55–60.

[87] See Venice Report, para.16; ICOM Study, Annex 1, para.5; Dakar Report, para.4; and Dakar Final Report, paras.12ff.

[88] See E. Eyo, Nigeria (1979) 31 *Museum* 18; and Thomason, 'Rolling Back', 72–76.

[89] Dakar Final Report, para.14. This objective was balanced by the need for adequate technical and financial resources for the care of the physical aspects of cultural materials – 'the primacy of the object': paras.20–22; and ICOM Study, para.12.

objects it covers is a précis of Article 1 of the 1970 Convention.[90] Nonetheless, the Committee has confined itself to restitution claims related to 'objects'. However, there was a growing appreciation of the need to protect all forms of cultural expression, from movable to immovable, tangible to intangible elaborated during the 1982 World Conference on Cultural Policies (Mondiacult).[91] From the 1990s onwards, UNESCO and the UN Working Group on Indigenous Populations have extrapolated upon this broader notion of 'cultural heritage'.

The Statute of the Intergovernmental Committee makes repeated references to the 'country of origin'. The ICOM Study noted that there were often difficulties in defining 'country of origin' because objects usually have a complicated 'life' history and may be important to several communities for varying reasons.[92] ICOM advocated the need for extensive and detailed documentation supporting any application to show that the goal of restitution is to '[reassemble] essential parts of a dispersed heritage'.[93]

The Statute provides that a return request can 'be made for any cultural property which has a fundamental significance from the point of view of the spiritual values and the cultural heritage of the people' (Article 3(2)). The Intergovernmental Committee has used the terms 'State',[94] 'nation',[95] and 'peoples' interchangeably.[96] Like the 1970 UNESCO Convention, it privileges the State. Only States that are Member States or Associate Members of UNESCO can make a claim or sit on the Committee.[97] By contrast, the United States has consistently opposed the exclusive right of governments to claim restitution of cultural objects.[98] Indigenous communities and minorities are wholly reliant on relevant States to represent their interests effectively before it.[99] By privileging the State within its operational framework, the

---

[90] See Venice Report, para.20; Art.3(1), Committee Statute (Statutes of the Intergovernmental Committee for Promoting the Return of Cultural Property); and Art.1, 1970 UNESCO Convention.

[91] UNESCO, World Conference on Cultural Policies (Mondiacult), Mexico City, 26 July–6 August 1982, UNESCO Doc.CLT/MD/1; and Final Report of the World Conference on Cultural Policies, Extract from the Report of Commission II, UNESCO Doc.CLT-83/CONF.216/5, Annex 1, paras.8–15, and Annex 2, Recommendations 51–56.

[92] See ICOM Study, paras.13–14; Dakar Final Report, paras.15–16; and H. Abranches, Report on the Situation in Africa, UNESCO Doc.CLT-83/CONF.216/2, Annex 2, 6–7. See also Art.4, 1970 UNESCO Convention, and Prott and O'Keefe, *Movement*, p.737, §1416; Art.149, United Nations Convention on the Law of the Sea, Montego Bay, 10 December 1982, in force 16 November 1994, 1833 UNTS 3; and (1982) 21 ILM 1261; and Arts.9(5), 11(4), 18(3) and (4), Convention on the Protection of the Underwater Cultural Heritage, Paris, 2 November 2001, UNESCO Doc.MISC/2003/CLT/CH/4; (2002) 41 ILM 37.

[93] ICOM added the words 'without discrimination on socio-cultural, religious or regional grounds on the part of the country of origin': ICOM Study, para.16.

[94] See Intergovernmental Committee for Promoting the Return of Cultural Property to its Countries of Origin or its Restitution in Case of Illicit Appropriation, First Session, Report by the General Conference on the discussions concerning the working methods and functions of the Committee, 9 October 1979, UNESCO Doc.CC-79/CONF.206/4, Annex, para.334.

[95] Report of the Intergovernmental Committee for Promoting the Return of Cultural Property to its Countries of Origin or its Restitution in Case of Illicit Appropriation, 11 August 1980, UNESCO Doc.21C/83, para.3.

[96] See UNESCO Doc.21C/83, paras.11 and 14; and Records of the Twenty-First Session of UNESCO General Conference, Belgrade, September-October 1980, UNESCO Doc.CC-81/CONF.203/4, Annex 1, para.251.

[97] Art.3(2), Committee Statute. See UNESCO Doc.CC-79/CONF.206/4, Annex, para.343.

[98] See UN Doc.A/C.3/31/SR.27, para.6; and UN Doc.A/46/PV.35, 52, Rockefeller (USA).

[99] Dakar Final Report, para.35.

Committee significantly undermines the ability of non-State groups to exercise the collective right of all peoples to self-determination and economic, social and cultural development.

UNESCO demonstrated a marked preference for bilateral negotiations between State members or their institutions to resolve claims for the restitution of cultural objects removed prior to the operation of the 1970 UNESCO Convention.[100] The Guidelines for the Use of the Standard Form concerning Requests for Return or Restitution drafted by ICOM and adopted by the Committee presupposes two parties and requires the failure of bilateral negotiations to trigger the Committee's intervention.[101] The primary reason for this bias was the belief that each claim was unique and could only be dealt with on a case-by-case basis.[102] This method of resolving such claims has been the preferred Anglo-American position since the mid-century. It arguably suppresses the context, particularly the colonial policies and processes, which led to the removal of the objects from their communities of origin. This exclusive reliance on former metropolitan powers voluntarily entering bilateral agreements is extraordinary given the reluctance historically of these States to consider restitution claims. In addition, the power between former metropolitan powers and the newly independent States remains unequal. This position is exacerbated by the Committee's declaration that 'moral and ethical matters not legal' govern its work.[103] Given the consistent State practice covering the restitution of cultural objects following territorial redistribution since 1815, the reference of the Committee to moral rights is regressive and counterproductive.

The inability of the Committee to resolve claims for objects removed during colonisation was flagged by the defeat of the Latin American push for the recognition of alternate relief. Augusto Ferrero suggested certain objects are so intrinsic to the identity of a nation that their acquisition by another State or individual as a result of conquest, occupation or illicit trade is a violation of the right of a State to exist.[104] Further, he maintained that a State that is an aggressor or beneficiary incurs a liability because of a breach of a duty, and is obligated to make reparation for any resulting injury. He advocated that peoples whose cultural heritage has been depleted by colonial or foreign occupation should be entitled to compensation or the provision of an object of like value when restitution is not viable. The first option was denounced by

---

[100] Res.3.428; Venice Report, para.26(a); ICOM Study, para.37(e); Dakar Report, paras.17–19; Dakar Final Report, para.5; and Art.4(1) and (2), Committee Statute.

[101] Intergovernmental Committee for Promoting the Return of Cultural Property to Its Countries of Origin or Its Restitution in Case of Illicit Appropriation, Fourth Session, Draft Guidelines for the Use of the 'Standard Form Concerning Requests for Return or Restitution', 22 February 1985, UNESCO Doc.CLT-85/CONF.202/3, 1.

[102] Venice Report, para.23; and ICOM Study, 9–10.

[103] UNESCO Doc.CC-79/CONF.206/4, Annex, para.348.

[104] A. Ferrero, Studying the possibility of supplying, by way of compensation, a piece of cultural property of different origin and of similar value when the restitution of cultural property claimed appears impracticable or does not correspond to the wishes of the requesting country, 15 November 1979, UNESCO Doc.CC-79/CONF.206/3, Add., Annex. See *Factory at Chorzów, Merits, (1928) PCIJ, ser.A, No.17*, p.47; and Arts.31, 34–37, Articles on Responsibility of States for Internationally Wrongful Acts, UNGA Res.58/83, 12 December 2001; and J. Crawford, *The International Law Commission's Articles on State Responsibility: Introduction, Text, and Commentaries* (Cambridge, 2002), pp.201–39.

several African and Asian delegates in the General Assembly. The Madagascar representative maintained restitution was 'an obligation' of holding States and compensation could not be a 'final solution' because it could be construed as a 'renunciation [by] some States of their legitimate rights'.[105] Ferrero argued compensation did not mean an abandonment of the principle of restitution of cultural objects. Rather, it is a form of restitution that should be available in specific circumstances and where agreed between the parties.

Conversely, former metropolitan powers and market States strove for a clear delineation of the application of the term 'restitution'.[106] These States resented the 'psychological aspects of the feelings of guilt associated with the act of restitution' and illicit acquisition.[107] They lobbied for the use of the more neutral term 'return' for objects acquired prior to the operation of the 1970 UNESCO Convention, with 'restitution' applying to objects removed illegally following its operation. Hence, the convoluted title of the UNESCO Committee. This division was a calculated effort by officials from some museums in former metropolitan capitals to depoliticise and de-historicise the circumstances surrounding the formation of their collections. Officials from holding museums were at pains to argue that their title to these objects was validly obtained in accordance with laws applicable at the time of acquisition.[108] The Allied governments had explicitly rejected such arguments in respect of Nazi confiscations, especially when cultural objects were removed pursuant to discriminatory and genocidal policies.

The UNESCO Committee dismissed the application of restitution-in-kind on grounds that have become familiar in claims for restitution of cultural objects. It maintained that such relief was akin to reparations. It added that its duty was above all to deal with requests from States seeking to assemble a representative collection of their cultural heritage.[109] The Committee's rejection of these remedies was a measure of the continued strength of universal survey museums in the national imagining of certain former metropolitan powers. Nonetheless, compensation has been endorsed recently, as an alternative, in a number of fora. The UK Spoliation Advisory Panel, which considers applications against British national collections for objects removed during the Nazi era, recommended an *ex gratia* payment in the first claim before it.[110] Also, the UNESCO Draft Principles relating to Cultural Objects Displaced in relation to the Second World War endorse compensation, either monetary or contribution to cultural development, where an object has been destroyed and a replacement cannot be found or agreed upon by the parties.[111] In addition, under the 2001 Yugoslav Succession Agreement compensation must be paid for tangible

[105] UN Doc.A/C.3/35/SR.41, para.29. See UN Doc.A/C.3/35/SR.39, para.7 (Senegal).
[106] Venice Report; and ICOM Draft Guidelines for Standard Form, 10ff.
[107] UN Doc.A/CN.4/322, para.51.   [108] See ICOM Study, para.27.
[109] UNESCO Doc.21C/83, paras.29, 31. The Peruvian draft resolution covering compensation (UNESCO Doc.DR.346) was unsuccessful: UNESCO Doc.CC-81/CONF.203/4, Annex 1, 2, para.257. Cf. UNESCO Committee of Experts recommendations for Second World War claims above.
[110] Report of the Spoliation Advisory Panel in respect of a Painting now in the Possession of the Tate Gallery (2001 HC 111), p.19.
[111] UNESCO Doc.CLT-2002/CONF/602/3, 10–11.

movable property removed without appropriate authorisation and which cannot be returned.[112]

The ICOM Study recommended that the Committee have two guiding principles: coherence of reconstituted heritage; and the primacy of the object.[113] In defining the Committee's goals in these terms, the Study neutralised the politically charged nature of the restitution debate during the 1970s and 80s by merging the concerns of the source and market States. Holding museums in former metropolitan capitals steadfastly maintained that preservation of the object according to acceptable (Western) standards must be the primary objective. They pointed to the lack of facilities and resources in developing States, to repel restitution claims.[114] By the 1970s, source States directly challenged these suppositions by arguing that this underdevelopment was a legacy of the colonial policies. Therefore, they maintained that developed States and the international community had a duty to assist them in reversing the effects of these past policies. In pursuing this course, however, they strove to observe standards of preserving, displaying and interpreting their cultures set by former metropolitan powers.[115]

The ICOM Study espoused a holistic approach to restitution that included the return of related data, the financing and construction of facilities and the training of staff. During the 1970s, this notion of restitution as a process began to permeate relations between Australian museums, Papua New Guinea and indigenous peoples in Oceania generally.

Working towards a new international cultural order

The plea by the UNESCO Director-General Amadou-Mahtar M'Bow, quoted in part at the commencement of this chapter, was delivered on the eve of the Committee's first session. For M'Bow, the first and to date the only African Director-General, the appeal became part of a wider push for cultural renewal and the (re)claiming of cultural memory by formerly colonised peoples. His call had particular resonance in the Asia Pacific because of the scale of cultural loss visited upon communities in this region by European colonisation.

Like the first phase of empire dismantling following the First World War, the establishment of a national museum and the possession of certain cultural objects fuelled the rhetoric of the independence era. Jim Specht of the Australian Museum keenly observed that during this latter period the act of repatriating cultural objects was as politicised as the act of requesting restitution.[116] This dynamic was set against a period of growing nationalism in the Asia Pacific, a form of nationalism

---

[112] Art.3(3), Annex A, Yugoslav Succession Agreement.

[113] See ICOM Study, Annex 1, paras.9–20.

[114] Museum practitioners and communities from requesting States argue holding museums are not necessarily the best equipped to conserve the cultural heritage of non-European States because they lack funding and the requisite knowledge to properly conserve materials peculiar to these cultures: Abranches, 'Report', 8. Tellingly, the 1990s refit of the Victoria and Albert Museum Asian galleries was funded by the relevant Asian governments and private benefactors.

[115] See UN Doc.A/34/PV.51(1979), para.60 (Ecuador).

[116] Interview with J. Specht, Head of Anthropology Department, Australian Museum, Sydney, 24 February 1999.

Figure 7.2 Aboriginal Gallery, Australian Museum, Sydney, 1958.

distinguishable from that exhibited in Europe. In their haste to build a unified sense of nation, these newly independent States often internalised their former colonial occupier's means of preserving and developing their own cultures.

This final section examines how Australia, and its museums, responded to changing relations with the inhabitants of its external colonial territories and indigenous peoples within its own borders. It is shown that, although most Asian Pacific States have been slow to ratify the 1970 UNESCO Convention, it instigated an intense debate concerning the past and present acquisition policies of museums.[117] Specht and MacLulich note that this discussion inevitably led to 'the failure of former colonial powers to exercise their power and responsibilities to prevent illegal exports during their time of colonial domination'.[118] This climate had a significant effect on the national cultural policies of Papua New Guinea and Australia, and these international preoccupations affected Australia's relationship with Papua New Guinea even after the grant of independence.

[117] As at 2005, there were 106 State parties to the Convention with 18 from the Asia Pacific region, at http://www.unesco.org/culture.
[118] J. Specht and C. MacLulich, Changes and Challenges: The Australian Museum and Indigenous Communities, in P. McManus (ed.), *Archaeological Displays and the Public* (London, 1996), p.27 at p.29.

Figure 7.3 Aboriginal Gallery, Australian Museum, Sydney, 1958.

Papua New Guinea and Australia

In 1977, the National Museum and Art Gallery was opened in Port Moresby with financial and technical assistance provided by the administering power, Australia.[119] Papua New Guinea has approximately 700 linguistic and tribal groups and has experienced multiple waves of foreign and colonial occupation.[120] The PNG government developed several institutions to nurture a national identity based on a combination of indigenous elements. Tribal groups were encouraged to maintain their distinctive cultures as living entities with the creation of a number of regional museums.[121]

---

[119] See R. Kaiku, Restoration of national cultural property: The case of Papua New Guinea, in R. Edwards and J. Stewart (eds.), *Preserving Indigenous Cultures: A New Role for Museums* (Canberra, 1980), p.175 at pp.179ff; Specht, 'Australian'; B. Craig, Samting Bilong Tumbuna: The Collection, Documentation and Preservation of the Material Cultural Heritage of Papua New Guinea, Ph.D thesis, Flinders University of South Australia (1996), pp.216ff; and M. Busse, The National Cultural Property (Preservation) Act, in K. Whimp and M. Busse (eds.), *Protection of Intellectual, Biological and Cultural Property in Papua New Guinea* (Canberra, 2000), pp.81–94.

[120] See L. Groube, The Ownership of Diversity: The Problem of Establishing a National History in a Land of Nine Hundred Ethnic Groups, in I. McBryde (ed.), *Who Owns the Past? Papers from the Annual Symposium of the Australian Academy of Humanities* (Melbourne, 1985), pp.49ff.

[121] See A. L. Kaeppler, Paradise Regained: Envisaging Culture as National Identity, in F. E. S. Kaplan (ed.), *Museums and the Making of 'Ourselves': The Role of Objects in National Identity* (London, 1994), p.34; Kaiku, 'Restoration', p.180; and D. Smidt, Establishing Museums in Developing Countries: The Case of Papua New Guinea, in S. M. Mead (ed.), *Exploring the Visual Art of Oceania* (Honolulu, 1979), p.392.

The development of a national museum with a representative national collection of objects was a central plank in the assertion of an autonomous national identity for newly independent States. Like many new States endeavouring to build a national collection, Papua New Guineans became increasingly aware of large gaps in their holdings which could only be remedied through recourse to repatriation requests, increased emphasis on curbing illicit traffic of cultural property and active field-collecting programmes.[122]

During the mid 1960s, the exponential increase in cultural losses caused sufficient alarm to result in the passage of the Papua New Guinea National Cultural Property (Preservation) Act 1965.[123] This Act entrusted the trustees of the National Museum with the authority to control the acquisition and transfer of cultural objects. However, there was little effective implementation of this Act until the mid 1970s when nationals were appointed to representative positions in the government and on the boards of cultural institutions. The opening of the National Museum and Art Gallery, the employment of locally trained nationals, and the education of the populace led to an increased consciousness at all levels of society of the effects of illicit trade.[124]

Following PNG independence, the Australian government acknowledged its continuing obligations to protect the cultural heritage of its former colonial territory. The Australian Customs Service and numerous Australian museums assisted the PNG authorities, especially the National Museum and Art Gallery, in their efforts to curb illicit traffic in cultural materials.[125] However, Australian museums were more reticent in their response to restitution claims.[126]

The effort to negotiate the return of collections from Australian institutions recommenced in earnest following PNG independence and the passage of the Papua New Guinea Cultural Development Act 1972.[127] Chief Minister Michael Somare acknowledged that restitution was only one part of the campaign to reverse the effects of colonialism and revitalise the national culture. He noted:

> Many of our ways, our arts and our beliefs have already been forgotten . . . I believe that the Museum has a vital role to play in preserving that culture. The museum must not be a place where our past is stored and displayed, but must act as an inspiration to our people in the effort to keep our culture alive.[128]

Yet, what was being (re)collected by these museums were national cultures without memory. They strove to collect and display the cultural objects of indigenous groups to signify the vitality, diversity and unity of PNG national identity. These cultural resources were deployed to manufacture a collective national memory and cultural identity which had not previously existed.

---

[122] See Kaiku, 'Restoration', p.175; and Smidt, 'Establishing', p.392.
[123] See Craig, 'Samting', pp.109ff; Kaiku, 'Restoration', pp.178–81; and S. Eoe, Papua New Guinea, in L. V. Prott and J. Specht (eds.), *Protection or Plunder? Safeguarding the Future of Our Cultural Heritage* (Canberra, 1989), pp.53ff.
[124] See Kaiku, 'Restoration', pp.179–81; and Craig, 'Samting', p.154.
[125] See R. Hope, *Report on the National Estate* (Canberra, 1974), p.252, para.8.134; interview with J. Specht; Specht, 'Australian', 30; and Eoe, 'Papua', p.54.
[126] See Specht, 'Australian', 28–29.   [127] See Craig, 'Samting', pp.304ff.
[128] D. Newton, Old Wine in New Bottles, and the Reverse, in Kaplan (ed.), *Museums*, p.269 at p.273.

Indigenous Australians and Australian national identity

Like that of its newly independent neighbour, Australian national cultural policy was undergoing a significant shift during the mid 1970s. Australia's altering national self-identity was reflected in the federal government's transfer of focus away from (colonial) British ties to the Asia Pacific region.[129] The Whitlam Labor government instigated a series of initiatives that stressed the importance of legislative and governmental protection of Australia's national cultural and natural heritage.[130]

In the face of a growing indigenous civil rights movement, the federal government pursued a pluralist cultural agenda. The impetus in Australia for indigenous cultural renewal was fuelled not by sympathetic non-indigenous policymakers but by Indigenous Australians themselves. They demonstrated against the representation of their cultures by state museums and demanded the return of ancestral remains to their communities.[131] As with other occupied peoples, Indigenous Australian efforts to repossess their traditional culture and history were entwined with claims for self-determination and land rights.

The formation of the Aboriginal Arts Board (AAB) in 1973 marked a significant step in the campaign to rebuild and strengthen indigenous cultures.[132] The Board was made up of Indigenous Australians and was funded by the Australian government. The AAB's policies and initiatives perceived Indigenous Australian cultures as 'living cultures' that were not suspended in a primordial past. It strove to encourage indigenous communities' decision-making in the preservation, interpretation and development of their cultures.

Australia's altering relations with its indigenous peoples was reflected in the federal government's proposal for a national museum contained in the 1975 Report of the Committee of Inquiry on Museums and National Collections (Pigott Report).[133] The report marked an early move on the road to remembering and acknowledging past relations between indigenous and non-indigenous peoples within Australia. It bore the hallmarks of the increased indigenous activism and the Australian government's responsiveness to indigenous concerns. It has had ongoing ramifications for the relationship between Indigenous Australians and Australian museums to the present day.

Before the 1970s, while indigenous peoples themselves were literally 'not counted' as part of the Australian nation, the legislative protection of 'Aboriginal' cultural objects was considered essential for the Australian national patrimony.[134] The

---

[129] See T. Bennett, *Out of Which Past? Critical Reflection on Australian Museum and Heritage Policy* (Brisbane, 1988); and T. Griffith *Hunters and Collectors: The Antiquarian Imagination in Australia* (Cambridge, 1996), pp.195–278.

[130] See Hope, *Report*; and P. H. Pigott, *Museums in Australia 1975: Report of the Committee of Inquiry on Museums and National Collections including the Report of the Planning Committee on the Gallery of Aboriginal Australia* (Canberra, 1975).

[131] R. Edwards, Introduction, in Edwards and Stewart, *Preserving*, p.2.   [132] *Ibid.*

[133] See Pigott, *Museums*; and M. Anderson and A. Reeves, Contested Identities: Museums and the Nation in Australia, in Kaplan (ed.), *Museums*, pp.45ff. Pigott recommended ratification of the 1970 UNESCO Convention and the passage of enabling legislation: *Museums*, pp.94–99.

[134] See E. Roberts, *The Preservation of Australia's Aboriginal Heritage: Report of National Seminar on Aboriginal Antiquities in Australia May 1972* (Canberra, 1975); and UNESCO Doc.CUA/123, Add.1, 1–3.

consent of Indigenous Australians was not requested either for their 'acceptance' as Australian citizens or for the physical and theoretical absorption of their cultural objects in the formation of Australian cultural identity. Indigenous cultural material continued to figure prominently in the Australian national narrative espoused by the Pigott Report.

The report proposed a Gallery of Aboriginal Australia as part of the national museum.[135] When he announced the Pigott Inquiry, Senator Lionel Bowen recalled that: '[N]either the Aboriginal people nor more recent Australians can draw much pride or encouragement from existing displays of their unique history, culture or achievements'.[136] It was hoped the gallery would enable Indigenous Australians to re-collect their cultural heritage and identity, and to unify all Australians in their appreciation of these cultures and its peoples. To have the former without the latter was, in the report's words, 'merely a gesture of restitution – repairing a guilty conscience'.[137]

The gallery had a lengthy gestation period and tumultuous reception. The National Museum of Australia opened its doors in 2001 with Indigenous Australian Dawn Casey as its director. The Gallery of Aboriginal and Torres Strait Islander Peoples stretches from so-called pre-history to the present covering the effects of European contact on Indigenous Australians and their environment, as recommended by the report.[138] The new museum quickly came under sustained attack from conservative commentators and politicians who argued that it reflected the so-called 'black-arm band' view of Australian history. These criticisms led to a review and revision of some displays.[139]

Pigott conceded the aversion many Indigenous Australians felt towards existing museums and cultural institutions whose actions have often caused offence, especially in relation to secret sacred material.[140] For this reason, the report strongly recommended community liaison and the employment of Indigenous Australians by the gallery. It also recommended that they be trained in current (Western) conservation techniques and that traditional indigenous conservation practices be respected and observed where applicable.[141] These goals were reaffirmed in the 1993 national museums policy detailed in Chapter 9. Although the report did not refer directly to repatriation, it envisaged that the large collection of Indigenous Australian artefacts and skeletal remains held by the Australian Institute of Aboriginal Studies would be transferred to the new gallery under the care of indigenous employees. Today, the museum has a specialist repatriation unit to facilitate the return of ancestral remains and secret sacred objects to Indigenous Australian communities. Also, it is

---

[135] D. J. Mulvaney, Report for Proposed Gallery of Aboriginal Australia: Report of the Planning Committee in Pigott, *Museums*, n.p. See W. E. H. Stanner, Gallery of Southern Man (1965), in W. E. H. Stanner, *White Man Got No Dreaming: Essays 1938–1973* (Canberra, 1979), pp.192ff; D. J. Mulvaney, The Proposed Gallery of Aboriginal Australia, in Edwards and Stewart (eds.), *Preserving*, pp.72ff; and T. Bennett, *The Birth of the Museum: History, Theory, Politics* (London, 1995), pp.148–152.

[136] Mulvaney, *Report*, p.5.   [137] See Mulvaney, *Report*, p.7, para.2.2.

[138] See Pigott, *Museums*, p.16; and Mulvaney, *Report*, pp.10–11.

[139] NMA, *Review of the National Museum of Australia Its Exhibitions and Public Programs* (Canberra, 2003), p.20.

[140] See Mulvaney, *Report*, p.16, para.3.12.   [141] See Mulvaney, *Report*, pp.15–18.

the 'prescribed authority' for the safekeeping of remains where appropriate indigenous custodians cannot be located.[142]

Prior to 1978, Australian museums had generally been slow to respond to changes which were occurring at national and international levels. In an effort to encourage interaction between museums and Indigenous Australians, the Aboriginal Arts Board with the Australian National Commission for UNESCO organised a conference entitled 'Preserving Indigenous Cultures: A New Role for Museums' (1978 Adelaide Conference).[143] Specht noted that criticisms levelled by indigenous participants from the Asia Pacific and Canada during the seminar put Australian museums on notice that they could no longer unilaterally determine how indigenous cultures represented in their collections were preserved and displayed.[144] Pacific Island delegates argued that they should be guardians and promoters of their own cultures. They demanded that their national museums be organised by nationals and not expatriates. Also, they must be recognised as active research collaborators, not as passive objects of research.[145] The seminar concluded that for most Pacific peoples, museums needed to address key issues including: loss of cultural identity; lack of representative collections; and inadequate resources to establish suitable institutions to encourage revitalisation of local cultural traditions.[146]

The seminar recommended the passage of legislation and provision of adequate funding by all levels of government to ensure: the establishment of community museums by indigenous peoples; the regulation of transfer of national cultural property; the training of indigenous peoples in museums; the development and marketing of indigenous arts and crafts under the control of the communities themselves; and the establishment of a regional fund for the repatriation of cultural materials from private and overseas collections. Member States of UNESCO were encouraged to return items of national cultural heritage to countries of origin. Finally, the assimilation of indigenous cultures by the dominant culture was opposed and the recognition of land rights claims was viewed as essential to the prevention of assimilation.[147]

Indigenous delegates condemned national museums of UNESCO Member States, particularly those in Australia, because of their colonial collecting practices. These delegates maintained that their core concerns were the same whether the State was newly independent or a settler State. Further, they noted that this dynamic was not limited to formal colonial relations but extended to third-party States whose institutions were also beneficiaries of colonial policies.

---

[142] Aboriginal and Torres Strait Islander Heritage Protection Act 1984 (Cth) (ATSIHP Act), ss.20–21.
[143] See Edwards and Stewart (eds.), *Preserving*.
[144] See J. Specht, Museums and the Cultural Heritage in the Pacific Islands, in M. Spriggs *et al.* (eds.), *A Community of Culture: The People and Prehistory of the Pacific* (Canberra, 1993), p.185; and Specht and MacLulich, 'Changes', p.30.
[145] See E. Bonshek, Objects, People and Identity: An Interplay between Past and Present at the Australian Museum, in T. Lin (ed.), *Proceedings of the International Conference on Anthropology and the Museum* (Taipei, 1995), p.261 at p.267.
[146] See Edwards, 'Introduction', pp.6–7; and A. Wendt, Reborn to Belong: Culture and Colonialism in the Pacific, in Edwards and Stewart (eds.), *Preserving*, pp.25ff.
[147] See Seminar Recommendations, in Edwards and Stewart (eds.), *Preserving*, pp.9–17.

Figure 7.4 Aboriginal Gallery, Australian Museum, Sydney, early 1980s.

Australian Museum: change in policy and practice

In response to the 1970 UNESCO Convention and the ICOM General Assembly Code of Professional Ethics 1986,[148] in the mid-1970s the Australian Museum's Board of Trustees approved a Code of Acquisition of Cultural Property.[149] The trustees acknowledged the Convention was ineffective because most market States, including Australia, had not ratified it. The museum articulated obligations that went beyond those contained within the 1970 UNESCO Convention. It refused to value, authenticate or accept loans of objects illicitly removed from the country of origin. At a State's request, it would take steps to acquire and return the item to the legal owner in the country of origin; or hold it on trust until the owner became

---

[148] ICOM, *Ethics of Acquisition* (Paris, 1970). See J. A. R. Nafziger, Regulation by the International Council of Museums: An Example of the Role of Non-Governmental Organizations in the Transnational Legal Process (1972) 2 DJILP 231.

[149] Anon., The Acquisition of Cultural Property: New Australian Museum Policy (1975) 10 *Mankind* 279. See T. D. Nicholson, The Australian Museum and the Field Museum adopt Policy Statements governing Collections (1975) 18 *Curator* 296; Bonshek, 'Objects', pp.261–82; and J. Specht *et al.*, Working Together on Issues of Access: Indigenous Peoples and the Australian Museum, in CAMA, *Something for Everyone: Access to Museums* (Adelaide, 1991), pp.185–88. The Australian Museum policy drew heavily from the University of Pennsylvania Museum of Archaeology and Anthropology declaration handed down the preceding year: personal communication, Jim Specht, 27 March 2005.

known. However, the policy affected objects exported or excavated from the country of origin only after 1 January 1975.[150]

The policy was applicable explicitly to the cultural heritage of Indigenous Australians and peoples in administered territories. It noted that communities whose cultural heritage was at greatest risk were unable to ratify the Convention because of their continued occupation. It approved initiatives designed to address indigenous concerns raised during the 1978 Adelaide Conference.[151] For example, it sought federal funding to employ and train Indigenous Australians in the museum and outlying cultural centres. In addition, the trustees resolved to increase community liaison in respect of the disposal of secret sacred material and museum displays generally.

During the 1970s, the Australian Museum received a number of requests from various Pacific Island States for the restitution of cultural materials. As a consequence of extensive negotiations, the museum's trustees granted several 'gifts' from its collections to Papua New Guinea, the Solomon Islands and Vanuatu following their independence.[152] The terms of return, often predicated on the attainment of facilities judged on Western standards, and the choice of objects to be returned were almost exclusively dictated by the holding museums during these early restitution negotiations. The Australian Museum's governing legislation empowers its trustees to dispose of its property as they see fit, subject to certain guidelines.[153] To date, the museum has conducted all negotiations concerning restitution on a direct museum-to-museum basis without recourse to diplomatic channels.[154]

In 1972, Dirk Smidt, Director of the National Museum and Art Gallery in Port Moresby, approached the Council of Australian Museum Directors with a request for the return of the MacGregor collection of Papuan artefacts collected in the 1890s. The collection had been housed at the Australian Museum from 1915 to 1934. Smidt also flagged other possible restitution claims. Various events prior to the request made it difficult for officials of the Australian Museum to refuse the request outright.[155] Consequently, Smidt was advised by the Australian Museum's director Frank Talbot that the museum would return selected objects once new facilities were completed. On 27 June 1977, at the opening of the National Museum and Art Gallery in Port Moresby, a representative of the Australian Museum delivered seventeen artefacts from its anthropological collections to the museum.[156] Like many developing States, Papua New Guinea sought a collaborative approach to restitution requests beyond the mere act of physically transporting an object from one institution

---

[150] The museum would consult with the competent authorities of that State before acquiring objects illegally removed prior to that date: Anon., 'Acquisition', 279.

[151] Australian Museum, *Annual Report 1979–1980* (Sydney, 1980), p.13.

[152] Interview with J. Specht; Specht, 'Australian', 28–30; and Specht and MacLulich, 'Changes', pp.37–38.

[153] See Australian Museum Trust Act 1975 (NSW), ss.9 and 10; and Specht, 'Australian', 29–30.

[154] Interview with J. Specht.

[155] Including the opportunistic collecting expeditions of Australia's Commonwealth Arts Advisory Board, the increased effectiveness of the territory's customs officials to control illicit trade, and the Australian grant for the development of a purpose-built museum: Specht, 'Australian', 28–29; and Craig, 'Samting', pp.195ff.

[156] Australian Museum, *Report of the Australian Museum Trust for the year ending 30 June 1977* (Sydney, 1978), p.28.

to another.[157] The museum officials of some former metropolitan powers, like the Australian Museum, were slowly taking steps towards the realisation of this equitable dialogue.

The initial returns were objects selected by the Australian Museum, and approved by the PNG National Museum, to 'fill known gaps or deficiencies in its collections'.[158] Far from depleting the museum's collections, the Australian Museum received a gift from Papua New Guinea 'maintaining a balanced reciprocity in accordance with Melanesian custom'.[159] The museum acknowledges that: '[its] experience is that repatriation is not about losing collections. It is about building mutual respect and goodwill, with positive outcomes for all parties.'[160]

In practice, this shift in attitude by the Australian Museum during the 1970s primarily benefited newly independent States in Oceania rather than Indigenous Australians.[161] The driving force of the debate concerning the restitution of cultural objects removed during colonisation in the international arena came from newly independent States. These States, and UNESCO, did not primarily rationalise these claims on the basis of State succession or State responsibility for past international wrongs. Instead, restitution was justified for the (re)constitution of 'representative' national collections, viewed as intrinsic to their right to self-determination and cultural development. Yet, newly independent States, when articulating a unified national identity, internalised standards of preserving, displaying and interpreting their cultures that had been set by former metropolitan powers.

The cultural objects of indigenous peoples and minorities within their borders became a cultural resource to be reclaimed from the State's colonial predecessor in the pursuit of national economic and cultural development. For indigenous communities, decolonisation replaced one occupier, the former colonial power, with the newly independent State. Increasingly, the claims by national museums to such cultural objects were challenged by indigenous communities and minorities from whom they were originally collected. By the close of the 1970s, the restitution debate had shifted from newly independent States to indigenous communities within and across existing States. Indigenous peoples themselves agitated for a process of national (re)collection of the effects of colonial policies and practices on indigenous communities, individuals and cultures. This renegotiation of the relationship between museums and indigenous peoples from the 1980s onwards is explored in the following chapter.

---

[157] See G. Mosuwadoga, Restitution of Collections (1980) 5 *COMA Bulletin* 6–8.
[158] See Specht, 'Australian', 29. Objects which had been returned since this initial restitution have been selected by mutual agreement between the two institutions: interview with J. Specht.
[159] See Specht and MacLulich, 'Changes', p.37.
[160] Australian Museum, 'Repatriation at the Australian Museum' (display panel), entrance foyer, 2004.
[161] Specht, 'Australian', 30.

Figure 8.1 Aboriginal Australia gallery, Australian Museum, Sydney, 1985.

8

Indigenous peoples and restitution as a process

> How shall we redeem it from the guilty awareness that these acts of genocide and attempted genocide were being enacted most vigorously at the very time when our own white Australian culture was being conceived and born, and that its very growth presupposed the termination of a black culture.[1]

> [Y]ou have come as invaders, you have tried to destroy our culture, you have built your fortunes upon the lands and bodies of our people . . . We say that it is our past, our culture and heritage and forms part of our present life. As such it is ours to control and it is ours to share on our terms.[2]

In the late twentieth century, indigenous peoples built upon the developments of the decolonisation period to remind the international community that their colonial occupation had not ceased, nor had their right to self-determination been realised. Their campaign for self-determination included the return of land, ancestral remains and cultural heritage. This broader understanding of the restitution of cultural objects as an essential part of the process of cultural renewal and development is the subject of this chapter.

Indigenous peoples strove to reclaim their place and identity, by reversing the 'mechanisms of forgetfulness' that were fostered by colonial expansion.[3] It was suggested earlier that newly independent States and former metropolitan powers were 'cultures without memory'. Following independence, new States sought to unify all territories and peoples through the creation of a national identity, whilst metropolitan powers often resisted acknowledging the impact of colonial policies on their former subjects. Their aversion to claims for the restitution of cultural objects held by their museums exemplified this resistance.

However, the restitution claims of indigenous communities forced these States to confront policies and practices of discrimination, assimilation and genocide which had ongoing effects on their peoples and cultures. The revisiting of the post-Second World War Allied restitution programme with the re-emergence of the claims of Holocaust survivors and their heirs from the 1990s reinforced calls for moral restitution as well as material restitution. The adoption of this second rationale for the restitution of cultural objects in international law – as a means of ameliorating or

---

[1] B. Smith, *1980 Boyer Lectures: The Spectre of Truganini* (Sydney, 1980), p.10.
[2] R. Langford, Our Heritage – Your Playground (1983) 16 *Australian Archaeology* 1 at 2.
[3] Smith, *Boyer*, p.17.

reversing internationally wrongful acts – is also fundamental to the claims of indigenous peoples.

This chapter details how the initiatives of the 1970s were gradually implemented by States in a manner which acknowledged their duty to indigenous peoples but also reaffirmed central tenets of colonialism. First, there is an explanation of how indigenous groups pushed for a voice within existing international structures to address their claims for self-determination and the restitution of their cultural heritage. Second, there is an examination of the work of the UNESCO Intergovernmental Committee and its response to the claims of indigenous peoples and Holocaust survivors and their heirs. Next, the implementation of the 1970 UNESCO Convention into domestic law by the United States, Australia and United Kingdom is considered. Finally, the early efforts of Indigenous Australians to renegotiate their relationship with the Australian museum community, as part of their campaign for cultural autonomy and revitalisation, is briefly examined.

Indigenous peoples, self-determination and cultural rights

The development of international law following the Second World War privileged the State and the individual as subjects. Individual members of non-State groups were to be protected within the international human rights framework. However, the exclusivity of this dichotomy compromised the protection of the collective identity of such groups. This deficiency was exacerbated with the restrictions placed on the exercise of self-determination during decolonisation. The compromises imposed on these developments in international law were aligned with the integration and assimilation policies of certain States. These policies were primary 'mechanisms of forgetfulness' fostered to de-historicise and depoliticise the differences between indigenous peoples and the dominant culture.

By the late twentieth century, indigenous peoples challenged these mechanisms nationally and internationally. This section outlines the earlier responses by the United Nations to these challenges. It is clear that from this early stage, the question of restitution of indigenous cultural heritage, held by former metropolitan and national museums, was a central concern. Indigenous organisations confronted their exclusion from participation in international organisations and the development of international law on several fronts, including:

(1) disputing the limitations of the decolonisation process;
(2) utilising the principles of non-discrimination to expose their plight within existing States;
(3) agitating for the establishment of an international forum and declaration to address their concerns and rights; and
(4) advocating the resuscitation of the notion of collective or group rights.

In short, indigenous peoples used the existing international law discourse to expose the adverse effects of ongoing colonial occupation on their communities and cultures.

The circumstances in which the international community would tolerate the exercise of the right to self-determination during decolonisation thwarted the aspirations of indigenous peoples and other groups within existing States. During the 1970s, indigenous organisations were becoming increasingly vocal on the international stage.[4] They challenged the new international order which was created by the unfinished project of decolonisation and which reaffirmed their colonial occupation. They maintained that the definition of 'peoples' in Chapter XI of the UN Charter must include indigenous peoples.[5] Indigenous representatives argued that their relations with the State or States in which they found themselves should be governed by international law not domestic law. To symbolically drive home this point, in January 1972, the Aboriginal Tent Embassy was erected on the lawns of the Australian federal Parliament House. In the years that followed, Indigenous Australians have unsuccessfully lobbied for the negotiation of a treaty with the Australian federal government.

Indigenous organisations were acutely aware of Western States' aversion to minority guarantees and therefore pursued their objectives within the human rights framework, particularly racial discrimination. Settler States had promoted the principle of non-discrimination and individual human rights to neutralise the claims of indigenous peoples and minorities within their borders. However, the UN investigation of discriminatory practices became an important catalyst for the international and national indigenous peoples' movement.[6]

In 1971, the Sub-Commission on Prevention of Discrimination and Protection of Minorities authorised a study by Special Rapporteur José R. Martínez Cobo on 'The Problem of Discrimination against Indigenous Populations'.[7] Cobo concluded that the existing human rights standards were 'not fully applied' to indigenous peoples and, moreover, were 'not wholly adequate' to the task.[8] Significantly, the Special Rapporteur was persuaded that 'self-determination, in its many forms, must be recognised as the basic precondition for the enjoyment by indigenous peoples of their fundamental rights and the determination of their own future'.[9] He affirmed the link between the aspirations of indigenous communities and the New International Economic Order (NIEO) interpretation of self-determination that stresses cultural development.

---

[4] See J. R. Martínez Cobo, Study of the Problem of Discrimination against Indigenous Populations, Final report (First part), 17 June 1981, UN Doc.E/CN.4/Sub.2/476/Add.5; S. J. Anaya, *Indigenous Peoples in International Law* (New York, 1996), pp.45ff; D. Sanders, The Re-Emergence of Indigenous Questions in International Law [1983] CHRY 3 at13ff and R. Neizen, *The Origins of Indigenism: Human Rights and the Politics of Identity* (Berkeley, 2003), p.29.

[5] See R. L. Barsh, Indigenous North American and Contemporary International Law (1983) 62 OLR 73 at 84–90; G. Bennett, *Aboriginal Rights in International Law* (London, 1978), pp.12–13; and L. E. Chávez, Report of the Working Group established in accordance with CHR Res.1995/32, Ninth Session, 7 January 2004, UN Doc.E/CN.4/2004/81, para.74.

[6] See B. Kingsbury, Reconciling Five Competing Conceptual Structures of Indigenous Peoples' Claims in International and Comparative Law, in P. Alston (ed.), *Peoples' Rights* (Oxford, 2001), p.69 at pp.71ff.

[7] See J. Martínez Cobo, The Study of the Problem of Discrimination Against Indigenous Populations, UN Doc.E/CN.4/Sub.2/1986/7, and Add.1–6 (citations from UN Doc.E/CN.4/Sub.2/1983/21/Adds.1–8 and UN Doc.E/CN.4/Sub.2/1983/2/Add.3 and 7); Sub-Comm. Res.8(XXIV), 18 August 1971; and ECOSOC Res.1589(L), 21 May 1971, para.7.

[8] UN Doc.E/CN.4/Sub.2/1983/21/Add.8, paras.624, 625 and 628.

[9] UN Doc.E/CN.4/Sub.2/1983/21/Add.8, para.580.

The Cobo Report served as a vehicle for increasing international interest in indigenous problems. He recommended the formulation of a declaration leading to a convention on the rights of indigenous peoples. This task was taken up by the UN Working Group on Indigenous Populations (WGIP). In 1982, following lobbying from indigenous organisations, a pre-sessional working group of the Sub-Commission was approved by the Economic and Social Council.[10] The mandate of the WGIP includes the review of developments relating to the protection of human rights and fundamental freedoms of indigenous peoples and the articulation of international standards for indigenous rights.

Maivân Clech Lâm argues that the WGIP 'is doing on a small scale for indigenous and tribal peoples what the General Assembly once did for the Third World'.[11] In respect of recent deliberations concerning the draft Declaration on the Rights of Indigenous Peoples, it is clear the forum is not the General Assembly. States have signalled their intent to pare back the Draft UN Declaration significantly. Most States tolerate the expression of indigenous rights, and specifically the exercise of self-determination, only within the confines of existing international law. The United Nations Permanent Forum on Indigenous Issues held its first session in May 2002. WGIP Chair Daes expressed the hope that the permanent forum would enable 'the next 50 years . . . to be truly a United Nations of all the peoples, including indigenous peoples, and thus reflect within itself, at last, the equality and solidarity of humankind'.[12]

During the 1980s, the International Labour Organization set in train the revision of the Convention (No.107 of 1957) concerning the Protection and Integration of Indigenous and Other Tribal and Semi-Tribal Populations in Independent Countries (ILO Convention No.107) which reflected States' preoccupations with integration policies.[13] Despite indigenous groups initially reticent about the review, there was unprecedented indigenous involvement in the drafting process.[14] It resulted in the ILO Convention (No.169 of 1989) concerning Indigenous and Tribal Peoples in Independent Countries (ILO Convention No.169).[15]

Yet, ILO No.169's exclusion of the right of political self-determination became a central criticism of the Convention by indigenous organisations and legal commentators (Article 1(3)). The preamble recognises:

[10] Sub-Comm. Res.2(XXXIV), 8 September 1981; Comm. Res.1982/19, 10 March 1982; and ECOSOC Res.1982/34, 7 May 1982. See C. Tennant, Indigenous Peoples, International Institutions and International Legal Literature from 1945–1993 (1994) 16 HRQ 1 at 16–23, 32–36; R. L. Barsh, Indigenous Peoples: An Emerging Object of International Law (1986) 80 AJIL 369 at 372–385; and H. Hannum, *Autonomy, Sovereignty and Self-Determination: The Accommodation of Conflicting Rights* (Philadelphia, 1990), pp.84–91.

[11] M. C. Lâm, Making Room for Peoples at the United Nations: Thoughts Provoked by Indigenous Claims to Self-Determination (1992) 25 CILJ 601 at 619.

[12] E.-I. Daes, Report of the Working Group on Indigenous Populations on its Thirteenth Session, 10 August 1995, UN Doc.E/CN.4/Sub.2/1995/24, para.28.

[13] 26 June 1957, in force 2 June 1959, 328 UNTS 247; and ILO, *Conventions and Recommendations Adopted by the International Labour Convention, 1919–1966* (Geneva, 1966), p.901.

[14] Observation Russel Barsh, 15 October 2002 (copy on file); and E.-I. Daes, The Participation of Indigenous Peoples in the United Nations System's Political Institutions, 27 May 2004 at http://www.law.monash.edu.au/castancentre/daes-paper.html.

[15] Geneva, 27 June 1989, in force 5 September 1991, 1650 UNTS 383; (1989) 28 ILM 1382.

[T]he aspirations of these peoples to exercise control over their own institutions, ways of life and economic development and to maintain and develop their identities, languages and religions, within the framework of the States in which they live.[16]

The general thrust of the ILO Convention No.169 is predicated on the supposition that indigenous and tribal peoples will continue as distinctive components of the State, and that the government will deal with them in accordance with the standards laid down in the Convention. These standards relate mainly to economic, social and cultural rights, rather than political rights. The ILO Convention No.169 acknowledges the collective right of indigenous and tribal peoples to preserve and develop their cultural identity.[17] The Convention's recognition of collective rights of indigenous peoples, even though highly qualified, is significant because it remains the only multilateral treaty to date to do so. This is augmented by the ILO's enforcement mechanism which implements the standards contained in its conventions.[18] The efforts of the WGIP to build on these developments in the 1993 Draft UN Declaration are examined in Chapter 9.

International law has inextricably linked the right of self-determination to the control of land and resources, and the return of cultural objects since the early nineteenth century. It is therefore no coincidence that indigenous peoples would make similar claims in United Nations' fora and, in addition, their claims be built upon the broader notion of restitution articulated by the NIEO.

Special Rapporteur Cobo affirmed the right of indigenous individuals and communities to cultural development, free of assimilation or integration policies imposed by the dominant culture.[19] He reiterated the NIEO interpretation of the 'right to culture', that is the right for societies emerging from colonial rule, to the 'recovery, protection and further development of cultural heritage'.[20] He noted that although indigenous communities continued to suffer loss of cultural objects, some States had made efforts to regulate the excavation and export of such items.[21] The efforts of two settler States, the United States and Australia, in this area are examined below.

Although Cobo stated that his study was not concerned with archaeological sites or objects, he did make specific recommendations covering relations between museums and indigenous peoples, including:

---

[16] Fifth recital, Preamble, ILO 169. See Arts.7(1) and 8(2).

[17] See Arts.2(2)(b) and (c), 4, 5, 7, 23, 26–31, ILO 169. See B. Kingsbury, 'Indigenous Peoples' in International Law: A Constructivist Approach to the Asian Controversy (1998) 92 AJIL 414 at 439; and R. L. Barsh, An Advocate's Guide to the Convention on Indigenous and Tribal Peoples (1990) 15 OCULR 209 at 229–31.

[18] See Anaya, *Indigenous Peoples*, pp.18–24 and 62–75; and J. Anaya, Indigenous Rights – Norms in Customary International Law (1992) 8 AJILC 1 at 5.

[19] UN Doc.E/CN.4/Sub.2/1983/21/Add.8, para.486.

[20] UN Doc.E/CN.4/Sub.2/1983/21/Add.3, para.18. See L. Prott, Cultural Rights as Peoples' Rights in International Law, in J. Crawford (ed.), *The Rights of Peoples*, (Oxford, 1988), pp.93ff; and H. Nieć (ed.), *Cultural Rights and Wrongs* (Paris, 1998).

[21] UN Doc.E/CN.4/Sub.2/1983/21/Add.8, para.147.

- there must be effective access, preservation and protection of sacred objects for indigenous groups;
- museums must not acquire cultural objects of current religious significance to indigenous peoples. Further, they should advise relevant communities of the appearance of such objects on the market;
- museums must return objects when requested by the community of origin because they require them for their 'current religious practices';
- until such objects are returned, museums must consult with community leaders concerning their exhibition, labelling, conservation, and storage; and
- museums must allow relevant community members to 'give necessary ritual treatment' to such objects.[22]

These recommendations formed the core of Indigenous Australian demands in their early renegotiations with museums. The Sub-Commission labelled the Cobo Report 'a reference work of definitive usefulness' and directed the WGIP to utilise it when setting standards.[23]

At its fourth session in 1985, the WGIP focused its efforts on the preparation of draft principles concerning indigenous rights based on relevant national legislation, international instruments and other juridical criteria.[24] Before the 1987 session, the Indigenous Peoples Preparatory Meeting adopted a Declaration of Principles which asserted that indigenous peoples 'continue to own and control their material culture' and 'have a right to regain items of major cultural significance'.[25] During the session, indigenous observers argued that this course was necessary because museums frequently misrepresented and offended their cultures, and retained sacred objects.[26]

In mid 1988, WGIP Chair Daes tabled a draft Universal Declaration on Indigenous Rights and invited comments from States and indigenous organisations. Article 6 of this 'preliminary first draft' affirmed that the 'right to the manifestations of their cultures, including archaeological sites, artefacts, designs, technology and works of art, lie with the indigenous peoples or their members'.[27] Importantly, the draft made an explicit connection between the return of traditional lands, cultural objects and traditional knowledge for cultural survival and development. Also, indigenous groups challenged the State-centric nature of most international instruments by emphasising the need to recognise collective and individual human rights

---

[22] UN Doc.E/CN.4/Sub.2/1983/21/Add.8, paras.599–600, 604–08; and paras.594–598 (related to sites).

[23] Sub-Comm. Res.1985/22, para.4(a), 29 August 1985; and Barsh, 'Indigenous', 371.

[24] E.-I. Daes, Report of the Working Group on Indigenous Populations on its Fourth Session, 27 August 1985, UN Doc.E/CN.4/Sub.2/1985/22, paras.71ff.

[25] E.-I. Daes, Report of the Working Group on Indigenous Populations on its Fifth Session, 24 August 1987, UN Doc.E/CN.4/Sub.2/1987/22, Annex 5. See points 13 (archaeological excavations) and 14 (sacred sites).

[26] UN Doc.E/CN.4/Sub.2/1987/22, para.62.

[27] E.-I. Daes, Report of the Working Group on Indigenous Populations on its Sixth Session, 24 August 1988, UN Doc.E/CN.4/Sub.2/1988/24, Annex 2, 33.

in respect of such cultural rights.[28] The WGIP Chair maintains that her work complements, rather than duplicates, the mission of the UNESCO Intergovernmental Committee. Daes's Study on the Protection of the Cultural and Intellectual Property of Indigenous Peoples is considered in the following chapter.

Assessment of the work of the UNESCO Intergovernmental Committee

As detailed in Chapter 7, the working methods of the UNESCO Intergovernmental Committee accommodated the interests of former metropolitan powers and States, thereby curtailing its application and accessibility to non-State groups. The Committee's work over the last two-and-a-half decades indicates that despite these restrictions, it has nevertheless evolved to facilitate the claims of non-State groups. It has promoted a multilayered approach to restitution originally advocated by newly independent States. Accordingly, the Committee has increasingly promoted cooperation between States, rather than the transfer of knowledge and resources from one State to another.

The Committee's work, especially with the re-emergence of the claims of Holocaust survivors and their heirs and the campaigns of indigenous peoples, has mirrored a process of remembering within the museum community and the general public. In particular, there is an emerging recognition of how museums both facilitated and benefited from the policies of the past.

Bilateral negotiations

The Committee has emphasised bilateral negotiations as the primary method of resolving claims for the return of cultural objects. Museum officials in holding States have stressed repeatedly the need for the development of relations with the requesting institution or community prior to any consideration of a restitution request.[29] In equal measures, newly independent States maintain that restitution is not simply the physical act of return but a process necessitating an equitable dialogue between cultures.

However, the Committee's ability to encourage bilateral negotiations is severely constricted by its legalistic approach.[30] This approach sits incongruously with its promotion of moral rather than legal rights of parties. As at 2005, the Committee's intervention had been sought only in a handful of cases and there is yet to be

---

[28] See E.-I. Daes, Report of the Working Group on Indigenous Populations on its Seventh Session, 25 August 1989, UN Doc.E/CN.4/Sub.2/1989/36, para.57.

[29] See K. Myles, Should Finding Mean Keeping? UNESCO Radio, Paris, June 1982, UNESCO Doc.PI/R/1825, 7; interview with J. Specht, Head of Anthropology Department, Australian Museum, Sydney, 24 February 1999; and interview with A. Herle, Senior Assistant Curator, Cambridge University Museum of Archaeology and Anthropology, Cambridge, 3 November 1999.

[30] For example, a Member State must complete a 'Standard Form' stating that bilateral negotiations have been exhausted. The application will not proceed if the holding State is not a Member of UNESCO. If the holding State does not respond within a year of the form's lodgement, the Committee can extend its good offices to mediation but it has no coercive authority. See Intergovernmental Committee for Promoting the Return of Cultural Property to its Countries of Origin or its Restitution in Case of Illicit Appropriation, Second Session, 7 August 1981, UNESCO Doc.CC-81/CONF.203/3, para.16; and Report of Director-General of UNESCO on the Return or Restitution of Cultural Property, 9 September 1987, UN Doc.A/42/533, Annex, para.10.

a successful resolution of a claim using the Committee's intervention alone. The UNESCO Director-General is currently preparing a strategy to strengthen the mandate of the Committee by extending its function to include mediation and conciliation which would be voluntary and non-binding on Member States.[31]

Case-by-case negotiations are favoured by holding States because this method avoids any consideration of the wider context of their collecting practices. Yet, the range of claims raised before the Committee over the last two decades reflects an appreciation of involuntary removal of cultural objects from communities beyond the narrow political agenda of the decolonisation era. The types of claims brought before the Committee may be divided into three phases:

(1) from the establishment of the Committee to the present day, there has been a fusion of claims for cultural objects removed during colonisation and those removed illicitly following the 1970 UNESCO Convention. Greater regard is paid to curbing present-day illicit traffic and restoring objects removed as a consequence of such trade.[32] This trend reflects the NIEO agenda by appreciating that the circumstances causing cultural loss during colonial occupation did not cease following independence.

(2) from the 1990s the Committee focused its attention on cultural objects which had been removed and destroyed as a result of armed conflict, and restitution claims of successor States following the dissolution of federations.[33] At its behest, a committee of experts presented a set of guiding principles to govern the recovery of cultural objects displaced during the Second World War. This has led to appreciation of the link between removal and destruction of cultural objects of a group and discriminatory and genocidal policies.

(3) from the late 1990s, there was increased understanding of the complex nature of European colonialism and its legacy concerning cultural objects.[34] The Committee noted the efforts of some States to protect the cultural heritage of indigenous peoples within their territory.[35] The restitution claims of indigenous peoples also have an affinity with earlier phases of the Committee's work.

[31] UNESCO Doc.32C/Resolution 38, para.9. See F. Shyllon, The Recovery of Cultural Objects by African Status through the UNESCO and UNIDROIT Conventions and the Role of Arbitration [2002] 2 ULR 219.

[32] Including the Law Ministers of the Commonwealth proposal; and the European Community Directive on Illegally Exported Cultural Objects: Report of the Director-General of UNESCO on the action taken by the organisation on the return or restitution of cultural property to the countries of origin, 7 October 1993, UN Doc.A/48/466, Annex, paras.15 and 16.

[33] Intergovernmental Committee for Promoting the Return of Cultural Property to its Countries of Origin or its Restitution in case of Illicit Appropriation, Thirteenth Session, 7–10 February 2005, Secretariat Report, UNESCO Doc.CLT-2005/CONF.202/2, paras.28–38; UN Doc.A/48/466, Annex, paras.11 and 12; UN Doc.A/48/PV.47 (2 November 1993), 8–11; and UN Doc.A/54/PV.72 (7 December 1999), 3–4.

[34] Namibian claim for the Cape Cross Padrão: Report of the Director-General of UNESCO on the action by the organisation on the return of cultural property to the countries of origin or its restitution in case of illicit appropriation, 4 October 1999, UN Doc.A/54/436, Annex, para.12; South Korea's claim for the Oe-Kyujanggak Archives from France: Intergovernmental Committee for Promoting the Return of Cultural Property to its Countries of Origin or its Restitution in case of Illicit Appropriation, Twelfth Session, 25–28 March 2003, Secretariat Report, UNESCO Doc.CLT-2003/CONF.204/2, para.8; and Ethiopia–Italy negotiations: CLT-2003/CONF.204/2, para.7.

[35] See UN Doc.A/54/436, Annex, para.8.

This gradual understanding of the multifaceted circumstances resulting in the removal of cultural objects during occupation, and efforts of the international community and museums to address these restitution claims, can only assist indigenous peoples and other non-State groups.

The Committee has also developed a more multifaceted approach to its other functions than that originally intended at its inception.

Public information

Initially, various preparatory reports and the Committee emphasised the need to educate people, especially museum officials and the local media, in holding States about the issues surrounding the return of cultural objects to countries of origin.[36] The organiser of the first British symposium covering restitution from Western institutions to former colonies found that museums were not only reticent about 'debat[ing] the issues but often [showed] a marked reluctance to recognise that there was any issue to be debated'.[37] Yet, by 1991, this campaign was so successful that delegates were advising of returns finalised following the involvement of the domestic media.[38]

However, this focus on holding States failed to concede that whilst requesting States had familiarised their populace with the political arguments surrounding restitution, there was still much work to be done to address the escalation in illicit trade.[39] By the 1980s, the Committee began to promote heavily the need for States to ratify and implement the 1970 UNESCO Convention.[40] This strategy targeted the Asia Pacific region, in particular.[41]

The re-emergence of claims of Holocaust survivors and their heirs in the national and international consciousness exposed the complex relationship between public education and restitution. Since the 1990s, these claimants have stressed the need for education programmes which enable the general public to understand that the systematic removal and destruction of cultural objects was an essential component of Nazi discriminatory and genocidal policies.[42] Museums have become an important

---

[36] See Dakar Final Report, UNESCO Doc.20C/86, Annex 2; and Art.4(4), Committee's Statute, UNESCO Doc.20C/86, Annex 1, 2.

[37] J. McKenzie, Opening Address, in I. Staunton and M. McCarthy (eds.), *Lost Heritage: A Report of the Symposium on the Return of Cultural Property held at the Africa Centre, 21 May 1981* (London, 1981), p.3.

[38] See UNESCO, General Conference, 26th session, Report by the Intergovernmental Committee for Promoting the Return of Cultural Property to its Countries of Origin or its Restitution in Case of Illicit Appropriate, 19 July 1991, UNESCO Doc.26C/92, 6, para.33.

[39] See ICOM, Study on the Principles, Conditions and Means for the Restitution or Return of Cultural Property in View of Reconstituting Dispersed Heritages, UNESCO Doc.CC-78/CONF.609/3, Annex 1, 5–6.

[40] UN Doc.A/36/651 [561], Annex, paras.20–29.

[41] See UNGA, Report of the Director-General of UNESCO on the action taken by the Organisation to promote the return or restitution of cultural property, 30 September 1991, UN Doc.A/46/497, Annex, para.23; and UN Doc.A/48/PV.47 (2 November 1993).

[42] See Principle A of the Statement of Principles, Report of the Association of Art Museum Directors (AAMD), Task Force on the Spoliation of Art During the Nazi/World War II Era (1933–1945), 4 June 1998 at http://www.aamd.org/guideln.shtml, and N. Palmer, *Museums and the Holocaust: Law, Principles and Practice*, (Leicester, 2000), p.280; American Association of Museums (AAM) Guidelines Concerning the Unlawful Appropriation of Objects During the Nazi Era, November 1999, amended April 2001, at http://www.aam-us.org/museum resources/ethics/nazi_guidelines.cfm,

forum for this process of individual and collective 'remembering' within several States. Later in this chapter, there is an examination of how indigenous peoples have insisted that museums in settler States reflect the effects of colonial occupation on their communities and cultures through their exhibitions and public programmes.

Inventories

The Committee's emphasis on the preparation of inventories facilitated this greater understanding of the collecting practices of metropolitan powers and the scale of cultural loss sustained by their former subjects. During negotiations for the 1970 UNESCO Convention, the United States was reticent about the provision covering inventories.[43] However, the work of various museum professionals in respect of Oceanic collections, and the claims of Holocaust survivors and indigenous peoples, led Anglo-American States to become more amenable to this process and to making the data accessible to prospective claimants.

The Venice Report maintained that inventories were crucial to 'the reconstitution of cultural heritages' by identifying gaps in national collections and the location of objects in foreign institutions.[44] Equally, the UNESCO Intergovernmental Committee argued inventories were necessary for the preparation of restitution claims and encouraging possible offers. A methodology for the compilation of inventories was eventually developed by non-indigenous museum practitioners, following extensive research on Oceanic collections held in Australia, Canada, New Zealand, United Kingdom and United States.[45] For requesting States in the Pacific region, the goal was to create an archive of photographs and documentation relating to the traditional material culture of each Pacific Island group. This objective was based on a right to access their cultural heritage and cultural revitalisation. Importantly, the data were returned to the national collection and the particular group to which it applied.[46]

and Palmer, *Museums*, p.286; Parliamentary Assembly of the Council of Europe (PACE) Resolution 1205: Looted Jewish Cultural Property, 4 November 1999, in *Official Gazette of the Council of Europe* (November 1999), and Palmer, *Museums*, p.275; Vilnius Forum Declaration, 5 October 2000, at http://www.vilniusforum.lt/media/declaration.htm; Museums & Galleries Commission (MGC) Statement of Principles, 1999, para.2.4, in J. Legget, *Restitution and Repatriation: Guidelines for Good Practice* (London, 2000), Appendix 3, pp.34–38; and National Museum Directors' Conference (NMDC), Statement of Principles and Proposed Actions, Palmer, *Museums*, p.290, and at http://www.nationalmuseumsorg.uk/spoliation/principles.html.

[43] UNESCO, Means of Prohibiting and Preventing the Illicit Import, Export and Transfer of Ownership of Cultural Property, Final Report, 27 February 1970, UNESCO Docs.SHC/MD/5, Annex 1, 21; and P. M. Bator, An Essay on the International Art Trade (1982) 34 Stan. LR 275 at 381.

[44] See UNESCO, Committee of Experts to Study the Question of the Restitution of Works of Art, Venice, Final Report, 21 April 1976, UNESCO Doc.SHC-76/CONF.615/5, 6.

[45] See J. Specht and L. Bolton, Pacific Islands' Artefact Collections: The UNESCO Inventory Project (2005) 17 *Journal of Museum Ethnography* (forthcoming); P. Gathercole, Recording Ethnographic Collections: The Debate on the Return of Cultural Property (1986) 38 *Museum* 187–92; L. Bolton, Collection of Inventories and the Return of Information to Oceania: The Australian Experience, 18 March 1985, UNESCO Doc.CLT-85/CONF.202/5; and A. L. Kaeppler and A. K. Stillman, Pacific Island and Australian Aboriginal Artifacts in Public Collections in the United States of America and Canada, Paris, 1985, UNESCO Doc.CLT-85/WS/12.

[46] See E. Bonshek, Objects, People and Identity: An Interplay between Past and Present at the Australian Museum, in T. Lin (ed.), *Proceedings of the International Conference on Anthropology and the Museum* (Taipei, 1992), p.261; and ICOM Study, para.26.

Within this schema, the identification of objects as a preliminary step in the restitution process was a secondary aim. The survey of Oceanic material in Australian public collections led to many enquiries for further information, but few requests for repatriation. This result can be explained in part by the limited involvement of the communities of origin, the non-inclusion of photographs of objects, and their description in terms foreign to these communities.[47] In addition, the compilation of inventories required expertise and resources usually not readily available in newly independent States. ICOM recommended that developed States provide expertise and training courses to assist these States.[48] Gradually, the preparation of inventories was subsumed within the wider programme of technical cooperation.[49]

Inventories were primarily of benefit to scholars and museums in holding States, not the communities whose cultures were represented in the collections. These museums were able to view their collections in perspective and appreciate their comparative size and importance.[50] Australian Museum staff became aware that information gaps existed in a large proportion of their collections and consequently approached community members who retained knowledge about the artefacts in question.[51] The process, in turn, strengthened the museum's educational role and its ability to facilitate indigenous cultural renewal through activities within the museum.

The Committee argues correctly that inventories contribute to the exchange of knowledge and the promotion of 'inter-cultural dialogue' independently of any request for restitution.[52] Up until this period, little was done to consider the meaning of objects in their original cultural context, the circumstances of their removal and ongoing importance to the communities of origin. The presentation and organisation of information and cultural objects by museums had continued to reflect Western taxonomic systems established in the nineteenth century. As a consequence there was a vast gulf between the categories in which museums organise their collections and those in which the original owners perceive these objects.

The Committee's efforts in promoting inventories focused gradually on the obligation under the 1970 UNESCO Convention to stem the illicit traffic in cultural objects. The United States, the United Kingdom and, to a lesser degree, Australia resisted this obligation during treaty deliberations. However, from the 1990s onwards, museums in these States have been required to inventory their collections in response to various restitution claims for objects acquired prior to the operation of the Convention. First, in the United States and Australia, federal government

---

47 See L. Bolton, Recording Oceanic Collections in Australia: Problems and Questions (1984) 36 *Museum* 32 at 35; B. Meehan, The National Inventory of Aboriginal Artefacts (April 1988) 20 *COMA Bulletin* 7; interview with J. Specht; and interview with B. Craig, Head, Division of Foreign Anthropology, South Australian Museum, Adelaide, 17 February 1999.
48 See UNESCO Doc.CC-78/CONF.609/3, Annex 1, 10; and J. Specht, Report on a Consultation of Specialists on Ways and Means of Safeguarding the Cultural Heritage of the Pacific Region (1981) 7 *COMA Newsletter* 32 at 34.
49 See UNESCO, General Conference, 23rd session, Report of the Intergovernmental Committee for Promoting the Return of Cultural Property to its Country of Origin or its Restitution in Case of Illicit Appropriation, 9 August 1985, UNESCO Doc.23C/87, 6.
50 Interview with B. Craig.
51 Australian Museum, *Annual Report 1983/84* (Sydney, 1984), pp.12–13; and interview with J. Specht.
52 UNESCO Doc.23C/87, 6.

incentives addressing the claims of Native Americans and Indigenous Australians respectively require museums to compile inventories of specific items, consult relevant indigenous communities and repatriate objects in their collections. Similar recommendations have been made recently in respect of UK national collections.[53]

Second, fuelled by greater accessibility to public archives in Western States and following the fall of the Communist bloc in Eastern and Central Europe, investigations were reignited concerning the fate of cultural objects confiscated during the 1930s and 40s.[54] Museums and museum organisations in numerous former metropolitan powers have deployed significant resources to provide prospective claimants with accessible information concerning objects in their collections of potentially questionable provenance.[55] Importantly, the process goes beyond the listing and cataloguing of existing museum collections by emphasising the provenance of every cultural object whether it is offered for sale, bequest or loan.[56]

These inventories have proved more successful in prompting museums worldwide to confront the history of objects in their collections and review their acquisition policies than stimulating repatriations.[57] The physical and theoretical decontextualisation of cultural objects of non-European peoples and centralisation in imperial collections was an essential component of European colonial and capitalist expansion. This increasing awareness of the 'history of the ownership' of an object, aided by the compilation of inventories, directly challenges these primary 'mechanisms of forgetfulness' of former colonial powers and their museums.[58]

Training of personnel and museum development

Pursuant to its governing Statute, the UNESCO Intergovernmental Committee is required to encourage 'the establishment or reinforcement of museums or other institutions for the conservation of cultural property and the training of the necessary scientific and technical personnel' (Article 4(6)). It was initially presumed that objects would be returned to facilities that met standards dictated by Western museum officials. However, the ICOM Study maintained that a lack of resources and facilities could not be a justifiable pretext for refusing a restitution request.[59]

---

[53] N. Palmer, *Report of the Working Group on Human Remains in Museum Collections* (London, 2003), Recommendation XIV.

[54] Palmer, *Museums*, Chapter 9.

[55] See Washington Conference Principles on Nazi-Confiscated Art, December 1998, Principles 2–6, at http://www.comartrecovery.org/policies/es3.htm; and Palmer, *Museums*, Appendix 7, p.278; AAMD Guidelines, Principles D and E, and Part 3; MGC Statement of Principles, Part 3; AAM Guidelines, Part 2A and 2C; ICOM Recommendation concerning the Return of Works of Art Belonging to Jewish Owners, Press Release, 14 January 1999, at http://www.icom.org/worldwar2.html; and CE Res.1205, para.11.

[56] See CE Res.1205, para.15; AAMD Guidelines, Part F; AAM Guidelines, 2B and 2F; and MGC Statement of Principles, Part 4, para.2.3; and DCMS Report, Part 3, paras.30ff.

[57] First Report of the Culture, Media and Sport Select Committee (2003–2004 HC 59), Q322; and A. Riding, Foot Dragging on the Return of Art Stolen by the Nazis, *New York Times*, 18 May 2004.

[58] Seventh Report of Select Committee on Culture, Media and Sport (1999–2000 HC 371), vol.1, para.35.

[59] UNESCO Doc.CC-78/CONF.609/3, Annex 1, 5.

Newly independent States acknowledged that there was a need for adequate facilities and trained personnel but criticised the Western concept of development and its effect on local cultural identity.[60] Many States argued against the mimicry of Western modes of preservation and presentation of their cultures.[61] They emphasised the importance of 'locally relevant' training programmes and regional centres, and the utilisation of traditional technologies for the production and protection of cultural objects.[62] Accordingly, the UNESCO Intergovernmental Committee uses the term 'technical cooperation' rather than 'technical assistance' to reflect the need for input from the receiving country and the importance it places on cross-cultural dialogue. This shift emphasises the growing appreciation of restitution as a process which enables the communities of origin to once again determine how their cultures are preserved, protected and developed. A UNESCO Intergovernmental Committee member noted:

> [A] cultural artefact is not merely something which is more or less dead, beautiful and scientific . . . It is something that, for a particular people, is a living thing which enables a people to achieve confidence in itself and is, thus, able to imagine its future.[63]

While Australian museums continued to assist indigenous communities with training and technical assistance, they have disavowed imposing conditions on requesting communities prior to effecting return.[64]

There has also been an increased awareness that museum officials in developed States required 'training' in observing due diligence in acquisitions and loans, and appreciating the effect of cultural losses on communities of origin. In 1986, the ICOM General Assembly adopted a Code of Professional Ethics that regulated the future acquisition and authentication of cultural objects by its members to inhibit illicit trade, as well as the handling of restitution requests.[65] Recently, international organisations and various States have adopted guidelines for museum professionals governing the restitution claims arising from the Holocaust and Second World War.[66] These guidelines, together with those concerning the claims of indigenous peoples examined in Chapter 9, are significant because they govern past, as well as future, acquisitions of cultural objects.

---

[60] See UNGA, Report of the Director-General of UNESCO on the preservation and further development of cultural values, including the protection, restitution and return of cultural and artistic property, 8 September 1980, UN Doc.A/35/349, Annex, para.106.

[61] UNESCO, General Conference, 24th session, Report by the Intergovernmental Committee for Promoting the Return of Cultural Property to its Countries of Origin or its Restitution in Case of Illicit Appropriation, 27–30 April 1987, UNESCO Doc.24C/94, 8.

[62] See UNESCO Doc.23C/87, 6, para.31.

[63] S. Stetie, The view of UNESCO's inter-governmental committee, in Staunton and McCarthy (eds.), *Lost Heritage*, pp.8–10.

[64] Cf. British position: MGC Statement of Principles, para.3.1.14.

[65] ICOM, *Statutes: Code of Professional Ethics* (1986) (Revised, Paris, 2001 and 2004). See Legget, *Restitution*, pp.7–10.

[66] 1999 ICOM Recommendation; Holocaust Commission Act of 1998, Pub. L. No.105–86; AAMD Guidelines; AAM Guidelines; and UK Spoliation Advisory Panel, Constitution and Terms of Reference, in Palmer, *Museums*, Appendix 12, p.300; and MGC Statement of Principles.

Funding restitution

Most previous examples of peace treaty provisions and international instruments sanctioning restitution of cultural objects required that the requesting party bear the cost of return.[67] For newly independent States and indigenous communities such costs are usually prohibitive. The 1977 ICOM Study recommended the establishment of a fund to assist a requesting country to purchase objects on the international art market.[68] At the Committee's first session in 1980, it was argued that certain States would react most unfavourably if they were required to return the cultural objects and finance the cost of such claims.[69] However, some States like Australia have assisted former colonial territories and indigenous peoples within its borders, financially and technically, during the restitution process.

In 2000, UNESCO finally launched a fund which finances the verification by experts of cultural objects in their countries of location, their transportation, insurance of objects, and the 'establishment of suitable exhibition facilities and training of museum professionals in countries of origin'.[70] By contrast, the WGIP Chair has proposed the establishment of a fund by UNESCO to act as a global agent for the recovery of, or compensation for, the unauthorised or inappropriate use of indigenous cultural heritage.[71]

The experience of Australian museums has shown that beside the initial purchase price, the holding State may expend substantial monies when returning objects even to territories under its control.[72] Further, a holding State may be required by its domestic laws to compensate a bona fide purchaser prior to the objects being returned to the requesting State. There has been limited recognition that the holding State should be compensated for the conservation and safekeeping of an object whilst in its possession. The UK Spoliation Advisory Panel considered the conservation and insurance costs expended by the Tate Gallery, offsetting it against the benefit it derived by having the requested painting in its collections for forty years.[73] By contrast, the Danish Supreme Court held that the Arne Magnussen Foundation had a right protected by the constitution in a repatriation claim brought against it, which forbade expropriation of property except where it was in the public interest and subject to compensation. However, the court found in that case there was no substantial loss, therefore no compensation was payable.[74]

---

[67] See Art.7(b)(ii), Convention on the Means of Prohibiting and Preventing the Illicit Import, Export and Transfer of Ownership of Cultural Property, Paris, 14 November 1970, in force 24 April 1972, 823 UNTS 231; (1971) 10 ILM 289.

[68] See ICOM Study, 9–11.   [69] See UNESCO Doc.21C/83, 4.

[70] See Report by the Intergovernmental Committee for Promoting the Return of Cultural Property to its Country of Origin or its Restitution in Case of Illicit Appropriation on its Activities, 9 August 2001, UNESCO Doc.31C/REP/16, para.10.

[71] See E.-I. Daes, Study on the Protection of the Cultural and Intellectual Property of Indigenous Peoples, 28 July 1993, UN Doc.E/CN.4/Sub.2/1993/28, para.176.

[72] Interview with J. Specht; and interview with R. Stack, Indigenous Heritage Officer, Macleay Museum, University of Sydney, Sydney, 3 May 2001.

[73] Report of the Spoliation Advisory Panel in respect of a Painting now in the Possession of the Tate Gallery (2001 HC III), p.19.

[74] *Arne Magnussen Foundation (Arnamagnaean Institute)* v. *The Ministry of Education* Supreme Court of Denmark, Case No.107/1966, (November 1966); and *Ministry of Education* v. *Arne Magnussen's*

Implementing the 1970 UNESCO Convention

For many newly independent States and indigenous peoples, the stemming of further cultural losses is as significant an objective as the restitution of cultural objects. Indeed, NIEO proponents maintained that circumstances leading to such losses do not end with the cessation of occupation. This argument has effectively blurred these two objectives. The 1970 UNESCO Convention was the culmination of efforts by 'source' States to formulate international legislation for the effective enforcement of domestic export controls after objects are illicitly removed from their territory.

States involved in the Convention negotiations were acutely aware that its effectiveness rested heavily on its ratification and implementation by 'market' States. For many years, these countries resisted the enforcement of foreign export laws. However, by 2004, most major market countries had become State parties to the Convention. This section considers the implementation of the 1970 UNESCO Convention into their domestic law by the United States and Australia during the 1980s, and United Kingdom in 2003. There is an examination of the respective national legislative schema designed to protect the movable cultural heritage of other States, and the cultural objects of indigenous peoples within their own borders.

The implementation of the Convention's obligations into domestic law by each of these three States reflects their differing concerns and the instrument's corresponding effectiveness in tackling illicit trade. The United States and United Kingdom as major market States adopted a restrictive implementation of the Convention's obligations into their domestic law, particularly in respect of foreign export controls. By contrast, whilst also a market State, Australia is sensitive to potential cultural loss to overseas collections. This position is reflected in Australia's more expansive interpretation of the Convention and application into its domestic law.

Regulating importation

US input during the negotiation for the 1970 UNESCO Convention and its subsequent ratification and implementation into domestic law significantly limited the operation of the instrument. The importance of these limitations cannot be underestimated, given the size of the US art market. A member of the US delegation, Mark Feldman, noted that by 1970 the United States could no longer ignore the concerns of source States.[75] However, for many US commentators the initial UNESCO draft placed too much emphasis on the protection of national patrimony whilst ignoring other (competing) interests, including the free-trade agenda.[76] The United States lobbied for redrafts which it believed struck a compromise between the perceived rigidity of the scheme favoured by source States and the self-described 'multilayered' approach of market States.[77]

Foundation (Arnamagnaean Institute) Eastern High Court of Denmark, Case III No.57/1967, (March 1970), in J. Greenfield, *The Return of Cultural Treasures*, (Cambridge, 1989), Appendix 1.

[75] M. B. Feldman, in L. D. DuBoff *et al.*, Proceedings of the Panel of the US Enabling Legislation of the UNESCO Convention on the Means of Prohibiting and Preventing the Illicit Import, Export and Transfer of Ownership of Cultural Property (1976) 4 SJILC 97 at 112.

[76] UNESCO Doc.SHC/MD/5, Annex 1, 20ff (US); and Bator, 'Essay', 372.

[77] See Nafziger, in DuBoff *et al.*, 'Proceedings', 102.

Non-retroactivity was a primary US concern during the 1970 UNESCO Convention deliberations.[78] The United States also listed it as an 'understanding' of its 'acceptance' of the Convention.[79] Resistance to any provision that threatened to scrutinise the provenance of existing collections remains a central 'mechanism of forgetfulness' for former metropolitan powers. As explained, this resistance is becoming increasingly unsustainable. Further, the US 'acceptance' of the Convention was made subject to its 1983 domestic legislation, the Convention on Cultural Property Implementation Act (CCPIA).[80] The constrictive translation of the Convention obligations into US domestic law reflects a continuation of US aversion to the enforcement of foreign laws by its domestic courts.[81] The major limitations can be summarised as follows.

First, the Act primarily addresses Articles 7 and 9 of the 1970 UNESCO Convention. Only the first part of Article 7(b) is included in the CCPIA, restricting it to the importation of objects removed from museums or similar institutions.[82] Since such acts are already prohibited by the criminal provisions contained in the National Stolen Property Act (NSPA), the civil provisions in the CCPIA added little to the existing law except to enable action by customs officials in addition to private litigation or prosecution under this Act.[83] According to some US commentators, Article 9 provides for cooperation on an ad hoc basis by State parties with other State parties whose cultural property, of importance to its national patrimony, is 'in jeopardy'.[84] Under the CCPIA, the US President is authorised under specific stringent conditions to negotiate bilateral and multilateral agreements to impose temporary US import restrictions on designated objects. The CCPIA requires a State to make a case that an 'emergency condition' exists concerning the illicit transfer of such material.[85] This term is not used in the 1970 UNESCO Convention. The US position clearly avoids a general undertaking as set out in Article 9 and effectively renders the 1970 UNESCO Convention an 'agreement to agree'.[86]

[78] UNESCO Doc.SHC/MD/5, Annex 1, 22.

[79] See UNESCO Doc.LA/Depository/1984/3 Annex 3; L. V. Prott and P. J. O'Keefe, *Law and the Cultural Heritage, Volume 3: Movement* (London, 1989), pp.794–95, §1492; and P. J. O'Keefe, *Commentary on the UNESCO 1970 Convention on Illicit Traffic* (Leicester, 2000), p.107. Cf. *Republic of Austria v. Altmann*, 372 F 3d 1246 (9th Cir. 2003); 539 US 987 (2004), 124 S. Ct. 46.

[80] Pub. L. No.97–446, 96 Stat. 2329 (1983); amended by Pub. L. No.100–204; 101 Stat. 1331 (1987), codified at 19 USC §§2601–13 (2000). See UNESCO Doc.LA/Depository/1984/3 Annex 1. Mexico maintained the US legislation and reservations were not adequate compliance with the Convention. UNESCO also sought clarification from the US government: UNESCO Doc.LA/Depository/1984/3, Annex 5 and 6; and LA/Depository/1985/40.

[81] See UNESCO Doc.SHC/MD/5, Annex 1, 21; Feldman, in DuBoff *et al.*, 'Proceedings', 114–15; and P. M. Bator, International Trade in National Art Treasures: Regulation and Deregulation, in L. DuBoff (ed.), *Art Law: Domestic and International* (South Hackensack, 1975), p.295 at pp.300–01.

[82] 19 USC §§2607. This limitation is exacerbated by the failure of the US to implement Art.13.

[83] 18 USC §§2314 *et seq* (2000). See Prott and O'Keefe, *Movement*, pp.373–79, §§712–20; and F. D. Struell, Cultural Property: Recent Cases under the Convention on Cultural Property Implementation Act (1997) 31 *The International Lawyer* 691.

[84] See Nafziger, in Duboff *et al.*, 'Proceedings', 104ff.

[85] 19 USC §2603(a). See Feldman, in Duboff *et al.*, 'Proceedings', 124–125; Bator, 'Essay', 379; R. D. Abramson and S. B. Huttler, The Legal Response to the Illicit Movement of Cultural Property (1973) 5 LPIB 932 at 962; and J. Gordon, The UNESCO Convention on the Illicit Movement of Art Treasures (1971) 12 HILJ 537 at 552–53.

[86] See O'Keefe, *Commentary*, p.108; and Feldman, in Duboff *et al.*, 'Proceedings', 114–15.

Second, the CCPIA substantially pares down the interpretation of cultural objects covered, compared to Article 1 of the 1970 UNESCO Convention. The limited import controls contained in the Act apply only to 'archaeological or ethnological material' or 'object[s] of archaeological interest', which are at least 250 years old.[87]

Although the effectiveness of the US enabling legislation has been questioned, it does represent limited recognition by the United States of the detrimental effect of its pursuit of an unfettered free trade policy in cultural objects.[88] This shift coincided with growing local appreciation of the effect of this international traffic on Native American sites and objects.[89] The US federal government recently reaffirmed its commitment to prosecute persons under the NSPA in respect of objects removed from excavations or monuments contrary to the laws of the relevant State. Also, despite their historic resistance to do so, US courts are increasingly recognising, in defined circumstances, the assertion by States of title over 'undiscovered' cultural objects removed from archaeological sites for the purposes of such criminal proceedings.[90]

Australia enacted the Protection of Movable Cultural Heritage Act 1986 (Cth) (PMCHA) as part of its fulfilment of obligations under the 1970 UNESCO Convention. The PMCHA operates to impose import and export controls in addition to those already existing under the Customs Act 1901 (Cth).[91] The PMCHA covers cultural objects imported into Australia in contravention of other States' laws (Section 14). The provision is invoked only where the State concerned makes a complaint to the Australian authorities (Section 41). It is not restricted to State parties to the 1970 UNESCO Convention. Significantly, the PMCHA applies to objects imported into Australia after 1 July 1987 'but which were previously exported from another country at any time when there was a cultural heritage protection law in

---

[87] 19 USC §2601(2)(A), (B), and (i)(II). The 2003 Iraq Cultural Heritage Protection bill (HR 2009) sought to amend the CCPIA to objects of archaeological interest older than 100 years thereby bringing it in line with the 1970 UNESCO Convention; and to countries generally, rather than just State parties to the convention.

[88] Senate Report No.97–654 on Implementing Legislation for the Convention on the Means of Prohibiting and Preventing the Illicit Import, Export and Transfer of Cultural Property, at http://exchanges.state.gov/culprop/problem.html.

[89] See A. M. DeMeo, More Effective Protection for Native American Cultural Property through Regulation of Export (1994) 19 AILR 1 at 8–10, 70; and V. Canouts and F. P. McManamon, Protecting the Past for the Future: Federal Archaeology in the United States, in N. Brodie, J. Doole and C. Renfrew (eds.), *Trade in Illicit Antiquities: The Destruction of the World's Archaeological Heritage* (Cambridge, 2001), pp.97–110.

[90] See *United States v. Hollinshead*, 495 F 2d 1154 (9th Cir. 1974); *United States v. McClain*, 545 F 2d 988 (5th Cir. 1977); Rehearing denied, 551 F 2d 52 (5th Cir. 1977); app. 593 F 2d 658 (5th Circ. 1979); cert denied 444 US 918, 100 S. Ct 234 (1979); *United States v. An Antique Platter of Gold*, 991 F Supp. 222 (SDNY 1999), affd 184 F 2d 131 (2nd Cir. 1999); and *United States v. Schultz*, 178 F Supp. 2d 445 (SDNY 2002), 333 F 3d 393 (2nd Cir. 2003); and Statement of US Secretary of State C. Powell, Press Release, 14 April 2003 (regarding Iraqi cultural objects).

[91] *Hansard*, Senate, vol.S113, cols.2233–34, 1 March 1986, Robertson; Customs Act 1901 (Cth), s.112. See B. Boer, Cultural and Natural Heritage: Protection of Movable Cultural Heritage (1987) 6 EPLJ 63; J. Battersby, Legislative Developments in Australia, in L. V. Prott and J. Specht (eds.), *Protection or Plunder? Safeguarding the Future of Our Cultural Heritage* (Canberra, 1989), p.92; O'Keefe, *Commentary*, pp.106ff; and H. H. Jamieson, The Protection of Australia's Movable Cultural Heritage (1995) 4 IJCP 215.

force, contrary to the provision of that law'.[92] Whilst the PMCHA is an important development in the protection of movable cultural heritage, it should be noted that it deals only with the movement of objects across national boundaries. It does not address the removal or destruction of cultural objects within Australia. This is contrasted with recent British legislation.

The United Kingdom became a State Party to the 1970 UNESCO Convention two decades after the United States. During the twentieth century, it had resisted any international instrument to curb the illicit trade in cultural objects by arguing that the burden should not fall on importing countries and that its implementation would require the passage of complicated domestic legislation.[93] Ironically, when it acceded to the 1970 UNESCO Convention the Blair Labour government announced that existing domestic laws complied with the treaty obligations.[94] Nonetheless, the UK parliament passed the Dealing in Cultural Objects (Offences) Act 2003 'designed to combat the traffic in unlawfully removed cultural objects . . . worldwide by removing the commercial incentive to those involved in the looting'.[95]

Under the 2003 Act, it a criminal offence to acquire or transfer an object removed from a structure or site located on or below land or water (Section 2(4)–(7)). It applies to acts committed within the United Kingdom (Section 2(3)(a)). There is no age restriction on the cultural objects or monument from which it is removed. Unlike the US NSPA, the prosecution needs to show only a breach of the national heritage law, of Britain or the relevant State (Section 2(3)), as opposed to theft.[96] Therefore, like the Australian law, the Dealing in Cultural Objects (Offences) Act goes beyond the protection of proprietary interests. However, the operation of the Act is constricted in a number of areas. First, the definition of the objects to which it applies is significantly narrower than the 1970 UNESCO Convention (Section 2(1)). Secondly, it relates only to objects removed or excavated after the Act came into force on 30 December 2003 (Section 2).[97] Thirdly, the prosecution must prove that the defendant knew or believed the object was tainted and his or her dealings with it were dishonest (Section 1(1)). This threshold is so onerous that the UK government estimated there would be one prosecution every two to three years.[98] Despite these

---

[92] J. F. Ley, *Australia's Protection of Movable Cultural Heritage: Report on the Ministerial Review of the Protection of Movable Cultural Heritage Act 1986 and Regulations* (Canberra, 1991), p.125. Cf. *Hansard*, HR, vol.145, col.3741, 27 November 1985, Cohen.

[93] See UNESCO, Final Report for Special Committee of Governmental Experts, 21 March 1964, UNESCO Doc.CUA/123/Add.1, Annex 1, 22–23; *Attorney-General of New Zealand* v. *Ortiz* [1982] QB 349 (QB), [1983] 2 WLR 809; [1984] AC 1 (HL); and Seventh Report of Select Committee on Culture, Media and Sport (1999–2000 HC 371), vol.1, para.76.

[94] Dealing in Cultural Objects (Offences) Act 2003, Explanatory Notes, para.6. See Report of Ministerial Advisory Panel on the Illicit Trade in Cultural Objects, May 2000, p.27, para.61.

[95] Explanatory Notes, para.7. The legislation's effectiveness has been questioned: First Report of the Select Committee on Culture, Media and Sport (2003–2004 HC 59).

[96] *Hansard*, HC, vol.402, col.1225, 4 April 2003, Allan. See Theft Act 1968; *Bumper Development Corporation* v. *Commissioner of Police for the Metropolis* [1991] 1 WLR 1362, [1991] 4 All ER 638 (CA); and *R.* v. *Tokeley-Parry* [1999] Crim. LR 578.

[97] When the removal is theft under local law the defendant could be prosecuted for handling stolen goods regardless of the date of removal or excavation: DCMS, *Guidance on the Dealing in Cultural Objects (Offences) Act 2003* (London, 2004).

[98] M. Bailey, A New UK Law to Fight Illicit Trade, *The Art Newspaper*, 11 January 2004, p.8.

limitations, it is clear the passage of the 2003 Act was driven by heightened awareness of London's central role in the illicit international art trade.[99]

Regulating export of indigenous cultural objects

The State-centric nature of current international protection of cultural heritage means that indigenous peoples and other non-State groups rely heavily on the relevant State for the protection of their cultural objects. The indigenous campaign for the restitution of cultural heritage at the international and national levels emerged following agitation for the return of ancestral remains for reburial. The earliest implementation of domestic laws pertaining to the control of indigenous cultural heritage by the communities themselves reflects this pattern.

The CCPIA does not address export controls of cultural heritage even though Article 6 of the 1970 UNESCO Convention places such an obligation on State Parties. US promotion of free trade of cultural objects has resulted in few restrictions on the export of its own cultural patrimony. Indeed, a US judge noted in 1990 that the United States has a 'short cultural memory'.[100] This position arises because of the United States' perceived imperviousness, because of its economic strength, to the loss of significant national cultural objects to overseas collectors.

However, as explained in Chapter 4, the US federal government did pass the Antiquities Act of 1906 which prohibits the export of Native American cultural objects under specific circumstances. Tellingly, the cultural objects to be protected were designated not by the indigenous communities but by the US President with guidance from archaeologists and anthropologists. The US federal government finally acknowledged the right of Native Americans to determine the preservation and protection of their cultural heritage with the passage of the Archaeological Resources Protection Act of 1979 (ARP Act) and, more particularly, Native American Graves Protection and Repatriation Act of 1990 (NAGPRA).[101] The ARP Act effectively replaced the 1906 Antiquities Act. Native Americans are to be advised of excavations on non-Native American public land that could result in harm to their religious or cultural sites. Any Native American complaints are advisory only and need not be heeded. The NAGPRA scheme is examined in Chapter 9.

Unlike the US enabling legislation, the Australian law does control the export of Australian cultural objects. The relevant federal Minister may refuse an export permit when he or she is satisfied that the object is of such importance to Australia, or 'part of Australia', that its loss would 'significantly diminish the cultural heritage of Australia' (Section 10(6)(b), PMCHA).[102] The Act sanctions the establishment of a fund for the purchase of objects to ensure their accessibility to the Australian

---

[99] See N. Brodie, J. Doole and P. Watson, *Stealing History: The Illicit Trade in Cultural Material* (Cambridge, 2000).

[100] *Autocephalous Greek-Orthodox Church of Cyprus and the Republic of Cyprus* v. *Goldberg & Feldman Fine Arts Inc.*, 917 F 2d 278, 297 (7th Cir. 1990). See P. Gerstenblith, Identity and Cultural Property: The Protection of Cultural Property in the United States (1995) 75 BULR 559 at 572–85.

[101] Pub. L. No.96–95, 93 Stat. 721 (1979), codified at 16 USC §470aa (2000).

[102] The Minister is advised by the National Cultural Heritage Committee. It advises the Minister, either of its own motion or pursuant to a ministerial request: ss.15–24, PMCHA.

public (Section 25). Further, the Act allows for a National Heritage Control List that designates objects which are subject to export control with no disadvantage to an owner (Section 8). Under the Act, certain types of Aboriginal and Torres Strait Islander cultural items are barred from export and the Minister may also designate further objects for protection and export control.[103]

The protection of Indigenous Australian cultural objects within Australia is governed by the Aboriginal and Torres Strait Islander Heritage Protection Act 1984 (Cth) (ATSIHP Act). This Act allows the federal government to step in to protect significant indigenous sites and objects, when State or Territory laws are ineffective. During the bill's second reading, Minister for Aboriginal Affairs Clyde Holding recognised that European settlement of Australia had resulted in 'pillage', 'attempted genocide' and 'systematic and unsystematic destruction of [Indigenous Australian] culture'.[104]

The purpose of the ATSIHP Act is to preserve and protect from injury or desecration areas and objects, including human remains, of particular significance to Indigenous Australians in accordance with Aboriginal traditions (Section 4).[105] By acknowledging the significance of these objects in indigenous customary law, the Act aids in the reversal of a 'mechanism of forgetfulness' by Australian museums and laws that privileged their importance to the scientific community and the national cultural identity. This shift is reflected in the 1993 national guidelines governing relations between Indigenous Australians and Australian museums.

While the ATSIHP Act provides legal protection for Indigenous Australian cultural heritage, the role of Indigenous Australians is limited. These restrictions betray their place within the Australian State. Aboriginal and Torres Strait Islander peoples can request the Minister to make a declaration to protect an object that is under threat of injury or desecration (Section 12). However, the Minister is required to consider the effects of the declaration on the proprietary or pecuniary interests of non-indigenous persons (Section 12(1)(c)). In 1989, the Australian federal government established the Aboriginal and Torres Strait Islander Commission (ATSIC) to facilitate the economic, social and cultural development of Indigenous Australians.[106] ATSIC provided early action and advice to the Minister on applications under the ATSIHP Act. However, the Commission operated within the legislative and political boundaries of the Australian State and its effectiveness was extremely sensitive to the policy agenda of the federal government. This was highlighted with ATSIC's abolition in 2005 (Aboriginal and Torres Strait Islander Commission Amendment Act (2004) Cth). The implications of this lack of autonomy for the capacity of indigenous

---

[103] See ss.7–13A, PMCHA; and Protection of Movable Cultural Heritage Property Regulations 1986 (Cth).

[104] *Hansard*, HR, vol.137, col.2133, 9 May 1984, Holding.

[105] See s.3(1), PMCHA; and E. Evatt, *Review of the Aboriginal and Torres Strait Islander Heritage Protection Act 1984* (Canberra, 1996), p.110.

[106] Aboriginal and Torres Strait Islander Commission Act 1989 (Cth). With federal allocated funds, ATSIC provided monies to establish and operate keeping places, community museums and cultural resources centres and facilitated the return of items of cultural property to Australia from overseas collections.

communities to determine how their cultural heritage is protected and developed are examined in Chapter 9.

During most of the last century, the United Kingdom steadfastly resisted export controls in the face of mounting losses of cultural objects to overseas collections. However, today, it operates an export licensing scheme for cultural objects which is designed to provide the State with an opportunity to retain items of outstanding national importance. The scheme seeks to balance the interests of the British nation, the individual owner, the exporter or purchaser, and the UK's position in the international art market.[107] Moreover, customs authorities are restricted in their capacity to halt the export of objects originally stolen or illicitly exported from a non-EU State.[108]

Unlike Australia and the United States, the United Kingdom is primarily tasked with facilitating rather than preventing the export of items from its collections to indigenous groups in settler States. It has been slow to accede to indigenous repatriation requests. Despite persistent resistance from some scientists and museum officials, a 2003 government-commissioned report on the repatriation of human remains from British national collections recommended export controls be clarified and amended, if necessary, to enable cross-border returns to the originating countries.[109]

Renegotiating relations between Indigenous Australians and museums

The current manager of the Aboriginal Heritage Unit at the Australian Museum, Phil Gordon, described his first year there, in 1980, as starting in 'complete ignorance' and finishing with 'doubts about whether it [was] doing it[s work] in the correct manner'.[110] His observation captures the tenor of the tentative renegotiation of relations between Indigenous Australians and Australian museums during the 1980s.

Up until this period, Australian museums were primarily concerned with the collection and preservation of objects, and the promotion of the dominant culture's viewpoint. However, increasing indigenous activism forced these institutions to gradually redefine their relations with Indigenous Australians and their role generally. This reflected the transition occurring in the indigenous policies of many settler States, away from the integration policies of the post-war period to the so-called 'self-determination' era.[111] Museums became essential to the broader campaign of

---

[107] DCMS, UK Export Licensing for Cultural Goods, Procedures and Guidelines for Exporters of Works of Art and Other Cultural Goods (Revised), 28 February 2003, p.1.

[108] See First Report of the Culture, Media and Sport Select Committee (2003–2004 HC 59), Recommendation 7; Government Response to Report of the 'Cultural objects: developments since 2000' (HC 59), Cm 6149 (2004), p.4; Council Directive 1993/7/EEC of 15 March 1993, as amended, on the return of cultural objects unlawfully removed from the territory of a Member State, OJ 1993 No.L74, 27 March 1993, p.74; and Return of Cultural Objects Regulations 1994.

[109] Palmer, *Report*, p.153, Recommendation X (xxxv).

[110] P. Gordon, From Ignorance to Doubt: My first year at the Australian Museum (1981), 7 *COMA Newsletter* 15.

[111] In Australia, this included the establishment of the Aboriginal Development Commission (Aboriginal Development Commission Act 1980 (Cth)) and ATSIC: J. Crawford, *The Recognition of Aboriginal Customary Law*, Australian Law Reform Commission, Report No.31, (3 vols., Canberra, 1986), vol.I, pp.22–23. In the US context: F. S. Cohen, *F S Cohen's Handbook of Federal Indian Law*, ed. R. Strickland (Charlottesville, 1982), pp.180ff.

Figure 8.2 Aboriginal Australia gallery, Australian Museum, Sydney, 1985.

cultural autonomy and revitalisation by indigenous peoples. This role also entailed the implementation of the process of restitution, including the education of the general public of the effects of colonial occupation on indigenous individuals, communities and cultures.

This final section examines early efforts to redefine relations between Indigenous Australians and Australian museums. First, the link between indigenous claims for the return of cultural heritage and the campaigns for land rights and repatriation of ancestral remains is detailed. Then, there is an explanation of how these events affected the changing relationship between the Australian Museum and Indigenous Australians. Finally, the impact of this process is described in respect of the changing nature of the Museum's exhibition programme. It becomes clear that whilst the number of successful returns was limited during the period, the relationship

Figure 8.3 Aboriginal Australia gallery, Australian Museum, Sydney, 1985.

between Indigenous Australians and the museum community, and the function of these institutions, was being irrevocably altered.

Return of land, return of cultural identity
In the early 1980s, formal requests and legal action by indigenous organisations concerning ancestral remains and cultural objects held by museums in Tasmania, Victoria and South Australia became turning points in the relationship between Australian museums and Indigenous Australians.[112] The ensuing debate gradually

---

[112] See Anon., Tasmanian Museum and Art Gallery: The Skeletal Debate, (1983) 12 *COMA Bulletin* 18; R. Weatherall, Aboriginals, Archaeologists and the Rights of the Dead (1989) 19 *Australian Archaeology* 122; T. Griffiths, *Hunters and Collectors: The Antiquarian Imagination in Australia* (Cambridge, 1996), 94–100; and P. Turnbull, Indigenous Australian People, Their Defence of the Dead and Native Title, in C. Fforde, J. Hubert and P. Turnbull (eds.), *The Dead and Their Possessions: Repatriation in Principle, Policy and Practice* (London, 2002), p.63.

led to the formulation of a national museum policy concerning Aboriginal and Torres Strait Islander peoples.

In early 1982, a group of Aranda elders from Central Australia and a representative from the National Aboriginal Conference visited the South Australian Museum seeking the return of *tjurunga* (secret sacred objects) to Central Australia. The Board of Trustees advised the claimants that it would 'balance the sincere, sustainable wishes of responsible tribal elders against the role of the Board, which acts as trustee on behalf of the whole South Australian community'.[113] The trustees also expressed concern about the precedent any such return would create within the general Australian museum community and its own limited financial resources in resolving such claims. Steven Hemming, who was involved in the negotiations on behalf of the museum, recorded that younger indigenous men referred to the *tjurunga* as 'title deeds to the Land'.[114] The correlation articulated by the Aranda men echoes that made by the British delegation during the 1815 Congress of Vienna. Their words reaffirm the 'sacred' link between peoples, land and cultural objects. When seeking to reverse their dispossession, Indigenous Australians, like other occupied peoples, assert the right to determine the preservation and development of their cultures as part of the right to self-determination.[115]

Indigenous Australian land rights claims have been closely aligned with this exercise of self-determination and cultural development. In 1963, the Yirrkala people were increasingly anxious about the impact of mining development on their sacred sites and presented a bark petition detailing their claim for land rights.[116] In response, the Federal Court of Australia in 1971 affirmed the applicability of the principle of *terra nullius* (uninhabited land) in Australian common law.[117] To address indigenous claims, the federal Labor government in 1983 unsuccessfully attempted to pass a national land rights scheme through the Australian parliament.[118] When introducing the bill, Clyde Holding stated:

> This generation of non-Aboriginal Australians may ask why they should be the ones to right the wrongs of their forebears. The answer is that, until this great issue is settled, and these legacies of the past are redressed, Australians – all of us – can never be truly free, never live in harmony and with a sense of equality.[119]

[113] South Australian Museum, *Annual Report of the South Australian Museum Board for the Year Ending 30 June 1983* (Adelaide, 1983), p.8. See P. Jones, Museums and Sacred Materials: The South Australian Museum's experience, I: History and Background (1989) 16 *COMA Bulletin* 16.

[114] S. Hemming, Museums and Sacred Materials: The South Australian Museum's experience, II: Development of the Issue (1985) 16 *COMA Bulletin* 22 at 30.

[115] See H. Goodan, *Invasion to Embassy: Land in Aboriginal Politics in New South Wales, 1770–1972* (Singapore, 1996), pp.1–19.

[116] See W. E. H. Stanner, The Yirrkala Land Case: Dress-Rehearsal, in W. E. H. Stanner, *White Man Got No Dreaming: Essays 1938–1973* (Canberra, 1979), pp.275ff, and N. Pearson, Mabo: Towards Respecting Equality and Difference, in *Voices from the Land: 1993 Boyer Lectures* (Sydney, 1994), p.89 at pp.95–96.

[117] *Milirrpum* v. *Nabalco Pty Limited and Anor* (1971) 17 FLR 141.

[118] See H. McRae *et al.*, *Indigenous Legal Issues: Commentary and Materials* (Erskenville, 1997), pp.171 and 205–07.

[119] *Hansard*, HR, vol.134, col.3489, 8 December 1983.

This central 'mechanism of forgetfulness' of Australian national domestic law remained intact until the 1992 *Mabo (No.2)* case which 'recognised' the existence of native title to land.[120]

In late 1984, the South Australian Museum Board issued a policy statement advising that 'material of ceremonial significance will be returned to living "owners" who are descendants of people who have a right pursuant to customary law to such material, if that was their wish'.[121] Chris Anderson, a social anthropologist employed by the museum in the wake of the Aranda request, maintained that museums needed to foster long-term relationships with indigenous communities regardless of whether they had received a restitution request or not. During the 1990s, as director of the South Australian Museum, Anderson became instrumental in the formulation of the 1993 national museums policy, which reflected this aim.

Redefining return and the role of museums
The 1980s marked a significant period of renegotiation of relations between the Australian Museum, Sydney and Indigenous Australians leading to a redefining of the role of the museum generally. The museum responded to increasing pressure from indigenous organisations within Australia and the Pacific region, and the work of the UNESCO Committee and UN Working Group on Indigenous Populations. It was also guided by the 1978 Adelaide Seminar recommendations,[122] 1980 Conference of Museum Anthropologists (COMA) recommendations,[123] and 1993 Council of Australian Museums Association (CAMA) national policy (1993 CAMA policy).[124] This section examines how the Australian Museum strove to provide training and resources to indigenous communities to facilitate cultural revitalisation and economic self-sufficiency. Then, there is a detailing of how it facilitated increased accessibility to indigenous peoples and the general public. Finally, the limitations on the museum's repatriation programme during the period are outlined.

Since the 1970s, the Australian Museum has engaged in technical cooperation with indigenous peoples of New South Wales and the Pacific States, inside and outside the walls of its institution. The importance of employing indigenous people in positions of responsibility within existing state and national museums, to reshape the mindset of these institutions, was recognised during the 1978 Adelaide Conference. This stance was reaffirmed by the 1993 CAMA policy which also referred to existing

---

[120] *Mabo & Ors v. Queensland (No.2)* (1992) 175 CLR 1, 107 ALR 1.
[121] C. Anderson, Research and the Return of Objects as a Social Process (1986) 19 *COMA Bulletin* 2 at 3.
[122] Seminar Recommendations, in R. Edwards and J. Stewart (eds.), *Preserving Indigenous Cultures: A New Role for Museums* (Canberra, 1980), pp.9ff.
[123] COMA, Recommendations concerning the UNESCO Seminar (1980) 5 *COMA Bulletin* 4.
[124] CAMA, *Previous Possession, New Obligations: Policies for Museums in Australia and Aboriginal and Torres Strait Islander Peoples*, 1993 (Reprint, Melbourne, 2000). It was recently superseded by Museums Australia, *Continuous Cultures Ongoing Responsibilities: A Comprehensive Policy Document and Guidelines for Australian museums working with Aboriginal and Torres Strait Islander Cultural Heritage* (Canberra, 2005).

anti-discrimination legislation.[125] In 1989, CAMA president Barrie Reynolds argued that '[i]ndigenisation will steadily advance so that by the end of the century we shall perhaps find a majority of curatorial positions held by Aboriginal and Torres Strait Islander people'.[126] Reynolds's prediction has not come to fruition. However, the indigenous people who were employed have had a profound influence on reshaping relations between communities and museums and defining the role of these institutions. These changes are detailed in Chapter 9.

The push to establish keeping places within indigenous communities arose from the Homelands or outstations movement of the 1960s and 70s.[127] Initially, non-indigenous Australians encouraged the growth of keeping places as a means of indigenous cultural renewal and economic self-sufficiency.[128] They made a strong link between the preservation and display of indigenous cultural objects in keeping places or local museums and the repatriation process.[129] The 1993 CAMA policy recommended that museums support the establishment and ongoing funding of keeping places and cultural centres in local indigenous communities.[130] Kelly, Gordon and Sullivan suggest that whilst keeping places augmented the repatriation process, they also enabled indigenous communities to teach non-indigenous Australians and Indigenous Australians about the vitality and diversity of indigenous cultures through exhibitions, public education and research programmes.[131] Indeed, they were quickly tailored to the needs of individual communities where they were located and gradually bore little resemblance to the function contemplated by their non-indigenous co-founders.[132] These needs range from protecting their culture from the assimilatory tendencies of the dominant culture, to the promotion of local employment.[133]

The Australian Museum's Aboriginal Heritage Unit runs an outreach programme that provides indigenous participants throughout New South Wales with training in museum-based skills, to develop and operate a keeping place within their regional

[125] See CAMA, *PPNO*, Principles 10 and 11, policies 5.1–5.2; and MA, *CCOR*, Principle 11 and 12, and guidelines, 3.1–3.4, 5.2.

[126] B. Reynolds, Museums in Anthropology: Anthropology in Museums (1989) 22 *COMA Bulletin* 11 at 13.

[127] See H. C. Coombs, Decentralisation Trends amongst Aboriginal Communities (1973) 1 *Aboriginal News* 14; P. Brokensha and C. McGuirgan, Listening to the Dreaming: The Aboriginal Homelands Movement (1977) 19 *Australian Natural History* 119; and J. Isaacs (ed.), *Renewing the Dreaming: The Aboriginal Homelands Exhibition. Anniversary Exhibition 1827–1977* (exh. cat., Sydney, 1997).

[128] See M. K. C. West, Keeping Places v. Museums – the North Australian Example (1981) 7 *COMA Bulletin* 9.

[129] See M. Simpson, *Making Representations: Museums in the Post-Colonial Era* (London, 2001), p.241; and C. Samson, Aboriginal Keeping Places (1988) 20 *COMA Bulletin* 20. Cf. West, 'Keeping'; and C. Anderson, Comments on 'Aboriginal Keeping Places' (1988) 20 *COMA Bulletin* 24.

[130] CAMA, *PPNO*, policy 4.5; and MA, *CCOR*, guideline 5.7. See Adelaide Seminar Recommendations, (1978 Adelaide Conference), p.13; and COMA Recommendation no.5.

[131] See L. Kelly, P. Gordon and T. Sullivan, 'We Deal with Relationships Not just Objects': An Evaluation of *Previous Possessions, New Obligation*, Green Paper, Museums Australia, revised 20 February 2001 (copy on file), p.16.

[132] See Samson, 'Aboriginal'; and Simpson, *Making*, pp.120–22.

[133] Interview with P. Gordon, Manager, Aboriginal Heritage Unit, Australian Museum, Sydney, 26 February 1999; and P. Gordon, Community Museums: The Australian Experience, in R. Ogawa (ed.), *Community Museums in Asia, Report on a Training Workshop* (Tokyo, 1998), p.132.

communities. It harnesses the experiences of those with an existing keeping place to encourage and assist those planning to establish one in their own locale. By the late 1990s, keeping places had become the focus of a plethora of community-inspired cultural and social activities such as language preservation and oral history recording.[134]

For indigenous communities, cultural renewal is essential to their exercise of the right to self-determination. The 1978 Adelaide Conference recommended that indigenous communities determine the development and marketing of their arts and crafts.[135] Cultural objects repatriated from museum collections to local communities often inspire indigenous artists and craftspeople producing contemporary works.[136] The 1993 CAMA policy requires museums to actively promote recognition of all forms of contemporary Indigenous Australian culture as 'vital, living, diverse and changing'.[137] The Australian Museum collects contemporary indigenous works in traditional and Western media.[138] Such initiatives are crucial in reversing the time-worn practice of natural history museums presenting indigenous cultures as static and 'dying', as well as assisting the communities economically.

Technical cooperation and increased accessibility between Australian museums and indigenous communities led to the redefinition of the role of these institutions and a re-evaluation of their functions and methodologies. By the late 1980s, museum officials were increasingly receptive to indigenous expectations that keeping places be established within existing major state museums, with restricted access to ancestral remains and secret sacred objects.[139] Accessibility to Indigenous Australian collections held by Australian museums was central to the renegotiation of relations between museums and the indigenous communities whose cultures were represented in their collections.[140] For indigenous peoples, the question of accessibility was divided between the relevant indigenous community and the general public.

---

[134] Aboriginal Heritage Unit, Keeping Culture: Achieving Self-determination through the Development of Aboriginal Cultural Centres and Keeping Places (CD-ROM), (Sydney, 2001); P. Gordon, Museums, Indigenous Peoples and the 21st Century: Or Is there a Place for Museums in this Brave New World?, in Ogawa (ed.), *Community*, p.34 at p.40; Simpson, *Making*, pp.107ff and 221ff; J. Specht and C. MacLulich, Changes and Challenges: The Australian Museum and Indigenous Communities, in P. McManus (ed.), *Archaeological Displays and the Public* (London, 1996), p.27 at p.36; and S. Thomsett, The Australian Museum's Training Programme for Community Museums (1985) 16 *COMA Bulletin* 39.

[135] 1978 Adelaide Seminar Recommendations, (1978 Adelaide Conference), pp.13–14. Aboriginal Arts Board of the Australia Council (later Aboriginal and Torres Strait Islander Arts Board), Aboriginal Arts and Crafts Pty Ltd and later ATSIC's Arts and Crafts Industry Support Strategy drove this agenda.

[136] See Edwards and Stewart, *Preserving*, p.13.

[137] CAMA, *PPNO*, policy 4.4; and MA, *CCOR*, guideline 1.2.1.

[138] See Australian Museum, *Annual Report 1983/84* (Sydney, 1984), p.13; and Australian Museum, *Annual Report 1985/86* (Sydney, 1986), p.11.

[139] Interview with P. Gordon; Australian Museum, *Annual Report 1987/88* (Sydney, 1988), p.13; and C. Anderson, The Economics of Sacred Art: The Uses of a Secret Collection in the South Australian Museum (1990) 23 *COMA Bulletin* 31.

[140] See J. Specht *et al.*, Working Together on Issues of Access: Indigenous Peoples and the Australian Museum, in *Something for Everyone: Access to Museums* (Adelaide, 1991), p.185.

The accessibility afforded to the general public was modified in two important respects:

(1) access to ancestral remains, secret sacred materials and culturally significant objects was determined by the relevant indigenous community;[141]
(2) museums were to make Indigenous Australian cultures more accessible to the general public. Through exhibitions, publications and new technologies, museums were required to improve national awareness of the vitality and diversity of contemporary indigenous cultures. In addition, exhibitions would address contemporary indigenous issues and ways of life.

This shift was reinforced by recommendations that Indigenous Australians be actively consulted and involved in the public programmes through their appointment as curators, administrators and trustees as well as through the establishment of indigenous advisory bodies in museums.[142]

The latter recommendation fed into the question of the accessibility afforded indigenous communities, including the ability to determine physical access to relevant collections and related data, availability of comprehensive and comprehensible information concerning museum holdings, and determining the storage, display and interpretation of their cultures.[143] The Australian Museum noted that '[w]e do not set "limits" to access . . . [W]e share a country . . . with indigenous people for whom the artefacts . . . still play important roles'.[144] However, for many museum professionals these restrictions on accessibility negated the role of museums. Nevertheless, there can be little doubt that indigenous demands for accessibility to museums and their collections irrevocably altered the mandate of these institutions. Chris Anderson noted that they moved away from 'museology's basic premise of the sanctity and primacy of the object' to 'focus on the human relationships that cultural objects have always represented'.[145]

The examples of return finalised by the Australian Museum during the 1980s reflected a growing awareness of the role of museum collecting practices within the larger European colonial enterprise in the Asia Pacific.[146] At the opening of the 1988 'Pieces of Paradise: Pacific Artefacts through Many Eyes' exhibition, three culturally significant objects were returned by the Museum Trust to national museums

---

[141] See C. Anderson, Aboriginal People and Museums: Restricting Access to Increase It (1992) 12 *Artlink* 11.

[142] Adelaide Seminar Recommendations, (1978 Adelaide Conference), pp.13–15; COMA Recommendation Nos.1, 2 and 11; CAMA, *PPNO*, principle 12, policies 4.1–4.4, 6.1, 7.1–7.2; and MA, *CCOR*, Principles 5–8, and guidelines 1.2.1–1.2.3. The Australian Museum appointed its first indigenous trustee, Faith Bandler in 1985; an Aboriginal Liaison Officer who established the Aboriginal Heritage Unit; and an Aboriginal Advisory Committee to represent the views of indigenous communities in New South Wales in 1990.

[143] CAMA, *PPNO*, principles 5 and 6.   [144] Specht *et al.*, 'Working', p.188.

[145] C. Anderson, Australian Aborigines and Museums: A New Relationship (1990) 33 *Curator* 165 at 170. See T. Naranjo, Musing on Two World Views, in B. Meister (ed.) *Mending the Circle: A Native American Repatriation Guide* (New York, 1996), pp.27ff.

[146] See Specht and MacLulich, 'Changes', pp.38–39; and Bonshek, 'Objects', pp.247ff.

in Papua New Guinea, Vanuatu and the Solomon Islands.[147] The exhibition was a centrepiece of the museum's commemoration of the bicentenary of the British settlement of Australia. In his foreword to the exhibition catalogue, Director Des Griffin wrote:

> These artefacts reflect to a large degree Australia's previous colonial relationship with the region . . . [W]e are neither ashamed nor frightened to present images of these artefacts, for the circumstances under which many of them came to our Museum belong to a past that cannot be changed.[148]

The exhibition's curator Jim Specht detailed the collecting history of local material cultures by colonial powers. He also noted that the illicit transfer of cultural objects from this region, and their reappearance on the international art market, had escalated exponentially following decolonisation.[149]

Restitution of cultural objects to indigenous communities in Australia was limited during the 1980s, however, and was effected on the basis of loans to indigenous communities for display in suitable local facilities. Ownership of these items still lay firmly with the museum. The Australian Museum also commenced negotiations with overseas institutions for the return of indigenous cultural objects representative of New South Wales communities.[150] These returns were made to the museum itself and not the relevant community.

'Aboriginal Australia' representing the transition

The transition in the relationship between the Australian Museum and Indigenous Australians during the 1980s was evidenced in the development of the semi-permanent exhibition entitled 'Aboriginal Australia'. The exhibition's planning commenced after the 1978 Adelaide Conference and it was opened in 1985. From the inception of the planning process, the gallery's curator Ronald Lampert insisted on consultation with indigenous communities.[151] The communities and their leaders highlighted the need to depict contemporary indigenous ways of life and the ongoing effects of colonisation on indigenous people and cultures. This resulted in a number of fundamental alterations to the original plans, with the indigenous viewpoint being given priority in the overall layout of the exhibition. For example, aspects of religious and burial practices were not exhibited pursuant to Indigenous Australian requests.

At the opening of the new gallery, Griffin argued that museums were a means of educating the general public of the need 'that ordinary human rights, ordinary

---

[147] Australian Museum, *Annual Report 1987/88* (Sydney, 1988), pp.4, 5 and 11; Australian Museum, *Annual Report 1988/89* (Sydney, 1989), p.12; Specht and MacLulich, 'Changes', pp.37–38; and M. Spriggs, Fragments of What? Thoughts on the 'Pieces of Paradise' exhibition at the Australian Museum (1989) 20 *Australian Archaeology* 66.

[148] D. J. G. Griffin, Foreword, in J. Specht, *Pieces of Paradise* (Sydney, 1988), p.2.

[149] J. Specht, Introduction, in Specht, *Pieces*, pp.4–7.

[150] See Australian Museum, *Annual Report 1980/81* (Sydney, 1981), p.12.

[151] See R. Lampert, The Development of the Aboriginal Gallery at the Australian Museum (1986) 18 *COMA Bulletin* 10; The Australian Museum – New Aboriginal Australia Exhibition – A Report to the Sponsor (1982), CRS 1437–3 Aboriginal Gallery 1982–1985, Australian Museum Archives, Sydney (AMA); Specht and MacLulich, 'Changes', pp.31–33; and Specht *et al.*, 'Working', p.186.

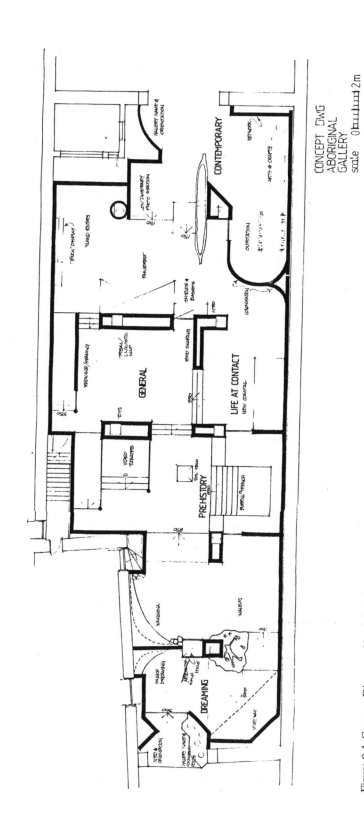

Figure 8.4 Concept Diagram, Aboriginal Gallery, Australian Museum, 1982.

human dignity, be guaranteed to all Aboriginal people'.[152] This process involved the renunciation of the 'scale of civilisation' that had for so long been promoted by museums:

> [T]he aim of counteracting the following attitudes that reinforce racist perceptions of aboriginal peoples . . . that aboriginal people are stone age and that human development is a climb from barbarism to Western materialism and industrialisation.[153]

For Lampert, the exhibition had an intellectual purpose of providing information about indigenous cultures, their history, diversity and 'survival against the odds'. He also noted its social purpose of improving the attitude of the public towards indigenous peoples.[154]

The gallery was composed of five thematic areas, including:

(1) the Dreaming – being an indigenous interpretation of their own and the continent's past. This was represented by rock paintings created by David Mowaljarlai;
(2) and by contrast, a Western scientific interpretation of the same period was represented in a three-dimensional reproduction of an archaeological dig;
(3) the effects of British colonisation on indigenous society. There was acknowledgement of the devastating effects of assimilation, removal from traditional lands, confinement on government reserves and removal of half-caste children on the physical and cultural development of indigenous peoples;[155]
(4) various indigenous ways of life which existed at the time of European settlement; and
(5) the contemporary lifestyles of Indigenous Australians in the bush and cities. It included a photographic display of prominent Indigenous Australians with their biographical details and space designed to change periodically to accommodate small displays by indigenous communities themselves.[156]

In some ways, 'Aboriginal Australia' echoed d'Harnoncourt's efforts to promote Native American arts and crafts through the 1941 MoMA exhibition, 'Indian Art of the United States'. However, cultural development and economic self-sufficiency were not the primary goals here. The Australian Museum exhibition overtly encouraged its audience to remember the relations between indigenous and non-indigenous Australians and the influence of colonialism on the daily lives of indigenous individuals, communities and their cultures.

The manner in which official governmental policies, international and domestic laws, and museums marginalised indigenous peoples and de-contextualised their

---

[152] D. J. G. Griffin speech for Aboriginal Gallery Opening, 1 March 1985, in CRS 1437-3 Aboriginal Gallery 1982–1985, AMA.
[153] Aims of the Aboriginal Gallery Update, 1982, Box 1, AN93/36, Aboriginal Gallery 1982–1985, AMA.
[154] Lampert, 'Development', 16.
[155] The Dreaming – Draft Four and Topics, Box 1, AN93/36, Aboriginal Gallery 1982–1985, AMA.
[156] Specht and MacLulich, 'Changes', p.32.

cultural heritage is a recurring theme of this book. In the last decades of the twentieth century, indigenous organisations strove to ensure that States and the international community remembered their peoples whose 'essence' they had for so long striven to expunge from the collective national memory. The reversal of these 'mechanisms of forgetfulness' was crucial to indigenous peoples' efforts to preserve, protect and develop their cultural identities on their terms.

The assertion of the right to self-determination, and claims for the restitution of cultural heritage by indigenous peoples, was built upon the notion of restitution as a process developed by newly independent States during the 1960s and 70s. However, despite the achievements of the campaigns of indigenous organisations in the 1980s, there was a central failure of this restitution agenda. Whilst indigenous communities increasingly determined accessibility, display and storage of their cultural objects, thereby gradually redefining the role of museums, the museums of States and former metropolitan powers continued to possess and own these objects. This result is emblematic of their continuing occupation – their internal colonisation.

By the late 1980s, indigenous peoples' claims for the restitution of their cultural heritage could not be ignored by States or former colonial powers. Griffin noted:

> Museums have a major role to play in placing the artistic products of Aboriginal and other indigenous peoples in context, to explain how such material relates to the sacred and profane aspects of Aboriginal life.[157]

The next chapter considers the return of indigenous cultural heritages from the profane to the sacred, from the museums of metropolitan powers to the communities of origin.

---

[157] See 'Aboriginal Gallery Opening', 2.

Figure 9.1 Indigenous Australians, gallery entrance, Australian Museum, Sydney, 1997.

9

Indigenous peoples, States and reconciliation

> History teaches us that the way to genocide is to take a culture and destroy its credibility so it can no longer reflect itself.[1]

> [T]he nation as a whole must remain diminished unless and until there is an acknowledgment of, and retreat from, those past injustices.[2]

> Fundamentally the reconciliation process has to involve recognition of what happened rather than simple acceptance of it.[3]

For indigenous peoples, the right to self-determination must include the ability to determine how their cultures and its manifestations are protected, preserved and developed. Their ongoing contemporary campaign for the return of ownership and control of cultural objects held in metropolitan museums is essential to the effective exercise of this right. This chapter considers the significance of the right to restitution of cultural heritage in promoting cultural diversity – ensuring 'each people makes its contribution to the culture of the world'.[4]

Indigenous peoples' claims for the physical and intellectual control of their cultural objects challenge the foundational premise of international law and museum collections. The claim for indigenous control sets up a confrontation between rival collective memories and narratives within States. For States, the integrity of national collections and the retention of indigenous cultural objects were fundamental to their national cultural identity. The assimilation of indigenous peoples, their lands and cultural objects was critical to the formation of settler States and their national economic and cultural development.[5] For indigenous peoples, these objects embody the negation of the 'dying race' theories of the dominant culture through the revitalisation of their own cultures. The recognition of indigenous control and ownership of these cultural objects reaffirms their presence prior to European settlement. It acknowledges the continuation and development of their cultures and communities despite the policies and practices of colonialism.

---

[1] R. Merritt, cited by H. Fourmile, Submission on behalf of Aboriginal and Torres Strait Islander Social Justice Commissioner, in *Culture and Heritage Inquiry: Submissions, Report of the Standing Committee on Aboriginal and Torres Strait Islander Affairs* (Canberra, 1997), p.S0929.

[2] *Mabo & Ors* v. *Queensland (No.2)* (1992) 175 CLR 1, at 109, Deane and Gaudron JJ.

[3] D. J. G. Griffin, Necessity: The Plea for Every Infringement of Human Freedom, 2, D. J. G. Griffin Papers, Australian Museum Archives, Sydney (AMA).

[4] Second recital, Preamble, Convention for the Protection of Cultural Property in the Event of Armed Conflict, The Hague, 14 May 1954, in force 7 August 1956, 249 UNTS 240.

[5] 175 CLR 1 at 69, Brennan J.

Indigenous peoples invite States and their citizens to recognise indigenous narratives, customs and laws, thereby subverting the apparent exclusivity and objectivity of those of the dominant culture. This moral restitution, it is argued, would facilitate the reconciliation of indigenous and non-indigenous peoples within States and the international community.

This chapter examines current measures to accommodate the rights of indigenous peoples to the restitution of their cultural heritage within existing international and national legal frameworks. It is shown that the 'acknowledgment, and retreat from past injustices' has been tentative and incremental. First, there is an explanation of the interrelation between the right to self-determination and the right to restitution of cultural heritage in the Draft UN Declaration on the Rights of Indigenous Peoples (1993 Draft UN Declaration). Next, the rationale and parameters of the right to restitution are outlined in the context of the draft declaration and Daes's Principles and Guidelines. Third, recent efforts to accommodate the right of indigenous peoples to restitution of cultural heritage are examined in relation to the 1995 UNIDROIT Convention on Stolen or Illegally Exported Cultural Objects and the national responses of the United States, Australia and the United Kingdom. Finally, there is a brief description of how museum collections and archives are being utilised to reconcile the narratives and memories of indigenous and non-indigenous peoples.

Self-determination and the 1993 Draft UN Declaration

The UN Working Group on Indigenous Populations (WGIP) agreed on the final text of the Draft UN Declaration on the Rights of Indigenous Peoples (1993 Draft UN Declaration) in 1993.[6] The WGIP views this text as 'comprehensive and reflect[ing] the legitimate aspirations of Indigenous peoples as a whole'.[7] The draft declaration is being considered presently by a working group, established by the Commission on Human Rights Working Group (CHRWG).[8] The CHRWG eventually agreed to work from the 1993 draft. However, its 'reworking' of the provisions reflects the greater involvement of States and the increased impediments to effective indigenous input in this phase of the declaration's development.[9] The declaration was not adopted by the UN General Assembly in 2004 as was originally intended.[10]

For indigenous organisations, the right to self-determination of all peoples, including indigenous peoples, is the foundation of the document.[11] They tie the right to the restitution of their cultural heritage inextricably to the right to self-determination. Equally, the interpretations and limitations placed on the right to self-determination

---

[6] Approved 26 August 1994, UN Doc.E/CN.4/Sub.2/Res/1994/56; and (1995) 34 ILM541.

[7] See E.-I. Daes, Report on the Working Group on Indigenous Populations on its Twelfth Session, 17 August 1994, UN Doc.E/CN.4/Sub.2/1994/30, para.133.

[8] CHR Res.1995/32, UN Doc.E/1995/23, 110; and Sub-Comm. Res.1994/45, 26 August 1994.

[9] See R. Barsh, Indigenous Peoples and the UN Commission on Human Rights: A Case of the Immovable Object and the Irresistible Force (1996) 18 HRQ 782 at 783–86.

[10] UNGA Res.50/157 of 21 December 1995.

[11] See S. Pritchard, *Setting International Standards: An Analysis of the UN Declaration on the Rights of Indigenous Peoples and the First Six Sessions of the Commission on Human Rights Working Group* (3rd edn, Sydney, 2001), pp.52–58.

by some States mirror their apprehension concerning the inclusion of a right to restitution of cultural heritage.

While settler States like Australia and the United States support the incorporation of the right to self-determination into the 1993 Draft UN Declaration, they have stridently reiterated the application of the principles of State sovereignty and territorial integrity.[12] They argue that indigenous communities – like all other peoples in independent States with representative governments – have a right to self-determination not a right to statehood. The form of self-determination advocated by these States as exercisable by indigenous peoples is reminiscent of the inter-war minority guarantees. They contend that the right includes the right to participate in national affairs on an equal basis like other citizens; and the right to preserve and develop their distinct cultural identity 'with a power to take decisions over their own affairs'.[13]

Indigenous peoples have vigorously rejected the application of the term 'minorities' to their communities by States. They argue that it decontextualises the impact of colonial occupation on their present circumstances.[14] However, indigenous peoples have implicitly invoked Article 27 of the International Covenant on Civil and Political Rights (ICCPR) despite its intrinsic limitations.[15]

WGIP Chair Erica-Irene Daes explained the delineation between internal and external self-determination thus:

external self-determination entails determination of a people's international status and liberation from foreign rule; and

internal self-determination refers primarily to determination of the system of government and administration, and 'to preserve its cultural, ethnic, historical or territorial identity' through the promotion of individual and collective political participation, democratic governance and cultural diversity.[16]

Indigenous organisations, however, stress the need to move beyond the preoccupation with the internal/external dichotomy and whether secession attaches to the

---

[12] L.-E. Chávez, Report of the Working Group Established in Accordance with CHR Res.1995/32, Fifth Session, 6 December 1999, UN Doc.E/CN.4/2000/84, paras.49, 50 and 62; Eighth Session, 6 January 2003, UN Doc.E/CN.4/2003/92, paras.22 and 24; Ninth Session, 7 January 2004, UN Doc.E/CN.4/2004/81, para.68; and UN Doc.E/CN.4/2004/WG.15/CRP.1, p.5. See J. Crawford, The Right to Self-Determination in International Law: Its Development and Future, in P. Alston (ed.), *Peoples' Rights* (Oxford, 2001), p.7; and M. C. Lâm, Indigenous Peoples' Conception of Their Self-Determination in International Law, in C. Lynch and M. Loriaux (eds.), *Law and Moral Action in World Politics* (Minneapolis, 2000), p.205.

[13] See Information received from the Government of Australia, Self-Determination – The Australian Position, 30 November 1995, UN Doc.E/CN.4/1995/WG.15/2/Add.2, para.12.

[14] See A. Eide and E.-I. Daes, Working Paper on the Relationship and distinction between the Rights of Persons Belonging to Minorities and Those of Indigenous Peoples, 19 July 2000, UN Doc.E/CN.4/Sub.2/2000/10; R. Barsh, Indigenous Peoples: An Emerging Object of International Law (1986) 80 AJIL 369 at 373–374; and H. Hannum, *Autonomy, Sovereignty and Self-Determination: The Accommodation of Conflicting Rights* (Philadelphia, 1990), pp.88–91.

[15] See B. Kingsbury, Reconciling Five Competing Conceptual Structures of Indigenous Peoples' Claims to International and Comparative Law, in Alston, *Peoples*, p.69 at p.78; J. Crawford, *The Recognition of Aboriginal Customary Law*, Law Reform Commission, Report No.31 (3 vols., Canberra, 1986), vol.I, pp.128ff; and Human Rights Committee, General Comment No.23, UN Doc.HRI/GEN/1/Rev.1 at 38 (1994), paras.3.2, 7.

[16] E.-I. Daes, Explanatory Note concerning the Draft Declaration on the Rights of Indigenous Peoples, 19 July 1993, UN Doc.E/CN.4/Sub.2/1993/26/Add.1, paras.17 and 19.

right.[17] They challenge the international community and its member States to recognise the tenacious durability of colonialism and its effects, and to rethink current international and national structures to facilitate the realisation of the right to self-determination of all peoples. The right is viewed as a process, involving a renegotiation of political, economic, social and cultural arrangements with States to provide an agreed form of autonomy.[18]

Indigenous peoples have consistently maintained that their current circumstances arise from their ongoing colonial occupation and 'dispossession of their lands, territories and resources'.[19] Daes acknowledges that during decolonisation, indigenous peoples were usually not invited to participate in the drafting of the constitutions of new States, nor do they have any 'meaningful' role in national decision-making.[20] She maintains that existing States have a duty through constitutional reform to 'accommodate' the aspirations of indigenous peoples for democratic power-sharing. Indigenous peoples, she argues, also have a duty to negotiate in good faith with the existing State in the pursuit of such aims.[21] The persistent discriminatory and assimilatory policies of many States, and the continuing denial of some Asian States of the existence of indigenous communities in their territories, compromise this process.[22]

For indigenous peoples, the right to self-determination contained within the first part of the 1993 Draft UN Declaration 'is the river in which all other rights swim'.[23] Draft Article 3 replicates the right as enunciated in Common Article 1 of the ICCPR and International Covenant on Economic, Social and Cultural Rights.[24] However, the deference to 'constitutional accommodation' inherently privileges the laws and customs of the relevant State and thereby restricts the right to self-determination of indigenous peoples. Indigenous organisations insist that the right to self-determination is *jus cogens*, a rule from which no State can derogate.[25] Therefore, they argue that the denial of the full exercise of this right for indigenous peoples, including the option of secession, is

---

[17] UN Doc.E/CN.4/2000/84, paras.43–47; UN Doc.E/CN.4/2001/85, para.78; and UN Doc.E/CN.4/2003/92, para.24. See K. Knop, *Diversity and Self-Determination in International Law*, (Cambridge, 2002), pp.255–274.

[18] See Art.31, 1993 Draft UN Declaration; and E.-I. Daes, Some Considerations on the Rights of Indigenous Peoples to Self-Determination (1993) 3 TLCP 5.

[19] Fifth recital, Preamble, 1993 Draft UN Declaration.

[20] UN Doc.E/CN.4/Sub.2/1993/26/Add.1, para.24.

[21] UN Doc.E/CN.4/Sub.2/1993/26/Add.1, para.25. See Twelfth recital, Preamble, 1993 Draft UN Declaration.

[22] See J. Urrutia, Report of the Working Group Established in Accordance with CHR Res.1995/32, Third Session, 15 December 1997, UN Doc.E/CN.4/1997/106, para.37; Barsh, 'Irresistible', 788 and 791; and B. Kingsbury, 'Indigenous Peoples' in International Law: A Constructivist Approach to the Asian Controversy (1998) 92 AJIL 414.

[23] M. Dodson cited in C. Scott, Indigenous Self-Determination and Decolonisation of the International Imagination: A Plea (1996) 18 HRQ 814.

[24] ICCPR, 16 December 1966, in force 23 March 1976, UNGA Res.2200A(XXI), 21 UN GAOR Supp.(No.16), p.52, UN Doc.A/6316 (1966), 999 UNTS 171, and (1967) 6 ILM 368; and ICESCR, 16 December 1966, in force 3 January 1976, 21 UN GAOR Supp.(No.16), p.49, 993 UNTS 3, (1967) 6 ILM 360. See UN Doc.E/CN.4/2004/81, paras.68–78.

[25] See E.-I. Daes, Report of the Working Group on Indigenous Populations on its Eleventh Session, 23 August 1993, UN Doc.E/CN.4/Sub.2/1993/29, para.57.

discriminatory.[26] It is a perpetuation of the scale of civilisation, which it is argued is a foundational element of international law. Daes has reassured that the right to self-determination accorded to indigenous peoples is a 'new' type of self-determination, not a second-class version.[27]

Indigenous peoples maintain that their right to self-determination, especially in respect to autonomy and self-government, is not derivative from the constitutional grant of an existing State but is inherent in their origins as autonomous nations, with unique social and legal traditions.[28] Moreover, they contend they must look to the international community and international instruments to protect their rights because they cannot rely on the relevant State which is founded on their dispossession.[29] Therefore, indigenous peoples seek recognition as subjects of international law and international guarantees to protect the 'very essence of their being'.[30]

WGIP and restitution of indigenous cultural heritage

Since the WGIP's inception, indigenous organisations have emphasised that their right to self-determination entails the right to determine how their cultures are preserved and developed. Indeed, the final Aboriginal and Torres Strait Islander Commission (ATSIC) Chair Geoff Clark noted: '[W]e do not accept that our freedom from oppression means leaving behind our cultural heritage . . . [I]t is in our own heritage that we can find our source of power and liberation'.[31] Closely tied to the evolving recognition of this right to preservation and development of cultural identity is the right to restitution of cultural heritage.

Restitution and the 1993 Draft UN Declaration

Indigenous organisations have insisted strenuously on the importance of maintaining the integrity of the 1993 Draft UN Declaration.[32] Indeed, only by reading Article 12 (covering the right to restitution of cultural heritage) in the context of the preamble and other provisions are we able to appreciate its lineage to preceding rationales for the restitution of cultural objects in international law.

The 1993 Draft UN Declaration seeks from the outset to ensure the equal enjoyment by indigenous peoples of rights prescribed to all peoples by the international human rights framework.[33] Pre-eminent amongst these rights is the right to self-determination. The ability to determine how their cultures are preserved and

---

[26] See Scott, 'Indigenous', 816ff; Daes, 'Considerations', 6; and E.-I. Daes, Equality of Peoples under the Auspices of the United Nations Draft Declaration on the Rights of Indigenous Peoples (1995) 7 St Thomas LR 493.

[27] Daes, 'Considerations', 10.   [28] Sixth recital, Preamble, 1993 Draft UN Declaration.

[29] M. Dodson, *Aboriginal and Torres Strait Islander Social Justice Commission, Annual Report* (Canberra, 1993), p.49. See P. Keal, *European Conquest and the Rights of Indigenous Peoples: The Moral Backwardness of International Society* (Cambridge, 2003).

[30] *Minority Schools in Albania case* (1935) PCIJ, ser.A/B, No.64, p.17.

[31] G. Clark, The Frank Archibald Memorial Lecture, 5 September 1994, University of New England (copy on file).

[32] UN Doc.E/CN.4/Sub.2/1994/30, para.133.

[33] First recital, Preamble, 1993 Draft UN Declaration. See 14th and 16th recitals, Preamble.

developed is an essential component of this right (and duty).[34] The preamble also recognises the right of 'all peoples to be different'. Accordingly, indigenous peoples maintain that the international community and States have a positive obligation to ensure that they are able to preserve and develop their cultural difference. Included in this obligation is the restitution of cultural heritage. This is the essence of the third rationale for restitution of cultural objects in international law.

For indigenous peoples, positive protection of the difference of groups is particularly relevant because of the legacy of colonial policies. The 1993 draft Declaration categorically repudiates the underlying racialised mindset espoused by international law, anthropology and the Western art canon to justify and facilitate the colonisation of indigenous peoples. The preamble affirms such doctrines are 'racist, scientifically false, legally invalid, morally condemnable and socially unjust'. While WGIP Chair Daes conceded that museum collecting practices were complex, she nonetheless placed the loss of indigenous cultural heritage within a 'colonial context'.[35] As detailed in earlier chapters, assimilation and integration policies of European metropolitan powers and settler States were accompanied by systematic and unsystematic destruction or removal of indigenous cultural sites, objects and practices. Daes noted that indigenous cultural heritages are the 'manifestations of an ancient and continuing relationship between the peoples and their territory'. She added that it was 'inconceivable that . . . [any] element of the people's collective identity . . . could be alienated permanently or completely'.[36] This recognition and restoration of the link between people, land and cultural objects has been a recurring rationale for restitution in international law.

The 1993 Draft UN Declaration also reaffirms the importance of cultural diversity and contribution of all peoples and their cultures to the 'common heritage of mankind'.[37] The preamble recalls the sentiment invoked during the mid-twentieth century to rationalise the restitution of cultural objects as a means of ameliorating or reversing discriminatory and genocidal policies. As explained in Chapter 6, this phrase – the contribution of all peoples to the cultural heritage of mankind – drew from the minority protection tradition in international law. It is in this tradition that indigenous peoples firmly install their right to the restitution of cultural heritage. Article 12, which defines the right to restitution of cultural heritage, is consolidated

---

[34] See Art.1, UNESCO Declaration of the Principles of Cultural Co-operation, adopted 4 November 1966, UNESCO Doc.14C/Resolutions, and UNESCO, *Cultural Rights as Human Rights* (Paris, 1970), p.123; and Y. Yokota and the Saami Council, Guideline for the review of the draft principles and guidelines on the heritage of indigenous peoples, 17 July 2004, UNESCO Doc.E/CN.4/Sub.2/AC.4/2004/5, para.18.

[35] E.-I. Daes, Working Paper on the Question of the Ownership and Control of the Cultural Property of Indigenous Peoples, 3 July 1991, UN Doc.E/CN.4/Sub.2/1991/34, paras.9ff. Daes noted that these cultural losses continue unabated because of the activities of non-European States, transnational corporations and increased penetration by non-indigenous tourism: E.-I. Daes, Study on the Protection of the Cultural and Intellectual Property of Indigenous Peoples, 28 July 1993, UN Doc.E/CN.4/Sub.2/1993/28, paras.87–89.

[36] UN Doc.E/CN.4/Sub.2/1993/28, para.22.

[37] Second recital, Preamble, 1993 Draft UN Declaration. See E.-I. Daes, Final Report in conformity with Sub-Comm. Res.1993/44 and CHR Dec.1994/105, 21 June 1995, UN Doc.E/CN.4/Sub.2/1995/26, Annex: Revised Text of the Principles and Guidelines for the Protection of the Heritage of Indigenous Peoples, Principles 1 and 2; and UNESCO Universal Declaration on Cultural Diversity, 2 November 2001, UNESCO Doc.31C/Res.25, Annex I; (2002) 41 ILM 57.

into Part III (Cultural Rights) of the 1993 Draft UN Declaration.[38] Indigenous peoples affix this right firmly to the right of a group to preserve and develop their cultural identity. Part III of the 1993 Draft echoes, and tailors to indigenous concerns, the right articulated in Article 27 of the ICCPR.[39] It seeks to confer positive and collective rights. Yet, Article 27 with its various compromises makes reliance upon it for such rights problematic.

Article 12 of the 1993 Draft UN Declaration states:

> Indigenous peoples have the right to practise and revitalize their cultural traditions and customs. This includes the right to maintain, protect and develop the past, present and future manifestations of their cultures, such as archaeological and historical sites, artifacts, designs, ceremonies, technologies and visual and performing arts and literature, as well as the *right to the restitution of cultural, intellectual, religious and spiritual property taken without their free and informed consent or in violation of their laws, traditions and customs.*[40] (emphasis added)

The ambit of the right is considered below with the 1995 Daes Principles and Guidelines. However, it is important to note here that indigenous organisations maintain that the draft declaration must recognise the indigenous peoples' ownership of their cultural heritage (Article 29).[41]

The CHRWG deliberated and redrafted Article 12 at its second (1996), sixth (2000) and tenth (2004) sessions.[42] Currently, various settler States are addressing indigenous claims for restitution of ancestral remains and cultural heritage at the national level. Yet, during CHRWG discussions, States have revisited their concerns regarding the right to self-determination generally and apprehensions aired during the 1970 UNESCO Convention deliberations. Some States, including Australia, objected to the use of the term 'restitution', preferring instead the term 'return'.[43] They argued that 'restitution' raises issues of compensation, non-retroactivity, and possible conflict with third-party rights or the national interest. They maintained that such a right must be clearly defined and conform with domestic laws that apply equally to indigenous peoples and other nationals.

More fundamentally, they seek to weaken the link between the right to preserve and develop cultural identity and the restitution of cultural heritage by proposing

---

[38] See also Arts.7(2) and 10(3), Draft Inter-American Declaration on the Rights of Indigenous Peoples, approved by the Inter-American Commission on Human Rights on 26 February 1997, 1333rd session, 95th regular session.

[39] See Art.12 of the 1993 Draft UN Declaration (the right to enjoy their own culture); Art.13 (to profess and practise their own religion); and Art.14 (to use their own language).

[40] Art.12, 1993 Draft UN Declaration (emphasis added). Earlier drafts dealt with the subject matter of Arts.12 and 13 in one provision. See P. Thornberry, *Indigenous Peoples and Human Rights* (New York, 2002), pp.25–26, 370–76.

[41] See ATSIC, *Annual Report 1994–1995* (Canberra, 1995), pp.102–08.

[42] See J. Urrutia, Report of the Working Group established in accordance with CHR Res.1995/32, Second Session, 10 December 1996, UN Doc.E/CN.4/1997/102; and UN Doc.E/CN.4/2001/85.

[43] UN Doc.E/CN.4/1997/102, paras.66–67; UN Doc.E/CN.4/2001/85, paras.145–48; and Letter P. Ruddock, Attorney-General of Australia to author, 12 August 2004.

they be relegated to two separate paragraphs. The present form of Article 12(2), prepared by the CHRWG, reads:

> States should/shall [make[best][appropriate]efforts], [to][promote][facilitate] the return to indigenous [peoples] of their *cultural, [intellectual], and religious [and spiritual] property [taken without their free and informed consent]* [after the present Declaration comes into effect], [*or in violation of [their] laws, traditions and customs*] [and][or][in violation of relevant laws and regulations].[44]
>
> (emphasis added)

By the 2004 session, some States had proposed a return to the original text, but with the crucial deletion of the words 'as well as the right to restitution of' and their replacement with: 'States shall provide mechanisms for redress with respect to'.[45] No longer referred to as a right to restitution, these redrafts expose the continuing resistance of former metropolitan powers and market States to any international instrument that disturbs legal title to cultural objects collected by their museums during colonial occupation. As explained below, the current domestic schemes of certain Anglo-American States do not provide for restitution of all indigenous cultural materials.

In response, indigenous organisations have reaffirmed the link between the right to self-determination and the right to preserve and develop their cultures that form the 'common heritage of mankind'.[46] They, and some States, charged that Article 12 must not be subject to domestic laws or third-party rights because their cultural rights require international protection against the policies and practices of States and transnational corporations.[47] They stress that this international protection must include restitution and compensation, unlimited by non-retroactive application. In addition, they argued that the proposed splitting of Article 12 renders the right to restitution of their cultural heritage illusory. The CHRWG redraft of Article 12 (to be contained in a non-binding declaration) is clearly regressive when compared to past and present international restitution initiatives, current domestic programmes and existing international obligations.

A more restrictive recognition of restitution is incorporated in Article 13 of the 1993 Draft UN Declaration, covering the right of indigenous peoples to profess and practise their religion.[48] Consistent with developments in several Anglo-American States examined below, the Article recognises 'the right to the use and control of [their] ceremonial objects' and 'right to repatriation of human remains'. During CHRWG negotiations, some States strove to 'balance' the Article with protection for third-party rights.[49] Yet, current Anglo-American States' schemes are based on

---

[44] L.-E. Chávez, Report of the Working Group established in accordance with CHR Res.1995/32, Seventh Session, 6 March 2002, UN Doc.E/CN.4/2002/98, Annex 1, 25 (1993 Draft text is in italics).

[45] UN Doc.E/CN.4/2004/WG.15/CRP.1, p.7.

[46] UN Doc.E/CN.4/2001/85, paras.148, 150, 151 and 153.

[47] See UN Doc.E/CN.4/2002/98, Annex 2, 30.

[48] See Art.18(1), ICCPR; and Pritchard, *Setting*, pp.131–32. Earlier drafts dealt with the subject matter of Articles 12 and 13 as one provision.

[49] UN Doc.E/CN.4/2002/98, para.51; and UN Doc.E/CN.4/2004/81, para.54.

an acknowledgement of the precedence of indigenous peoples' right to religious expression over the rights and interests of third parties, such as scientists and museums. Unlike these schemes, Article 13 does not recognise indigenous peoples' right to restitution of 'sacred' or 'culturally significant' objects.

1995 Daes Principles and Guidelines

The 'right to restitution' of cultural heritage articulated in the 1993 Draft UN Declaration is augmented by the work of WGIP Chair-Rapporteur Daes. Leading up to her 1993 'Study on the Protection of the Cultural and Intellectual Property of Indigenous Peoples', Daes had noted that restitution uncovered 'a variety of historical, political, legal, and moral questions, some of which are of a delicate and legally complicated nature'.[50] Nonetheless, she emphasised that the return of human remains, sacred materials and cultural objects is essential to indigenous peoples' 'right to their own culture', to practise their religious beliefs and to 'preserve their group identity'.[51]

Daes was subsequently called upon to prepare draft Principles and Guidelines for the Protection of the Heritage of Indigenous People.[52] When presenting her draft Principles and Guidelines to the Sub-Commission in 1995, she expressed the hope that it would encourage States to pass more effective legislation and that the UN General Assembly would adopt it as a declaration by 2004.[53] They were not adopted. Instead, a review was launched and Yokota and the Saami Council presented substantive proposals on the guidelines at the 2005 WGIP session.[54]

In her 1993 Study, Daes found that contemporary national and international schema for the protection and restitution of cultural objects were formulated without reference to indigenous laws and customs.[55] In Chapter 2, it was noted that with the universalisation of European international law from the early nineteenth century, the limited number of States making up the family of nations determined the definition of culture and its 'international' protection. However, as the membership of the international community expanded, the definition of culture and its protection evolved in international law. Daes emphasises that indigenous peoples have facilitated the growing acceptance of a holistic notion of cultural heritage and the tying together of the return of land, cultural objects, cultural practices and knowledge.[56] Indeed, this understanding of cultural heritage is increasingly reflected in

---

[50] UN Doc.E/CN.4/Sub.2/1991/34, para.2. See Sub-Comm. Res.1990/25, 31 August 1990; UN Doc.E/CN.4/Sub.2/1991/34; Sub-Comm. Res.1991/32, 29 August 1991; Sub-Comm. Res.1992/35, 27 August 1992; CHR Dec.1992/114; ECOSOC Dec.1992/256, 20 July 1992; UN Doc.E/CN.4/Sub.2/1993/28; and UN Doc.E/CN.4/Sub.2/1993/29, paras.153–76.

[51] UN Doc.E/CN.4/Sub.2/1991/34, para.28.

[52] Sub-Comm. Res.1993/44, 26 August 1993; and CHR Dec.1994/105, 4 March 1994.

[53] UN Doc.E/CN.4/Sub.2/1995/26, paras.19 and 32.

[54] Expanded Working Paper presented by Y. Yokota and the Saami Council on the substantive proposals on the Draft Principles and Guidelines on the Heritage of Indigenous Peoples, 21 June 2005, UN Doc.E/CN.4/Sub.2/AC.4/2005/3.

[55] UN Doc.E/CN.4/Sub.2/1991/34, paras.4–8 and 14; and UN Doc.E/CN.4/Sub.2/1993/28, para.32.

[56] See UN Doc.E/CN.4/Sub.2/1995/26, at Guidelines 11 and 12; E.-I. Daes, Protection of the Heritage of Indigenous People, Preliminary Report submitted in conformity with Sub-Comm. Res.1993/44 and CHR Dec.1994/105, 8 July 1994, UN Doc.E/CN.4/Sub.2/1994/31, paras.8–10; and UN Doc.E/CN.4/Sub.2/1993/28, paras.21ff. See T. Janke, *Our Culture, Our Future, Report on Australian Indigenous Cultural and Intellectual Property Rights* (Canberra, 1998).

international instruments like the 2003 UNESCO Convention for the Safeguarding of the Intangible Cultural Heritage.[57]

Daes also noted that the word 'heritage' is more appropriate than 'property' to define that which 'belongs to the distinct identity of a people'.[58] This transition from scientific and commodity-value to religious and spiritual value (or profane to sacred) is crucial to domestic debates concerning the restitution of cultural objects from national museums to indigenous communities. Yet, as the 2004 Yokota and Saami Council review guideline notes, the definition of 'cultural heritage' remains problematic. Certain States highlight that if there is to be a legally binding instrument 'parties should be clear as to the exact scope of the protection'.[59]

Indigenous peoples maintain that international and national legal systems must recognise that they have their own laws and customs which govern the care and custody of and access to their cultural heritage.[60] The 1995 Daes Principles and Guidelines and Article 12 of the 1993 Draft UN Declaration affirm this position.[61] The United States and other settler States have long resisted the recognition of collective rights, a central characteristic of indigenous claims.[62] However, from the 1990s onwards, various settler States have endeavoured to accommodate indigenous laws, customs and collective rights into international instruments and national frameworks for the protection and restitution of cultural objects. The 2004 review guideline suggested that rules be established to protect indigenous peoples against the disposal of their cultural heritage by individual members of the group, in circumstances where it may be legal pursuant to national laws but contrary to indigenous customary law.[63]

Indigenous peoples stressed that they are the primary custodians and interpreters of their cultures, their past, present and future manifestations.[64] Daes maintained that the recognition of indigenous peoples' ownership of their cultural heritage was imperative.[65] The 1995 Daes Principles and Guidelines state that consent is always revocable because the continuous, collective right to manage their cultural heritage is crucial to the identity, survival and development of each community.[66]

---

[57] Paris, 17 October 2003, UNESCO Doc.MISC/2003/CLT/CH/14.

[58] UN Doc.E/CN.4/Sub.2/1993/28, para.24. See L. V. Prott and P. J. O'Keefe, 'Cultural Heritage' or 'Cultural Property'? (1992) 1 IJCP 307; and R. J. Coombe, The Properties of Culture and the Politics of Possessing Identity: Native Claims in the Cultural Appropriation Controversy (1993) 6 CJLJ 249.

[59] UN Doc.E/CN.4/Sub.2/AC.4/2004/5, para.17.

[60] Including Declaration of the World Conference of Indigenous Peoples on Territory, Environment and Development, Kari-Oca, 30 May 1992; and Declaration on Cultural and Intellectual Property Rights of Indigenous Peoples, Mataatua, 18 June 1993. See UN Doc.E/CN.4/Sub.2/1994/31, para.6; and UN Doc. E/CN.4/Sub.2/1993/29, paras.163–68.

[61] See UN Doc.E/CN.4/Sub.2/1995/26, Annex, Principles 4 and 5, and Guideline 13; and UN Doc.E/CN.4/2002/98, paras.34–37.

[62] See UN Doc.E/CN.4/2002/98, Annex 2, pp.28–30; and Pritchard, *Setting*, pp.82–84.

[63] UN Doc.E/CN.4/Sub.2/AC.4/2004/5, para.20. See *Attorney-General of New Zealand* v. *Ortiz* [1982] QB 349 (QB); [1984] AC 1 (HL).

[64] UN Doc.E/CN.4/Sub.2/1995/26, Annex, Principle 3.

[65] UN Doc.E/CN.4/Sub.2/1993/28, paras.171–75. See M. F. Brown, *Who Owns Native Culture?* (Cambridge MA, 2004).

[66] UN Doc.E/CN.4/Sub.2/1993/28, paras.28, 30 and 68–80; and UN Doc.E/CN.4/Sub.2/1995/26, Principles 5 and 10. See *Foster* v. *Mountford* (1976) 29 CLR 233, 14 ALR 71.

Nonetheless, Canada suggested that the application of retroactivity and revocable consent in respect of objects or knowledge in widespread general usage would have 'an adverse impact on science, medicine and art'.[67] Daes advised that this assumption against the extinguishment of the rights of indigenous peoples could be overcome through the demonstration of the exercise of free and informed consent. It is no coincidence that Daes and Article 12 of the 1993 Draft UN Declaration implicitly recall the Declaration of London. She expected that States were not concerned with 'compelling museums or other institutions to return materials that were acquired in the past by force, fraud or deception'.[68] The 2004 review guideline recommended that the WGIP debate whether the burden of proving consent should rest with indigenous communities or the third party claiming legal acquisition.[69]

Indigenous peoples remain dependent on the benevolence of States to ensure the establishment and implementation of legal and administrative frameworks to protect, preserve and develop their cultures and their manifestations. Daes concluded that the established UNESCO mechanisms for the return of cultural objects provide inadequate protection of indigenous peoples' rights concerning their cultural heritage because they privilege the State as subject.[70] She noted the UNESCO Intergovernmental Committee on Return or Restitution effectively excludes indigenous participation and does not consider intra-State disputes. Equally, the 1970 UNESCO Convention requires indigenous peoples to rely on the relevant State party to enforce the instrument's obligations.[71] Significantly, recent UNESCO instruments make specific reference to the interest of non-State groups, including indigenous peoples, to cultural heritage.[72]

Daes found that States requesting the restitution of indigenous cultural objects from overseas institutions usually returned them to national museums, rather than the relevant indigenous community, although this is not current Australian and US practice. In 2004, the International Law Association recommended that holding institutions respond 'in good faith' to requests by indigenous peoples for the return of cultural heritage, even if they are 'not supported by the government of the state in whose territory [they] are principally domiciled or organized'.[73]

---

[67] E.-I. Daes, Supplementary Report of the Special Rapporteur submitted pursuant to Sub-Comm. Res.1995/40 and CHR Res.1996/63, 24 June 1996, UN Doc.E/CN.4/Sub.2/1996/22, para.11.

[68] UN Doc.E/CN.4/Sub.2/1996/22, paras.19–20.

[69] UN Doc.E/CN.4/Sub.2/2004/5, para.19.

[70] UN Doc.E/CN.4/Sub.2/1993/28, paras.123–27.

[71] Regional agreements like the 1976 Convention on the Protection of the Archaeological, Historical and Artistic Heritage of the American Nations are similarly deficient. Cf. 1995 UNIDROIT Convention.

[72] 2003 UNESCO Convention for the Safeguarding of the Intangible Cultural Heritage, sixth preambular recital, Arts.1(b), 2(1), 11(b) and 15; Declaration concerning the Intentional Destruction of Cultural Heritage, adopted by the 32nd session of the UNESCO General Conference, Paris, 17 October 2003, fifth preambular recital; and UNESCO Universal Declaration on Cultural Diversity, Art.4.

[73] ILA, *Report of the Cultural Heritage Law Committee* (London, 2004), p.8 (refers to the draft UN Declaration).

The Revised Draft Principles and Guidelines (2000)[74] made the following recommendations concerning 'recovery and restitution of heritage' already removed from indigenous communities:

Human remains and related funerary objects must be returned to their descendants and territories in a manner determined by the relevant indigenous people. Related documentation can only be retained or displayed in the form and manner agreed to by them (Guideline 19). Likewise, human remains and secret sacred objects cannot be displayed without their approval (Guideline 22).

Movable cultural objects should be returned where possible to the traditional owners, particularly when it is of cultural, religious, or historical significance to the people. An individual or institution may retain these objects only pursuant to written agreement with the traditional owners, covering custody and interpretation (Guideline 20).

Where the traditional custodians cannot be identified, the indigenous peoples of the territory from which it originated are presumed to be the custodians (Guideline 21).

Researchers and scholarly institutions, including museums, must immediately provide indigenous peoples with comprehensive inventories of the cultural objects (and related documentation) in their possession (Guidelines 27 to 29). Further, they must take steps to return items to the traditional owners on demand. If items are retained, formal agreements on shared custody, use and interpretation must be completed. Finally, they may only acquire such objects with the knowledge of the traditional owners.

National governments, in cooperation with international organisations, should assist indigenous peoples in recovering control and possession of their cultural heritage (Guidelines 17, 23 and 24). Furthermore, they must enact domestic legislation which guarantees indigenous peoples 'prompt, effective and affordable' judicial or administrative assistance to prevent, punish, restore and compensate for the unauthorised 'acquisition, documentation or use' of their cultural heritage. Such laws must be developed in consultation with persons designated by indigenous peoples.

The 2000 Revised Guidelines emphasise the need for effective coordination between the United Nations, its agencies, international institutions and governments to ensure indigenous peoples' capacity to protect and develop their cultures (Guidelines 18 and 54).[75] It calls on the United Nations to urgently consider the draft of a convention for the protection of indigenous heritage (Guideline 55).[76] This recommendation was reaffirmed by the 2004 review guideline and the International

---

[74] E.-I. Daes, Report of the Seminar on the Draft Principles and Guidelines for the Protection of the Heritage of Indigenous Peoples, 19 June 2000, UN Doc.E/CN.4/Sub.2/2000/26, Annex 1. See E.-I. Daes, Report of the Technical Meeting on the Protection of the Heritage of Indigenous Peoples, 24 June 1997, UN Doc.E/CN.4/Sub.2/1997/15.

[75] Daes had originally recommended the establishment of a specialised committee similar to the existing UNESCO Committee for Return or Restitution: UN Doc.E/CN.4/Sub.2/1993/28, paras.175. See also Mataatua Declaration, para.2.13.

[76] Daes originally recommended a convention providing international jurisdiction for the recovery of indigenous peoples' heritage: UN Doc.E/CN.4/Sub.2/1995/26, Annex, Guideline 60.

Law Association.[77] Indigenous organisations have indicated their commitment to the Daes Revised Draft Principles and Guidelines of 2000.[78] These Guidelines reflected the developments occurring within certain settler States and anticipated trends at the international level, including the 1995 UNIDROIT Convention.

Restitution and the 1995 UNIDROIT Convention

The UNIDROIT Convention on Stolen or Illegally Exported Cultural Objects (1995 UNIDROIT Convention) provides a mechanism in private international law for the restitution of stolen or illegally exported cultural objects during peacetime or war.[79] Indigenous peoples were not involved directly in the treaty negotiations. Nonetheless, UNESCO and several settler States strove to ensure that the rights, laws and customs of indigenous peoples were accommodated in the final text.[80]

Four aspects of the Convention are particularly relevant for our present purposes:

(1) The inclusion of 'national, tribal, indigenous or other communities';
(2) States and individuals as claimants;
(3) Non-retroactivity; and
(4) The inclusion of the 'due diligence' requirement.

The preamble of the 1995 UNIDROIT Convention explicitly concedes the 'irreparable damage' caused to the 'cultural heritage of national, tribal, indigenous or other communities' and all peoples by illicit trade in cultural objects. The Convention then goes on to acknowledge at particular junctures the importance of this cultural heritage not only to States and humankind but to the relevant 'community' also.[81] Anglo-American States adhering to a free trade agenda have objected consistently to any international provision requiring the enforcement of another State's export controls. The differentiation between rights and obligations relating to stolen cultural objects (Chapter II) and illicitly exported cultural objects (Chapter III) by the Convention was a significant concession extracted by these States.

Nonetheless, the following provisions were redrafted to accommodate the interests of indigenous and tribal communities as follows. First, the more generous time limit applicable to objects stolen from public collections is extended to include 'a sacred or communally important cultural object belonging to and used by a tribal or indigenous community' (Article 3(8)). Next, a 'holding' State must order the return

---

[77] UN Doc.E/CN.4/Sub.2/AC.4/2004/5, para.33; and ILA, *A Blueprint for the Development of Cultural Heritage Law: First Report* (London, 2000), p.4.

[78] See UN Doc.E/CN.4/Sub.2/2000/26, paras.46–47.

[79] Rome, 24 June 1995, in force 1 July 1998, (1995) 34 ILM 1322. Australia is currently considering becoming a party to the Convention: Letter, Ruddock to author.

[80] See L. V. Prott, *Commentary on the Unidroit Convention* (Leicester, 1997), p.17; and Prott and O'Keefe, 'Cultural Heritage'.

[81] Prott suggests that the Convention seeks to subvert the alleged dichotomy between 'internationalism' (free-trade agenda) and 'retentionism' (national controls): Prott, *Commentary*, pp.19–20 and 52. See ICOM, *Code of Ethics for Museums*, 2001, para.4.4; and 2004, para.6.3 at http://icom.museum/ethics.html, sanctions returns to 'country or people of origin'. The definition of 'indigenous' and 'tribal' peoples reflects UN and ILO documents in the area: Prott, *Commentary*, p.40.

of an illicitly exported object after a requesting State establishes that its removal impairs 'the traditional or ritual use of the object by a tribal or indigenous community' (Article 5(3)(d)).[82] And finally, the exception in respect of illicitly exported objects produced by contemporary artists does not apply to objects made by a member of an indigenous or tribal group for traditional or ritual use by that community (Article 7(2)).

The 1995 UNIDROIT Convention covers only international transactions, not those within States (Article 1(a)). This is a significant limitation for indigenous peoples. For, as detailed in Chapters 4 and 7, the centralising and assimilating policies of States and their museums are as disruptive and destructive to indigenous cultures as those pursued by metropolitan powers. Some concessions are made to non-State claimants. In contrast to the 1970 UNESCO Convention, objects do not have to be 'specifically designated by each State' under the 1995 UNIDROIT Convention. This arises because the latter deals with private international law. Also, a claim for return of a stolen cultural object may be lodged by an individual or State Party[83]; whilst a claim concerning illicitly exported cultural objects may only be lodged by a State Party to the Convention. Significantly, objects removed from clandestine excavations are designated as 'stolen' and included in Chapter II of the Convention if it can be proven that they were 'unlawfully excavated or lawfully excavated but unlawfully retained' (Article 3(2)).[84] Regardless, the rights arising under the 1995 UNIDROIT Convention cannot be exercised without the instrument's ratification by the relevant State.

Following intense lobbying from former metropolitan powers and market States, the Convention includes a provision affirming non-retroactivity (Article 10).[85] States that had already suffered significant cultural losses expressed concern that the provision would legalise illicit transfers completed before the operation of the Convention. To allay their fears, the Convention clearly pronounces that nothing in its text should be interpreted as conferring 'approval of legitimacy upon illegal transactions' finalised prior to its operation.[86] Nor does it limit any right of a State or individual to make a claim for return available outside the Convention (Article 9(1)).

Although not relevant to acts of removal prior to the operation of the 1995 UNIDROIT Convention, the vexed question of the bona fide purchaser is significant

---

[82] The UNIDROIT Secretariat noted that the interests listed in Art.5(3) are alternative and not cumulative, and the list is not exhaustive: Prott, *Commentary*, p.58. Prott suggests that objects removed from an indigenous community without its consent, prior to the operation of the Convention, and kept in a private collection may attract the operation of the provision.

[83] Daes observed that indigenous peoples lacking the financial means of pursuing legal actions in other States are usually reliant on the support of the relevant national government: UN Doc.E/CN.4/Sub.2/1993/28, para.158.

[84] If there is evidence that the requested objects were exported without the requisite export permit, it falls under Art.5(3): Prott, *Commentary*, pp.32–34; and L. V. Prott, Unesco and Unidroit: A Partnership against Trafficking in Cultural Objects, in N. Palmer (ed.), *The Recovery of Stolen Art: A Collection of Essays* (The Hague, 1998), p.205 at p.210.

[85] See Prott, *Commentary*, pp.78, 81; Prott, 'UNESCO', p.213; and C. Fox, The Unidroit Convention on Stolen or Illegally Exported Cultural Objects: An Answer to the World Problem of Illicit Trade in Cultural Property (1993) 9 AUJILP 225 at 265ff.

[86] Sixth recital, Preamble and Art.10(3), 1995 UNIDROIT Convention.

because of ongoing cultural losses suffered by indigenous and tribal peoples.[87] In response to lobbying by ICOM, UNESCO and professional archaeological associations, Civil Law countries gradually acknowledged that the bona fide purchaser principle facilitated the illicit trade in art and antiquities. The 1995 UNIDROIT Convention therefore provides a compromise for these States. It allows a purchaser to pursue compensation where he or she can show they exercised due diligence to avoid acquiring stolen cultural objects (Article 4(1) and (4)).[88] The publication by indigenous organisations of guidelines pertaining to the transfer and use of their cultural heritage is an essential means of placing potential purchasers on notice for this purpose.[89]

National models for restitution to indigenous peoples

From the 1990s onwards, several States that had engaged in Anglo-American imperialism began addressing the demands by indigenous peoples for the restitution of their ancestral remains and cultural heritage. In each case, this process has resulted in an acknowledgement of:

(1) the significant cultural losses suffered by indigenous peoples because of colonial occupation and its attendant policies;
(2) that the religious and cultural interest of indigenous peoples in their heritage must take precedence over its scientific and national importance; and
(3) that the ability of indigenous peoples to determine how their cultures are preserved and developed is an intrinsic part of the right to self-determination.

These States have accommodated (rather than reconciled) the rights, laws and customs of indigenous peoples to cultural objects held by national museums.

This section examines the national responses of the United States, Australia and United Kingdom to the restitution claims of indigenous peoples. First, the US legislative framework for the repatriation of items held by museums to indigenous communities is considered. By contrast, Australia has adopted a voluntary national policy that seeks to redefine relations between Indigenous Australians and the museum community. In addition, the Australian government is facilitating indigenous efforts to repatriate objects from local and overseas collections. This leads, finally, to a description of current British efforts to address the claims of indigenous peoples from former colonial territories.

Legislative model – United States

The Native American Graves Protection and Repatriation Act of 1990 (NAGPRA) signalled the reluctant acceptance by the United States of the primacy of indigenous peoples' interests in their movable cultural heritage. Peter Welsh of the Heard Museum described it as marking the transition from paternalism to recognition of

---

[87] See Prott, 'UNESCO', pp.212–13; and L. V. Prott, The Preliminary Draft Unidroit Convention on Stolen or Illegally Exported Cultural Objects (1992) 41 ICLQ 160 at 166.
[88] See Prott, *Commentary*, pp.41–51.   [89] UN Doc.E/CN.4/Sub.2/1993/28, para.156.

indigenous human rights and cultural diversity.[90] The US legislative model of repatriation of cultural objects from national and federally funded institutions to Native American communities under the NAGPRA is examined with reference to: (1) its origins; (2) the mechanics of the scheme; (3) assessments of its implementation; and (4) the facilitation of international repatriation.

The NAGPRA framework had its genesis in two particular developments within the United States during the late twentieth century. First, Native Americans pursued repatriation claims as part of their civil rights movement that included campaigns for effective religious freedom.[91] The Native American reburial movement challenged the precedence given to scientists and the US national interest over indigenous peoples' ability to dictate how (and whether) ancestral remains and cultural heritage were preserved, displayed and interpreted.[92] The campaign drew upon the international human rights regime, including the right to self-determination that evolved following the Second World War.[93]

Second, diplomatic pressure from its American neighbours and increasing public awareness of the US role in illicit traffic of cultural objects led the United States to temper its strident adherence to a free-trade policy in cultural 'resources'. The US museum community became accustomed to constraints on their acquisition policies following the implementation of the 1970 UNESCO Convention into domestic US law and the adoption of ethical acquisition policies by international organisations and US institutions.[94] For Native Americans, it was untenable that the US

---

[90] P. H. Welsh, Repatriation and Cultural Preservation: Potent Objects, Potent Pasts (1992) 25 UMJLR 837 at 839. See A. Gulliford, *Sacred Objects and Sacred Places: Preserving Tribal Traditions* (Boulder, 2000), p.23.

[91] Prior to the enactment of the NAGPRA framework, Native Americans had unsuccessfully sought to rely on the American Indian Religious Freedom Act 1978, Pub. L. No.95–341, §1, 92 Stat. 469 (1978), codified at 42 USC §1996 (2000); *Lyng v. Northwest Indian Cemetery Protective Association*, 485 US 439 (1988); and *Crow v. Gullett*, 541 F Supp. 785 (DSD 1982); affd 706 F 2d 856 (8th Cir. 1983). See R. Hill Sr, Reflections of a Native Repatriator, in B. Meister (ed.), *Mending the Circle: A Native American Repatriation Guide* (New York, 1996), and at http://repatriationfoundation.org/MTC.html, p.81 at pp.84ff.

[92] See V. Deloria Jr, *Custer Died For Your Sins: An Indian Manifesto* (Norman, 1969); M. B. Bowman, The Reburial of Native American Human Remains: Approaches to the Resolution of a Conflict (1989) 13 HELR 147; J. Riding In, Without Ethics and Morality: A Historical Overview of Imperial Archaeology and American Indians (1992) 24 ASJL 11; J. F. Trope and W. R. Echo-Hawk, The Native American Graves Protection and Repatriation Act: Background and Legislative History (1992) 24 ASLJ 33; P. Gerstenblith, Identity and Cultural Property: The Protection of Cultural Property in the United States (1995) 75 BULR 559 at 583–86 and 622–42; and D. Hurst Thomas, *Skull Wars: Kennewick Man, Archaeology, and the Battle for Native American Identity* (New York, 2000), pp.198–208.

[93] See S. S. Harjo, Native Peoples' Cultural and Human Rights: An Unfinished Agenda (1992) 24 ASLJ 321; R. Strickland, Implementing the National Policy of Understanding, Preserving and Safeguarding the Heritage of Indian Peoples and Native Hawaiians: Human Rights, Sacred Objects and Cultural Patrimony (1992) 24 ASLJ 175; and D. B. Suagee, Human Rights and the Cultural Heritage of Indian Tribes in the United States (1999) 8 IJCP 48.

[94] See American Anthropological Association, *Resolution on Acquisition of Cultural Properties* (Washington DC, 1973); American Association of Museums, *Museum Ethics* (Washington DC, 1978); P. Parker, *Keepers of the Treasures: Protecting Historic Properties and Cultural Traditions on Indian Lands* (Washington DC, 1990); J. Raines, One Is Missing: Native American Graves Protection and Repatriation Act: An Overview and Analysis (1992) 17 AILR 639 at 650; J. A. Nason, Beyond Repatriation: Cultural Policy and Practice for the Twenty-First Century, in B. Ziff and P. V. Pao (eds.), *Borrowed Power: Essays on Cultural Appropriation* (New Brunswick, 1997), p.291; and J. A. R. Nafziger and R. J. Dobkins, The Native Americans Graves Protection and Repatriation Act in its First Decade (1999) 8 IJCP 77 at 80–81.

government enabled the protection and restitution of cultural objects of indigenous peoples outside the United States, and ignored its 'special relationship' with their communities.[95]

However, US museum organisations opposed the imposition of binding national legislation in favour of self-regulated ethical policies. Their opposition to the draft NAGPRA was founded on several familiar grounds. They continued to insist that any restitution request could be resolved through informal case-by-case negotiations.[96] In addition, they argued that scientific knowledge benefiting all humankind would be sacrificed for the religious beliefs of a minority.[97] The potential loss of repatriated items through their decay or destruction was also said to be contrary to museums' role of collecting and preserving objects for educational purposes.

With the passage of the Native American Grave Protection and Repatriation Act of 1990, the US Congress finally recognised the pre-eminence of the rights of Native American tribes and Hawaiian organisations to their cultural heritage over the interests of the scientific and museum communities.[98] Significantly, unlike current international instruments, the Act sanctioned investigation of the provenance and restitution of cultural objects removed before and since its operation.

NAGPRA vests ownership or control of Native American and Hawaiian ancestral remains and cultural items – excavated or found on federal or tribal lands after 16 November 1990 – with the lineal descendants, Native American tribe or Hawaiian organisation.[99] In respect of items removed prior to that date (and located in a federal agency or a federally funded museum) the Act provides the following framework for resolution of restitution claims.

Affected institutions were to inventory Native American *human remains and associated grave goods* in their possession or control and identify the geographical and cultural affiliation of each object (Section 5(a)). The process was to be undertaken in consultation with appropriate Native American and Hawaiian representatives. After completing the inventory, they were required to notify appropriate indigenous

[95] See North American Indian Museums Association, Suggested Guidelines for Museums in Dealing with Requests for Return of Native American Materials, in *Directory of North American Indian Museums and Cultural Centers* (Niagara Falls, 1981).

[96] See Nason, 'Beyond', p.295; and AAM, Policy Regarding the Repatriation of Native American Ceremonial Objects and Human Remains, Washington, 1987 (1988) 7 IJMMC 310.

[97] See L. Zimmerman, Archaeology, Reburial and the Tactics of a Discipline's Self-Delusion (1992) 16 AICRJ 37; and L. Zimmerman, A New and Different Archaeology (1996) 20 AIQ 297. NAGPRA improved scientific knowledge and output from museum collections. Whilst museums notified the relevant indigenous group before research was undertaken, this trend is not replicated in the reporting of results: T. J. Sullivan, M. Abraham and D. J. G. Griffin, NAGPRA: Effective Repatriation Programs and Cultural Change in Museums (2002) 43 *Curator* 231 at 239–48.

[98] Pub. L. No.101-601, 104 Stat. 3048 (1990), codified at 25 USC §§3001 *et seq* (2000); and NAGPRA Regulations, 43 CFR Part 10. See Meister (ed.), *Mending*; C. Williams, *American Indian Sacred Objects, Skeletal Remains, Repatriation and Reburial: A Resource Guide* (Washington, 1994); and http://www.cr.nps.gov/nagpra.

[99] Section 3, NAGPRA (details order of priority accorded to persons or groups); and *Pueblo of San Ildefonso* v. *Ridlon* (1996, CA 10 NM) 103 F 3d 936 (10th Cir., 1996). A review committee appointed by US Secretary of the Interior supervises compliance with and administration of the Act: s.8. Federal grants are authorised to assist indigenous groups and museums in making use of or complying with the Act: s.10; and C. T. McKeown, NAGPRA Grants, in Meister (ed.), *Mending*, pp.21–22.

groups (Section 5(d)). Items were to be returned expeditiously to the lineal descendant, relevant tribe or organisation upon their request (Section 7(a)).

Information requirements in respect of *sacred items, items of cultural patrimony and funerary items* unrelated to human remains were less stringent.[100] Sacred objects are defined as items required by 'traditional Native American religious leaders for the practice of traditional Native American religions by their present day adherents' (Section 2(3)(C)), while 'cultural patrimony' must have 'ongoing historical, traditional or cultural importance' to an indigenous group who consider it inalienable (Section 2(3)(D)). Lineal descendants or appropriate indigenous groups can request the repatriation of these items (Section 7(a)(5)). The requesting group must present a *prima facie* case that the institution does not obtain possession of the item with the voluntary consent of the individual or group with authority to alienate it (Sections 2(13) and 7(c)).[101] The burden then shifts to the holding institution to establish that it does have the right of possession.

The Act 'accommodates' indigenous law and custom at three particular points: first, in the consideration of what constitutes 'cultural patrimony'[102]; secondly, in determining whether a holding institution has the right to possess an object (unrelated to ancestral remains), it must be shown that voluntary consent was obtained from the individual or group who had authority under indigenous law to alienate it (Section 2(13)); and thirdly, it is used in the determination of 'cultural affiliation' (Section 7(a)(4)).[103]

The operation of the NAGPRA framework is limited in several significant areas. First, the Act covers only a portion of the relationship between Native Americans and US museums, namely the ownership, repatriation and illicit trade of certain cultural items.

Second, NAGPRA is exclusively concerned with 'federally recognised' tribes (Section 2(7)). The Act ignores internal disputes within tribes concerning custodianship. It fails to address the relocation and destruction of tribal groups caused by assimilation and relocation policies.[104] This is exacerbated by the 'cultural affiliation' requirement whereby a requesting Native American tribe or Hawaiian organisation

---

[100] Only a written summary detailing the scope of the collection, type of objects, details of acquisition and geographical location and cultural affiliation is required: s.6(a).

[101] This is not an issue in respect of human remains and associated funerary objects which can not be 'owned' or transferred: Gerstenblith, 'Identity', 629.

[102] See *United States v. Corrow* 941 F Supp. 1553 (DNM 1996); affd 11 F 3d 796 (10th Cir. 1997); cert. denied 522 US 1133, 118 S Ct 1089 (1998); and D. E. Goldman, The Native American Graves Protection and Repatriation Act: A Benefit and a Burden, Defining NAGPRA's Cultural Patrimony Definition (1999) 8 IJCP 229.

[103] See D. B. Suagee, Building a Tribal Repatriation Program: Options for Exercising Sovereignty, in Meister (ed.), *Mending*, p.32.

[104] See T. L. Bray, Repatriation, Power Relations and the Politics of the Past (1996) 70 *Antiquity* 440; and S. Russell, The Legacy of Ethnic Cleansing: Implementation of NAGPRA in Texas (1995) 19 AICRJ 193. A holding institution may retain an item requested by multiple claimants until they agree upon its disposition or the dispute is resolved by procedures prescribed by the review committee or federal courts: s.7(e). See National Park Service, *National NAGPRA FY04 Midyear Report* (Washington DC, 2004), pp.31–44; Nafziger and Dobkins, 'First Decade', 92–98; and T. Naranjo, Musings on Two World Views: The NAGPRA Review Committee, in Meister (ed.), *Mending*, p.27.

must link itself to an identifiable earlier group (Section 7(a)(4)).[105] The privileging of traditional cultures perpetuates the stasis of indigenous cultures promoted by early anthropologists and impedes the protection and development of living cultures.[106]

Third, the operation of the Act is limited to federal agencies and federally funded museums (includes state, federal, educational and other institutions containing such items) (Section 2(8)). It has no impact on cultural objects in private collections unless they were obtained from a museum after 16 November 1990 or the items were found on federal or tribal lands (Section 3(a)(1)).

Finally, NAGPRA is susceptible to 'redefinition' by those claiming third-party rights in such items. Under the Act, repatriation can be delayed for ninety days if the items are 'indispensable for completion of a specific scientific study the outcome of which would be of major benefit to the United States' (Section 7(b)). In *Bonnichsen* v. *US Department of the Army*, the court held for the applicant scientists, finding that, because of their physical characteristics and age, the remains bore no relationship to any 'existing tribe, people or culture' and the Act was not applicable.[107] The transfer to the tribe for immediate reburial was barred and the scientists were permitted to study them pursuant to the ARPA 1979. Some museums have also begun to actively reassert their interests in indigenous cultural objects. For example, the Bishop Museum Hawai'i had claimed that it was a 'Native Hawaiian organisation' for the purposes of NAGPRA, thereby potentially enabling it to retain cultural objects in its collections and make restitution claims for items held by other institutions.[108] These recent developments reveal starkly the vulnerability of Native Americans and Hawaiians' 'controlling voice' in determining the fate of their cultural heritage under US domestic laws.[109]

NAGPRA itself states that it 'reflects the unique relationship between the Federal Government and Indian tribes and Native Hawaiian organisations'.[110] In their assessment of its first decade of operation, Nafziger and Dobkins described it as an 'expression of civil rights and ethnic reconciliation', and its implementation is

---

[105] See 43 CFR Part 10, Subpart A, 10.2(c). Appropriate evidence in support of cultural affiliation claims can include geographical, kinship, biological, archaeological, anthropological, linguistic, folklore, oral tradition, historical, and other relevant information or expert opinion: 43 CFR Part 10, Subpart A, 10.14(d); and Nason, 'Beyond', p.300.

[106] See Welsh, 'Repatriation', 844.

[107] 969 F Supp. 628 (D. Or. 1997) (preliminary ruling); 217 F Supp. 2d 1116 (D. Or. 2002); aff. 357 F 3d 962 (9th Cir. 2004); 367 F 3d 864 (9th Cir., 2004). Cf. *Idrogo* v. *United States Army*, 18 F Supp. 2d 25 (DDC 1998). See D. W. Owsley and R. L. Jantz, Kennewick Man – A Kin? Too Distant, in E. Barkan and R. Bush (eds.), *Claiming the Stones, Naming the Bones: Cultural Property and the Negotiation of National and Ethnic Identity* (Los Angeles, 2002), p.141.

[108] Bishop Museum, Interim and Proposed Final Guidance: Native American Graves Protection and Repatriation Act, 30 June 2004, at http://www.bishopmuseum.org/NAGPRAGuidelines.html.

[109] L. Zimmerman and R. N. Clinton, Case Note: Kennewick Man and Native American Graves Protection and Repatriation Act Woes (1999) 8 IJCP 212 at 225. See P. Gerstenblith, Cultural Significance and the Kennewick Skeleton: Some Thoughts on the Resolution of Cultural Heritage Disputes, in Barkan and Bush (eds.), *Claiming*, p.162; and W. Aila Jr *et al.*, Bishop Museum leadership must change, *The Honolulu Advertiser*, 13 June 2004.

[110] Section 12, NAGPRA (adds it 'should not be construed to establish a precedent with respect to any other individual, organisation or foreign government').

'redress[ing] historic grievances against the dominant culture'.[111] The US museum community initially viewed the Act as an additional legislative burden but now identifies it as 'a sweeping force for cultural change'.[112] In combination with the re-emergence of the claims of Holocaust survivors and their heirs, the Act has forced museums to consider the provenance of objects in their collections and their acquisition policies.

For Native Americans and Hawaiians, NAGPRA is a crucial step in their ability to determine how their cultures are preserved and developed.[113] Following passage of the Act, there has been a proliferation of tribal museums and cultural centres. Yet, there is increasing concern that the focus on the repatriation process has led to decreased vigilance concerning ongoing cultural losses caused by illicit trade and clandestine excavations.[114]

Native Americans also hoped that NAGPRA would aid in redefining their relations with the US museum community.[115] There has been increased consultation in respect of interpretation policies, including displays and exhibitions, and employment in curatorial positions.[116] However, indigenous representatives argue that there has been little progress in respect of 'co-authority' arrangements.[117] The Act's impact on the exercise of the right to self-determination and cultural development by indigenous peoples – outside US museums – has been restrained. US museums allocated resources only to programmes over which they 'maintained effective control and extracted direct and tangible benefit'.[118] They were less likely to provide technical and financial resources to assist initiatives within indigenous communities with the same goals, and are reluctant to loan cultural materials to local indigenous cultural centres.[119] This trend is problematic for indigenous peoples because NAGPRA places additional strains on the limited resources and personnel of tribal organisations.[120] Nonetheless, the Act has encouraged Native Americans, at the

---

[111] Nafziger and Dobkins, 'First Decade', 82. See M. A. Fred, Law and Identity: Negotiating Meaning in the Native American Graves Protection and Repatriation Act (1997) 6 IJCP 199 at 212; C. T. McKeown, Implementing a 'True Compromise': The Native American Graves Protection and Repatriation Acts after Ten Years, in C. Fforde, J. Hubert and P. Turnbull (eds.), *The Dead and Their Possessions: Repatriation in Principle, Policy and Practice* (London, 2001), p.108.

[112] Sullivan et al., 'NAGPRA', 252; and M. Abraham, T. J. Sullivan and D. J. G. Griffin, Implementing NAGPRA: The Effective Management of Legislated Change in Museums (2001) 40 *Management Decision* 35 at 39, 48. See Gerstenblith, 'Kennewick', p.179; and W. R. West et al., NAGPRA at 10: Examining a Decade of the Native American Graves and Protection and Repatriation Act (2000) 79 *Museum News* 42 at 67 (McKeown) and 68 (Harjo).

[113] See Nason, 'Beyond', 300; and R. W. Hill Sr, Regenerating Identity: Repatriation and Indian Frame of Mind, in T. Bray (ed.), *The Future of the Past: Archaeologists, Native Americans and Repatriation* (London, 2001), p.127.

[114] See West et al.,' NAGPRA at 10', 44 (Lomawaima); and V. Canouts and F. P. McManamon, Protecting the Past for the Future: Federal Archaeology in the United States, in N. Brodie, J. Doole and C. Renfrew (eds.), *Trade in Illicit Antiquities: The Destruction of the World's Archaeological Heritage* (Cambridge, 2001), p.97.

[115] See D. K. Inouye, Repatriation: Forging New Relationships (1992) 24 ASLJ 1.

[116] See J. A. R Nafziger, The New Fiduciary Duty of United States Museums to Repatriate Cultural Heritage: The Oregon Experience (1995) 29 UBCLR 37 at 41.

[117] West et al., 'NAGPRA at 10', 67 (Isaac). See Sullivan et al., 'NAGPRA', p.8; and J. Haas, Power, objects, and a voice for anthropology (1996) 37 *Current Anthropology* S1.

[118] Abraham et al., 'Implementing', 39.   [119] Sullivan et al., 'NAGPRA', 250–53.

[120] See Nason, 'Beyond', pp.304ff; Nafziger and Dobkins, 'First Decade', 82; and D. Drake Wilson, California Indian Participation in Repatriation: Working Toward Recognition (1997) 21 AICRJ 191.

tribal level and internationally with other indigenous organisations, to formulate their own codes covering principles and procedures for the management of their cultural heritage.[121]

NAGPRA offers Native American groups limited assistance for the repatriation of human remains and cultural objects located outside US jurisdiction. Objects in international collections may be subject to the Act if they were removed from land under the control of a federal agency. Indeed, items originally removed from federal lands in Alaska have been repatriated by Swiss and Danish institutions.[122] To this end, US museum officials provide communities with information about culturally affiliated collections located in other US and international institutions.[123]

Although NAGPRA is a national legislative framework, it does facilitate repatriations to indigenous groups outside the United States in two ways. First, indigenous groups in Canada have obtained access to inventories and collections and had items repatriated to them because they meet the Act's 'cultural affiliation' requirement to the objects and present-day tribes in the United States.[124] The objects are returned to the relevant US tribe who then transfer them to the requesting affiliated group.

Second, US museums have utilised NAGPRA as a model for foreign repatriation requests. For instance, the National Museum of the American Indian (NMAI) has adapted its national programme for international repatriations to indigenous communities in Canada, Cuba and Peru.[125] The NMAI determines the 'cultural affiliation' of items to present-day indigenous groups. Then, through the US State Department, it establishes government-to-government relations before it officially contracts the relevant indigenous group. This procedure ensures negotiations are conducted with authorised representatives if there are competing, indigenous claimants. Significantly, the NMAI supports repatriation directly to the 'descendant indigenous community'.[126]

---

[121] Nason, 'Beyond', p.306; Suagee, 'Building', pp.31ff; and R. Strickland and K. Supernaw, Back to the Future: A Proposed Model Tribal Act to Protect Native Cultural Heritage (1993) 46 Ark. LR 161.

[122] Notice of Inventory Completion by the Bureau of Land Management, Alaska State Office, FR Doc.96-22495; and Notice of Inventory Completion by US Forest Service, Alaska, FR Doc.97-20634.

[123] Personal communication, S. Makseyn-Kelley, Repatriation Program Specialist, NMAI, Suitland MD, 23 June 2004.

[124] Personal communication, M. Downs, NAGPRA Program Officer, National Park Service, Washington DC, 16 and 28 July 2004; Notices of Inventory Completion by NPS, FR Doc.01-9753, FR vol.66, no.77, 20 April 2001, p.20329; and FR Doc.98-14575, FR vol.63, no.105, 2 June 1998, p.30019; and Notices of Intent to Repatriate by NPS, FR Doc.03-26580, FR vol.68, no.204, 22 October 2003, p.60413; FR Doc.00-10464, FR vol.65, no.82, 27 April 2000, p.24712; FR Doc.96-11791, FR vol.61, no.92, 10 May 1996, p.21486; and FR Doc.94-17599, FR vol.59, no.138, 20 July 1994.

[125] Personal communication, S. Makseyn-Kelley, 30 April 2002 and 4 February 2005; NMAI, Beyond the Medicine Line: International Repatriation and the NMAI (Washington DC, n.d.) (copy on file); and NMAI, National Museum of the American Indian Policy Statement on Native American Human Remains and Cultural Materials, revised 1991 (copy on file). The Smithsonian Institution is excluded from NAGPRA's operation. It is covered by the National Museum of the American Indian Museum Act of 1989, Pub. L. No.101-85, codified at 20 USC §§80q-80q-15.

[126] NMAI, 'Beyond', p.2.

Figure 9.2 Indigenous Australians, Australian Museum, 1997.

Voluntary model – Australia

Since 1993, Australian museums have voluntarily chosen to abide by a policy prepared by its peak body in consultation with indigenous peoples. Like the Daes Principles and Guidelines, it not only covers restitution but also strives to redefine relations between indigenous peoples and museums generally. Nevertheless, recent evaluations of its implementation reveal that the limitations exhibited by the US model are replicated in Australia. While the Australian federal government is assisting Indigenous Australian claims for the restitution of ancestral remains and cultural heritage held in domestic and foreign institutions, problems remain. The Howard federal government has pursued a policy agenda that leaves it vulnerable to the charge that it is less than committed to ensuring indigenous peoples' right to preserve and develop their cultural identities.

On 1 December 1993, the Council of Australian Museums Association (CAMA) launched a statement of principles and guidelines covering relations between museums and Indigenous Australians entitled 'Previous Possessions, New Obligations' (PPNO).[127] Des Griffin, CAMA president and director of the Australian Museum, noted that, by the 1990s, indigenous activism and international developments rendered it untenable for museums to continue to claim that they alone could determine public programmes and management of Indigenous Australian collections.[128]

---

[127] CAMA, *Previous Possession, New Obligations: Policies for Museums in Australia and Aboriginal and Torres Strait Islander Peoples* (1993) (Reprint, Melbourne, 2000).

[128] D. J. G. Griffin, Previous Possessions, New Obligations: A Commitment by Australian Museums (1996) 39 *Curator* 45 at 46ff. Including World Archaeological Congress, First Code of Ethics (1990) 6 *Anthropology Today* 24; NAGPRA; and Assembly of First Nations and Canadian Museums Association, *Turning the Page: Forging New Partnerships between Museums and First Peoples* (3rd edn, Ottawa, 1994).

CAMA formally recognised Indigenous Australians as the original inhabitants and 'owners' of the territories of present-day Australia.[129] The policy details the significant and ongoing role of museums in the colonisation of Indigenous Australians, and its effects on their communities, lands and cultures.[130] While affirming the importance of cultural diversity in Australia, CAMA pronounced that Indigenous Australians have a 'unique, distinctive and different' culture from non-Indigenous Australians.[131] PPNO recognises as its primary principle the right of Indigenous Australians to self-determination 'in respect of cultural heritage matters'. The policy acknowledged that Indigenous Australian cultures 'are living cultures: there are fundamental links between cultural heritage, traditional belief and land'.[132]

In his statement before the WGIP in 1993, Des Griffin noted that 'museums today must address fundamental issues of ownership of cultural heritage'.[133] However, whilst the US legislation deals directly with the question of ownership, the Australian policy skirts around this issue. Indigenous representatives consulted during the formulation of PPNO recommended the recognition of Indigenous Australian control and ownership of all past, present and future cultural and intellectual material.[134] Although PPNO concedes that the issue of ownership of cultural heritage is a 'strongly held' view by Indigenous Australians, the final text did not incorporate this recommendation.[135] Instead, the policy stipulates that existing collections were acquired legitimately according to 'Australian law' and museums 'are entitled to do with them as they see fit in accordance with their enabling legislation'.[136] The rights of indigenous peoples to their cultural heritage are defined as 'special rights' or 'primary rights'.[137] It affirms the pre-eminence of indigenous interests in Indigenous Australian collections over those of the general scientific community.[138] Nonetheless, the policy only acknowledges the moral claims of indigenous peoples without resolving their legal title.[139] Indigenous Australian organisations, particularly ATSIC, were critical of PPNO's formulation of their 'title' to indigenous items within Australian museum collections.[140]

[129] D. J. G. Griffin, Previous Possessions, New Obligations: A New Policy for Australian Museums, 1994, p.2, Griffin Papers, AMA.
[130] Preamble, CAMA, *PPNO*, pp.3–4.   [131] Griffin, 'New Policy', p.2.
[132] Introduction, and Principle 1, CAMA, *PPNO*, pp.2 and 6; and Griffin, 'New Policy', p.19.
[133] D. J. G. Griffin, Written statement on behalf of the Council of Australian Museums, in ATSIC, *UN Working Group on Indigenous Populations, Eleventh Session, 19–30 July 1993, The Australian Contribution*, (Canberra, 1993), p.93.
[134] Griffin, 'New Policy', p.11. See Part IIA, Aboriginal and Torres Strait Islander Heritage Protection Act 1984 (Cth).
[135] CAMA, *PPNO*, p.4.   [136] CAMA, *PPNO*, p.6.
[137] Ownership is recognised in respect of intangible cultural heritage: CAMA, *PPNO*, p.1; and Griffin, 'New Policy', p.20. Cf. Australian Aboriginal Affairs Council, National Principles for the Return of Aboriginal and Torres Strait Islander Cultural Property, October 1993, in Griffin, 'New Policy', Appendix 3.
[138] CAMA, *PPNO*, Guideline 3.8. Contrary to PPNO, Australian museums are unlikely to advise the relevant indigenous community of proposed research or results in respect of general collections: L. Kelly, P. Gordon and T. Sullivan, 'We Deal with Relationships: Not Just Objects', An Evaluation of *Previous Possessions, New Obligations*, Green Paper, (Sydney, 2001), pp.3–4, 12 and 17.
[139] CAMA, *PPNO*, p.7. See CAMA, *PPNO*, Guideline 3.9; C. Anderson, Australian Aborigines and Museums – A New Relationship (1990) 33 *Curator* 165 at 172; and D. J. G. Griffin, Meaning in the Bones: Museum Futures and Indigenous Australians (November 1996) *Museum National* 11 at 13.
[140] Fourmile, 'Submission', pp.948–49.

The policy's failure to recognise Indigenous Australians' ownership and control of their cultural heritage reflects the effort of the dominant culture to 'accommodate' indigenous claims within its existing museological and legal frameworks. This legal/moral rights dichotomy revives the terminology of the 'sacred trust of civilisation' formulated originally by the colonial powers. If PPNO is part of a process of recognising past wrongs, then Australian museums must desist from asserting their legal title to indigenous collections by cloaking themselves in the validity of laws that perpetuated colonialism.

PPNO addresses the handling of requests for return of human remains,[141] secret sacred material,[142] general collections,[143] and archives.[144] In addition, guidelines concerning custodianship and access, display, documentation and research are provided for each category.

In respect of *secret sacred objects*, PPNO recognises custodianship in accordance with indigenous law and custom.[145] Museums must consult traditional custodians to identify secret sacred items and decide whether repatriation is desired. Museums may retain custodianship of these objects if requested to do so by the traditional custodians. These items must be stored separately from the general collections and in accordance with the reasonable conditions stipulated by the traditional custodians. Museums will not acquire nor display such objects except with the permission of the traditional custodians.

In respect of *collections in general*, including items of contemporary cultures, museums will 'incorporate where appropriate' the views of the indigenous community of 'whose cultural traditions the items form part'.[146] When return of such items is requested their provenance will be considered by the museum. Even where the museum finds that the object has been legally acquired, 'the primacy of Aboriginal and Torres Strait Islander interests will guide decisions'.[147]

PPNO encourages museums to loan cultural material to museums and 'other appropriate venues' (like keeping places and culture centres) 'subject to appropriate conditions concerning conservation and security of the items'.[148] Indigenous groups reject conditional 'returns' because, as Daes noted, ownership of these items could not be relinquished by indigenous communities. However, Australian museums do not place any conditions on successful restitution claims.[149]

---

141 CAMA, *PPNO*, Guidelines 1.1–1.10. See Museums (Aboriginal Remains) Act 1984 (Tas.).
142 CAMA, *PPNO*, Guidelines 2.1–2.10.   143 CAMA, *PPNO*, Guidelines 3.1–3.10.
144 CAMA, *PPNO*, Guidelines 3.5, 3.9–3.10.
145 See E. Evatt, *Review of the Aboriginal and Torres Strait Islander Heritage Protection Act 1984* (Canberra, 1996), pp.109ff.
146 CAMA, *PPNO*, Guideline 3.1. Australian museums will not copy or replicate the objects being returned unless specifically offered by the relevant community: CAMA, *PPNO*, Guideline 3.5.
147 CAMA, *PPNO*, Guideline 3.8. See Griffin, 'New Policy', p.17.
148 CAMA, *PPNO*, Guideline 3.3.
149 Interview with R. Stack, Indigenous Heritage Officer, Macleay Museum, University of Sydney, Sydney, 3 May 2001; and interview with RICP Project Group, Museum Victoria, Melbourne, 29 January 2002. See Museums Australia, *Continuous Cultures Ongoing Responsibilities: A Comprehensive Policy Document and Guidelines for Australian Museums Working with Aboriginal and Torres Strait Islander Cultural Heritage* (Canberra, 2005), Guidelines 1.4.6 (Ancestral remains), and 1.5.5 (Secret sacred material).

Following the 'recognition' of native title to land by the High Court of Australia in 1992, the federal Labor government fostered a policy of reconciliation between indigenous and non-indigenous Australians which replaced the recurring but failed efforts for a negotiated treaty.[150] Various reports prepared to address the effects of indigenous dispossession universally emphasised the importance of the protection, development and return of indigenous cultural heritage.[151] In February 1998, the Australian Cultural Ministers Council approved limited funding for the Return of Indigenous Cultural Property (RICP) Program.[152] Under the programme, Indigenous Australian communities are advised of ancestral remains and secret sacred objects from their particular group held by Commonwealth, state and territory museums, and have them repatriated by those museums. The initiative also aims to provide appropriate storage within museums for items not subject to a restitution request. The programme does not include formal principles and guidelines for these processes. Instead, Australian museums have formulated their own policies, which generally reflect PPNO.[153]

ATSIC welcomed PPNO for setting standards in 'the day-to-day management of indigenous material culture collections', despite its shortcomings.[154] In 2000, CAMA's successor, Museums Australia, commissioned a review of PPNO's implementation. It concluded that PPNO's principles had been internalised in 'everyday practice and institutional policies' by the major collecting and research museums but less so by rural institutions.[155] However, it found that, generally, Australian museums did not provide adequate financial and human resources to facilitate indigenous repatriation claims. They did loan objects from their collections to keeping places and provide advice and training to indigenous communities.[156]

Following on from the review in February 2005, Museums Australia endorsed its new principles and guidelines, 'Continuous Cultures Ongoing Responsibilities' (CCOR). CCOR was prepared in the wake of a number of significant political, social and technological developments in the intervening decade since PPNO. Its

[150] See Department of the Prime Minister and Cabinet, *Aboriginal Reconciliation: An Historical Perspective* (Canberra, 1992); Council for Aboriginal Reconciliation, *Addressing the Key Issues for Reconciliation* (Canberra, 1993), p.14; and M. Grattan (ed.), *Essays on Australian Reconciliation* (Melbourne, 2000), pp.60–64. The decade-long formal reconciliation process ended in 2001. Thereafter, ATSIC recommenced its push for a negotiated treaty between the Australian federal government and Indigenous Australians.

[151] See Council for Aboriginal Reconciliation, *Addressing*, pp.24–25; Council for Aboriginal Reconciliation, *Valuing Cultures: Recognising Indigenous Cultures as a Valued Part of Australian Heritage* (Canberra, 1994), pp.44–45; ATSIC, *Recognition, Rights and Reform: Report of the Government on Native Title Social Justice Measures* (Canberra, 1995), Recommendations 76–77 and paras.6.22–6.23 at pp.23–39 and 104–09; and Council for Aboriginal Reconciliation, *Going Forward: Social Justice for First Australians* (Canberra, 1995), Recommendations 56–60, pp.80–82.

[152] Cultural Ministers Council, 14th meeting, Communiqué, 11 August 2000, p.4.

[153] K. Gosling, General Manager, Cultural Development, Department of Communications Information Technology and the Arts to the author, 8 April 2002 (copy on file).

[154] Fourmile, 'Submission', p.948. See ATSIC, Protection and Return of Significant Aboriginal and Torres Strait Islander Cultural Property, 1994, and revised November 2001 (copy on file).

[155] Its authors included the Australian Museum's Phil Gordon and Lynda Kelly. See Kelly *et al.*, 'Relationships', 3–4, 20; and L. Kelly and P. Gordon, Developing a Community of Practice: Museums and Reconciliation in Australia, in R. Sandell (ed.), *Museums, Society and Inequality* (London, 2002), p.153 at pp.156ff.

[156] See Kelly *et al.*, 'Relationships', pp.4 and 13, and Recommendation 14.

re-titling is intended to reflect 'a greater emphasis on relationships and partnerships' between indigenous peoples and museums.[157] CCOR builds upon and modifies the principles and guidelines of its predecessor. First, it calls on museums to recognise contemporary indigenous cultural practices. It acknowledges the broader political and social importance of museum collections for indigenous self-determination, land claims and reconciliation.[158] Second, it recognises the diversity of indigenous cultures and multiplicity of viewpoints within these communities.[159] Third, it adopts a more holistic interpretation of culture including movable cultural property, human remains, art works, photographs, film and sound recordings 'as cultural objects in their own right as well as being documentation of cultural practices'.[160] And fourth, it affirms museums are bound to respect the cultural and intellectual property rights of Indigenous Australians and 'relevant customary law'.[161]

However, CCOR reaffirms a central limitation of the voluntary approach. Australian museums continued to be bound by a 'moral imperative' rather than legal obligations. Nonetheless, it acknowledges that museums are custodians rather than owners of indigenous cultural materials. CCOR reiterates that the objects are held according to Australian law and Indigenous Australians have an 'inherent' interest in the 'spiritual and practical care and control of their cultural property'.[162] Furthermore, it concedes that the guidelines pertaining to general collections apply to items 'acquired by open and legal means', that is 'legal' according to the laws and customs of the dominant culture, and not those of indigenous peoples. Yet, restitution requests for cultural items, even those legally acquired, 'must be given serious consideration' by the holding institution.[163] Repatriation of ancestral remains and secret sacred material, under CCOR, is exercisable without reference to 'legal' title.

This limited commitment by the Australian museum community to facilitating the broader right of indigenous peoples to preservation and development of their cultural identities is accentuated by the vulnerability of this right in the wider national context. Whilst the current Australian government supports indigenous repatriation campaigns, it has repeatedly sacrificed the rights of indigenous peoples to self-determination and 'religious freedom' in order to pursue national economic development.[164]

---

[157] MA, *CCOR*, p.9, and Guideline 5.1.

[158] MA, *CCOR*, pp.6–7, Principle 16 and Guidelines 1.3.5–1.3.8 and 5.1–5.6. See Kelly *et al.*, 'Relationships', p.21 and Recommendation 5.

[159] MA, *CCOR*, p.11, Principle 4 and Guidelines 1.2.1, 1.2.3 and 1.5. See M. Harris, The Narrative of Law in the Hindmarsh Island Royal Commission, in M. Chancock and C. Simpson (eds.), *Law and Cultural Heritage* (Melbourne, 1996), p.115.

[160] *Ibid.*

[161] MA, *CCOR*, pp.8, and Principles 3 and 15. See T. Janke, *Our Culture', Our Future.* (Canberra, 1998)

[162] MA, *CCOR*, pp.7, 9.   [163] MA, *CCOR*, p.15–16, Guideline 1.1.8.

[164] See Report of the Mission to Kakadu National Park, 29 November 1998, UNESCO Doc.WHC-98/CONF.202/INF.18; *Kartinyeri v. Commonwealth* (1998) 195 CLR 337; (1998) 152 ALR 450 Aboriginal and Torres Strait Islander Social Justice Commissioner, *Native Title Annual Report 2000* (Canberra, 2000), Chapter 4; UN, Concluding Observations of the Human Rights Committee, 69th session, 28 July 2000, UN Doc.CCPR/CO/69/AUS, para.11; Council for Aboriginal Reconciliation *Final Report*; and *Yarmirr v. Northern Territory & Commonwealth* (1999) 101 FRC 171, 168 ALR 426 affd (2001) 208 CLR 1, 184 ALR 113.

In her 1996 review of the Aboriginal and Torres Strait Islander Heritage Protection Act 1984, Elizabeth Evatt recommended the establishment of a uniform national legal framework for the protection and development of Indigenous Australian cultures.[165] She advised that in accordance with the right of self-determination, indigenous peoples must be substantially involved in decisions relating to their cultural heritage.[166] She recommended a holistic interpretation of cultural heritage contained in the 1993 Daes Study.[167] Evatt also reiterated the urgent need to recognise indigenous law and custom concerning cultural heritage.[168] She did not make specific recommendations covering ownership and restitution, stating instead that it should be the subject of further review.[169] Ironically, however, the report reproduced Article 12 of the 1993 Draft UN Declaration on its frontispiece.

The federal Liberal government has acknowledged that indigenous rights and interests in their heritage 'arise from their spirituality, customary law, original ownership, custodianship, developing Indigenous traditions and recent history'.[170] Yet, its Aboriginal and Torres Strait Islander Heritage Protection bill 1998 (Cth) deviated from Evatt's recommendations in two significant respects. The protection of indigenous cultural heritage would be deferred to State and Territory laws, subject to a Commonwealth accreditation scheme. The federal government would intervene only if the Minister considered it to be 'in the national interest'. Also, the bill diminishes existing indigenous participation in relevant decision-making processes. Indigenous autonomy was weakened further with ATSIC's demise and the assumption of its role under the existing Act by the Office of Indigenous Policy Coordination.[171] Where ATSIC was made up of representatives elected by Indigenous Australians, the new body is selected by the federal government.

International restitution has particular resonance for indigenous peoples in Oceania because of the large-scale collecting practices of various colonial forces during the nineteenth and twentieth centuries. Museum organisations have consistently stressed the workability of museum-to-museum negotiations.[172] By contrast, Evatt, like Daes, recommended the federal government enter into diplomatic negotiations for repatriation from overseas institutions to fulfil its obligations to Indigenous Australians.[173] In March 2000, the Australian Prime Minister John Howard and British Prime Minister Tony Blair issued a joint statement announcing that their respective governments 'agreed to increase efforts to repatriate human remains to Australian indigenous communities'.[174] It was projected that this new cooperative arrangement

---

[165] Evatt, *Review*, pp.42–44 and 231, paras.3.62–3.68 and 12.24 and Recommendations 3.1–3.3.
[166] *Ibid.* See Evatt, *Review*, Recommendations 11.1–11.17.   [167] Evatt, *Review*, p.232, para.12.27.
[168] Evatt, *Review*, pp.41 and 47, para.3.59 and Recommendations 4.1–4.4, 5.4, 6.1 and 8.1–8.9.
[169] Evatt, *Review*, p.227, para.12.13. See Fourmile, 'Submission', pp.940 and 934–936.
[170] *Hansard*, HR, vol.9, col.4543, 27 June 2002, Kemp.
[171] Aboriginal and Torres Strait Islander Commission Amendment Act 2005 (Cth); and Ruddock to author.
[172] See ICOM, *Code*, 2004, para.6.2.
[173] See Evatt, *Review*, pp.232–33, para.12.28 and Recommendation 2.4. See Council of Aboriginal Reconciliation, *Addressing*, pp.81 and 13–14, paras.56–58; and Commonwealth of Australia, *Creative Nation: Commonwealth Cultural Policy* (rev. edn, Canberra, 1994), n.p.
[174] Office of the Prime Minister of Australia, *Prime Ministerial Joint Statement on Aboriginal Remains*, 4 July 2000.

between the two countries would include protocols for information-sharing between institutions and indigenous peoples; inventorying indigenous collections; and identifying traditional custodians and their aspirations for the collections.

ATSIC advocated the replacement of individual returns with unconditional, 'whole-of-collection' repatriations to Australia, which it hoped would precipitate similar agreements with other European States. It also counselled that the repatriation of ancestral remains could not be separated from the restitution of 'sacred objects', which are critical to the maintenance of the 'collective identity' of Indigenous Australians.[175]

Developing a response – United Kingdom

Although several European metropolitan powers had formalised agreements with their former colonies for return of cultural objects, there has been no such arrangement concluded with Britain and its former colonies.[176] Indeed, the unstinting aversion of successive British governments and the museum community to the question of restitution has long impacted on the development of international instruments in the field. Indigenous Australian organisations have approached British holding institutions for the return of ancestral remains and cultural objects since the 1980s, with limited success.[177] However, by the mid 1990s, various factors combined to sway the Blair Labour government and UK museum organisations to rethink their intransigence and formulate policies governing restitution requests.[178]

In 2000, the Museums and Galleries Commission published guidelines to encourage museums to become proactive in the development of institutional policies for the handling of restitution requests.[179] The guidelines are the current voluntary framework which governs restitution claims in Britain. They do not address the rights of indigenous communities in respect of items held in British institutions or recognition of indigenous laws and customs.[180] Instead, they reaffirm that the final decision concerning restitution lies with the holding institution's governing body and that 'each request needs to be dealt with on a case-by-case basis, while mindful of the implications for the wider museum community'.[181] This individual application scheme is viewed as 'humiliating' by indigenous peoples and it often results in the return of well-provenanced items only.[182]

The MGC Guidelines, which deal exclusively with the question of restitution, must be contrasted with its 1999 Statement of Principles in respect of Nazi

---

175 ATSIC, Submission November 2001, in N. Palmer, *Report of the Working Group on Human Remains in Museum Collections* (London, 2003), paras.34–36, 100.
176 See M. Simpson, *Museums and Repatriation: An Account of Contested Items in Museum Collections in the UK, with Comparative Material from Other Countries* (London, 1997), pp.57ff.
177 See ATSIC, 'Submission', paras.53–54; and M. Simpson, *Making Representations: Museums in the Post-Colonial Era* (rev. edn, London, 2001), pp.276–77.
178 These included the claims of indigenous peoples, and Holocaust survivors and their heirs; lobbying by British archaeological organisations; and the experience of settler States and domestic institutions negotiating repatriation claims.
179 J. Legget, *Restitution and Repatriation: Guidelines for Good Practice* (London, 2000).
180 Customary law may be a consideration in determining the status of claimant or the circumstances of acquisition: Legget, *Restitution*, pp.15 and 18.
181 J. Joll, Foreword, in Legget, *Restitution*, p.5.   182 ATSIC, 'Submission', para.86.

Spoliation.[183] The latter policy covers restitution and the compilation of inventories, access to museum records, acquisitions and incoming loans, funding and public education. The distinction made by British museum and governmental approaches between spoliation (objects removed between 1933 and 1945) and restitution generally has been challenged.[184]

The Blair government advised a House of Commons Select Committee Inquiry in 2000 that 'objects which have been legitimately and properly acquired in the past should remain in the institutions which legally own them'.[185] Nonetheless, in response to the Select Committee's recommendations, the government announced the formation of the Working Group on Human Remains (WGHR).[186] The WGHR critically examined the 'legitimate and proper' circumstances under which human remains were acquired in the past. The WGHR report, released in November 2003, recognised that British institutions were the beneficiaries of colonial expansion and their collections were deployed to legitimise British imperial ambitions.[187] It observed that removal of human remains and associated objects rarely occurred with the consent of originating communities and was accompanied by the loss of traditional lands, self-determination and customary rights.[188] It stressed that 'effective' restitution was intimately connected to indigenous peoples' assertion of self-determination and cultural revitalisation.[189]

As in the United States and Australia, the WGHR recognised the oft competing interests of the originating and scientific communities.[190] It recommended that no holding institution retain them or 'perform any other act' without the consent of the genealogical descendants or those with equivalent status within the culture or religion of the originating community.[191] The working group noted that their retention by metropolitan museums, contrary to the wishes of relevant communities, is a 'continuing wrong'. It suggested indigenous communities could bring an action under the Human Rights Act 1998 for the ongoing human rights violations, and discrimination.[192] Indigenous Australian representatives have indicated they would seek to enforce these rights in the courts if holding institutions continue to reject repatriation claims.[193]

Nonetheless, the WGHR rejected the need for legislation requiring mandatory return. Instead, it recommended holding institutions formulate, publicise and

---

[183] MGC, Spoliation of Works of Art during the Nazi, Holocaust and World War II Period – Statement of Principles, 1999, in Legget, *Restitution*, Appendix 3, pp.34–38.

[184] Palmer, *Report*, para.470; and First Report of the Culture, Media and Sport Select Committee (2003–2004 HC 59), QQ41–49.

[185] Memorandum of DCMS, Seventh Report of Select Committee on Culture, Media and Sport (1999–2000 HC 371), vol.2, para.20, (8 June 2000). See First Report, QQ37–39.

[186] *Hansard*, HC, vol.368, col.115W, 8 May 2001, A. Howarth; and *Hansard*, HL, vol.625, Part 75, col.WA240, 10 May 2001, Lord McIntosh of Haringey; and Seventh Report of Select Committee on Culture, Media and Sport (1999–2000 HC 371), vol.1, paras.1, 163 and 166.

[187] Palmer, *Report*, pp.16–24, 126.   [188] Palmer, *Report*, Chapter 7.

[189] Palmer, *Report*, pp.22, 60–61.

[190] Palmer, *Report*, Chapter 9, and pp.134–35. See dissenting statement of N. Chalmers, pp.162–68.

[191] Palmer, *Report*, p.156, Recommendation 15.

[192] Palmer, *Report*, pp.22, 86–87 and 152. See WAC, Media Release 198/03.

[193] ATSIC Media Release, Repatriation Report Update, 26 November 2003.

implement 'externally approved' procedures for the resolution of restitution requests.[194] Significantly, it drew some parallels between restitution claims arising from the Nazi era and those of formerly colonised peoples. It recommended the establishment of a national Human Remains Advisory Panel along the lines of the Spoliation Advisory Panel.[195] Reference to the panel would be by consent of the parties to the dispute, and its recommendations would not be binding. Presumably, the panel would also be required to consider 'any moral consideration rest[ing] on the institution taking into account in particular the circumstances of its acquisition of the object'.[196] In 2005, the Spoliation Advisory Panel and the High Court found that such moral obligation did not override the prohibition on restitution in the governing legislation of the British Library and British Museum respectively.[197] They recommended that the British parliament enact legislation to permit these institutions to return objects in their collections.

Despite its terms of reference, the WGHR's recommendations specifically excluded 'associated objects'.[198] This is a substantial shortcoming. Repatriation schemes in the United States and Australia evolved from claims by indigenous peoples for the return of ancestral remains. The WGHR's findings and recommendations concerning human remains are equally applicable to the restitution of 'sacred' or 'culturally significant' objects.[199] The report must serve as a catalyst for the ongoing renegotiation of relations between British institutions and indigenous communities whose cultures are represented in their collections, thereby reaffirming the UK government's stated commitment to 'righting historic wrongs'.[200]

Australian museums and the recollection of colonialism and reconciliation

In Chapter 8, it is shown how the claims of indigenous peoples, together with the re-emergence of the claims of Holocaust survivors and their heirs, have highlighted the importance not only of material restitution, but moral restitution. Moral restitution has been described as an open-ended process of 'confronting the past honestly

---

[194] Palmer, *Report*, p.148–49, Recommendations 2(5) and 4.

[195] Palmer, *Report*, pp.137–39, 150, and Recommendation 5. Palmer foreshadowed the possibility of a single body dealing with all repatriation claims: First Report, Q237.

[196] UK Spoliation Advisory Panel, Constitution and Terms of Reference, in N. Palmer, *Museums and the Holocaust: Law, Principles and Practice* (London, 2000), Appendix 12, p.300, at para.7(g).

[197] Report of the Spoliation Advisory Panel in respect of a 12th Century Manuscript now in the Possession of the British Library (2005 HC 406), paras.72ff; and *Attorney-General* v. *The Trustees of the British Museum* [2005] EWHR 1089 (Ch), paras.40 and 45.

[198] Palmer, *Report*, pp.157–158, Recommendation 17. It recommended the establishment of a ministerial advisory group for 'sacred objects', with a comparable mandate to the WGHR. In the interim, it suggested holding institutions adhere to the MGC guidelines. Cf. ATSIC, 'Submission', paras. 51–52.

[199] See Palmer, *Report*, p.117, para.388 and Appendix 3, para.52; ICOM, *Code of Ethics for Museums*, 2001, Article 6.6 at http://icom.museum/ethics.html. Cf. British government position, at First Report, Q46.

[200] See A. Herle *et al.*, Objects, agency and museums: continuing dialogues between the Torres Strait and Cambridge, in A. Herle, N. Stanley, K. Stevenson and R. L. Welsch (eds.), *Pacific Arts: Persistence, Change and Meaning* (Adelaide, 2002), p.231.

and internalising its lessons'.[201] Many settler States and former metropolitan powers have gradually begun to confront their colonial past and its ongoing effects on
indigenous peoples and their cultures. Des Griffin was confident that the Australian
Museum's 'Indigenous Australians' gallery would aid the reconciliation process by
'recognis[ing] the wrongs of the past, acknowledg[ing] those wrongs and injustices
and try[ing] to move forward in a new way with Aboriginal people, to recognise that
they have rights to self-determination'.[202]

This final section examines how Australian museum collections, created as part
of the British colonial project, are used to counter the effects of colonial occupation
by promoting recollection by the dominant culture, thereby facilitating reconciliation.[203] First, there is a brief description of the (re)presentation of relations between
indigenous and non-indigenous peoples within Australian museums today. Second,
there is an explanation of how museum collections and archives are used to stymie
the land claims of indigenous communities. Finally, the way in which these same collections are ameliorating the ongoing effects of assimilation policies is considered.

From the nineteenth century onwards, international law and museums became
significant vehicles for the European colonisation of non-European peoples and
their territories. Today, however, they are scrutinised and deployed to unravel and
remedy the legacies of European colonial occupation by indigenous peoples and
non-indigenous peoples in settler States. In the last decade, these States have witnessed a proliferation of new national museums opening their doors at a rate not
witnessed since the late nineteenth century.[204] These museums aim to include differing voices, narratives and memories of the past, present and future of the nation,
in particular those of indigenous peoples.

Long-established museums (including the V&A, MoMA and Australian Museum)
have undertaken substantial renovations of their premises, particularly the exhibition spaces, during this period. Such transition is more overt for institutions like
the Australian Museum which have sought to recollect and redefine their own histories and relations with indigenous peoples and other communities represented
by their collections. From the mid-1990s onwards, successive state museums in
Australia have opened discrete but significant exhibition spaces within their institutions devoted to Indigenous Australians and their cultures.

Two distinct trends are discernible in these new galleries:

• Object-focus – These galleries portray the diversity of Indigenous Australian cultures, but they rely primarily on the display of cultural objects from historic

---

[201] E. Bronfman to US President, 15 December 2000, in US Presidential Advisory Commission, *Plunder
and Restitution: Findings and Recommendations of the Presidential Advisory Commission on Holocaust
Assets in the United States and Staff Report* (Washington DC, 2000).
[202] A Conversation with Dr Des Griffin, 1997, D. J. G. Griffin Papers, AMA.
[203] See D. S. Mundine, Black my Story (Not History), (1993) 24 *COMA Bulletin* 12; and Simpson,
Making, pp.247ff.
[204] Including the Canadian Museum of Civilisation (1988), Te Papa the Museum of New Zealand
(1998), National Museum of Australia (2001) and the National Museum of the American Indian,
Smithsonian Institution (2004).

Figure 9.3 Indigenous Australians, Australian Museum, 1997.

anthropological collections to convey their message to visitors.[205] The South Australian Museum gallery's purpose is to 'highlight the achievements of Australian Aboriginal people before their material culture and traditions were significantly affected by European contract'.[206] The installations convey the impression of static, timeless cultures reminiscent of early anthropological exhibitions and modern art displays.

- Narrative-focus – These exhibitions strive to provide a space within the museum where Indigenous Australians can convey their narratives and concerns to the general public.[207]

The Australian Museum's current gallery 'Indigenous Australians: Australia's First Peoples' opened in March 1997. By consulting indigenous communities from its earliest planning stages, the exhibition marked a shift from the museum's interpretation of Indigenous Australians' heritage to the community themselves; and from an object-focus to themes designated by Indigenous Australians of New South Wales.[208]

---

[205] Including Aboriginal Cultures Gallery, South Australian Museum (March 2000–); and djamu gallery, offsite exhibition, Australian Museum (2000).

[206] Aboriginal Cultures Gallery, Ingarnendi: Material Culture of Aboriginal Australia, South Australian Museum at http://www.ingarnendi.samuseum.sa.gov.au.

[207] Including 'Indigenous Australians: Australia's First Peoples', Australian Museum (1997–); Bunjilaka, The Aboriginal Centre at Melbourne Museum, Melbourne Museum (October 2000–); and First Australians: Gallery of Aboriginal and Torres Strait Islander Peoples, National Museum of Australia (2001–). In the US context: A. Kawasaki, *The Changing Presentation of the American Indian* (Washington DC, 2000).

[208] Interview with P. Gordon, Manager, Aboriginal Heritage Unit, Australian Museum, 26 February 1999; Kelly *et al.*, 'Relationships', 159; and Australian Museum, Aboriginal Australian: Planning Report, October 1995, pp.2, 8–10, AMA.

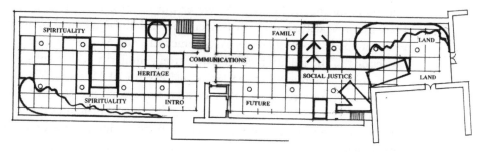

EXHIBITION LAYOUT PLAN
CONCEPT AREAS 1:200

Figure 9.4 Exhibition Layout Plan, Indigenous Australians gallery, Australian Museum, August 1996.

Two characteristics of the 'Indigenous Australians' gallery reflect the renegotiation of relations between indigenous and non-indigenous peoples covered in this chapter. First, there is an emphasis on the promotion of cultural diversity and the need to ensure the 'long-term sustainability' for 'future generations' of cultures, especially indigenous cultures. This forms part of the Australian Museum's formal mission and projects like the 'Indigenous Australians' gallery and the Aboriginal Heritage Unit are essential to its fulfilment.[209] Through the gallery, the museum aimed to provide Indigenous Australians with a forum to tell their 'experiences and stories . . . in their own words' and 'to demonstrate the cultural and material diversity of indigenous cultures and the diversity of impacts of European colonisation'.[210] This purpose was facilitated by the inclusion throughout of audio and video recordings of indigenous peoples and a designated area for temporary exhibits installed by local indigenous communities. Cultural objects are deployed to challenge existing public perceptions.[211]

Secondly, the Australian Museum's mission is also guided by the principle of 'learning from the past to understand the present to shape a sustainable future'.[212] Components of the Museum's gallery bear a strong affinity with 'memorial museums'. ICOM has described these museums as 'commemorat[ing] victims of State, socially accepted or ideologically motivated crimes' and 'convey[ing] information of historical events in order to put the present into perspective'.[213] The 'Indigenous Australians' gallery reflects the political, historical and social context in which it was developed.[214] The dispossession visited on Indigenous Australians with European colonisation and its ongoing effects on indigenous communities and cultures was the subject of a series of high-profile Australian government inquiries and judicial

---

[209] Australian Museum, *Annual Report 2002/03*, (Sydney, 2003), p.2.
[210] Australian Museum, 'Aboriginal Australia Exhibition', August 1996, Second Referral Meeting Report, 2, AMA.
[211] Interview with P. Gordon.   [212] Australian Museum, *Annual Report 2002/03*.
[213] Anon., Museum News (2001) 54 *ICOM News* 2. In July 2001, the International Committee of Memorial Museums for the Remembrance of Victims of Public Crimes was established under the auspices of ICOM. These spaces address various other reconciliation processes within States worldwide, including Berlin's Holocaust Museum and Chile's Peace Park.
[214] Interview with P. Gordon; and Kelly *et al.*, 'Relationships', 158ff.

decisions during the 1990s.[215] However, during the gallery's planning, the Museum's research revealed gaps or misconceptions in knowledge held by its patrons about indigenous issues and concerns. Significantly, the Museum's assessment of visitor reactions to the gallery highlighted a strong similarity with results recorded in visitor surveys conducted at the Holocaust Memorial Museum, Washington DC. In addition, visitors registered an increased understanding of and 'empathy' for the past treatment of Indigenous Australians.[216] CCOR promotes the role of museums in the ongoing process of reconciliation between indigenous and non-indigenous Australians.[217]

Indigenous communities consulted during the planning of the gallery emphasised 'land' and 'family' as important issues that they expected would be examined by the new gallery. Both areas are central to the current renegotiation of relations between indigenous and non-indigenous peoples in Australia. Museum collections and archives have played a significant role in these renegotiations.

Any assertion of autonomy by occupied peoples is usually accompanied by the demand for the restitution of their cultural heritage – the restoration of the link between peoples, land and cultural identity.[218] The decision of the High Court of Australia in *Mabo and Others* v. *Queensland (No.2)* (1992) is viewed as a seminal moment in the Australian nation's acknowledgement of past wrongs.[219] The Court afforded limited recognition of indigenous interest in land by accommodating 'native title' (and indigenous law and custom) within Australian Common Law.[220] Brennan J explained that: 'We can modify our legal system to make it conform to contemporary notions of justice and human rights, but we must not destroy it.'[221] In response to the decision, the Australian federal government passed the Native Title Act 1994 (Cth) which reaffirmed the non-applicability of *terra nullius*, acknowledged Indigenous Australian rights to the land and established a judicial framework for the determination of Native Title claims. However, the vulnerability of the rights of Indigenous Australians within this national framework was again exposed with the passage of the Native Title Amendment Act 1998 (Cth), in response to the *Wik* case.[222]

Also, Indigenous Australians have found that museum collections are being used once again to reaffirm the dispossession visited upon them by European settlement. Under the present framework, claimants must be able to establish a continuing

[215] Including E. Johnston, *National Report, Overview and Recommendations, Royal Commission into Aboriginal Deaths in Custody* (Canberra, 1991); HREOC, *Bringing Them Home: Report of the National Inquiry into the Separation of Aboriginal and Torres Strait Islander Children from their Families* (Sydney, 1997); and *Mabo & Ors* v. *Queensland (No.2)* (1992) 175 CLR 1.

[216] Personal communication L. Kelly, Australian Museum Audience Research Centre, Australian Museum, Sydney, 19 February 2002; Kelly *et al.*, 'Relationships', 159–63.

[217] See MA, *CCOR*, Principle 16. In the British context: Palmer, *Report*, pp.37–39, paras.128–34.

[218] See Aboriginal and Torres Strait Islander Social Justice Commissioner, *Native*; and E.-I. Daes, Indigenous Peoples and their Relationship to Land: Final Working Paper, 11 June 2001, UN Doc.E/CN.4/Sub.2/2001/21.

[219] (1992) 175 CLR 1.

[220] See N. Pearson, The Concept of Native Title at Common Law, in G. Yunupingu (ed.), *Our Land is Our Life* (St Lucia, 1997), p.150 at p.153.

[221] (1992) 175 CLR 1 at 43.   [222] *Wik Peoples v. Queensland* (1996) 187 CLR 1.

association or customary usage to the land claimed. This requirement has resulted in documentary evidence collected by anthropologists, missionaries and settlers (and held in museums and archives) often being pitted against the oral evidence of indigenous community members. The situation is particularly problematic when courts fail to examine critically the context in which the museum collections and archives were created. This was a central concern in *Members of the Yorta Yorta Aboriginal Community* v. *State of Victoria & Ors.*[223] Black CJ, in his dissenting opinion, warned of 'the particular difficulties and limitations of historical assessments' especially those written 'with their own cultural preconceptions and for their own purposes'.[224] However, the majority reaffirmed the trial judge's finding, based largely on non-indigenous documentary sources, that European colonisation and 'the tide of history had indeed washed away any real . . . observance' of their 'traditional' laws and customs by the Yorta Yorta people. Accordingly, their native title rights had similarly 'disappeared' and 'could not be revived'.[225]

By insisting that indigenous communities demonstrate 'continuous' adherence to 'traditional' cultures, national legislatures and courts' efforts to correct 'past wrongs' have two major shortcomings. First, they reaffirm the notion of indigenous cultures as static and primordial, rather than living, diverse and developing. Second, they do not address the dominant culture's culpability in causing cultural discontinuity and disintegration through its policies of discrimination, assimilation and genocide.

Official Australian government policies requiring the removal of indigenous children from their families during the twentieth century fuelled cultural discontinuity. The 1997 *Report of the National Inquiry into the Separation of Aboriginal and Torres Strait Islander Children from Their Families* (HREOC Report) defined these policies as systematic racism and cultural genocide.[226] The report found that a principal aim of the policy was the elimination of Indigenous Australian cultures as 'distinct entities'.[227]

Since the 1990s, Australian museum collections and archives have been accessed increasingly by Indigenous Australians affected by these policies.[228] Like the current claims by Holocaust survivors and their heirs, archives and museum collections have played a significant role in providing material and moral restitution for the victims of these policies. Three distinct means can be highlighted in which

---

[223] (2001) 110 FCR 244; (2001) 180 ALR 655; App. (2002) 214 CLR 422, 194 ALR 538, HCA 58 (12 December 2002).

[224] [2001] FCA 45, para.55, Black CJ. See *Commonwealth of Australia* v. *Yarmirr* (1999) 101 FCR 171, FCA 1668 (December 3, 1999) at 342–352, Merkel J; and *Delgamuukw* v. *British Columbia* (1997) 153 DLR (4th) 193 at 231, Lamer CJC.

[225] [2001] FCA 45, para.26. See [2001] FCA 45, para.61 Black CJ; and J. Clifford, Identity of Mashpee, in J. Clifford, *The Predicament of Culture: Twentieth Century Ethnography, Literature and Art* (Cambridge, 1988), p.342.

[226] HREOC, *Bringing*, pp.266ff. See Art.2(e), Convention on the Prevention and Punishment of the Crime of Genocide, 9 December 1948, in force 12 January 1951, UNGA Res 260 A(III), 78 UNTS 277.

[227] HREOC, *Bringing*, p.273.

[228] See H. Fourmile, Who owns the past? – Aborigines as captives of the archives (1989) 13 *Aboriginal History* 1; HREOC, *Bringing*, pp.324–356; and Simpson, *Making*, pp.256–59.

they aid the restitution process. First, they can aid in the amelioration or reversal of the effects of assimilation policies. Anthropological collections and archives contain genealogies and photographic collections created during the assimilation period. The HREOC Report recommended that access to Commonwealth, State and Territory archives be improved to assist Indigenous Australians to re-establish familial and community ties.[229] Many major Australian museums have developed specialist units and programmes to assist the reunion of indigenous families.[230]

Second, museum collection can facilitate education, remembrance and research to 'strengthen humanity's ability to absorb and learn from the dark lessons of the past'.[231] Indigenous Australians have impressed upon Australian museums the need to educate the general public about colonialism and its ongoing effects.[232] In 1993, the Australian Museum hosted the 'Between Two Worlds' exhibition.[233] Organised by the Australian Archives, it aimed to 'correct' the national memory by raising Australian public awareness of the consequences of government assimilation policies on indigenous families.[234]

Third, they can provide information and resources for reparation claims arising from internationally wrongful acts and gross violations of human rights, including racial discrimination and genocide. Settler States and former metropolitan powers have long resisted the application of 'restitution' in this sense. However, indigenous organisations are demanding that States review their historical record to account for 'assets' they acquired and injuries inflicted on indigenous communities with such practices.[235]

Particularly in the last quarter century, indigenous organisations have campaigned to ensure that the right to self-determination 'of all peoples' includes indigenous peoples. They contend that this right is not a political act but a process incorporating the ability of a people to determine how their cultural identity is preserved and developed. Integral to that process is the right to restitution of cultural heritage removed 'without their free and informed consent or in violation of their laws, traditions and customs'.

---

[229] Recommendation 21–30, HREOC, *Bringing*, pp.408–15 and 655–57. See Recommendation 53, Johnston, *National Report*.

[230] See N. Grzybowicz, D. Kartinyeri and B. Craig, The Aboriginal Family History Project at the South Australian Museum (1990) 23 *COMA Bulletin* 12; Simpson, *Making*, pp.256–59; and Anderson, 'Australian', 176.

[231] Declaration of the Task Force for International Cooperation on Holocaust Education, Remembrance and Research, Washington DC, 1998. See HREOC, *Bringing*, pp.284ff and Recommendations 5a, 5b, 6, 7a, 7b, 8a, 9a and 9b; and Guidelines 44–47, Daes Revised Draft Principles and Guidelines.

[232] See Kelly *et al.*, 'Relationships', 160; and interview with P. Gordon.

[233] See R. MacDonald, *Between Two Worlds: The Commonwealth Government and the Removal of Aboriginal Children of Part Descent in the Northern Territory* (Alice Springs, 1996).

[234] MacDonald, *Between*, p.ix.

[235] See HREOC, *Bringing*, pp.247ff and Recommendations 3, 4, 5a, 6, 7a, 7b. The report also recommended the establishment of a national fund to provide compensation for the loss of cultural rights and fulfilment: Recommendation 14.

Indigenous organisations maintain that 'past injustices' can be reversed or ameliorated only with recognition by settler States and former metropolitan powers of the persistent impact of discriminatory and genocidal policies. Such recognition is fundamental to indigenous claims to an autonomous place and identity within and across States. Indigenous peoples do not seek the negation of States, their laws and knowledge systems, but the recognition by the dominant culture that they are neither exclusive nor objective. They stress that only in these circumstances will dialogues between indigenous and non-indigenous peoples commence, and the continuing contribution of indigenous communities and their cultures be assured.

Figure C.1 Galarrwuy Yunupingu (Yolgnu) drawing attention to two laws following his delivery of the 1998 Vincent Lingari Memorial Lecture.

CONCLUSION

> These spoils . . . impede a moral reconciliation between France and the countries she has invaded . . . [W]hilst these objects remain in Paris, constituting, as it were, the title deeds of the countries which have been given up, the sentiments of reuniting these countries again to France, will never be altogether extinct.[1]

> While in theory closure can be obtained on material restitution, moral restitution is an open-ended process that ought not be limited in time, as there can be no point at which we stop trying to confront the past honestly.[2]

From 1815 to the present day, the framers of restitution programmes have been acutely aware that the return of cultural objects is not merely a physical act. Instead, it is an integral component of 'an open-ended process' of material and moral restitution addressing the effects of policies and practices that fuelled the removal (and destruction) of cultural heritage. Three distinct rationales for the restitution of cultural objects in international law have been identified in this book. These rationales, and their interrelation to each other, reinforce the role of restitution of cultural objects within this broader, open-ended process.

The first rationale for restitution of cultural objects seeks to restore the 'sacred' link between people, land and cultural heritage. Lord Castlereagh acknowledged perceptively the symbolic value of these objects as: 'the title deeds of the countries'. In the colonial relationship, the possession of these cultural objects was central to the collective imaginings of the occupier and the occupied. For colonial occupiers, these objects represented the possession of people, territories and resources within an empire. Their centralisation and public display reinforced and projected a national imperial imagining. Conversely, for colonised peoples, the removal of these cultural objects represented the dispossession of their lands, autonomy and identity. Independence movements were often accompanied by claims for the restitution of cultural objects held in imperial collections, in order to reconstitute and revitalise an autonomous collective cultural identity.

---

[1] Note 15, Memoir of Lord Castlereagh [to Allied Ministers], Paris, 11 September 1815, PRO FO 92/26, 115 at 121; and Parl. Deb, vol.32, ser.1, p.298 at p.300, (1816).

[2] E. Bronfman, Chair to US President, 15 December 2000, in US Presidential Advisory Commission, *Plunder and Restitution: Findings and Recommendations of the Presidential Advisory Commission on Holocaust Assets in the United States and Staff Report* (Washington DC, 2000).

The second rationale promotes the restitution of cultural objects as a means of ameliorating or reversing internationally wrongful acts, including discrimination and genocide. Those seeking to eliminate a group usually target its cultural manifestations – 'the very essence of its being' – through its systematic destruction and confiscation.[3] The Allied restitution programme, following the Second World War, affirmed the importance of restitution of cultural heritage as a means of addressing the effects of such policies and ensuring the continuing contribution of the group to the 'cultural heritage of all (hu)mankind'.

The third rationale for restitution of cultural objects in international law is intimately tied to the broader notion of the right to self-determination that evolved following decolonisation. It is argued that restitution of cultural objects held by the museums of former metropolitan and national capitals is an essential component of a people's ability to maintain, revitalise and develop their collective cultural identity. This rationale draws from the preceding two rationales for restitution. It emphasises that self-determination is a process that includes the return of land, ancestral remains, cultural heritage and resources. In addition, these claims also call for the recognition and amelioration of the ongoing effects of colonial policies of discrimination, assimilation and genocide.

The advocates of the third rationale, in particular, have exposed the importance of the process of restitution. The removal and destruction of cultural objects was part of the process of colonisation and genocide. Therefore, efforts to reverse or ameliorate their effects must also involve a multilayered process. Fundamental to each of these rationales for restitution is the requirement that the holding parties 'confront the past honestly'. Moral restitution is an essential step on the path to reconciliation between the claimant and the holding party. However, material restitution is also crucial. In 1815, Castlereagh charged: 'If the French people be desirous of treading back their steps, can they rationally desire to preserve this source of animosity between them and all other Nations [?]'.[4]

The underlying purpose that binds all rationales for the restitution of cultural objects in international law is ensuring the continuing contribution of a people and their culture – not cultural objects *per se* – to the cultural heritage of all humankind.

It is no coincidence that, in the last two centuries in international law, the question of restitution of cultural heritage has directly or indirectly arisen when the international community has resolved to guarantee the 'very essence of [the] being' of minorities within and across States. The importance of protecting peoples' ability to preserve and develop their cultural identity, to the stability of the international community, States and the sustainability of these groups and their cultures was recognised by the European powers from at least the nineteenth century. However, the implementation of discriminatory, assimilationist and genocidal policies that accompanied the European colonial and capitalist expansion meant this recognition was often selectively applied or ignored.

From the mid-twentieth century onwards, the international community has gradually abandoned cultural Darwinism and its supporting race-based theories in favour

---

[3] *Minority Schools in Albania case* (1935) PCIJ, ser.A/B, No.64, p.17.
[4] Castlereagh to the Allied Ministers.

of cultural diversity. The barbarism of fascist regimes during the 1930s and 40s, the independence movements of colonised peoples and the campaigns for self-determination by indigenous peoples led to the repudiation of the unilinear 'progression' of civilisation. There has also been an increasing recognition of the supremacy of peoples' interest in their own cultural heritage over external scientific, artistic, commercial and national interests.

The international community is tentatively addressing the following key areas of reform in international law to ensure the ongoing contribution of all peoples to the cultural heritage of humankind. These four overlapping areas represent compromises forged in response to the anxieties of certain States, fuelled by the Cold War and secessionist fears during decolonisation.

First, the absence of the cultural elements of genocidal practices from the definition of genocide in the 1948 Convention on the Prevention and Punishment of the Crime of Genocide has become a matter of contention once again.[5] Recently, the International Criminal Tribunal for the former Yugoslavia conceded that, although the international community has not accepted any alteration to the 1948 definition, there are multiple means of eliminating a group beyond the physical extermination of its individual members.[6] It is a sentiment implicit in the 2003 UNESCO Declaration concerning the Intentional Destruction of Cultural Heritage adopted following the destruction of the monumental Buddhas of Bamiyan, Afghanistan by the Taliban in 2001.[7] The confiscation and destruction of the cultural and religious manifestations of the targeted group has consistently been a primary mode of implementing such policies. The ongoing silence of the 1948 Genocide Convention regarding the cultural aspects of genocidal programmes ignores their threat to the continuing contribution of the group to the common heritage of all humankind. In addition, it diminishes the applicability of restitution of cultural heritage to ameliorate or reverse their effects.

Second, the effective exercise of the right to self-determination by all peoples, including indigenous peoples, must be recognised by States and facilitated by the international community. Indigenous peoples and minorities were denied the effective exercise of this right during decolonisation. The unequal application of this foundational human right perpetuates the scale of civilisation originally formulated to justify and facilitate European colonial and commercial expansion. To counteract this legacy, the UN General Assembly must adopt, as a matter of urgency, the 1993 Draft UN Declaration on the Rights of Indigenous Peoples recognising indigenous peoples' right to self-determination including their cultural development.[8]

Third, there is a trepid acknowledgement that the ability of non-State groups, including indigenous peoples, to maintain and develop their cultural identity must

---

[5] 9 December 1948, in force 12 January 1951, UNGA Res.260A(III), 78 UNTS 277.
[6] *Prosecutor v. Radislav Krstić*, Trial Judgment, No.IT-98-33-T, Trial Chamber I, ICTY (2 August 2001), 574.
[7] Adopted by the 32nd session of the UNESCO General Conference, Paris, 17 October 2003.
[8] M. A. Martínez, Report of the Working Group on Indigenous Populations on its 22nd Session, 3 August 2004, UN Doc.E/CN.4/Sub.2/2004/28, para.71; and Report of the Secretary-General on the preliminary review by the Coordinator of the International Decade of the World's Indigenous People on activities of the United Nations system in relation to the Decade, 24 June 2004, UN Doc.E/2004/82, para.66.

be recognised and enforceable in international law as group and individual right. This right must impose a positive obligation on the international community, States and transnational corporations to guarantee the continued cultural sustainability of these groups and cultural diversity generally. Indigenous peoples and other non-State groups must be able to invoke and seek enforcement of rights and obligations expounded under the existing international and regional frameworks for the protection and restitution of cultural heritage.[9]

Fourth, the international community must recognise that legal ownership and control of their cultural heritage by a group is crucial to the right to determine the preservation and development of that group's cultural identity. The international community, particularly former metropolitan powers and settler States, must 'confront their [colonial] past honestly' and acknowledge the role of their museums in the cultural losses sustained by colonised peoples. Whilst settler States have shown a degree of willingness to engage this process, by contrast, former metropolitan powers and their holding institutions have been reticent about doing so, especially when compared to their eventual response to the claims of Holocaust survivors and their heirs. Effective mechanisms must be established at the international and national levels for the restitution of cultural objects removed, at any time, from these peoples 'without their free and informed consent or in violation of their laws, traditions and customs'.[10] The urgency of this requirement has been raised recently in several quarters.[11] These mechanisms must form part of broader legislative frameworks encompassing the right to self-determination and economic, social and cultural development and embracing a holistic interpretation of cultural heritage.

The history of museums shows that these institutions have facilitated, justified and benefited from colonialism and related policies of discrimination, assimilation and genocide. They have also often served to inform and engage broader societal concerns. The present-day 'commitment to righting historic wrongs' by former metropolitan powers and their museums must include the restitution claims of indigenous and other colonised peoples.[12] Museums must be actively involved in reversing and ameliorating the ongoing effects of these policies and practices. This 'open-ended process' should include the education of the general public about colonialism, and discriminatory, assimilation and genocidal policies which support it and

---

[9] See generally UNESCO Universal Declaration on Cultural Diversity, Paris, 2 November 2001, UNESCO Doc.31C/Res.25, Annex I, and (2002) 41 ILM 57; Declaration on the Rights of Persons Belonging to National or Ethnic, Religious and Linguistic Minorities, UNGA Res. 47/135 (1995), 18 December 1992, UN Doc.A/Res/47/135, and (1993) 32 ILM 911; Framework Convention for the Protection of National Minorities, Council of Europe, Strasbourg, 1 February 1995, ETS No.157 and the Lund Recommendations on the Effective Participation of National Minorities in Public Life, Foundation on Inter-Ethnic Relations, September 1999.

[10] Art.12, 1993 Draft UN Declaration on the Rights of Indigenous Peoples, UN Doc.E/CN.4/Sub.2/1994/56; and (1995) 34 ILM 541.

[11] Working Document for Discussion on a Strategy to Facilitate the Restitution of Stolen or Illicitly Exported Cultural Property, January 2005, UNESCO Doc.CLT-2005/CONF.202/4; Y. Yokota and the Saami Council, Guideline for the review of the draft principles and guidelines on the heritage of indigenous peoples, 17 July 2004, UNESCO Doc.E/CN.4/Sub.2/AC.4/2004/5, para.33; and ILA, *Report of the Cultural Heritage Law Committee* (London, 2004) (certain recommendations run contrary to the demands of indigenous peoples).

[12] UK Department of Culture, Media and Sport, Press Release, 84/2000, 13 April 2000.

its effects on individuals, communities and their cultures. Also, they must provide active support (technically and financially) for the realisation of indigenous peoples' right to self-determination and cultural development within and outside the walls of their institutions. This process must involve the formal recognition of indigenous peoples' ownership of their cultural heritage held in museum collections. In addition, museums, archives and other collecting institutions must facilitate the claims of indigenous, and other colonised peoples, for reparations and related relief arising from international wrongful acts perpetrated during colonial occupation.

It is imperative that the international community generally, and museums specifically, acknowledge the pre-eminence of the rights, laws and customs of indigenous peoples in their cultural heritage over those of the scientific or artistic communities, or national interests and laws of the relevant State. Indigenous peoples must be involved in and approve the development of any international and national frameworks for the protection and restitution of their cultural heritage.

This book has concentrated on the impact of Anglo-American colonialism on indigenous peoples in the Asia Pacific region, from the nineteenth century to the present day. However, this colonial project has been neither uniform nor is it exclusive. Investigation of the effects of Anglo-American colonialism on other regions, the impact of rival contemporaneous colonial projects and Civil Law tradition would enrich our understanding of the development of the pertinent areas of international law and museum practices. In addition, the current wave of globalisation and the overlapping and growing impact of transnational corporations on the cultural sustainability of all peoples must be compared and contrasted with these earlier waves of 'globalisation'.[13]

Indigenous peoples, too, are transcending State boundaries by increasingly turning to international organisations and by formalising relations with other indigenous groups within and across existing States to achieve their goals. Indigenous organisations have recently indicated their intent to formulate their own international principles and guidelines concerning the protection and restitution of their cultural heritage.[14] The response of States and museums, nationally and internationally, to these international principles and guidelines will need to be monitored and assessed in the future.

This work has deliberately focused on issues arising from the return of cultural objects removed during colonisation. As explained, the cultural losses sustained by affected communities escalated, rather than dissipated, following decolonisation. Most of the States which host the centres of the international art market have recently accepted the 1970 UNESCO Convention. Perhaps this development may encourage source States not already party to it to follow suit. Indigenous organisations have stressed continually, and the proposed framework of rationales highlights, that restitution of cultural objects is a process intimately entwined with the return of land,

---

[13] El-H. Guissé, Working Paper on Globalization and Economic, Social and Cultural Rights of Indigenous Populations, 15 June 2003, UNESCO Doc.E/CN.4/Sub.2/AC.4/2003/14.

[14] E.-I. Daes, Report of the Seminar on the Draft Principles and Guidelines for the Protection of the Heritage of Indigenous Peoples, 19 June 2000, UN Doc.E/CN.4/Sub.2/2000/26, para.39.

ancestral remains and protection of intangible cultural heritage, including 'traditional' knowledge. Accordingly, it would be beneficial to examine whether the trends in international law relating to the protection and restitution of cultural objects of indigenous peoples are replicated or distinguishable in respect of these other elements of cultural heritage. For example, the 2003 Convention for the Safeguarding of the Intangible Cultural Heritage, in combination with the Convention for the Protection of the World Cultural and Natural Heritage (1972 World Heritage Convention) on which it is modelled, could conceivably provide a more effective international legal framework for the protection of various forms of cultural heritage, including cultural objects, of these groups.[15] Significantly, the 1972 World Heritage Convention has a far greater take-up rate in the Asia Pacific region than the 1970 UNESCO Convention.

The restitution of cultural objects in international law has progressed in fits and starts in the last two centuries, with the pendulum swinging away from cultural Darwinism accompanied by genocide, assimilation and the confiscation and destruction of the cultural manifestations of groups and towards cultural diversity accompanied by expansive restitution and cultural reconstruction programmes. International law and museum collections and practices are 'document[s] of civilisation' and at the 'same time document[s] of barbarism'.[16] Despite unspeakable regressions, one lesson has not been and can not be unlearnt – the need for the international community to ensure the continuing contribution of all peoples and their cultures to the common heritage of humankind.

Current international circumstances leave States vulnerable to the seduction of policies and practices promoting cultural Darwinism. Yet, it is at this very moment that the international community, its member States and their populace must 'confront the past honestly and internalise its lessons'. This process must include recognition of their positive obligation to enable all peoples to preserve and develop their cultural identities.

---

[15] Paris, 17 October 2003, UNESCO Doc.MISC/2003/CLT/CH/14; and Convention concerning the Protection of the World Cultural and Natural Heritage, Paris, 16 November 1972, in force 17 December 1975, 1037 UNTS 151, and (1972) 11 ILM 1358.

[16] W. Benjamin, *Illuminations*, trans. H. Zohn (London, 1992), p.248.

Aboriginal and Torres Strait Islander Commission. *Recognition, Rights and Reform: Report of the Government on Native Title Social Justice Measures* (Canberra, 1995)

Aboriginal and Torres Strait Islander Social Justice Commissioner. *Native Title Annual Report 2000* (Canberra, 2000)

Abraham, M., T. J. Sullivan and D. J. G. Griffin. Implementing NAGPRA: The Effective Management of Legislated Change in Museums (2001) 40 *Management Decision* 35

Abrams, G. H. J. The Case for Wampum: Repatriation from the Museum of the American Indian to the Six Nations Confederacy, in F. E. S. Kaplan (ed.), *Museums and the Making of 'Ourselves': The Role of Objects in National Identity* (London, 1994), p.351

Abramson, R. D., and S. B. Huttler. The Legal Response to the Illicit Movement of Cultural Property (1973) 5 LPIB 932

Abranches, H. Report on the Situation in Africa, UNESCO Doc.CLT-83/CONF.216/2

Adachi, S. The Asian Concept, in S. Nahlik (ed.), *International Dimensions of Humanitarian Law* (Paris, 1988), p.16

A Guide to the Great Exhibition; containing a description of every principal object of interest (London, 1851)

Alison, A. *Lives of Lord Castlereagh and Sir Charles Stewart the Second and Third Marquesses of Londonderry. With annuals of contemporary events in which they bore a part from the original papers of the family* (3 vols., Edinburgh, 1861)

Althusser, L. *Montesquieu, Rousseau, Marx* (London, 1972)

Altick, R. D. *The Shows of London* (Cambridge, 1978)

Alvarez, A. International Life and International Law in America (1940) 74 *Bulletin of the Pan American Union* 232

The New International Law (1929) 15 TGS 35

American Anthropological Association. Resolution on Acquisition of Cultural Properties (Washington DC, 1973)

Statement on Human Rights (1947) 49 *American Anthropologist* 539–43

American Association of Museums (AAM). Guidelines Concerning the Unlawful Appropriation of Objects During the Nazi Era, November 1999, at http://www.aam-us.org/museumresources/ethics/nazi_guidelines.cfm

Policy Regarding the Repatriation of Native American Ceremonial Objects and Human Remains, Washington, AAM, 1987 (1988) 7 IJMMC 310

Museum Ethics (Washington DC, 1978)

American Association of Museum Directors (AAMD). Report of Taskforce on the Spoliation of Art During the Nazi/World War II Era (1933–1945), 4 June 1998, at http://www.aamd.org/guideln.shtml

Anaya, J. S. *Indigenous Peoples in International Law* (New York, 1996, 2004)

Indigenous Rights – Norms in Customary International Law (1992) 8 AJICL 1

Anderson, B. *Imagined Communities: Reflections on the Origin and Spread of Nationalism* (rev. edn, London, 1991)

Anderson, C. Aboriginal People and Museums: Restricting Access to Increase It (1992) 12
Artlink 11

Australian Aborigines and Museums: A New Relationship (1990) 33(3) *Curator* 165

The Economics of Sacred Art: The Uses of a Secret Collection in the South Australian
Museum (1990) 23 *COMA Bulletin* 31

Comments on 'Aboriginal Keeping Places' Document from Department of Aboriginal
Affairs (1988) 20 *COMA Bulletin* 24

Research and the Return of Objects as a Social Process (1986) 19 *COMA Bulletin* 2

Anderson, J. Treasure Trove (1904) 1 SHR 74

Anderson, M. and A. Reeves. Contested Identities: Museums and the Nation in Australia,
in F. E. S. Kaplan (ed.), *Museums and the Making of 'Ourselves': The Role of Objects in
National Identity*, (London, 1994), p.45

Anghie, A. Finding the Peripheries: Sovereignty and Colonialism in Nineteenth Century
International Law (1999) 40 HIJL 1

Human Rights and Cultural Identity: New Hope for Ethnic Peace? (1992) 33 HIJL 339

Anker, P. M. The Mandate System: Origin – Principles – Application, LN Doc.IV.A.Mandates
(Geneva, 1945)

Anon. Museum News (2001) 54 *ICOM News* 2

Tasmanian Museum and Art Gallery: The Skeletal Debate (1983) 12 *COMA Bulletin*, 18

A Brief History of the Creation by UNESCO of an Intergovernmental Committee for
Promoting the Return of Cultural Property to its Countries of Origin or its Restitution
in Case of Illicit Appropriation (1979) 31 *Museum* 59

The Acquisition of Cultural Property: New Australian Museum Policy, (1975) 10 *Mankind*
279

Rocky Road to Art, *Newsweek*, 18 July 1966, p.90

US Seeks to Replace Cultural Property Displaced during World War II (1951) 25(635)
Department of State Bulletin 345

Art of the South Seas (May 1946) *The Architectural FORUM*

Removal of German Art Objects to the United States (1945) 13(327) *Department of State
Bulletin* 499

The Spanish Government's Gifts to the Fogg Art Museum, *Harvard Alumnae Bulletin*
(15 September 1933), n.p.

Indian Tribal Arts (April 1931) 22 *The American Magazine of Art* 303

The Loan Exhibition of Mexican Arts (1930) 25 *Bulletin of the Metropolitan Museum of Art*
210

American Precedents for Mandates (January 1920) *Review of Reviews* 20

Reorganisation at South Kensington – I, II (1908–9) 14 *Burlington Magazine* 129

Indian Collections at South Kensington (1908–09) 8 *Museums Journal* 449

Archer, M. *The India Office Collections of Paintings and Sculpture* (London, 1986)

Archuleta, M. and R. Strickland (ed.). *Shared Visions: Native American Painters and Sculptors
in the Twentieth Century* (Phoenix, 1992)

Ashton, L. (ed.). *The Art of India and Pakistan* (London, 1948)

Assembly of First Nations and Canadian Museums Association *Turning the Page: Forging New
Partnerships between Museums and First Peoples* (3rd edn, Ottawa, 1994)

Attwood, B. and A. Markus. *The Struggle for Aboriginal Rights: A Documentary History* (Sydney,
1999)

Auer, P. de. The Protection of National Minorities, in International Law Association, *Report
of the 30th Conference, 1921* (London, 1922), vol.I, p.113

Auerbach, J. A. *The Great Exhibition of 1851: A Nation on Display* (New Haven, 1999)

August, T. G. *The Selling of Empire: British and French Imperialist Propaganda 1890–1940*
(Westport, 1985)

Australian Museum. *Annual Report 2002/03* (Sydney, 2003)
  Annual Report 1988/89 (Sydney, 1989)
  Annual Report 1987/88 (Sydney, 1988)
  Annual Report 1985/86 (Sydney, 1986)
  Annual Report 1983/84 (Sydney, 1984)
  Annual Report 1980/81 (Sydney, 1981)
  Annual Report 1979–1980 (Sydney, 1980)
  Report of the Australian Museum Trust for the Year Ending 30 June 1977 (Sydney, 1978)
Babbage, C. *The Exposition of 1851; or, the view of the industry, the science and the government of England*, 2nd edn (1851) (Reprint, Farnborough, 1969)
Baddeley, O. and V. Fraser. *Drawing the Line: Art and Cultural Identity in Contemporary Latin America* (London, 1989)
Baedeker. *London and its Environs* (Leipzig, 1889)
Baker Bart, S. *Halleck's International Law or Rules Regulating the Intercourse of States in Peace and War* (London, 1878)
Baker, M. *The Cast Courts* (London, 1982)
Barr Jr, A. H. *Painting and Sculpture in the Museum of Modern Art, 1929–1967* (New York, 1967)
Barringer, T. The South Kensington Museum and the Colonial Project, in T. Barringer and T. Flynn (eds.), *Colonialism and the Object: Empire, Material Culture and the Museum* (London, 1998), p.11
Barsh, R. L. Indigenous Peoples and the UN Commission on Human Rights: A Case of the Immovable Object and the Irresistible Force (1996) 18 HRQ 782
  An Advocate's Guide to the Convention on Indigenous and Tribal Peoples (1990) 15 OCULR 209
  Indigenous Peoples: An Emerging Object of International Law (1986) 80 AJIL 369
  Indigenous North America and Contemporary International Law (1983) 62 OLR 73
Barsh, R. L. and J. Youngblood Henderson. *The Road: Indian Tribes and Political Liberty* (Berkeley, CA, 1980)
Barthes, R. *Mythologies*, trans. A. Lavers (London, 1993)
Baslar, K. *The Concept of the Common Heritage of Mankind in International Law* (The Hague, 1998)
Bateson, G. Exhibition Review: Art of the South Seas (June 1946) 28 *The Art Bulletin* 119
Bathurst, M. E. The United Nations War Crimes Commission (1945) 39 AJIL 565
Bator, P. M. An Essay on the International Trade in Art (1982) 34 Stan. LR 275
  International Trade in National Art Treasures: Regulation and Deregulation, in L. DuBoff (ed.), *Art Law: Domestic and International* (South Hackensack, 1975), p.295
Battersby, J. Legislative Developments in Australia, in L. V. Prott and J. Specht (eds.), *Protection or Plunder? Safeguarding the Future of Our Cultural Heritage* (Canberra, 1989), p.92
Bedjaoui, M. *Towards a New International Economic Order* (New York, 1979)
Benjamin, W. *Illuminations*, trans. H. Zohn (London, 1992)
Bennett, G. *Aboriginal Rights in International Law* (London, 1978)
Bennett, T. *The Birth of the Museum: History, Theory, Politics* (London, 1995)
  Out of Which Past? Critical Reflection on Australian Museum and Heritage Policy (Brisbane, 1988)
Bentham, J. *The Works of Jeremy Bentham, published under the superintendent of his executor, John Bowring*, ed. J. Bowring (11 vols., Edinburgh, 1843)
Bentwich, N. de Mattos International Aspects of Restitution and Compensation for Victims of the Nazis (1955–56) 32 BYIL 204
  The Mandate System (New York, 1930)
Berlo, J. C. (ed.). *The Early Years of Native American Art History* (Seattle, 1992)

Berlyn, P. *A Popular Narrative of the Origin, History, Progress and Prospects of the Great Industrial Exhibition 1851* (London, 1851)

Berman, M. *All that is Solid Melts into Air: The Experience of Modernity* (New York, 1988)

Bhabha, H. K. *The Location of Culture* (London, 1994)

Biddick K. *et al.* Aesthetics, Ethnicity and the History of Art: A Range of Critical Perspectives (1996) 78 *Art Bulletin* 594

Bishop Museum. Interim and Proposed Final Guidance: Native American Graves Protection and Repatriation Act, 30 June 2004, at http://www.bishopmuseum.org/NAGPRAGuidelines.html

Blackstone, W. *Commentaries on the Laws of England* (1765–69) (4 vols., New York, 1978)

Blake, J. On Defining the Cultural Heritage (2000) 49 ICLQ 61

Blumer, M.-L. Catalogue des peintures transportées d'Italie en France de 1796 à 1814, in *Bulletin de la société de l'histoire de l'art française* (Paris, 1936)

Bluntschli, J.-C. *Le droit international codifié* (Paris, 1870)

Boas, F. *Race, Language, and Culture* (1910) (Reprint, New York, 1940)

Some Principles of Museum Administration (1907) 25 *Science* 921

Bodkin, T. *Dismembered Masterpieces: A Plea for their Reconstruction by International Action* (London, 1945)

Boer, B. Cultural and Natural Heritage: Protection of Movable Cultural Heritage (1987) 6 EPLJ 63

Bolton, L. Recording Oceanic Collections in Australian: Problems and Questions (1984) 36 *Museum* 32

Collection of Inventories and the Return of Information to Oceania: The Australian Experience, 18 March 1985, UNESCO Doc.CLT-85/CONF.202/5

Bonnet, H. Intellectual Co-operation (1942) *World Organization* 189

Bonshek, E. Objects, People and Identity: An Interplay between Past and Present at the Australian Museum, in T. Lin (ed.), *Proceedings of the International Conference on Anthropology and the Museum* (Taipei, 1992), p.261

Bonython, E. *King Cole: A Picture Portrait of Sir Henry Cole, KCB 1808–1882* (London, 1982)

Bonython, E. and A. Burton. *The Great Exhibitor: The Life and Work of Henry Cole* (London, 2003)

Bordwell, P. *The Law of War between Belligerents: A History and Commentary* (Chicago, 1908)

Bossuyt, M. J. *Guide to the 'Travaux Préparatoires' of the International Covenant on Civil and Political Rights* (Dordrecht, 1987)

Bowman, M. B. The Reburial of Native American Human Remains: Approaches to the Resolution of a Conflict (1989) 13 HELR 147

Boylan, P. J. Culture and World Trade (2002) 55 *ICOM News* 4

Review of the Convention for the Protection of Cultural Property in the Event of Armed Conflict (The Hague Convention of 1954), Paris, UNESCO, 1993, UNESCO Doc.CLT-93/WS/12

Brailsford, H. N. The Rise of Nationalism in the East (1927) 2 *Problems in Peace* 318

Brain, R. *Into the Primitive Environment: Survival on the Edge of our Civilisation* (London, 1972)

Brain, R. (ed.). *Going to the Fair: Readings in the Culture of the Nineteenth-Century Exhibitions* (Cambridge, 1993)

Bray, L. Repatriation, Power Relations and the Politics of the Past (1996) 70 *Antiquity* 440

Breckenridge, C. A. and P. van der Veer (eds.), *Orientalism and the Postcolonial Predicament: Perspectives on South Asia* (Philadelphia, 1993)

Breen, L. M. The Osage of Oklahoma, in D. Fane, I. Jacknis and I. M. Breen, *Objects of Myth and Memory: American Indian Art at The Brooklyn Museum* (exh. cat., New York, 1991), p.281

Brierly, J. L. The Shortcoming of International Law (1924) 5 BYIL 14

Brittlebank, K. Sakti and Barakat: The Power of Tipu's Tiger: An Examination of the Tiger Emblem of Tipu Sultan of Mysore (1995) 29 *Modern Asian Studies* 257

Brodie, N., J. Doole and P. Watson. *Stealing History: The Illicit Trade in Cultural Material* (Cambridge, 2000)

Brody, J. J. *Indian Painters & White Patrons* (Albuquerque, 1971)

Brokensha, P. and C. McGuirgan. Listening to the Dreaming: The Aboriginal Homelands Movement (1977) 19 *Australian Natural History* 119

Brophy, W. A. and S. D. Aberle. *The Indian. America's Unfinished Business: Report of the Commission on the Rights, Liberties and Responsibilities of the American Indian* (Norman, 1966)

Brown, G. Baldwin. *The Care of Ancient Monuments, An Account of the Legislative and Other Measures Adopted in European Countries for Protecting Ancient Monuments and Objects and Scenes of Natural Beauty, and for Preserving the Aspect of Historical Cities* (Cambridge, 1905)

Brown, M. F. *Who Owns Native Culture?* (Cambridge, MA, 2004)

Brownlie, I. *Basic Documents in International Law* (4th edn, Oxford, 1995)

Bruegel, J. W. A Neglected Field: Protection of Minorities (1971) 4 HRJ 413

Buell, R. L. The Protection of Minorities (1926) 222 *International Conciliation* 348

Burnett, P. Mason. *Reparation at the Paris Peace Conference from the Standpoint of the American Delegation* (2 vols., New York, 1940)

Burnham, B. *The Protection of Cultural Property: A Handbook on National Legislations* (Paris, 1974)

Burton, A. *Vision and Accident: The Story of the Victoria and Albert Museum* (London, 1999)
  The Image of the Curator (1985) 4 *The Victoria and Albert Museum Album* 373

Burton, B. International Exhibitions and National Identity (1991) 7 *Anthropology Today* 5

Busse, M. The National Cultural Property (Preservation) Act, in K. Whimp and M. Busse (eds.), *Protection of Intellectual, Biological and Cultural Property in Papua New Guinea* (Canberra, 2000), pp.81–94

Butler, G. *A Handbook to the League of Nations* (London, 1919)

Buxton, C. R. *The Alternative to War* (London, 1936)

Cahill, E. H. America has its Primitives (1920) 75 *International Studio* 80

Calderwood, H. Black. The Protection of Minorities by the League of Nations (1931) 2 *Geneva Research Information Committee Special Studies* 17

Cameron, D. F. The Museum, a Temple or the Forum (1971) 14(1) *Curator* 11

Canouts, V. and F. P. McManamon. Protecting the Past for the Future: Federal Archaeology in the United States, in N. Brodie, J. Doole and C. Renfrew (eds.), *Trade in Illicit Antiquities: The Destruction of the World's Archaeological Heritage* (Cambridge, 2001), p.97

Cardoso, R. D. Teaching by Example: Education and the Formation of South Kensington's Museums, in M. Baker and B. Richardson (eds.), *A Grand Design: The Art of the Victoria and Albert Museum* (London, 1999), p.107

Carducci, G. *La restitution internationale des biens culturels et des objets d'art volés ou illicitement exportés* (Paris, 1997)

Cassese, A. Political Self-Determination – Old Concepts and New Developments, in A. Cassese (ed.), *UN Law/Fundamental Rights* (Sijthoff and Noordhoff, 1979), p.137

Castel, J. G. Polish Treasures in Canada – 1940–1960: A Case History (1974) 68 ASILP 121

Çelik, Z. *Displaying the Orient: Architecture of Islam at Nineteenth-Century World's Fairs* (Berkeley, CA, 1992)

Chamberlin, E. R. *Preserving the Past* (London, 1979)

Chamberlin, R. *Loot! The Heritage of Plunder* (London, 1983)

Chapman, W. R. Ethnology in the Museum, Ph.D thesis, University of Oxford (1981)
  Arranging Ethnology: A. H. L. F. Pitt Rivers and the Typological Tradition, in G. Stocking (ed.), *Objects and Others: Essays on Museums and Material Culture* (Madison, 1985), p.15

Charles, G. M. *Independence of Africa* (New York, 1960)

Charlot, J. All-American (8 February 1941) 8 *The Nation* 165

Chatterjee, A. *Representation of India, 1740–1840: The Creation of India in the Colonial Imagination* (Basingstoke, 1998)

Chaudhuri, J. American Indian Policy: An Overview, in V. Deloria Jr (ed.), *American Indian Policy in the Twentieth Century* (Norman, 1985), p.15

Chippindale, C. The Making of the First Ancient Monuments Act, 1882, and its Administration under General Pitt-Rivers (1983) 86 *Journal of the British Archaeological Association* 1

Chklaver, G. Projet d'une convention pour la protection des institutions et monuments consacrés aux arts et aux sciences (1930) 6 RDI 589

Choay, F. *The Invention of the Historic Monument* (Cambridge, 2001)

Chrzaszczewska, J. Un exemple de restitution: Le traité de Riga de 1921 et la patrimoine artistique de la Pologne (1932) 17–18 *Mouseion* 205

Claude, I. L. *National Minorities: An International Problem* (Cambridge, MA, 1955)

Clemen, P. (ed.). *Protection of Art During the War: Reports concerning the Condition of Monuments of Art at the Different Theatres of War and the German and Austrian Measures taken for their Preservation, Rescue and Research* (Leipzig, 1919)

Clifford, J. *The Predicament of Culture: Twentieth-Century Ethnography, Literature and Art* (Cambridge, MA, 1988)

Clifford, J. and G. E. Marcus. *Writing Culture: The Poetics and Politics of Ethnography* (Berkeley, CA, 1986)

Clunas, C. The Imperial Collections: East Asian Art, in M. Baker and B. Richardson (eds.), *A Grand Design: The Art of the Victoria and Albert Museum* (London, 1999), p.230

China in Britain: The Imperial Collection, in T. Barringer and T. Flynn (eds.), *Colonialism and the Object: Empire, Material Culture and the Museum* (London, 1998), p.42

Codrington, K. de B. Introduction, in L. Ashton (ed.), *The Art of India and Pakistan* (London, 1948), p.3

Coggins, C. Illicit Traffic in Pre-Columbian Antiquities (1969) 29 *Art Journal* 94

Cohen, F. S. *F. S. Cohen's Handbook of Federal Indian Law*, ed. R. Strickland (Charlottesville, 1982)

Americanizing the White Man (1952) 21 *The American Scholar* 177

Cohn, Bernard S. *Colonialism and its Forms of Knowledge: The British in India* (New Jersey, 1996)

Cohn, E. J. A Novel Chapter in the Relations between Common Law and Civil Law (1955) 4 ICLQ 493

Cohodas, M. Washoe Innovators and Their Patrons, in E. Wade (ed.), *The Arts of the North American Indian* (New York, 1986), p.203

Cole, H. On the National Importance of Local Museums of Science and Art, *Journal of the Society of the Arts* (23 January 1874), 167

Art of Savage Nations and People considered Uncivilised, *Journal of the Society of Arts* (21 January 1870), 183

Public Galleries and Irresponsible Boards (January 1866) 251 *The Edinburgh Review* 69

Collier, J. *From Every Zenith: A Memoir and Some Essays on Life and Thought* (Denver, 1963)

The United States Indian, in J. B. Gittler (ed.), *Understanding Minority Groups* (New York, 1956), p.33

The Indians of the Americas (New York, 1947)

The Red Atlantis (October 1922) 2 *Survey Graphic* 15

Colonial and Indian Exhibition 1886. *Her Majesty's Colonies, A Series of Original Papers issued under the Authority of the Royal Commission* (London, 1886)

COMA Recommendations concerning the UNESCO Seminar (1980) 5 *COMA Bulletin* 4

Commission on the Responsibility of the Authors of the War and on Enforcement of Penalties Violation of the Laws and Customs of War: Reports of Majority and Dissenting Reports of American and Japanese Members of the Commission of Responsibilities, Conference of Paris, 1919 (1920) 14 AJIL 95

Commissioner of Indian Affairs *Annual Report, 1954* (Washington, 1955)

Commonwealth of Australia *Creative Nation: Commonwealth Cultural Policy* (rev. edn, Canberra, 1994)

Conforti, M. The Idealist Enterprise and the Applied Arts, in M. Baker and B. Richardson (eds.), *A Grand Design. The Art of the Victoria and Albert Museum* (London, 1999), p.23

Conn, S. *Museums and American Intellectual Life, 1876–1926* (Chicago, 1998)

Conway, M. The South Kensington Museum (1875) 51 *Harper's New Monthly Magazine* 486 *Travels in South Kensington* (London, 1882)

Coombe, R. J. The Properties of Culture and the Politics of Possessing Identity: Native Claims in the Cultural Appropriation Controversy (1993) 6 CJLJ 249

Coombes, A. E. *Reinventing Africa: Museums, Material Culture and Popular Imagination, in Late Victorian and Edwardian England* (New Haven, 1994)

Ethnography and the Formation of National and Cultural Identities, in S. Hiller (ed.), *The Myth of Primitivism: Perspectives on Art* (London, 1991), p.189

Museums and the Formation of National and Cultural Identities (1988) 11 OAJ 57

Coombs, H. C. Decentralisation Trends Amongst Aboriginal Communities (1973) 1 *Aboriginal News* 14

Council for Aboriginal Reconciliation *Final Report* (Canberra, 2000)

Going Forward: Social Justice for First Australians (Canberra, 1995)

Addressing the Key Issues for Reconciliation (Canberra, 1993)

Valuing Cultures: Recognising Indigenous Cultures (3 vols., Canberra, 1986)

Council of Australian Museum Associations (CAMA). *Previous Possession, New Obligations: Policies for Museums in Australia and Aboriginal and Torres Strait Islander Peoples*, Melbourne, Council of Australian Museum Associations Inc., 1993 (Reprint, Melbourne, 2000)

Craig, B. Samting Bilong Tumbuna: The Collection, Documentation and Preservation of the Material Cultural Heritage of Papua New Guinea, Ph.D thesis, Flinders University of South Australia (1996)

Crawford, J. *The International Law Commission's Articles on State Responsibility: Introduction, Text and Commentaries* (Cambridge, 2002)

The Right of Self-Determination in International Law: Its Development and Future, in P. Alston (ed.), *Peoples' Rights* (Oxford, 2001), p.7

The Rights of Peoples: 'Peoples' or 'Governments'? in J. Crawford (ed.), *The Rights of Peoples* (Oxford, 1988), p.55

The Recognition of Aboriginal Customary Law, Law Reform Commission, Report No.31 (3 vols., Canberra, 1986)

The Creation of States in International Law (Oxford, 1979)

Crawford, J. (ed.). *The Rights of Peoples* (Oxford, 1988)

Creech Jones, A. and R. Hinden. *Colonies and International Conscience: Report of the Fabian Colonial Bureau* (London, 1945)

Crockford, J. *The Journal of the Great Exhibition of 1851: Its Origins, History and Progress* (London, 1851)

Crowe, S. E. *The Berlin West African Conference 1884–1885* (Westport, 1970)

Culin, S. The Road to Beauty (1927) 14 *The Brooklyn Museum Quarterly* 41

Curtin, P. *The Image of Africa: British Ideas and Action 1780–1850* (Madison, 1964)

Daes, E.-I. Equality of Peoples under the Auspices of the United Nations Draft Declaration on the Rights of Indigenous Peoples (1995) 7 St Thomas LR 493

Some Considerations on the Rights of Indigenous Peoples to Self-Determination (1993) 3 TLCP 5

Protection of Minorities under the International Bill of Human Rights and the Genocide Convention, in *Xenion: Festschrift für Pan J Zepos anlasslich seines 65* (2 vols., Athens, 1973), vol.II, p.35

Davies, H. J. C. Robinson's work at the South Kensington Museum, Part I and Part II (1998)10 JHC 169; and (1999) 11 JHC 95

Davies, W. J. The Preservation of Ancient Monuments (1913) 20 JRIBA 533

Davis, R. H. *Lives of Indian Images* (Princeton, 1997)

Deloria, P. J. *Playing Indian* (New Haven, 1998)

Deloria Jr, V. *Red Earth, White Lies: Native Americans and the Myth of Scientific Fact* (New York, 1995)

Custer Died for Your Sins: An Indian Manifesto (New York, 1969)

Deloria Jr, V. and C. Lytle *The Nations Within: The Past and Future of American Indian Sovereignty* (New York, 1984)

DeMeo, A. M. More Effective Protection for Native American Cultural Property through Regulation of Export (1994) 19 AILR 1

Department of Culture, Media and Sport (DCMS). *Guidance on the Dealing in Cultural Objects (Offences) Act 2003* (London, 2004)

Department of the Prime Minister and Cabinet. *Aboriginal Reconciliation: An Historical Perspective* (Canberra, 1992)

Desmond, R. *The India Museum 1801–1879* (London, 1982)

D'Harnoncourt, R. Challenge and Promise: Modern Art and Modern Society (1948) 41 *Magazine of Art* 250

Indian Arts and Crafts and Their Place in the Modern World, in O. La Farge (ed.), *The Changing Indian* (Norman, 1942), p.144

Living Arts of the Indians (1941) 34 *Magazine of Art* 72

All-American Art (1 January 1941) *Art Digest* 15

North American Indian Arts (1939) 32 *Magazine of Art* 164

Four Hundred Years of Mexican Art (1932) 13 *Art and Archaeology* 71

Exhibition of Mexican Arts (1931) 4(8) *The Carnegie Magazine*, 227

Mexican Arts (New York, 1930)

Dockstader, F. Directions in Indian Art, in *Proceedings of a Conference held at the University of Arizona, March 20–21, 1959* (Tucson, 1959), p.13

Dodson, M. *Aboriginal and Torres Strait Islander Social Justice Commission, Annual Report* (Canberra, 1994)

Douglas, F. H. and R. d'Harnoncourt *Indian Art of the United States* (exh. cat., New York, 1941)

DuBoff, L. (ed.). *Art Law: Domestic and International* (South Hackensack, 1975)

DuBoff, L. *et al.* Proceedings of the Panel on the US Enabling Legislation of the UNESCO Convention on the Means of Prohibiting and Preventing the Illicit Import, Export and Transfer of Ownership of Cultural Property (1976) 4 SJILC 97

Duncan, C. *Civilising Rituals* (London, 1995)

Duncan, C. and A. Wallach. The Universal Survey Museum (December 1980) 3 *Art History* 447

Eagleton, C. Self-Determination and the United Nations (1957) 47 AJIL 88

Edwards, R. (ed.). *The Preservation of Australia's Aboriginal Heritage* (Canberra, 1975)

Edwards, R. and J. Stewart (eds.). *Preserving Indigenous Cultures: A New Role for Museums* (Canberra, 1980)

Eisenmann, L. Rights of Minorities in Central Europe (1926) 222 *International Conciliation* 315

Eisler, W. and B. Smith (eds.). *Terra Australis: The Furthest Shore* (Sydney, 1988)

El-Ayouty, Y. *The United Nations and Decolonization: The Role of Afro-Asia* (The Hague, 1971)

Eoe, S. Papua New Guinea, in L. V. Prott and J. Specht (eds.), *Protection or Plunder? Safeguarding the Future of Our Cultural Heritage* (Canberra, 1989), p.53

Ermacora, F. The Protection of Minorities before the UN (1983-IV) 182 RCADI 251

Evans, A. J. On a votive deposit of the Gold Objects found on the North-West Coast of Ireland (1897) 55 *Archaeologia or Miscellaneous Tracts relating to Antiquity* 391

Evans, I. L. The Protection of Minorities (1923–24) 4 BYIL 95

Evatt, E. Individual communications under the Optional Protocol to the International Covenant on Civil and Political Rights, in S. Pritchard (ed.), *Indigenous Peoples, the United Nations and Human Rights* (Sydney, 1998), p.113

   Review of the Aboriginal and Torres Strait Islander Heritage Protection Act 1984 (Canberra, 1996)

Exhibition of the Works of Industry of All Nations 1851. *Reports by the Jurists on the Subjects in the Thirty Classes into which the Exhibitions were divided, Presentation copy* (London, 1852)

Eyo, E. Nigeria (1979) 31 *Museum* 18

Fabian Society. *International Action and the Colonies: Report of a Committee of the Fabian Colonial Bureau* (London, 1943)

Fabian, J. *Time and the Other: How Anthropology Makes its Object* (New York, 1983)

Fane, D. New Questions for 'Old Things': The Brooklyn Museum's Zuni Collection, in J. C. Berlo (ed.), *The Early Years of Native American Art History* (London, 1992), p.62

   The Language of Things: Stewart Culin as Collector, in D. Fane, I. Jacknis and I. M. Breen, *Objects of Myth and Memory: American Indian Art at The Brooklyn Museum* (exh. cat., New York, 1991), p.13

Fane, D., I. Jacknis and I. M. Breen. *Objects of Myth and Memory: American Indian Art at The Brooklyn Museum* (exh. cat., New York, 1991)

Fanon, F. *The Wretched of the Earth*, trans. C. Farrington (London, 1990)

Farmer, W. I. Custody and Controversy at the Wiesbaden Collecting Point, in E. Simpson (ed.), *The Spoils of War: World War II and Its Aftermath: The Loss, Reappearance and Recovery of Cultural Property* (New York, 1997), p.131

Feliciano, H. *The Lost Museum: The Nazi Conspiracy to Steal the World's Greatest Works of Art* (New York, 1997)

Ferrero, A. Studying the possibility of supplying, by way of compensation, a piece of cultural property of different origin and of similar value when the restitution of cultural property claimed appears impracticable or does not correspond to the wishes of the requesting country, 15 November 1979, UNESCO Doc.CC-79/CONF.206/3, Add., Annex

Ffrench, Y. *The Great Exhibition, 1851* (London, 1950)

Field, D. Dudley. *Projet d'un code international proposé aux diplomats, aux hommes d'état, et aux jurisconsultes du droit international: Contenant en outre l'exposé de droit international actuel sur les matrières les plus importantes* (Paris, 1881)

Findling, J. E. and K. D. Pelle (eds.). *Historical Dictionary of World's Fairs and Expositions, 1851–1988* (New York, 1990)

Fisher, D. Rockefeller. Philanthropy and the Rise of Social Anthropology (1986) 2 *Anthropology Today* 5

Fishman, J. J. and S. Metzger Protecting America's Cultural and Historical Patrimony (1976) 4 SJILC 57

Fitzmaurice, C. G. The Juridical Clauses of the Peace Treaties (1948-II) 81 RCADI 327

Fixico, D. L. *Termination and Relocation: Federal Indian Policy, 1945–1960* (Albuquerque, 1986)

Foster, H. *Recodings: Art, Spectacle, Cultural Politics* (Seattle, 1985)

Foster, W. *A Descriptive Catalogue of the Paintings, Statues &c, in the India Office* (3rd edn, London, 1906)

Foucault, M. *The Order of Things: An Archaeology of the Human Sciences* (London, 1994)

The Archaeology of Knowledge (London, 1972)

On Governmentality (1979) 6 *Ideology and Consciousness* 5

Foundoukidis, E. L'activité de l'office International des Musées, septembre 1932 – septembre 1933, rapport à la commission internationale de coopération intellectuelle (1933) 23–24 *Mouseion* 242

Fourmile, H. Submission on behalf of Aboriginal and Torres Strait Islander Social Justice Commissioner, in *Culture and Heritage Inquiry: Submissions, Report of the Standing Committee on Aboriginal and Torres Strait Islander Affairs* (Canberra, 1997), p.S0929

Who Owns the Past? – Aborigines as Captives of the Archives (1989) 13 *Aboriginal History* 1

Fox, C. The Unidroit Convention on Stolen or Illegally Exported Cultural Objects: An Answer to the World Problem of Illicit Trade in Cultural Property (1993) 9 AUJILP 225

Franc, H. M. The Early Years of the International Program and Council, in J. Elderfield (ed.), *The Museum of Modern Art at Mid-Century: Art Home and Abroad* (New York, 1994), p.108

Franck, T. Postmodern Tribalism and the Right to Secession, in C. Brölmann, R. Lebefer and M. Zieck (eds.), *Peoples and Minorities in International Law* (Boston, 1993), p.3

Fraoua, R. *Le trafic illicite des biens culturels et leur restitution* (Fribourg, 1985)

Fred, M. A. Law and Identity: Negotiating Meaning in the Native American Graves Protection and Repatriation Act (1997) 6 IJCP 199

Fredericksen, B. B. (ed.). *The Index of Paintings Sold in the British Isles during the Nineteenth Century* (4 vols., Los Angeles, 1988–95)

Frigo, M. Cultural property v. cultural heritage: A 'battle of concepts' in international law? (2004) 86(854) IRRC 367

Fritz, H. *The Movement for Indian Assimilation 1860–1890* (Philadelphia, 1963)

Gardner, H. *Art Through the Ages: An Introduction to Its History & Significance* (rev. edn, New York, 1936)

Art Through the Ages: An Introduction to Its History & Significance (New York, 1926)

Garmhausen, W. *History of Indian Arts Education in Santa Fe: The Institute of American Indian Arts with Historical Background 1890–1962* (Santa Fe, 1988)

Garner, J. Wilford. *International Law and the World War* (2 vols., London, 1920)

Gathercole, P. Recording Ethnographic Collections: The Debate on the Return of Cultural Property (1986) 38 *Museum* 187

Gathii, J. Thuo International Law and Eurocentricity (1998) 9 EJIL 184

Gerig, B. *The Open Door and the Mandates System: A Study of the Economic Equality before and since the Establishment of the Mandate System* (London, 1929)

Gerstenblith, P. Cultural Significance and the Kennewick Skeleton: Some Thoughts on the Resolution of Cultural Heritage Disputes, in E. Barkan and R. Bush (eds.), *Claiming the Stones, Naming the Bones: Cultural Property and the Negotiation of National and Ethnic Identity* (Los Angeles, 2002), p.162

Identity and Cultural Property: The Protection of Cultural Property in the United States (1995) 75 BULR 559

Goldman, D. E. The Native American Graves Protection and Repatriation Act: A Benefit and a Burden, Defining NAGPRA's Cultural Patrimony Definition (1999) 8 IJCP 229

Goldwater, R. *Primitivism in Modern Art* (1938) (Enlarged edn, Cambridge, 1986)

Gong, G. *The Standard of 'Civilization' in International Society* (Oxford, 1984)

Gonzalez, M. A. New Legal Tools to Curb the Illicit Traffic in Pre-Columbian Antiquities (1973) 12 CJTL 316

Goodan, H. *Invasion to Embassy: Land in Aboriginal Politics in New South Wales, 1770–1972* (Singapore, 1996)

Goodwin, M. Objects, Belief and Power in Mid-Victorian England – the origins of the Victoria and Albert Museum, in S. Pearce (ed.), *New Research in Museum Studies no. 1: Objects of Knowledge* (London, 1990), p.33

Gordon, J. The UNESCO Convention on the Illicit Movement of Art Treasures (1971) 12 HILJ 537

Gordon, P. Community Museums: The Australian Experience, in R. Ogawa (ed.), *Community Museums in Asia, Report on a Training Workshop, 26 February–10 March 1997* (Tokyo, 1998), p.118

Museum, Indigenous Peoples and the 21st Century: Or Is there a Place for Museums in this Brave New World?, in R. Ogawa (ed.), *Community Museums in Asia, Report on a Training Workshop, 26 February–10 March 1997* (Tokyo, 1998), p.34

From Ignorance to Doubt: My First Year at the Australian Museum (1981) 7 *COMA Newsletter* 15

Gosden, C. and C. Knowles. *Collecting Colonialism: Material Culture and Colonial Change* (Oxford, 2001)

Gould, C. *Trophy of Conquest, the Musée Napoléon and the Creation of the Louvre* (London, 1965)

Goy, R. Le retour et la restitution des biens culturels à leur pays d'origine en case d'appropriation illégale (1979) 83 RGDIP 962

Grattan, M. (ed.). *Essays on Australian Reconciliation* (Melbourne, 2000)

Grautoff, O. Foreign Judgments on the Preservation of Monuments of Art, in P. Clemen (ed.), *Protection of Art during the War. Reports concerning the Condition of Monuments of Art at the Different Theatres of War and the German and Austrian Measures taken for their Preservation, Rescue and Research* (Leipzig, 1919), p.129

Green, L. C. Protection of Minorities in the League of Nations and the United Nations, in A. Gotlieb (ed.), *Human Rights, Federalism and Minorities* (Toronto, 1970), p.180

Greenfield, J. *The Return of Cultural Treasures* (1989; 2nd edn, Cambridge, 1995)
The Return of Cultural Treasures (Cambridge, 1989)

Greenhalgh, P. Education, Entertainment and Politics: Lessons from the Great Exhibitions, in P. Vergo (ed.), *The New Museology* (London, 1989), p.74

Ephemeral Vistas: The Expositions Universelles, Great Exhibitions and the World's Fairs 1851–1931 (Manchester, 1988)

Gregorian, R. Unfit for Service: British Law and Looting in India in the Mid-Nineteenth Century (1990) 13 *South Asia* 63

Grewe, W. G. *The Epochs of International Law*, trans. and rev. M. Byers (Berlin, 2000)

Griffin, D. J. G. Meaning in the Bones: Museum Futures and Indigenous Australians (1996) 5 *Museum National* 11

Previous Possessions, New Obligations: A Commitment by Australian Museums (1996) 39 *Curator* 45

Written statement on behalf of the Council of Australian Museums, Des Griffin, President of CAMA, in ATSIC, *UN Working Group on Indigenous Populations, Eleventh Session 19–30 July 1993, The Australian Contribution* (Canberra, 1993), p.93

Griffiths, T. *Hunters and Collectors: The Antiquarian Imagination in Australia* (Cambridge, 1996)

Gritton, J. L. *The Institute of American Indian Arts: Modernism and US Indian Policy* (Albuquerque, 2000)

Grotius, H. *De Jure Belli Ac Pacis Libri Tres*, trans. F. W. Kelsey (Oxford, 1925)
De Iure Praedae Commentarius (Commentaries on the Law of Prize and Booty) (1604), trans. G. L. Williams (Oxford, 1950)

Groube, L. The Ownership of Diversity: The Problem of Establishing a National History in a Land of Nine Hundred Ethnic Groups, in I. McBryde (ed.), *Who Owns the Past?*

Papers from the Annual Symposium of the Australian Academy of the Humanities (Melbourne, 1984), p.49

Grzybowicz, N., D. Kartinyeri and B. Craig. The Aboriginal Family History Project at the South Australian Museum (1990) 23 *COMA Bulletin* 12

Guha-Thakurta, T. *The Making of a New 'Indian' Art: Artists, Aesthetics and Nationalism in Bengal, c.1850–1920* (Cambridge, 1992)

Gulliford, A. *Sacred Objects and Sacred Places: Preserving Tribal Traditions* (Boulder, 2000)

Guy, J. and D. Swallow (eds.). *Arts of India 1550–1900* (London, 1990)

Hall, A. R. The Recovery of Cultural Objects Dispersed During World War II (1951) 25(635) *Department of State Bulletin* 339

   Return of Looted Objects of Art to Countries of Origin. Memorandum by the State Department (1947) 16 (399) *Department of State Bulletin*, (1947) 358

   The US Program for the Return of Historic Objects to Countries of Origin, 1944–54 (1954) 31(797) *Department of State Bulletin* 493

Hall, H. Duncan. *Studies in the Administration of International Law and Organization: The League Mandate System and the Problem of Dependencies* (Washington, 1948)

Hall, W. E. *A Treatise on International Law* (4th edn, Oxford, 1895)

Halleck, H. W. *Elements of International Law and Law of War* (Philadelphia, 1866)

Handler, R. Who Owns the Past? History, Cultural Property, and the Logic of Possessive Individualism, in B. Williams (ed.), *The Politics of Culture* (Washington, 1991), p.63

Hanke, L. *All Mankind is One: A Study of the Disputation between Bartolomé de las Casas and Juan Gines de Sepúlveda in 1550 on the Intellectual and Religious Capacity of the American Indians* (DeKalb, 1974)

Hannum, H. *Autonomy, Sovereignty and Self-Determination: The Accommodation of Conflicting Rights* (Philadelphia, 1990)

Harjo, S. S. Native Peoples' Cultural and Human Rights: An Unfinished Agenda (1992) 24 ASLJ 321

Harris, M. The Narrative of Law in the Hindmarsh Island Royal Commission, in M. Chancock and C. Simpson (eds.), *Law and Cultural Heritage* (Melbourne, 1996), p.115

Hartley, M. Red Man Ceremonials: An American Plea for American Esthetics (1920) 9 *Art and Archaeology: The Arts throughout the Ages* 7

Havell, E. B. *Indian Sculpture and Painting* (London, 1908)

Hemming, S. Museums and Sacred Materials: The South Australian Museum's experience, II: Development of the Issue (1985) 16 *COMA Bulletin* 22

Henkin, L. (ed.) *The International Bill of Rights: The Covenant on Civil and Political Rights* (New York, 1981)

Herle, A. *et al.* Objects, agency and museums: continuing dialogues between the Torres Strait and Cambridge, in A. Herle, N. Stanley, K. Stevenson and R. L. Welsch (eds.), *Pacific Arts: Persistence, Change and Meaning* (Adelaide, 2002), p.231

Heyking, B. The International Protection of Minorities: The Achilles' Heel of the League of Nations (1927) 13 TGS 31

Hill, G. *Treasure Trove in Law and Practice from the Earliest Time to the Present Day* (Oxford, 1936)

Hill Sr, R. W. Regenerating Identity: Repatriation and Indian Frame of Mind, in T. Bray (ed.), *The Future of the Past: Archaeologists, Native Americans and Repatriation* (London, 2001), p.127

   Reflections of a Native Repatriator, in B. Meister (ed.), *Mending the Circle: A Native American Repatriation Guide. Understanding and Implementing NAGPRA and the Official Smithsonian and other Repatriation Policies* (New York, 1996), p.81

Hill, S. McCalmont. The Growth and Development of International Law in Africa (1900) 63 LQR 249

Hiller, S. *The Myth of Primitivism: Perspectives on Art* (London, 1991)

Hinsley, C. M. *The Smithsonian and the American Indian: Making a Moral Anthropology in Victorian America* (Washington, 1994)

Collecting Cultures and Cultures of Collecting: The Lure of the American Southwest 1880–1915 (1992) 16 *Museum Anthropology* 12

Digging for Identity: Reflecting on the Cultural Background of Collecting (1996) 20 AIQ 180

The World as Marketplace: Commodification of the Exotic at the World's Columbian Exposition, Chicago, 1893, in I. Karp and S. D. Lavine (eds.), *Exhibiting Cultures: The Poetics and Politics of Museum Displays* (Washington, 1991), p.344

Hirst, D. *Report of the Spoliation Advisory Panel in respect of a Painting now in the Possession of Glasgow City Council* (London, 2004)

Report of the Spoliation Advisory Panel in respect of a Painting now in the Possession of the Tate Gallery (London, 2001)

Hitchens, C. (ed.). *The Elgin Marbles: Should they be Returned to Greece?* (London, 1997)

Hobbes, T. *Leviathan, or The Matter, forme or power of a common-wealth ecclesisticall and civill* (London, 1651)

Hobsbawm, E. *Nations and Nationalism since 1780: Programme, Myth, Reality* (2nd edn, Cambridge, 1997)

The Age of Empire 1857–1914 (London, 1996)

Hobsbawm, E. and T. Ranger (eds.). *The Invention of Tradition* (Cambridge, 1997)

Hobson, J. A. *Towards International Government* (New York, 1915)

Hobza, A. Questions de droit international concernant les religions (1924-IV) 5 RCADI 371

Hollander, B. *The International Law of Art for Lawyers, Collectors and Artists* (London, 1959)

Hooper-Greenhill, E. *Museums and the Shaping of Knowledge* (London, 1992)

Hope, R. *Report on the National Estate* (Canberra, 1974)

House, E. Mandell and C. Seymour (eds.). *What Really Happened at Paris: The Story of the Peace Conference, 1918–1919 by American Delegates* (New York, 1921)

Howard, J. *The Paris Agreement on Reparations from Germany* (Washington, 1946)

HREOC. *Bringing Them Home: Report of the National Inquiry into the Separation of Aboriginal and Torres Strait Islander Children from Their Families* (Sydney, 1997)

Hudson, M. O. *International Legislation: A Collection of the Texts of Multipartite International Instruments of General Interest* (9 vols., Washington, 1919–1950)

The Protection of Minorities and Natives in Transferred Territories, in E. Mandell House and C. Seymour (eds.), *What Really Happened at Paris: The Story of the Peace Conference, 1918–1919 by American Delegates* (New York, 1921), p.208

Huxley, J. *Memories II* (New York, 1973)

ICOM. *Ethics of Acquisition* (Paris, 1970), http://icom.museum/acquisition.html

Statutes: Code of Professional Ethics (1986) (Rev., Paris, 2001 and 2004)

Study on the Principles, Conditions and Means for the Restitution or Return of Cultural Property in View of Reconstituting Dispersed Heritage (1979) 31 *Museum* 62

Ilsley, L. L. The Administration of Mandates by the British Dominions (1934) 28 APSR 287

Inouye, D. K. Repatriation: Forging New Relationships (1992) 24 ASLJ 1

International Group of Organisers of Large-Scale Exhibitions Declaration on the Importance and Value of Universal Museums, Munich, October 2002 (2004) 57 *ICOM News* 4

International Law Association (ILA) *Report of the Cultural Heritage Law Committee* (London, 2004)

A Blueprint for the Development of Cultural Heritage Law: First Report (London, 2000)

International Military Tribunal (IMT) *Trial of the Major War Criminals before the International Military Tribunal, Nuremberg, November 14, 1945–October 1, 1946* (42 vols., Nuremberg, 1947–1949)

Isaacs, J. (ed.). *Renewing the Dreaming: The Aboriginal Homelands Exhibition: Anniversary Exhibition 1827–1977* (exh. cat., Sydney, 1997)

Jacknis, I. The Road to Beauty: Stewart Culin's American Indian Exhibitions at The Brooklyn Museum, in D. Fane, I. Jacknis and I. M. Breen, *Objects of Myth and Memory: American Indian Art at The Brooklyn Museum* (exh. cat., New York, 1991), p.29

Franz Boas and Exhibits: On the Limitations of the Museum Method of Anthropology, in G. W. Stocking (ed.), *Objects and Others: Essays on Museums and Material Culture* (Madison, 1985), p.75

Jamieson, H. H. The Protection of Australia's Movable Cultural Heritage (1995) 4 IJCP 215

Janis, M. W. Jeremy Bentham and the Fashioning of 'International Law' (1984) 78 AJIL 405

Janke, T. *Our Culture, Our Future: Report on Australian Indigenous Cultural and Intellectual Property Rights* (Canberra, 1998)

Johnston, E. *National Report, Overview and Recommendations, Royal Commission into Aboriginal Deaths in Custody* (Canberra, 1991)

Jonaitis, A. Creations of Mystics and Philosophers: The White Man's Perceptions of Northwest Coast Indian Art from the 1930s to the Present (1981) 5 AICRJ 1

Jones, M. Gardiner. National Minorities: A Case Study in International Protection (1949) 14 LCP 599

Jones, P. Museums and Sacred Materials: The South Australian Museum's experience, I: History and Background (1989) 16 *COMA Bulletin* 16

K. C. Obituary: Eric Maclagan (1951) 93 *Burlington Magazine* 358

Kaeppler, A. L. Paradise Regained: Envisaging Culture as National Identity, in F. E. S. Kaplan (ed.), *Museums and the Making of 'Ourselves': The Role of Objects in National Identity* (London, 1994), p.34

'Artificial Curiosities': Being an Exposition of Native Manufactures Collected on the Three Pacific Voyages of Captain James Cook R.N. (exh. cat., Honolulu, 1978)

Kaeppler, A. L. and A. K. Stillman, Pacific Island and Australian Aboriginal Artifacts in Public Collections in the United States of America and Canada, Paris, 1985, UNESCO Doc.CLT-85/WS/12

Kaiku, R. Restoration of national cultural property: The case of Papua New Guinea, in R. Edwards and J. Stewart (eds.), *Preserving Indigenous Cultures: A New Role for Museums* (Canberra, 1980), p.175

Kaplan, F. E. S. (ed.). *Museums and the Making of 'Ourselves': The Role of Objects in National Identity* (London, 1994)

Karp, I. and S. Lavine (eds.). *Exhibiting Cultures: The Poetics and Politics of Museum Display* (Washington, 1991)

Kastl, L. Colonial Administration as an International Trust (1930) 5 *Problems in Peace* 132

Kawasaki, A. *The Changing Presentation of the American Indian* (Washington DC, 2000).

Keal, P. *European Conquest and the Rights of Indigenous Peoples: The Moral Backwardness of International Society* (Cambridge, 2003)

Kellock, H. Colonies after the War (1943) 1(17) *Editorial Research Papers* 287

Kelly, L. C. *The Assault on Assimilation: John Collier and the Origins of Indian Policy Reform,* (Albuquerque, 1983)

Kelly, L. and P. Gordon. Developing a Community of Practice: Museums and Reconciliation in Australia, in R. Sandell (ed.), *Museums, Society and Inequality* (London, 2002), p.153

Kelly, L., P. Gordon, and T. Sullivan. 'We Deal with Relationships: Not just Objects': An Evaluation of Previous Possessions, New Obligations, Green Paper (Sydney, 2001)

Kennedy, D. International Law and the Nineteenth Century: History of an Illusion (1997) 17 *Quinnipiac Law Review* 99

Primitive Legal Scholarship (1986) 27 HILJ 1

Kenyon, F. G. *Museums & National Life: The Romanes Lecture* (Oxford, 1927)

Kiernan, V. G. *The Lords of Human Kind: European Attitudes to the Outside World in the Imperial Age* (London, 1969)

Kimmelman, M. Revisiting the Revisionists: The Modern, its Critics and the Cold War, in J. Elderfield (ed.), *The Museum of Modern Art at Mid-Century: At Home and Abroad* (New York, 1994), p.38

King, J. Tradition in Native American Art, in E. Wade (ed.), *The Arts of the North American Indian: Native Traditions in Evolution* (New York, 1986), p.65

Kingsbury, B. Reconciling Five Competing Conceptual Structures of Indigenous Peoples' Claims in International and Comparative Law, in P. Alston (ed.), *Peoples' Rights* (Oxford, 2001), p.69

'Indigenous Peoples' in International Law: A Constructivist Approach to the Asian Controversy (1998) 92 AJIL 414

Sovereignty and Inequality (1998) 9 EJIL 599

Klüber, J. L. *Droit des gens modernes de l'Europe* (Paris, 1874)

Klukhohn, C. and R. Hackenberg. Social Science Principles and the Indian Reorganization Act, in W. Kelly (ed.), *Indian Affairs and the Indian Reorganization Act, The Twenty Year Record* (Tucson, 1954), p.29

Knop, K. *Diversity and Self-Determination in International Law* (Cambridge, 2002)

Kopytoff, I. The Cultural Biography of Things: Commodification as Process, in A. Appadurai (ed.), *The Social Life of Things: Commodities in Cultural Perspective* (Cambridge, 1986), p.64

Koskenniemi, M. *The Gentle Civilizer of Nations: The Rise and Fall of International Law, 1870– 1960* (Cambridge, 2002)

From Apology to Utopia: The Structure of International Legal Argument (Helsinki, 1989)

Kowalski, W. W. Repatriation of Cultural Property Following a Cession of Territory or Dissolution of Multinational States (2001) 6 AAL 139

Art Treasures and War: A Study on the Restitution of Looted Cultural Property pursuant to Public International Law, ed. T. Schadla-Hall (London, 1998)

Kroeber, A. L. *The Nature of Culture* (Chicago, 1952)

Kurtz, M. The End of the War and the Occupation of Germany, 1944–52, Laws and Conventions Enacted to Counter German Appropriations: The Allied Control Council, in E. Simpson (ed.), *The Spoils of War. World War II and Its Aftermath: The Loss, Reappearance and Recovery of Cultural Property* (New York, 1997), p.112

Nazi Contraband: American Policy on the Return of European Cultural Treasures 1945–1955 (New York, 1985)

Lachs, M. Address at Thirtieth Anniversary Celebration for the Protection of Cultural Property in the Event of Armed Conflict, 14 May 1984, in UNESCO, *Information on the Implementation of the Convention for the Protection of Cultural Property in the Event of Armed Conflict* (Paris, 1984), p.13

Lafiti, A. *Effects of War on Property Being Studies in International Law and Policy* (London, 1909)

Lâm, M. C. Indigenous Peoples' Conception of their Self-Determination in International Law, in C. Lynch and M. Loriaux (eds.), *Law and Moral Action in World Politics* (Minneapolis, 2000), p.205

Making Room for Peoples at the United Nations: Thoughts Provoked by Indigenous Claims to Self-Determination (1992) 25 CILJ 601

Lampert, R. The Development of the Aboriginal Gallery at the Australian Museum (1986) 18 *COMA Bulletin* 10

Langen, E. and E. Sauer *Die Restitution im internationalen Recht* (Dusseldorf, 1949)

Langford, R. Our Heritage – Your Playground (1983) 16 *Australian Archaeology* 1

Lansing, R. Notes on Sovereignty in a State (1907) 1 AJIL 105

LaRiviere, A. L. New Art by the Oldest Americans (1973) 65 *Westways* 23

Lauterpacht, H. *International Law and Human Rights* (London, 1950)
  An International Bill of the Rights of Man (New York, 1945)
LaViolette, F. E. *The Struggle for Survival* (Toronto, 1961)
Lawrence, T. J. *The Principles of International Law* (4th edn, London, 1913)
  The Principles of International Law, (London, 1895)
Lee, R. F. The Antiquities Act (2000) 42 *Journal of the Southwest* 1
Legget, J. *Restitution and Repatriation: Guidelines for Good Practice* (London, 2000)
Lehman, A. L. and B. Richardson (eds.). Preface: A Point of View, in M. Baker and B.
  Richardson (eds.), *A Grand Design: The Art of the Victoria and Albert Museum* (London,
  1999), p.9
Lemkin, R. Genocide: A New International Crime: Punishment and Prevention (1946) 17
  Revue internationale de droit pénal 360
  Axis Rule in Occupied Europe, Laws of Occupation, Analysis of Government, Proposals for Redress
  (Washington DC, 1944)
Leuprecht, P. Minority Rights Revisited: New Glimpses of an Old Issue, in P. Alston (ed.),
  Peoples' Rights (Oxford, 2001), p.111
Ley, J. F. *Australia's Protection of Movable Cultural Heritage: Report on the Ministerial Review
  of the Protection of Movable Cultural Heritage Act 1986 and Regulations* (Canberra,
  1991)
Lindley, M. F. *The Acquisition and Government of Backward Territory in International Law: Being
  a Treatise on the Law and Practice Relating to Colonial Expansion* (London, 1926)
Linstrum, D. The Sacred Past: Lord Curzon and the Indian Monuments (1995) 11 *South
  Asian Studies* 1
Linton, R. and P. S. Wingert *Arts of the South Seas* (exh. cat., New York, 1946)
Locke, J. *Two Treatises on Government, Of Civil Government*, ed. P. Lastlett (1690) (Reprint,
  Cambridge, 1960)
Lorimer, J. *The Institutes of the Law of Nations. A Treatise of the Jural Relations of Separate Political
  Communities* (2 vols., Edinburgh, 1883)
Lowenthal, D. *The Past is a Foreign Country* (Cambridge, 1985)
Lubbock, J. *Addresses, Political and Educational* (London, 1879)
Lugard, F. D. *The Dual Mandate in British Tropical Africa* (Hamden, 1965)
Lynes, R. *Good Old Modern: An Intimate Portrait of the Museum of Modern Art* (New York,
  1973)
Macartney, C. A. *National States and National Minorities* (1934) (Reprint, New York, 1968)
MacDonald, R. *Between Two Worlds: The Commonwealth Government and the Removal of
  Aboriginal Children of Part Descent in the Northern Territory* (Alice Springs, 1996)
McGrath, A. (ed.). *Contested Ground: Australian Aborigines under the British Crown* (Sydney,
  1999)
Mackay Quynn, D. The Art Confiscations of the Napoléonic Wars (1945) 50 AHR 439
McKean, J. Joseph Paxton: Crystal Palace, London 1851, in B. Dunlop and D. Hector (eds.),
  Lost Masterpieces (London, 1999), n.p.
McKean, W. *Equality and Discrimination under International Law* (Oxford, 1983)
Mackenzie, G. J. *Propaganda and Empire: The Manipulation of British Public Opinion 1880–1960*
  (Manchester, 1984)
McKenzie, J. Opening Address, in I. Staunton and M. McCarthy (eds.), *Lost Heritage. A
  Report of the Symposium on the Return of Cultural Property held at the Africa Centre, 21 May
  1981* (London, 1981), p.3
McKeown, C. T. Implementing a 'True Compromise': The Native American Graves Pro-
  tection and Repatriation Acts after Ten Years, in C. Fforde, J. Hubert and P. Turn-
  bull (eds.), *The Dead and Their Possessions: Repatriation in Principle, Policy and Practice*
  (London, 2001), p.108

NAGPRA. Grants, in B. Meister (ed.) *Mending the Circle: A Native American Repatriation Guide. Understanding and Implementing NAGPRA and the Official Smithsonian and other Repatriation Policies* (New York, 1996), p.21

McLaughlin, R. H. The Antiquities Act of 1906: Politics and the Framing of an American Anthropology and Archaeology (1998) 23 OCULR 61

Macpherson, C. P. *The Political Theory of Possessive Individualism: Hobbes to Locke* (Oxford, 1962)

McRae, H. *et al. Indigenous Legal Issues: Commentary and Materials* (Erskenville, 1997)

Makinson, D. Rights of Peoples: Point of View of a Logician, in J. Crawford (ed.), *The Rights of Peoples* (Oxford, 1988), p.69

Makkonen, T. *Identity, Difference and Otherness: The Concepts of 'People', 'Indigenous People' and 'Minority' in International Law* (Helsinki, 2000)

Margalith, A. *The International Mandates* (Baltimore, 1930)

Marks, G. C. Indigenous Peoples in International Law: The Significance of Francisco de Vitoria and Bartolomé de las Casas (1992) 13 AYIL 1

Martin, A. Private Property, Rights and Interests in the Paris Peace Treaties (1947) 24 BYIL 277

Martin, T. *The Affirmative Action Empire: Nations and Nationalism in the Soviet Union, 1923–1939* (Ithaca, 2001).

Martin, W. Treasure Trove and the British Museum (1904) 77 LQR 27

Mastalir, R. W. A Proposal for Protecting the 'Cultural' and 'Property' Aspects of Cultural Property under International Law (1992–93) 16 FILJ 1033

Maurer, E. The Role of the State Department regarding National and Private Claims for the Restitution of Stolen Cultural Property, in E. Simpson (ed.), *The Spoils of War. World War II and Its Aftermath: The Loss, Reappearance and Recovery of Cultural Property* (New York, 1997), p.142

Maxwell, A. *Colonial Photography and Exhibitions: Representations of the 'Native' and the Making of European Identities* (London, 2000)

M'Bow, A.-M. A Plea for the Return of an Irreplaceable Heritage to Those Who Created It: An Appeal by the Director-General of UNESCO (1979) 31 *Museum* 58

Meehan, B. The National Inventory of Aboriginal Artefacts (April 1988) 20 *COMA Bulletin* 7

Meister, B. (ed.). *Mending the Circle: A Native American Repatriation Guide. Understanding and Implementing NAGPRA and the Official Smithsonian and other Repatriation Policies* (New York, 1996); and at http://repatriationfoundation.org/MTC.html

Meriam, L. *The Problem of Indian Administration* (Baltimore, 1928)

Merryman, J. H. (ed.). *Thinking about the Elgin Marbles: Critical Essays on Cultural Property, Art and Law* (The Hague, 1999)

Note on the Marquis de Somerueles (1996) 5 IJCP 319

Two Ways of Thinking About Cultural Property (1986) 80 AJIL 831

Thinking of the Elgin Marbles (1985) 83 Mich. LR 1880

International Art Law: From Cultural Nationalism to a Common Cultural Heritage (1983) 15 NYUJILP 757

Messenger, P. M. (ed.). *The Ethics of Collecting: Whose Culture? Cultural Property: Whose Property?* (Albuquerque, 1989)

Meyer, K. *The Plundered Past: The Traffic in Art Treasures* (New York, 1973)

Michaelis, A. *Ancient Marbles in Great Britain*, trans. C. A. M. Fennell (Cambridge, 1882)

Mill, J. S. *Considerations on Representative Government* (1861), ed. C. Shield (Reprint, New York, 1958)

Miller, D. Hunter *The Drafting of the Covenant* (2 vols., New York, 1928)

Miniham, J. *The Nationalization of Culture: The Development of State Subsidies to the Arts in Great Britain* (London, 1977)

Mitter, P. The Imperial Collections: Indian Art, in M. Baker and B. Richardson (eds.), *A Grand Design: The Art of the Victoria and Albert Museum* (London, 1999), p.222

   Much Maligned Monsters: A History of European Reactions to Indian Art (Oxford, 1997)

   Art and Nationalism in Colonial India, 1850–1922: Occidental Orientations (Cambridge, 1994)

Mitter, P. and C. Clunas The Empire of Things: The Engagement with the Orient, in M. Baker and B. Richardson (eds.), *A Grand Design: The Art of the Victoria and Albert Museum* (London, 1999), p.221

MoMA. *René d'Harnoncourt 1901–1968: A Tribute* (New York, 1968)

   The Family of Man (exh. cat., New York, 1955)

   Twenty Centuries of Mexican Art (exh. cat., New York, 1940)

Moore, J. B. *A Digest of International Law* (8 vols., Washington, 1906)

Morris, G. T. In Support of the Right of Self-determination for Indigenous Peoples under International Law (1987) 29 GYIL 277

Mosuwadoga, G. Restitution of Collections (1980) 5 *COMA Bulletin* 6

Moustakas, J. Group Rights in Cultural Property: Justifying Strict Inalienability (1984) 74 Cornell LR 1179

Mower, E. C. *International Government* (Boston, 1931)

Mullin, M. The Patronage of Difference: Making Indian Art as Art, Not Ethnology (1992) 7 *Cultural Anthropology* 395

Mulvaney, D. J. The Proposed Gallery of Aboriginal Australia, in R. Edwards and J. Stewart (eds.), *Preserving Indigenous Cultures: A New Role for Museums* (Canberra, 1980), p.72

   Report for Proposed Gallery of Aboriginal Australia: Report of the Planning Committee, in P. H. Pigott, *Museums in Australia 1975: Report of the Committee of Inquiry on Museums and National Collections*, AGPS (Canberra, 1975), n.p.

Mundine, D. S. Black My Story (Not History) (1993) 24 *COMA Bulletin* 12

Munro, R. The Recent Case of Treasure Trove (1903) 15 *Juridical Review* 267

Müntz, E. Les invasions de 1814–1815 et la spoliation de nos musées (1897) 105 *Nouvelle Revue* 706

   Les annexions de collections d'art ou de bibliothèques et leur rôle dans les relations internationales (1895) 8 RHD 481; (1895) 9 RHD 375; and (1895) 10 RHD 481

Murray, G. National Tolerance as an International Obligation (1930) 5 *Problems in Peace* 132

Murray, T. The History, Philosophy and Sociology of Archaeology: The Case of the Ancient Monuments Protection Act (1882), in V. Pinsky *et al.*, *Critical Traditions in Contemporary Archaeology: Essays in the Philosophy, History and Socio-politics of Archaeology* (Cambridge, 1989), p.55

Museums Australia. *Continuous Cultures Ongoing Responsibilities: A Comprehensive Policy Document and Guidelines for Australian museums working with Aboriginal and Torres Strait Islander Cultural Heritage* (Canberra, 2005)

Myles, K. Should Finding Mean Keeping? UNESCO Radio, UNESCO Doc.PI/R/1825, (Paris, 1982)

Nafziger, J. A. R. The New Fiduciary Duty of United States Museums to Repatriate Cultural Heritage: The Oregon Experience (1995) 29 UBCLR 37

   Comments on the Relevance of Law and Culture to Cultural Property Law (1983) 10 SJILC 323

   Regulation by the International Council of Museums: An Example of the Role of Non-Governmental Organizations in the Transnational Legal Process (1972) 2 DJILP 231

Nafziger, J. A. R. and Dobkins, R. J. The Native Americans Graves Protection and Repatriation Act in its First Decade (1999) 8 IJCP 77

Nahlik, S. E. (ed.), *International Dimensions of Humanitarian Law*, (Paris, 1988), p.203

The Case of the Displaced Art Treasures (1980) 23 GYIL 255

La protection internationale des biens culturels en cas de conflit armé (1967-I) 120 RCADI 62

Naranjo, T. Musing on Two World Views, in B. Meister (ed.), *Mending the Circle: A Native American Repatriation Guide. Understanding and Implementing NAGPRA and the Official Smithsonian and other Repatriation Policies* (New York, 1996), p.27

Nason, J. A. Beyond Repatriation: Cultural Policy and Practice for the Twenty-First Century, in B. Ziff and P. V. Pao (eds.), *Borrowed Power: Essays on Cultural Appropriation* (New Brunswick, 1997), p.291

National Museum of the American Indian (NMAI). Beyond the Medicine Line: International Repatriation and NMAI, Washington, NMAI, n.d.

National Museum of the American Indian. Policy Statement on Native American Human Remains and Cultural Materials, revised 19 February 1991

National Museum of Australia (NMA). *Review of the National Museum of Australia, its Exhibitions and Public Programs* (Canberra, 2003)

National Museum Directors' Conference (NMDC) *International Dimensions* (London, 2002)

National Park Service. *National NAGPRA FY04 Midyear Report* (Washington DC, 2004)

Nelson, R. A. and J. F. Sheley. Bureau of Indian Affairs Influence on Indian Self-Determination, in V. Deloria Jr (ed.), *American Indian Policy in the Twentieth Century* (Norman, 1985), p.177

Netherlands Archaeological Society Pays-bas. La protection des monuments et objets historiques et artistiques contre les destructions de la guerre (1919) 26 RGDIP 329

Newton, D. Old Wine in New Bottles, and the Reverse, in F. E. S. Kaplan (ed.), *Museums and the Making of 'Ourselves': The Role of Objects in National Identity* (London, 1994), p.269

Nicholas, L. *The Rape of Europa: The Fate of Europe's Treasures in the Third Reich and the Second World War* (London, 1995)

Nicholson, T. D. The Australian Museum and the Field Museum adopt Policy Statements governing Collections (1975) 18 *Curator* 296

Nieć, H. Human Rights to Culture (1979) 44 YAAA 109

Nieć, H. (ed) *Cultural Rights and Wrongs* (Paris, 1998)

Nieciówna, H. Sovereign Rights to Cultural Property (1971) 4 PYIL 239

Niezen, R. *The Origins of Indigenism: Human Rights and the Politics of Identity* (Berkeley, 2003)
  Spirit Wars: Native North American Religions in the Age of Nation Building (Berkeley, 2000)

Njoya, A. Ndam. The African Concept, in S. Nahlik (ed.), *International Dimensions of Humanitarian Law* (Paris, 1988), p.8

North American Indian Museums Association Suggested Guidelines for Museums in Dealing with Requests for Return of Native American Materials, in *Directory of North American Indian Museums and Cultural Centers* (Niagara Falls, 1981)

Northedge, F. S. International Intellectual Co-operation within the League of Nations: Its Conceptual Basis and Lessons for the Present, PhD thesis, University of London, (1953)

Nussbaum, A. *A Concise History of the Law of Nations* (rev. edn, New York, 1954)

'O'. International Arbitrations under the Treaty of St Germain (1923–24) 4 BYIL 124

O'Brien, S. Tribes and Indians: With Whom Does the United States Maintain a Relationship? (1991) 66 NDLR 1461
  Federal Indian Policies and the International Protection of Human Rights, in V. Deloria Jr (ed.), *American Indian Policy in the Twentieth Century* (Norman, 1985), p.35

OIM *Manual on the Techniques of Archaeological Excavations*, (Paris, 1940)

OIM and E. Foundoukidis *Final Act of the International Conference on Excavations* (Paris, 1937)

O'Keefe, P. J. *Commentary on the UNESCO 1970 Convention on Illicit Traffic* (Leicester, 2000)

O'Keefe, P. J. and L. V. Prott. *Law and the Cultural Heritage, Volume 1: Discovery and Excavation* (London, 1984)

O'Keefe, R. Law, War and 'the Cultural Heritage of All Mankind', Ph.D thesis, University of Cambridge (2000)

The Meaning of 'Cultural Property' under the 1954 Hague Convention (1999) 46 *Netherlands International Law Review* 26

Olivier, S. *The League of Nations and Primitive Peoples* (London, 1918)

Oppenheim, L. *International Law: A Treatise*, H. Lauterpacht (ed.) (3rd edn, 2 vols., London, 1920)

International Law: A Treatise (2nd edn, London, 1912)

The Science of Inernational Law: Its Task and Method (1908) 2 AJIL 313 at 328–330.

International Law: A Treatise (London, 1906)

Osman, D. N. Occupiers' Title to Cultural Property: Nineteenth Century Removal of Egyptian Artifacts (1999) 37CJTL 969

Owsley, D. W. and R. L. Jantz. Kennewick Man – A Kin? Too Distant, in E. Barkan and R. Bush (eds.), *Claiming the Stones, Naming the Bones: Cultural Property and the Negotiation of National and Ethnic Identity* (Los Angeles, 2002), p.141

Palmer, A. Land Claims: The use of Museum collections by traditional owner claimants (1980) 4 *COMA Bulletin* 13

Palmer, N. *Report of the Working Group on Human Remains in Museum Collections* (London, 2003)

Museums and the Holocaust: Law, Principles and Practice (Leicester, 2000)

Palmer, N. (ed.). *The Recovery of Stolen Art: A Collection of Essays* (The Hague, 1998)

Panel for a National Dialogue on Museum/Native American Relations. Report of the Panel for a National Dialogue on Museum/Native American Relations (1990) 14 *Museum Anthropology* 6

Pankhurst, R. The Case of Ethiopia (1986) 38 *Museum* 58

Parker, P. *Keepers of the Treasures: Protecting Historic Properties and Cultural Traditions on Indian Lands* (Washington DC, 1990)

Parsons, D. Tipu's Tiger (1979) 1 *Antique Machines and Curiosities* 47

Peabody Museum *Annual Report* (Cambridge, MA, 1890)

Pearson, N. The Concept of Native Title at Common Law, in G. Yunupingu (ed.), *Our Land is Our Life* (St Lucia, 1997), p.150

Mabo: Towards Respecting Equality and Difference, in *Voices from the Land: 1993 Boyer Lectures* (Sydney, 1994), p.89

Pechota, V. The Development of the Covenant on Civil and Political Rights, in L. Henkin (ed.), *The International Bill of Rights: The Covenant on Civil and Political Rights* (New York, 1981), p.32

Petch, A. 'Man as he Was and Man as he Is': General Pitt River's Collections (1998) 10 JHC 75

Phillips, T. (ed.). *Africa: The Art of a Continent* (exh. cat., New York, 1995)

Phillipson, C. *Termination of War and Treaties of Peace* (London, 1916)

International Law and the Great War (London, 1915).

Philp, K. *John Collier's Crusade for Indian Reform 1920–1954* (Tucson, 1977)

Physick, J. *The Victoria and Albert Museum: The History of its Building* (Oxford, 1982)

Pigott, P. H. *Museums in Australia 1975: Report of the Committee of Inquiry on Museums and National Collections including the Report of the Planning Committee on the Gallery of Aboriginal Australia* (Canberra, 1975)

Pinsky, V. A. Archaeology, Politics and Boundary-Formation: The Boas Censure (1919) and the Development of American Archaeology during the Inter-War Years, in J. E. Reyman (ed.), *Rediscovering our Past: Essays on the History of American Archaeology*, (Aldershot, 1992), p.161

Pitt Rivers, A. H. L. F. *Catalogue of the Anthropological Collection lent by Colonel Lane Fox for exhibition in the Bethnal Green branch of the South Kensington Museum June 1874 Parts I and II* (London, 1874)

Platzman, S. Objects of Controversy (1992) 41 AULR 517

Politis, N. *The New Aspects of International Law, A Series of Lectures delivered at Columbia University in July 1926* (Washington, 1928)

Pomerance, M. The United States and Self-Determination: Perspectives on the Wilsonian Conception (1976) 70 AJIL 1

Potter, P. B. Origin of the System of Mandates under the League of Nations (1922) 16 APSR 563

Pradier-Fodéré, P. *Traité de droit international public européen et américain: Suivant les progrès de la sciènce et de la pratique contemporaines* (9 vols., Paris, 1885–1906)

Price, S. *Primitive Art in Civilized Places* (Chicago, 1989)

Pritchard, S. *Setting International Standards: An Analysis of the UN Declaration on the Rights of Indigenous Peoples and the First Six Sessions of the Commission on Human Rights Working Group* (3rd edn, Sydney, 2001)

Prott, L. V. Understanding One Another on Cultural Rights, in H. Nieć (ed.), *Cultural Rights and Wrongs* (Paris, 1998), p.161

UNESCO and Unidroit: A Partnership against Trafficking in Cultural Objects, in N. Palmer (ed.), *The Recovery of Stolen Art: A Collection of Essays* (The Hague, 1998), p.205

Commentary on the Unidroit Convention (London, 1997)

The Protocol to the Convention for the Protection of Cultural Property in the Event of Armed Conflict (The Hague Convention) 1954, in M. Briat and J. A. Freedberg (eds.), *Legal Aspects of International Trade in Art* (Paris, 1996), p.163

Principles for the Resolution of Disputes Concerning Cultural Heritage Displaced during the Second World War, 1995, UNESCO Doc.CLT-99/CONF.203/2, Annex I

The Preliminary Draft Unidroit Convention on Stolen or Illegally Exported Cultural Objects (1992) 41 ICLQ 160

Cultural Rights as Peoples' Rights in International Law, in J. Crawford (ed.), *The Rights of Peoples* (Oxford, 1988), p.93

Prott, L. V. and P. J. O'Keefe. 'Cultural Heritage' or 'Cultural Property'? (1992) 1 IJCP 307

Law and the Cultural Heritage, Volume 3: Movement (London, 1989)

Prucha, F. P. (ed.). *Documents of United States Indian Policy* (2nd edn, Lincoln, 1975)

Przyborowska-Klimczak, A. Les notions de 'biens culturels' et de 'patrimoine culturel mondial' dans le droit international (1989–90) 18 PYIL 51

Radin, M. J. Property and Personhood (1982) 34 Stan. LR 957

Raines, J. One Is Missing: Native American Graves Protection and Repatriation Act: An Overview and Analysis (1992) 17 AILR 639

Rappard, W. E. Minorities and the League (1926) 222 *International Conciliation* 330

Reynolds, H. *Frontier: Aborigines, Settlers and Land* (Sydney, 1987)

Richards, T. *The Imperial Archive: Knowledge and Fantasy of Empire* (London, 1993)

Riding In, J. Without Ethics and Morality: A Historical Overview of Imperial Archaeology and American Indians (1992) 24 ASLJ 11

Rigby, D. Cultural Reparations and a New Western Tradition (1943–44) 13 *The American Scholar* 284

Rigg, V. Curators of the Colonial Idea: The Museum and the Establishment as Agents of Bourgeois Ideology in Nineteenth Century NSW (1994) 4 *Public History Review* 188

Riles, A. Aspiration and Control: International Legal Rhetoric and the Essentialization of Culture (1993) 106 HLR 723

Roberts, E. *The Preservation of Australia's Aboriginal Heritage: Report of National Seminar on Aboriginal Antiquities in Australia May 1972* (Canberra, 1975)

Roberts Commission. Resolution of the American Commission for the Protection and Salvage of Artistic and Historic Monuments in War Areas, 20 June 1946, (1951) 11 CAJ 34

Robinson, J. International Protection of Minorities: A Global View (1971) 1 IYHR 61

The Genocide Convention. A Commentary (New York, 1960)

From the Protection of Minorities to the Promotion of Human Rights (1949) 1 JYIL 115

Minorities (1942) *World Organisation* 231

Robinson, J. C. English Art Connoisseurship and Collecting (October 1894) *Nineteenth Century* 523

Our National Art Collections and Provincial Art Museums (June 1880) *Nineteenth Century* 988

Our Public Art Museums: A Retrospective (December 1897) *Nineteenth Century* 940

Robinson, N. Reparations and Restitution in International Law (1949) 1 JYIL 186

Rocher, R. British Orientalism in the Eighteenth Century: The Dialectics of Knowledge and Government, in C. A. Breckenridge and P. van der Veer (eds.), *Orientalism and the Postcolonial Predicament: Perspectives on South Asia* (Philadelphia, 1993), pp.215–49

Roerich Museum *Third International Convention for the Promotion of the World Wide Adoption of the Roerich Pact and Banner of Peace* (New York, 1933)

Roerich Pact Banner of Peace. *Proceedings Third International Convention for the Roerich Pact and Banner of Peace, 17 and 18 November, 1933 Washington DC* (2 vols., New York, 1934)

Rogers, W. D. The Legal Response to the Illicit Movement of Cultural Property (1973) 5 LPIB 936

Roht-Arriaza, N. Of Seeds and Shamans: The Appropriation of Scientific and Technical Knowledge of Indigenous and Local Communities, in B. Ziff and P. Rao (eds.), *Borrowed Power: Essays on Cultural Appropriation* (New Brunswick, 1997), p.255

Roosevelt, E. Foreword, in F. H. Douglas and R. d'Harnoncourt, *Indian Arts of the United States* (exh. cat., New York, 1941), p.8

Roosevelt, T. *Colonial Policies of the United States* (Garden City, 1937)

Rosting, H. Protection of Minorities by the League of Nations (1923) 17 AJIL 641

Rouček, J. *The Working of the Minorities System under the League of Nations* (Prague, 1929)

Rousseau, J. J. *The Social Contract*, trans. M. Cranston (Harmondsworth, 1968)

Royal Institute of International Affairs. *The Colonial Problem: A Report by a Study Group of Members of the Royal Institute of International Affairs* (London, 1937)

Rubin, W. (ed.), *'Primitivism' in 20th Century Art: Affinity of the Tribal and Modern* (New York, 1984), p.1

Rushing, W. J. *Native American Art and the New York Avant-Garde: A History of Cultural Primitivism* (Austin, 1995)

Marketing the Affinity of the Primitive and the Modern: René d'Harnoncourt and 'Indian Art of the United States' in J. C. Berlo (ed.), *The Early Years of Native American Art History: The Politics of Scholarship and Collecting* (Seattle, 1992), p.191

Russell, R. B. and J. E. Munther. *A History of the United Nations Charter: The Role of the United States, 1940–1945* (Washington, 1958)

Russell, S. The Legacy of Ethnic Cleansing: Implementation of NAGPRA in Texas (1995) 19 AICRJ 193

Rydell, R. *All the World's a Fair: Visions of Empire at American International Expositions 1879–1916* (Chicago, 1984)

Said, E. *Orientalism: Western Conceptions of the Orient* (London, 1995)

Culture and Imperialism (London, 1993)

Samson, C. Aboriginal Keeping Places (1988) 20 *COMA Bulletin* 20–21

Sanders, D. The Re-Emergence of Indigenous Questions in International Law (1983) CHRY 3

Saumarez Smith, C. National Consciousness, National Heritage and the Idea of 'Englishness', in M. Baker and B. Richardson (eds.), *A Grand Design: The Art of the Victoria and Albert Museum* (London, 1999), p.275

Saunders, F. Stonor *Who Paid the Piper? The CIA and the Cultural Cold War* (London, 1999)

Sax, J. L. Heritage Preservation as a Public Duty: The Abbé Grégoire and the Origins of an Idea (1990) 88 Mich. LR 1142

Is Anyone Minding Stonehenge? The Origins of Cultural Property Protection in England (1990) 78 Cal. LR 1543

Schabas, W. A. *Genocide in International Law* (Cambridge, 2000)

Schindler, D. and J. Toman (eds.). *The Laws of Armed Conflicts: A Collection of Conventions, Resolutions and Other Documents* (3rd edn, Dordrecht, 1988)

Schmoeckel, M. The Internationalist as a Scientist and Herald: Lassa Oppenheim (2000) 11 EJIL 699

Schrader, R. F. *The Indian Arts and Crafts Board: An Aspect of New Deal Indian Policy* (Albuquerque, 1983)

Scott, C. Indigenous Self-Determination and Decolonisation of the International Imagination: A Plea (1996) 18 HRQ 814

Scott, J. Brown Intellectual Coöperation (1930) 24 AJIL 762

(ed.). *The Spanish Origins of International Law: Lectures* (Washington DC, 1928)

The Proceedings of the Hague Peace Conferences. Translation of the Official Texts (3 vols., New York, 1921)

Seabrook, J. B. Legal Approaches to the Trade in Stolen Antiquities (1974) 2 SJILC 51

Seeley, J. R. Introduction, in Colonial and Indian Exhibition 1886, *Her Majesty's Colonies, A Series of Original Papers issued under the Authority of the Royal Commission* (London, 1886), p.i

Seferiades, S. La question du repatriement des 'Marbres d'Elgin' considérée plus spécialement au point de vue de droit des gens (1932) 3 RDI 52

Shimazu, N. *Japan, Race and Equality: The Racial Equality Proposal of 1919* (London, 1998)

Shyllon, F. The Recovery of Cultural Objects by African Status through the UNESCO and UNIDROIT Conventions and the Role of Arbitration [2002] 2 ULR 219

Simpson, E. (ed.) *The Spoils of War. World War II and Its Aftermath: The Loss, Reappearance and Recovery of Cultural Property* (New York, 1997)

Simpson, M. *Making Representations: Museums in the Post-Colonial Era* (rev. edn, London, 2001)

Museums and Repatriation: An Account of Contested Items in Museum Collections in the UK, with Comparative Material from other Countries (2nd edn, London, 1997)

Simpson, T. *Indigenous Heritage and Self-Determination: The Cultural and Intellectual Property Rights of Indigenous Peoples* (Copenhagen, 1997)

Sinha, P. *New Nations and the Laws of Nations* (Leyden, 1967)

Skelton, R. The Indian Collections: 1798–1978 (1978) 120(902) *Burlington Magazine* 134

Sljivic, A. Why do You Think it's You? An Exposition of the Jurisprudence underlying the Debate between Cultural Nationalism and Cultural Internationalism (1997–1998) 31 GWJILE 393

Smidt, D. Establishing Museums in Developing Countries: The Case of Papua New Guinea, in M. Mead (ed.), *Exploring the Visual Art of Oceania* (Honolulu, 1979), p.392

Smith, A. Lord Elgin and his Collection (1916) 36 *Journal of Hellenic Studies* 163

Smith, B. *European Vision and the South Pacific* (New Haven, 1992)

Imagining the Pacific in the Wake of the Cook Voyages (Carlton, 1992)

1980 Boyer Lectures: The Spectre of Truganini (Sydney, 1980)

Smith, C. Harcourt The Future of Craft Museums (1916–17) 16 *Museum Journal* 152

Smith, T. *Making the Modern: Industry, Art and Design in America* (Chicago, 1993)

Snow, A. H. *The Question of Aborigines in the Law and Practice of Nations* (New York, 1921)

Snow, F. *Cases and Opinions on International Law with Note and A Syllabus* (Boston, 1893)

South Australian Museum *Annual Report of the South Australian Museum Board for the year ending 30 June 1983* (Adelaide, 1983)

Specht, J. Museums and the Cultural Heritage in the Pacific Islands, in M. Spriggs *et al.* (eds.), *A Community of Culture: The People and Prehistory of the Pacific*, Occasional papers in Prehistory 21 (Canberra, 1993), p.185

Pieces of Paradise (exh. cat., Sydney, 1988)

The Australian Museum and the Return of Artefacts to Pacific Island Countries (1979) 31 *Museum* 28

Specht, J. and L. Bolton. Pacific Islands' Artefact Collections: The UNESCO Inventory Project (2005) 17 *Journal of Museum Ethnography* (forthcoming)

Specht, J. and C. MacLulich. Changes and Challenges: The Australian Museum and Indigenous Communities, in P. McManus (ed.), *Archaeological Displays and the Public* (London, 1996), p.27

Specht, J. *et al.* Working Together on Issues of Access: Indigenous Peoples and the Australian Museum, in CAMA, *Something for Everyone: Access to Museums* (Adelaide, 1991), p.185

Spinden, H. J. Fine Art and the First Americans, in J. Sloan and O. La Farge (eds.), *Introduction to American Indian Art to accompany the first exhibition of American Indian Art selected entirely with consideration to esthetic value* (1931) (Reprint, Glorieta, 1970), p.69

Indian Art on its Merits (1931) 3 *Parnassus* 12

Spriggs, M. Fragments of What? Thoughts on the 'Pieces of Paradise' Exhibition at the Australian Museum (1989) 20 *Australian Archaeology* 66

Stahn, C. The Agreement on Succession Issues of the Former Socialist Federal Republic of Yugoslavia (2002) 96 AJIL 376

Staniszewski, M. A. *The Power of Display: A History of Exhibition Installations at the Museum of Modern Art* (Cambridge, 1998)

Stanner, W. E. H. *White Man Got No Dreaming: Essays 1938–1973* (Canberra, 1979)

Staunton, I. and M. McCarthy (eds.). *Lost Heritage: A Report of the Symposium on the Return of Cultural Property held at the Africa Centre, 21 May 1981* (London, 1981)

Stetie, S. The View of UNESCO's Inter-governmental Committee, in I. Staunton and M. McCarthy (eds.), *Lost Heritage: A report of the symposium on the return of cultural property held at the Africa Centre, 21 May 1981* (London, 1981), p.8

Stocking, G. W. Jr. Philanthropoids and Vanishing Cultures: Rockefeller Funding and the End of the Museum Era in Anglo-American Anthropology, in G. W. Stocking (ed.), *Objects and Others: Essays on Museums and Material Culture* (Madison, 1985), p.112

Ideas and Institutions in American Anthropology: Thoughts toward a History of the Interwar Years, in G. W. Stocking (ed.), *Selected Papers from the American Anthropologists* (Washington DC, 1976), p.1

Stocking, G. W. (ed.) *Objects and Others: Essays on Museums and Material Culture* (Madison, 1985)

Strati, A. Deep Seabed Cultural Property and the Common Heritage of Mankind (1991) 40 ICLQ 859

Strickland, R. Implementing the National Policy of Understanding, Preserving and Safeguarding the Heritage of Indian Peoples and Native Hawaiians: Human Rights, Sacred Objects and Cultural Patrimony (1992) 24 ASLJ 175

Strickland, R. and K. Supernaw. Back to the Future: A Proposed Model Tribal Act to Protect Native Cultural Heritage (1993) 46 Ark. LR 161

Struell, F. D. Cultural Property: Recent Cases under the Convention on Cultural Property Implementation Act (1997) 31 *The International Lawyer* 691

Suagee, D. B. Human Rights and the Cultural Heritage of Indian Tribes in the United States (1999) 8 IJCP 48

    Building a Tribal Repatriation Program: Options for Exercising Sovereignty, in B. Meister (ed.), *Mending the Circle: A Native American Repatriation Guide. Understanding and Implementing NAGPRA and the Official Smithsonian and other Repatriation Policies* (New York, 1996), p.32

Sugerman, D. 'A Hatred of Disorder': Legal Science, Liberalism and Imperialism, in P. Fitzgerald (ed.), *Dangerous Supplements: Resistance and Renewal in Jurisprudence* (London, 1991), p.47

Sullivan, T. J., M. Abraham and D. J. G. Griffin. NAGPRA: Effective Repatriation Programs and Cultural Change in Museums (2002) 43 *Curator* 231

Sultan, H. The Islamic Concept, in S. Nahlik (ed.), *International Dimensions of Humanitarian Law* (Paris, 1988), p.38

Szarkowski, J. The Family of Man, in J. Elderfield (ed.), *The Museum of Modern Art at Mid-Century: At Home and Abroad* (New York, 1994), p.13

Tallis, J. *Tallis's History and Description of the Crystal Palace, and the Exhibition of the World's Industry in 1851* (3 vols., London, 1852)

Tasmanian Aboriginal Centre. Memorandum, in Seventh Report of Select Committee on Culture, Media and Sport (1999–2000 HC 311) vol. 3, Appendix 58.

Taylor, F. H. *The Taste of Angels: A History of Art Collecting from Rameses to Napoleon* (Boston, 1948)

Taylor, G. D. *The New Deal and American Indian Tribalism: The Administration of the Indian Reorganization Act, 1934–45* (Lincoln, 1980)

Temperley, H. W. V. *History of the Peace Conference of Paris* (1920–24) (Reprint, 6 vols., London, 1969)

Tennant, C. Indigenous Peoples, International Institutions and International Legal Literature from 1945–1993 (1994) 16 HRQ 1

Thomas, D. Hurst *Skull Wars: Kennewick Man, Archaeology and the Battle for Native American Identity* (New York, 2000)

Thomas, N. *Colonialism's Culture: Anthropology, Travel and Government* (Cambridge, 1994)

    Entangled Objects: Exchange, Material Culture and Colonialism in the Pacific (London, 1991)

Thomason, D. N. Rolling Back History: The United Nations General Assembly and the Right to Cultural Property (1990) 22 CWRJIL 47

Thompson, C. T. *The Peace Conference Day by Day* (New York, 1920)

Thomsett, S. The Australian Museum's Training Programme for Community Museums (1985) 16 *COMA Bulletin* 39

Thornberry, P. *Indigenous Peoples and Human Rights* (New York, 2002)

    International Law and the Rights of Minorities (Oxford, 1991)

Thullen, G. *Problems of the Trusteeship System: A Study of Political Behaviour in the United Nations* (Geneva, 1964)

Tietze, H. L'accord Austro-Hongrois sur la répartition des collections de la maison des Habsbourg, (1933) 23–24(III-IV) *Mouseion* 92

Todman, T. A. Note to Rodolfo Silva, Chairman of the Permanent Council of the OAS concerning the Convention of San Salvador, in *Digest of United States Practice in International Law 1977* (New York, 1964), p.880

Toman, J. *The Protection of Cultural Property in the Event of Armed Conflict: Commentary on the Convention for the Protection of Cultural Property in the Event of Armed Conflict and its Protocol* (Paris, 1996)

Trachtenberg, A. *The Incorporation of America: Culture and Society in the Gilded Age* (New York, 1982)

Treue, W. *Art Plunder: The Fate of Art in War and Unrest*, trans. B. Creighton (New York, 1961)

Trope, J. and W. R. Echo-Hawk. The Native American Graves Protection and Repatriation Act: Background and Legislative History (1992) 24 ASLJ 33

Turnbull, P. Indigenous Australian People, their Defence of the Dead and Native Title, in C. Fforde, J. Hubert and P. Turnbull (eds.), *The Dead and their Possessions: Repatriation in Principle, Policy and Practice* (London, 2002), p.63

Turner, M. L. Art Confiscations in the French Revolution (1976) 4 *Proceedings of the Annual Meeting of the Western Society for French History* 274

Twiss, T. *The Law of Nations considered as Independent Political Communities on the Rights and Duties of Nations in Time of War* (Oxford, 1863)

The Law of Nations considered as Independent Political Communities on the Rights and Duties of Nations in Time of Peace (Oxford, 1861)

Tyler, S. *Indian Affairs: A Study of Changes in Policy of the United States towards Indians* (Provo, 1964)

UNESCO. *Conventions and Recommendations of UNESCO concerning the Protection of the Cultural Heritage* (Paris, 1983)

The Cultural Heritage of Mankind: A Shared Responsibility, Paris, 1982, UNESCO Doc.CLT-82/WS/27

Moving Towards Change: Some Thoughts on the New International Economic Order (Paris, 1976)

Cultural Rights as Human Rights (Paris, 1970)

Intergovernmental Conference on the Protection of Cultural Property in the Event of Armed Conflict – The Hague, 1954: Records of the Conference (The Hague, 1961)

Statutes of the Intergovernmental Committee for Promoting the Return of Cultural Property to its Countries of Origin or its Restitution in Case of Illicit Appropriation, at http://www.unesco.org/culture/laws/committee/html_eng/statuts.shtml

UNWCC. *History of the United Nations War Crimes Commission and the Development of the Laws of War* (London, 1948)

Law Reports of Trials of War Criminals (15 vols., London, 1947–49)

US Department of State *Treaty of Versailles and After* (Washington, DC, 1947)

US Department of State and United States Holocaust Memorial Museum. Washington Conference on Holocaust-Era Assets in the United States (Washington, DC,) 30 November – 3 December 1998, at http://www.state.gov/www/regions/eur/holocaust

US Presidential Advisory Commission on Holocaust Assets. *Plunder and Restitution: Findings and Recommendations and Staff Report* (Washington DC, 2000)

Valliant, G. C. *Indian Arts in North America* (New York, 1939)

Vane, C. (ed.). *Correspondence, Despatches and other Papers of Viscount Castlereagh, Second Marquess of Londonderry* (London, 1853)

Varnedoe, K. The Evolving Torpedo: Changing Ideas of the Collections of Painting and Sculpture of the Museum of Modern Art, in J. Elderfield (ed.), *The Museum of Modern Art at Mid-Century: Continuity and Change* (New York, 1995), p.12

Vásárhelyi, I. *Restitution in International Law* (Budapest, 1964)

Vattel, M. de *Le droit des gens, ou principes de la loi naturell, appliqués à la conduite et aux affaires des nations et des souverains* (1758) (3 vols.; Reprint, Washington DC, 1916)

Veatch, R. Minorities and the League of Nations, in Graduate Institute of International Studies and UN Library, *The League of Nations in Retrospect: Proceedings of the Symposium* (Berlin, 1983), p.396

Canada and the League of Nations (Toronto, 1975)

Vergo, P. *The New Museology* (London, 1989)

Vincent, P. J. Racial Equality, in H. Bull and A. Watson (eds.), *The Expansion of International Society* (Oxford, 1984), p.239

Visscher, C. de. International Protection of Works of Art and Historic Monuments, Washington, *US Documents and State Papers*, International Information and Cultural Series, No.8, June 1949, Washington, 821

Rapport de l'office international des musées a la commission internationale de coopération intellectuelle (juillet 1933) et texte du premier projet de convention internationale, in (1939) 1 *Art et archéologie: recueil de législation comparée et de droit international* 47

Nouvelle rédaction des articles 1er et 17 (1939) 1 *Art et archéologie: recueil de législation comparée et de droit international* 75

Le projet définitif établi en 1939 en vue de la conférence diplomatique (1939) 1 *Art et archéologie: recueil de législation comparée et de droit international* 78

La protection des patrimoines artistiques et historiques nationaux: nécessité d'une réglementation internationale (1938) 43–44 *Mouseïon* 7

La conférence internationale des fouilles et l'oeuvre de l'office international musées (1937) 18 RDILC 700

La protection internationale des objets d'art et des monuments historiques (1935) 16 RDILC 32

Vitoria, F. de. *De Indies et de jure belli relectiones*, ed. E. Nys (Washington DC, 1917)

Wagner, R. *The Invention of Culture* (rev. edn, Englewood Cliffs, 1975)

Walker, T. A. *The Science of International Law* (London, 1893)

Washburn, W. E. *Red Man's Land/White Man's Law: The Past and Present Status of the American Indian* (2nd edn, Norman, 1995)

Washburn, W. E. (ed.). *The Indian and the White Man* (Garden City, 1964)

Watson, J. Forbes. *On the Measures required for the Efficient Working of the India Museum and Library, with Suggestions for the Foundation, in connection with them, of an Indian Institute for Enquiry, Lecture and Teaching* (London, 1874)

International Exhibitions (London, 1873)

Weatherall, R. Aboriginals, Archaeologists and the Rights of the Dead (1989) 19 *Australian Archaeology* 122

Webster, C. K. *The League of Nations in Theory and Practice* (London, 1933)

Weihe, H. K. Licit International Trade in Cultural Objects for Art's Sake, in M. Briat and J. A. Freedberg (eds.), *Legal Aspects of International Trade in Art* (The Hague, 1996), p.54.

Wellington, Duke of. *Selections from the Dispatches and General Orders of Field Marshall the Duke of Wellington*, ed. L. Gurwood (London, 1842)

Welsh, P. H. Repatriation and Cultural Preservation: Potent Objects, Potent Pasts (1992) 25 UMJLR 837

Wendt, A. Reborn to Belong: Culture and Colonialism in the Pacific, in R. Edwards and J. Stewart (eds.), *Preserving Indigenous Cultures: A New Role for Museums* (Canberra, 1980), p.25

Wengler, W. Conflicts of Laws, Problems relating to Restitution of Property in Germany (1962) 11 ICLQ 1133

West, M. K. C. Keeping Places v. Museums – the North Australian Example (1981) 7 *COMA Bulletin* 9

West, W. R. *et al.* NAGPRA at 10: Examining a Decade of the Native American Graves and Protection and Repatriation Act (2000) 79 *Museum News* 42

Westlake, J. *Chapters on the Principles of International Law* (Cambridge, 1894)

Wheaton, H. *Elements of International Law*, ed. G. Wilson (8th edn, 1866) (Reprint, Washington DC, 1964)

Elements of International Law, ed. R. H. Dana Jr (8th edn, 1866), (Reprint, London, 1964)

Elements of International Law: With a Sketch of the History of the Science (1836) (Reprint, New York, 1972)

Whiting Jr, F. A. The New World Is Still New, *Magazine of Art* 32 (November 1939) 613

Wilkins, D. E. *American Indian Sovereignty and the US Supreme Court: The Masking of Justice* (Austin, 1997)

William, F. E. *The Collection of Curios and the Preservation of Native Culture* (Port Moresby, 1923)

Williams, C. *American Indian Sacred Objects, Skeletal Remains, Repatriation and Reburial: A Resource Guide* (Washington, 1994)

Williams, J. A. *Politics of the New Zealand Maori: Protest and Cooperation* (Auckland, 1969)

Williams, J. Fischer *Some Aspects of the Covenant of the League of Nations* (London, 1934)

Williams, S. *The International and National Protection of Movable Cultural Property* (Dobbs Ferry, 1978)

The Polish Art Treasures in Canada: 1940–60 (1977) 15 CYIL 292

Willoughby, W. F. *Territories and Dependencies of the United States: Their Government and Administration* (New York, 1905)

Wilson, D. Drake. California Indian Participation in Repatriation: Working Toward Recognition (1997) 21 AICRJ 191

Wippman, D. (ed.). *International Law and Ethnic Conflict* (Ithaca, 1998)

Woolley, C. L. Antiquities Law, Iraq (1935) 9(33) *Antiquity* 84

World Archaeological Congress WAC First Code of Ethics (1990) 6 *Anthropology Today* 24

Wright, Q. *Mandates under the League of Nations* (Chicago, 1930)

Yonke, C. *The Life and Administration of Robert Banks, Second Earl of Liverpool KG, Late First Lord of the Treasury* (3 vols., London, 1868)

Young, R. *White Mythologies: Writing History and the West* (London, 1990)

Zimmerman, L. A New and Different Archaeology (1996) 20 AIQ 297

Archaeology, Reburial and the Tactics of a Discipline's Self-Delusion (1992) 16 AICRJ 37

Zimmerman, L. and R. N. Clinton. Case Note : Kennewick Man and Native American Graves Protection and Repatriation Act Woes (1999) 8 IJCP 212

INDEX